A HISTORY OF EUROPE
Volume I

Herbert Albert Laurens Fisher O.M., F.R.S. was born
in London in 1865 and educated at Winchester
and New College, Oxford. Apart from his
academic career he had a long and distinguished
public life. He was a member of the Royal
Commission on the Public Services of India, 1912-
15; a member of the Government Committee on
Alleged German Outrages, 1915; a Member of
Parliament, 1916-26; President of the Board of
Education, 1916-22; and a British delegate to the
League of Nations, 1920-2. He was Vice-
Chancellor of Sheffield University from 1912-16;
Warden of New College, Oxford, from 1925; and
Governor of the BBC from 1935-9. He died in
1940.

His other publications include *The Medieval
Empire* (1898), *A Political History of England*
(1906), *The Republican Tradition in Europe* (1911),
Studies in History and Politics (1920), *The Common
Weal* (1924), *Whig Historians* (1928), and *Pages
from the Past* (1939).

D1642880

£2·95

H. A. L. FISHER

A HISTORY OF EUROPE

VOLUME I

From the Earliest Times to 1713

FONTANA/COLLINS

First published by Eyre & Spottiswoode 1935
First issued in Fontana 1960
Nineteenth impression February 1982

© H. A. L. Fisher, 1935

Made and printed in Great Britain by
William Collins Sons & Co. Ltd, Glasgow

PUBLISHER'S NOTE

The Author's Preface to the one volume edition of 1936
has been printed in the present edition
The bibliographies have been revised by Mr. Neil McKendrick
of Gonville and Caius College, Cambridge.

PREFACE

I BEGIN this book with neolithic man and conclude with Stalin and Mustapha Kemal, Mussolini and Hitler. Between these rough and rugged frontiers there are to be found some prospects flattering to human pride which it is a pleasure to recall to memory, the life-giving inrush of the Aryan peoples, the flowering of Greek genius, the long Roman peace, the cleansing tide of Christian ethics, the slow reconquest of classical learning after the barbaric invasions, the discovery through oceanic travel of the new world, the rationalism of the eighteenth, and the philanthropy and science of the nineteenth centuries. One intellectual excitement has, however, been denied me. Men wiser and more learned than I have discerned in history a plot, a rhythm, a predetermined pattern. These harmonies are concealed from me. I can see only one emergency following upon another as wave follows upon wave, only one great fact with respect to which, since it is unique, there can be no generalizations, only one safe rule for the historian: that he should recognize in the development of human destinies the play of the contingent and the unforeseen. This is not a doctrine of cynicism and despair. The fact of progress is written plain and large on the page of history; but progress is not a law of nature. The ground gained by one generation may be lost by the next. The thoughts of men may flow into the channels which lead to disaster and barbarism.

My opening themes are Greece and Rome, barbarism and Christianity. The discovery and colonization of the new world, the rise of nation states and the full development of the capitalistic system, belong to a later but still, having regard to the six thousand years of civilized life upon the planet, relatively recent period. Steam and electricity are more recent still. It is possible that two thousand years hence these two scientific inventions may be regarded as constituting the "Great Divide" in human history.

Book III describes The Liberal Experiment, using the adjective Liberal in no narrow party sense, but as denoting the system of civil, political and religious freedom now firmly established in Britain and the Dominions as well as among the French, the Dutch, the Scandinavian and American peoples. And if I speak of Liberty in this wider sense as experimental, it is not because I wish to disparage Freedom (for I would as soon disparage Virtue herself), but merely to indicate that after gaining ground through the nineteenth century, the tides of liberty have now suddenly receded over wide tracts of Europe. Yet how can the spread of servitude, by whatever benefits it may have been accompanied, be a matter for congratulation? A healthy man needs no narcotics. Only when the moral spine of a people is broken may plaster of Paris become a necessary evil.

For extended bibliographies the reader is referred to the Cambridge Ancient, Mediaeval and Modern Histories, to the authorities cited in J. B. Bury's edition of Gibbon's *Decline and Fall of the Roman Empire*, Lavisse's *Histoire de France*, Stubbs' *Constitutional History of England*, and other standard histories. I have confined myself to drawing attention at the end of each chapter to a few illustrative books, choosing by preference those which are modern and accessible in the English or French languages.

I have to thank my wife, Mr. Leopold Wickham Legg and Mr. David Ogg for their great kindness in reading the proofs; Mr. D. A. Reilly, of All Souls College, for several useful suggestions with respect to the opening chapters; and, for much valuable counsel in the later part of the work, my old friend Sir Richard Lodge, who at eighty years retains unimpaired his remarkable gifts of historical judgment and information.

H. A. L. FISHER

January, 1936

CONTENTS

CONTENTS

MAPS IN THE TEXT

LAETITIAE SACRUM

INTRODUCTION

Our civilization Hellenic. At present Europe is a creditor, formerly it was a debtor. Rome transmits the legacy of Greece. Oriental religions penetrate the west. Christianity the white man's religion. Its severance from Judaism and submission to Greek influence. The Christian test. Its acceptance by Bulgars, Hungarians, and Finns, its rejection by Jews, Arabs, and Turks. Civilization of Europe spiritual not racial. The problem of European unity.

WE EUROPEANS are the children of Hellas. Our civilization, which has its roots in the brilliant city life of the eastern Aegean, has never lost traces of its origin, and stamps us with a character by which we are distinguished from the other great civilizations of the human family, from the Chinese, the Hindus, the Persians, and the Semites. Scholars may explain to us that the languages spoken by the formative races of Europe are akin to Sanscrit and Persian, that the west has borrowed from the east, and the east from the west, and that the interpenetration of east and west has been so complex and subtle and continuous that any attempt to disentangle the European elements in our civilization from those which are foreign and adventitious must be a forlorn enterprise. Nevertheless, the broad fact remains. There is an European civilization. We know an European when we meet him. It is easy to distinguish him from a native of Pekin, of Benares, or of Teheran.

Our civilization, then, is distinct: it is also all-pervading and preponderant. In superficial area Europe is surpassed by Asia, Africa, and America, in population by the vast stable peasantry of Asia, which outnumbers not Europe only, but the rest of the world put together. Yet if a comprehensive survey of the globe were to be made, it would be found that in almost every quarter of it there were settlements of European men, or traces of the operation of the European mind. The surviving aboriginal peoples in the western hemisphere are a small, unimportant, and dwindling element in the population. The African negroes have been introduced by white men as an economic convenience. Northern and southern America are largely populated by colonists from Europe. Australasia is British. The political direction of Africa has fallen, with the ambiguous exception of the lower reaches of the Nile, into European hands. In Asia the case is not dissimilar. The political influences of Europe are apparent, even where they are not, as in India or Palestine, embodied in direct European control. The ideas of nationality and responsible government, of freedom and progress, of democracy and democratic education, have passed from the west to the east with revolutionary and far-reaching consequences.

It is, moreover, to European man that the world owes the incomparable gifts of modern science. To the conquest of nature through knowledge the contributions made by Asiatics have been negligible and by Africans (Egyptians excluded) non-existent. The printing press and the telescope, the steam-engine, the internal combustion engine and the aeroplane, the telegraph and telephone, wireless broadcasting and the cinematograph, the gramophone and television, together with all the leading discoveries in physiology, the circulation of the blood, the laws of respiration and the like, are the result of researches carried out by white men of European stock. It is hardly excessive to say that the material fabric of modern civilized life is the result of the intellectual daring and tenacity of the European peoples.

Yet this astounding supremacy in the field of scientific discovery has not always existed and may not always continue. Judged by the length of years during which human life has existed on this planet, the intellectual ascendancy of the white European races is a very recent phenomenon. Europe has not always been the tutor, nor Asia always the pupil. There was a time when these relations were reversed, and the men of Europe (the land of the setting sun) were deeply influenced by the far older and more sumptuous civilizations of Babylon and Egypt.

It is not my purpose to discuss the extent to which the civilization of Hellas was influenced by oriental sources. Let it be sufficient to note that an imposing mass of archaeological evidence can now be adduced in support of the proposition that the arts and crafts of the Orient were widely known to the peoples dwelling round the Mediterranean basin long before our earliest written records of Ionian civilization. Yet when the dawn of European literature begins to shine it reveals a society which is not oriental. The Homeric poems are a sufficient proof that round the eastern shores of the Mediterranean there was about 1200 B.C. a distinctive civilization of the west.

From that moment the survival value of the European mind was assured. The civilization of Greece, which was rooted in the religion of the Homeric age, grew from strength to strength. It repelled the might of Persia; and when the free cities of Greece were extinguished by the power of Macedon the influence of Hellenism was spread eastwards to the Indus by the armies of Alexander.

The mantle of the great Macedonian ultimately devolved on the Roman Empire, which for four hundred years defended western civilization against the dangers which assailed it from the barbarians without. But if the Roman legions could hold the frontiers against external foes, they afforded no protection against the penetration of the west by oriental beliefs. The old classical deities gave ground before the cults of Isis and Mithras and the Sun God, and these in turn ceded to Christ.

The founder of Christianity was a Galilean, speaking the Aramaic language, and nurtured in the Jewish traditions; but the Christian religion struck no deep roots in the country of its origin. Almost from the first it became a European creed, winning the souls of the poor as well as by its simple Galilean piety and democratic ideals as by its ardent claim, inherited from the Hebrews, to be the one truth and the sole means of salvation from a terrible and impending doom. A religion springing from a Jewish root, but how quickly in the Hellenic atmosphere of the first century severed from the legal rigours of Jerusalem and woven into the texture of Greek thought! The language of its Scriptures was Greek. So, too, remains the distinctive vocabulary of its creed, its ritual, its organization—the words apostle, evangel, church, diocese, bishop, priest, deacon, and countless others, for the Christian Church, even in Rome, was Greek before it was Latin, Greek in its theology, its official language, its local organization. The oriental rite of circumcision, which Paul of Tarsus, the greatest Greek writer of his age, rejected as a fatal obstacle to the spread of the Gospel through the gentile world, drew a clear line of division between two sects which in the Roman mind were at first apt to be confounded. Christian and Jew sprang apart. As time went on, the story of the Crucifixion, told with exquisite simplicity and pathos, and becoming widely known wherever Christians met together, deepened the gulf, and the crime of a handful of priests and elders in Jerusalem was visited by the Christian Churches upon the whole Jewish race. It is thus that St. Mark, the earliest evangelist, appears to many Jews today as being, although without malice, the first of the line of anti-Semite authors.

Here, then, in Christianity as sharply distinguished from Judaism, was a new test, a new principle of organization for European society. To be a Christian was to be admitted, as it were, into the fellowship of the European nations. To be a non-Christian was to be an outcast and an enemy. Much of European history consists in the secular conflict between east and west, which, beginning with the wars of Greece and Persia, was resumed in the form of the long duel between Christianity and Islam, the most recent phase of which was closed by the Treaty of Lausanne in 1923. What famous names are connected with that secular struggle—Urban II and Godfrey de Bouillon, Saladin and Richard Coeur de Lion, St. Louis and the Cid, Soleyman the Magnificent and Prince Eugène, Mustapha Kemal and Venizelos! The action and interaction of the Moslem and Christian world is one of the great themes of European history.

The acceptance of the Christian test as a mark of European fellowship has necessarily determined the relations between the old-established European races and those Asiatic peoples who at one time or another have effected a lodgment in the European continent. The Bulgars, the Hungarians, and the Finns accepted with varying degrees of readiness the European religion. The fact that in language and physical type they bore marks of an oriental and savage origin did not injure them. Religion atoned for an alien origin, and gave them the rights of the European confraternity. It was otherwise with the three oriental races, which continued to maintain upon European soil a non-Christian faith.

The Jews were persecuted, the Arabs by degrees driven from Spain, and the Turks, after a long-drawn struggle, expelled from the Greek mainland and islands, and from all but a small fraction of the Balkan peninsula.

Of these three sharply contrasted peoples only one has exercised a major and permanent influence on European life The Turks have been barren of ideas, and retained until the present generation the modes of thought and life appropriate to the nomads of the Asiatic highlands. From the Arab peoples mediaeval Europe learnt something of medicine, science, history, and philosophy which served its turn for the moment and is now superseded. But to the Jews Europe owes the Old Testament, which, being translated into Greek and becoming an accepted part of the Christian canon, has entered more deeply perhaps than any other book into the lives of the western peoples. From this great body of sacred literature, some of it rising to heights of sublime moral beauty, while other parts reflect the morals of a barbarous age, generation after generation of European men have drawn their ideas, not only of an historical order governed by divine providence, but of extreme antiquity, and of the lineaments of oriental society in distant times. The influence of the Old Testament has not been wholly good. If it has given courage and consolation to the saint, it has too often nerved the arm of the persecutor.

Apart from the power of their sacred literature, and despite the cruel persecutions to which they have been exposed, the Jews have achieved for themselves a singular position in the economy of Europe. Dispersed after the conquest of Palestine by the Roman Emperor Titus in A.D. 70, this shrewd and gifted oriental people have spread themselves through the Christian society of the world, and now number some eleven millions in Europe and four millions in America.

For many centuries the gates of mercy were closed upon them. They were regarded as outcasts, debarred from the most honourable callings and responsibilities, and constrained to the pestilential squalors of the ghetto. Always despised, periodically plundered, and in times of public calamity or fear exposed to the blood lust of murderous and ignorant mobs, the Jews of Europe endured through the middle ages unspeakable miseries. The eighteenth century brought the dawn of happier things. As the sunshine of religious toleration spread through central and western Europe the Jews were admitted to civic rights. The hospitality of the Christian state was amply repaid in noble contributions to art, science, and literature. Receiving at last encouragement from the vigorous and thriving populations of the west, the Jew rose to the level of the society around him, educated himself in its spirit, took on its colour, and ministered to some of its needs. Yet the difference between east and west, between Aryan and Semite, between Jew and Gentile, still remained, as sensible after more than eighteen hundred years as when the Hebrews were first driven from their small sunbaked home in Palestine to seek an asylum and a future in the west, and is liable even yet, as in the violent paroxysm of racial hysteria which has shaken the Germans, to give rise to bursts of savage oppression.

Race, then, has never entered as a unifying factor into European history. The races of Europe have always felt themselves to be different from one another, and have acted as if they were so. Attempts to give to Europe some form of organization or coherence have never been based on racial unity, or limited in scope to the geographical area which we have agreed to describe as European. The Empire of Alexander stretched to India, the Empire of Rome to the Euphrates, the claims of the Pope to the uttermost parts of the earth. The League of Nations, which incidentally supplies Europe with an organization for peace, is so framed as to include Asia and Africa, South America, Canada, and Australasia.

It follows that the kind of civilization which we specifically designate as European reposes not upon a foundation of race, but on an inheritance of thought and achievement and religious aspirations.

To this inheritance every race in Europe has made its distinct and specific contribution. That is why Europe is interesting. Its civilization has a certain character to be distinguished from that of the Semites, the Hindus, or the Chinese, and yet as we examine that character it dissolves under our eyes into a thousand different colours and shades, race differing from race, country from country, shire from shire, the men of Wiltshire sharply opposed in certain particulars to the men of Dorset, and even neighbouring villages eyeing one another as foreigners.

These differences are unresolved. One by one the great attempts to impose a common system upon the energetic self-willed peoples of Europe have broken down. The Roman Empire was foiled by the Germans. The Christian Church, by far the most powerful of the influences which in historical times has worked for union, was ruptured first by the quarrel between the Greeks and Latins, and then by the revolt of the Protestant north. Nor has any system of secular ideas been more successful in obtaining universal acceptance. Europe refused to be unified by the egalitarian plan of the French Revolution. Equally it now declines to accept the iron programme of Russian Communism. Yet ever since the first century of our era the dream of unity has hovered over the scene and haunted the imagination of statesmen and peoples. Nor is there any question more pertinent to the future welfare of the world than how the nations of Europe, whose differences are so many and so inveterate, may best be combined into some stable organization for the pursuit of their common interests and the avoidance of strife.

CHAPTER I

ORIGINS

Geographical and climatic changes. Evidence of craniology. Peasantry of the neolithic and bronze age. The coming of the Aryans. Mixed races of Europe. The Aegean culture of archaic times. Its debt to Babylon and Egypt. Difference between east and west.

IN THE last three thousand years there has been little change in the geographical conformation or climatic conditions of Europe. Here and there the sea has gained upon the land, or the land encroached upon the sea. Here and there a harbour has been silted up, a river has changed its course, a hill has subsided. But the broad currents of history have not been and could not be altered by such slight changes as these. In its physical outlines the Europe of the Homeric age was practically the same as the Europe of today.

This has not always been so. Geographical evidence shows that at earlier periods in the world's history the area which is now described as Europe went through transformations remarkable in scale. though effected by minute gradations spread over long periods of time. The climate was now much colder, now much warmer, than that which we experience at the present day. At one time herds of reindeer wandered over France and Britain; at another the shy hunter in the forests of western Europe would track the elephant, the hippopotamus, and the sabre-toothed tiger—animals now to be found only in the tropical or semi-tropical regions of the world. There was an age during which the Scandinavian peninsula, the British Isles, and the greater part of northern Germany were covered by a vast sheet of ice, an age when men might cross the Irish Sea, the German Ocean, and the British Channel dryshod, and walk into Africa or China without the use of oar or sail. In this long period of human history, extending perhaps for three hundred thousand years, there was a time when Europe pushed out a shelf a hundred miles to the west of its present limits, when the Baltic was a fresh-water lake, and the Atlantic had not yet burst into the Mediterranean, nor the Mediterranean established a marine connection with the Black Sea. At one point or other in geological time it would seem that every part of Europe wore an aspect wholly at variance with our present experience of it. The islands of the Aegean were eminences in a stretch of land inhabited by the elephant, the rhinoceros, and the mastodon. The plain of Hungary was a waste of salt water stretching to the Caspian; the Harz mountains were an island; Britain was broken up into a number of little pieces floating in an icy inhospitable sea. The site of imperial Rome was hidden beneath a floor of untravelled waters. Only after many experiments, continued into upper miocene times, were the main lines of Europe, as we now know it, decided.

The new structure of Europe was of capital importance. The waterways opened from the Atlantic into the Mediterranean in the south, and into the Baltic in the north, the establishment of a maritime connection between the Aegean and the Black Sea through the Dardanelles, the Sea of Marmora, and the Bosphorus have given to Europe a climate so temperate and subject to such modest variations of heat and cold as to provide the most favourable physiological stimulus to activity and enterprise. The sea is a source of infinite refreshment. The penetration of the continent of Europe by the long arms of inland seas has not only en-

couraged intercommunication, with all its consequences for
the development of trade and society, but has prevented, at
least in that part of Europe which lies west of the Pripet
marshes, the social and political stagnation which prevails in
the heart of great land continents. But the favours of nature
are distributed unequally. The vast plain of Russia is, save
on its southern fringes, too remote from the mitigating
influences of a great body of temperate sea water to enjoy
the benefits of its western neighbours. The cold, dark winters
of the Russian plain are inimical to the spirit of activity,
vigilance, and criticism. In such a climate man easily becomes
the victim of narrowing localism and deadening routine. The
gloom of geographical uniformity, combined with a harsh
climate, exercises its effect on the mind. An all-pervading
spirit of resignation and acquiescence saps initiative and
lames resource.

In the western half of Europe man has been assisted both by
climate and by geography. Rolling hills or mountain ranges
relieve the monotony of the level spaces. Comparatively
speaking, the cleansing sea is always a neighbour. Save in
northern Germany there is no long stretch of monotonous
plain, and here the plain is comparatively narrow, and
bounded on one side by the waters of the Baltic. In all this
western part of Europe, nature seems to have been bent on
providing every form of variety calculated to refresh and
encourage the human race. Hill and valley are intermingled;
mountain ranges are intersected by passes, and never so high
as to oppose an insuperable barrier to the passage of men.
The plains are well watered. In the Scandinavian north,
where the winter cold is extreme, there is always the sea and
always the mountains. In Greece or Spain, where the summer
heat is strongest, it is never, as in India, almost unbearable.
Everything facilitates the movement of men, the intermixture
of races, and the development of an active habit of thought
and enterprise.

Long before the age of history proper, man had made his
appearance in Europe. Some think that he came from Africa,
others from southern Russia, others again that the original
habitat of the human race is to be found in the highlands of
Asia. We do not know. But if the origin of man and the
course of his early migrations are wrapped in obscurity, we
know something of his physical properties, something of the

stages of civilization through which he passed, and something of the racial types existing in Europe when he first emerged into the light of history.

At the beginning of the neolithic age, when the great ice sheets had receded from the continent of Europe, and the climate had become tolerable to the human species, it would seem that European men fell into three main types, the Mediterranean, the Nordic and the Alpine; the Mediterranean and the Nordic agreeing with one another in the important particular of being long-headed, but the Nordic, probably under the stress of climatic influences, being fairer, slower to achieve maturity, and more muscular than the Mediterranean. In sharp contradistinction to these two long-headed races, the one resembling the modern Berber and the other the modern Swede, is a race of round-headed, thick-set people, sometimes, as in the Illyrian Alps, tall and dark, elsewhere, as in the Swiss and French Alps, short and stocky, who appear to have come into Europe from the east, and are known to ethnologists as Alpines from the fact that they are to be found thickly occupying the mountain chains which divide northern from southern Europe. It is not, however, to be supposed that these races were possessed of any developed sense of race consciousness or exclusiveness. Alpine mixed freely with Nordic, Nordic with Mediterranean. Almost everywhere we find evidence of intermediate types, or of survivals from an earlier age. In the British Isles, for instance, "the population was long-headed, and 'intermediate' in character between the two differentiated races, tall, gaunt, and dark in parts of the Scottish Highlands and North Wales, short and almost Mediterranean in parts of South Wales and Ireland, and 'betwixt-and-between' almost everywhere." In Finland, Asiatic broadheads mingled with long-headed men of the Nordic stock.

In a word, as Europe is a patchwork of differing landscapes, so it is a miscellany of differing physical types.

As the ice age came to an end, and mile after mile of Europe was retrieved from frosty desolation, the hunting men of the south came drifting northwards through the evergreens of bay and myrtle and box, through the thick forests of beech and oak, with their flint arrows and spears in pursuit of game. *Homo sapiens* had entered upon his long struggle with nature. Peril and want sharpened his wits and gave him reliance. He

learned to spin, to weave, to clothe himself against the cold.
By degrees he perfected his weapons against the wild beasts
in the forests, exchanging stone for bronze, and bronze for
iron. The sail, the wheel, the domestication of animals, three
of the most important inventions in human history, belong
to this unrecorded period. Gradually the hunter acquired
the arts of stock keeping and farming, so that thousands of
years before the dawn of history a peasantry was settled upon
the soil of Europe, and there, for century after century, bent
to the unchanging cycle of the seasons, sowing, ploughing,
and reaping, tending the ox, the goat, the sheep, and the pig,
practising with such skill as they might command the arts
and crafts of weaving and building, carving and pottery, and,
since religion is well-nigh universal, worshipping nature in
its manifold forms, whether terrible or benignant. Into this
passive civilization of scattered huts and villages there was
injected somewhere in the course of the second millennium
before Christ a new and disturbing force. Out of hither Asia,
we know not by what successive waves or driblets, there
streamed a people who had tamed the wild horse to the needs
of man and had found in the use of iron the convincing secret
of the slashing sword. With these two commanding advantages the new race or combination of races imposed itself as
a dominating authority upon the archaic Europe of the
bronze age and was the exciting cause of new and far reaching
developments. Not that the newcomers obliterated the old
sedentary population of the continent, or that they were able
to efface the primitive beliefs which haunt the imagination
of rustic men. That population, those beliefs, endure to this
day, but refashioned and overlaid by the higher and more
spirited culture of the new tribal aristocracy, which had come
so far and moved so fast. What these new peoples called
themselves or were called by others when they dwelt in their
original home (wherever that may have been) and spoke their
original tongue is a mystery, for in historical times they were
divided into separate races, which had lost the memory of a
common origin: but since they share with the Persians and
Indians a common linguistic pedigree, they are called by
philologists Indo-Europeans or Aryans. From the mixture
of these conquering intruders with the bronze-using peoples
of archaic Europe, the races which bear the burden of
European history, the Greeks and Latins, the Celts, Teutons,

and Slavs, derive their origin. Purity of race does not exist. Europe is a continent of energetic mongrels.

In certain regions, and most notably in the eastern Aegean, civilization had touched high points of luxury and craftsmanship long before the Aryan invasions. The exhumed treasures of Crete and the Cyclades, of Mycenae and the Troad, suffice to show that the human hand has gained nothing in dexterity from the lapse of ages. In Crete, that long and beautiful island, surmounted by the snowy crest of Ida, which of all European islands lies nearest to Egypt, there was for near two thousand years (3000-1400 B.C.) a flourishing civilization which spread its influence far and wide through the lands washed by the Aegean seas or westward to the shores of Sicily.

The ruins of the palace of Minos at Cnossos afford astonishing evidence of the comfort and luxury to be procured in that distant age. The system of heating and draining, and even some of the women's fashions, as depicted in the frescoes, have a thoroughly modern air. The source of Minoan luxury is not obscure. Cnossos, planted at the northern end of the great south road across the island, received and distributed the merchandise of the east. In that distant age this city, which may have contained a hundred thousand inhabitants, acted as a centre of exchange between east and west, playing the same part in the economy of European trade as afterwards devolved on Venice. Then a sudden destruction came upon it. The place was burned and sacked, the town was destroyed. The Minoan dynasty and the Minoan power pass out of history, leaving only among the Greeks a memory of half-magical skill, luxury, and cruelty.

No clue has been discovered to the Minoan script, nor has any book belonging to this age survived the catastrophe of the Greek conquest. The mysterious people, who worshipped a woman, a man, and a child, and for whom the cross appears to have been a religious symbol, cannot speak to us, and could not, so it would seem, speak to the fair-haired Achaeans, who at Mycenae and elsewhere settled in the shell of their castles and palaces. The break seems absolute. Yet it has been suggested, despite the silence of records, that something precious may yet have been handed down to posterity from this brilliant race. The Minoan gems are of exquisite workmanship, and fragments of the art of that distant age, unearthed by the spade in Hellenic times, may have helped to inspire the aesthetic consciousness of Greece in the greatest period of its artistic achievement.

The secret of this rich Aegean culture is to be found in its contact with the yet older and more advanced civilization in the alluvial valleys of the Euphrates and the Nile. Here it is that we find the first evidence of a developed urban life, of temples and priestly corporations, of written records and correspondence, of schools and codes of law, and of a leisured class raised above the urgency of material wants and dedicated to the pursuit of learning. While all Europe was yet rude and unlettered, geometry, astronomy, engineering, and land-surveying were cultivated by the Sumerians of Mesopotamia. Here, too, more than three thousand years before Christ mankind had carried to a point of perfection, as the most recent investigations at Ur of the Chaldees have shown, the arts of the jeweller, the carver, and the cabinet maker. Great centres of culture and wealth are never self-contained. From the Sumerians, shafts of light spread in every direction to the Hittites and Cretans, to the Philistines and Egyptians, and ultimately through many different channels to the Aryan Greeks. Yet, though the west borrowed from the east, a deep chasm divides the settled hieratic society and theocratic governments of Mesopotamia and Egypt from the free world of warriors, minstrels, pirates, and adventurers, which is depicted in the poems of Homer, and out of which, as the wild Greek clans took to city life, the distinctive civilization of the European world was in due course developed.

BOOKS WHICH MAY BE CONSULTED

Christopher Dawson: *The Age of the Gods.* 1928.

John Joly: *The Surface History of the Earth.* 1925.

W. J. Sollas: *Ancient Hunters and their Modern Representatives.* 1924.

V. G. Childe: *The Aryans.* 1926.

V. G. Childe: *The Dawn of European Civilization.* 1925.

T. Rice Holmes: *Ancient Britain.* 1907.

G. Glotz: *The Aegean Civilization.* 1925.

J. L. Myres: *The Dawn of History.* 1911.

Arthur Evans: *The Earlier Religions of Greece in the Light of the Cretan Discoveries.* Frazer Lecture, 1931.

G. Elliott Smith: *The Migrations of Early Culture*. 1915.
H. J. Fleure: *The Peoples of Europe*. 1922.
Ebert: *Reallexikon der Vorgeschichte*. 14 vols. 1924-9.
C. S. Coon: *The History of Man*. 1955.
V. G. Childe: *What Happened in History*. 1942.

CHAPTER II

THE DAWN OF HELLAS

The coming of the Greeks. The Homeric age. Geographical features. The city states. Absence of theocracy. Successive stages of political development. Athens and Sparta. The Ionian cities. The colonial movement.

BY AN astonishing dispensation of fate the one people of genius in the annals of the world is the earliest of the European races to emerge into the full light of history. The Greeks of history believed themselves to be one in race, origin, language, and institution, and in all these respects were misled; but the fact that they thought of themselves as one, and as distinguished by a superior culture from the dark background of the barbarian world around them, is more important than the truth, discerned by modern analysts, that like all the great peoples of the world, the Greeks drew their wealth from many quarters. Who they were and whence ultimately they came, are matters rather of learned conjecture than of certain knowledge. We only know that when the dawn breaks about 1000 B.C. men of Aryan stock are established, as a result of a long series of tribal infiltrations, which may have lasted many hundred years, in the coastlands of Asia Minor, in the islands of the Aegean, and in the land which is now called Greece.

In the western portions of this sunlit corner of the Mediterranean, in the islands, and on the mainland of Greece, the invaders found a civilization long established, and distinguished as far back as the fifteenth century B.C. by an advanced degree of accomplishment in the arts of life. With these older Minoan or Aegean peoples, the Achaeans and Dorians (for such were the names of successive tribal migrations of the

Greek-speaking invaders) mingled in varying proportions, taking whatever culture the autochthonous settlers had to give, but everywhere imposing their own rich and flexible language, their political ideas, and their worship of Zeus. But how little do we know of those distant times! No chronicle records the sequence of these early migrations (1200-900 B.C.) and confused struggles, of this widespread displacement and readjustment of peoples, while the Aegean civilization was broken up under the pressure of immigrants from the north, and the Ionians and others were forced out of mainland Greece and formed settlements on the coast of Asia Minor. We do not even know whether the later sovereigns of Mycenae were Greek. Legend and conjecture must take the place of true knowledge.

Yet one incomparable monument remains of this period of vast and adventurous agitation. In Greece everything invites to the seafaring life, the scant living to be obtained from the sun-baked hills and little level plains, the abundance of small, well-sheltered harbours, the constellation of islands, forming, as it were, a pathway between Greece and Asia Minor. The Greeks took to the sea. They crossed the Aegean, and made settlements on the further shore, they stole up to the mouths of the Hellespont, challenging, when a challenge was needed, the peoples of hither Asia. One such encounter (1194-84 B.C.), between a great Achaean confederacy and the Phrygian inhabitants of Troy, supplied to the minstrels of the Greek world a theme upon which the poetic imagination of many subsequent generations embroidered unending tapestries. In the Iliad of Homer the blind poet of Chios, which embodies, transmutes, and enlarges the poetical material of the Achaean minstrels, the facts of history are obscured in a haze of legend. The actors take on heroic form, the gods participate in the struggle and the issue is portrayed as a contest between the gathered strength of Hellas and an Asiatic power. To the modern antiquary the Iliad, which depicts in vivid colours the Aegean civilization of the bronze age, is full of instruction. In the ruins of Tiryns, the port of Mycenae, he discovers the regal halls of Homer; but to ancient Greece this splendid body of epical verse was much more than a repertory of curious detail; it was the Bible of a vanished and more heroic world, the book of books, containing the traditions and beliefs of a race, the testament of that great age of conflict, migration, and discovery, out of which a triumphant civilization was destined to emerge.

To us this great Ionian poem is precious not only by reason of its artistic beauty, but also as the earliest surviving specimen of European speech.[1] Our common culture derives from Homer. In certain broad particulars his outlook on the world is also ours. Though it seems probable that he spent most of his life on the Asiatic coast, for the Iliad shows him to be familiar with the landscape round Smyrna and Ephesus, and but dimly cognizant of the west, there is no touch of orientalism in the Homeric poems. The scene of action in the Iliad is not laid in the Asiatic hinterland, into which Greek mercenaries had already penetrated, but in the eastern Mediterranean, and always within sight of the foaming seas. The joy of life, a sense of the dignity of man, the eager desire for personal pre-eminence, the cheerfulness, curiosity, and love of adventure, which are characteristics of the Greek genius and were destined to make the fortunes of Europe, are to be found in Homer. Man was essentially proud and free, on happy terms with himself, with the world, and with Olympus. The gods were his friends and partners, very human, amusing men and women, not monstrous animals as in Egypt or India. The King was no eastern despot, but the first in an equal company of princes. Speech was free. Agamemnon, the King, was balanced by Thersites the demagogue.

The landscape of Greece, one of the loveliest in the world, conceals beneath its manifest seductions of line and colour a harsh discipline for man. In the temperate north the seasons melt into one another by insensible gradations, summer is not too hot, winter is not too cold, and the daily flow of human activities proceeds with little interruption through the year. In such climes rivers flow level, or nearly level, with their banks, and woods of well-grown timber clothe the rounded hills or are interspersed with the tillage and spreading pastures of the plain. Greece offers a complete contrast. Here a winter of piercing cold is sharply distinguished from a practically rainless summer, the heat of which is only tempered by the north-north-east winds which blow at that season. In place of rivers in our northern sense there are torrents rushing

[1] Though the Homeric poems seem to have assumed their final form only in the sixth century, the Iliad and Odyssey were probably in existence c. 800 B.C. The society which they depict is much earlier—c. 1200-1100 B.C.

and brawling during the winter's rains, a silent bed of dry
boulders under the long summer drought. Here and there,
amid the tumbled mass of barren mountains, there is a
small level plain of cultivated soil. But of forest timber there
is little. It is a land of olives and tamarisks, of juniper trees
and oleanders. The plane, the lime, and the oak are less
abundant.

A land thus stinted is a perpetual invitation to plunder and
piracy, to colonization and war. The Greek settlers, hibernating through the winter cold, but with the first spring flowers
resuming their active life of open-air discussion and hard
agricultural or mechanical toil, felt the stress of a niggard
world. The gaiety of the Greek scene, its sharp mountain
outlines cut against a sky of azure, did nothing to soften the
uphill struggle with the spectre of want. The frontier foray
for sheep and goats, leading perhaps to a regular little summer
campaign, was, in these early centuries, as common an
incident as the raid of a pirate craft or the more lawful quest
for wealth by the peaceful methods of trading. The quest of
supplies by war or plunder was a necessary supplement to the
tillage and pasturage of the community. It was not so much a
crime as a part of state economy. Man must eat to live. If
crops ran short, he must steal, fight, or emigrate.

Before any organized colonizing movement had begun
(750 B.C. to 550 B.C.) the public life of the Greeks had assumed
the form which has given it a permanent value in the education
of man. The early settlers had lived in scattered villages,
half-nomads, half agriculturalists; but by degrees convenience
and defence pointed to concentration. Cities were built, on
high, defensible crags, and at a distance from the shore, so
that they might not be surprised by a pirate raid; and with a
city there was developed a political consciousness of such
rare power and intensity that the world has never been able
to forget it. The Greek city state owes much to the favouring
circumstances of climate and geography. Set in a girdle of
hills it lived a life apart from its neighbours, developed its
own institutions, and acquired a character so well marked
that, despite all the common ties of language and religion, a
Spartan, an Athenian, and a Theban could as little be confused as the Marseillais with the Parisian, or the Yorkshire
tyke with the Somersetshire yokel.

The aloofness imposed by geography over against the neighbour on the other side of the hill was set off by a closeness of association among the citizens themselves for which we can find no parallel in the northern latitudes of Europe. The Greek citizen lived in the public eye. All day during the fine months he was out of doors, talking with his neighbours, acting as a juror, sitting in the theatre, or carrying on his employment. Never was there a society so favourable to the clash of intellects, the dissemination of scandal, or the development of political liberty and civic pride; never an audience more delighting in eloquence, more keen in criticism, more open to the persuasive arts of the great advocate, never a patriotism more happily tempered, or in its greater moments more passionate and entire. Jealousy and detraction flourished side by side with a degree of political idealism which has never been surpassed.

It is perhaps a consequence of this frank open-air existence that the Greeks escaped the paralysing control of an organized priestcraft. At no time were they enslaved to a book or to a church, or embarrassed by the quarrels of civil with sacerdotal authorities. Neither the mysteries of Eleusis nor the priests of Delphi were able to crush the free curiosity or luxurious imagination of this quick-witted race. Superstition they had in abundance, some of it dark and primitive, but much of it lightly held and sublimated by the genius of poetry, for they found divinities everywhere, in sky and sea, stream and grove, as well as in the half-legendary figures of their distant past, and peopled Olympus with beings of like passions and appetites with themselves. Indeed, whatever seemed to them to be precious, august, or formidable was likely to receive divine honours—the snakes of Aesculapius, which were regarded by the invalid visitors to Epidaurus as sound ministers of health, no less than the divine Apollo, mediator between earth and heaven, or Aphrodite, that primitive goddess of love, who, long before the Greeks had touched the Aegean shores, had secured her empire over the hearts of Mediterranean men. But more particularly was devotion due to the tutelary god or goddess of the city itself.

Religion, then, entered into patriotism, but not to any great extent into politics. The great wars of ancient Greece were fought not upon religious but upon secular issues. It was not Athena who brought Athens her enemies, but the jealousy of an imperial and ambitious power felt by her rivals in trade and arms.

So in the miniature states of the Greek world there grew up an art and practice of secular politics which, despite social revolutions such as the abolition of slavery, and great changes of scale and power, has still a meaning for modern men. In that lively and mutable society forms of government were quickly made, altered, discarded. Every experiment was possible, every idea was open to discussion. In the comprehensive treatise on Politics in which Aristotle sums up the experience gained from the study of a hundred and fifty-eight Greek constitutions, the world has a manual of political wisdom which can never be obsolete. The roots of European political philosophy are to be found in the practice and speculation of this distant age.

Monarchy, aristocracy, plutocracy, and thereafter tyranny leading to democracy—such, broadly speaking, were the five successive stages in the political development of the Greek city states. A long catalogue, it will be urged, yet marked by one instructive omission. Despotism of the old Asiatic type, theocratic, hereditary and absolute, was absent. The typical Greek tyrant did not, like Napoleon afterwards, or like some Sicilian tyrants in ancient times, cleave his way to power by arms and violence. He came forward as the champion of the oppressed and as the enemy of aristocratic privilege. If he was a despot, he was also a demagogue who broke the crust of custom, promoted commerce and wider relations with foreign states and paved the way for democratic freedom. In the development of Athenian culture and liberty, Peisistratus the enlightened tyrant had his contribution to make as well as Solon, the wise legislator who preceded him, and Cleisthenes the founder of Athenian democracy, who rose to to power when the absolutism of the Peisistratid family had done its work.

It was a great step forward in the rational ordering of human affairs when political decisions came to be taken by a majority vote after a peaceful discussion. This discovery, the root of all civilized political life, was made by the cities of Greece, and most notably by Athens, where the institutions of liberty were earliest and most fully developed. There are many points in Athenian democracy, such as the use of the lot, and the ostracism or banishment of prominent men, the popular law courts and the swift rotation of office and responsibility, which bring a smile to the lips of modern critics. How childish, they exclaim, how amateurish, how inconsistent with efficiency! Yet the more closely these things are examined, the more evident does it become that such was the necessary price of political freedom. Democracy was a lottery only made attractive by lavish opportunities of reward. The principle of equal opportunity so logically carried out in Athenian institutions appealed to the sense of justice which is inherent in human nature itself, and made up for the sacrifice of primitive passion which is involved in the acceptance of majority rule.

To the general course of political development which had now been evolved Sparta offered a notable exception. Ever since their victory over the Messenians at the end of the seventh century the Spartans had been the foremost people in the Peloponnesus. No state enjoyed so high a reputation for the steadfastness of its temper, the simplicity of its living, or the antiquity and harmony of its constitution as this old-fashioned, unwalled city in the rich and secluded valley of the Eurotas. Here it would seem that a great alarm, probably connected with Helot revolts and Messenian risings, had converted a society once easy, luxurious, and artistic to the need of a grim and grinding military discipline founded on the entire abnegation of self. The Spartan citizen, living in the midst of mutinous subjects or hostile serfs, was trained from early childhood to the arts of war. Private luxury was forbidden, weakling children were exposed, even the girls were submitted to gymnastic exercises. The whole state was a military barrack governed on communal principles, and taking no account of private tastes and inclinations. A community ordered on so clear a plan evoked the enthusiasm of contemporary philosophers. Here was primitive and heroic virtue preserved and regulated. Here was a pattern of human character exempt from the weakness bred of liberty. But war is not the true end of human life, and being organized solely for war, Sparta had no contribution to make to the arts of peace. Nor was she apt for far-flung enterprise. The first military power in Greece was too keenly alive to her domestic perils eagerly to respond to the attractions of empire or to venture her famous hoplites in distant fields.

It was not, however, either in Sparta or in Athens, but

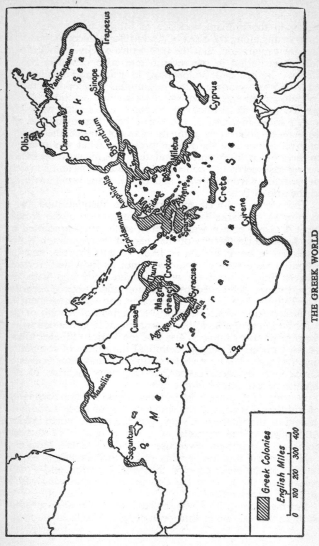

THE GREEK WORLD

rather in the brilliant necklace of Ionian cities, which had been strung along the coast of Asia Minor as a consequence of the great migration, that the true centre of Greek civilization was to be found in the seventh and sixth centuries before Christ. In art and philosophy, in trade and civilization, Miletus was a pioneer in that astounding development of the human faculties, speculative, artistic, and practical, which we recognize as distinctively Hellenic. At a time when the rough tribal invaders of the north were destroying the old Mycenaean civilization in the mainland of Greece, the Ionians of Asia Minor and the islands preserved what was precious in the older culture, and assimilating also the customs of the nearer east, deriving a coinage from the Lydians and a system of astronomy from Babylon and Egypt, made rapid advances in the arts of peace,

The Greek colonial movement was distinguished by a feature which marks it off from the emigration of the present age. A Greek colony was an act of state, often prompted by the desire to rid the city of that part of its population which appeared to be redundant or likely to give trouble, and the colonists were sped on their way, not as individual fortune seekers, but as members of a daughter city and with the circumstance demanded by a solemn and public enterprise. The Delphic Oracle gave its sanction and encouragement to an undertaking which without the goodwill of Apollo or the information available to her priests might have seemed to err from rashness or impiety, and like the Vatican in later times, or the Concert of Europe, delimited the sphere of competing undertakings. Under such favouring circumstances bodies of Greek citizens were despatched to every quarter of the Mediterranean and Pontic coasts.

A string of colonies from Miletus tapped the rich corn lands of southern Russia and the spoils of the fur traders and gold miners of the interior. Cyrene was the key to north Africa, Marseilles to the markets of Gaul, a cluster of thriving colonies, Corinthian Syracuse, Rhodian Gela, Megarian Selinus to the limitless fertility of the Sicilian vales. By the middle of the sixth century the Mediterranean and Pontic coasts from the Ebro to the Dnieper were surrounded with a girdle of Greek cities.

For many centuries it was the habit of Europeans, or rather of that small section of European peoples who lived along the

shores of the Mediterranean, to consider that they alone
constituted the civilized world. Outside the sacred circle of
Hellas they saw nothing but a penumbra of barbaric darkness.
Very little was known of further Asia, either in antiquity, or
until the voyages of Marco Polo the Venetian were published
at the end of the thirteenth century. Even Alexander the
Great did not suspect the existence of China. Vast tracts of
desert separated the great orderly society of land-owning
Chinese from the active mariners and traders of the Mediterranean basin. The two chief civilizations of the planet grew
up in mutual ignorance. Dante, reflecting the common view
of the geographers of the thirteenth century, places Jerusalem
at the centre of the earth.

BOOKS WHICH MAY BE CONSULTED

M. Rostovtzeff: *A History of the Ancient World.* 2 vols. 1926-7.
Grote: *A History of Greece.* Condensed and edited by J. M.
    Mitchell and M. A. B. Caspari. 1907.
J. B. Bury: *A History of Greece.* 1922.
A. E. Zimmern: *The Greek Commonwealth.* 1911.
G. Glotz: *The Greek City.* Tr. N. Mallinson. 1929.
Gilbert Murray: *History of Ancient Greek Literature.* 1897.
Gilbert Murray: *Rise of the Greek Epic.* 1924.
C. M. Bowra: *Tradition and Design in the Iliad.* 1930.
C. M. Bowra: *Ancient Greek Literature.* 1933.
Walter Leaf: *Homer and History.* 1915.
S. H. Butcher: *Some Aspects of the Greek Genius.* 1904.
E. Abbott: *Hellenica.* 1898.
E. Cavaignac: *Histoire de l'Antiquité.* 3 vols. 1913-9.
M. I. Finley: *The World of Odysseus.* 1956.
H. L. Lorimer: *Homer and the Monuments.* 1950.

CHAPTER III

GREECE AND PERSIA

Lydia conquered by the Persians. The Carthaginian challenge. The Ionian revolt. The Persian War. Real significance of the Greek victory. Rise of the Athenian Empire. Pericles.

UNTIL THE sixth century was half spent the Greek world had met no peril more formidable than its own internal dissensions. The dispersion of the Greek race had nowhere been seriously contested. Their settlements in Sicily and Magna Graecia, in Tripoli and in Egypt, had successfully survived the perils of youth. Even in Asia Minor, with its vast hinterland of barbaric peoples, the Ionian coast towns had been permitted a period of almost unmolested prosperity. On the sea, the Phoenicians, a Semitic people, long familiar with the southern routes of Europe, were compelled to admit a rival. On land the Lydia of Alyattes and his son Croesus owned the fascination of a culture more refined than its own. So long as the Lydian kingdom survived, the hither parts of Asia Minor were probably more open to Greek influence than at any period previous to the conquests of Alexander. Greek travellers frequented Sardis, the Lydian capital. Greek oracles were appealed to and lavishly remunerated by the Lydian monarch. Perhaps if another half-century had been conceded to the kingdom of Croesus the Lydian, Asia Minor would have been largely hellenized. But there supervened one of those catastrophes which abound in the violent history of Asia. Suddenly (546 B.C.), to the surprise of the Greeks, the Lydian Croesus, long regarded as a miracle of wealth and authority, was overthrown and his capital stormed and conquered. The victor was Cyrus (Kurush) the Persian, whose vast empire, not long afterwards to be augmented by the conquest of Egypt, was built on the ruins of Assyrian power. With the disappearance of the Lydian buffer state the Greek world was brought face to face for the first time with an organized and aggressive oriental monarchy. For the next two hundred years the Persian menace was a governing factor in Greek politics. It was a rivalry between east and west, between despotism and liberty, between Iranian fire-worship and the free and various play of Hellenic polytheism. To the generation of Greeks who experienced its opening phases the stakes appeared to be freedom, law, progress. The history of Herodotus, who was a youth during the great days when Hellas repelled the might of Darius the Persian and his son Xerxes, is full of the exaltation caused by the triumph of Athenian democracy over oriental barbarism.

For it so happens that when the clash came Athens had become, thanks to the reforms of Solon and Cleisthenes, a democratic state; and since she was at once the naval and intellectual capital of Hellas, and from her geographical position exposed to the first onset of the invader, it seemed to contemporaries that the force opposed to the legions of Asia was not so much the collective energies of Greece as the power released by the new-found liberties of Athens.

While the drama of the Persian War was proceeding in the east, the Greeks of Sicily were confronted by an oriental power long schooled in trade and commerce, and now embarked on a course of political expansion. The Phoenicians of Carthage were making rapid strides in the western Mediterranean. They were established on the coast of Spain, their influence was predominant in Sardinia, they were at once allied with the pirates of Etruria and in close communication with the Persian court. It is then no mere chance that a Carthaginian attack on the Greeks in Sicily should have coincided with a Persian invasion of Greece. The glorious year of Thermopylae and Salamis in the east also witnessed the Carthaginian over-throw at the battle of Himera in Sicily. On each front the Greeks were assailed by an Asiatic people; in each case it was the Asiatic power which sustained defeat. Yet though Greece after the victory of Salamis was never subjected to a Persian occupation, nor Sicily after the battle of Himera left undisputed to the Carthaginians, there was no settlement in either sphere. The Persian War dragged on with intermissions until Persia was finally conquered by Alexander the Great. And not all the wealth and military power of the tyrants of Syracuse were able to sweep the Carthaginians out of western Sicily.

The Persian War arose out of the help afforded by Athens

480
B.C.

and Eretria to a revolt of the Ionian cities of Asia Minor against the satraps of Darius (521-485).

The opening phases of this famous struggle were big with a sense of impending calamity for Hellas. Darius stamped out the Ionian revolt with ruthless thoroughness. Miletus, birth-place of Thales, the parent of European philosophy, was stripped bare of its populace, its men slain, its women and children deported to Susa, and after Asia Minor had been thus cruelly tranquillized and Thrace and Macedonia reduced to the Persian obedience, a powerful armada proceeded east-ward to effect the chastisement of Eretria and Athens.

Had Greece been united, the problem of repelling the in-vader might still have appeared grave and even desperate; but neither then nor at any subsequent time in her history were all the forces of Greece combined under a single leader, with undivided loyalty upon a common enterprise; and in that critical summer of 490 B.C. it fell to nine thousand Athenians only, aided by a small contingent from the little town of Plataea, to assail and beat the Persian army on the famous field of Marathon.

This surprising victory concluded the campaign. Finding Athens defended, the Persian fleet sailed for home, and ten years elapsed before Xerxes, the successor of Darius, was in a position to resume the attack. In that precious decade Athens, inspired by the rare insight of Themistocles, and aided by the discovery of silver at Laureion, fortified the Piraeus and strengthened her navy, so that when the blow fell in 480, she was among the cities of Greece as supreme at sea as was Sparta on land.

The new invasion was marked by every circumstance calcu-lated to alarm the Greeks into comprehensive and concerted measures of defence. The vast Asiatic army, magnified by rumour to a host of five million men, drawn from forty-three races variously armed and accoutred, the bridge of boats across the Hellespont, the canal to pierce the peninsula of Athos—these formidable preparations announced perils transcending all former experience.[1] Yet even so, not all Greece was of one mind. A congress of thirty-one cities summoned to the Isthmus of Corinth was remarkable for the sparse representation of the north. Here some were hostile,

[1] The army could not have exceeded 150,500 combatants, 60,000 followers and 75,000 animals (Sir F. Maurice. *Journal of Hellenic Studies*, 1931).

others afraid to venture their future. Even Sparta was more concerned with the defence of her own position in the Peloponnesus than with measures to arrest the invader on the threshold of Hellas. The Pass of Thermopylae, the gateway into eastern Greece, was held not by an army but by a detachment whose valour and unavailing sacrifice are among the immortal memories of Europe.

When the last of the brave Spartans had paid the toll, the Persians marched into Attica without let or hindrance, for the main body of the Peloponnesians, instead of contesting their advance, were engaged in building a wall across the isthmus. It was then that the Athenians took one of the great resolutions in history. Unsheltered and unprotected on the landward side, with no assurance of Spartan help and with a very clear determination that they would not share the fate of Miletus, they decided to find their salvation on the sea. The population, save a small garrison left in the acropolis, was embarked, and while the old, the women, and the children, were distributed in the neighbouring islands, the valid men of Athens were with the fleet and eager to try conclusions with the enemy. A cowardly decision to retreat to the isthmus was overcome by the arts of Themistocles, the Athenian. To him it is due that the united navy of the Greek allies sailed out to challenge the Persians in the narrow straits between Salamis and the sea.

In this battle, in which two hundred Athenian triremes were supported by smaller but still substantial contingents from Sparta and other members of the Confederacy, the Persians, fighting under the eyes of the great King himself, experienced an irreparable disaster. But though Xerxes withdrew to Asia, his army, after a winter in Thessaly, renewed the offensive in 479. The issue was joined at Plataea. Again the Greeks attacked, the Spartans this time bearing the brunt of the battle, and again the orientals were defeated. Outgeneralled and outfought, their leader Mardonius slain, and their numbers depleted, the army of Asia evacuated Greece, and the great peril, which for more than ten years had hung over the country, was finally overpast. The later stages of the war were fought on the sea or on the soil of Asia.

Marathon, Salamis, Plataea have each been accounted among the world's decisive battles. Decisive indeed they were, but not in the accepted political sense. Had Darius won at

Marathon or Xerxes at Plataea, it is difficult to believe that the free and distinctive life of the Greek cities would have suffered a final eclipse. Susa was far away, and to govern Greece from Susa would have exceeded the resources of any state of the ancient world. The Persians had already seen the wisdom of conferring some form of liberty on the conquered Ionian Greeks, and what was politic in Asia Minor was far more politic in Europe. It may be assumed that the great King, if victorious, would not have been wanting in an obsequious band of Greek supporters. Darius would have restored the tyrant Hippias to the governance of Athens from which he had been ejected. Xerxes would have discovered Thessalian princes or Boeotian oligarchs amenable to his nod. A loose Persian suzerainty exercised through philo-Persian Greeks might have been compatible with the preservation of many of the essential liberties and institutions of Hellas.

But the real significance of the Greek victories in this great decade is to be found not so much in the field of politics as in the domain of spirit. A tiny people had defeated a great empire. Something spiritual had, by the help of the favouring gods, vanquished wealth, numbers, material strength. Insolence had been curbed; the pride of power had received a fall. The goddess Athena had protected her chosen people in the hour of need. The exaltation which ensued bred great designs and a body of achievement in literature and art so astonishing in its beauty, its variety, and the permanence of its human appeal, that of all the elements which have entered into the education of European man, this perhaps has done most for the liberation of thought and the refinement of taste.

The forty-seven years which succeeded the battle of Plataea are marked by the rise of the Athenian empire and by the opening phases of that great movement of the artistic imagination which has secured for Athens the undying gratitude of mankind. It was in this period that Aeschylus, who fought as a hoplite at Marathon, produced the "Persae" and afterwards (in 458) his famous trilogy the "Oresteia." It was now that the genius of Sophocles was first manifested on the Athenian stage. To the Athenians of that golden age everything must have seemed possible after Marathon and Salamis. The Greeks of the Aegean looked to the foremost naval power in Greece for protection, and allowed themselves to be combined in the Confederacy of Delos, which implied acceptance of Athenian leadership and monetary contributions to the support of the fleet. It is given to few victorious peoples to make moderate use of a brilliant fortune, and Athens cannot be acquitted of the charge of having in some directions overstrained her strength and in others exercised it to the oppression of her subject cities. An expedition to Egypt ended in inevitable failure, and the transference in 454 of the Confederate Treasury from Delos to Athens gave rise to the well-founded suspicion that the funds of the Confederacy would be spent on the embellishment of the metropolis. Still, with all deductions it is a brilliant page in the history of Greece. The Persians were again beaten by land and sea at the Eurymedon (468) and in 448 brought to the signature of peace. The acquisition of Thasos, an island rich in minerals, strengthened the financial basis of the Empire. To the islanders who grumbled at the tribute, to the prudent who challenged the expense, the directors of Athenian policy could reply that, popular or no, the Empire had at last realized its mission. It had made the coasts of the Aegean safe for the Greeks.

Moreover, the conduct of Athenian affairs had from 462 onwards fallen into the hands of a visionary of genius. Pericles was a democrat and an imperialist, and was therefore in full sympathy with the two main currents of political thought which prevailed in Athens at that time; but he appears to have had also what is a rarer gift—a clear-cut ideal for his state, not only in its political and economic aspect, but also in relation to human conduct and character and artistic achievement. He wanted the influence of Athens to be widespread, and so planted out Athenian settlers far and wide from the shores of the inhospitable Euxine to the vine-clad hills of southern Italy; but it was also part of his philosophy that the mother city should occupy a position of commanding pre-eminence from the splendour and beauty of her public monuments. In a moment of inspiration he determined to restore the temples of Athens and Eleusis which had been destroyed by the Persians and to make of this act of restoration a demonstration, not merely of Athenian, but of Hellenic magnificence. A great architect and a great sculptor were at hand to serve his ambition. The famous statue of Athena has long since been destroyed, but the sculptured frieze of

Pheidias may be seen in the British Museum, and we may still admire the genius of Ictinus, who contrived the exquisite proportions of the Parthenon.

BOOKS WHICH MAY BE CONSULTED

G. B. Grundy: *The Great Persian War*. 1893.
R. W. Livingstone (*ed.*): *The Legacy of Greece*. 1921.
Cambridge Ancient History, Vol. IV.
Herodotus. Tr. A. D. Godley. (Loeb Classical Library.) 4 vols. 1921-4.
G. Glotz and R. Cohen: *Histoire Grecque*. 1925.
E. Cavaignac: *Histoire de l'Antiquité*. 3 vols. 1913-19.
H. D. Kitto: *The Greeks*. 1951.

CHAPTER IV

ATHENS AND SPARTA

Causes of the Peloponnesian War. Athens and Sparta. First decade of the war. The Syracusan expedition. The Athenian defeat. Permanent effects. Lustre and fame of Athenian literature.

HARDLY HAD Athens established herself under the enlightened rule of Pericles as the capital of Hellenic civilization than she was drawn into a war which, though marked by initial success, ultimately led to great disasters and to the extinction of Athenian political influence in the Mediterranean world.

The Athenian empire, the brilliant growth of two generations, shared the fate of every polity which arises by the repression of local liberties. From within it was exposed to the discontents of unwilling subjects, from without to the enmity of jealous rivals. To the more conservative states of Greece there was something alarming in the spectacle of so much power placed at the disposal of a single city. Athens ruled the waves. Her ships convoyed the harvests of the Crimea and Cyprus, of Egypt and Cyrene; they could close and open the Dardanelles, they pressed forward into the waters of the western Mediterranean. The need of finding food for a constantly increasing foreign population enjoined a policy of expansion, and apprehensions such as Japan now inspires in Australia and New Zealand were entertained by the citizens of Sparta and Corinth when confronted by the marine empire of Periclean Athens, so recent in its origin, so swift in its development, so formidable in its possibilities of pressure or offence.

When a war atmosphere is once created the particular circumstances out of which war arises are relatively indifferent. A quarrel broke out between Dorian Corinth and her powerful colony Corcyra. Both parties appealed to Athens for assistance, and Athens found it in her interest to support Corcyra against a strong commercial rival for the markets of the west. A naval battle was fought at Sybota, off the coast of western Greece, in which Athenian ships were engaged on one side and Megarian ships on the other. Then the quarrel widened ominously. Megara and Corinth were members of the Lacedaemonian Confederacy, of which Sparta was the honoured chief. Both were grievously affronted by Pericles. Megara was interdicted from the ports of the Athenian empire. Corinth was wounded through an attack on Potidaea, a tributary ally of Athens, but also a Corinthian colony which had refused, on the demand of Pericles, to dismiss its Corinthian magistrates or to raze its walls. The obstinacy with which Pericles persisted in these severe courses provided so remarkable a contrast to a record of peacefulness spread over fifteen years that strange theories were invented to account for it, as that the woman Aspasia was at the bottom of the Megarian decree, or that the great statesman plunged into war to divert the force of a private attack. It is more probable that his patience gave way, and that, deeming war to be inevitable, he chose his own occasion for precipitating the crisis.

It would be hardly possible to imagine a sharper contrast than that which distinguished the two leading states of Hellas who were now about to enter upon a twenty-seven years' war. A deliberate prudence was the mark of the Spartan, a vivacious and enterprising audacity of the Athenian character. The Spartan loved his home, the Athenian sought adventure far and wide in foreign lands. All the oligarchical parties in the Greek cities looked to conservative Sparta as their natural leader and the principal prop and support of the aristocratic cause. To the democrats, on the other hand, whether on the mainland of Greece or in the islands or in the distant cities of Thrace, Sicily, or Asia Minor, Athens stood out, not indeed as the champion of liberty, but as the exponent of equality at home; so that the war between Athens and Sparta, involving as it did not merely a conflict of interests and customs, but an opposition of political principle, in addition to its own evils, raised the temperature of local factions throughout Greece, and led to revolutions, some of which were shamed by great atrocities.

It might have been expected that a war between peoples so opposed to one another in every particular of character and temperament would in that age of costly battles have been sharp and short. But Sparta was a continental, Athens a maritime power. The Athenians had no army capable of mastering the Spartans on land, and Sparta, during the earlier years of the war, possessed no navy strong enough to try conclusions with the Athenians at sea. In effect Athens was an island. Her treasure, her foodstuffs, her shipbuilding materials came to her from overseas. A revenue-bearing Empire supported her democratic fleet and kept in repair her invulnerable fortifications. A power so equipped was in a strong position. The enemy might ravage the harvests of Attica, but he could neither starve Athens to submission nor compel her against her wish to accept battle on land. At the end of ten years of costly struggle no decisive advantage had been gained. The Athenians had fought a number of successful actions both by sea and land, mainly on the north-western coast of Greece; had established three bases on the Peloponnese, and captured a Spartan force on the island of Sphacteria. These were for Athens important advantages, but they were offset by severe trials, an annual invasion of Attica by a Spartan army, resulting, through the overcrowding of the city, in the great plague of 430, and, six years later, a severe defeat in the plains of Boeotia (battle of Delium) coupled with the loss of Amphipolis, an important and wealthy colony in Chalcidice. Sensible men like Nicias, a wealthy conservative slave-owner, had long seen the folly of a war out of which no material advantage could be gained; but since the death of Pericles in 429 B.C. the control of Athenian policy had fallen into the hands of a new type of politician, rougher, more violent, nearer to the common crowd than the wise aristocrat and philosopher who has given his name to an age of literary and artistic triumphs. To Cleon the leather merchant, and Hyperbolus the lampmaker, a popular war fought to a finish was the wine of life. So the war went on, waged somewhat reluctantly by Sparta, but as a matter of life and death by Corinth and Athens, until in an interval of good sense, and through the influence of Nicias, a peace was ultimately signed. But it was one thing to sign a peace and 421 another to secure its observance. Before the ink was dry on B.C. the Treaty of Nicias it became clear that some of Sparta's most important allies, notably Corinth, Megara, and Boeotia, refused to be bound, and that Sparta either could not, or would not, hold them to the bond. Still, had the peace mind really prevailed in Athens it would have been an easy task to avoid giving fresh provocation to the principal enemy. But a new and dazzling star had risen above the political horizon in Athens. Alcibiades was young and beautiful, brilliant and persuasive. He had learned from his master Socrates to challenge accepted conventions, and a gay audacity of thought and speech, blending with the natural grace of his person, marked him out in the eyes of the Demos for high responsibilities. In 420 Alcibiades was chosen to be a general, and it is probably due to his restless spirit that Athens sought new allies in the Peloponnese and sent an army into the Argolis to attack Epidaurus, afterwards a famous health resort, but in this connection solely important as the friend of Sparta. The enterprise resulted in failure. The Athenian and Argive armies were routed at Mantinea, and Athens was compelled to look outside the Peloponnese for her next military adventure.

Prominent among the Greek cities in Sicily, and consequently the cause of fear and jealousy among its neighbours, was the Corinthian colony of Syracuse. To wound Corinth by the conquest and occupation of the greatest of her daughter cities was a thought which naturally occurred to the war party in Athens. What indeed might not follow from the acquisition of so great a prize? The mastery of Syracuse might lead to the control of Sicily, and this in turn to the capture of Carthage and a naval supremacy in the western Mediterranean. In 427, moved by the eloquence of Gorgias of Leontini, the Athenians sent an expedition to Syracuse; but the work was done with half a heart, and nothing came of it.

Very different was the response given nine years later to the appeal of another Sicilian city. The glowing imagination of Alcibiades was now at play, and on the call of Segesta the greatest armada yet seen in Greek waters set sail from the Piraeus for the west.

There was nothing desperate in this design. An army of thirty thousand Athenians backed by a large fleet was quite capable of taking Syracuse by a prompt and resolute attack; but the Athenians made the fatal mistake of entrusting the chief command to Nicias, who was as inept in his prosecution of the campaign as he was averse from its inception. To his long catalogue of errors, more than to any other cause, the catastrophe which ensued must be ascribed.

There was another blunder which proved to be equally serious. On the eve of the expedition the public mind of Athens had been deeply stirred by the mutilation of certain ancient statues known as the Hermae. To whom, it was asked, was this foul impiety to be ascribed? Alcibiades sailed with the expedition. He had many enemies, he was known to be a freethinker, and during his absence the cloud of detraction thickened till it was resolved to recall him for trial.

Alcibiades, however, was not the man to allow himself to be led like a sheep to the slaughter. He left Sicily, not, however, for Athens but for Sparta, and during the next eight years devoted his great abilities to procuring the humiliation of his native city. It was on his advice that Sparta seized and fortified Decelea, a strong post on the soil of Attica, which enabled her to deprive Athens of the resources derived from the mines and farms of her territory. It was Alcibiades, again, who told the Spartans that if they wished to save Syracuse they must send a general to conduct the defence. His advice was taken, and the skill of Gylippus, assisted by the incompetence of Nicias, brought down upon Athens and upon the whole Athenian connection the greatest disaster which they sustained during the war.

The repercussion of this event was felt throughout the civilized world. Rebellion beginning in Chios spread among the island allies of Athens, but what was even more serious, Persia re-entered the war on the side of Sparta. The scales were now weighted more heavily than ever against the Athenians. While their silver mines were closed, a new source of supply was open to their adversaries. The Spartans had no

hesitation in sacrificing the Ionian cities to their new allies,
and, having discovered in the person of Lysander an admiral
distinguished alike for military and political talent, were in
a position to drive home their advantage. Meanwhile political
and constitutional changes succeeded one another in Athens
as the sky lowered or brightened. An oligarchy was tried
and discarded, and it was under the rule of the demagogues,
who declined two fair offers of peace, that Athens experienced
that final overthrow of the fleet at Aegospotami which concluded the war. Deprived of her navy and her foreign
possessions, and with her fortifications razed to the ground,
the city of Pericles tasted the bitterness of frustrated hopes.
The victors imposed a government to their liking, and an
oligarchy was established in place of that desperate democratic faction which had played so high for victory and lost
the stakes.

405
B.C.

The losses of Athens during this long and melancholy
struggle were far in excess, having regard to the population
of Attica at that time, of those experienced even by the most
highly tried country in the great war of 1914-1918. The
plague alone is estimated to have carried off seventeen thousand soldiers. Forty thousand men were lost in Sicily; and
besides these outstanding catastrophes, every year brought
its sad tale of casualties, "ships lost by tens and fives and more,
and men that died by the thousand and ten thousand." Even
if we make allowances for the fact that a considerable proportion of the rowers of the Athenian fleet may have been
hired slaves and that there were subject ally contingents and
mercenaries in the Athenian army, the casualties were
formidable. The old aristocratic families which had played so
great a part in the Persian war were extinguished in this baser
controversy, and aliens in increasing numbers were inscribed
upon the civic rolls, so that, in the words of Isocrates, there
was in Athens "a new people." When we reflect upon the
brilliant contributions to art, letters, and philosophy which
we owe to the Athenians of the fifth century B.C., the destruction through war of a large part of this gifted population
must be accounted one of the grave and irretrievable calamities of history.

The needless tragedy of the Peloponnesian war has received
more than its fair share of attention from the fact that it
forms the theme of one of the world's great historical master-

pieces. The genius of Thucydides has conferred immortality upon many a trifling detail attending the declension of Athenian
power. The long series of disastrous errors by which the
Athenians threw away their great initial advantage is recounted in terms of grave and moving eloquence by this
Athenian, writing in exile, but raised above the exile's narrow-
ness by a native austerity and greatness of soul. The story of
the revolution in Corcyra, of the plague at Athens in the
second year of the war, of the capture of Sphacteria, and of
the Syracusan expedition, and the speeches with which the
moral issues underlying the conflict are brought before the
reader's mind, give to the pages of Thucydides the colour of
a tragic drama. Yet in reality it is not the ruin of Athens in
the Peloponnesian War which has been important for mankind, but its survival; not its political failures, but its intellectual and artistic triumphs. While the deathly struggle with
Sparta was proceeding, Socrates, the stonecutter, was
challenging the accepted conventions of mankind, and laying
the basis of moral and metaphysical science. It was during
this same period of agonizing strain that Athenian audiences
were crowding to the open-air theatre of Dionysus to delight
in the exquisite poetry of Euripides, the rationalist, or the
brilliant wit of Aristophanes, the critic of rationalism,
demagogy, and jingoism. It was in the first year of the
struggle that Euripides produced the Medea, in the second
that Herodotus completed his History, and, while no less than
fourteen out of the twenty-seven years of the war are similarly memorable in the annals of the stage, it has been noted
that the two blackest moments were marked each by the
production of plays which still preserve their freshness and
brilliance for the world. In 413, when the Spartans fortified
Decelea and the Athenians were disastrously beaten in a
great naval action in the harbour of Syracuse, Euripides produced the Iphigenia in Tauris and the Electra. The fatal year
of Aegospotami (405) was similarly distinguished. It is the
year of the Bacchae, the beautiful swan song of Euripides, and
of the Frogs, perhaps the most delightful of ancient comedies.

The services of Athens to the education of Hellas were
recognized and requited. When her fleet had been destroyed
at Aegospotami at the end of a long and bitter war, Sparta
might have applied to Athens the same terrible penalty which
in a spasm of passionate wrath, Athens had meted out to the

little island of Melos. She might have razed the city to the ground, she might have slaughtered or enslaved its inhabitants. In the fierce hatred inspired by Athenian tyranny these cruelties would have been popular and were, in fact, recommended; but Athens was saved by the respect which even Sparta was compelled to feel for the brightest ornament of Hellenic civilization. The city was spared in consideration of her virtues, and not on one occasion only. Seventy years later, when Alexander of Macedon had destroyed Thebes, saving only the house of Pindar, and Athens, which had designed to send help to the Thebans, was exposed to his attack, the same sentiment of homage to the shrine of so much genius interposed its mediation—

> and the repeated air
> Of sad Electra's poet had the power
> To save the Athenian walls from ruin bare.

BOOKS WHICH MAY BE CONSULTED

Thucydides. Tr. Crawley. (Everyman's Library.) 1910.
E. Abbott: *Pericles and the Golden Age of Athens.* 1891
Grote: *A History of Greece.*
J. B. Bury: *A History of Greece.* 3rd Ed. revised by R. Meiggs. 1951.
A. E. Zimmern: *The Greek Commonwealth.* 5th Ed. 1931
Cambridge Ancient History, Vol. V.
B. W. Henderson: *The Great War between Athens and Sparta.* 1927

CHAPTER V

GREECE AND MACEDON

*Disunion of Greece. Macedon. Philip II. Alexander. The
hellenistic age. Religion. Philosophy. The Epigoni. Political
legacies of the Macedonian age. Empire worship. Bureaucracy.
The divisions of Greece are the opportunity of Rome. Character
of the Greeks. Hellenic influences on Christianity.*

THE FOURTH century, which opens with the condemnation and
death of Socrates (399 B.C.), is chiefly memorable as the great
age of Greek prose writing, and for the rise and spread of the
Macedonian empire. The accusation preferred against Socrates, that he did not believe in the gods recognized by the
city, that he introduced strange supernatural beings, and that
he corrupted the youth, marks the honest fears inspired in
vulgar minds by the application of free, logical questioning to
the loyalties, conventions, and traditions of a people. For,
indeed, Greece was moving swiftly into a new intellectual
climate, in which the individual counted for more, and the
city for less, and old inhibitions of custom and religion were
fast breaking down. Socrates, who taught that life was an art
and knowledge the key to it, was behind these changes, and
was condemned to drink the cup of death; but it is idle to
suppose that the influence of a great liberating mind can be
stayed by persecution. The glory of Socrates was enhanced
by the tragedy of his end. He was revered as a saint of rationalism and virtue; and the beautiful fabric of the Platonic
philosophy is the homage of a pupil to a master, and an
imperishable monument to his fame.

Hellenic politics during the sixty-six years which divided the
Spartan conquest of Athens from the Macedonian conquest
of Greece were marked by a continuation, with some aggravations, of the old evils of the Peloponnesian War. Factions
were as furious, fighting was as fierce, but mercenary troops
tended to replace citizen levies. So far from profiting from the
lessons of the past, Sparta repeated all the faults which had
been charged against Athens during her period of domination,

with none of her redeeming graces. The old ideal of Pan-hellenic unity in opposition to Persia seems to have survived chiefly in the orations of the wise Isocrates. All parties were willing to help themselves from the Persian till and to move at the Persian behest. Xenophon, a pupil of Socrates and an accomplished gentleman, thought it no shame to serve with a band of Spartan mercenaries under the Persian Cyrus and after-wards even to fight with a Spartan army against Athens, the nursing mother of his mind. When Sparta was opposed to Per-sia, Athens was Persia's friend, and an Athenian admiral, com-manding a Persian fleet, and aided by Persian funds, defeated the Spartans at sea and rebuilt the fortifications of his city. When, on the other hand, Sparta made friends with Persia, and even went so far as solemnly to betray to her the interests of the Ionian Greeks (Peace of Antalcidas, 387), the attitude of Athens was correspondingly reversed. The spirit of the soldier of fortune, snatching at luck, wherever it might be found, dominated the scene.

Isocrates is probably right when he claims that the curse of Hellenic politics at this time was the desire for empire. Athens, Sparta, Thebes, Phocis, all in turn, strove for suprem-acy, and as each state mounted on the crest of fortune, it was pulled back into the trough by its jealous rivals. Even 420? Epaminondas of Thebes, the ablest and the most disinterested -362 soldier of his age, could not see beyond Boeotia, and was B.C. incapable of great political combinations.

The solution of the Greek question came from an unsus-pected quarter. To the north of Thessaly, in the coastlands round the Thermaic gulf, there was established a Greek people, rougher and less civilized than the inhabitants of Athens or Corinth, and regarded by the southern Greeks much as a Parisian views a provincial from Brittany or Languedoc. These were the Macedonians, deep drinkers, lusty fighters, passionate in pursuit of the bear and the wolf through the forests and glens of their mountain home, and still living in the Homeric stage of civilization, of whom not much that is important can be related until Philip of the royal house, returning at the age of twenty-four from Thebes, where he had learned the art of war from Epaminondas, made himself master of his native country. In the whole range of European history few statesmen have been more effective than this strenuous clear-sighted man (359-336). Macedonia at the time of his accession was poor, but became, through the exploitation of the gold-mines of Mt. Pangaeus, the richest state in Europe. Out of this country, which was scarcely more than a geographical expression (for the wild Illyrian hillmen, though nominally vassals of the crown, were as little congenial to the lowland Greeks as were the highland reavers of the seventeenth century to the farmers in the vales of Perth or Stirling), Philip made a nation and an army—a nation wholesomely compounded, and an army at once national in spirit and professional in aim, and moreover, in its combination of the cavalry with the infantry arm and of light with heavy troops, superior to any force which the states of Hellas could put into the field. The Macedonian phalanx changed the history of the world. It was the creation of Philip. Loyal to their punctual paymaster, the spearmen of Macedonia marched into action in open array and held the enemy while the cavalry charged in upon the wings in wedge-like squadrons and decided the issue.

What would be the attitude of the Greek states towards this new half-barbarian power in the north? Philip was anxious to be friendly. Despite his rough animal nature he reckoned himself to be a Greek, set a value on culture and knowledge (engaging Aristotle of Stagira, the son of a Macedonian court doctor, as tutor to his son), and desired to be accepted as suzerain of a Greek confederacy. A true realist comparing his resources with those of the Greek cities would have advised them to seek his goodwill. Even contemporaries asked whether a captain had not now arisen who could lead the Greeks against Persia, and provide for their hungry and redundant numbers new fields for colonial settlement in Asia Minor. Athens certainly had much to gain from a firm understanding with the master of Macedonia and Thessaly and the conqueror of Thrace: but at this juncture of her history Athenian policy was swayed by an orator who saw in the growing power of the Macedonians a menace to the traditional liberties of Hellas, which must be resisted to the death. The speeches of Demosthenes rank among the classics of political liberty, and cannot even now be read without emotion: but they led only to the bloodstained field of Chaeronea. Here Philip, defeating the joint army of Thebes and Athens, made himself by that one blow master of Greece. Two years later the conqueror fell by the hand of an assassin. At a synod of

338
B.C.

Greek cities at Corinth he had announced his intention of making war upon Persia on behalf of Greece and the gods, of liberating the Greek cities in Asia Minor, and of punishing the barbarians for acts of sacrilege committed in the reign of Xerxes; and it was on the eve of his departure on this vast enterprise that the founder of Macedonia met his end.

336 B.C.

Alexander, his son by the violent Olympias, succeeded to his throne and vast ambitions. In a short reign of thirteen years this wonderful young man reasserted the Macedonian authority in Hellas and Thrace, levelled Thebes to the ground, conquered, with his small, mobile, and most effective army, Asia Minor, Syria, Egypt, and Persia, and marched his Macedonian veterans over the Khyber Pass into the plains of India. No military career, not even that of his imitator Napoleon, has exercised a wider influence on history, opening out as it did the whole of hither Asia to Hellenic speech and culture, and bringing to the west a flood of new facts relating to oriental lands and peoples, which is only equalled by those later additions to knowledge which Europe owes to the Crusades. Moreover, it must be recollected that Alexander embarked upon his enterprise as the elected generalissimo of Greece. Steeped in Greek legends and literature, believing himself to be sprung from Achilles, the fair young Macedonian descended upon Asia as the successor of the heroes who fought against Troy; but if he came as the missionary of Hellas, crowning the statue of Achilles at Troy and founding a temple of Zeus at Sardis, he was a missionary untouched by fanaticism. Despite the advice of Aristotle he refused to regard the orientals as an inferior race, nor did he proscribe their religious beliefs. A wise toleration, social, religious, political, informed the government of his conquered provinces. The great landowning nobles of Persia won from him the sympathy and respect which the spectacle of a gentleman and a sportsman never fails to evoke in the hearty nature of the open-air man. While he lost nothing of his conviction of Hellenic excellence, founding, as it is said, seventy Greek cities, and carrying the Iliad as the constant companion of his travels, he wedded his Macedonian paladins to the heiresses of Asia, himself married a Persian princess, and assumed the state of an oriental monarch. In idea his empire was coterminous with the world and founded on the doctrine of the equality of man, a universal society designed to con-

356-23 B.C.

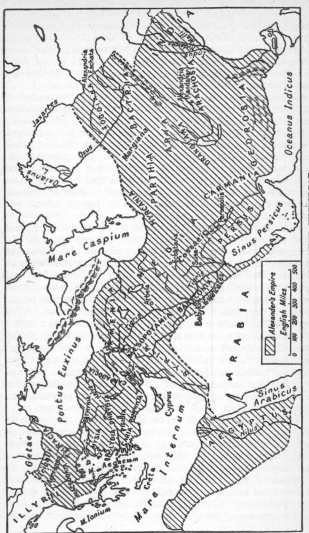

THE EMPIRE OF ALEXANDER THE GREAT

form to a common standard and subjected to a sovereign who, as the supreme benefactor of mankind, was rightly accorded divine honours, in fine a Holy Greek Empire foreshadowing the Holy Roman Empire of later times. In fact, he created the conditions under which Greek civilization could flourish in Asiatic or north African soil, and gave to Europe a vast new province, comprising Asia Minor, Syria, and Egypt, which remained subject to Macedonian dynasties until it was absorbed by the Roman empire.

The story of the conquests of Alexander, while it falls outside the scope of a history of Europe, contains two connected incidents which have a close relation to the fate of the Mediterranean peoples, the destruction of Tyre and the foundation of Alexandria, the one marking the eclipse of Phoenician power, the other the establishment of a new centre of Hellenic culture and commerce on the coast of Egypt, which was destined to vie with Athens herself.

It was not easy for the cities of Hellas to realize the change which was coming over the world. Could it be that these tiny states, which had been so passionately loved, so affectionately adorned, for which men had been willing to sacrifice life and even honour, were finally to lose their independence and their dream of empire? Men were reluctant to believe it. The wise Aristotle, who was teaching in Athens, under the slopes of Mt. Lycabettus, while his pupil was overrunning Asia, writes of the science of politics as if it were contained in the experience of cities small enough "to hear the voice of one herald," and based on the distinction of slave and free. Even the greatest thinker of antiquity, with a sphere of interests ranging from the anatomy of a fish to the ultimate verities of the human soul, failed to discern in the Macedonian empire the birth of a new era, and the coming of cosmopolitan thought.

384-22 BC.

The age into which we now pass is still Hellenic, but Hellenic with a difference. It was a great age of sculpture, of mathematics, of widespread education. The Attic tongue, prevailing over rival dialects, is the language of international commerce and polite society, spoken from Marseilles to Antioch, from Pella to the Cataracts, penetrating even the Jewish synagogues, and found to be so indispensable by that conservative people that by degrees the Old Testament is rendered into Greek. But the great masters of poetry and philosophy have passed away, having bequeathed to posterity almost every *genre* of the literary art and an introduction to almost every branch of philosophical and scientific enquiry. Their place is taken by writers of popular fiction and by learned poets and specialists congregating where great libraries are to be found and a government capable of protecting the studious from piracy and the disturbance of war. Under the rule of the Ptolemies and Attalids such libraries were founded at Alexandria and Pergamum, the rival capitals of paper and parchment.

Another feature of this age which is called Hellenistic is that, without being fanatical, men and women are feeling everywhere for religion. It is the property of polytheism to be tolerant, and while the Greeks had preferences in the matter of gods and goddesses, they practised no exclusions. As the old Olympian divinities lost their appeal, new worships and beliefs surged in from the religious east: astrology, magic, the mystery religions with their rites of initiation and purification, the imposing and popular cult, proximately derived from Egypt, of Serapis and Isis. More particularly significant was the worship of Isis, for two centuries the Holy Mother of the Mediterranean world. Isis "all-seeing and all-powerful, the star of the sea, the diadem of life, the law giver and saviour," was the woman's goddess. She was figured as a young matron, crowned with the blue lotus or the crescent moon, bearing the infant Horus in her arms. Not seldom were the statues of Isis made afterwards to serve as images of the Madonna.

For the higher minds there were the religious philosophies of Zeno and Epicurus. In 311 Zeno, a Phoenician from Cyprus, came to Athens and took up the teaching of philosophy in the painted portico or Stoa. He preached the doctrine of a World State ruled by a Supreme Power, all-wise and all-good, of equality and human brotherhood, of conscience and duty, of harmony with the divine purpose only to be obtained through wisdom and virtue, and of an inner peace proof against the outward agitations of fate to be found in a retreat within the fortress of the soul. Little remains of the original writings of this noble thinker, bnt the hymn of Cleanthes (rendered into English prose by Walter Pater in *Plato and the Platonists*), the Meditations of Marcus Aurelius and the singularly beautiful body of moral teaching which survives in the works of Epictetus, attest the wide and prolonged influence of Stoicism over the best minds and characters of the Pagan world in its decline. Epicurus was the philosopher of happiness, as Zeno of duty.

In the field of politics the Hellenistic period is distinguished by a difference of scale from the centuries which preceded it. Large kingdoms, vast cities, greater ships and engines of war, imposing private fortunes, are the marks of the new age. The Greek world waxes prosperous on the pillage of the east and the opening of new markets, despite the fact that the sea is infested by pirates, and that few years pass without fighting in some part or other of the Macedonian empire. War, infanticide, and perhaps even malaria take their toll. The true Greek population steadily dwindles, and the cities of Hellas in the first century must have been largely filled by Greek-speaking aliens.

Alexander left no will, and the prize of the Macedonian empire fell to be disputed by his marshals. The tie of race counted for nothing with these able and ambitious adventurers: and the disappearance of the great captain is followed by a long series of wars between Egypt and Syria, and Egypt and Macedonia, until a new power enters the eastern scene, and the vast estate which the Macedonians had squandered in their quarrels was taken over and administered by Rome. Yet, despite the grave drawback of their civil dissensions, the Macedonian dynasts conferred upon European civilization two great services, for the absence of which the world today would be immeasurably the poorer. For a century and a half they defended the fabric of Greek civilization from the Illyrians and Thracians, from the Parthians in the east, and from the pressure of the hungry and savage denizens of the fens and forests of central Europe. Their armour was sometimes pierced: their defence was not always loyal. They had to retreat from India. The Gauls or Galati penetrated to Delphi, crossed into Asia Minor, and at one time threatened to plunge that flourishing region into chaos. Yet in the end the power of these formidable barbarians was checked and confined within territorial limits by princes of the Macedonian house. The Gauls were beaten in Europe by Antigonus Gonatas, "the second founder of Macedonia," and in Asia by Attalus of Pergamum. It is easy to see that the Galatians, to whom St. Paul writes his Epistle, had long been fitted into the fabric of hellenistic society.

318-
242
B.C.

Within the irregular frontier which they thus guarded the descendants of Alexander upheld, and often promoted vigorously, the interests of Greek civilization. The Ptolemies, who established themselves in Egypt, if they failed to hellenize the country or even seriously to mitigate the violent superstitions of its native inhabitants, developed in the royal quarter of Alexandria a centre of learning and taste which has exercised a critical influence on the progress of Europe.

Here it was that the masterpieces of Greek thought and poetry were collected and stored in a great library, copied by slaves, and annotated by scholars; here that the Old Testament was translated from Hebrew into Greek, the text of Homer fixed, and the love-story and the pastoral added to the categories of western literature. Here, finally, was born a mystical philosophy founded on the writings of Plato, which has exercised a profound influence on the theology of the Christian Church.

Nor was the vast Asiatic empire which Seleucus and his descendants ruled from the great pleasure city of Antioch to be regarded otherwise than as part of a world in which culture and Greek were synonymous terms. If there was no centre in this so-called Syrian kingdom so predominant in science and letters as Alexandria, there was no part of Egypt so thoroughly hellenized as Syria. The delicate lyrics of Meleager and the simple eloquence of the synoptic gospels attest the vitality of the Greek language in a land where the speech of the common folk was Aramaic.

The Macedonian sovereigns gave to the world a new principle of authority, which was one of the most important of the means of binding the Roman Empire together in the first two centuries of its existence. Alexander and his descendants claimed and received the worship due to divinity. Since they could find no place in the constitution of the Greek city state, they entered with general acclamation the Greek Pantheon. Where better than in worship could a force be found to bind together a heterogeneous kingdom and to give sanctity and legitimacy to a usurping rule? The idea of a universal state appealed to the philosophers, the worship of the monarch excited and satisfied the mob.

Another element important to the future governance of Europe may be traced back to Macedonian times. Statistics and bureaucracy were familiar in Egypt. In this archaic civilization exact knowledge, more particularly with regard to revenue, had long been regarded as a perquisite of government. Here was a regular and minute administration depending on an army of scribes and a mountain of documents. The lessons to be derived from such a spectacle were not lost upon the conquerors of Egypt. If the Romans took their literature from Greece, they borrowed the civil service of their Empire from the valley of the Nile.

It might perhaps have been expected that the Antigonids of Macedonia, whose state proved to be so useful a protection against the barbarians of the north, would have been able to count upon the support and sympathy of the Greek cities. This was not to be. There was no political sentiment deeper in the Greek mind than aversion from the monarchy, and Macedon was a monarchical state. Yet though the underlying sentiment of Greece, too often stimulated by Egyptian gold, was anti-Macedonian, the Greeks were at no time prepared with a united mind to resist their suzerain. Athens, among whose democratic leaders the spirit of Demosthenes burned brightly, gave up the struggle just when Achaia and Aetolia were prepared to take it up. The civic attachments, jealousies, and passions, which were at once the spiritual force and political weakness of Hellas, continued to the end. The honourable expedient of federation was tried by the Achaeans, and, in a less hopeful form, by the bandit villages of Aetolia. But federation in any full sense involved sacrifices which no member of a Greek League was prepared to make. The Achaean League, which fought Antigonus and his successor Demetrius II (251-229), was itself the object of a destructive attack by Cleomenes III of Sparta, and neither the brilliance of its leaders nor the value of the political principle upon which it was founded won for it the allegiance of a united country or brought to its counsels the wider vision. So Greece, fretting for home rule, but not sufficiently united within itself effectually to throw off the light yoke of Macedonia, waited for a deliverer, and hailed with expectation and delight the growing influence of Rome.

The peoples who described themselves as Hellenes were quick-witted, hardy, and frugal, and, as Herodotus observed, marked off from the barbarians around them as more intelligent and more emancipated from silly nonsense; but they lived in an insecure world. The barriers against want, plague, war, and revolution were frail and easily overthrown. At any moment plenty might give way to starvation, peace to war. Merely to keep alive required wit and energy. In such a society some virtues which we find easy were very difficult. The Greeks, though an extraordinary people, were not perfect. They exposed their new-born infants. Some of them tortured slaves. Many practised, without adverse comment, vices which excite our abhorrence. Their religion, which was un-fettered by a sacred book, was compatible with the belief in magic and with a luxuriant growth of primitive and violent superstitions. A strange callousness to suffering seems to have been accepted as a necessary, if lamentable, part of the human lot. Great as was their wealth in political ideas, they lacked the power of combination, so that the history of their cities is a long tale of faction, which was apt to degenerate into that "competition in perfecting the fine art of con-spiracies and atrocities" of which Thucydides writes in his account of the sedition in Corcyra. They loved freedom, but from time to time, as in the famous case of Socrates, took fright for the safety of their cherished conventions and persecuted an honest thinker to the death.

Yet almost everything which is to be valued in modern civilization is owing to the ancient culture of that part of the Mediterranean world which spoke and thought in Greek—our science and philosophy, our epic and drama and lyrical poetry, our standards in sculpture and architecture, our medicine and mathematics, our theory of humane education, the form of our Christian theology, and that ideal of the rule of law which distinguishes western from Chinese civilization. The Greeks loved beauty and pursued reason. They lived close to nature. Their taste in art was austere and simple. They thought greatly about great things. The profound question of the ultimate constitution of matter, which vexes the minds of modern physicists, was raised as early as the sixth century B.C. by Thales of Miletus (c. 585), who regarded the four elements as states of one substance. Our theory of numbers is to be traced to Pythagoras, our moral science to Socrates, our biology to Aristotle. The spirit of free enquiry, which we sometimes describe as rationalism because it leads men to search by the light of reason for natural causes rather than to acquiesce in popular superstitions, was distinctively Greek. The curiosity of the Greeks was lively and universal.

No problem suggested by the contemplation of the mysterious universe was too remote, too sacred, or too abstruse, to abash their refreshing audacity. Centuries before Copernicus discovered the heliocentric theory a Greek thinker had inferred that the earth was a globular body revolving round the sun, and had reached conclusions, differing little from the reality, as to its exact girth.

It has sometimes been contended that while the science and literature of the modern world derive from the Greeks, the religion of Europe is in its origin essentially Jewish. This states the contrast too strongly. Greece has exercised a profound influence on religion no less than on science and literature. We know little of the life of Jesus. His disciples were not chiefly concerned to record it. When at last, more than a generation after the Crucifixion, Mark took up his pen to write, it was not that he might trace the life course of the Master and Prophet, who had filled his soul with a new enchantment, but that he might reveal Him from the story of the Passion and the Resurrection, and from the recital of His many proofs of miraculous power, as a divine and predestined figure, as the Messiah foretold in Jewish Scriptures, who was come to judge the world and to call sinners to repentance. We cannot, therefore, follow the development of Christ's teaching in chronological order, or reconstruct His life for any given year, month, week, or day. Save for the detailed story of the Passion, we are much at a loss for chronological guidance.

Precious fragments of ethical teaching are contained in the Gospels, and in scattered sayings, some of which have only recently been recovered from a buried library in Egypt; but the spread of Christianity in the Apostolic age was not so much due to the conviction that only the Christian life was perfect as to the belief that in Christ the divine power was manifested. The disciples did not ask their hearers to imitate Christ, but to accept His Messianic authority. They represented Him as healing the sick, casting out devils, working miracles, and preaching repentance, believing in common with many of their generation that the end of the world was at hand and that Jesus was the anointed one, the Man from Heaven, who was sent to recall mankind to righteousness before the Last and terrible Day.

The early disciples did not, then, dream of a permanent

4
B.C.-?
A.D.
33 ?

universal Church. For them the end of the world was near
at hand, the number of the elect necessarily small. They were
content to preach the message of their Master in the little
Jewish synagogues of Palestine.

Paul of Tarsus, who brought Christianity to the Gentiles,
was a Jew of the Dispersion. He belonged to a society which
spoke and thought in Greek. The Epistles to the Colossians
and Ephesians clearly show that he was acquainted, as indeed
could hardly fail to be the case, with the allegories and
mysteries of the Greek religion and that he was influenced
by them; and since his message was addressed, not to the
Jews of Palestine, but to the Gentiles who derived their
culture from Greece, the fact that he was a member of two
worlds, of the narrow Jewish as of the wider Hellenic brotherhood, served to commend his message to the Greek-speaking
city populations of the west. If he never saw Jesus in the
flesh, this meant the less for him since in a sudden flash,
after persecuting Christians with Jewish fanaticism, he had
reached the conviction that the spirit of Christ had entered
into possession of his own soul. This burning faith gave wings
to his eloquence. Wherever he travelled in his missionary
journeys he made converts and established little communities
of Christian men and women bound together by ties of worship, self-surrender, and affection. Passing from Asia into
Europe, he preached at Salonika, at Athens, at Corinth, and
in Rome, everywhere creating intense spiritual excitement,
both by his free treatment of the Jewish Law and by the sharp
contrast he presented to the current beliefs of pagan society.
Under the powerful impulsion of his fervent genius a small
Judaic sect, spurned by the priests and scribes of Jerusalem,
became a religion so large and human in its appeal that no
European race, however rude and brutal, has altogether
escaped its spiritual influence.

By the second century the chief seaport towns of the Mediterranean basin, and many upland towns also, contained
little groups of Christians, who were now, and even as early
as A.D. 65, when Nero singled them out for persecution in
Rome, recognized to be distinct from the Jews, with whom
they were at first commonly confounded.

With the Jews, however, they had in common a prophetical
and exclusive religion. They lived a life apart, based on principles of belief and conduct, upon which they refused to

d.
A.D.
67?

compromise. "We," wrote Justin Martyr, "who formerly re- d.c.
joiced in uncleanness of life and now love only chastity; who A.D.
also used magic arts and have now dedicated ourselves to the 165
good and unbegotten God; we who loved resources of money
and possessions more than anything, and now actually share
what we have and give to everyone who is in need; we who
hated one another and killed one another and would not eat
with those of another race, and now since the manifestation
of Christ have a common life, and pray for our enemies
and try to win over those who hate us without just cause."
But while the Christians were thus sharply severed from the
pagan world it was a source of strength to them that
they never regarded their religion as a reversal of human
history, but rather as its divinely ordained fulfilment. Christian apologists were equally willing to find authority for their
religion in the Jewish Scriptures, in Greek philosophy, and
in the prophecies of the Sibyl. It was one of the secrets of
the success of the Christian Church that, while it offered
salvation to the outcasts of the world, it did not shrink from
challenging the wise upon their own ground, nor hesitate
to call to its aid the speculations of the ancients. Nothing
certain is known of the origin of the Fourth Gospel or of the
circumstances in which it was written. The better opinion
appears to be that it was composed by John the Presbyter in
Ephesus early in the second century. But whether this be so or
not, there is little doubt that the author of this wonderful
book, without which the substance of Christian belief would
be far other than it is, was influenced by St. Paul and perhaps
also by the doctrine of Philo of Alexandria, a learned Jew b 20
who evolved from the philosophy of Plato a warrant for the B.C. ?
truths of his inherited faith. Philo was the first of a long line
of theologians and philosophers who believed that Plato
was divinely inspired, and addressed themselves to the congenial task of harmonizing the exalted teaching of the Athenian thinker with the Jewish or Christian message. For
nearly thirteen centuries the theology of the Christian Church
in the west was moulded by the thought of Plato. There
followed an age of intellectual disturbance. The metaphysical
and physical writings of Aristotle were restored through the
Arabians of Spain. Christian theology was confronted by
pagan science, Christian idealism by a philosophy based on
experience. There was a moment of anxiety, of free thinking

on fundamentals, when even doctors in the Paris University dallied with Pantheism and challenged the orthodox view of the creation of the world. Albert the Great and Thomas Aquinas, two great Dominican doctors, restored the situation by harnessing the new Aristotle to the chariot of the Catholic Church. The teaching of Christ was a sublime and original contribution to the moral improvement of mankind. But it is doubtful whether the Christian religion would have made the conquest of Europe had it not been of all oriental religions the most Greek and the most nearly akin alike to the best thought of the Greek philosophers and to those popular notions of purgatory and purification, of eternal bliss and eternal torment, of a divine mediator between God and man, and of some sacramental ceremony whereby the sinner might be cleansed of his sin and assured of his salvation hereafter, which were already current among the Greeks, and the basis of solemn religious observance over that wide tract of the Mediterranean basin in which Greek civilization prevailed.

BOOKS WHICH MAY BE CONSULTED

Cambridge Ancient History, Vols. VI. and VII.

D. G. Hogarth: *Philip and Alexander of Macedon.* 1897

W. W. Tarn: *Hellenistic Civilisation.* 3rd Ed. 1952.

E. Bevan: *The House of Seleucus.* 1902.

Gilbert Murray: *Four Stages in Greek Religion.* 1912.

W. S. Ferguson: *Greek Imperialism.* 1913.

A. E. Taylor: *Plato.* 1929.

A. E. Taylor: *Aristotle.* 1919.

C. Bailey: *Epicurus.* 1926.

W. S. Ferguson: *Hellenistic Athens.* 1911.

B. Jowett: *The Dialogues of Plato.* 5 vols. 1892.

J. A. Smith and W. D. Ross: *The Works of Aristotle translated into English.* 1908-31.

E. Barker. *The Political Thought of Plato and Aristotle.* 1906.

G. Glotz: *Ancient Greece at Work.* 1926.

A. D. Nock: *Conversion, the Old and New in Religion from Alexander the Great to Augustine of Hippo.* 1933.

W. W. Tarn: *Alexander the Great.* 2 vols. 1950-1.

A. Andrewes: *Greek Tyrants.* 1957.

K. R. Popper: *The Open Society and its Enemies.* 2 vols. 1957.

C. M. Bowra: *The Greek Experience.* 1957.

CHAPTER VI

ROME AND CARTHAGE

Rise of the Roman Republic. Character of its legal and constitutional growth. The Roman conquest of Italy. Cisalpine Gaul and Carthage. Romans and Etruscans. The Punic Wars and conquest of Cisalpine Gaul. Hannibal. P. Cornelius Scipio. Destruction of Carthage. Roman prestige. Growing influence of Rome in the east. Subjection of Macedonia and Greece. Absence of a predetermined plan of conquest.

GREECE LOOKS to the rising, Italy to the setting sun. On the west of the Italian peninsula are wide and fertile plains, ample streams, and sheltered ports. On the east the stiff spine of the Apennines runs close to an inhospitable coast for the greater part of its course, so that, save for the two good Apulian harbours of Brindisi and Otranto, there is little shelter for the mariner against the storms of the Adriatic. Thus a sharp difference established itself between the centre and south of the Italian peninsula. While the southern littoral became the scene of a brilliant Greek culture, and of an immigration which has left a still discernible mark upon the character and appearance of the south Italian people, the Latin heart of the country was sheltered from these alien influences. Between Hellas and the yellow waters of the Tiber there was interposed, apart from the Adriatic, a barrier of rude and difficult hills.

Behind that barrier the Roman Republic, originally a small state, developed an aptitude for government and war which owed little to the practice and precepts of Greece. A supremacy, greater than that for which Athens, Sparta, and Thebes had in turn striven, came to the Romans as the prize of tenacious warfare and wise discipline, of moderation and good sense, of sound family life and strong legal instincts, and of a certain stern and simple gravity of bearing, which was rooted in the ancient pieties of the homestead and the soil. A sharp revolution, the expulsion of a dynasty of foreign kings in 510 B.C., made upon the Roman memory an impression which was all the deeper because revolutions were not in the Roman fashion. The constitution of the Republic developed slowly, insensibly adapting itself to successive changes of social pressure and the imperious calls of expanding duty.

A system of law gradually developed out of a mass of primitive custom and sacerdotal usage, growing with the enlarging life of the community, helping itself from the decrees of popular assemblies, the edicts of praetors, the opinions of jurisconsults, the systems of philosophers, until it became adequate to the practical needs of the civilized world. Inner social and political discords were solved by protest and compromise, by sagacious, face-saving expedients and constitutional laws rather than by bloodshed or the clash of arms. In the long struggle between the patricians and the plebeians (510-287 B.C.) the successive victories of the plebeian party appear to have left no mortal wound or implacable resentment. Compelled to surrender privilege after privilege the patricians never went into exile nor yielded their claim to render honourable service to the Roman state. Vital liberties were early conquered, as early as the Twelve Tables, but the Senate, though partially recruited from the Plebs, remained in essence and outlook a patrician body. Domestic tension was never so grave as to sap the patriotism of the Romans or to weaken them in face of a foreign foe.

450
B.C.

One by one all her Italian antagonists were made to acknowledge the power of Rome, the Latins of the plain, the mysterious non-Aryan Etruscans within whose kingdom Rome herself was once embodied, the sturdy Samnites of the hills, the formidable Gauls who had sacked Rome in 390, leaving behind them a memory of terror, and finally the Greek cities of the south aided by the phalanx and the elephants of Pyrrhus the Epirot. By the beginning of the third century B.C. Rome was supreme in Italy. But while other cities of the ancient world had conquered and lost, what Rome conquered in Italy she held and welded into a compact state. There was a method in her aggrandizement. She built military roads, such as only the Persian Empire had witnessed, and upon these planted at strategic points fortified cities garrisoned by Roman citizens. Other Italian communities she united by ties of exclusive alliance and carefully graded privilege to herself.

Yet she was not secure. The Gauls, established in the valley of the Po, occupied the largest and richest plain in the Mediterranean basin: but a peril even greater than the Gauls was the naval power of Carthage, disputing the fertile island of Sicily with the Greeks, contesting Sardinia, and exercising through her experienced fleets an unchallenged supremacy in the Tyrrhenian Sea.

With this great Semite power, then the commercial capital of the world, Rome waged a struggle lasting more than 100 years (264-146 B.C.), which changed the political complexion of Europe. At the end of this desperate contest, conducted on a scale far exceeding all previous experience, Carthage was obliterated from the scroll of history. Her navies were sunk, her empire reft from her, her proud and populous capital was levelled to the ground. Rome, entering the contest without a military navy or a yard of territory beyond the seas, had become by the logic of war a world power. The commerce of the Mediterranean was in her hands. Sicily, Sardinia, Spain, Africa had become Roman provinces. Every part of the widespread Carthaginian Empire in the west had passed into her control.

Character rather than culture supplied the key to the understanding of these victories. In point of artistic taste and achievement the Etruscans, who invaded Italy from Asia Minor at the end of the ninth century, and reached their highest point of power and prosperity three hundred years later, distanced their rude and virile conquerors. Central Italy is still full of the monuments of a gifted and luxurious aristocracy who spoke a non-Indo-European language, which we cannot read, who rode and drove, hunted and farmed, and bequeathed much secret lore concerning the arts of divination to the great Roman families, who were proud to reckon an Etruscan among their ancestors. If there was any Etruscan literature, it has perished long ago, but the Apollo of Veii and the Orator of Lake Trasimene are among the glories of European statuary. The Romans of the young Republic had nothing which could compare with these masterpieces in terra-cotta, or with the ivories and jewelry of this accomplished people who, while borrowing freely from the art of Assyria, Egypt, and Greece, had nevertheless something distinctive of their own to contribute. It was not then a barbaric Italy which was subdued by the Romans, but as to a third of its area an Italy imbued with the arts and crafts of Hellas and the east. But while Rome was united and tenacious, the Etruscans suffered from a fatal lack of combination. The Tarquins were expelled from the Seven Hills on the Tiber (510 B.C.). The Etruscan navy went down before the Greeks at Cumae (476). It was permitted that Veii, a principal shrine of Etruscan statuary, should sustain unfriended a war of eighty years against her inveterate enemy. Yet, if Etruria disappeared as an empire, the Tuscans survived as a race, substantially identical with itself through millennia, and now and again, as in the thirteenth and fifteenth centuries, revealing a genius for beauty which touches the summit of human excellence.

The First Punic War ended after twenty-three years of intermittent and disjointed struggle with a peace which transferred the island granary of Sicily from Carthage to Rome. That the contest lasted so long and was productive of no more decisive result may be attributed, partly to the conditions under which the war was waged, and also to a certain indistinctness of aim in the minds of each of the combatants. In days when a warship must be propelled by oars, when only in the summer months could it safely put to sea, and when, in the absence of long-range weapons, the ship which had not been grappled and boarded might easily escape unharmed, swift decisions were not difficult to avoid. Rome had to learn the lessons of salt water; Carthage, experienced at sea, but hampered at home, found difficulty in sparing mercenary troops sufficient for the needs of the Sicilian campaign. Neither party was as yet fully resolved upon a war of destruction. The Romans invaded Africa, but left the army of Regulus without support, and made no attempt to retrieve his defeat. Nor did the Carthaginians make use of their sea power to molest the coasts of Italy. In the end the Romans won, because, having learnt from their adversary a disagreeable and unfamiliar technique, they were able by a supreme effort of private patriotism to build a fleet capable of victory at a moment when Carthage was weary of the contest.

There followed an interval of twenty-three years which has left its mark upon the history of Europe. In that interval, Rome seized Sardinia, curbed the Illyrian pirates in the Adriatic, effecting in that process, through the conquest of Corcyra, her first lodgment on Grecian soil, and, greatest and

264-
241
B.C.

241-
218
B.C.

most important achievement of all, conquered Cisalpine Gaul and extended her frontiers to the Alps. Not less memorable is the work of Carthage during the same period. Apart from the suppression of a serious revolt in Africa it consisted in the establishment of a new empire in Spain.

It is then to Carthage that Spain owes its introduction into the political history of Europe. In Spain, with its wealthy mines and factories, its fertile littoral, its numerous population of hardy and warlike tribes distributed in the high central plateau, where the wind is searching and the sun scorches, and the breed of man is tough and wiry, a Carthaginian of genius descried a new source of power for his state and a new base of operations against Rome. Hamilcar Barca, a soldier well proved in the Sicilian War, had determined to dedicate the remainder of his days to a war of vengeance. The idol of the Carthaginian democracy, he obtained a free hand in the Iberian peninsula, and there, in eight years of crowded and brilliant energy, built up a state, a treasury, and an army. A son-in-law and a son continued and consolidated his work. The son was Hannibal. To him, inheriting power in 221 B.C., Hamilcar had bequeathed his gifts, his energies, and his revenge.

Among the captains of the ancient world Hannibal alone in point of genius ranks with Alexander the Great. If he lacked the engaging radiance of the Macedonian, he was his superior in sobriety and concentration of purpose. His daring was extreme, his resource infinite, and his gifts of personal magnetism were such as in passages of extreme hardship and peril evoke and sustain the devotion of an army. He was quick to discern and to profit by the weakness of an adversary. Nothing was too great or too small for his attention.

His plan was simple, audacious, and, had all gone well, of deadly efficiency. It was to pick a quarrel with Rome, which he did by attacking Saguntum, a Spanish town under Roman patronage, and then to march with his African and Spanish levies overland to Italy, and to strike the Republic at the heart. He was not, of course, so foolish as to suppose that he could accomplish his purpose unaided. He counted upon the Cisalpine Gauls, still writhing under their recent defeat, on the cities of Italy presumed to be resentful of Roman dominion, on Philip of Macedon, young, ambitious, headstrong, who might be lured to emulate the career of Pyrrhus under happier circumstances, and to win from the Romans the control of the south.

Despite an amazing march, followed by three brilliant and annihilating victories, the plan failed. There was no general rising of the Gauls, no revolt in central Italy, no invasion from Macedonia, no abatement in the resolution of the Roman Senate never to treat with an enemy standing on Italian soil, nor was there from Carthage that measure of support which Hannibal had a right to expect. Yet for years he held the field with his small army of 30,000 in a populous enemy country and against a foe who had the call on forces more than thirty-three times as numerous as his own.

In the ruses and stratagems of war, in the handling of cavalry as well as in the moral gift of leadership which inspires the devoted loyalty of troops, Hannibal was supreme. A magical aura seemed to surround him. Though he had no siege train, and could never have taken Rome by force, he created in his adversaries a paralysing sense of their inferiority. Again and again, after Lake Trasimene, after Cannae, and when it was known that his brother Hasdrubal had crossed the Alps with Spanish reinforcements, a deadly anxiety clutched at the heart of Rome. But Hasdrubal was beaten at the Metaurus. In truth, ever since Fabius had discerned that the best way of dealing with Hannibal was to avoid engaging him, a Roman victory was only a matter of time.

What finally brought the war to a conclusion was the discovery by Rome of a gifted commander. While Hannibal was overrunning Italy, P. Cornelius Scipio was engaged in evicting the Carthaginians from Spain. The lustre of this considerable achievement, which has fixed the mould of Spanish civilization, gave to Scipio a unique place in the confidence of the Roman people. He was permitted to conduct an expedition to Africa the surest way of relieving the Italian peninsula of the incubus of a Punic army; in 204 B.C. he crossed the sea, and two years later, meeting Hannibal on the field of Zama, routed his elephants, his foot, and his horse, and secured a peace (201) which stripped Carthage of her overseas possessions and left her the tributary vassal of Rome.

Still, while Carthage remained, a fortified city on the gulf of Tunis with a population of some 700,000 inhabitants, rich, enterprising, industrious, resilient, Rome was uneasy.

Fear and jealousy possessed her of a rival whose deadly fault was a too swift recovery from defeat. "Carthage must be destroyed," she began to repeat to herself. The incantation worked, pretexts were found, the apologies and excuses of compliant Semites were brushed aside. Carthage, it was urged, had attacked Massanissa, the Numidian ally of Rome. So fifty-two years after the field of Zama another Roman expedition crossed to Africa. This time there was to be no weakness. After a long and terrible siege the city of Carthage was stormed and burned to the ground, and Africa incorporated as a province in the dominions of Rome.

The surprising fortunes of the Roman Republic had long been followed with anxiety and wonder by the intelligent peoples of the east. An honourable pedigree was invented for this rude community of formidable supermen, and the Romans learned that they were descended through Aeneas from King Priam of Troy, and linked to the most splendid legends of Hellenic antiquity. As the Punic Wars proceeded, the great qualities of the Roman character, never more brilliantly exhibited than in the dark hours of defeat, impressed themselves with increasing force upon the Greek-speaking world. Was it not to Rome, a Republic, and the inveterate foe of monarchy, that the city states of Greece and Asia Minor might look for the protection of their liberties and the preservation of their alliance, to Rome, which had chastised the Gauls and curbed the Illyrian pirates and was now, after desperate vicissitudes, vanquishing the stubborn oligarchy of Carthage? Such, at least, was the view of Polybius the Arcadian, whose wise history is the capital authority for these critical times, when Rome was bringing east and west into the orbit of her controlling power.

It will readily be imagined that, amid the strain and exhaustion of the Carthaginian struggle, Rome was in no mood to embark upon a course of aggression in the east. Her policy was to foster commercial relations with Egypt, and to grasp the hand of friendship, where it was freely offered, as by the wealthy house of Pergamum, the powerful island state of Rhodes, and the university city of Athens, and by such connections to paralyse the activities of any power who might be tempted to intrude on the western theatre of war.

This policy was successful. Neither Antiochus III of Syria nor Philip V of Macedon was in a position to send a ship or a man to Italy. Each of these eastern friends of Carthage, operating without combination, was defeated in detail and in his own territory, Antiochus in the great slaughter of Magnesia (190 B.C.), Philip in the soldiers' battle at Cynoscephalae. The cumbrous phalanx of spearmen, which had helped Alexander to conquer his vast empire of the east, had shown itself unequal to the Roman legion and the Spanish sabre. Antiochus was compelled to withdraw behind the Taurus, and the hegemony of Asia Minor henceforth devolved upon Rome.

Still the Greeks were unhappy. Home rule they had asked for, and home rule they had received. The Macedonians had been expelled from the key fortresses of Greece, the Romans had been acclaimed as liberators; but the harmony and union of Hellas were no further advanced. Roman commissioners were called in to arbitrate Greek quarrels, making enemies as well as friends with every award, and if it be true that unscrupulous Romans fomented Greek discords, it is no less certain that disaffected Greeks intrigued secretly with Perseus, King of Macedonia, as they found him steadily drifting into enmity with Rome.

So the final destruction of Macedonian power after the battle of Pydna in 168 B.C. was followed by the deportation to Italy of the leading Greek sympathizers with the vanquished cause. L. Aemilius Paulus was one of the best of Romans, a soldier, a statesman, a friend of good letters, a character raised above pecuniary temptation; but the vengeance which he exacted after his crowning victory at Pydna lacked nothing in completeness. Every Macedonian notable from the king downwards was deported to Italy. A great part of the population was enslaved, the country broken into four fragments, and reduced to such a state of helpless misery that its subsequent conversion into a Roman province was by comparison a blessing.

But the stern lesson was lost on Greece. An insurrection broke out, cruelly conducted, cruelly suppressed; and when the last desperate rally of the Achaean League had been crushed by L. Mummius on the field of Corinth (146 B.C.), and the men of Corinth had been slain and the women and children sold into slavery, and the city had been razed to the ground, Greece at last had a rest of fifty years under her Roman master. Long before this, war, infanticide and malaria had depleted her population and carried off the descen ants of the men who had given her an immorta name and that burning love of liberty which had brought her to her doom.

The subjection during the space of a single lifetime of the whole inhabited world to the rule of Rome struck contemporaries as being, which indeed it was, the crowning miracle of history. Yet, while the political power of the Roman Republic was felt from Cadiz to the Euphrates, the limits of its deeper influence were more strictly drawn. Upon Sicily and Spain the image of Rome was ineffaceably stamped; but east of the Adriatic the peoples of the Mediterranean remained, as they were before, a world apart, half Greek, half oriental, influencing their conquerors deeply by their refined and more exquisite culture, but receiving nothing in return save a measure of order, discipline, and protection, and not until the mediaeval crusades seriously invaded by the Latin culture of the west.

It would appear that Rome was drawn into empire not indeed in a fit of absentmindedness, but half reluctantly and of no set plan. The successive stages of her conquest of Italy were forced upon her because, as England afterwards experienced in India, an orderly power ringed round by turbulence always finds itself compelled to establish peace and security upon its frontiers. The struggle with Carthage indeed began with a moment of popular war fever, but that was short-lived. Rome went to Spain to cut off Hannibal, to Gaul much later that she might keep open her communications with Spain. There is no substance in the view that commercial and financial interests pushed Rome into conquest and annexation, except possibly in the cases of the destruction of Carthage and Corinth, until the first century B.C., when Pompey's annexation of Syria was probably due to the influence of the *equites*, the capitalistic class. More particularly did Rome show great reluctance to annex the Hellenistic kingdoms. She broke their power, practically destroyed their capacity to rule the east, and then shirked the task of administration herself. It is a remarkable fact that she had been the dominating power in the eastern Mediterranean for a hundred and fifty years before she finally, after suffering immense inconvenience from chaos and piracy, took over the direct rule of the whole area.

BOOKS WHICH MAY BE CONSULTED

T. Mommsen: *History of Rome.* Tr. W. P. Dickson. 5 vols. 1894.

H. F. Pelham: *History of Rome. Outlines of Roman History.* 4th Ed. 1905.

D. Randall McIver: *The Etruscans.* 1927.

G. Dennis: *Cities and Cemeteries of Etruria.* 1878.

H. Stuart Jones: *A Companion to Roman History.* 1912.

W. E. Heitland: *Short History of the Roman Republic.* 1911.

L. P. Homo: *L'Italie Primitive et les Débuts de l'Impérialisme Romain.* 1925.

Cambridge Ancient History, Vol. VIII.

Tenney Frank: *An Economic History of Rome till the End of the Republic.* 1927.

M. Cary: *A History of Rome down to the reign of Constantine.* 2nd Ed. 1957.

CHAPTER VII

REPUBLIC AND EMPIRE

The Roman Senate. Flaws in the Republican constitution. Ill effects of rapid conquest. Maladministration in the provinces. The last century of the Republic. The Gracchi. Idea of Italian freedom. Marius and Sulla. The challenge of Mithradates. Sulla's victories in the east and at home. His proscriptions. The unsolved military and police problems of the later Republic. Pompey. His compact with Caesar and Crassus. Julius Caesar. Early reputation and campaigns in Gaul. Rift with Pompey. Victories and death. The spirit of his rule. Its adaptation to the needs of the time.

THE FORM of government under which the Romans conquered Italy and weathered the storms of the Punic Wars was, like many constitutions which are the growth of time, one thing in theory and another in practice. In theory sovereignty rested with the assemblies of the Roman people organized in their centuries or their tribes. In practice government was carried on by the Senate, an aristocracy of birth and service, recruited according to established rules from men who had held offices of state or had distinguished themselves in war. It is to this remarkable assembly of patriotic and disciplined citizens that we must principally ascribe the successes of republican Rome. Armies might suffer defeat, fleets might be lost at sea, but the Senate, drawn for the most part from the members of patrician or ennobled families, grave, proud, resolute, accustomed to consider dishonour more terrible than death, never flinched in the hour of danger and created in the Roman colonies and in many of the allied cities of Italy a spirit as courageous and patriotic as their own.

Yet even at this period, when the republican government was working at its best, it was subject to many drawbacks. Of these the gravest was the organization of the executive power, which was neither concentrated in the hands of a single person, nor divided between a soldier and "civilian," nor granted for a term of years. By a singular arrangement, prompted by the strong and continuing fear of monarchy which had existed in Rome ever since the expulsion of its foreign kings, the supreme authority both in peace and war was confided to two annual officers known as consuls, each possessed of plenary power, and each entitled to veto the other's decisions. The evils of such a system, patent at all times, were specially manifest in times of war. No state is so rich in military talent as to be able to furnish an annual supply of excellent generals. The Romans of the third century before Christ, despite their martial habits, were no exception to this rule, and save on those occasions which justified the appointment of a dictator, submitted to a system under which good generals were retired too soon and bad generals appointed too often.

Another defect almost equally serious was the absence of any effective machinery for financial administration and control. There was no Board of Finance. The *quaestors*, to whom the management of the public Treasury was confided, so far from being the most experienced, were the least experienced members of the official hierarchy. Living on war plunder, the state could afford to dispense with direct taxation and to farm out its public lands to companies of tax farmers.

Upon a state so governed the burden of an empire descended

with an almost unbearable shock. The vast plunder of Africa and Asia, of Macedonia and Greece, produced upon the Roman character the evil effects which suddenly acquired wealth always exerts upon minds unprepared to receive it. The old virtues of rustic simplicity and patriarchal discipline, of honest toil and pecuniary integrity, gave way before the overwhelming temptations of the new luxury. The flower of the Italian yeomanry had been used up in the armies, slaves were abundant, for every Roman victory brought a fresh consignment of slaves to the Roman market, and slavery, here as elsewhere, produced its demoralizing results. In the countryside great ranches tilled by gangs of slaves began to supersede the small holdings which before the terrible devastations of the Hanniballic wars had been the pride and mainstay of Italy. In Rome itself a vast slave population, ministering to the necessities and enjoyments of the free, constituted an invitation to idleness, frivolity, and vice. Moreover, as Rome became the capital and chief money-making centre of the world, it acted as a magnet upon the fortune hunters and adventurers of the Levant. To the influences of Greece, as to those of a civilization admittedly superior, the Romans of this and the succeeding centuries were more particularly open, but it was not the highest part of the Greek message which made the widest appeal in Italy, but rather the superficial cleverness, the attractive and effeminate vices, and the supple adaptability of conscience for which the average Greek of the period was then noted.

With these demoralizing influences abroad it is little to be wondered at that the first experiment of republican government overseas was attended by calamitous abuses. It was the custom of the Senate, on the establishment of a Roman province, to lay down in a written document known as the *Lex Provinciae* the principles in accordance with which the province was to be administered. In general, however, there was the sharpest opposition between the Provincial Law, which was often enlightened and humane, and the administration, which was for the most part characterized by cruel and shameful extortions. In a very short space of time the proconsuls of the Republic bled the provinces white. They ruined Sicily and the province of Asia and carried their depredations through every part of Greece. Neither the law courts nor the Senate were strong enough to check the evil. A fierce hatred of the Italian spread round the Mediterranean basin and threatened the new foundations of his rule.

To the disaffection bred of extortion and misgovernment abroad there was added a long catalogue of formidable evils threatening to shatter the fabric of empire which had been built up under senatorial rule: slave revolts in Sicily and Italy, a fierce fight in Rome between the popular and senatorial party which widened out into a bitter and destructive civil war, a dangerous rebellion of the Italian allies, and, reacting fiercely on domestic politics, the pressure of external enemies on every frontier. The last century of the Roman Republic is an age of violent internal convulsions associated with and exasperated by foreign wars. A succession of great captains, a gift of fortune upon which no community has a right to reckon, saved the state again and again, and maintained and greatly extended the boundaries of Roman rule. Gaius Marius ended the Jugurthine war, and by his two great victories over the Teutons and Cimbri saved northern Italy from barbaric invasions for five hundred years. L. Cornelius Sulla reconquered Greece from Mithradates, King of Pontus, and compelled him to restore his Asiatic conquests. The names of Lucullus and of Pompey are associated with a series of brilliant Asiatic campaigns, which left Rome mistress of Syria and Asia Minor, and with no serious enemy in the east save the distant monarchy of Parthia. Gaul was conquered, Britain was invaded by Julius Caesar, yet the age which witnessed these dazzling feats of arms was one of the most unhappy and uncomfortable in Roman history. It was marked, indeed, by a great advance in wealth and luxury, by the growth of huge private fortunes, and by a concern for art, letters, and philosophy which has left an enduring mark upon civilization. It is the age of Lucretius, of Catullus, and of Cicero. Yet the contemporaries of these three fine human spirits had witnessed the clash of contending armies in the streets of Rome, had heard the cries of Sulla's victims as they were beheaded in their thousands in the Campus Martius, and in their walks among the glistening marbles of the sacred city were compelled to endure the grisly spectacle of severed heads, a ferocious but not unusual symptom of a party victory in the last century of the Republic. From these miseries bred of civil discord and external peril Italy was eventually delivered by the foundation of the Empire and by the Augustan Peace.

The first blows in the long domestic struggle were struck by two brothers, well born, for they were the grandsons of Scipio the elder, and well-to-do, but each touched by the spirit of reform and fated to atone for his dreams and ambitions by a violent end.

d. 133
B.C. Tiberius Gracchus was killed in a vulgar riot by his political enemies of the senatorial party. Ten years later his younger brother Gaius, defeated, disillusioned, and desperate, fell in the same cause. The programme of Tiberius was to restore the decaying agriculture of central Italy by planting out settlers upon the public lands. His object was admirable, but since the proposals for carrying it out involved a widespread disturbance of vested interests, they were hotly resisted by the Senate. It was now that the vehement Tiberius developed a procedure, archaic in form but revolutionary in substance, which threatened to undermine the authority of the Senate and to give a new complexion to the Roman constitution.

In the course of the struggles between the patricians and plebeians during the fourth century there had been developed, over and above the assembly of the whole people voting by tribes (*Comitia Tributa*) and of the more plutocratically organized assembly of the whole people voting by centuries (*Comitia Centuriata*), which had the right of appointing the chief magistrates, of making the laws, and of deciding on the questions of war and peace, another more democratic legislative body, the *concilium plebis*, which was served by officers known as tribunes of the people. Each of these assemblies was sovereign, but each was hampered by archaic restrictions, meeting only when convened by a magistrate, opining only upon questions which the convening magistrate had laid before them, and with characteristic Roman conservatism giving their votes standing and in groups (centuries or tribes) like the primitive armed levies of the Roman people. It was this cumbrous machinery which first Tiberius and then Gaius set in motion against the Senate. Each was a tribune, and saw that in the exercise of the tribunician power he could submit measures to the *concilium plebis* without reference to the Senate and pass them into law in spite of its resistance. Neither was a stickler for constitutional forms. When the constitution served their purpose it was obeyed; when it presented obstacles it was strained or broken.

Men once embarked on the ocean of political strife are apt to be carried further than they originally intended. In the hands of the younger Gracchus the programme of the popular party went far beyond the agrarian policy which first brought Tiberius into the arena against the Senate. Excellent schemes for colonization overseas were accompanied by plans in which the alloy of political profit was copiously blended with the gold of philanthropy. To conciliate the world of commerce and finance, and at the same time to abase the Senate, the equestrian order were put in charge of the Law Courts and accorded the lucrative privilege of farming the taxes and destroying the prosperity of the province of Asia. The favour of the Italian cities enjoying Latin rights was sought by the offer of the Roman franchise, that of the Roman proletariat by one of those fatal bribes so easy to offer and so difficult to withdraw, a dole of Sicilian corn from the granaries of the state.

Yet despite his skilfully combined programme, his popular gifts, and his ardent industry, the position of Gaius Gracchus was essentially insecure. His activities had been purely civilian. He had no army at his back. He was a tribune of the people, dependent for his office, his authority, and his life on the popular vote. He was elected twice. On the third occasion the *Comitia* turned against him. A private citizen who had made so many enemies as he could hardly hope to survive in that climate of furious hatred when the luck turned.

The idea of the Italian franchise had a great future. Though the Italian allies could seldom expect to vote in Roman assemblies, they learned from the lips of Roman orators to resent their inferior status, and to claim equality with Roman citizens. For a time progress was blocked. The enfranchisement of the despised Italian was opposed by all that was selfish and narrow in the Senate and people of Rome. At last the Italian allies rose in revolt, chose a capital, sketched out a constitution, and involved Rome in a serious war; and then only did the Senate concede a privilege which, once asked, should never have been denied. In the history of political enfranchisement one step leads to another. Out of the policy originally promulgated by the Gracchi there sprang

91
B.C.

a long series of enfranchising and equalizing measures culminating in the great edict of Caracalla (A.D. 212), which conferred Roman citizenship on all freeborn members of the Roman Empire. Yet though in theory political equality was conceded first to Italy and then to the whole Empire, no organ was created through which the provinces could make an effective use of their rights. The idea of representative government was foreign to antiquity. The first parliament of united Italy met in 1870.

With this one exception of the Italian franchise nothing so far had been done to increase the stability of republican government. A new peril was, in fact, already disclosed, the full bearing of which neither faction could justly measure. The rôle of popular hero, which had been played by the civilian Gaius, had now fallen to a soldier, who had recruited a volunteer army from the lowest class of the community and was universally and rightly regarded as the saviour of his country. Gaius Marius, the hero of the Jugurthine and Cimbrian Wars, the rude soldier from Arpinum, who had been selected to defend Italy from the gravest peril by which it had yet been assailed, and after five years of vigilant soldiering had wiped out the German victories at Arausio on the fields of Aquae Sextiae (102) and Vercellae (101), had the Roman state in the hollow of his hand.

106-110 B.C.

In the plenitude of their thankfulness for these two crowning triumphs there was no political boon which Rome would have denied him. But in the field of home politics Marius was a child, with little in his head save the abasement of the Senate through the demagogic activities of his turbulent friends, so that although he was seven times elected consul, and may thus be regarded as a forerunner of the Emperors, he left no mark on the structure of Roman government. The task which he might have accomplished devolved upon his nephew Caius Julius Caesar.

By a curious accident of history the next great Roman general who might have upset the Republic was a conservative only anxious to preserve it. L. Cornelius Sulla had begun his military career as the lieutenant of Marius in Africa. The two men were opposed to one another in almost every point of circumstance and temper. Marius was a plebeian and a savage, Sulla an aristocrat of fine culture and licentious manners. The art of politics as understood by Marius was a

107 B.C.

course of violent demagogy directed to no coherent end.
Sulla cherished a distinct scheme, articulated in every part,
for the restoration of the Senate to the position of ascendancy
which it had enjoyed during the Punic Wars. Each was reckless of bloodshed; but whereas the later cruelties of Marius
were tinged with insanity, Sulla's butchery was done upon a
system. A special cause of rancour envenomed the relations
of the two soldiers thus differently disposed, for Sulla
had procured the betrayal of Jugurtha, which had given
Marius his reputation, and lost no occasion to advertise the
fact.

Fourteen years after Marius had won his last great victory in
the Cimbrian War, Rome was called upon to face a serious
danger in the east. Mithradates Eupator, the King of Pontus,
was an oriental of remarkable force and large ambitions who
viewed himself as the leader and patron of an Hellenic
world burning to free itself from Roman shackles. The
territory of this Philhellenic barbarian was attacked by
Nicomedes of Bithynia, a client of Rome, and, since satisfaction was refused him, Mithradates declared war upon the
Roman Republic. In the challenge of this fiery potentate the
Greek cities of the Levant saw an opportunity of wreaking
vengeance on the Italians, by whom they had been merci-
lessly pillaged and oppressed. There was a great massacre
in which it is said that a hundred thousand Latin residents in
Asia, in Delos, and on the mainland, perished at the hands
of outraged or envious Greeks. Asia Minor was won for
the King. His armies, generalled by Greeks, occupied Athens
and Boeotia. Was the Empire of Alexander the Great to live
again and to be ruled from Sinope by an eastern tyrant served
by eunuchs and soothed by a harem?

The Roman Senate commissioned Sulla to take up the
eastern command, and no better choice could have been
made. Sulla was in the prime of life. His military service had
been varied and distinguished. As Propraetor in Cilicia he
had fought and bargained with orientals. He was the only
Roman officer of high mark who had a first-hand knowledge
of Asia. But the idea of so great a prize going to a political
opponent stirred the fury of the Roman democrats. The
tribune Sulpicius Rufus introduced a decree depriving Sulla
of his command and appointing Marius, now grown old 88
and impotent, in his place. That was the signal for civil war. B.C.

At the head of 30,000 men, Sulla marched to Rome, dispersed the disorderly horde of the Marians, and, having executed many prominent democrats and hunted Marius out of Italy, crossed the sea with five legions to deal with Mithradates.

A lurid light was then thrown upon the extent to which party passion had corrupted the political life of Rome. Sulla's campaign was brilliant. He stormed Athens and the Piraeus, crushed, with infinitesimal loss to himself, the swollen oriental armies of Mithradates in two great battles, and after **84 B.C.** four years of successful fighting, forced his adversary to a humiliating peace. Yet in all these operations he was acting, not only without the support, but with the active opposition of the government of Rome. In his absence the *populares* had seized the helm; and while Sulla was winning victories in the east, his friends at home were exposed to the remorseless rage of Marius and his associates.

Then Sulla returned to Italy, rich with spoils and indemnities, and with a well-paid, seasoned army at his heels to deal with his enemies. Mingling force with blandishments, defeating one army, seducing another, he marched to Rome, while two able young members of his party, Gnaeus Pompeius and Marcus Crassus, emerging from their hiding places, **82 B.C.** created diversions in his favour. Yet even the possession of Rome did not end the war. The democrats had appealed to the Samnites for help, and, while Sulla was engaged in Etruria, an army inspired by the fierce old Samnite spirit marched against Rome, Caius Pontius of Telesia, the national leader of these mountain levies, proclaiming that the tyrant city must be destroyed to her foundations and that the Roman wolves, the bane of Italian liberty, would never be got rid of until their land was laid waste. Sulla hurried back, and, just in time, threw his weary legions against the enemy at the Colline Gate. The fight was long and hard; but in the end the veterans of the east, aided by the levies of Crassus, won a decisive victory.

The proscriptions of the victor, undertaken on a scale and with a fierceness beside which the cruelties of the Marians seemed mild, inflicted an irreparable harm on the senatorial cause. Italy could not be made safe for the Senate either on these or on any other terms. It was easy for Sulla to draw up a new constitution, depriving the assemblies of their initiative, the tribunate of its importance, the equestrian order of their new judicial privileges, and precluding the continuous exercise of the higher offices of the state in order that the Senate might shine with an unchallenged lustre. What neither Sulla nor anyone else could do was to fight against the stars in their courses. In quiet times an oligarchical assembly, served by annual magistrates, might survive the jealousy of the populace and the envy of the world of business and finance. An ambitious soldier or a great emergency were lethal. Sulla died in 78 B.C. Eight years later Pompey and Crassus, each in command of a victorious army, undid his work.

Swiftly, but imperceptibly, the world was slipping into a new phase of history in which the old forms and methods of the Roman Republic were no longer effective. In the days before Marius a Roman army was composed of peasant proprietors enlisted from their farms for a summer campaign and afterwards, when the fighting was over, well content to return to the pleasant livelihood which awaited them at home. Levies so composed and so supported constituted no danger to the republican state, But as the march of Roman conquest advanced and the military problems confronting the Republic increased in scale, this old-fashioned domestic way of levying war no longer sufficed. The military reforms of Marius marked a revolution. The Roman army became in practice a long-service force of professional soldiers. A vast change was imposed by the stern pressure of circumstance, the implications of which, since they were costly and unpleasant, were, as often happens when novelty is disagreeable, never boldly faced. The Senate failed to realize that, unless the Republic controlled the professional armies by making itself responsible for their pay and pensions, the professional armies would master the Republic. It failed to see that, while an army recruited in the old short-service way from the farms was already provided for, a professional army recruited in the new long-service way was not. It refused to listen to the demands which came from the commanders that the soldiers under their command should receive the guerdon of their services. And since it declined to work out a system of military pensions, it taught the armies to look, not to the state, but to the military chiefs who had promised rewards to the troops under their command, and were alone in a mood and a position to secure them.

One reason, therefore, why the Republic gave way to the Empire was that it provided no solution of the military problem created by the span of its conquests.

Another was its incapacity to police the streets of Rome. The idea of a professional police force, which is at once the friend of the people and the impartial protector of law and order, was alien to the conceptions both of the ancient and of the mediaeval world. Rome knew nothing of the kind. At no time, however, was the capacity of the government to keep order in the streets at a lower point of efficiency than during the period which is described in the letters of Cicero. The republican government in its last days was not only unable to control the commanders of the legions, it was not strong enough to put down the armed gangs of the political factions who were struggling for power in the streets of the capital itself.

Pompey was not one of those men who swing instinctively with the spirit of the masses, or apprehend the approach of great revolutions. By early association he was a member of the *optimate*, or aristocratic, party, but he had affiliations with the democrats, and was fitted by a certain moderation of temper and haziness of view to occupy an arbitral position between the two rival factions. He had no taste for party management, no base absorption in money getting, none of the eloquence or literary culture which gave to Cicero his unique position in the Senate and the Forum. But he was a soldier, a gentleman, and a patriot, well content to be the servant of the Republic on condition that no rival aspired to be its master.

The great opportunity which was given to this able but somewhat enigmatic figure came to him in 67 B.C. He was then called upon by popular acclaim to put down the Cilician pirates, whose depredations had even caused a famine in Rome. The task, estimated to last three years, was accomplished brilliantly and once for all in seven months, but on its heels came a wider and more important commission. The crushing victories of Sulla had failed to satisfy Mithradates of his inferiority. The irrepressible monarch was still in the field, and still capable, despite many reverses, of inflicting upon a Roman army the ignominy of a defeat. Pompey was commissioned to retrieve the situation, and endowed under the Manilian law with the largest powers.

The confidence of the Roman people was not misplaced. The eagles were carried to the Caspian and the Euphrates, Mithradates was driven into the Crimea. Cilicia, Syria, and Bithynia Pontus were annexed to the Republic. In a short five years Pompey had made Rome mistress of hither Asia, leaving behind him the name, not only of a successful general, but of a founder of cities, a friend of civilization, a wise and humane administrator. His work was not seriously disturbed till the coming of Islam.

Fresh from this resplendent achievement, he asked the Senate to confirm his Asian treaties and to make a grant of land to his veterans. His requests were refused. Though he had disbanded his armies, he was still suspect, confronted by that strong spirit of republican puritanism which has been a force in European politics from Cato to Robespierre, and by the vanity of politicians, unable to measure the size of men and events. But what the Senate refused, the democratic leaders were prepared, upon terms, to grant. He entered (60 B.C.) into a compact with Crassus, the millionaire manager of the democratic party, and with Caesar, his brilliant lieutenant. The consideration for Caesar was a year of the consulate to be followed by five years of the Gallic and Illyrian commands.

No one would have predicted that the youngest member of this triumvirate would outrange Pompey in military renown and change the face of Europe. Save for a year's soldiering in Spain, when he was already past forty, Caesar had no experience in the handling of troops. As an "intellectual" trained under the best Greek masters, as an eloquent advocate in the forum, and a skilful manager of democratic intrigues, he was well known in the capital. His gallantries, his lavish spectacles and entertainments, his debts, were famous, and since he was the nephew of Marius and son-in-law of Cinna, rumour was prompt to associate him with every dark plot to upset the Republic.

Something of the true scale of the man appeared during his year of consulship. He passed a decree to put down extortion, swept aside constitutional fetters, and showed that he meant to have his way in Rome: but it was eight wonderful campaigns in Gaul which revealed for the first time his full range as a 58-51 soldier and a statesman. Everything he set out to accomplish B.C. was secured. The frontiers of Rome were extended to the ocean and the Rhine, and, so defined, the Gaul of Caesar remains graven this day on the heart of France.

It is no deduction from his renown that the Celtic tribes of Gaul were ill armed, ill disciplined, and honeycombed with rivalries. Caesar knew how to avail himself of every weakness. He could cajole as well as threaten, conciliate as well as coerce. In the early stages of his Gallic war he was helped by the Aedui and the Remi. Later, when his old allies had turned against him, the Gallic cavalry, in the critical fight before Alesia, was routed by a body of German horsemen, whom, with a prompt sense of the military value of these giants of the north, Caesar had enlisted in the Roman army. It was perhaps also a fortunate incident that he first appeared rather as the defender than as the assailant of the Celtic tribes of Gaul, repelling a great popular migration from Helvetia, and then a formidable intrusion from the German forests. But no one can read the sober narrative in which Caesar himself describes his Gallic campaigns without realizing the breadth and audacity of his conceptions, his personal courage, his wonderful combination of patience and velocity, and the fidelity and skill with which he was served. At every extremity of Gaul he gave evidence of Roman power. He crossed the Rhine to impress the Germans, the Channel twice to overawe the Britons, and built a fleet on the lower waters of the Rhine to help the Celtic mariners of the channel to realize that Rome was mistress of the seas. Three great barbarian leaders, Ariovistus, the German, Cassivelaunus, the Briton, and Vercingetorix, the Arvernian noble who headed the last and most formidable rally of the Gauls, went down before him.

It is easy to conceive the thrill of excitement which these conquests must have caused in the Roman world. Southern Gaul had long been overrun by Roman farmers and graziers, moneylenders and contractors. But now a vast territory, contiguous to the "province," but hitherto little explored, rich in flocks and herds, suitable for tillage, abounding in potential slaves, and providing almost inexhaustible opportunities for trade and commerce, was laid open to the Roman view. And beyond Gaul lay another reservoir of slave labour, the mysterious island of Britain, long famous for its tin mines, but otherwise little visited even by the adventurous seamen of Marseilles, and now shown to be easily accessible to the Roman legions. In comparison with this spectacular development of exploration and conquest at the very door of Italy, the distant triumphs of Pompey lost something of their original lustre.

There was, however, in Rome itself a clique of hard-bitten republicans, in whose eyes the very scale of these achievements constituted an offence. The *optimates* had never trusted the mercurial chieftain of the popular party. They hated his hardy spirit, his mocking defiance of established creeds and customs, his patent contempt for constitutional pedantries, and after the Gallic conquests they feared the sharp edge of his sword. They were therefore resolved that when, on March 1, 49 B.C., the time should come for Caesar to lay down his proconsular command, he should for a time at least be depressed to the station of a private citizen, unprotected by the sacrosanctity of public office, and deprived of all possibility of public harm.

Into these busy machinations Pompey allowed himself to be drawn by men whose party passions were probably a good deal more violent than his own. Detaching himself from Caesar, his father-in-law and former ally, and perhaps influenced by accidents of personal history, such as the death of Julia, his wife, and his remarriage to the daughter of a severe republican, Pompey drifted into the headship of the conservative party. As time proceeded, the quarrel became malignant. Clodius, Caesar's political agent in Rome, was murdered by Milo, the bravo of the opposite faction. A reasonable proposal for compromise was rejected by the Pompeians. It became plain to Caesar that his enemies were implacable and that they wanted his blood. The long renown of the Roman Republic, for Pompey was sole consul and the lawful ruler of that ancient state, had no terrors for the master of the Gallic legions. Crossing the Rubicon in January, 49 B.C., he marched his famous veterans, amid the acclamations of the countryside, down the Adriatic coast, drove Pompey out of Italy, and upset the constitution which had served Rome for five hundred years and even yet commanded the passionate loyalty of some of her noblest sons.

Much fighting lay still before Caesar. There were enemy legions in Spain, in Epirus, in Africa; and Roman republicans of the iron stamp of Cato were not the men to cede their cherished ideals without a struggle. But at the end of four years the favourite of fortune had triumphed over all his enemies in the field. He had beaten Pompey at Pharsalus, vanquished the republican levies in Africa and Spain, and even found time to dally with Cleopatra in Egypt, and to punish a king of Pontus in his distant home on the Euxine.

Then, in July, 45 B.C., he returned to Rome, bringing to the task of reorganization the greatest civil intelligence which had yet been seen in Europe.

Seven months later, at the age of fifty-eight, he fell by the hands of two republican fanatics.

In that brief space of time Caesar laid the foundations of the Roman Empire. There were no proscriptions or confiscations. The new ruler intended himself to be regarded, not as the victorious head of a vindictive faction, but as the healer of civic wounds, as the master of a united society. All power, civil and military, was concentrated in his hands. The commanders of the legions and the rulers of the provinces were no longer the nominees of the Senate or assemblies, but the legates of the great soldier, who, after the crowning victory of Munda, was also created dictator for life. Yet the old constitution, the centre of so many loyalties and affections, was still in name preserved. The Senate, enlarged and diluted, the Comitia, the republican magistracies, continued to function, but as instruments in the hands of a military commander, who at the same time was consul and had the sacrosanctity of a tribune for life. Indications were also given that the supreme power so constituted would be used for wise and beneficent ends. Decency was restored to the capital by the dissolution of the factious guilds and the limitation of the corn dole; but with the recognition of the cogent need for discipline went a large vision of the wants of Italy. The generous ideas of the Gracchi were taken up by their political heir, but worked out with greater prudence and on an ampler scale. The franchise was granted to Cisalpine Gaul. Every city government in Italy was the better for Caesar's touch.

The world was in need of such a man. There was no outrage to the civilian conscience in a government which, though created by the sword and contemptuous of republican forms, enthroned the civil above the military power. In our age, the ideals of Caesarism would be sharply challenged by national sentiment and democratic doctrine. Neither of these great fashioning forces existed in the civilized world during this century. There were no nations, no democracies, not even a general intellectual interest in politics, but on the one side an old-fashioned civic Republic, unable even to police the streets of Rome, and on the other a vast society of men and women hungering for peace that it might meditate on religion or philosophy, or taste the sweets of its fast expanding wealth.

BOOKS WHICH MAY BE CONSULTED

T. Mommsen: *History of Rome. Tr.* W. P. Dickson. 5 vols. 1894.

H. F. Pelham: *History of Rome. Outlines of Roman History.* 4th Ed. 1905.

Sir Charles Oman: *Seven Roman Statesmen.* 1902.

J. L. Strachan Davidson: *Cicero and the Fall of the Roman Republic.* 1894.

Warde Fowler: *Julius Caesar, and the Foundation of the Roman System.* 1892.

W. E. Heitland: *Short History of the Roman Republic.* 1911.

Gaston Boissier: *Ciceron et ses Amis.* 1877.

C. Bailey: *Phases in the Religion of Ancient Rome.* 1932.

C. Bailey (*ed.*): *The Mind of Rome.* 1926.

C. Bailey (*ed.*): *The Legacy of Rome.* 1925.

H. D. Leigh and W. W. How: *History of Rome to the Death of Caesar.* 1898.

Cambridge Ancient History, Vol. IX.

T. Rice Holmes: *The Roman Republic.* 1923.

G. Ferrero: *Greatness and Decline of Rome. Tr.* A. E. Zimmern and H. J. Chaytor. 5 vols. 1907-09.

Tenney Frank: *An Economic History of Rome till the End of the Republic.* 1927.

M. Cary: *A History of Rome down to the Reign of Constantine* 2nd Ed. 1957.

R. E. Syme: *The Roman Revolution.* 1939.

N. Lewis and M. Reinhold: *Roman Civilisation.* 2 vols. 1951.

CHAPTER VIII

STRENGTH AND WEAKNESS OF
THE ROMAN EMPIRE

The end of the Civil War. Actium. Augustus and Virgil. Bounds of the Empire. Absence of fixed rule of succession. Expansion of the Empire. Romanization of the provinces. Roman tolerance. The age of the Antonines. The third century. Barbaric pressure and imperial defence. Growth of religious interest. Stoicism. Oriental cults. The Christians. Decay of patriotism. Roman education. Its defects and merits. Absence of scientific and technical progress. Gradual impoverishment. Currency. Decline of the population in numbers and quality. The army: its composition and numbers.

THE MURDER of Julius Caesar plunged everything once more into chaos and uncertainty. There was a war between the Caesarians and the Republicans, and again a war of succession between the Caesarians themselves. The blood of Cicero, the last prophet of the Roman Republic, the greatest orator and humanist of his age, was shed in an orgy of retribution for the crime of the Ides of March. Nor was the quarrel confined to Italy. It extended to every quarter of the Empire, which threatened to disrupt. Parthians fought at Philippi for Brutus and Cassius. Greeks commanded the pirate fleet of Sextus Pompeius, which for seven years held the seas for the republican cause. The fleets and treasures of Egypt were thrown into the scale in the last deciding phase of the conflict.

Eventually and by slow degrees light broke through the clouds. Octavius, the adopted son and great-nephew of Julius Caesar, was at his great-uncle's death in his nineteenth year; but though young in years, and with little aptitude for the profession of arms, he was old in prudence and heir to a famous name. From the first he determined to have everything, but from the first was wise enough to see that he was not strong enough to have everything at once. Mark Antony, formerly Caesar's Master of the Horse, was, on the date of his patron's murder, sole consul and *de facto* ruler of Italy,

63
B.C.-
A.D.
14

and, had the brilliance of a soldier been supported by the gifts of a statesman, his authority would have been difficult to shake. But Antony met more than his match in the youth who was destined to establish on firm foundations the empire of the Caesars. Octavius fought him, treated with him, used him as an ally against Brutus, and then quieted him with the lure of the east, while he employed his own sagacious energies on the problems of Italy, Spain, and Gaul. The seductions of the Levant worked on the emotional temperament of Antony. While the prudent Octavius was deepening his hold on the affections of the Italian people, Antony drifted into the vices, the languors, the credulities of the east. Vast nebulous ambitions floated before his brain, fostered, per aps, by Cleopatra, his Egyptian siren, who captured his love and for nine years corrupted his will. He claimed to be the god Dionysus, and, having mastered the east, to extend his domination to Italy. At the sea fight at Actium his dream *Sept. 2* was shattered. Octavius, with a fleet organized by his friend 31 Agrippa and all the resources of the west behind him, was B.C. stronger than any power which could then be recruited in the Levant. The consequences of his victory were momentous. The presumption of Cleopatra was avenged by the annexation of Egypt, with its great wealth, its advanced methods of accountancy, business, and finance; and the Roman Empire, which seemed likely to split into an eastern and a western half, was soldered together during those critical centuries, when the establishment of a world state seemed providentially designed to give support to the aspirations for a world religion.

The new government set itself to work to cure the evils which had been bequeathed by two centuries of war. The empire of Augustus, as Octavius now (January 16, 27 B.C.) came to be called, stood for peace and clemency, order and justice. It was a symbol of the new era that thirty-two legions were demobilized and rewarded without confiscations. The frontiers were defended by standing armies, the administration placed upon a business footing by the formation of a bureaucracy, by a statistical survey, and by the introduction, most probably from Egypt, of a regular system of public accounts. Ignorant amateurs were no longer entrusted with unlimited powers to enrich themselves at the expense of the provinces which had been submitted to their charge. The legates of Augustus were experts, flanked by independent financial officers responsible only to the Emperor, and if they proved themselves worthy were continued in their province. So organized the provincial system of the Roman Empire stood the test of centuries and stamped itself deeply on the life of Europe.

It was part of the prudence of Augustus to preserve the forms of liberty so dear to a proud and conservative people. If his person was sacrosanct, it was because at stated intervals he solicited and received at the hands of the people the tribunician power; if his authority was unchallenged, it was because the people had given him the legions, the provinces, and the proconsular authority in Rome itself. His innovations, which were vast, but harmless because they were gradual, were concealed under the guise of a republican restoration, and the master of the civilized world was content to be known as Princeps, the first citizen of a free state.

There has never been a more valuable government than that of this thrifty, respectable, long-headed, and long-lived representative of the Italian middle class. Under Augustus power for the first time became consistently helpful, benign, and even paternal. The odious extortions of the capitalist oligarchy who in the last days of the Republic had ruined the provinces were at an end. The Princeps made war on irreligion and race-suicide and attempted to restore the wholesome morals and immemorial pieties of the Italian race. It was noted of him that he had a full measure of the countryman's superstitions, that he loved truth and hated flattery, that he was discreet in the choice of counsellors, affable to his friends, and intolerant of pride in his associates. Agrippa, the contriver of his victories, and Maecenas, the discerning patron of the arts, gave lustre and variety to his court. A society just escaped from the galling trials of civil war was little disposed to quarrel with a prince so accessible and considerate, or with a system which afforded to every class in the community an honourable career in the public service. The modest Augustus, who was rightly hailed as a saviour of his country, could not escape the divine honours which had actually been accorded to his brilliant uncle; and the worship of the Emperor, gently insinuated into the family and local cults of Rome and with some ostentation practised in the provinces, was soon regarded as a helpful bond of union in a providential state.

Yet, important as was the achievement of Augustus, it would have meant far less for the world but for the image which the spectacle of Roman greatness created in the minds of two writers of genius.

It so happens that Virgil, the inspired poet of Italy, and Livy, the romantic historian of the Roman Republic, were both born in that Cisalpine region which had so lately been incorporated in the Roman state—Virgil at Andes, near Mantua, in 70 B.C., and Livy at Padua in 59 B.C. But if there was Celtic blood in either writer, it was compatible with an ardour of Italian patriotism so strong as to kindle for all time a sense of Roman virtue and greatness in the imagination of mankind. The beautiful landscape of Italy is painted in the Georgics, the historic mission of Rome unfolded in the Aeneid. Upon that age these two wonderful works of a shy poet, nature lover, scholar, savant, patriot, fell with the force of a revelation. A supreme master of Latin letters, inviting comparison with Homer himself, had burst upon the scene, giving lessons to grammarians in language, to rhetoricians in eloquence, to ritualists in ceremonial, to poets in music. Moreover, this great artist had a message. He preached the love of Italy, the mission of Rome, the gospel of patriotic duty. He discerned in the rise of the Roman Empire a new hope for the human race, a hope of peace, of order, of civilization. So long dominant was his gospel in Europe that Dante, writing in the spirit of the great concluding passage of the first Georgic, assigns Brutus and Cassius, the murderers of Julius Caesar, to the lowest pit of the Inferno with Judas Iscariot, the betrayer of Christ.

The empire, as it was finally shaped by Augustus, included Spain, Gaul, Italy and the Balkans, the north coast of Africa, Palestine, Syria and Asia Minor. The Mediterranean was a Roman lake. Every people who had contributed to the sum of western civilization was now subjected to Rome. In the north and north-west, the two quarters from which the pressure of the barbarian world was most to be feared, the empire was defended by the Danube and the Rhine, a long river frontier behind which were ranged in uncalculated numbers the valiant tribesmen of Germany. The conquest of this tumultuous people, had it been achieved by Augustus, would have changed the course of European history, for a

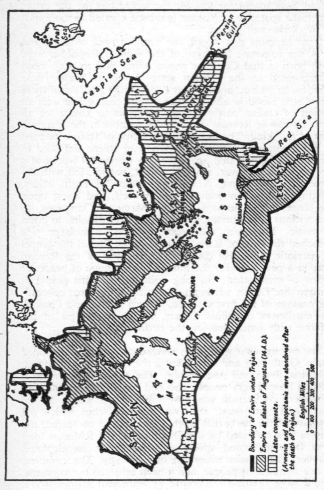

THE ROMAN EMPIRE AT ITS GREATEST EXTENT UNDER TRAJAN

Boundary of Empire under Trajan.

Empire at death of Augustus (14 A.D.).

Later conquests.

(Armenia and Mesopotamia were abandoned after the death of Trajan.)

English Miles

0   100   200   300   400   500

frontier drawn from the Baltic to the Danube by the line of
the Elbe and the Morava would have been relatively short
and easy to defend. But a single military disaster in a German
forest was sufficient to deter the Emperor from further
adventures in a difficult, unexplored, and uninviting land.   A.D. 9

After the loss of Varus and his legions, Augustus resolved
to stand on the defensive. His decision was wise. The world
needed peace. The laborious pacification of Spain was in
itself a task sufficient to employ the energies of the young
Empire, and the legions stationed on the Rhine could not be
expected at one and the same time to police Gaul and conquer Germany. Yet, however wise and inevitable it may have
been, the determination to refrain from a resolute attempt
to include the Germans within the Empire was none the less
momentous. The long new frontier was not permanently
held, and Italy and Gaul were overwhelmed before Rome
had civilized its Teutonic conquerors. Six centuries of intellectual darkness were the tremendous penalty consequent upon
the premature breakdown of the Imperial defences.

The work of Augustus was continued by his stepson and
successor Tiberius, an excellent soldier and administrator,   A.D.
whose reign of twenty-three years, odious as it appeared to   14-37
the aristocratic *frondeurs* of Rome, did much to consolidate
the Imperial system. That the Empire responded to a general
need is sufficiently evidenced by its survival despite the almost
inconceivable crimes and vices of many of its rulers. The
three immediate successors of Tiberius were a madman, a
pedant, and a monster. Yet it is probable that the freaks of
Caligula, the pedantries of Claudius, and the atrocities of
Nero, distasteful as they must have been to the better elements
of Roman society, made little impression upon the larger life
of the Empire. What was more serious was the absence of
any fixed rule of succession. Such was the prejudice against
the mere thought of an hereditary monarchy that despite the
manifold evils of a system which often remitted the choice of
an Emperor to the clamour of the troops and more than
once involved the Empire in civil discords, the idea of
Caesarism as an autocracy founded on popular election was
never lost sight of. The death of Nero, the last representative   A.D.
of the Julio-Claudian house, was the signal for the emergence   68
of four rival Emperors and for a year of anarchy during which
a battle was fought in Rome itself which is said to have cost

fifty thousand lives. Then ensued a happier century inaugurated by Vespasian (A.D. 69-79), a rude Sabine soldier, and
lasting until the death of Marcus Aurelius (A.D. 180), during
which the transmission of the supreme power was peaceably
effected at first through heredity and afterwards through the
sensible practice of adoption. It is to this last practice that
Rome owes the choice of Trajan, the great Spanish conqueror
of Dacia, of Hadrian, the universal genius, and of Antoninus
Pius, the embodiment of the best virtues of the Italian country
gentleman. But these standards were not maintained. The
elevation of Pertinax, who was the choice of the Praetorian
Guard, set an evil example to every legionary camp on the
frontier. The diadem became the prize of ambitious soldiers
and its transmission the occasion of civil strife. The results
were such as might be expected from a system under which
military leaders chosen by distant troops and imposed by
violence were suddenly called upon to undertake the greatest
political responsibility in the world. The rulers of Rome in
the third century were often bad and always insecure. Of
the twenty-three Emperors who preceded Diocletian (A.D.
284), all but three died violent deaths.

d.
193

It was said of the wise Augustus that he left a solemn injunction upon his successors to be content with the existing
frontiers of the Empire. All experience, however, shows that
nothing is so difficult as to arrest the enterprise of a people
once infected with ideas of conquest and exploration. While
Christ and His disciples were preaching the gospél of renunciation, the Italians, animated by a spirit as far removed as
possible from that of the Galilean, were pushing into new
markets, developing new enterprises, exploring new lands,
and clamouring for new conquests. Claudius, the boorish,
self-indulgent invalid, yielding to the exalted spirit of his
times, began the serious conquest of Britain and added
Thrace, Mauretania, and Judea to the Roman provinces.
Even under Nero, to whom nothing was serious save his
own reputation as an actor and a vocalist, places so far
distant as the flats of Anglesea and the highlands of Armenia
were subjected by Roman arms. To the Flavian Emperors
belongs the credit of seizing the strategical importance of
Vienna and of connecting the Danube with the Rhine by a
chain of fortified posts.

Nor was it until the later part of the second century, under the reign of Marcus Aurelius, the noblest of the Emperors, that the Roman guard at length gave way. In 161 A.D. a horde of barbarians, the Marcomanni from Bohemia, the Quadi from Moravia, forcing the north-eastern barrier of Italy at its lowest and most vulnerable point, besieged Aquileia—a symptom of worse things to come, and a warning to the Italians that they could no longer count upon the Augustan peace.

Meanwhile the Roman legions, defending the Imperial frontiers as they did during the two centuries which followed the battle of Actium, preserved to posterity the priceless gift of Greco-Roman civilization. It is to the respite from external invasion so obtained that we must ascribe the permanent romanization of France and Spain, and that most important though more superficial romanization of Britain which, though almost wholly obliterated by the Saxon conquest of the fifth century, has bequeathed to us the city of London and our Roman roads. Behind the spears and shields of the legions Iberian and Gaulish schoolboys blundered through the Latin Grammar, henceforward the quickest passport to worldly success, as their parents learnt from the conquering people the manner of its baths and theatres, its meals and festivals, its amphitheatres and law courts, or the empty and elegant ritual demanded by its gods. Behind the buckler of Roman valour the knowledge of Latin spread as English has spread in India, or supersedes for the Greek or Italian immigrant to the United States the use of his native tongue. Latin was the avenue to public employment, public dignity, literary renown. The members of the senatorial order, a kind of imperial peerage, spoke Latin and lived as Latins did. The humble German or Briton who waited upon the rich Roman invalid as he took the cure at Wiesbaden or Bath would doubtless furnish himself with some scraps of a vocabulary which the student of Terence and Plautus may recognize today; and upon a higher scale, as new towns sprang up and received colonists from Rome, men of distinguished talent would come forward, a Seneca or a Lucan from Corduba, an Apuleius from the Roman province of Africa, and add to the splendour of Latin letters.

Grim and terrible as was the process of Roman conquest, it brought happiness and prosperity in its train. If some provinces like Rhaetia and Britain were backward, in others, notably in Gaul and southern Spain, the progress was amazing. Here there was developed during the two hundred years of the Augustan peace a flourishing city life which vied with that of Italy itself. Old towns were expanded and glorified, new towns grew up round legionary camps or in response to the needs of expanding commerce, so that the Empire became a great association of municipalities, tending to be assimilated, so far as their rights and privileges went, to the colonies and *municipia* of Italy. To the provincials of Lyons or Toledo, of Autun or Saragossa, Rome was the glass of fashion. The amusements, the occupations, the studies of the capital were followed in the provinces. If a book were popular in Rome, copies would be eagerly awaited by the reading public in Lyons, and many a well-appointed villa in Baetica or Provence must have afforded to the wealthy Italian visitor a cuisine and a library not wholly unworthy of his pleasant country home among the Alban hills.

Tacitus said of his countrymen, "They value the reality of the Empire, but disregard its empty show." It was part of the Roman strength to mingle diplomacy with force, to make no more disturbance of local customs than was necessary, to attack only such forms of religious belief as, like the worship of the Druids, were political in their object, and to preserve old laws and institutions where, as in Egypt or in Sicily, they adjudged them to be good. When the soldiers had done their butchers' work, military predominance was kept in the background. The legions were employed to make roads, to build amphitheatres and aqueducts, and generally to assist in making as rapidly as possible the material fabric within which the common life of a civilized community could proceed; but they were not obtruded The great legionary camps were on the frontiers, and a traveller might voyage from Marseilles to Boulogne without catching the glint of a Roman helmet. To outward seeming Rome's handsome estate might be held together by nothing but the invisible ties of good humour and good will.

The age of the Antonines was selected by Gibbon as that in which the state of the human race in the west was happier than at any period either before or since. The full weight of the barbaric pressure upon the frontiers had not yet made itself felt. The burden of taxation was still light. A large cultivated middle class enjoyed a rich inheritance of literature in circumstances of great material comfort. Amusements on a lavish scale were provided for the many, the chariot races in the circus, the gladiatorial games and combats of wild beasts in the amphitheatre, an easy access to the public baths. A pleasant intercommunion, unvexed by the modern fanaticisms of creed and race, of nationality, language and colour, spread from one end of the Empire to the other. In the service of Rome, Syrians and Spaniards, Africans and Britons mingled together without difficulty or wounding discrimination. A wide and indulgent tolerance was the mark of the age. The peoples of the Empire were too close to the Romans in race and too quick to assimilate Roman culture ever to be regarded in the light of natural inferiors. The cities were self-governing and much left to themselves. Of religion as such there was no persecution, for the Roman Pantheon was hospitable to every god. Social customs were embodied in the growing fabric of Roman law, local languages—Punic, Lycaonian, Celtic—permitted to coexist with the *lingua franca* of the Empire which was Latin. Cruelty, indeed, existed then as it exists now; but the humanitarian might reflect that the slave trade had died down, that freedmen could win their way to wealth and authority, and that even a slave might exercise an influence as an author in a society where careers were open to talent. Of the ultimate fate of the Empire there were as yet no apprehensions. It was the universal and comforting belief that Roman rule would endure for ever.

A change came with the third century A.D. After the strain of the Marcomannic War certain ominous symptoms made themselves for the first time increasingly evident. Already in the time of Augustus grave anxiety was felt as to the falling birthrate of Italy. Legislation was attempted, but while the natality of Jews, Egyptians, and Germans steadily advanced, the Italian birth-rate continued to fall. The wastage of almost incessant warfare, the practice of infanticide, the growth of luxury and self-indulgence, the inability of science, as then conceived, to cope with the sanitary problems of large towns, were among the causes which contributed to the depletion of the man power in the two leading countries in the Mediterranean. By the age of Marcus Aurelius there was little left of the virile population of ancient Greece or of the best breeding stocks of Rome and Italy. Even among the Emperors and their relations the will to found large families seems to have been absent. And to these unhappy tendencies there was added a series of devastating plagues, beginning in 166 A.D. with the return of the troops of Avidius Cassius from the east, and observed to be specially fatal to Italians.

It was idle to expect that the defence of the Empire could be entrusted to Italians only. Nor was this in fact ever the practice. Auxiliary troops, drawn from every quarter of the compass, from Palmyra and the Balearic Islands, from Germany and Illyria, had assisted the legions in their vigils and excursions. But after the Marcomannic War it was found that these measures no longer sufficed to meet the growing difficulties of the state. A policy was then for the first time initiated of directly opening the Empire to colonization. Blocks of barbarian warriors were invited to settle on the waste places behind the Roman frontiers. Once inaugurated, the process of infiltration continued. From the opening of the third century the great traditions of Greek and Roman civilization were protected almost entirely by troops of alien origin, living with their wives and families a half-civilian life in the standing camps along the confines of the Empire. The most responsible posts in the army and the state might be filled by men devoid of any drop of Italian blood. The two best generals of Marcus Aurelius were Syrians. During the third century one Emperor was a Syrian, another an Arab, a third an African, springing from a family whose familiar speech was Punic. The African was Septimius Severus, who was raised to the purple by the Pannonian legions in 190 A.D., and died in York in 212 A.D. His name should be known in England, for by repairing Hadrian's wall, between the Solway and the Tyne, he secured for Britain a century of peace.

The third century of the Christian era is memorable for the work of two great Roman jurists, Ulpian and Papinian, both of Asiatic origin, and for a late and brilliant flowering of Greek literature, illustrated by the profound mystical writings, harmonizing Christian belief with Platonic thought, of the Alexandrian philosopher Plotinus. It was an age of great distraction and unhappiness, during which the pressure of the barbarian tribes upon the defences of the Empire became increasingly severe, reaching a climax in the middle of the century when the Goths, a northern people of fair-haired giants, sacked most of what was worth plundering in the Balkans, seized the Crimea, and, after pillaging many flourishing cities in the Euxine and Asia Minor, crowned their pirate course by burning to the ground the great Temple of Artemis at Ephesus. It was an age in which Tarragona, in the heart of Spain, was sacked by a wandering band of Franks from Germany, when the Alemanni carried fire and sword through the valleys of the Rhone and Po, and Antioch, the key of Roman power in the east was held, now by a King of Persia, and now by a rebel Queen of the desert city of Palmyra. It was an age also of sharp civil discords, of clashes between rival emperors and rival armies, the main centre of power lying throughout with the Pannonian legions, schooled in the hard life of the Danube frontier, and with the Illyrian soldiers whom from time to time it was their pleasure to raise to the purple. Yet grave as were the dangers which assailed the Roman Empire in the third century, often as it must have seemed likely to contemporaries either that Gaul would fall away on the one side, or that the east would pass out of Roman control on the other, or that the whole Greco-Roman world would be overwhelmed and ruined by the barbarism of the north, the task of defence was in fact accomplished. Advanced positions were, indeed, abandoned. From the Black Forest and the plain of Transylvania the legions fell back to the Rhine and the Danube, the old frontiers of Augustus; and it is significant of the increased insecurity that Aurelian, the brilliant soldier, who drove the Germans out of Italy and restored Gaul and the east to a common obedience, thought it prudent to fortify Rome.

A.D.
270
?

Meanwhile in this time of general strain and anxiety the Mediterranean world was becoming increasingly occupied with the thought of a life beyond the grave.

The old paganism of the Roman people, which had still a long life before it in the hill villages of Italy, was a pleasant, unmoral, tolerant creed, free from the control of clerics or the vexation of inquisitors, and easily harmonized with those popular festivals and amusements of which it was, indeed, an integral part; but it had long since ceased to claim the allegiance of the finer natures or the better minds. It responded to none of the deeper needs of conscience. It answered to none of the claims of intellect. To thinking men and women, philosophy, which ever since the days of Zeno and Epicurus had become increasingly occupied with problems of conduct, offered a stronger and more satisfying diet. Before Christianity had become a European religion, educated people in the Roman Empire were familiar with the conception of a monotheistic faith and of a dedicated life.

In the society of the second century the philosopher filled a definite place, as a spiritual counsellor, a healer of inward distress, performing many functions which were afterwards discharged by the father confessors of the Roman Church. Under the worst of the Roman tyrants Stoic philosophers had been found brave enough to speak their minds and to defend the full dignity of man, and, were reason a sufficient support for human frailty, Stoicism, the noblest contribution which the pagan world had to offer to the art and science of righteous living, would have secured for itself a permanent influence in human society.

To Mediterranean men, athirst for colour, imagery, and consolation, a system of austere monotheism and reasoned ethics could never bring full satisfaction. The Roman world turned with increasing interest to the ardent cults of the east, like those of Isis and Serapis, and Mithras, the soldier's god, which offered to all, however humble in station or mean in intellect, the boon of purifying mysteries and the hope of eternal life. It is in reality with these eastern creeds, rather than with the Olympian gods of Homer, that the eventual battle of Christianity was fought. The worshippers of the Egyptian Isis, the Phrygian Cybele, and the Persian Mithras shared many beliefs which were afterwards to be found in the Christian system. They believed in a sacramental union with the divine being, either through a ritual marriage, or more simply through a ceremonial eating of the god's flesh. The old riddle of birth and death, of fertility and decay, of the seed which flowers, and of the flower which returns to seed, was ever present to the religious imagination of the east. A god dying amid wails and lamentations, but resurgent amid cries of welcoming joy, was a central feature in these oriental mystery cults. In such symbolism the devotees of Mithras and of Isis found warrant for a faith in ultimate deliverance from the grave.

It is easy, even were the evidence of monuments less abundant, to account for the wide popularity of such beliefs. No attempt was made to check them. Marcus Aurelius instituted a temple to Mithras on the Vatican hill. Aurelian made sun-worship the official religion of the state. "The worship of Isis," writes Dean Inge, "was organized in a manner very like that of the Catholic Church. There was a kind of Pope, with priests, monks, singers, and acolytes. The images of the Madonna were crowned with true or false jewels, and her toilette was dutifully attended to every day. Daily matins and evensong were said in her chief temples. The priests were tonsured and wore white linen vestments." Before Rome became Christian, it had become clerical, a city of temples and images, of priests and religious processions, of cynic philosophers in cowls and coarse woollen gowns like the begging friars of the middle ages, of astrologers and magicians, such as always thrive amid public misfortunes. When, under the reign of Diocletian, Rome ceased to be a political capital, it was not perhaps difficult to foresee that one day the place of the absent Emperor would be taken by a Roman priest. A.D. 284-305

From this pagan effervescence the sectaries of the Christian religion stood austerely apart. As a secret society professing pacifist opinions and refusing to do sacrifice to the Emperor, the Christians were suspect to authority, and from time to time, as under Decius and Valerian, were exposed to severe persecutions. The odium which in many quarters now attaches to the opponent of militarism and blood sports, and in a lesser degree to the feminist and the communist, was easily aroused by the spectacle of these eccentric fanatics, who denounced the cruel abominations of the amphitheatre, claimed equal treatment for the woman and the slave, and, spurning the delights of wealth and comfort, professed themselves the sole depositaries of truth. A body offering so strong a challenge to the social and political convictions of the world was bound to be unpopular and to be misunderstood. The Christians were accused of atheism because they did not accept the pagan gods, of misanthropy because they denounced the debased amusements of the people, and of immorality because they were not comprehended. Yet the Church grew steadily, fostered rather than hindered by persecution, which was never sufficiently systematic or continuous to be deadly. By the time of Aurelian Christian beliefs had spread widely through the east, and in Rome itself were firmly rooted, a A.D. 249-253 A.D. 270-3 rival influence to the established worship of the unconquerable sun.

It is perhaps to this growing concern for religion that we should in part ascribe a curious feature of the life and policy of the Empire in the fourth and fifth centuries. The more people thought about the inner life, the less they cared about the outward accidents. The more they became involved in the new religious excitements, the less were they attracted by the laborious routine of secular duty. In that mobile cosmopolitan society there was little left of the old flame of Roman patriotism. A new allegiance was beginning to claim an increasing number of earnest and valuable men and women in Gaul, in Italy, and in the Greek world. The state offered careers, but had ceased to speak to the soul. As outward difficulties accumulated, government became more costly, more nervous, and more exacting. The pressure of the state upon the individual increased in a steadily diminishing temperature of political obedience. The spirit of evasion, of reluctance to pay the taxes in blood, in money, and in commodities, which the state demanded, spread through all classes. It was found in the peasants, in the traders, in the town councils, and it was met by a policy of repression which converted peasants, traders, and town councillors into the hereditary bondsmen of a servile state.

The educational outlook of antiquity was necessarily coloured by the institution of slavery. Even for the most generous minds a sharp line was drawn between the small number of studies and pursuits which a free man might follow without loss of dignity, and the more utilitarian occupations from which he would properly shrink. Plato thought that retail trade was degrading. Lucian, while admiring the statues of Praxiteles, was thankful that he had not been called upon to produce them. The conception which most generally prevailed was that the world consisted of a civilized society whose economic needs were provided by slaves and freedmen, foreigners and mechanics, for whom nature had ordained a life of service, and who stood outside the charmed circle of the city. It followed that the education of civilized men concerned itself with those branches of knowledge which ministered to happiness or success in a society thus circumscribed.

In so far as it was not physical, education was concerned

with the appreciation of poetry, philosophy, and the fine arts. It trained taste, afforded a discipline in eloquence, and exhibited the ethical and political lessons of the past. Further it did not go. Nature, history, and religion found no place in the curriculum. There was nothing in the ordinary education of the Roman clearly calculated to direct his mind to the grave social and economic problems which lay around him. In the first century of the Empire slaves were so abundant that they revolutionized the agrarian economy of Italy; but no attempt was made to measure the productiveness of slave as compared with free labour. Indeed, Varro even goes so far as to advise the landowner to send freemen rather than slaves to work on unhealthy land, as the loss of a freeman would be less crippling than the death of a slave. Again, the steady depreciation of the currency during the third century was productive of manifold evils and of a violent remedial measure in the reign of Aurelian, over which men fought and died by the thousand in the streets of Rome. Yet no one put out a theory of currency or realized that bad money drives out good. So little were the elements of economic science understood that Diocletian, one of the wisest of the Emperors, issued an edict fixing prices all over the Empire, and found, as many have found since his day, that not all the laws or penalties in the world can prevent men from buying in the cheapest and selling in the dearest market.

The Eton master of the eighteenth century flogged his boys. The Roman youth of the second and third centuries flogged his masters. A system under which the education of youth is mainly entrusted to slaves cannot be wholesome; yet under favouring circumstances the literary training of a young Roman was probably as good as that which was received by an English boy in the reign of George III. In the sphere of grammar and literary criticism a tradition of scholarly competence long outlived the glories of the Augustan age. The Latin classics were studied with care. An effort, not often successful, was made to teach Greek as a subsidiary language. Education, however, cannot be carried on with success in airless compartments, but depends for its healthy growth upon fresh currents of thought and interest sweeping in from the active intellectual life of the world outside. If great motives vanish from poetry and prose, they will disappear also from the teaching of the young. The singular decay of

Latin language and literature, which set in during the third century, was accompanied by a corresponding decline in the serious effectiveness of western education. Here there was no ferment comparable to that exciting influence of Plato and Aristotle, which so long sustained the intellectual life of the University of Athens. The pagan world of the west was ailing for lack of a popular literature. The Christian movement was regarded by its teachers as vulgar, foreign, and remote. It was, perhaps, a misfortune that the dominant intellectual influence in Latin education was that of a master of golden eloquence, for the ghost of Cicero hovered over every classroom. The imitation of his rounded periods became a schoolboy industry, and when the Empire was starving for statesmen and thinkers, the typical product of its schools was a shallow rhetorician.

To this narrow literary convention we may perhaps attribute the great lack of inventiveness in the practical arts which is characteristic of the Roman people. There was no science after the reign of Hadrian, there were no technical improvements. Even in the art of war, so well understood and so brilliantly practised for many centuries, the Romans were curiously un-inventive. The Carthaginians taught them how to handle ships at sea. The Parthians taught them the value of mounted archery, the Balearic Islanders the use of the sling, the Goths the penetrating power of heavily armed cavalry. But with the exception of the "raven," a moving platform constructed to enable ships to be boarded, which was discovered in the First Punic War, and Greek fire, which was first put to decisive use in the sea fight at Actium, no important innovation in the mechanics of war was discovered by the most warlike of the Mediterranean peoples. The Roman legion inherited a long tradition of discipline. It was sturdier than its barbarian opponents, less subject to wild panics, handier in manoeuvre: but it never enjoyed the mechanical advantages which in modern times have given to European troops a commanding ascendancy against uncivilized armies.

Most curious is the fact, only recently brought out by a French enquirer, that the true art of harnessing draft horses was unknown to antiquity and only discovered in the west in the age of Charlemagne. Much as the Greeks and Romans valued horses, skilful as were their charioteers, they failed to see that no horse can pull its proper weight if the harness

A.D. 117-38

presses against the windpipe. The industrial consequences of a wrong method of harnessing were far reaching. The transport of heavy material by road was made eight times as costly as it need have been, and the concentration of material for the purposes of large-scale production was proportionately hindered.

Although the Roman Empire was an association of towns, the Romans were never an industrial people. With some few exceptions the cities of Italy, Gaul, or Spain did not produce wealth for the surrounding country, still less did they attempt to supply a world market. The wealth which was squandered in Rome during the first century had not been manufactured in the west, but was derived from the spoils of the conquered east, and once dissipated, was not replaced. By the reign of A.D. Vespasian the impoverishment of the old senatorial class was 69-73 already marked, and though happier times came under the Antonines, and large fortunes could still be made, the general level of prosperity continued to descend. Gradually the towns shrank in size and population, and being walled to meet the hazards of the third century, lost something of the abundance and expansiveness of their earlier life. The spreading suburbs, with their pleasant gardens and marble villas, were no longer appropriate to those grim times. A stern fortress crowned the hill or dominated the plain. And long before the Roman Empire went down, its cities had adopted the mediaeval livery of fear.

The absence of any organized system of industrial production in Roman society, accompanied as it was by a lack of economic forethought, had serious consequences, of which one example may here be given The devaluation of the coinage during the third century brought about the ruin of the middle class. In recent times a similar cause has produced a similar effect in one of the most advanced nations in Europe. But deadly as were the immediate effects of the fall of the German mark in 1923, these effects were soon repaired by the productive energies of the German people assisted by the application of capital to industry. The Roman Empire possessed no such powers of recuperation. There was no organized system of credit, no elaborate industrial plant, or skilled industrial or commercial leadership. The conditions under which a great economic reverse could be promptly retrieved did not exist.

More important was a decline in morale, a loss of heart, evident even in the Senate, the body which should have led the Commonwealth in the civic virtues of honour and independence, courage and patriotism. No contrast can be more tragic than the picture which Livy paints of the Roman Senate in the days of its glory during the Punic Wars, and the image of the same assembly abasing itself in servile adulation before the sombre Tiberius, which Tacitus presents to his readers. In that loss of moral dignity and independence we may read the terrible price which Rome was compelled to pay for the civil wars and proscriptions which had decimated her ruling class, and extinguished the flame of republican liberty. Demoralization was not, however, confined to the senators of Rome. Polybius, writing a hundred years before the days of Augustus, had pointed out the disastrous effects of luxury and immorality on the population of Greece. The causes which operated there were present throughout the Mediterranean littoral. Everywhere save in Egypt there was a dearth of men, and everywhere the immediate reason was the same, a reluctance to bring children into the world.

As the old families which had been the mainstay of the Roman state died out, new stocks came to the front, some of them sound and wholesome, but the greater number bearing little resemblance either in character or mentality to the men who fought in the Sabine or Punic Wars. Even in the first century, Juvenal had complained of the alien immigration into Rome. "The Orontes," he writes, "has flowed into the Tiber." The evil denounced by the satirist did not diminish. Apart from the slaves and freedmen, who were for the most part non-Italic, Levantine crews manned the commercial navy, bringing Levantine usurers and merchants into every western mart where money could be made. By the fourth century much alien blood, Greek, Asiatic, Punic, Iberian, must have mingled with the native strain in Rome and the largest cities of Italy. The admixture did not help to preserve a high standard of public duty. We receive the impression of an unhappy, superstitious, nervous society, depressed by a sense of calamity, which it has not the calmness or thinking power to diagnose. It is significant that when the armies of A.D. Aurelian returned to Europe, bringing with them the terrible 270-5 eastern plague, no attempt was made to explore the cause or to find a remedy. Analysis was bankrupt. In place of thought, superstition indicated imaginary foes and administered its damaging opiates. When political troubles were unusually grave, as under Decius, it was thought prudent to persecute the Christians.

The fighting spirit which had made the fortunes of the Republic had already by the age of Hadrian deserted the Italians. They were well content that their battles should be fought by Illyrian and Anatolian highlanders or by barbarian mercenaries from beyond the frontiers. In the old republican days, when the fighting was for the most part under the blue Italian sky, in a land of vines and olives, and campaigns were short and plunder was good, war was a national pastime; but life in a legionary camp on the Danube or the Rhine or by the Roman wall in Britain was a different matter. It did not attract the Latin race. The Italians vanished from the legions, which in the fourth century were chiefly composed of and even officered by Germans.

Since the most populous and civilized parts of the Empire had ceased by the beginning of the third century to contribute fighting men to the legions, the number of troops available for frontier defence was far smaller than it should have been, having regard to the total population of the Empire, which in the time of Constantine may have reached 70,000,000. A modern state containing 70,000,000 inhabitants might be expected in a great war to put 6,000,000 soldiers in the field. Of such an effort the Empire was incapable. Even after its reorganization by Diocletian and Constantine the total strength of the Roman army did not exceed 650,000 men, one-third belonging to the mobile force and two-thirds to the garrisons. In view of the length of the frontier to be defended these figures were dangerously low. As the defending force came in the end to be composed mainly of Germans they were such as to lead to inevitable disaster.

BOOKS WHICH MAY BE CONSULTED

H. Stuart Jones: *The Roman Empire*. 1908.
Rostovtzeff: *Social and Economic History of the Roman Empire*. 1926.
J. W. Mackail: *History of Latin Literature*. 1895.
J. W. Mackail: *The Aeneid of Virgil*. 1930.

W. W. Capes: *The Roman Empire of the Second Century or, The Age of the Antonines.* 1876.

J. B. Bury: *History of the Later Roman Empire.* 2 vols. 1889.

J. B. Bury: *Invasion of Europe by the Barbarians.* 1928.

Christopher Dawson: *The Making of Europe.* 1932.

Ferdinand Lot: *La Fin du Monde Antique et le Début du Moyen Age.* 1927.

Lefebvre des Noëttes: *L'attelage, le cheval de selle à travers les âges.* 1931.

W. R. Inge. *The Philosophy of Plotinus.* 1918.

G. Boissier: *La Fin du Paganisme.* 2 vols. 1891.

E. Renan: *Marc Aurèle.* 1882.

L. P. Homo: *L'Empire Romain.* 1925.

G. Ferrero: *Greatness and Decline of Rome.* Tr. A. E. Zimmern. 1907.

J. S. Reid: *Municipalities of the Roman Empire.* 1913.

T. Rice Holmes: *The Architect of the Roman Empire.* 1928-31.

N. M. P. Nilsson: *Imperial Rome.* Tr. G. C. Richards. 1926.

T. Mommsen: *The Provinces of the Roman Empire.* Tr. W. P. Dickson. 2 vols. 1886.

Cambridge Ancient History, Vol. X.

Tenney Frank: *Roman Imperialism.* 1914.

Tenney Frank: *An Economic History of Rome till the End of the Republic,* 1927.

M. Cary: *A History of Rome down to the Reign of Constantine.* 2nd. Ed. 1957.

J. Carcopino: *Daily Life in Ancient Rome.* Tr. E. O. Lorimer. 1956.

M. P. Charlesworth: *The Roman Empire.* 1951.

CHAPTER IX

DIOCLETIAN AND CONSTANTINE

*Reforms of Diocletian. Constantine as soldier and organizer.
He embraces Christianity. Consequences of the Imperial
recognition of the Christian Faith. Close association of Church
and State under Constantine. His choice of Byzantium as a
capital. East and west drift apart. Less Greek culture in the
west. The continuing influence of Latin classics. Difference
between the Roman and the Greek church.*

THE NEW despotism was inaugurated by two great Illyrian
Emperors, Diocletian and Constantine. To every lover of
liberty their work would seem to have grave faults, for it
was conceived in a spirit most hostile to individual initiative and
executed in an atmosphere poisoned by spies and sycophants.
Moreover, the last eight years of Diocletian's reign are marked
by a bitter and memorable persecution of the Christians.

A.D.
297-
305

Yet, despite these shortcomings, few statesmen have been so
successful in giving to the world in which they were born what
it seemed to want and was content to preserve. The administrative system of Diocletian governed eastern Rome for a
thousand years. The reformed coinage of Constantine[1]
lasted till the eleventh century. And the whole course of
European history would have been otherwise, had Constantine declined to accept Christianity as an authorized
religion, or failed to summon the Council of Nicaea, which
defined the doctrine of the divinity of Christ, or had he not,
with the instinct of the higher strategy, determined to transfer
the capital of the Empire to that old Greek city on the
Bosphorus which still bears his name.

Diocletian, who was raised to supreme power by the Pannonian legions in 284, brought an atmosphere of saving
novelty into the management of affairs. Through his long
reign of twenty years he applied the resources of a powerful
and restless mind to the tasks of government. To contemporaries the course of this Dalmatian peasant may have appeared

[1] A gold aureus or solidus, roughly equalling 12s. 6d. of our money.

inconsistent and wayward, and too often determined by impulse and superstition. He would build and unbuild, enact and recall his enactment: but posterity, regarding not so much the details as the general effect of his work, sees in him a man of system supervening on a planless state. He introduced centralization, administrative uniformity, the subdivision of powers and provinces. He saw the importance of severing political and military authority, of a strict and hierarchical civil discipline in a society which had lost the gift of political thinking. To him also is due the introduction of those servile forms of ceremonial which for many centuries afterwards continued to characterize the court life of European princes. In theory the Emperor was still the elected protector of the people, bound by laws which it was his duty to obey. In fact, he was an eastern sultan, claiming divine right, the directing engine of a vast bureaucratic machine with a long and careful graded hierarchy of officials depending on his nod. We pass from the Roman to the Byzantine age.

In another respect also the reign of Diocletian marks an epoch. He appreciated the fact that the defence of the Empire on four separate fronts could not be supervised by a single man, that defence must be mobile, not stationary, and directed from centres near the frontier, and that an end must be put to the system of military *pronunciamentos*, which had involved the Empire in so much chaos and bloodshed. His plan was that the Empire should be governed by two Augusti, himself and Maximianus, a Thracian peasant, and that these should be assisted by two younger men to be known as Caesars, who should succeed to the purple when the Augusti resigned, as they undertook to do after twenty years of rule. Rome ceased to be the capital. The rulers of the Empire held their courts at Trèves and Milan, at Sirmium and Nicomedeia. Diocletian himself selected Nicomedeia, and from that pleasant Asiatic station undertook to police the troublesome east.

Ingenious as was the device of entrusting the management of the Empire to a college of four, it failed to secure the desired effect. The retirement of the two Augusti in 305 was followed by a period of civil discord, memorable only at this distance of time as establishing upon unassailable foundations the name and the empire of Constantine the Great.

This outstanding man, the bastard son of a well-born

Illyrian officer by an innkeeper at Nish (in modern Serbia), was upon the death of his father Constantius at York proclaimed Emperor by the troops—the precise evil which the reforms of Diocletian had been framed to avert. Disastrous as such elections had too often been, the instinct of the British legionaries was here justified. The youth of thirty-two proved himself to be a consummate commander in the field. After a skilful defence of the Gallic frontier, he overthrew, in a succession of brilliant engagements, his two rivals, Maxentius, the ruler of Italy, and Licinius, the Emperor of the East. In all his military career he never suffered a reverse. The speed and energy of his offensives were characteristic of a man to whom physical fears were unknown, and the ever present world of spirits supplied cordials of intoxicating strength. Is it to be wondered that he regarded himself as the favoured son of the victory-bringing God, or that the despotic system of Diocletian received from his hands additional aggravations?

Only the strictest regard to the principles of justice and economy can save such a system from terrible abuses. The Roman administration in the fourth century, despite many improvements, was still lamentably deficient in justice and knowledge. Great wealth was lightly taxed, moderate fortunes were crippled by crushing exactions. Owing to the steady depreciation of the coinage, an important part of the revenue was levied in kind, a system leading on the one hand to irregularity and extortion, and on the other to a forlorn attempt to fix a money value to commodities. These things were bad enough. A vicious fiscal system was not the least among the causes which led to the downfall of the Roman empire; but what was equally serious was the all-pervading system of compulsion, by which the new despotism attempted to secure the upkeep of the state. The landlord was compelled to act as recruiting officer and tax collector for his neighbourhood. The peasant was tied to the soil. The *decurion*, a town councillor, was made responsible for the contributions due from his municipality and forbidden to leave his birthplace. Even trade was placed in fetters. Free commercial associations were turned into hereditary castes and saddled with definite obligations of state service.

More important even than these far-reaching changes were the two decisions which have given to Constantine a place among the small number of men who have changed the course of history. Nobody would be bold enough to contend that this vigorous and capable soldier was a Christian character. If he did not actually, as is attested, throw German captives to the beasts, he certainly put to death his wife and his son. But in a violent age crimes of violence are lightly condoned, and the failings of Constantine were soon overshadowed by the great achievement which caused him to be regarded in the eastern Empire as a thirteenth apostle.

In that rude age the truth of a religion was apt to be measured by its results. If it brought victory to its devotees, it was likely to be true; if defeat, it was probably false. It is to the credit of Constantine that at an early point in his long career, while he was policing the frontier of Gaul, he came to the conclusion that the Cross, a symbol alike of Christ and of the Sun God, was the bestower of victory. In a vision, reported at first hand to Eusebius, and by him recounted, not in his ecclesiastical history, but in a later biography, Constantine saw the standard of the Cross with the legend Ἐν τούτῳ νίκα (By this conquer), and, advancing with the Christian monogram on his banner, won four victories in succession against the forces of his rival Maxentius, and made himself master of Italy (A.D. 312). The secular fortunes of the Christian Church were henceforth assured. Though his baptism was delayed till 337, the conqueror of Maxentius threw the full weight of his influence on the side of the religion which had brought him victory at Turin, at Verona, at the Milvian bridge hard by the very gates of Rome. The Christians had given their proofs. They had survived persecution, they were organized. Active and energetic characters had been drawn into their fold. Constantine made up his mind to enlist the support, to control the activities, and to appease the dissensions of this influential society. It is true that the Christians were a small minority.[1] The barbarians, the legions, the vast proportion of the civilian population of the west, were still pagan. But there was this difference between paganism and Christianity, that while the pagans, with polytheistic hospitality, were willing to receive the Christian God, the Christians regarded the pagan divinities as malignant demons. A Christian bishop could not dispute the power of Apollo to foresee or of Aesculapius to heal. He did not

[1] Bury estimates one-fifth, *History of the Later Roman Empire*, p. 366.

contest the reality of these beings, but he contended that they were false and that it was wicked to consult them. Paganism was more tolerant. To a discerning prince a well-organized and convinced minority, fortified by sacred books and a clear-cut creed, might well seem to be a better ally than a superior number of indulgent and variously minded sectaries.

Yet it would appear that even after the crowning mercy A.D. of the Milvian bridge the purpose of Constantine was still 312 indistinct. He believed in Christ, but also in the unconquered sun. He tolerated the Christians but retained the office of Pontifex Maximus. His coins bore on one side the emblem of Christianity, on the other an attestation of sun-worship. More than a decade elapsed before soldiers were rebuked for sacrificing to Jupiter or pagan rites were eliminated from official ceremonies.

It can hardly be doubted that the adoption of Christianity as the official religion of the Empire gave a powerful impulse to the enlargement of the Christian community. To pass from Paganism to Christianity was not for many professors of the older creed to enter a climate altogether strange nor to experience a revolution altogether sudden. The process of conversion was gentle and assisted by infinite small gradations of feeling and experience. The sacraments of the new religion recalled the ancient mysteries, its preaching the newer philosophy. The doctrine of a mediator was familiar alike to the Persians and the Neoplatonics. The conception of a Trinity was a well-known religious idea proceeding from the acknowledged fact that three was the perfect number. Abstinence and poverty, ecstasy and calm, were no novelties to the pious adherents of the older creeds. Nor was the idea of the last judgment, with all its terrible consequences, a monopoly of the Christian Faith. The believers in Mithras and the professors of Stoicism were united in holding that the world was destined to perish in flame.

Yet when the pagan had completed his journey he found himself in a world of altered values. Old virtues were disparaged, new virtues, such as chastity, rose in the scale. Poverty was exalted above wealth, faith above works, humility above pride, equality above privilege. The gates of salvation were open to all. A strong inrush of ethical feeling from the underworld pervaded the Empire, dashing itself against the vices and cruelties which were the shadow side of that old civilization, cleansing away many foul impurities, but also obliterating in its passionate course much that in ancient ideals of conduct and expression was noble, temperate, and wise.

From such enthusiasms Constantine, for all his superstition, was exempt. His motto was unity. A church divided against itself would be of little value to the state. So, though he had small personal interest in theological discussions, he was drawn from considerations of policy to be a convener and president of Church councils, a mediator in Church disputes, an influence in the determination of Church dogma. The defeat of the Donatists (a sect of African Puritans) at the Western Council at Arles (314) and of the Arians at the far more important Ecumenical Council at Nicaea (325) were signs of a new association between the Catholic Church and the Roman State, which has coloured the destinies of all Christian peoples. The importance of Constantine's decision is clear; its consequences are variously estimated. To the friends of institutional religion the sovereign who brought the Roman Empire over to Christianity is one of the greatest benefactors of mankind. Others see in that close association of church and state a principal source of the secular pride and ambition which for so many centuries has obscured the original candour of the Christian life.

The second great decision of Constantine was prompted by personal pride blended with military and religious considerations. Like Romulus and Alexander he must build a capital. But he was a son of the Balkans. He knew, as the Austrians knew so well at a later time, how rich in recruits were the wild Illyrian hills of his native home. He was aware that for more than a hundred years the chief danger to the Empire had come from the barbarian tribesmen north of the Danube, and from the oriental monarchies east of the Euphrates. If he were well placed for the defence of the Balkans he saw that he would be in the best position to save the Empire. Already Diocletian had realized that on strategical grounds the capital should be near the frontier between Asia and Europe. Guided by a sure instinct, Constantine, when he had defeated his rival, Licinius, at Chrysopolis, decided on Byzantium, than which no town was better defended by nature or by art.

The new city was to be both Christian and Latin. Christian

it remained, Latin it soon ceased to be. The Emperor may
have reflected that it was easier to make a Christian capital
on the Bosphorus than in a great centre of historic paganism
like Rome, where every temple and statue challenged attack
or defence. He can as little have foreseen the dominance of
the Greek language in Constantinople as that Rome, which
he regarded as the chief fortress of paganism, should become
the leader of the Christian world.

The eastern city rose like an exhalation. Palaces and
mansions, porticos, law courts, and public baths were constructed with feverish celerity. The whole Empire was ran-
sacked for treasures wherewith to decorate the fame of
Constantine. While the serpent column reft from Delphi
recalled the victory of Plataea, the basilica of the Roman law
court crowned with the Persian dome gave to the new
Christian churches their characteristic form, a blend of the
eastern and the western spirit. On May 11, 330, the work was
complete. The new Rome had been built in less than six years.

The foundation of Constantinople marks the beginning of
a new era, during which the Greek and Roman worlds drift
further and further apart until the unity of the Empire becomes nothing more than a theory and a hope. Roman
government as reconstructed by Diocletian and Constantine
survived in the east and was not seriously shaken until the
Frankish conquest of Constantinople in 1204. Far different
was the future of western Europe. Here after a hundred and
fifty years of weakened and precarious existence the Empire
went down under the German invasions, leaving to the Church
the office of preserving as best it might the legacy of ancient
culture in a barbaric world.

Much of that ancient culture was lost or rejected. The free
spirit of rationality which was characteristic of Hellenism
disappeared in a world which had come to believe with St.
Augustine that Time was a brief course of passing moments A.D
created by God and destined at God's pleasure in the twink- 354-
ling of an eye to pass away and to give place to eternity. In 430
this frail, uncertain, and crumbling dispensation, so full of
wickedness and misery, the Christian held that all mundane
interests paled before the awful problem of the soul's salvation.
The reward of the righteous was everlasting blessedness.
Sinners (including unbaptized infants) would burn for ever

in the fires of hell. Sacred books, interpreted by a Providential Church, illumined the path to heaven. Following those lamps, and those alone, and constraining others to pursue the same course, the believer would be saved. False opinion would mean ruin. He must neither dally with it nor suffer it in others. Had not Jesus said, "Compel them to come in"? On this text St. Augustine founded the doctrine of religious persecution which fenced in the mind of Europe during the centuries of Faith.

Though St. Augustine was saturated with the thought of Plato, as later St. Thomas with the speculations of Aristotle, a first-hand knowledge of Greek language and literature died out in the west. Some time in the course of the third century, by an obscure revolution in literary history, Greek ceased to be used by Roman Christians in the celebration of their rites. In time the language fell under suspicion as a vehicle of heresy. Ovid and Terence were taught. Homer and Aeschylus were forgotten, and the knowledge of Greek, the key to the most original and valuable portion of the ancient culture, was not recovered in the west till the fifteenth century. The consequences were serious both for culture and for religion. The effective unity of the Christian Church was broken on the rock of vocabulary and syntax. Greek Christianity, in a climate of Greek metaphysics and imperial despotism, took one course. Latin Christianity, in an undisciplined and barbaric world, but using the language and sharing the spirit of Roman Law, took another. In the east the church was subject to the state; in the west, under the leadership of the Bishop of Rome, it made pretensions to be an independent, if not a superior authority.

The culture of the Latin Church in the west was founded partly upon the Christian and Jewish Scriptures and partly upon the tradition of Latin learning which was maintained in the schools of rhetoric, and which survived the disappearance of the pagan empire. It is this interfusion of literary influences which characterized the intellectual life of western Europe during the early middle ages, when the Church alone preserved and multiplied manuscripts and schooled its barbarian pupils in the elements of Latin grammar and style. At no time has European civilization been so deeply in the debt of Virgil and Cicero as during the first fierce and gloomy centuries of the Christian Empire, when almost alone they represented, in a society which but dimly apprehended their greatness, the healing spirit of ancient humanism.

In curious contrast to the rationalistic spirit of ancient Greek philosophy, the Greek Church of the East Roman, and afterwards of the Russian Empire, has felt little temptation to challenge secular power or ecclesiastical tradition. No great liberating movements for the improvement of the human lot are traceable to its agency. It has been a department of state, stiff, hieratic, constitutional, and conservative, in art no less than in belief. The annals of the Roman Church in the tumultuous and disorganized west present a very different picture, for here during the long abeyance of the western Empire the Church stood out from the licence of the times as heir to the discipline and influence of Rome.

BOOKS WHICH MAY BE CONSULTED

Christopher Dawson: *The Making of Europe*. 1932.

N. H. Baynes: *Constantine the Great and the Christian Church*. (Proceedings of the British Academy, Vol. XV., 1931.)

N. H. Baynes: *The Byzantine Empire*. 1926.

S. Dill: *Roman Society in the Last Century of the Western Empire*. 1899.

Charles Oman: *Short History of the Byzantine Empire*. 1892.

F. Lot: *The End of the Ancient World and the Beginnings of the Middle Ages*. Tr. P. and M. Leon. 1931.

A. H. M. Jones: *Constantine and the Conversion of Europe*. 1949.

F. W. Walbank: *The Decline of the Roman Empire in the West*. 1946

CHAPTER X

THE GERMANIC INVASIONS

Two currents of migration. The east Germans or Goths. They become Arians. The west Germans described by Tacitus. Main characteristics of German society. The impact of the Huns. The Visigoths cross the Danube. Alaric. Dislocation of the western Empire. Continuing prestige of Rome. Gaul in the fifth century. Fall of the Visigothic Kingdom. Vandal conquest of Africa. Attila, his rise and fall. Deposition of Romulus. Theodoric in Italy. Clovis in Gaul. He becomes a Roman Catholic. The darkest age in Britain. The Saxon Conquest. Multiplicity of states. Conversion to Roman Christianity.

So FAR the history of Europe has been dominated by the three great forces of Hellenic civilization, the Roman empire, and the Christian religion, the first two clearly interlinked, but the last deriving from the east and challenging at many crucial points the conduct, beliefs, and interests of the ancient world. A further influence now comes upon the scene and changes for all subsequent time the course of European history. The Latin world of the west, after successfully defeating and absorbing the continental Celts, is overcome by the Germans.

We know very little of the early history of this remarkable race save that they were originally settled in the Scandinavian north, where some remained to form the parent stock of the present Swedish, Norwegian, and Danish nations, while others wandered through Germany in search of food or warmth, or from mere love of adventure and fighting, until one group of these southward-trending peoples reached the waters of the Rhine, while a second, pursuing a more eastern course, descended ultimately on the Danube and the coast of the Black Sea. It is with these two diverging currents of German migration that the Roman Empire was brought into contact. It was the West Germans who fought with Marius and Julius Caesar, who under Augustus defeated Varus and his legions, and whose habits and institutions are described in one of the classics of ethnology, the *De origine, situ, moribus et populis Germaniae* of Tacitus. Finally, it is to two West German peoples, the Saxons and the Franks, that we must ascribe the formation of the mediaeval kingdoms of England and France.

The career of the eastern or Gothic branch of this vigorous race[1] differs in certain important particulars from the future of its western cousins. The Goths burst later into the sunlight of history,[2] struck harder, and built more swiftly, but their work, though arresting and spectacular, was ephemeral and soon undone. Whereas the Franks and Saxons have left a permanent memorial of their passage through time in two powerful and ordered modern states, the name Gothic, save where it is used in relation to a form of architecture originating in a region which the Goths never controlled, is synonymous with all that is dark, barbaric, and destructive. Yet on two occasions the shaping of Europe seemed likely to be confided to the Goths. In the middle of the third century it might have appeared to contemporaries that the fabric of the Roman Empire was destined to perish under the mighty hammer of this formidable people. With an equal show of probability it might have been contended two hundred years later that from the Gothic kingdoms of Italy and Aquitaine there was destined to proceed a continuous and promising civilization blending the vigour and piety of the Goth with the long inherited culture of the Roman. Yet each of these predictions, had it been made, would have been falsified in the event. The terrible crisis of the third century (235-268) was mastered by the courage and resource of three Illyrian commanders, Claudius II, Aurelian, and Probus; and two centuries afterwards, by the strange irony of fortune, the Goths of the west were undone by their very eagerness to receive the spiritual gifts of the Roman world. The Visigoths who were settled in the Balkan peninsula were the first of all the German peoples to accept Christianity. Ulfila, a great missionary of Cappadocian extraction, translated the Bible into Gothic and so spread the Christian message among his adopted people that Ostrogoths and Visigoths alike accepted the faith, and attempted, as far as their rough natures permitted, to understand its meaning. Unfortunately the sacred message had reached the Goths in its Arian form. The poor barbarians

A.D. 310-80

---

[1] Goths, Vandals, Gepids, Burgundians, Lombards, Rugians, etc.
[2] Goths had reached the Black Sea under Caracalla (A.D. 214).

had learned that though Christ was divine, he had been
created by God and was inferior to his Father. Many pious
divines, many famous statesmen, including Constantine the
Great himself, had shared these opinions, first promulgated
in Alexandria by the presbyter Arius, as to the nature of
Christ.

The Goths can hardly be blamed if they believed what they
were told about a mystery so abstruse by leading oracles of
contemporary wisdom. But Arianism, despite brilliant spells
of official favour, finished in the blackest disgrace. It was
condemned by the Council of Nicaea. It was condemned by
the Bishop of Rome. It was reprobated by the western clergy
in Italy, Gaul and Spain, who represented to congregations
unversed in theological subtleties that the Arian was the
enemy of Christ ($\chi\rho\iota\sigma\tau\acute{o}\mu\alpha\chi\circ\varsigma$) and that Arianism was a
challenge to Christ's divinity In the troubled theological
atmosphere of the fifth century, when success in this world
and in the world beyond was thought to depend on the
accuracy of faith, there was no issue more passionately or
widely debated than the nature of the Second Person of the
Trinity, which few were fitted to discuss, and none were able
to understand.

So the Gothic kingdoms of Italy and Aquitaine, which had
been founded by the sword, perished of a heresy, and the
more barbarous West Germans, who were converted later,
but to the orthodox faith, entered upon a long inheritance of
power, with the applause and support of the western Church.

C.A.D.   Of these West Germans, Tacitus, writing in the time of
98 Trajan, has drawn a picture more remarkable perhaps for its
moral purpose than for its fidelity to fact. It is the aim of the
Roman historian to contrast the idealized simplicity of the
German life with the degenerate luxury of Italian society,
and to find in the free ways of the noble savage material for
the chastisement of civilized man.

It is probable, therefore, that the virtues of the Germans
were here exaggerated, as it is certain that no Roman would
willingly have exchanged the vivid life of the forum for the
lonely clearings, the forbidding forests, and the leaden skies
of Germany. Tacitus, however, was right in thinking that the
Germans had something new and valuable to give to European
civilization. He seems to have divined in this barbaric people
a refreshing and renovating power, to have seen that they

had the secret of political liberty, which Rome had forgotten, the passion for individual initiative which Rome had suppressed, the habit of rearing large families, which Rome had chosen to neglect and despise. The last of these characteristics gave to the Germans a decisive superiority in the struggles which were to come. Again and again in the course of history the Latin world has had cause to tremble before the irrepressible fecundity of this wholesome and monogamous race.

Save that the West Germans had by the time of Tacitus taken to a settled agricultural life, while the easterners with their waggons and herds were still trekking through pathless forests, one part of the Teuton world much resembled another. The violent, blond, beer-swilling giant with fierce blue eyes and long fair hair, drinking and dreaming, fighting and gambling, singer and song lover, his strong loyalty to chieftain and clan only mastered by his still greater passion for warlike adventure, was a type well known in the fourth century to every legionary camp on the northern frontier. It is true that during two centuries of internecine war and forest clearance the clans of Germany had undergone many changes of size, shape, and appellation. Small clans had disappeared, greater aggregations had been formed round some heroic figure, or in response to some warlike necessity, and then dissolving, as men died or fell, had entered into new combinations. The little tribes mentioned by Tacitus had vanished by the age of Constantine, and were replaced by larger people, the Franks, the Saxons, the Alemans of south Germany. But the main characteristics of German life and society were little changed, and might be found anywhere in central Europe—the chieftain and his chosen band of warrior comrades, the popular assembly of free tribesmen, the ancient royal families, from which kings might be chosen, the great herds of small cattle, the open field tillage of corn and barley, the predial serfs, and the absence not only of towns but even of villages or hamlets with close-set houses and sheltered streets. Yet despite their common origin and similar manners the Germans were wholly devoid of national feeling. Tribe fought with tribe, family with family. By some the Roman Empire was regarded as an enemy, by others as a possible paymaster or host. Accordingly the armies which this fecund race could put into the field at any one time were ludicrously dispro-

portionate to its numbers. If the Roman armies were, as
we have seen, dangerously under strength, their German
antagonists were not to any marked degree more numerous.
It is not, then, to a series of conflicts in which some twenty
thousand men were involved on either side that we must look
for an explanation of the decline and fall of the Roman
Empire. That great structure was not brought down to the
ground by a frontal attack, but by a process of infiltration
extending over a hundred years which ended by placing the
government of Italy, Gaul, Spain, and Africa in German
hands.

A wild Mongolian people riding on stout ponies out of
central Asia had in the later part of the fourth century made
its way over the steppes into south-eastern Europe. Slaying
and plundering as they rode, these ugly merciless creatures,
known as Huns, swept every obstacle before them like chaff
before an eastern gale. Alans, Ostrogoths, and Visigoths felt
successively the force of a thrust spreading tremors through
the whole German world, and leading to those great but
obscurely chronicled movements of the German peoples,
which had for a time submerged Gaul and Britain, Spain,
Africa, and Italy, and bequeathed to mediaeval Germany the
heroic memories of the Niebelungenlied.

The first effect of this new disturbing force was felt upon the
north-eastern bastion of the Empire. By 376 the Huns had
penetrated into Dacia (the beautiful country of Transylvania
which has recently passed to the Roumans) and there
defeated the Visigoths, who had themselves some years before
evicted the descendants of that Roman province, from which
Trajan has obtained an undying renown, and modern
Roumania a disputed title.

Uprooted from this pleasant home the Visigoths appealed
for Roman shelter. They were permitted to cross the Danube
and to form an encampment in lower Moesia. Eighty thousand
alien immigrants are not easily absorbed even by the best
organized community. The Visigoths were uncomfortable,
and as discomfort ripened into suspicion and suspicion into
hate, they took up arms against their imperial host. The
issue was joined on the field of Adrianople (378), when the
mailed cavalry of the invaders defeated the imperial army,
slew Valens, the Emperor, and established for a thousand

years the predominance of the cavalry arm in European warfare.

The man who was called upon to deal with this desperate situation was a fine Spanish soldier, claiming descent from the family of Trajan. Theodosius I, being ready to apply persecution to the support of orthodoxy, has received from ecclesiastical historians the title of "great"; and the Emperor under whose rule the mysteries of Eleusis and the Olympian games were celebrated for the last time deserves a special place in the annals of the Christian Church. But the reputation of Theodosius has a better foundation than the bigotry with which he persecuted the pagans and the heretics. By skilfully converting the Goths into federates of the Empire and providing them with an assured settlement on imperial territory, he purchased a peace of thirteen years for his harassed dominions.

Had Theodosius been succeeded by a son as resolute as himself, it is possible that the Goths might have been converted into loyal and obedient servants of the east Roman state; but there ensued upon his death, at the age of fifty in 395, a calamity from which the Empire never recovered. At this critical juncture two feeble and inexperienced youths, Arcadius and Honorius, were called respectively to rule the eastern and western Empire. The first of these shadow sovereigns was governed by the eunuch Eutropius, the second by the Vandal Stilicho.

Though bound to defend the Empire under the terms of the recent treaty, the Visigoth retained in his Thracian home the heart and speech of a German savage. A cultured visitor from Africa saw the impolicy of admitting these armed and predatory aliens into the body of the Roman state. In a spirited allocution to Arcadius, Synesius of Cyrene pleaded for the formation of a national army to cope with the Gothic peril. The farmer should be called from his farm, the philosopher from his study, the craftsman from his craft, the salesman from his shop, the city drone from his beloved theatre, and all should be enrolled in a force for national defence. The speech, if ever delivered, fell upon idle ears. While Arcadius did nothing effective, the Visigoths elected as their King a fighting man of thirty, Alaric the Bold.

The career of this Christian savage is in many respects of great significance. All through his life Alaric appears to have had for his object not the destruction of the Empire, which would have been to him unthinkable, but his own elevation in the Imperial Service, and the assignment of an attractive settlement to his people. To obtain these ends there was no form of blackmail to which he would not resort, no impiety which he was not prepared to commit. He held Athens to ransom, took Corinth and Sparta, ravaged Thessaly and the Peloponnese, and then, passing into Italy, besieged Rome three times, and finally (410) gave it over to his barbarians to sack.

This great calamity striking a city which for many centuries had been regarded as the pre-ordained centre of human authority on earth created a profound impression of dismay. Was this, then, the result of Christianity, and the vengeance of the ancient shrines? Was this the reward of the Christian Faith? The answer came in the *De Civitate Dei*, begun in 412 and finished in 427. In this, perhaps the greatest of patristic writings, St. Augustine of Hippo replied that over and against the city of man was the city of God, unaffected by material things, without frontiers and embracing the entire body of the faithful all over the world.

Yet the sack of Rome was but a minor element in a great developing calamity. The Gothic attacks on Italy initiated nine years before had only been repelled by the depletion of the imperial garrisons on the Rhine. Sueves, Alans, Vandals (the last an East German people already converted to Arian Christianity) swarmed over the ill-defended frontier of Gaul, and after three years of terrible pillage and slaughter crossed the Pyrenees into Spain. In these three years of memorable anarchy the whole complexion of the western Empire was changed; for not only was its authority finally shaken in Gaul and Spain, but a certain Constantine, raised to the purple by the legions of Britain, took most of the Roman garrison from that island, leaving it by so much the more exposed to the assaults of Saxon pirates in the south, and to the raids of Picts and Scots along the northern border.

A.D. 406-9

This preliminary hurricane was followed by a steady pressure of German tribes westward into Gaul. The Salian Franks occupied Belgium, the Ripuarian Franks took Trèves, the Alemanni encamped in Alsace, the Burgundians founded a kingdom with its capital at Worms, and finally the Visigoths, exchanging Italy for Gaul, settled in the region of Toulouse,

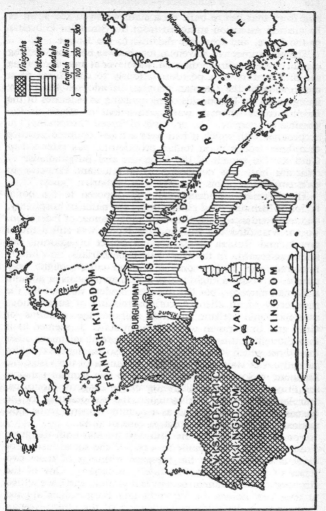

THE GOTHIC KINGDOMS AT THE HEIGHT OF THEIR POWER

and from that centre built up a state which at the point of its greatest extension stretched from the Straits of Gibraltar to the Loire, and from the Atlantic to the Rhone.

The government of Ravenna, for this was now the working capital of the Empire in the west, was never at any time during the fifth century in a position seriously to curb these mass movements of the German peoples. It adopted the policy inaugurated by Theodosius of recognizing as federates of the Empire tribes whom it was inconvenient to attack or impossible to conquer. The principle of forced "hospitality," in accordance with which it had been a time-honoured practice to quarter troops upon Italian proprietors, was extended to Gaul for the benefit of the Visigoths and Burgundians. A reluctant host was compelled by a reluctant Emperor to cede two-thirds of his property to a barbarian "guest."

The German intruders were well disposed to the polite fiction, which disguised pillage under the name of hospitality, and independence under the respectable banner of federation. To the Visigoths and Burgundians Rome was still a moral power, and Roman civilization an object of ignorant but admiring regard. In the eyes of these barbarians, now faintly tinctured with civility, only a Roman citizen might wear purple. A Visigoth might marry a Roman princess or acclaim a Roman emperor, but the imperial diadem was not for the rude brow of an alien. A curious mixture of superstitious reverence and defiant hostility marked the relations of Goth and Burgundian to the Roman state. It seemed as if they thought that against Rome there were no talismans other than those which Rome could supply. So among the trophies carried out of Italy by Ataulph, the founder of the Visigothic kingdom in South-Western Gaul, were two Roman persons, the Princess Galla Placidia, sister of the Emperor Honorius, and Attalus, an obscure rhetorician, the first designed for the barbarian's bed, the second as a counter emperor to be used against the court of Ravenna in case of need.

A.D. 411

For the remainder of the fifth century and until the great Frankish victory at Vouillê in A.D. 507 the social history of Gaul is dominated by the presence within it of these two states of "friendly" or "federate" barbarians. One of the strongest forces in human society is imitation, and once settled in their new homes the Visigoths and Burgundians applied themselves to the study and imitation of the Greco-Roman culture, which nowhere in that age was so fully maintained as in Gaul. The barbarian kings soon discovered that, however much they might despise the effeminacy of Mediterranean men, government could not be carried out in a Latin-speaking country without the employment of ministers and clerks who spoke the Latin tongue or of legists who knew the Roman law. It does not then appear that life was anywhere made intolerable to the Gallo-Roman provincial who lived in the kingdoms of Burgundy or Aquitaine. The great noble farmed and hunted, built and gardened, visited his friends and trifled in his library, enjoying a stately, unruffled existence, as if there were no barbarians to murder the beautiful Latin tongue, no need to think for the collective life-future of the Empire, no social problem or foreign menace, but an unending prospect of plenty and elegance for the fortunate and cultured members of the senatorial class. To the poor the yoke of a Theodoric or a Gondebaud sometimes seemed lighter than the grinding oppression of the imperial tax-gatherers.

By this time the Roman world had become so familiar with the German soldier in the legions, the German adventurers at court, and the German immigrant in the fields, that the true drift of the events of the fifth century went unperceived. The cultivated noble of Auvergne feared the defacement of the Latin tongue and the decay of Latin letters. What he did not apprehend was the dissolution of the Roman state. The political consequences of the great changes in the social texture of the population brought about by German immigration were as little present to his mind as were the lessons of American immigration statistics in the last quarter of the nineteenth century to the statesmen in Washington. When once the first agonies of the settlement were overcome, the Visigoths and the more cultivated Burgundians were regarded by the older inhabitants of Gaul as instruments rather than as enemies. With the assistance of their barbarian kings, with their robes of skin and their uncouth jargon, great Gallo-Roman nobles might be raised to the purple, and Gothic and Burgundian armies might protect and even extend the Empire. On a commission from Honorius, King Wallia led his Visigoths into Spain and reconquered the greater part of that peninsula from the Sueves, the Vandals, and the Alans; and later, when Aetius, "the last of the Romans," rallied the forces of Gaul against King Attila and his Huns, the Visigoth Theodoric, without whose army success would hardly have been won, laid down his life in the cause of the Empire.

In broad outline, then, the history of Gaul in the fifth century, though opening with a carnival of pillage and destruction, witnesses a certain retardation in the advance of intellectual darkness.

The Visigoths and Burgundians turned out to be better than might have been expected. The schools continued to teach, the lawyers to plead, the nobles to write verses, and the bishops to minister to the needs of their congregations. Until Euric, the A.D. Visigoth, exchanged the policy of religious toleration which 400- his predecessors had pursued for a campaign of active perse- 84 cution, the orthodox Church in Gaul had little to complain of from the presence of two Arian monarchies on Gallic soil. Euric, however, was intolerable. That he was the most powerful and aggressive of the Visigoth monarchs, that he attacked the Bretons and conquered the loyalist province of Auvergne, were errors less heinous in that theological age than his aggressive heresy. At Euric's death whatever store of popularity his house had secured in Aquitaine was effectively squandered, and when the Visigothic army went down before the orthodox Franks on the field of Vouillé, the old inhabitants of southern France looked on with indifference and relief.

Seventy-eight years before this, the Roman government suffered a startling reverse in an unexpected quarter. Africa, the principal source of the Roman corn supply and the seat of a flourishing Italian civilization, had already fired the ambition of two Gothic kings, and was now, on the invitation of a Roman governor, invaded by the Vandals of Spain. To the enfeebled strength of the western empire no blow could be more serious. Under the leadership of Gaiseric, the ablest barbarian chieftain of his age, the Vandals advanced from strength to strength. They took Carthage (439), built a fleet, and in a short time made themselves the greatest naval power in the western Mediterranean. For the first time since the close of the Punic Wars the Roman government was faced with the menace of a navy superior to its own, a navy capable of detaching Sicily, Sardinia, and Corsica, and of bringing an army of pillaging Vandals to loot and ravish, devastate and murder in Rome itself. A succession of treaties (435-442), each more favourable to the invader than the last, failed to convert these Arian barbarians into friendly or even valuable associates of the government in Italy. The Vandals were savages. They destroyed much, they constructed nothing, and of their hundred years of rule in Africa only memories of havoc remain. Yet their intervention in the theatre of European affairs was of critical importance. At the moment when it was most necessary that all the forces of Italy should be concentrated on checking the barbarian advance in Gaul and Britain, they were weakened and dispersed by the necessity of dealing with the formidable pirate state which had established itself in the richest corn-bearing province of the Empire. The consequences were far reaching. They comprise the final loss of Gaul, the withdrawal (442) of the last Roman garrison from Britain, the conquest of the south-eastern portion of the British island by the Saxons, and, on a lower scale of importance, the exodus of Celtic fugitives from the south-western regions of our island, which has given the name of Brittany to the ancient Armorican districts of Gaul.

The Mongolian invasion of eastern Europe, which had been the *primum mobile* in this long chain of shattering experiences for the Empire, had not yet exhausted its effects. It was one of the secrets of the longevity of the Roman state that it made a practice of recruiting from its most formidable enemies. The Franks were employed to defend the Rhine frontier in 407, the Huns to destroy the Burgundian kingdom of Worms in 435. But this policy, though it might be successful as a makeshift, offered no permanent protection against the hungry appetites of restless and fecund nations. In the middle of the fifth century one of the greatest dangers which assailed the Empire proceeded from the Huns, who a few years earlier had proved themselves to be valuable auxiliaries. This people, under the guidance of Attila, one of those remarkable leaders who from time to time arise to fashion the destiny of a race, or startle the world by a sudden revelation of violence or power, succeeded in obtaining for themselves for a period of nineteen years (435 to 454) an ascendancy which extended from the Rhine to the Urals. The eastern Empire paid them tribute; the German peoples of central

Europe (Gepids, Ostrogoths, Rugians, and Scirians) entered into their confederacy, submitted to their direction, and influenced their manners.

So vast an aggregation of peoples ruled by a powerful and unscrupulous savage sent a thrill of consternation through Europe. Upon whom would the thunderbolt fall? The western Empire, under the rule of Valentinian, the feeble nephew of the weak Honorius, offered the most tempting prey, and in 450 Attila made up his mind to seize it.

Then a striking illustration was afforded of the gulf which divides courage from strategy, numbers from science, and true political coherence from the magnetism of a name. Attila was no general. His vast and miscellaneous following was no army. His personal ascendancy was no substitute for the organized institutions of a state. The Mongolian invasion of Gaul in 451, dreadful as it appeared in prospect and retrospect, was foiled when Attila turned back from Orleans rather than attack a fortified and well defended city; and the battle of Troyes, which inflicted severe punishment on the retreating army, confirmed rather than decided the issue of the campaign. Nor was the invasion of Italy in the succeeding year marked by any evidence of intelligent design. After a brief spell of pillage and extortion, Attila withdrew north of the Alps, and that so swiftly that the pious have ascribed to the intercession of the Bishop of Rome a course more probably dictated by the prevalence of disease, the failure of supplies, and the intelligence of an advancing army from the east. Two years later the Hun king was in his grave and his empire broken (battle of Nedao, 454) by an insurrection of its German vassals.

From this moment the germanization of the west steadily proceeded. Ostrogoths poured into the Balkan peninsula, creating by their restless and turbulent activities a problem similar to that which had taxed the resources of the eastern Empire a century before. In Italy a succession of phantom and ephemeral emperors reached its close with a pathetic figure, named, by the supreme irony of providence, Romulus Augustulus, who was deposed by Odovacar, the East German master of the troops. Military revolutions were no novelty in the annals of the Roman Empire, and the act of Odovacar had many precedents. If he assumed the title of king, so, too, had Ataulph and his Visigothic successors. If he had risen to

A.D. 476

power by claiming for his troops a third part of the lands of Italy, he was entitled to invoke the old practice of hospitality so recently applied in Burgundy and Aquitaine. It is true that he deposed Romulus, but the lad was a usurper, unrecognized in Constantinople, and the deed condoned by the bestowal upon its author of the high imperial title of patrician. What was original in Odovacar's action was not that it was revolutionary, but that it was conservative. He refused to appoint a successor to Romulus, calculating that he would have more elbow room in a united Empire governed from Constantinople as in the days of Theodosius the Great. That unity was in fact and theory preserved until the coronation of Charlemagne as Emperor of the west in 800.

The age immediately succeeding is remarkable for the emergence of two great barbaric figures, Theodoric the Ostrogoth and Clovis the Frank, the first the founder of a short-lived Gothic monarchy in Italy, the second the creator of the medieval monarchy of France. A peculiarity common to each of these dynamic and experienced men, though more clearly marked in the Goth than in the Frank, was a recognition of the continuing authority of the Emperor. Theodoric was sent into Italy to overthrow Odovacar on a commission from the Emperor Zeno, and throughout his long reign (493-526) regarded himself not only as a Gothic king, but also as an Imperial official. Clovis received the insignia of the honorary consulship from Anastasius. But there was one critical difference. Theodoric, by far the more powerful and important figure throughout his life, was an Arian. Clovis became a militant Catholic. To this divergence we may principally ascribe the fact that Theodoric failed and Clovis succeeded in laying the foundations of an enduring state.

Yet a singular interest attaches to the experiment which failed in Italy. In the legends of Germany, Theodoric figures under the name of Dietrich of Bern as a great leader of the German peoples, the Achilles of a German Iliad playing his heroic part in a tempestuous and memorable age. And such a leader he was recognized to be by the Arian sovereigns, Vandal, Visigoth, and Burgundian, with whom he entered into bonds of alliance. The instinct of a people is never wholly wrong. There was a bigness of scale about Theodoric which redeemed many of the grosser vices, and may be set against illiteracy, cruelty, and craft. After three years' hard fighting he eliminated from Italy the Rugian army of Odovacar, and thereafter gave thirty-six years of golden peace to that much harassed land, enlarging its frontiers, encompassing it with a network of protective diplomacy, and holding or winning for it a circle of outlying territories, Provence, southern Germany, the Tyrol, part of Hungary, and Dalmatia, and exercising a kind of suzerainty over Spain. But it is probable that even so he would not have attained to mythical stature but for the fact that he, a German with all the qualities of his race, ruled as the Roman master of Italy, and from that central pivot directed his far-flung operations.

The beautiful city of Ravenna, besides other famous memorials of this age, still shows the tomb of Theodoric the Goth. His court and administration were Latin. He respected the Roman Senate and was studious to restore the ancient monuments of Italy. The folly of attempting to force the Gothic language upon Italy was far from his mind. It was no part of his policy to make changes in law or government, to force the pace of racial assimilation, or to affront the religious prejudices of Rome; he did not legislate, or issue coins without the Emperor's name. He repaired the aqueducts, maintained the public chairs of grammar and rhetoric, and even the Imperial laws which forbade intermarriage between Romans and barbarians; and it was only in his last years, and as an answer to an outbreak of persecution against his co-religionists in the east, that the Arian in him showed his teeth, and that he committed the crime of passion which is charged against the memory of many good deeds. Boethius, the last of the ancient thinkers and poets, whose *De consolatione Philosophiae* was one of the best books generally known to the middle ages, was a benefactor of mankind. His judicial murder is a blot on the fame of Theodoric.

A.D.
525

The reign of Clovis, founder of the Merovingian House and Architect of France (481-511) is marked by three great victories, over Syagrius, King of the Romans, at Soissons in 486, over the Alemans in Alsace ten years later, and lastly over Alaric, king of the Visigoths, on the field of Vouillé (near Poitiers) in 507. It was after the first of these triumphs, obtained over an officer who was representing the Roman cause in Gaul, that Clovis removed from Soissons to Paris and there established his capital; after the second that he exchanged paganism for the Catholic faith; after the third that he advanced his kingdom to the Pyrenees, driving the main body of his Visigothic enemies to find in Spain the centre of their power. Whether the conversion of Clovis was due to the influence of his Catholic wife Clotilda, a Burgundian princess, or to his conviction that Christ had delivered the Alemans into his hands, or to a long-headed calculation of political chances, is of little moment compared with the capital fact that in 496 the leader of the Salian Franks, the most renowned of all the Germanic tribes, became a protagonist of the Catholic cause.

The long alliance between the French monarchy and the Roman Church, which ended in 1830 with the flight of the last Bourbon King from the Paris mob, was baptized in the blood of that Alsatian battlefield more than 1,300 years earlier. It was a turning point in the history of Gaul, and indeed of Europe, when the Catholic Church was made supreme from the Mediterranean to the Channel and from the Atlantic to the Rhine, and a barbarian king accepted under the influence of the Church the machinery of government through bishops, count, and city, which was the legacy of later Rome to mediaeval France. A warrior chief had placed himself at the head of a militant church; and in the words attributed by the chronicler to Clovis, as he marched against the Visigoths, "It vexes me to see these Arians hold part of Gaul. Let us attack them with God's aid, and having conquered them, subject their land," we seem to hear a premonitory blast of the trumpet which called the Frankish chivalry to the Crusades, sounded the knell of the Albigensian heretics, and led to the Huguenot emigration from France in the seventeenth century, by which the Protestant countries of Europe were sensibly enriched.

It has been noted that among the consequences of the great tidal wave of Germanic conquest which swept into Gaul at the beginning of the fifth century was the snapping of the connection between Britain and Rome. The province was not formally abandoned. There was no official decision to relinquish territory which for four hundred years had been a source of affluence and pride to the Empire, territory covered by Roman roads, studded with Roman cities and luxurious villas, and long prized not only as a market for slaves, but for its minerals, its agriculture, its watering-places, and its oyster beds. The separation ensued from the force of events which Rome was unable to control. The provincials of Britain were left to their own resources, and before the double danger of the Picts and the Scots in the north and of the Saxon pirates in the south the provincials ultimately succumbed. How fierce or protracted their resistance may have been we can only conjecture.

What happened in Britain during the hundred and fifty years which elapsed between the final break with Rome and the coming of St. Augustine is shrouded in the deepest mystery. There are no contemporary chronicles or records or any gleam of authentic light. The spade of the archaeologist indicates extensive burnings in many important towns, such as Canterbury, which are thought to point to a violent contest, but may have other interpretations. The Anglo-Saxon Chronicle, which belongs to a much later date, contains so much that is clearly mythical that a tincture of doubt necessarily attaches to those portions of its narrative which may embody authentic facts.

A.D.
597

We cannot therefore reconstitute the chain of events through this dark period. It may be that a violent and destructive attack, ruining towns and exterminating, enslaving, or chasing away the provincial population, was followed by a quieter period of steady agricultural settlement. Nothing is certain but the result. When the darkness clears away with the coming of St. Augustine, England is a Saxon and a pagan country.

This astonishing change, pointing to some great unchronicled catastrophe, was quite consistent with the preservation in Britain of those earlier human types which Julius Caesar and Claudius had found in the island. The dark Iberians, who may be traced back to the neolithic age, the fair-haired Goidelic or Gaelic Celts of the Scottish highlands, whose weapons were of bronze, and the later wave (later, as we know, for their weapons were of iron) of the Brythonic Celts, who eventually settled in Wales and Cornwall, survived the shock and are still constituent elements of the British population. What was obliterated by the Saxon conquest was the living influence of Rome, its speech, its religion, its towns, its institutions.

In the shell of this old Roman province was a raw, Teuton, agricultural society, worshipping Odin, speaking a Germanic tongue, and living a life as far as possible removed from the routine of a provincial townsman under the Roman Empire. The Jutes, the Saxons, and the Angles, the three cognate peoples who are found firmly settled in England at the beginning of the seventh century, were quite untouched by Roman influence. Everywhere they lived in townships or villages, cultivated the land in common on the open field system, and retained in their hundred courts those forms of popular government and justice which had attracted the notice of Tacitus in the first century. Conquest, however, had brought in its train one important development. The leader in war had become a king, and traced his pedigree to the gods. He was assisted by a Witan, a body of counsellors.

Yet despite their strong family likeness, the invaders were far from being of the same mind. Vast tracts of marsh and impenetrable forest kept the settlers apart and obstructed communication. The estuary of the Humber was probably in the seventh century a greater obstacle between the north and south of England than are the Pyrenees today between Spain and France. East Anglia was an island surrounded by forests and fen. The Andredsweald, an intricate tract of marsh and forest, divided the North Downs and the South Downs. In a country so full of natural obstacles many years passed before the descendants of the original private adventurers grew together into a state, and many more before any local king dreamed of an all-England monarchy. Accordingly the early history of that part of our island which was colonized by the Saxons is marked by a tangle of internecine wars between various parties of invaders, who, helped by the geography of the country, had formed themselves into separate states. Now a kingdom rose, now it declined in the scale of superiority. The little Jutish kingdom of Kent, then as always the garden of England, and of all portions of our island the most advanced in civilization, saw its best days under Ethelbert, the patron of St. Augustine. Northumbria, quickened by its contact with Celtic Christianity, was supreme till 685, Mercia till the death of Offa in 796. It was while the country was thus distracted by internal rivalries that the Danes opened a new chapter in English history.

Meanwhile England had once again been called into the circle of the Roman Church. Here, as elsewhere, the conversion of the pagan is to be attributed not to any penitential movement of the heart, but to the pressure of the monarchy upon a submissive population. The men of Kent and the Kentish men followed Ethelbert into the Christian fold. In Northumbria, in East Anglia, in Mercia, and in Wessex the story was the same. The creed of the king became the creed of the people. A plain, unquestioning, superstitious people was content to take its religious fashions from the court.

The effect of the conversion was not the less profound and far-reaching by reason of its perfunctory and superficial operation on conscience and conduct. Britain was again knit to the Latin world, taught the advantage of written law, and fitted with an ecclesiastical organization which was strictly modelled on the imperial organization of Rome. The first national assemblies to be held in Britain were church councils. The first code of native laws was drafted in Kent under the influence of Augustine. The parish, which has played so large a part in English life, more particularly in the country, was the gift of the Roman churchmen to Saxon England. It was characteristic of the downright practical temper of the race that the Celtic form of Christianity, which had been brought from Ireland to Iona, and had thence with all its wayward graces penetrated to Northumbria, was not able to survive in the competition with its stern Roman antagonists. Both on the continent and in England the Saxons were noted for their submission to the papal see. The Latin education of the inhabitants of this island, which had been intermitted for a hundred and fifty years, was now begun again under the ferule of the Roman priest.

BOOKS WHICH MAY BE CONSULTED

C. W. Previté-Orton: *Outlines of Mediaeval History*. 1924.

L. Halphen: *Les Barbares* ([*Vol. V.,*] *Peuples et Civilisation. Ed.* Halphen et Saquac. 1926.)

A. Rambaud: *Histoire de la Russie*. 1884.

V. Kluchevsky: *History of Russia*. Tr. C. J. Hogarth. 5 vols. 1911-31.

T. Hodgkin: *Italy and her Invaders*. 1931.

T. Hodgkin: *Theodoric the Goth*. 1891.

S. Dill: *Roman Society in the Last Century of the Roman Empire*. 1899.

R. G. Collingwood: *Roman Britain*. 1921.

Sir Charles Oman: *A History of England before the Norman Conquest.* 1910.
G. M. Trevelyan: *History of England.* 1926.
E. Lavisse: *Histoire de France,* Vol. II. 1903.
Shorter Cambridge Medieval History, Vol. 1. 1952.
J. M. Wallace Hadrill: *The Barbarian West,* 400–1000. 1952.
Sir Frank Stenton: *Anglo-Saxon England.* 1943.
E. A. Thompson: *A History of Attila and the Huns.* 1948.

CHAPTER XI

THE AGE OF JUSTINIAN

Belief in the necessary continuance of the Empire. The Byzantine state. Justinian and Theodora. Western policy. The reconquest of Italy from the Goths. Effects of the Gothic wars. The destruction of the Gothic kingdom of Italy a mistake. The Lombards. Exhaustion of the eastern Empire at Justinian's death. The causes. Roman law. The Monophysite heresy and its influence in the east. Absolutism and orthodoxy of the Emperor.

THE BARBARIC conquests in the west, which to the modern eye are significant as leading to the replacement of the Roman Empire by other and more varied forms of political life, were very differently regarded by the Christian contemporaries of Clovis and Theodoric. Learned divines then taught to the full satisfaction of plain men that the world had entered into its sixth and last phase, and that beyond the Roman Empire there was nothing but Antichrist and the final catastrophe of all things. Such was the doctrine of Augustine in the fifth and of Bede in the eighth century, and from such teaching it followed either that the triumphs of the barbarians would be succeeded by an imperial restoration or else that they portended the coming of the judgment day. The one contingency which was ruled out was that the Roman Empire might perish and the world notwithstanding proceed.

Accordingly it is not surprising that in the century succeeding this great upheaval in the west, a serious attempt was made to restore the effective unity of the Empire. While all was fluid and tumultuous in Italy and Gaul, the great fabric of

Roman government was still maintained by the civil officials and mercenary armies of the eastern Empire. Here was a corrupt and intriguing court, a centralized but venal bureaucracy, a city mob living for the rival factions of the hippodrome, a church obscurantist, influential and umbrageous, and a line of Emperors owing their authority, not as did the barbarian kings to a divine origin, but as often as not to the workings of intrigue and to the tumultuous acclamations of the soldiers and the crowd. Amid the upheavals of Europe there was within the cincture of Constantinople an assured civilization and an atmosphere in the conduct of affairs so unwholesome, refined, and persistent that under the name of Byzantinism it survived both the Latin and the Turkish conquests, and was only dispersed by the vigorous blasts of Ottoman nationalism in our own age.

Though it experienced great alternations of fortune, sometimes brilliantly victorious, at other times driven to the lowest pit of abasement and misery, the east Roman Empire defended for a thousand years the cause of Greek Christianity in a world of enemies. Goths, Slavs, Avars, Bulgars, Persians, Saracens ravaged and despoiled, but failed to upset this enduring fabric of the ancient world. It persisted through every storm, renouncing nothing which had once been Roman, cherishing hopeless claims and outworn pretensions, and yet, despite its rags and tatters, so vital, that but for the shattering Latin conquest in the thirteenth century, it might have had strength to uphold the Cross against the Crescent into modern times. For century after century, this state, Roman in name and theory, but in reality part Greek and part oriental, maintained a standard of cultured refinement which shone like gold against the surrounding gloom. The classical scholar may smile at the Byzantines, yet they were the channel through which the rudiments of culture and Christianity were communicated to the Slavs of Russia and the Balkans, and the instructors of many rude Asiatic peoples in the ways and institutions of an ordered state.

On the death of the Emperor Anastasius in 518 the throne of Constantinople passed to an elderly and illiterate Illyrian soldier, who in later life developed an unpleasant passion for persecuting Arians. Justin was born in the village of Tauresium near Uskub, that swiftly contracting region of the Balkans in which Latin still survived as the spoken tongue.

Latin, then, he knew, and the soldier's trade, but little else. He had, however, a nephew from the same Latin-speaking region, whom, being childless, he adopted as his heir, and caused to be instructed in all the accomplishments then thought to be necessary for the formation of the princely mind. Justinian proved worthy of his uncle's regard. The young Illyrian peasant was endowed with that rare capacity for sustained and minute labour which is a sure sign of intellectual strength. Long after others were abed this passionate worker would be toiling over his files, or would be found restlessly striding down the corridors like a ghost. During Justin's reign he was the real ruler. Then in 527, a year after Theodoric's death, the heir-apparent, an experienced man in his forty-fifth year, succeeded to his uncle's place.

Before this he had looked into the gutter for a wife and picked out a diamond. Theodora was the daughter of a Cypriot bear keeper. She had been an actress and a courtesan, had wandered and suffered, and combined in her person every quality of station and experience certain to give offence to respectable people. But though a thousand scandals were woven round her name, though she was violent in her passions and vindictive in her hates, she appears to have been in a sense a noble being, beautiful and witty, with a high courage, a statesman's mind, and the precious gift of womanly compassion. When Constantinople was in the hands of the rioters in 532, and the Emperor and his councillors were in favour of flight, Theodora came forward and saved her husband's throne. "If you wish to protract your life, O Emperor, flight is easy; there are your ships and there is the sea. But consider whether, if you escape to exile, you will not wish every day that you were dead. As for me, I hold with the ancient saying that the imperial purple is a glorious shroud." Her piety was equal to her pluck. The first home for the rescue of fallen women to be erected in Europe is due to this fallen woman, who for twenty-one years shared an Emperor's throne and swayed his policy.

A peace with Chosroes I of Persia, struck in 532 after three years' indecisive fighting, released the energies of Justinian for the great task of imperial recovery in the west. An army under Belisarius, whose shining military talents had been equally proved in the riots at Constantinople and in the Persian War was sent to Africa to evict the Vandals, and after two pitched battles near Carthage so effectually accomplished his task that nothing more was heard of this barbarous and heretical people, whose fleets had been the terror of the western Mediterranean. Africa returned nominally to the Roman obedience and to undisputed enjoyment of the orthodox faith. But if Justinian expected to extend to the north African littoral a Roman peace he was soon disabused. The Moors, who had seriously strained the powers of the Vandals, began at once to molest the new government in Africa. The western provinces fell into their hands. What remained was only held after two exhausting wars which tested the resources of the best generals of the Empire.

For the moment, however, the Emperor had triumphed beyond all expectations. In a three months' campaign Belisarius had wiped one set of German heretics off the map, and it was reasonable to suppose that with hardly less expenditure of effort he could do equal execution on another. Accordingly the next objective was the Gothic kingdom of Italy, which had just lost a capable ruler by the murder of Amalasuntha, the daughter of Theodoric the Great. Since the murderer was Theodahat, the Gothic king whom Amalasuntha in her need for male support had selected as a colleague, and since the victim was a lady friendly to Roman ways and already in secret relation with the Imperial Court, a convenient pretext was offered for a premeditated invasion. In September, 535, the brilliant Belisarius was despatched to Sicily with a small army of 7,500 men.

There ensued a struggle of twenty-eight years, during which fortune favoured alternatively the Roman, the Gothic, and again the Roman cause. At first Belisarius, despite the exiguous force at his disposal, outmatched his opponents. Sicily fell to him almost without a struggle, Naples after a siege. He found Rome undefended and there successfully maintained himself for a year and nine days against the large but ill-led army of King Vitiges the Goth. So skilful was his management, so well did he compensate for inferior numbers by the efficiency of his mailed cavalry, by the command of the sea, and by a clever use of mounted archers that by 540 he appeared to have broken the enemy's resistance. Vitiges had been trapped into captivity. Ravenna had fallen into the hands of the imperialists. All central and southern Italy was recovered for the Empire. But then, when the Gothic fortunes appeared to be desperate and the great Roman general had returned in triumph to Constantinople, the wheel turned full circle. A young leader of genius, bold, humane, and enterprising, was elected to be king of the Gothic people in 541, and under Totila's inspiring command the Goths recovered all Italy save Ravenna and Ancona, exhibiting qualities of resilience and resource which might have inclined a less tenacious antagonist to thoughts of peace.

Peace Totila was anxious to have and had more than once offered, for he was willing, like Odovacar, to rule Italy as the servant of the Empire, and even to pay tribute. But Justinian was determined on victory, and in 551 sent Narses, an elderly Armenian eunuch, with a strong army of 35,000 men to secure it. On the field of Gualdo Tadino, a village in Umbria, Narses, a good soldier and a most prudent statesman, defeated his enemy, using against him that combination of dismounted archers and pikemen which was afterwards employed with success by English commanders against the chivalry of France. Totila was slain in the pursuit, and eleven years afterwards, but not before Italy had been exposed to the horrors of an invasion of Franks and Alemans, the last garrisons of the gallant Gothic army surrendered Brescia and Verona to the foe.

For Italy this long and bitter struggle was an unrelieved calamity. The armies of Belisarius and Narses were Roman only in name, and even more alien to the native population of Italy than the Gothic swordsmen who had been peaceably settled in the country for half a century. Great atrocities were committed on either side, none more notable than the destruction of the whole adult male population (300,000 according to Procopius) of Milan by the Goths and Burgundians in 539. We have pictures, which may perhaps be overdrawn, of the unspeakable misery of the countryside, of populations wasted, of peasants living on chestnuts and grasses and in some instances impelled to acts of cannibalism. For the city of Rome, five times besieged, the results of this calamitous struggle were decisive. At the end of the war the teeming capital with its luxurious public baths, its system of food doles and popular amusements had disappeared. In its place a few thousand impoverished beings, many of them clerics, lingered on among the monuments of ancient greatness, henceforth and for many centuries to come to be girdled by undrained and malarious wastes. No more was there a Roman Senate. The last circus had been held, the last triumph celebrated, the last consul elected. Trade and commerce were extinct, and since the Goths had cut the aqueducts which had given to ancient Rome as good a water supply as any modern city can boast, the reign of mediaeval squalor, which Roman example might have corrected, spread without resistance through the western world.

The conquest of Africa and Italy only spurred Justinian's ambition for further triumphs. "God," he said, "has granted us to bring the Persians to conclude the peace, to submit the Vandals, the Alemans, and the Moors, to recover all Italy and Sicily, and we have good hopes that the Lord will grant us the rest of the Empire which the Romans formerly extended to the limits of the two oceans and lost through indolence."

The satisfaction of these vast ambitions was far beyond Justinian's powers. His conquests in Africa, Italy, and Spain (for here too an imperial force was successful in its capture of seaports) were as impossible to maintain as the recovery of Gaul and Britain was impossible even to initiate.

Moreover, the whole policy of uprooting the Goths from Italy was a great disaster. A better course, both for Italy itself and for the Balkan peninsula, would have been to have supported this brave Teutonic people, as a bulwark against the ruder nations beyond the alpine barrier. As a Gothic envoy said to Belisarius, "We have observed the laws and constitutions of the Empire as faithfully as any of the Emperors of the past. Neither Theodoric nor any of his successors has ever enacted a law. We have shown scrupulous respect for the religion of the Romans. No Italian has ever been forcibly converted to Arianism, no Gothic convert has been forced to return to his old creed. We have reserved all the posts in the Civil Service to the Italians." A Gothic monarchy thus respectful of Italian sentiment and tradition might have saved Italy from the long series of invasions and civil wars to which that unfortunate land was condemned. The Goths were a virile race. They were capable of supplying to the defence of the peninsula those qualities of martial energy which the native population had lost for centuries. It was a profound error to destroy them. Had they been left in peace there might have been no Lombard invasions, no papal state, no revival of the Empire in the west, and the political unity

which Italy so painfully achieved in the reign of Queen
Victoria might have been realized in the reign of Ethelbert.

Had the Emperor been able to establish a strong government in Italy, the elimination of the Goths might have been
effected without evil results. But at no time was the Exarch
at Ravenna master of the whole country or able to defend its
frontiers against attack. The Lombards, the last great wave of
conquering Teutons to sweep down upon the Roman Empire,
poured into Italy under their King Alboin and effected a
permanent lodgment in the country. Little good can be said
of these fierce Arian barbarians at this early stage of their
history, but like all the Teutons they had in them the seeds of
discipline and decency, and if the Italian borders had been
guarded by Gothic spears the Lombards might have been
deflected to the Balkan peninsula. In that event the face of
history might have worn a different aspect. With a population
largely Teutonic established in the Balkans the eastern
question would have assumed another and perhaps easier
form.

A.D.
568

The ambitious western wars of Justinian were conducted
by a state which was never safe from hazards and humiliations.
During the reign of this laborious monarch the Huns nearly
took Constantinople, the Slavs captured Adrianople, and the
Persians sacked the brilliant city of Antioch. The government
which was ready to send an army to Spain and even cherished
gigantic designs on Gaul and Britain could not secure a
Balkan village against marauding barbarians. When every
effort should have been concentrated on domestic defence
much was fruitlessly expended on distant ventures involving,
if Procopius is to be trusted, a loss of ten million lives in
Italy and Africa alone. And so Justinian, dying in 565 at
the age of eighty-three, left his Empire poorer, weaker, and
less Roman than it was when he mounted the throne thirty-
eight years before.

It seems that the Cypriot Theodora took a sounder view
of the needs of the political situation than her Latin-speaking
husband. She saw that the strength of the eastern Empire
depended upon the degree to which it could command the
resources of Asia Minor, of Syria, and of Egypt, and that
no conquests in the west were likely to compensate the
government of Constantinople for the loss of the Anatolian

highlanders, the Egyptian harvests, and the wealth and sparkling talents of Syria. Yet the maladies of the reign must not
wholly be traced to errors of policy. In many respects the
Emperor showed a true perception of the problems of his
day, and made a courageous and indeed imaginative attempt
to cope with them. Realizing the weakness of the barbarians in
siege operations, he covered his Asiatic and European
dominions with castles, forts, and lines of defence. Since
armies were costly and money was difficult to raise, he tried
every device which diplomacy could suggest to cajole, to
divide, or to undermine his opponents. To some barbarians
he would pay regular tribute. Others he would enrol as
"federates" in his army or load, perhaps unwisely, with
sumptuous hospitality and costly gifts. Lombards were set
against Gepids, Avars against Huns, Greek missionaries
were scattered far and wide against the heathen. Yet even
so the government which began in a blaze of glory steadily
declined in strength.

The causes of this progressive exhaustion were partly
natural, the great plague of 542, which is reputed to have
carried off a third of the population, and the declining energies
of the Emperor himself during the last two decades of his
long life. But there was a third evil which, being moral, was
more serious. The government was cheated by all its agents.
Two-thirds of the revenue extorted from the taxpayers failed
to find its way to the Treasury. The evil was apparently
incurable: against the peculation of his tax-collectors the good
laws of Justinian were so ineffectual that a reign begun with
promise and continued with ambition closed in an atmosphere
of opprobrium and grinding discontent.

Yet there are few rulers in Europe whose work is still so
widely remembered as the sovereign who commissioned the
building of St. Sophia and that great series of legal compila-
tions, the Codex, the Digest, the Institutes, and afterwards
the Novellae, through which the legacy of Roman law has
been transmitted to posterity. The numerous buildings,
ecclesiastical, municipal, and military, with which Justinian
endeavoured to secure or embellish his dominions have been
described by the secretary Procopius, to whose brilliant
narrative we are indebted for our principal knowledge of the
campaigns of Belisarius his master. Many of these buildings
have perished, but there survive a sufficient number both in

Europe and hither Asia to impress the traveller with a sense of grandeur and force. The mosaics at Ravenna are famous. More renowned is St. Sophia, whose vast low dome crowning the lovely city of Constantinople exceeds the masterpieces of the Moslem architects who found in its mysterious proportions a challenge to their highest genius.

The final systematization of Roman law by Justinian exercised an immediate and continuous influence in the east and in those regions of Italy which remained under Byzantine control. It was not, however, until the foundation of the famous school of glossators at Bologna at the end of the eleventh century that the study of Justinian's civil code became an active influence in the intellectual history of western Europe. From that moment it would be difficult to overestimate its power as a factor in the moulding of intellectual, social, and political life. The Roman law expressed the ideas of a society more civilized and mature than the western Europe of the early middle ages. It was a society which had evolved clear-cut ideas about private property and possession, family rights and the sanctity of contract, and had come to regard law as a reasoned and intelligible system adapted to the needs of humanity as a whole. A great state with commercial dealings all over the world evolves a law capable of meeting the manifold occasions of its life. The Roman law though influenced by philosophy was close to reality. It was built up not so much by legislation as by custom and by the answers of jurisconsults upon the cases real and imaginary which were submitted to them. And so as western Europe emerged from mediaeval darkness it found in the Corpus Juris of Justinian a revelation of the great thing which European civilization had once been and might again become. The ferment of the mind thus occasioned was immense. Perhaps a faint analogy may be found in the exciting influence at a later stage of human development of Rousseau's *Contrat Social* or Darwin's *Origin of Species*.

All this lay in the future. For the moment the intellectual life of the eastern Empire was not legal but theological. The Council of Nicaea had failed to quench the curiosity of the Greek world as to the difficult problem of the Incarnation. Other questions in connection with this high mystery suggested themselves to ingenious minds, and, being involved in the pretensions of rival sees or attached to the proclivities of different races, excited the fiercest and most intolerant passions. If Nicaea had affirmed the divinity of Christ, it had left open for further examination the delicate matter of determining how the divine substance was related to the human nature. Was there one Nature or two? Was Mary the mother of the human Christ only or of the human and divine as well? In the fifth century no question was more passionately discussed than this of the single or dual nature of Christ, or than the formula by which that union of natures should be most correctly expressed. The controversy lasted long after its original protagonists, Cyril of Alexandria and Nestorius of Constantinople, were laid in their graves, influencing the debates of four Councils of the Church, and continuing, even after the Council of Chalcedon had decided, under the joint influence of Pope and Emperor, for the dual nature in 451, to envenom the impressionable peoples of the east. It followed that however orthodox the Emperor might desire to be, he was forced, if he were a wise man, to take account of the strong bodies of monophysite[1] opinion which were to be found in Constantinople, in Mesopotamia, in Syria, and in Egypt. Some Emperors essayed compromising formulae, others like Anastasius a policy of toleration. No statesman could be indifferent to a question which even excited the dangerous mobs of the hippodrome and threatened to disrupt the Empire.

Justinian was an orthodox bigot against whom it must be remembered not only that he closed the schools of Athens and silenced the voice of philosophy in the Greek world, but that he spent the concluding years of his life in sterile theological speculations and stern repression of heresies. Yet theology was a subject in which the beautiful Theodora had also her opinions. Her sympathies were monophysite, her interests oriental, her political sense enlisted on the side of a theological entente with a movement which defied persecution and was proving increasingly attractive to the peoples of the east. Justinian listened to the counsels of his wife. A substantial measure of toleration was extended to the monophysites, and to the delight of the anti-Roman party a miserable captive Bishop of Rome was compelled in a Council at Constantinople to condemn certain theses which had won the approval of the hated Council of Chalcedon. It was wise

[1] *I.e.*, in favour of the single nature of Christ

of Justinian thus to endeavour to plaster over the cracks which this heresy was driving through the eastern half of his Empire. Yet the cracks remained and steadily widened, weakening the sentiment of allegiance to Constantinople, more especially in Egypt and Syria, preparing, maybe, the way for the Saracen conquests, and so permanent that the Coptic Church in Egypt today stands on the ancient rock of the monophysite faith.

To Justinian it was given to display upon a great theatre and to an admiring world the two spectacles, not hitherto combined, of Roman absolutism and ecclesiastical tyranny. He was, says Agathias, "the first of the Roman Emperors to show himself by word and deed the absolute master of the Romans." Yet a man so jealous, vain, and irresolute, a man for whom no design was too great, no detail too small, no superstition too absurd, and no subject irrelevant or remote, cannot excite admiration. With almost infinite resources of skill and industry he appears to have lacked the higher gifts of statesmanship, the energetic will, the true sense of proportion, the capacity for taking unpleasant decisions. Few men, whose personality is so uncertain, fill a greater place in history. As for a moment we tread beside him through the corridors of the past we seem to see the shades of night battling with the blood-red sunset of imperial Rome.

BOOKS WHICH MAY BE CONSULTED

J. B. Bury: *History of the Later Roman Empire.* 2 vols. 1889.

N. H. Baynes: *The Byzantine Empire.* 1926.

Cambridge Mediaeval History, Vol. IV.

C. Diehl: *Byzance—Grandeur et Décadence.* 1919.

C. Diehl: *History of the Byzantine Empire.* Tr. G. B. Ives. 1925.

C. Diehl: *Une République Patricienne.* 1915.

O. M. Dalton: *Byzantine Art and Archaeology.* 1911.

W. G. Holmes: *The Age of Justinina.* 2 vols. 1905-7.

A. A. Vasiliev: *History of the Byzantine Empire.*

L. Bréhier: *Le Monde Byzantin.* 3 vols. 1947-50.

G. Ostrogorski: *History of the Byzantine State.* Tr. J. M. Hussey. 1956.

CHAPTER XII

ISLAM

Early obscurity of Arabia. The Arab conquests of the seventh century. Muhammad, his life and teaching. Rise and progress of Moslem civilization. The mystics of Islam. Shiites and Sunnites. The defence of Europe against Islam by Leo the Isaurian and Charles Martel.

WE HAVE now reached a point at which the history of Europe becomes complicated by the victories of the Moslem religion. For the first six centuries of the Christian era no European statesman had occasion to remember the existence of Arabia. It was a land of mystery, doing a little trade with Syria and Egypt and contributing some mercenaries to the Persian and Byzantine armies, but otherwise as remote and inhospitable as the frozen north. Nothing likely to be reported from this scorching wilderness would be calculated to disturb the bazaars of Damascus or Alexandria. Arabian society was still in the tribal stage, and the hawk-eyed Bedouin tribes might be confidently expected to rob and massacre each other till the crack of doom. Nowhere was there a vestige of an Arabian state, of a regular army, or of a common political ambition. The Arabs were poets, dreamers, fighters, traders; they were not politicians. Nor had they found in religion a stabilizing or unifying power. They practised a low form of polytheism, so low that some finer minds among them, touched perhaps by vague influences from Christianity or Judaism, had begun quietly to challenge it. At Mecca, their principal trading town, only fifty miles removed from the great highway of the Red Sea, they appeared to worship a black stone in a temple, called the Caba, or Cube. Such were the impressions likely to prevail about the population of Arabia in the year in which Heraclius, the Byzantine Emperor, concluded his Persian wars.

A hundred years later these obscure savages had achieved for themselves a great world power. They had conquered Syria and Egypt, they had overwhelmed and converted

Persia, mastered western Turkestan and part of the Punjab. They had wrested Africa from the Byzantines and the Berbers, Spain from the Visigoths. In the west they threatened France, in the east Constantinople. Their fleets, built in Alexandria or the Syrian ports, rode the waters of the Mediterranean, pillaged the Greek islands and challenged the naval power of the Byzantine Empire. Their successes had been won so easily, the Persians and the Berbers of the Atlas mountains alone offering a serious resistance, that at the beginning of the eighth century it must have seemed an open question whether any final obstacle could be opposed to their victorious course. The Mediterranean had ceased to be a Roman lake. From one end of Europe to the other the Christian states found themselves confronted with the challenge of a new oriental civilization founded on a new oriental faith.

To what causes are we to attribute this sudden and extra-ordinary outpouring of the Arab race? An answer which is often given is that the Arabs were propelled into the utter-most parts of the earth by the ferment within them of their new religion, and that they rode, battled, and conquered to extend the faith. But this explanation does not accord with the fact that, during the early years of the Arab expansion, the conquerors were at no particular pains to make converts. On the contrary, their success in government largely consisted in the wise policy of toleration which they practised towards Jews and Christians, presenting in this respect the happiest contrast to the persecuting practices of their successors. But if religion was not the primary motive which underlay this extraordinary movement, still less can it be ascribed to con-sistent design. The Bedouin horsemen did not ride out of Arabia with a clear-cut scheme for the conquest of the world and the establishment of new states. They made their empire as other states have made empires after them, blindly, without set purpose and with no near and immediate project other than plunder. They began by making plundering raids into Palestine and Irak at a time when the defences of those provinces were at their lowest point of efficiency, and finding victory easy and booty rich, they extended their operations. Success, beyond the utmost dreams of ambition, attended their attacks. In 636 they beat the last army of Heraclius at the Yarmak and conquered Syria. In 637 they entered Ctesi-phon and mastered Mesopotamia. In 639 they invaded

Egypt, and three years later entered Alexandria. Having discovered the weakness of the Empire, they were resolved to exploit it and to hold, administer, and extend their conquests. Not otherwise did the Elizabethan buccaneers throw themselves upon the wealth of the western hemisphere. Yet if religion was not the originating force in the expansion of Arabia, it gave to it a degree of animation and permanence which it would otherwise have lacked. Without the bond of a common religion the Arab horsemen would have lacked the cohesion failing which victories can seldom be won and never secured. Without some inspiration higher than mere appetite they could never have commended their rule to Syrians and Egyptians, Persians and Berbers. No small part of their success was due to the fact that there had been evolved in the heart of Arabia a form of religion which satisfied then, as it continues to satisfy now, the souls of men and women living under the burning skies of Asia and Africa, and that of this religion the Arabs were the armed and exultant missionaries.

The Hedjaz was that part of Arabia most exposed, by reason of its trade, to foreign influences. Here Jews and Christians might sometimes be found, more especially in Mecca, which was the commercial centre of the district and a town of pilgrimage, or at Yathrib, two hundred miles north, one of the few areas in that waterless land where the arts of agriculture were practised by a settled population.

Muhammad (c. 570-632) was born at Mecca of a family neither rich nor distinguished, but of the Kuraishite tribe, which controlled the local sanctuary. As a young man he entered the commercial house of Kadija, a wealthy widow, whom he subsequently married, nor perhaps is it irrelevant to his spiritual development that the pursuit of his calling involved caravan journeys across the desert and opportunities of converse with Christians and Jews. Muhammad was one of those men of whom religious history offers many examples, in whom a passionate animal nature is combined with the temper of a visionary. In many of the conventional virtues of western society he was wholly deficient. He was cruel and crafty, lustful and ignorant, lacking in physical courage and the gift of self-criticism; but despite these grave faults, which became intensified with age and success, he had the ardour of the mystic, the zeal of the ethical reformer, and that absorbing preoccupation with the things of the soul which comes most easily to men in the solitary places of the world. By degrees the mind of this Arab merchant became possessed of certain large religious and ethical ideas. He went into trances, and in these trances visions appeared to him. He had a vision of the one God, of a future life, of the sensual delights of paradise, of the material torments of hell, and of an impending day of retribution in which sinners would be punished. These visions, crude, vigorous, animated, he began to recite (Koran), first of all privately to a circle of intimates, then more widely. Mecca was sharply critical. Was he a madman, an impostor, a poet? Nevertheless he persevered, winning adherents by the flow and vehemence of his invective, by his apocalyptic threats of impending doom, and by the large and attractive appeal of the monotheistic faith and the practice of brotherly love. That he was influenced by Judaism and Christianity is certain; but his information with regard to these two religions, being derived from oral sources only, was dim, fragmentary, and confused. He regarded Christ as a prophet, born of a virgin mother, but neither had the story of the crucifixion reached him, nor yet does he appear to have been aware of the difference between the Jewish and Christian creeds. The Koran is a collection of utterances of an unlettered prophet preaching the message of God to the Arab race.

From the mockeries of his native town Muhammad escaped in 622 to Yathrib, henceforth known as Medinat en Nabi, the city of the Prophet. This is the famous *Hegira*, or flight, which is taken to mark the beginning of the Moslem era. In Medina, which was tormented by rival factions, the Prophet continued his pious labours, preaching the welcome doctrine of concord, of submission (*islam*) to the will of God (*Allah*) and developing many of those practical precepts which govern the conduct of the Moslem world to this day, the five daily prayers, the fasting in the month of Ramadan, the yearly pilgrimage, the abstention from wine. In all this side of his teaching the Prophet showed a shrewd insight into Arab nature. It would be an anachronism to ascribe to him the idea of attempting to impose upon Arabia a universalist religion. With that strong, practical sense which was in him so strongly combined with religious exaltation and self-hypnotism, he aimed at reform rather than at revolution. He did not attempt to change everything, but tolerated polygamy and slavery, institutions too secure to be assailed with success, and even temporized with the symbols of polytheism. Returning to Mecca in 631, after a long struggle marked by acts of brigandage and wholesale murder, he adopted the black stone, and declared that the Caba was the temple of Abraham. Before he died he had founded a little state by the sword, for in the last analysis his Universal God was an Arab, and Mecca was his Holy City.

The new religion had from the first a great political value. Into the wild, lawless, infinitely divided Arab world it brought unity of belief, submission to authority, a tranquillizing daily ritual of prayer and that abstinence from strong drinks which has given to Moslem armies throughout history a special advantage. Moreover, the monotheism of Islam was not so far removed from the monophysite forms of Christianity which were popular in Syria and Egypt as to interpose an obstacle in the way of the Arab conquest of those lands.

So the Moslem civilization spread. Under the Ummayyads its political centre was Damascus, under the Abbasids Bagdad, under the Fatimites Cairo. Syrians and Persians, Turks, Berbers, and Spaniards contributed to bring about the great age of Moslem literature and art which, for four centuries while the European mind was deep sunk in ignorance and sloth, gave to the peoples of Islam the intellectual leadership of the world. The memory of that epoch still survives. Still the Palestinian Arab proudly contrasts the literature of his golden age with the scriptures of the Jew. Still the Nigerian Emir dreams of the pilgrimage to Mecca, and of the day when all the world will acknowledge the true faith. Still from the Atlantic Ocean to the Himalayas the *muezzin* calls the faithful to prayer at sunrise and sunset, the mosques fill with shoeless worshippers, the little children learn the Koran by heart, and in the shaded alcoves of the great Cairene University of Al Azhar groups of white-robed students, seated on the floor, swing back and forth in a mood of fanatical ecstasy, as they intone the sacred words of the polygamous Prophet to whom all wisdom and all modern science were miraculously revealed.

Islam is a religion of warriors and shepherds, which, albeit without a clergy or a regular liturgy, has persisted for 1,300 years and now is thought to number some 300,000,000 adherents. Asceticism after the early Christian manner was not encouraged by the Prophet, who is reputed to have said that "two prostrations of a married Moslem are worth more than seventy of a celibate." Nevertheless Islam, like Christianity, reckons its fraternities of ascetics, its enraptured mystics, its nonconformist sectaries. The harsh creed of the Arabian desert has taken colour and content from the richer civilizations of Syria and Egypt, of Persia, India, and Spain, from which, at different times, it has drawn its votaries. The crude outpourings of the Koran do not exhaust its message. There is in Islam a body of mystical literature, which, in the purity of its religious emotion, vies with the spiritual masterpieces of the Jewish or Christian faith.

The period which succeeds the death of the Prophet, while distinguished for many dazzling achievements in war and policy, is also memorable for the emergence of that deep rift within the Moslem world which still envenoms the relations of the Shiite and the Sunnite sects. Under the able rule of Omar, the second of the Caliphs or Vicars and the true founder of the Arab state, the voice of discontent was silenced by the victories of the Arab generals. But his successor, Othman, was less fortunate, less able, less industrious, and perhaps also, since his government was hotly blamed for its extortions, less well served. A campaign was set on foot in favour of Ali, the son-in-law of the Prophet, which resulted in the assassination of Othman, and in the elevation of Ali to the caliphate in his place. From that moment the Moslem world was sharply sundered into two irreconcilable factions. The title of Ali was disputed by the experienced Moawya, the cousin of the murdered caliph and a member of the Ummayyad house, who, having ruled Syria for seventeen years, was in no mood to surrender the throne of power to the nominee of Medina.

The Shiites or partisans of Ali were strong in Arabia and Irak, the Sunnites adhered to Moawya in Syria and Egypt. The murder of Ali and later of his second son, Hosein, left in the hearts of their votaries a long memory of passionate regret such as has coloured the annals of Ireland and Serbia; but the strength lay with the caliphs of the Ummayyad house who ruled at Damascus. At the cost of two civil wars they established (692) their supremacy over the Arab world.

The divisions between the Shiites and the Sunnites, while

A.D. 634-43

A.D. 643-56

A.D. 661

temporarily arresting the Moslem offensive, brought no permanent relief to the Byzantine Empire. Its position was challenged in Asia Minor and in the islands. Its capital was exposed to the risk of capture. The defection of those of its Christian subjects who exalted the divine as opposed to the human side of Christ was always to be apprehended. Meanwhile no great figure appeared upon the Byzantine scene between the death of Heraclius in 641 and the accession of Leo the Isaurian in 717. Emperor succeeded emperor, assassination followed assassination. But though the state was shaken by palace revolutions and civil war and its annals stained by fratricidal intrigues, Asia Minor and Constantinople were held. The subdivision of the Empire into military districts or themes, garrisoned by army divisions and under entire subjection to military officers, may have helped to this end.

It is a commonplace of history to remark that the Saracen expansion in Europe was ultimately checked by the victory won by the Frankish sovereign, Charles Martel, over the great army of the Viceroy Abdur Rahman on the field of Poitiers in 732. The numbers engaged on either side in that famous conflict were high, the conflict between the huge Frankish footmen and the fiery cavalry of Spain and Africa was fierce and long, the victory of the Christian army was complete and decisive. But in the scale of importance the victory of Poitiers does not rank with the successful repulse by Leo the Isaurian of the formidable Saracen attacks on Constantinople in 717 and 718, not only because Constantinople was closer to the centre of Moslem power and therefore more likely, if taken, to be retained, but also because the Saracens once established in the Byzantine capital would have found among the rude and imperfect Christians of eastern Europe a free field for Moslem propaganda. If the Turkish conquest of Constantinople in the fifteenth century spread the Moslem creed far and wide through the Balkan peninsula, we may imagine the success which would have attended a Saracen conquest 700 years earlier, at a time when the peoples of Russia and the Balkans had received but a faint initial tincture of Christianity, and were still in a rude disorder of institutions and beliefs.

In the west the Saracens were confronted by an organized Christian society inheriting something of the strength of the

Roman Empire, and even had they won the day at Poitiers, would still have been far removed from the conquest and conversion of France. In eastern Europe it was otherwise. Here in Russia and Hungary, or among the Bulgarians and Slavs of the Balkan peninsula, there was no centre of moral and physical resistance comparable to the Gallo-Roman Church or to the Frankish monarchy. Had Leo the Isaurian failed to beat off the imposing armada of Moslemah, the Moslem faith might have spread like a prairie fire through the Balkans and the plain of Hungary and northwards and eastwards to the Urals. From this danger the great defence of Constantinople in 718, conducted by a young and capable Emperor, with the aid of stout fortifications, a superior navy, Greek fire, and the timely assistance of a Bulgar army, delivered European civilization. The name of Leo should be remembered. That the Russian Church is Greek and not Moslem today is one of the results, how fortunate we dare not say, which may, without a great stretch of probabilities, be attributed to his great and resounding triumph.

BOOKS WHICH MAY BE CONSULTED

W. Muir. *Mahomet and History of Islam.* 1894.

D. S. Margoliouth: *Mohammed and the Rise of Islam.* 1905.

H. Lammens: *Islam, Beliefs and Institutions. Tr.* E. Dennison Ross. 1929.

R. Bell: *The Origins of Islam in its Christian Environment.* 1926.

R. A. Nicholson: *A Literary History of the Arabs.* 1907.

Sir Thomas Arnold and A. Guillaume (edd.): *The Legacy of Islam.* 1931.

P. K. Hitti: *The Arabs.* 1956.

CHAPTER XIII

THE FRANKISH EMPIRE

Long duration of the house of Meroveus. Sources of its author-
ity. Survival of Latin culture in Gaul. Its disappearance in
Britain. Decomposition of public power under the Meroving-
ians. Survival of the idea of Frankish unity. Rise of the
Carolings. Charles Martel. Christian missions in Germany.
The Papacy quarrels with the Greeks and Lombards and in-
vokes the Franks. Pippin and Pope Stephen. Charles the
Great. First visit to Rome. Coronation in A.D. 800. Its
importance. The Carolingian renaissance. The debt to Ireland
and England. Alcuin. The Saxon wars. Central Europe
secured for the Latin Church. Strength and weakness of the
Frankish Empire. Its dissolution in the ninth century.

THE DESCENDANTS of King Clovis the Frank were for the most
part either cruel and treacherous barbarians or enfeebled
debauchees. Yet, despite their atrocities and lusts, their
fratricidal enmities and purposeless civil wars, the house of
Meroveus endured for nearly 300 years (481-716), outlasting
the Valois or the Bourbons, the Stuarts or the Hanoverians,
and in this point of endurance presenting the sharpest contrast to the short-lived ruling families of imperial Rome. So
strong was the prestige attaching to the stock of Clovis that
for seventy-eight years after all effective power had passed
into the hands of the mayors of the palace, members of the
Merovingian house were still solemnly crowned and accorded
honours of a phantasmal royalty. "Nothing," says Einhard,
writing of this last period of their rule, "was left the King,
except the name of King, the flowing locks, the long beard.
He sat on his throne and played at government, gave audience
to envoys, and dismissed them with the answers which he
had been schooled, or rather commanded, to give. He had
nothing to call his own except one estate of small value
where he had a residence and a not very numerous retinue.
He travelled, when occasion required it, in a waggon drawn
by oxen, and driven like a farmer's cart by a cowherd. In this

guise he came to the palace or to the annual assembly of his people. The Mayor controlled the administration and decided all issues of policy at home or abroad."

The explanation of this extraordinary reluctance to terminate the life of a bad dynasty is to be chiefly found in the field of religion. If the Merovingians were kings, they were also priests. If they were wicked, they were also holy. No steel must shear their flowing locks, for were they not, as the Frankish song writers knew, descended from the sea god or sea monster who begat Meroveus? An aura of sanctity, far older than Christianity, clung about this national priesthood of the Franks. They did not need the consecration of a Christian bishop to establish their authority, or to commend them to the loyalty of their Frankish warriors, Not that they failed to derive substantial and continuing advantages from the fact that Clovis, the founder, had adopted the faith and obtained the support of the Roman Church. Thereby they were not free from the obstacles which confronted the Arian Ostrogoths or Lombards in Italy, or the Visigoths during their government of Toulouse and the first heretical period of their Spanish rule. The only organized and educated body of men, surviving the wreck of the Empire in the west, instead of being inimical, was an ally. They could beat down the Arian and the Jew with the plaudits of the Church, and count every victory as a triumph of the orthodox, of the Roman faith.

Moreover, despite their Teuton origin, the early Merovingian kings were prone to regard themselves as the generals or magistrates of Rome. They accepted Roman insignia, made use of Roman coins, and appear, in the true imperial spirit, to have recognized no frontiers to the extension of their rule. In Constantinople they were, from time to time, regarded as auxiliaries. The Emperor Maurice, in 590, alluding to the ancient concord between the Franks and the Roman people, invoked the aid of Childebert II against the Lombards in Italy.

It is, therefore, easy to see how, despite the Teutonic origin of its Frankish conquerors, the land which is now known as France has remained part of the Latin world. The Franks, though they effected an occupation of Gaul, did not enter upon their inheritance as the enemies of the Gallo-Roman population, but rather as the foes of the Arian Visigoths and

Burgundians. It was against these, or against one another, that Clovis and his descendants were chiefly concerned to turn their arms, not against the Roman Church, which they regarded as a friend, nor the Gallo-Roman population which accepted their yoke, nor the Roman Emperor, who, from his distant throne on the Bosphorus, was disposed to regard them as potential allies. After a very few years the Church imposed its Latin culture on the conquerors. Chilperic, the grandson of Clovis, described by Gregory of Tours as the Nero and Herod of his age, composed Latin verses, and in the pride of his new won knowledge, added four Greek letters to the alphabet.

That the continuity of Latin civilization should have been thus secured in Gaul while it was broken in Britain is explained when we consider the comparative weight of the Roman influence in the two countries and the differing circumstances attending their conquest. In Gaul the Roman cities were numerous and comparatively large; in Britain they were few (some fifteen or sixteen in number) and exceedingly small. In the one country the Church was affluent and influential; in the other, as the tiny basilica in Silchester seems to indicate, it was weak and poor. The correspondence of Sidonius Apollinaris, taken in conjunction with the later evidence of Gregory of Tours, proves that in Gaul there was both before and after the Frankish invasion an influential country aristocracy of Gallo-Roman descent. No such aristocracy survived in those parts of Britain which were effectually conquered by the Saxons. But what was equally important was the contrasted character of the two invasions, in Gaul accepted by the larger part of the native population, in Britain fiercely contested, and leading to the replacement of the Latin-speaking Celts of England by their heathen and Teutonic conquerors, to the submergence of the Christian religion and the loss of the Latin speech.

With the Franks, as with the other Teutonic peoples, the old institutions of tribal liberty had failed to survive the ordeal of war. The popular assemblies were no longer held. The king's will, in so far as it was not contested in practice by the nobles, was law. Yet nothing was done to turn these initial advantages to account. The Merovingian kings had no idea of political responsibility or historical tradition. They applied to the Frankish monarchy the principles which in Teutonic society governed the regulation of private property. The inheritance was divided among the sons, and since the sons invariably quarrelled, the country was plagued for five generations by useless civil war.

From these contests, which were inspired by no principle higher then the violent appetities of an ill-conditioned child may supply, one consequence plainly followed, a progressive degeneration in the art and system of government. As we study the history of Gaul in the Merovingian age we are sensible of a steady decomposition of public power. Privileges are freely granted or freely taken, which are inconsistent with the exercise of state authority.

The tendencies which Sir Henry Spelman, an English jurist of the seventeenth century, summarized under the phrase "the feudal system," begin to make themselves increasingly apparent. The administration of justice, the levy of taxes, the obligation of raising fighting men for the army or the host, tend to fall into the hands of great landed proprietors, civil or ecclesiastical. Grants of "immunities" are made to churches or abbeys, which in effect exclude them from the normal responsibilities and duties of the citizen. The count, who is the public official in the city, may not enter the "immunized" territory to levy taxes, or to administer justice, or to raise men for the host. These functions, if they are still to be performed, belong henceforth to the territorial lord, upon whom, under the vague and ill-defined suzerainty of the king, the exercise of political power is in effect devolved. By the end of the Merovingian period a great part of the land of Gaul had fallen into the hands of the Church.

While this slow decompostion was taking place in the body politic of Frankish Gaul, while the monarchy was becoming weaker, the Church more wealthy, and in consequence more barbarous and corrupt, and the nobility more independent, the fabric of Christian society in the west was menaced by the Saracens, the Avars, and the Slavs. The pressure of foreign danger was sufficient to maintain in the ill-soldiered Frankish dominions a sense of unity which the partitions and civil wars of the Merovingian kings were unable to destroy. The frontiers were defended. A term was placed on fresh Teutonic invasions. The strong provincial feelings of Burgundy and Aquitaine, of Neustria and Austrasia (as the western and eastern parts of northern France had by 561 come to be termed), were not allowed altogether to efface the historic image of Rome. Even the fifty years of decadence and disorder which followed the death of Dagobert (638), the last Merovingian king to rule over a united country, failed to obliterate the idea of an undivided monarchy, Christian, Roman, and Frankish, governing the vast area which was once Gaul.

A new epoch opens with the rise to power of that vigorous and remarkable Teutonic dynasty which obtains an immortal lustre from the great name of Charlemagne. From being weak and contemptible the Frankish monarchy became, under the Carolings, the strongest instrument for government and conquest which Europe had seen since the great days of the Roman Empire. The whole landscape of public affairs was transformed by the strenuous activities of the Austrasian or eastern Franks. The Saracens were driven back into Spain, the Avars blotted from the map, and Pannonia, their latest home, made bare for the reception of the Hungarian people. A Papal state was created in Italy at the expense of the defeated Lombards, with the three important consequences of preventing, until 1870, the establishment of a unified Italian state, of widening the rift between Rome and Byzantium, and of giving to the Papacy a position of political independence, which was thought by some to be a temptation to worldliness and corruption, by others to be essential to its spiritual freedom and authority. These changes were important. To this day we experience their effects. But more important still was the conversion to Christianity of Frisia and Germany and the acceptance by Charlemagne of the Imperial crown from the hands of Pope Leo III on Christmas day, 800. A new world in central Europe was called into the Christian and Roman fold to redress the losses in Syria and Egypt, in Africa and Spain. A conquest for Rome greater than any single conquest since the days of Julius Caesar had been achieved by the co-operation of English and Irish missionaries, Frankish soldiery, and papal encouragement and support.

The Carolings sprang from the border land which has been disputed for centuries between the Latin and Teutonic races. Among the grandees who were prominent in the politics of

Austrasia at the beginning of the seventh century were a certain Pippin of Landen in Brabant, and a certain Arnulf, a duke, and subsequently a bishop of Metz. Pippin, who became mayor of the palace, and *de facto* ruler of Austrasia in 622, married his daughter to the son of Arnulf, and seldom can there have been a grander alliance in Austrasia than this union between the daughter of its foremost statesman and the son of a man who was in turn a duke, a bishop, and a saint, but most specially distinguished, if his genealogy can be trusted, for his connections with a Roman senatorial family in Narbonne. The child of this marriage won for himself a place in world history.[1]

Pippin II, Mayor of Austrasia in 681, master of Neustria in 687, a valiant fighter, and a zealous friend of missionary enterprise among the German and Frisians, was the father of Charles Martel and the great-grandfather of Charlemagne. Such in brief was the lineage of the illustrious Emperor, who is claimed as a national hero both by the Germans and by the French, but who was in truth neither German nor French as we now understand these terms, but an Austrasian Frank, Teutonic, no doubt, in origin and sentiment, but Latin in discipline, and regarded by himself and his contemporaries as the captain of Roman Christianity in the western world.

Charles Martel, or Charles "the Hammer," the bastard son of Pippin II, reigned over the two kingdoms of Austrasia and Neustria for twenty-six years, defeating all his neighbours in battle, and earning his title of the Hammer by his drastic and probably not unneeded handling of the Gallo-Roman Church. The tall, mail-clad infantry from the east who brought him victory on so many fields had not been softened by the luxuries of the town, and restored to the Frankish name a military lustre which had been lost since the days when Clovis first loosed his untamed Teutons on the fields of Gaul. Of the Hammer's achievements, one, though most insufficiently described, is specially memorable. On an October Sunday in 732 he defeated near Poitiers a great Moslem army under Abdur Rahman, the Arab Governor of Spain, with a loss to the invaders, if the figures of Paul the Deacon can be trusted (as they can not), of 375,000 lives. This resounding victory, though it did not prevent fresh Arab incursions into Gaul,

[1] Genealogical Table A.

for three years later the Arabs took Arles and Avignon. from each of which cities they were evicted by the Hammer, was nevertheless a decisive deliverance.

It is true that the Arabs would not have been strong enough to capture, still less to hold Gaul, and that quite apart from the conspiracies and intrigues which are the web and woof of oriental politics, they were confronted with troubles from the Berbers in Africa and the Christians in Spain. Still, if they could not have conquered, they could have persisted in destructive raids. In particular they could have opposed a serious obstacle to the prosecution of the greatest of all the improvements which was then, with the Hammer's material help, being carried out in Europe.

The conversion of Germany could never have been accomplished by the Frankish clergy in the state to which it had been reduced under the Merovingian régime. It is to the missionaries of Ireland and England, where Christianity shone with a purer light, that we must ascribe the spiritual impulse which prompted the German mission and revived the religious tone of the western Church. We have now reached the time when the British peoples, emerging from their northern mists, make their first great contribution to the advancement of civilized life in the larger world. The long roll of great Englishmen opens at the beginning of the eighth century with the names of a scholar and a missionary. Thus early did the Anglo-Saxons evince their passion for the improvement of mankind through religion and knowledge. The Ecclesiastical History of Bede, a Northumbrian monk, who took all knowledge for his province, retained for at least four centuries a pre-eminent place in the Latin literature of Europe, and is still valued as our prime source of information on the development of Christian society and institutions in Britain. Almost an exact contemporary of this famous polymath was Wynfrith, better known under his later name of Boniface, the apostle of Germany. The work of a missionary among barbarous people, living in dense and distant forests, may leave but little trace on the written memorials of his time. But the salient facts in the career of Boniface are eloquent of ardour and persistence, of capacity and success. Despatched by Pope Gregory II in 719 on a mission to the heathen in Germany, he put himself to school with his compatriot Willibrod, who was engaged upon the conversion of the

Frisians; and it was in Frisia, after thirty-five years of unremitting toil, that Boniface found a martyr's death. Meanwhile, labouring always in the service of the apostolic see, but also with the powerful assistance of the Frankish kings, he converted the Hessians and Thuringians, organized the Church in Bavaria, and being appointed to the Archbishopric of Mainz in 748, exercised a general supervision over the Christian communities which, mainly through his efforts, had been fashioned in southern and central Germany. That he was assisted by other valiant workers does not detract from his achievement. In the task of binding Germany to Rome he was a pioneer, and his the decisive and dynamic influence.

In one important particular the conversion of Germany differs from the earlier movement for the introduction of Christianity into Gaul. The humble Syrian traders who first brought the Christian message to Marseilles came into a highly civilized Roman province. Votaries of an obscure oriental sect, they could offer neither poetry nor metaphysics, neither law nor science, to a society far better instructed in all these matters than they. What they had to propound was a revolutionary way of life round which a new literature, wider and more practical than the old, and offering a fresh range of moral interests, was gradually built up in Greek and Latin. To the cultivated gentlemen of Gaul, even as late as the fifth century, Virgil was more melodious than Prudentius, Cicero more eloquent than Augustine. The new theology had a rival in the old literature, which to many a pious mind seemed to be dangerous just because it was seductive. But in Germany there was no such dualism. There the Christian missions did not at any point conflict with allegiance to an ancient and splendid literature, for Boniface and his fellow-workers preached to rude, unlettered barbarians. It was indeed to the missions and monasteries that Germany owed its knowledge of Latin and an introduction into the culture of the ancient world.

While the Venerable Bede was writing his immortal work in his cell at Jarrow and Boniface was preaching Christ to the wild Thuringians, and Charles the Hammer, but also the missionary, was hammering the bishops and abbots of Gaul, and secularizing their property, events were preparing a fresh rift within the Christian fold, and working up to that alliance between the Papacy and the Frankish kings which transformed the politics of western Europe.

It is part of the wisdom of the Roman Church to accept what it cannot prevent. It accepts and subordinates to its system the ineradicable polytheism of Mediterranean man. The pagan genius became the Christian angel, the pagan Isis the Christian Madonna, the pagan hero became the Christian saint, the pagan festival the Christian feast. And while canonizing this deep-seated popular craving for spiritual helpers and mediators, the Roman Church also welcomed the material modes, be they low or lofty, in which expression was sought to be given to these needs. It accepted statues and paintings, the worship of relics and the pilgrimage to shrines in which relics were placed. In the general debasement of mind and morals which characterized the seventh century this material or superstitious side of the Christian religion was greatly developed. Image worship was prevalent in the Roman, it was still more prevalent in the Byzantine Church. It was open to the critic to observe that the cult of a single God had been left to the Moslem and the Jew.

Such critics were to be found in plenty in the highlands of Armenia and Anatolia. The Paulicians, so called because they appealed to the authority of St. Paul, acknowledged only those principles of conduct for which they found a warrant in the Scriptures. They repudiated the commentaries of the Fathers. They denied the authority of the Church. They rejected the sacraments, the veneration of the Cross, the adoration of the Virgin. In the rigour of their puritanism they anticipated the Protestant reformers of the sixteenth century. It would seem that the Emperor Leo III, who came from the regions in Asia Minor where such beliefs prevailed, was impressed by the message of these highland sectaries. To his austere and soldierly mind the practices which may be summarized in the term "image-worship" were corrupting to the fibre of the body politic. The Empire was not to be saved from the Moslem by monks, relics, and incantations, but by civilian discipline and military valour. In 726 the Isaurian Emperor issued an edict commanding the destruction of images throughout his dominions.

At once a storm arose in Italy. To the many causes of dissension between Greek and Roman churches, the quarrel

over the single Nature, the quarrel over the single Will, the
claim that the Patriarch of Constantinople was on an equal
footing with the Pope of Rome, there was now added the
embittering circumstance that a Greek tyrant was seeking to
deprive the Italian people of their cherished religious images.
A revolt broke out in Ravenna, a Greek exarch was killed;
in a council of Italian bishops summoned in 731 by Gregory
III the iconoclasts were excommunicated. The defiance of
Rome was bold, popular, dangerous. Hopelessly at issue
with the Empire, the Popes were compelled to look elsewhere
for material support.

The stream of history would have run in different channels
if, at this juncture, the Papacy had elected to ally itself steadily
with the Lombard monarchy. There was much to be said for
such a course. The Lombards, after the first great explosion
of cruelty which marked their original settlement in Italy,
had shown some aptitude for civilization. They had abjured
Arianism and reduced some of their laws to writing, and
under the rule of the enlightened Liutprand were making 712-
swift advances in the arts of life. Moreover, in a contest with 43
the Greeks, Lombard sympathy could be counted on in
advance. From their first entry into Italy in 568 until the
peace of 680, the principal thread in Lombard history had
been the prosecution of a quarrel with the Greek Empire.
That antagonism, though intermitted for the time, was still
an underlying condition of Italian politics. No Lombard
king could rest content while an inch of Italian soil was held
by the Empire, and no Emperor could look upon the Lombards as other than pestilent intruders upon his sacred
preserves. A doubt can never have existed in the papal curia
but that the Lombards would prove to be zealous and effective allies against the Greek iconoclasts.

Yet the Papacy, showing that fine instinct for secular
diplomacy which belongs in a special degree to Italian statesmanship, decided, after some fluctuations of policy, that the
Lombards, despite their Catholicism and their improvements
in the arts and their hatred of the Greeks, were to be treated
not as friends but as enemies. Pavia was too near Rome. If
the Lombards became uncontested masters of Italy, the Papacy would be degraded to a Lombard bishopric. Rather than
rest upon the support of these warlike neighbours, the Popes
decided to appeal to the distant and powerful Franks. In

739 Gregory III sent the keys of St. Peter's tomb to Charles Martel, and asked him to replace the Emperor in the governance of Rome. That offer Charles declined, and two years afterwards the three great political figures on the stage— Leo, Gregory, and Charles—were dead.

The men changed, the policies continued. By the steady suction of circumstances the Pope of Rome and the Frankish king were drawn into fateful combination. Pippin the Short, the younger son of Charles, and after the retirement of his elder brother to a monastery the effective ruler of France, was the friend of Boniface the Englishman. To the mayor of the palace, as to the missionary, it was important to venerate the apostolic see, to promote the German missions, and to administer a much-needed correction to the Gallic Church. The piety of Pippin, whether real or assumed, met with its reward. In response to a prudent enquiry as to whether it was right that the real should not also be the nominal ruler, he was assured by Pope Zachary that he might depose the last of the Merovings and assume the crown himself. Pippin acted on that advice. In the cathedral at Soissons, Boniface, the Englishman, anointed him king.

For the enormous services of legalizing the Carolingian monarchy, the Pope was soon in a position to claim a commensurate recompense. The new Lombard king, Aistulf, was distinguished by an imprudent and intemperate ambition to conquer at one and the same time the exarchate and the Roman patrimony. His armies, directed against the imperialists, met with such success as to inspire the liveliest apprehensions in the heart of the Pope. At the invitation of Pippin, and possibly also with the connivance of the Emperor, Pope 753 Stephen crossed the Alps and made a memorable bargain with the Frankish king. He conferred upon him the imperial title of Patrician, anointed him afresh together with his two sons, and bound the Franks to choose their future kings from his descendants alone. In return, Pippin engaged to transfer the cities which the Lombard kings had taken from the Emperor, not to their lawful but iconoclastic master, but to the Roman Republic and to St. Peter. What the Frank promised he performed. In two brief campaigns he wrested from the Lombards all the country which they had won since the death of Liutprand, and made it over to the Papal See.

Thus was founded that extraordinary polity, governed for over eleven hundred years by clerics, and presenting over most of that long period an almost continuous spectacle of disorder. Such was the origin of the Papal States, so long a fatal obstacle to Italian unity and a perpetual invitation to foreign invasion and intrigue. It is perhaps reasonable to conjecture that even in the eighth century some scrupulous minds may have been exercised by the validity of a title resting on nothing better than two violent conquests. If so, a pious and timely forgery allayed such misgivings. It was discovered that the Emperor Constantine had, upon his conversion, made a donation to Pope Sylvester of all Italy and the west. The extravagance of the legend was no bar to its acceptance, even after many centuries, and by men violently hostile to the mundane ambitions of the Church. It is thanks to the forged donation that Constantine is eloquently denounced alike in Hell and Paradise by Dante, the imperialist, more than five hundred years after the pious forger had been sent to his last account.

Pippin died in 768. Among the blessings vouchsafed to Charles, his eldest son, was, as a pious monk once reminded him, the removal by death three years later of his younger brother Carloman. For forty-three years the deadly system of partition, which even Pippin had not been strong enough to discard, was interrupted by fate, and the stage was cleared for the unimpeded action of a powerful character. Charles was worthy of his opportunity. He was bold and yet deliberate, genial and yet exact, popular and yet formidable. A vast appetite for animal enjoyment was combined in him with the cardinal gifts of statesmanship, a spacious vision, strong common sense, a flawless memory, and a tenacious will. It was part of his strength that he attempted nothing impossible, and asked no more of his people than they were able to accomplish. To his Frankish warriors he was the ideal chief, tall and stout, animated and commanding, with flashing blue eyes and aquiline nose, a mighty hunter before the Lord. That he loved the old Frankish songs, used Frankish speech, and affected the traditional costume of his race—the high-laced boots, the cross-gartered scarlet hose, the linen tunic, and square mantle of white or blue—that he was simple in his needs, and sparing in food and drink, were ingratiating features in a rich and wholesome character. Yet if in the habits of daily life he was a Frank to the marrow, in all matters pertaining to culture and religion he was prepared to obey the call and to extend the influence of his Roman priests.

Not many years elapsed before the same political logic which brought about the close conjunction of Pippin with the Papacy worked to a similar conclusion for Charles. Again a Lombard king made an incursion into papal territory. Again a Pope appealed to the Frankish monarch for help, and again that help was accorded. In the second act of the drama, however, the incidents appeared to be heightened and intensified, the actors to be stronger, the dénouement to be decisive. Didier the Lombard and Charles the Frank were already estranged before Didier made his attack on Ravenna and the Pentapolis and menaced the walls of Rome. Charles had married, and on grounds of personal aversion divorced, the daughter of the Lombard king. Didier had given shelter to the infant nephews and possible rivals of Charles, and pressed the Pope to crown them. Nothing, however, was further from the mind of Pope Hadrian, a proud and steadfast Roman noble, than to purchase by a dishonouring alliance with the hated Lombard the dangerous enmity of the Frank. He appealed to Charles the Roman Patrician (773) and his appeal was not in vain. A great Frankish army marched into Italy and drove Didier off his throne. Nothing was wanting to the completeness of the Frankish triumph, neither the eclipse of the royal line of Lombards after two hundred years of rule in Italy, nor the assumption by Charles, the conqueror, of the Lombard crown, nor the final act of scorn which relegated the last of the Lombard kings to a lifelong imprisonment in a monastery.

In the midst of his Italian campaign Charles was solemnly received by the grateful and submissive ecclesiastics of Rome. He was thirty-two years of age; upon his fresh and experiencing, but naïvely superstitious, mind the marvels of Rome, its wealth in churches and wonder-working relics, its finished priestcraft, its Gregorian chants and well-ordered ritual, made a profound impression. A visit to Rome more than seven hundred years later drove Luther from the Catholic fold. Upon Charles the reaction of this extraordinary city was otherwise. He found it rich and incomparable in the favour of God. Here the awestruck visitor would be shown the very ark of the covenant and the heads of St. Peter and St. Paul. Here he could inspect two phials of blood and water from the side of Christ, the purple robe worn by the Saviour of mankind, and part of the cradle in which He lay when the Magi came to adore Him. Here was the very table at which He ate His Last Supper, here His portrait painted by the hand of Luke the Evangelist, or perhaps even, as some were bold to conjecture, by the divine brush of the Creator Himself. Moreover, the whole art and science of serving God was here better understood than anywhere in those northern lands with which Charles was familiar. The singing was more beautiful, the ritual more perfect, the churches richer and more numerous. Charles determined to bring this Roman art and science of priestcraft into his Frankish world. Making a lifelong friend of the Pope, he confirmed, perhaps with additions, that donation of mid-Italian territory by which his father had founded the Papal State.

Twenty-six years afterwards a yet graver problem connected with the Papacy brought Charles again to Rome. If a Pope were accused by his enemies of simony, adultery, and perjury; if he were set upon by his enemies in the streets of Rome (as was the fate of Leo III on April 25, 799) and beaten within an inch of his life; if then he were rescued by his friends and escorted to the great Frankish king as he held court at Paderborn, who was competent to try the issue? To what power was entrusted the solemn duty of passing judgment on the vicar of Christ?

Certainly, in the view of the wise men of the west, that function did not belong to the beautiful Athenian lady who, having caused her son Constantine VI to be blinded and imprisoned, now reigned supreme in Constantinople. Irene, despite her addiction to images, and the enthusiasm of her monkish following, was no more fit to try the Pope of Rome than her wretched, image-breaking boy. A woman, least of all a homicidal Greek woman, could not be Roman Emperor. Thus, in 800, men awoke to the fact that in the wide world there was neither a valid Emperor nor yet a valid Pope.

To the mind of that age a world so destitute was given over to ruin and chaos. Someone there must be to uphold the Christian Faith, to safeguard the Roman tradition, to preside over the trial of the dubious Pope, to balance the brilliant and menacing power of Abdur Rahman, the Caliph of

Bagdad, and to maintain in a comprehensive bond the sacred
unity of civilization. That person could only be Charlemagne.
It is an illustration of his wide renown that the Patriarch of
Jerusalem, despairing of protection from the eastern Empire,
despatched to him the keys of the Holy Places.

So when, in the late autumn of 800, Charles descended
into Italy, we cannot doubt that over and above the urgent
need of clearing the reputation of the Pope, there was present
to his mind that momentous void in the Roman Empire. A
Pope must be purged and an Emperor must be crowned. Yet
the precise method of reaching these two ends may have
been left to chance. On December 23 Pope Leo asserted his
innocence by a solemn oath taken on the Gospels in the
Basilica of St. Peter's, to the satisfaction of a great synod of
Roman and Frankish clergy. Two days later, as Charles
was rising from his knees at the end of the Christmas Mass,
the Pope placed upon his head the imperial crown, and the
congregation at St. Peter's, apparently not unprepared,
shouted, "Karolo piissimo Augusto a Deo coronato vita et
victoria." Once more there was a Roman Emperor in western
Europe.

It is possible that Charles was chagrined, as his biographer
hints, by the sudden mode of his coronation, for no Emperor
in the west had ever yet received his crown from the Pope.
But the superstructure of papal pretensions built upon that
Christmas Day ceremony was in the distant future. What
mattered at the time was not the mode, but the fact, of the
coronation. The imperial title brought with it neither treasure
nor territory. It did not give to Charles authority in Spain,
or Britain, or Africa, once flourishing provinces of the Roman
Empire; nor a yard of Lombardy, of which he was already
king and master; nor yet on the strength of it could he command the service of an additional soldier or ship of war. Yet
the revival of the Roman Empire in the west was none the
less important, for through it that deep inner sense of unity
which persists at the heart of European turmoils, and has given
rise to such institutions as the Concert of Europe and the
League of Nations, received for many centuries its secular
embodiment.

It is one of the highest titles of Charlemagne to fame that
he used his great authority to promote the revival of intellectual life on the illiterate continent of Europe. The Carolingian

Renaissance lacks all the qualities of charm, freedom, and audacity which distinguished the great liberating movement of the human spirit in the age which divides Petrarch from Galileo. To the orthodox mind of Charles literature was chiefly to be valued as the handmaid of faith. The learned men who were attracted from all quarters to his court were not expected to discover new verities for the service of man. The Holy Scriptures, though often circulating in corrupt and misleading texts, contained the whole key to the truth, the sovereign guide to conduct. These it was the province of the scholar to copy out, and if needful, to amend, to understand himself and to make clear to his pupils; and that a supply of men qualified to perform this learned office might never be lacking, every diocese and monastery of the realm was expected to take up the work of education.

The value of this intellectual movement must not be judged by the quality of Carolingian literature. This, with the exception of Einhard's Life of Charles, does not rise above mediocrity, and shines only by contrast with the preceding darkness. What is important to notice is the new place which, with the advent of Charles, learning and education are made to take in the life of the court and the country, the concentration of foreign men of learning round the person of the king, the travelling academy or school of the palace which follows him even on his campaigns, the equal terms on which he associates with his scholar friends, his strong insistence on literacy as a qualification for a clerical career and for preferment in the Church, the establishment of diocesan and monastic schools, and the encouragement given to the multiplication, correction, and gathering together of books. Far reaching novelties were not to be expected in that age. There was no idea of science, no close observation of the outer world, no instinct for discovery. The prime necessity of the moment was not to invent, but to recover what had been lost, to preserve what had been found, and to reconstitute in the midst of barbarism a literate society.

The task would have been rendered by many degrees more difficult but for the fact that there was one corner of western Europe in which the lamps of learning and literature were still burning with a relative brightness. The islands of Ireland and Britain, though far from peaceful, had been for a century immune from many of the grave calamities which had afflicted the continent. At Armagh and Iona, at Jarrow and York, knowledge and piety shone with a clear, if intermittent, lustre. In these two islands a scholar possessed of a good deal of Latin, a little Greek, and possibly some fragments of Hebrew was not altogether unknown. More particularly in Northumbria, where Roman and Irish influences were found in combination or in conflict, was the care for letters specially evident. It is probable that at the date of Charlemagne's accession the best store of books north of the Alps was the library at York.

It was from York that Charles took his spiritual counsellor. To Alcuin, a Northumbrian of noble lineage, born and educated in that city, there was vouchsafed the greatest educational opportunity ever opened to an Englishman. He was called in to prescribe for the intellectual wants of a great empire fallen from civilization to barbarism. To this task he brought a pure and ardent character, a communicative zeal, and a gift of eloquent but unoriginal writing. He composed complimentary Latin verses, moral and pedagogic treatises, and an extended controversial reply to those Spanish heretics who maintained that Christ was adopted by God. Nobody now reads the tedious writings of Alcuin. Yet he was one of those valuable men who, without being gifted with discovering genius, create by their energy, sociability, and enthusiasm an atmosphere favourable to intellectual advance. His school of the palace set a new standard of culture. To the influence of this robust, studious, and convivial Englishman we may fairly trace the legislation which defines the educational responsibilities of the Church and the episcopal and monastic schools which resulted from it. To him also is due the initiation of that immense labour in the transcription, the emendation, and the preservation of manuscripts, the best and most permanent contribution which that age was able to make to the relief of man's estate. The earliest copies of twelve of the great Latin classics are due to the scribes of the Carolingian Renaissance.

Notable among the achievements of a famous reign was the final inclusion of Germany within the sphere of the Frankish nation and the Roman Church. Since Julius Caesar conquered Gaul there had been no such augmentation of Latin influence in Europe. Einhard, whose brief biography of Charles is justly accounted a model, says not only that he almost doubled the Empire which he received from his father, but that all the tribes between the Rhine and the Vistula were subjected to his rule. The particular mode of his operation was to batter down with a persistence which no rebuff could weaken the two principal obstacles which arrested the advance of Christianity in central Europe. These were the Saxon block in Westphalia, and the Avars, whose barbarous power, enriched by the sack of the Balkan cities, lay athwart the middle Danube. The struggle was long, obstinate, and cruel. Thirty-three years of hard fighting were necessary to the reduction and forced conversion of the Saxons, eight campaigns to the destruction of the Avars, whose hoarded treasures are said to have raised their conquerors from prosperity to affluence. But once done, the work did not require to be done again. The Saxons passed into the Christian fold, the Avars vanished from the map, and the tide of Frankish influence, bearing with it the seeds of Christian and Latin culture, swept slowly but surely eastwards into lands which afterwards came to be known as Poland and Bohemia, Austria and Hungary.

Even had he desired to do so, Charlemagne could never have latinized Germany as Caesar latinized Gaul. That branch of the Saxon race which had not passed into Britain preserved among their untamed forests a fierce attachment to the faith of their ancestors. Under Widukind, their national leader, they offered a desperate resistance to the armed missionaries of the Christian Faith. In the end they suffered a decisive defeat. Their idols were broken, their sacred groves were burned; their independence was forfeit; they were compelled to accept the odious creed of their conquerors at the point of the sword. But notwithstanding they remained true to type. Wotan was nearer than Christ. The Latin outlook on the world, clear, orderly, precise, was never theirs. They preserved their language, and with it the spirit, vague, passionate, and tumultuous, which distinguishes the German from the Latin character.

There is no failure here as some French authors have surmised. The prodigal military energy of this extraordinary reign was not vainly expended. The purpose of the wars of Charlemagne, of his fifty-three campaigns fought upon every front, Danish, Slav, Saxon, Avar, Dalmatian, Lombard, Spanish, was not to give lessons in the Latin spirit, but to

defend the orthodox Christians of the west against the enemies
who assailed them on every side. The issue was not one between Latin and Teuton, Gallo-Roman and German, but
between the Latin Christians of the west, Germans, Gauls,
Romans, Spaniards, and the encircling forces of the anti-
Christian world. In that struggle Charlemagne emerged the
victor. He made central Europe safe for the Roman Church.
By admitting the conquered Saxons and Bavarians into his
empire on equal terms with the conquering Franks he made
Germany. And if he failed to break the Saracens in Spain,
and even suffered a reverse at the hands of the Gascons in
the pass of Roncesvalles, his one repulse shone with more
glory than many victories through the transforming power
of legend, which gave to his campaign in the Ebro Valley
the lustre of a crusade, and wove round the name of the fallen
Roland interminable garlands of song.

814   When the great Emperor passed away, his vast dominions
fell asunder, and in their severance gave rise to the nations of
the west. He did not succeed, fortunately perhaps for Europe,
in creating a centralized government strong enough to function in the absence of a dominating mind. His permanent
achievements must be sought elsewhere. Mounting the throne
at a time when the political future was dark and troubled,
when the idea of authority had grown faint, and the lamps of
learning and literature were flickering to extinction, he called
a vigorous halt to the forces of paganism, anarchy, and
ignorance. To him the domain of Latin Christianity owes
the geographical shape which it has since retained. To his
vigorous impulsion is due a remarkable revival of intellectual
activity. The idea of a strong civilized government, concerned
to promote religion, to secure justice, to listen to the complaints of all its subjects, to spread education, and to conserve
learning, was brought back into western Europe by this eager,
vital, and capacious spirit. The central institutions which he
alone could infuse with energy did not long survive him;
but under the protection of his lengthy reign, dukes and
counts and other feudatories made private fortunes and
built up for themselves centres of local government and
authority, little states capable of defending themselves against
hostile attack, and of preserving some part of the legacy of
Greece, of Syria, and of Rome.

The keynote of Charlemagne's rule was personal authority

but not despotism. A monarch without a paid regular army or a bureaucracy or a settled revenue payable in coin may exercise a widespread influence but cannot play the tyrant. At the great periodical gatherings of notables, the *placita Generalia*, when enquiry was held into the public needs, it was Charlemagne who represented the people at large, and not the officials by whom the poor were too often oppressed. Moreover, without organization no large state can be tyrannically governed, and the Frankish Empire, like every other mediaeval polity, was unorganized. Some necessary steps in decentralization were taken. The government of Italy was handed over to one son (Pippin), that of Aquitaine to another (Lewis). But the Civil Service, if this phrase may be used of administrators who did not regard themselves as belonging to a professional corps, was deficient in numbers, skill, and honesty. The business was unclassified, and since the king insisted on looking into everything, some grave matters passed unnoticed while trivialities attracted an earnest regard. This fundamental absence of method meant that the kingdom was undergoverned, that the imperial edicts or capitularies were imperfectly executed, and that the bishops and counts who conducted the local government were inadequately controlled. For a time the commanding energy of the Emperor mitigated the force of these evils. Constantly travelling from vill to vill, asking questions, redressing grievances, showing himself open and hospitable to all, and when he was unable himself to be present, sending imperial commissaries to represent him, the popular sovereign kept the august fact of government before the eyes of his subjects. Yet all through his reign tendencies, destructive as contemporary nationalism to the workings of effective empire, were gathering in strength. Fiefs, awarded on condition of public service, were becoming hereditary estates. Vassals were becoming independent chieftains. The pious or politic benefactions of the sovereign were building up for the German church a basis of material power so great as permanently to influence the balance of political forces in that country. It is to this reign that we trace the rise of the great abbeys which played so large a part in the development of German agriculture, commerce, and learning. It is to the munificence of Charlemagne that the Archbishops of Köln, Trier, and Mainz owed their princely estates and a position of worldly

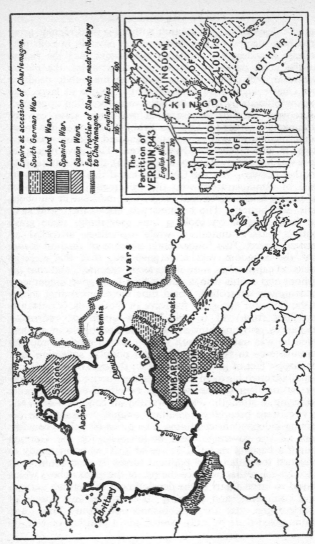

CHARLEMAGNE'S EMPIRE AND (INSET) THE PARTITION OF VERDUN

power and independence which lasted till the days of Napoleon.

Out of the energetic movement of the Frankish Empire Europe emerges in its mediaeval shape. Over against the Greek world ruled from Byzantium, and the Saracen world governed from Bagdad and Cordova, is the vast territory of Latin Christianity stretching from the Ebro to the Carpathians and acknowledging the rule of the Frankish Empire and the Pope of Rome. The Germans are now Christians, having been baptized in tribes, and are submitted to Roman bishops. The Czechs of Bohemia are drawn within the orbit of Frankish trade and Roman missionaries. Italy has become a geographical expression, linked to the Franks through the Lombard kingdom, and possessing in its very heart the paralysing structure of the Papal State. In Roman Gaul the races are now fused, the little, dark, prehistoric peoples of the Mediterranean littoral, the descendants of the Roman emigrants, the lively Celts, the vigorous Franks, in a common allegiance to the faith and discipline of the Church of Rome. Saracen Spain is no longer a conquering power, but stands on the defensive against the Christian colonies of the March out of which in after years grew the famous fighting kingdoms of Navarre and Aragon.

After the death of Charlemagne a break-up of the Frankish Empire was in some shape inevitable and wholesome. Territories so vast could never, save in exceptional times and under an exceptional man, be governed from one centre. There are, however, various way in which authority may be devolved and territories partitioned, and more than one manner in which devolution may be combined with the retention of some appropriate measure of central authority. But of all manners of subdividing an empire, the descendants of Charlemagne, who were mediocre where they were not degenerate, chose the worst. They adhered to the bad old system of family partitions, which had been the curse of Frankish politics from the first. As if no lessons were to be derived from history, they treated their kingdoms as private estates to be bequeathed and subdivided as family affection or convenience might dictate. To this disastrous custom many of the evils which affected western Europe during the ninth century may be clearly traced. Louis le Débonnaire would have been spared two depositions and a long spell of humiliating civil war if he had not attempted to make, at the expense of his elder sons, a territorial provision for Charles the Bald, the son of his old age.

To suppose that the policy of these sovereigns was in any way influenced by the principle of nationality would be to import into the politics of the ninth century ideas belonging to a later age. Yet it is true that in the Carolingian partitions of the ninth century we may discern the emergence of the nations of western Europe. After the death of Louis le Débonnaire in 840, civil war broke out between his sons, Charles the Bald, who ruled in Neustria, combining with Lewis the German, who ruled east of the Rhine, against Lothair their elder brother, who had been allotted Austrasia, Burgundy, and Italy. After the great battle at Fontenay, at which Lothair was defeated with huge losses, the three brothers came together at Verdun and agreed to divide their father's inheritance. To Charles the Bald were allotted Neustria, Aquitaine, and the Spanish March, a territory mainly, though not entirely, Romance in speech, and comprising all that part of modern France which is west of the Rhone and the Saône. Lewis the German received Austrasian Francia east of the Rhine, Bavaria, Swabia, Saxony, and Rhaetia, all save the last German-speaking districts, and all save the last comprised in the modern German Reich; while Lothair was assigned a long, intermediate, heterogeneous region comprising the two capitals of Aix-la-Chapelle and Rome, and stretching from Friesland to the border of Calabria. It would be possible to contend that Lewis the German ruled over a nation. It would be a tenable proposition to make the same claim for Charles the Bald, despite the fact that he exercised no real authority either in Brittany or in Aquitaine. But the share of the Emperor Lothair, with its mixture of Teutonic and Latin populations, is a flat contradiction of the racial principle and a proof that very little importance was attached to it by the members of the Carolingian house.

A subdivision of the Frankish dominions, clear, absolute, and regarded as permanent, would have served the cause of good government. The Partition of Verdun was none of these things. It was provisional, liable to change at every death in the family, and vitiated by the fact that each of the parti-

843

tioning brothers regarded himself as king of the Franks, as a
potential claimant to the undivided inheritance and imperial
authority of Charlemagne. Thus, although the idea of unity
survived, it was in the form most calculated to weaken
effective rule. The Partition of Verdun, so far from inaugura-
ting an era of peaceful government, was followed by new
partitions and fratricidal wars, by a steady decline in the
power of the Frankish kings, and a corresponding increase
in the power of the nobles.

In the western and middle kingdoms the anarchy was
appalling. In East Francia or Germany, where the inhabitants
were of one stock and language, where the level of civilization was uniform and low, where there was still a large class of
freeholders, and the institutions of feudalism were in an early
stage of development, the prospect of strong government
should have been more favourable. Yet government was no
stronger in Germany than it was in France. The tribes of
Germany, despite their common origin and speech, were as
little prepared to live together in amity as the Athenians and
the Spartans. The Saxons, the Franconians, the Bavarians,
and the Alemans lived their own law, went their own ways,
and were as ready to quarrel among themselves as to follow
the king against Danes and Slavs. The kingdoms were
partitioned and repartitioned. Even the imperial crown
failed to bring good fortune to its holder or to restore the
lost sentiment of a common allegiance. There is no more
significant fact in the Europe of the ninth century than the
fate of Charles the Fat, the third son of Lewis the German.
Upon this incompetent descendant of Charlemagne fortune
showered every blessing. He was crowned Emperor by the
Pope. A chapter of convenient family accidents made him
king of Italy, Germany, and France; a ruler, on paper at least,
such as Europe had not seen for seventy years. But the man
was a craven, his authority a figment, and on his deposition
in 887 there was a final break-up of the Carolingian Empire,
and save for the bastard Arnulf, a grandson of Lewis the
German, who was chosen to rule in East Francia, an end
to the long spell of authority exercised by the Carolingian
house.

In fairness to these later Frankish kings it should be remembered that all through the ninth century they were assailed by
external dangers from the Saracens, the Slavs, and the

Northmen. The outskirts of Rome itself were burned by the Saracens in 847. To these pirates who had succeeded in breaking down the guard of the Byzantines and in making themselves masters of Sicily the reply should have been the formation of a strong Frankish navy. Nothing of the kind was attempted; but to Pope Leo IV is due the credit of giving to the Vatican suburb that girdle of fortifications which has earned it the name of the Leonine City. The achievement of the Pope lives in the memory of the Italian people, while the well-meant endeavours of the Frankish Emperor Louis II to rid southern Italy of its Saracen pests are only known, and that imperfectly, to a handful of learned men.

BOOKS WHICH MAY BE CONSULTED

S. Dill: *Roman Society in Gaul in the Merovingian Age.* 1926.

O. M. Dalton: *Gregory of Tours (The History of the Franks).* 1927.

N. D. Fustel de Coulanges: *Histoires des Institutions Politiques de l'ancienne France.* 1888-92.

F. P. G. Guizot: *Histoire de la Civilisation en France.* 1851.

H. W. C. Davis: *Charlemagne.* 1900.

J. B. Mullinger: *The Schools of Charles the Great.* 1877.

J. Bryce: *The Holy Roman Empire.* 1904.

M. R. James: *Learning and Literature till Pope Sylvester II. (Cambridge Mediaeval History,* Vol. III.).

Einhard: *Life of Charlemagne. Ed.* H. W. Garrod and R. B. Mowat. 1915.

T. Hodgkin: *Charles the Great.* 1897.

E. Lavisse: *Histoire de France,* Vol. II. 1903.

E. S. Duckett: *Alcuin, Friend of Charlemagne.* 1951.

H. Fichtenau: *The Carolingian Empire. Tr.* P. Munz. 1957.

CHAPTER XIV

THE ROMAN CHURCH

The Primitive Church. Earliest Popes of Rome. Their creden-
tials. The Papacy helped by the breakdown of the imperial
power in the west. The early Christians not social reformers.
Effect of the Teutonic invasions on the position of the western
clergy. Social and educational work of the western Church.
Spread of monasticism.

RELIGIONS ARE founded by laymen and organized by priests.
The early Christian communities were societies of poor men
and women banded together for worship, charity, and discipline. The spirit was democratic, universalist, and egalitarian.
There was "neither Greek nor Jew, barbarian nor Scythian,
bond nor free." In the eyes of God all Christians were equal.
A bishop or overseer dispensed alms with the assistance of a
deacon, and came to be regarded as the successor of the
Apostle or missionary to whom the Church owed its original
foundation. Where religion was a common and intimate
concern and the body of the faithful was small and ardent
no very sharp line was drawn between laity and clergy. A
council of presbyters or elders was associated with the
bishop in the direction of the Church's affairs.

The story of the development of the Roman Catholic
Church from such democratic and simple beginnings may be
explained by the common human craving for authority and
direction in the conduct of life. As the Roman republic grew
into an autocratic empire, so out of the scattered churches
of the apostolic age there was gradually evolved the imposing
fabric of papal theocracy. The trend of the human spirit
being in the direction of despotism, the Church followed where
the State had led. Its organization was modelled on that
of the Empire. It became, in fact, after the conversion
of Constantine, the Roman Empire in its ecclesiastical
aspect.

From the logic then prevailing it followed that the Church,
like the Empire, must have a supreme head. Councils were

difficult to assemble and were better adapted to deal with great emergencies than with the current administration. If the unity of doctrine and practice was to be observed there must be a bishop of bishops, to whom in the last resort all questions of doubt could be referred, a single church dominated by a single head and embracing in its large hospitality all the Christian peoples of the world.

That this primacy should belong to the Bishop of Rome was an opinion more readily entertained by the Italians than by the Patriarchate of Constantinople, by the Christian bishops of Africa, or by the apostolic churches of Antioch, Jerusalem, or Alexandria. It was only by slow degrees that the papal claims, which have never been universally acknowledged by Christians, obtained a general acceptance from the churches of the west. The early Popes were mostly obscure men. They were not philosophers or theologians. They contributed nothing to the building up of church doctrine, and only with Gregory the Great entered the missionary field, which had been left to the saints and visionaries of Ireland. If here and there a Pope was eminent, his capacity was displayed in the sphere of statesmanship, not of religion. Yet the Church of Rome was able to put forth credentials which in that age brought conviction to minds prepared to accept whatever was traditional, miraculous, or flattering to Roman pride. It was contended on the strength of a famous text, "Thou art Peter. On this rock I will build my Church" (Matt. xvi. 17-19), that Christ had given to St. Peter the primacy over the Apostles, that St. Peter, who is known to have preached and suffered in Rome, handed on his divine commission to Linus, the first bishop of the see, and that from Linus there had descended through an unbroken chain of bishops the sublime charge of safeguarding St. Peter's knowledge of Christian truth. Of Roman bishops we have no list earlier than Irenaeus (*circa* A.D. 180), but the belief in a secret reservoir of ultimate verity, in an oral tradition only to be communicated to the initiate, was widely spread through the pagan and Christian world. To this belief was added the strong conviction, shared not only by Latin but also by Greek Christians, that the city of Rome derived a peculiar strength and sanctity from the possession of the bones of St. Peter and St. Paul. St. John Chrysostom, the most eloquent of the Greek Fathers, has expressed in a powerful sermon the sentiments excited by the

590-
610

contemplation of the privileges which were thus accorded to the city of Rome. "For this," he writes, "it is I love Rome: though I might praise her on other grounds, for her greatness, her antiquity, her beauty, her numbers, her power, her wealth, her victories in war; but passing over all these, I bless her because Paul, when living, wrote to the Romans, and loved them so much, and was among them, and spoke to them, and there ended his life. Whence also the city is more renowned for this than for all else; and like a great and mighty body, she has two eyes, the bodies of those two saints. The heaven is not so bright when the sun shoots forth his rays as the city of the Romans, shedding forth the light of these two lamps throughout the world. Thence shall Paul be caught up, thence Peter shall rise. Consider and be amazed! What a sight shall Rome then behold, when Paul suddenly shall arise with Peter from the tomb, and be caught up to meet the Lord. What a rose shall Rome send forth to Christ! What diadems are those two, with which the city is crowned, with what chains of gold it is girded; what fountains it hath! It is for this that I admire the city, not for its much gold, for its columns or any other phantasy, but because of these two pillars of the Church. Who will grant me to embrace the body of Paul, to cling to his sepulchre, and to see the dust of that body which 'filled up what was wanting' to Christ, which bore His stigmata, and sowed His teaching everywhere!"[1]

Had the emperors continued to reign in Rome the guardians of the Petrine tradition would hardly have escaped the servile destiny of the Byzantine patriarchs. The Popes would have been the agents of the emperors, and would have lost the moral authority which always attaches to the assertion of spiritual independence. From this danger, however, the Papacy was delivered by the two great political events which concurrently changed the face of western Europe—the breakdown of the imperial government and the barbaric invasions. As the emperor vanished from the west, the empty place was taken by the descendant of St. Peter. It was to the Pope that a bishop, condemned by a provincial council, was encouraged by the Fathers at Sardica (343) to appeal; it was the Pope and not the emperor who stood out as the champion of Italian civilization against the Huns and the

---

[1] Hom. 32 in Rom., 2, vol. ix., p. 678 (757). *Cf.* Chapman, *Studies in the Early Papacy*, p. 97.

Saracens, who defended Rome from the attacks of the
Lombards, and upon whom necessarily devolved the power
of writing letters or decretals on ecclesiastical issues which
had the force of law. In the dark and troubled age of the
barbaric invasions, in the days of Leo I and Gregory the
Great, the see of St. Peter stood out in western Europe like
a lighthouse in a storm.

The early Christians, though sharply opposed to many
ancient practices, never set out to reform mankind. It is a
mistake to imagine that any modern political label can be
safely attached to them. They were neither socialists, nor
communists, nor individualists. They had no philosophy
of the state or belief in the regeneration of society through
institutions. The idea that the framework of Roman politics
or society could be transformed by the agency of their small
and uninfluential congregations would never have occurred
to them. They knew that the world was wicked, for they
had learnt that man was fallen from grace and merited eternal
torment, and rather than act wickedly some of them were
willing to face a martyr's death. But they held that this evil
world was not destined to endure for long. At the second
coming of Christ, which many believed to be imminent and
none thought would be long delayed, righteousness would be
enthroned upon earth and all the flaws, wickedness,and im-
perfections of mankind be cleansed away. Why, then, should
the Christian labour to abolish slavery, or war, or trade, or
these great engines of physical force, which sustained the
weight of the Roman Empire? All this was fated soon to
vanish, and meanwhile each individual soul was confronted
with the problem, at once awful and instant, of how best to
avoid the everlasting torment which was the retribution of
God for the original sin of Adam in the garden.

The Christians, then, accepted what they could not change.
They offered up prayers for the Roman Emperor, though they
refused to burn incense to his image. They accepted and condoned slavery. So far were they from generally repudiating
force, that war among Christians became a melancholy feature
of European society from the fifth century onwards. In
none of their activities is it possible to discern any trace of
class conscious motives. Though the Christians of the
apostolic age were poor, their religion spread so swiftly
through every class that before the end of the first century

it had even penetrated into the circle of the Emperor's family.

One grave danger the new Christian community was enabled to avoid through the worldly wisdom of a bishop of Rome. Callistus (219-223) showed himself prepared to absolve the fornicator and adulterer from sin. His decision, though it ran counter to a large body of Christian feeling, was epoch-making in its consequences. Based on exclusive doctrine a Church is strong, limited by exclusive morality it is weak. Many will subscribe to a test. Few will lead the life of virtue. A Church confined in its membership to the saints and offering nothing to the sinners would never have effected the conquest of Europe.

The position of the clergy in western society was greatly changed by the influx into the Roman Empire of wave after wave of Teutonic barbarism. In the tragical eclipse of lay education and culture the intellectual advantages of the Church became for the first time conspicuous. The cleric could at least read and write, was familiar with Latin, had enough arithmetic to calculate the date of Easter and was often accustomed to the sedentary toil which is necessary to the regular despatch of business. Moreover, as the attractions of the imperial service had fallen away, the Church had begun to draw men of the highest social standing into its service. In Gaul the bishops of the fifth, sixth and seventh centuries were often noblemen of ancient lineage, of great wealth and widespread influence, who found in the discharge of official duties the only opportunity for the exercise of administrative gifts or the satisfaction of a public conscience. Accordingly it is not surprising that the Franks in Gaul and the Visigoths in Spain made a free use of this serviceable profession. The Teutonic sovereigns had a rich capacity for the pursuit of the boar and the stag and for the slaughter and pillage of their enemies. Without the aid of the Church they could not have governed.

The lively narrative of Gregory of Tours is sufficient to warn us against the temptation to idealize the Gallican Church in the sixth century. Its corruptions were numerous and flagrant. But comprising as it did all the little that was good in the French society of that time, it performed valuable functions which would not otherwise have been rendered. The fusion of the Latin and Teutonic elements in the state could not have been accomplished without the Church. The whole work of education was in its hands. If a river was to be embanked or an aqueduct was to be built, it was generally a bishop who supplied the initiative and controlled the funds. Despite much evidence of a cowardly compliance with wickedness, a bishop from time to time found the courage to rebuke or the authority to overawe a transgressing ruler. Nor in that age of violent autocracy was there elsewhere than in the Church a protection for the poor, the helpless, and the oppressed.

It is, indeed, to the circumstances of these turbulent centuries that we must ascribe the present position and authority of the priestly profession. The chaos of the Empire was the opportunity of the Church, the childish ignorance of the barbarian prepared the triumph of the priest. In an age when books were rare, everything depended on the voice and example of the teacher. The simple and superstitious barbarian was ready to tolerate a degree of interference in his private life which the cultivated Roman lady or gentleman would have resented as a vulgar intrusion. As the task of educating the barbarian world in the rudiments of the Christian Faith unfolded itself in all its vast and desperate proportions, the clergy became of necessity, like the school teachers of the United States during the spate of immigration from Europe, a well-marked and influential profession. In the sixth century it was ordained that the Latin clergy should wear a distinctive dress. While the German kept his tunic short and his hair long, the priest preserved the long robe and short hair of the ancient Roman.

The century which followed the conversion of Constantine is marked by the spread of monasticism through western Europe. Asceticism is a common feature of religious movements, and in Egypt, the original home of monkery, was apt to assume extravagant forms of self-torture and abasement. The good sense of the west avoided the eccentricities of the Egyptian solitary who, perched upon a pillar or a tree, exhibited the charms of his pious emaciation and squalor to the admiring pilgrim. The Latin genius was more practical, less speculative than the Greek. The rule of St. Benedict of Nursia (480-540) the great Italian visionary, who founded the monasteries of Subiaco and Monte Cassino, enjoined the intermingling of manual labour with study and devotional exercises, and as it became general through the west, enabled monasticism, which might otherwise have wrought nothing but evil, to make a positive contribution to human progress. It is to the credit of the Benedictine monks that they improved tillage and reclaimed waste land, that they undertook the work of relieving the poor, and that by preserving and copying manuscripts they rendered an important and necessary service to European culture. During the darkest age of Teutonic barbarism there was perhaps no other way in which the gentler natures of society might be turned to useful account.

The diffusion of Benedictine monasteries through the countries of the west proceeded during the next two centuries with a rapidity so amazing as to suggest that there must have been some special feature in the circumstances of that age to impel men and women to embrace in such great numbers a life of sheltered asceticism. Their motives, no doubt, were compounded of many elements, ranging from exaltation and heroic piety to cowardice, evasion, and hope of ease; but we can hardly doubt that what chiefly operated upon the imagination of those who were then drawn into the monastic movement was the difficulty of leading a Christian life in a world racked and disturbed by the barbarian invasions, a world of crime, lust, violence, and steadily increasing chaos. Their asceticism is intelligible; discerning little hope of improvement through human agencies, they withdrew from the darkness and turmoil around them into the tranquil light of the Christian paradise.

BOOKS WHICH MAY BE CONSULTED

C. Gore: *Jesus of Nazareth*. 1929.

E. Bevan: *Christianity* (Home University Library). 1932.

E. Bevan: *Hellenism and Christianity*. 1921.

L. Battifol: *Primitive Catholicism*. 1911.

J. Chapman: *Studies in the Early Papacy*. 1928.

F. H. Dudden: *Gregory the Great—His Place in History and Thought*. 1905.

H. H. Milman: *The History of Latin Christianity*. 1867.

Gibbon: *Decline and Fall of the Roman Empire*. Ed. Bury. 1896-1900.

C. Bigg: *The Origins of Christianity.* 1909.

C. Bigg: *The Church's Task under the Roman Empire.* 1905.

M. Deanesly: *A History of the Medieval Church,* 590-1500. 1954.

S. L. Greenslade: *Church and State from Constantine to Theodosius.*
    1954.

C. N. Cochrane: *Christianity and Classical Culture.* 1940.

CHAPTER XV

THE NORSEMEN

*Norse culture. The Norsemen on the Dnieper. Viking raids
in the west. Danes and Norwegians. Raids on Ireland,
England, France. Rise of Wessex. Alfred and his successors.
Danish Conquest of England. Canute leads Scandinavia into
the Christian fold. Edward the Confessor. The Normans in
Normandy. Their acceptance of Latin culture. The Normans
in Sicily. Splendour of Roger II. Exhaustion and poverty
of Scandinavia.*

ONE BRANCH of the Nordic race, hitherto withdrawn from the
zone of Latin and Teutonic influence, now made a violent
irruption into the political scene, and for more than two
centuries filled the world with noise and fury. The Norsemen
were pagans. The ideas of conscience and sin, of virtue in the
Christian sense of that term, were foreign in their ways of
thinking. There was nothing in the cult of Thor, the God of
Thunder, of Odin, the Lord of War and the inventor of song,
or of Frey, the God of Fertility, that might bring shame to
the murderer, the adulterer, or the pirate. The Norsemen loved
war and women, wassail and song, pillage and slaughter.
Their mythology, which was common to all the Nordic
races, was distinguished for a spirit of fatalism, fierce as the
northern seas, grave as the arctic skies. The gods they regarded not as guides to disciplined conduct, for of this they
had no sense, but as friends and allies in a great adventure,
leading, if a man was brave and fortunate, to death in battle
and to a passage into the halls of Valhalla, where heroes slain
in combat fight and feast to the end of time. Of false optimism
there is no trace in the prose sagas which were written down

in Iceland many centuries later. The Norsemen knew too A.D.
much about the wild elements of nature and the furious 1150-
passions of man to ask of life more than life could give. And 1250
so the old Norse literature, in which the record of this pagan
civilization is faithfully preserved, stands out among the
literatures of the world for its freedom from rhetoric and
sentiment, its closeness to the facts of life, its abstinence
from moral comment or literary embellishment, but above
all for the picture which it gives of a society at once aristocratic and anarchic, violent and tenacious of the past, but ennobled despite all its lusts and cruelties by a manly veracity
and a proud acceptance of inevitable fate.

To this very capable and strenuous race of mariners and
shipwrights, yeoman farmers and merchants, woodmen and
whalers, there was disclosed in the later half of the eighth
century the exciting secret that great tracts of the globe offered
the richest plunder on the cheapest terms. If the southward
route was blocked by the Saxons and Franks, eastwards and
westwards the paths lay open and almost undefended. While
the Swedish merchants exploited the virgin resources of the
Russian plain, the pirates of Denmark and Norway helped
themselves, with more fighting but less effort, to the glittering
treasures of the west. The Swedes established a factory near
Lake Ladoga, and from that central and convenient station,
close to the head waters of the Volga and the Dnieper, traded
down the great Russian waterways to the Caspian and the
Black Sea. Their settlements at Holmgarth or Novgorod, at
New Garth or Kiev, became, in the midst of the unpolitical
and disorganized Slavonic peoples, centres of guidance and
authority. To Ruric, the Swedish leader, fame assigns the
credit of having founded at Novgorod and at Kiev the
original centres of a Russian state. So powerful was the
Swedish influence, so patient and receptive were the Slavonic
populations, who accepted Swedish rule, that the name
(Ruotsi) by which the Swede was known to his Finnish
neighbours was soon transferred from the master to the
subject, and has become the common designation of the
Russian people.

It is, then, to the Norsemen, and more particularly to a
remarkable sequence of Swedish rulers in Kiev, that the
Slavs of the Russian plain owe their first experience of state
life. The Slavonic nature, dreamy, passionate, lethargic,

imaginative, more Asiatic than European, needed then, as often afterwards, the shock and stimulus of an alien discipline. Such a benefit at the threshold of their history the Scandinavian adventurers conferred upon the Russian race. Nor is it less important that the Principality of Kiev, the chief centre of Swedish power on the Dnieper, was taught by its rulers to look for its civilization, not to the north, but southwards to Constantinople. To the Swedish governors of Kiev Russia principally owes its introduction to the art and religion of the Byzantine world. For these merchant pirates the Dnieper was chiefly to be valued as the waterway to Middlegarth, the wealthiest and mightiest of cities, which it was their ambition to conquer and despoil. Four times (860, 880, 907, 914) did their powerful fleets menace the capital of the eastern Empire. Four times were their attacks frustrated by arms or parried by diplomacy. In the end Swedish mercenaries entered the imperial bodyguard and by their valour and detachment helped to sustain the Byzantine state. But Russia's ambition to be mistress of Constantinople, first inflamed by the robber pirates of Sweden, has survived through the ages, and has been, until the late revolution, an important factor in European policy.

While the Dnieper Swedes were feeling their way to the Bosphorus, and the Volga Swedes were chaffering their wares with the Transcaspian subjects of the Caliph of Bagdad, the Danes and Norwegians had embarked upon a course of highhearted rapine in the west. The monasteries of Ireland in particular, and in a lesser degree those of England and of France, were stored with gold and silver ornaments, with rich brocades and precious stones, and once discovered, were the first mark for Viking attack. A single shipload laden with the spoil of Lindisfarne or Noirmoustier is sufficient to explain all that followed. The Vikings were poor, the monasteries were rich. After the gloom of a northern winter it was a rare, and in the existing political distractions of the western kingdoms a not too dangerous amusement, to set sail with the first favouring breeze of summer in search of a quick fortune beyond the western sea. We need not look beyond common cupidity for the explanation of the Scandinavian expansion. The historians who descry in the Viking raids a pagan protest against the forced conversion of the Saxons by Charles the Great attribute to the Northmen a precise intolerance postulating a priesthood which they do not appear to have possessed, and in any case foreign to their cloudy theology.

Geography rather than design prescribed for these two plundering races differing routes and fields of activity. The Danes, being nearer to the Channel, threw themselves on Frisia, England, and France. The Norsemen, taking a wider and more westerly sweep, attacked the Orkneys and Shetlands, the Hebrides, and the Isle of Man, and effected settlements not only in these islands but in northern Scotland, Northumbria, and Ireland. Thereafter, when their long clinker built boats of stout Norwegian oak had been well tested in violent seas, these wonderful mariners performed feats more daring still, and never surpassed in the annals of seafaring men. Iceland and the Faroes were claimed and settled. The Atlantic was crossed. From Ireland as a base, the long Viking warships, driven by oar and sail, planted colonies on the bleak shores of Greenland and, six hundred years before the voyage of Columbus, explored the North American coast—the Vineland of Icelandic saga.

Apart from their skill in navigation the Vikings possessed the further advantage of alone understanding the value of swift movement in warfare. They would row up the Thames or the Loire, and, suddenly landing on some quiet inland field, seize the horses from the farms and scamper through the country burning, slaying, and robbing as they went, and be gone long before the slow-footed countrymen could combine to offer an effective resistance.

The long period of time during which these raids were successfully repeated, the immense havoc which they caused, and the panic which prevailed not on the seaboard only but in the heart of the continent, are a sufficient measure of the disorganization into which western Europe had fallen after the death of Charlemagne. Society seemed paralysed before an enemy so fierce, so mobile, and so ubiquitous as within the space of a few years to attack Cadiz and Seville, Hamburg and Bordeaux, Valence and Pisa.

It is foolish to imagine that everything which happens on a great scale in this world is for good. The raids of the Vikings were purely destructive. In the first half of the tenth century they went near to bringing down in complete ruin the whole fabric of civilization in western Europe. The old

Irish culture, once so distinctive and brilliant, never recovered from their widespread and persistent depredations, and with the sack of Iona, the principal channel through which Irish Christianity had flowed into England was finally obstructed. Yet such is human nature that great calamities provoke in the end counter-vailing efforts, and are found in the last account to have some compensations. The piracies of the Vikings led through conquests to settlements. If the Norsemen sacked the Irish monasteries, they founded the Irish trading towns. If they destroyed Armagh, they created Dublin and Wexford, Waterford and Limerick. Nor were their insults to the Gaelic-speaking Highlands barren of distant benefits. By their control of the Western Isles and the Irish Sea a barrier was interposed between Ireland and Scotland, preventing migration, obstructing fusion, and promoting the union of the Scottish people under a Scottish king.

An even deeper impression was left by the Danish dealings with England and France, by the startling shock of their terrible raids, by their conquest first of a Danelaw in England, then of a Danelaw to be known as Normandy in France, and finally by that critical period in the annals of our own country (1013-1042) during which England was ruled by Danish kings and became part of a great Scandinavian Empire. The Northmen, like the Anglo-Saxons and the Franks, were a Teutonic people. In essentials of character they resembled the Saxons and so much of the population of northern France as was Teutonic and not Celtic in origin. For this reason the effects of the Danish settlement of eastern England and of Normandy are of more enduring importance than the Moorish settlement of Spain. The conquerors and conquered influenced one another in a permanent way, not because they were unlike, but because they were like, and at one in the important particular of being intelligent and receptive. The Danes in Normandy became Frenchmen, the Danes in England became Englishmen. The conquerors accepted Christianity and the Latin culture which went with it. What they gave in return was an assemblage of spirited qualities, which, when once the first passion of destructiveness had been exhausted, made first of the Normans and then of the English the two leading peoples in the world.

To the student of English institutions the fundamental similarity between Saxon and Dane is the key to many riddles. The Anglo-Saxon people was distinguished above all other branches of the Teutonic family for a copious and continued output of written law. The stream which was eventually to broaden out into the great river of the English common law began under Ethelbert of Kent, at a time when Roman jurisprudence was speaking its valediction in the Institutes of Justinian, and received substantial additions to its volume under the kings of Wessex. But the last and most comprehensive Code of our island law, issued before the Norman Conquest, was the work of no Saxon but of Canute the Dane. To him as to the antiquarians of today it clearly seemed that while the differences of custom between Dane and Saxon were superficial the resemblances were profound. The word law is Norse; so too is that passion for litigation which is a distinctive feature of the English character; but each race was accustomed to public trials, to a procedure by oath helpers and ordeals, and to a tariff of compensations for acts of violence to be paid in whole or in part to the injured party. If the jury of inquisition is a Norman innovation it has analogies in the practice of the Saxons and the Danes.

A further consequence following the Danish invasions of France and England was a strengthening of the state in each of these countries by the emergence of a dynasty of efficient rulers. In France, after many weary decades of weakness and disorder, the house of Capet, first springing to eminence through its defence of Paris against the Northmen, superseded the effete epigoni of Charlemagne, and started upon a long career of modest but steady aggrandizement. Not very dissimilar was the course of events in England. Here at the climax of their destructive energies, with English government broken in Northumbria, East Anglia, and Mercia, and the fate of Saxon civilization trembling in the balance, the Danes met in the monarchs of the house of Egbert a series of stubborn and valiant opponents. The contest was long, savage, and marked by abrupt vicissitudes, but not wholly sterile. From it emerged the idea of a national monarchy, centred in Wessex, the sole surviving Teutonic power in the island which had escaped destruction at the hands of the Vikings.

It was in 866 that the Danish raids on England, which for thirty-two years had been steadily gathering in strength and destructiveness, were exchanged for a definite policy of conquest. In a brilliant and meteoric campaign Hingwar, the son of Ragnar Lothbrok, one of the most famous pirates of his age, carried everything before him from the Thames to the Clyde. The weak kingdoms of Northumbria and East Anglia crumbled under his hammer blows. He took Nottingham and besieged Dumbarton, and when he crossed over to Ireland in 868, leaving Halfdan, his brother, to continue his work, it seemed as if the whole island might swiftly become a Danish prize.

There was, however, in the kingdom of Wessex, which now extended from Land's End to the North Sea, a slow but stubborn population of nobles, farmers, and peasants, which was capable under the strong leadership of a native king of offering a brave and dogged resistance to the enemy. It was in 871, when the Danes were in the heart of his country, that Alfred at the age of twenty-three succeeded to the formidable responsibilities of the West Saxon kingship. Everything which relates to the life of this great national figure is of interest to Englishmen: his early visits to Rome; his delight in the songs and literature of his people; his concern for education; his encouragement of learning through the translations which he commissioned of the most popular Latin books of the time, such as the *De Consolatione* of Boethius or the *Pastoral Cure* of Gregory the Great; his patronage of foreign artists, craftsmen, and divines; his interest in travel and geography; his widespread international relations; his intrepidity in war; his zest in hunting; his zeal, carried almost to the point of morbidity, in the cult of relics and the exercises of religion. But what makes his career significant is not this evidence of width and versatility, but the fact that he drove the Danes out of Wessex, and that in saving Wessex he secured the survival of Anglo-Saxon civilization and laid the foundations of a national state in Britain.

The triumph of Wessex under the leadership of Alfred is thus memorable for two distinct reasons. It was the first serious check to the great heathen onslaught from the north, and the beginning of that reverse process which led to the christianization of the Scandinavian races and their acceptance as members of the polity of Europe.

This is the ecumenical significance of Alfred's life. But it is also a landmark in the history of England. The saviour of

Wessex has a claim on the loyalty of all men using the Saxon speech. Without any formal document, but from the march of events, he became the ruler of all that part of England which was not by express treaty ceded (878, 885) to the Danes. The fleet, the law, the capital of later England seem to be prefigured in his policies. He built long ships, issued a code based on Saxon, Mercian, and Kentish customs, restored a devastated London and incorporated it in his dominions.

Moreover, his work served as a foundation. From Wessex, as from a well-defended base, Alfred's son Edward reconquered the Danelaw, and his grandson Athelstan repulsed a combined attack from Ireland and Scotland in a battle so moving in its incidents and wide in its appeal (Brunanburh, 937) that it has inspired a great Anglo-Saxon poem and supplied a theme to one of the finest of the Icelandic Sagas. By 954 the king of Wessex ruled all England from the Channel to the Clyde.

So for seventy-seven years after the death of Alfred the Great the West Saxon monarchy preserved its predominance, extending its influence by steady degrees, ruling the Danelaw with a light hand, and with the help of the Church surviving the perils of a minority. Yet the unity of England, though proclaimed in theory, was still for various reasons insecure, and so remained till the consolidating work of the Norman Conquest. The Danish armies encamped and settled east of Watling Street, and the Norwegian armies who had established themselves in Northumbria were neither at one with one another nor completely fused with the Saxon population. The earlier traditions of the heptarchy were not altogether forgotten and under weak governance might again revive.

The crisis came under the long unhappy reign of Ethelred the Redeless (979-1016). The Danes now revived their attacks upon a country which after seventy-six years of comparative peace must, in contradistinction to the prevailing misery of the continent, have presented a spectacle of rare and tempting prosperity. To buy off these terrible enemies the government weakly resorted to the expedient of a danegeld, a tax so crushing in amount and so frequently imposed that under its weight the rural population lost its early character of freedom and, save in Danish East Anglia, sank into a condition of predial servitude. Some taxes are so heavy as to change the face of society, some are so lucrative that governments retain them long after the original occasion for their imposition has passed away. The danegeld belonged to both these categories. It promoted the development of feudalism and predial servitude. It was retained by Canute and William the Conqueror, and was the chief financial buttress of the Norman monarchy.

Heavy as was the danegeld it could not avert but only postpone a Danish conquest of England. Under Canute, the son of Sweyn, and the inheritor of his conquests, Britain became part of a Scandinavian empire, which ultimately included Denmark, Norway, and the Hebrides. A state divided by so wide a waste of stormy water could hardly hold together for long, and we may dismiss from the region of historical probabilities the vision of Britain as a permanent part of a greater Scandinavia. The reign of Canute was but an interlude, more important for Scandinavian than for British history. Not for the first time did the conquered peoples make a captive of their conqueror. In becoming a Christian Canute crossed from the Nordic into the Latin world. He made a pilgrimage to Rome, he married Norman Emma, the widow of Ethelred, his Saxon predecessor, and ruled England not as a foreign, but as a native, king. To a man of his forcible common sense there could be no comparison between the fertile plains of England, with their gentle full-brimmed rivers, their rich harvests and thriving merchant settlements, and the wild mountain scenery of Norway, or the wind-swept undulations of Denmark. Britain was the pleasanter, the more cultivated land. Canute made Britain his centre, and from it determined to bring the religion of civilized men into his Scandinavian dominions. In this effort he was not a pioneer. As early as 830, St. Anschar, a Picard trained in the monastery of Corvey, voyaged through Denmark, Norway, and Sweden preaching the Gospel, a gallant adventure soon overpowered by the might of the pagan tradition. At the great temple of Upsala in Sweden worship continued to be rendered to Odin, Thor, and Frey, with an immense sacrificial slaughter, in every ninth year, of animals and men. Then, at the end of the tenth century, the miracle of the Roman Empire began to work among the wild peoples of the north. The Scandinavians of the Danelaw, who had gone over *en bloc* to the new faith at the Peace of Wedmore in 878, submitted themselves in increasing measure to the ministrations of the Saxon Church, so that traders from Norway and Sweden found in our English ports Christian men of their own speech and blood. From such encounters some rough seafarers were actually converted; in others the hostile prejudice against Christianity was broken down. A demand arose for English priests. By one of those consentaneous movements of policy, which through the force of imitation happen from time to time in history, the reign of Canute coincided with a development of Christian propaganda in Norway and Denmark, initiated by two kings, Olaf the Saint and Olaf Sootkonning, who owed their conversion to English missionaries, and carried on their work with English help.

That Canute should have thrown his weight into the same religious scale is of critical importance. Of all Scandinavians he was by reason of his mastery of England the richest and most powerful. Had he resisted baptism and appealed to vast reserves of pagan sentiment in the hamlets of Norway and Sweden, he might have greatly retarded the settlement of Europe. He took the opposite course. In every way he was determined to show himself more Saxon than the Saxon, more Roman than the Pope, a pious and loyal member of the Christian polity. He restored St. Edmund's Bury in honour of the hero king who had been slain by the Danes, and sent English priests to Denmark to help the Danish Church. Though Thor and Odin were slow to die, his policy marks an end of the Scandinavian menace to Latin Christianity.

The historian will observe that the conversion of Europe to Christianity was, after the first heroic age of poverty and enthusiasm, mainly the result of material calculation or political pressure. The Goths, the Franks, the Saxons, the Scandinavians went over to Christianity, not as individuals directed by an inner light, but as peoples subject to mass suggestion and under the direction of political chiefs. That in every generation there were religious enthusiasts touched by the moral beauty of the Christian virtues or exalted by the contemplation of the Divine Nature will not be denied. There were conversions of the heart and of the mind. But the great mass of those who, under the Roman Empire or in the early middle ages, passed from Paganism to Christianity were little moved by considerations of pure religion or morality, and experienced no change of heart on conversion.

It is well to remember that the acceptance of Christian beliefs by the barbarian world entailed no such profound and sudden change as the word conversion may seem to imply. Europe still remained the scene of fierce passions, animal lusts, and degrading superstitions. The great task of educating a savage society in the Christian virtues was hardly begun; and after centuries of toil is still uncompleted. Yet even in the rude society of mediaeval Europe human sacrifice was stamped out, polygamy forbidden, and slavery put down.

The Anglo-Danish kingdom was personal to Canute. His sons were not of the calibre to sustain so difficult a structure. Our island, which had led Europe in culture in the eighth century, lost nothing of its native character under the brilli-

A.D.
1042-
66

ant Dane, reverted soon after his death to its ancient loyalties and recalled the son of Ethelred from his Norman exile. The character of Edward the Confessor was neither so saintly nor so weak as it has been portrayed by monkish chroniclers. He was an honest, well-meaning, mediocre man, handicapped by a youth spent abroad, by foreign ways, and by a foreign speech, and confronted by powerful factions fostered under Danish rule, which he had neither the force to control nor the subtlety to undermine. Moreover, he was childless. The uncertainty attaching to the succession, entering as an exciting element into the manoeuvres of the time, increased the difficulties of government. To whom would the Witan allot the prize? Would it send abroad for the infant grandson of Edmund Ironside? Would it place the crown upon the brows of Harold, the son and heir of the most powerful and ambitious noble of the realm, Godwin Earl of Wessex? Or would foreign ambitions play a part in deciding the fate of the masterless land? There were two vigorous aliens to whom the throne of England was a matter of close personal interest. The first of these was Harold Hardrada of Norway, the second was William the Bastard, Duke of Normandy, a man of devouring energy and ambition, who, through the marriage of his aunt Emma to the father of King Edward, could claim a family relationship with the house of Egbert.

The Viking dispersion which in England, Ireland, and Russia quickened the life of commerce and the growth of towns, and led in the remote valleys of Iceland to a wonderful flowering of original literature, also gave Normandy to

Europe. The Normans, as the Northmen settled since 911 in the Seine valley and its neighbourhood came to be called, grew to be the most brilliant of European races. All the virile energy of their northern origin they retained, much of the polish of the Latin races with whom their descendants mingled they succeeded in acquiring. Paganism was exchanged for Christianity, Danish for French, the tumultuous memories of the north for the defined traditions of the Latin world. They learnt to intone masses and to build churches, they listened to the *jongleur* as he recited the Chanson de Roland, and recalled in verses never to be heard without emotion the tragic death of the Paladin of Charlemagne. To the marine skill of the Scandinavians they added all that was then known of cavalry warfare and the poliorcetic art. The pastures of Normandy, like those of ancient Elis, were rich in horses. The Normans took as much pleasure in a horse as in a ship. So combative was their disposition that when they were not engaged in fighting a real enemy, they would slay one another, with the exhilaration of schoolboys at play, in the mailed encounters of the tourney.

Among the nominal subjects of the king of France none was so powerful as the leader of this strong and receptive race. The dukes of Normandy from their capital at Rouen were in a position to contend on even terms with the kings of France, whose headquarters were now fixed in Paris. Many a battle was fought over the Vexin, the disputed borderland between Normandy and the Ile de France, but the ambitions of the Normans were not confined within the borders of the duchy. A passion for adventure was blended with their gift for close and cautious calculation. In the eleventh century they conquered Sicily and England, in the fifteenth they discovered the Canary Isles, and two centuries later the Norman voyagers were the first to descend the mysterious waterways of the Mississippi.

By the middle of the eleventh century Normandy had become, under a dynasty of vigorous dukes, the strongest and most coherent principality in western Europe. Here, as nowhere else at that time so fully, feudalism was organized and controlled for public ends. Military service was fixed by custom and rendered in respect of the tenure of land by feudal vassals. Private war was limited, castle building conceded only under ducal licence, the coinage made a ducal monopoly, the local administration entrusted to a *vicecomes*, or sheriff, who represented the ducal or public, as opposed to the feudal or local, interest. Even the Church, seldom more powerful in Europe than in the eleventh century, was in Normandy controlled by the duke. Nor did the old leaven of aristocratic anarchy, which was characteristic of Norse society, finally prevail against the dominance of the ducal house. The last formidable rebellion of the Norman nobles was broken by William the Bastard on the field of Val és Dunes in 1047.

It is the more important to note these facts, because the slow rebuilding of Europe into an organized society after the cataclysm which succeeded the death of Charles the Great was rendered possible only by the development of small, well-organized feudal states. Of these Normandy was the earliest and best example. The practice of Normandy was carried over the Channel to England, and to all those regions of France which the kings of England and dukes of Normandy acquired by conquest or marriage. It spread to Maine and Anjou, to Aquitaine and Gascony, as well as to the islands of Scotland. In any part of this wide area, the Norman Empire as we may perhaps call it, justice came in the twelfth century to be administered with an eye to common principles and in a form of provincial French which would have been intelligible to every lawyer from the Forth to the Garonne.

That the Normans had become Frenchmen for at least half a century before the battle of Hastings was of great moment for the reconstruction of Europe. Had they retained their Norse language and ways and remained an insoluble element in the social fabric of France, they would have exercised as little general influence as the Basques or the Bretons, the Irish or the Welsh. As it was they carried with them in all their enterprises the attractive stamp of Latin civilization.

It is characteristic of this adventurous people that half a century before their conquest of England they had begun to hunt for fortune under an Italian sky. Norman pilgrims returning from the Holy Sepulchre in 1015 learnt that in the feuds which distracted southern Italy there was an opening for the surplus energies of many a younger son impatient of the dullness or poverty of home, and anxious for travel, sustenance, and renown. The news spread rapidly. Norman knights drifted southwards, took their part in the local struggles of south Italy, and proved their worth as fighting men. In 1030 the Duke of Naples accorded to his valiant corps of Norman mercenaries the county of Aversa. In his craft, courage, and domineering ambition, in his lust for gain and munificence in spending, in his industry and endurance, in his love of gaudy clothes and command of eloquent words, but above all in his mastery of the whole technique of fighting, the Norman knight appeared to the motley south Italian population, Greeks, Lombards, Saracens, Italians, and Jews, to be at once a figure of glittering brilliance and a paragon of efficiency. The prestige of these adventurers was out of all proportion to their numbers. The conquest of south Italy and Sicily was effected by a few hundred knights under the leadership of the twelve stalwart sons of Tancred of Hauteville.[1]

There are few more curious pages of mediaeval history than those which recount the rise of this famous house, which wrested south Italy from the Greeks, Sicily from the Saracens, Antioch from the Turks, and challenged the might of the Byzantine Empire. The figures of Robert Guiscard, "a man of great counsel, talent, generosity, and daring," an expert cattle thief and a born leader of horse, and of his youngest brother, Roger, the conqueror of Sicily, tall, handsome, eloquent, ambitious, live again in the pages of a Sicilian chronicler, who delights in abrupt vicissitudes of fortune. To this pious enthusiast it matters little that the sons of Tancred were capable of every devilry. The rough warfare of the Normans was redeemed by the possession of the Latin Faith. Though they handsomely defeated a papal army which was sent against them (1053), they made amends by the elaborate respect which they accorded to a captive legate. The Pope was quick to discern the advantage which might be derived from an alliance with this formidable body of muscular Christians, how they might rid Italy of the Greeks, redeem Sicily for the Faith, and make the Holy Father secure upon the Roman throne. A treaty was struck in 1058. Under the convenient authority of the forged donation of Constantine, Guiscard was accorded the duchy of Apulia as a papal fief. Forty years later his brother Roger

[1] Genealogical Table B.

received as the reward of his Sicilian crusade the singular honour of hereditary apostolic legate in that island.

So under the full glow of papal benediction these freebooters of the north laid the foundations of a civilized state in Mediterranean waters. With Norman flexibility the descendants of Tancred proved themselves equal to the responsibilities of conducting an organized government under new and difficult conditions and on original lines. In the kingdom of Roger II, who united the Norman territories on either side of the Straits of Messina, Europe witnessed a polity half-oriental, half-western, providing a shelter for Greek, Latin, Moor, and Jew, and better organized, seeing that it preserved the tradition of its Greek and Saracen past, than any other European government of that age. Among the orange groves of Palermo, Roger, the descendant of the Vikings, sat upon his throne, robed in the dalmatic of the apostolic legate and the imperial costume of Byzantium, his ministers part Greek, part English, his army composed as to half of Moors, his fleet officered by Greeks, himself a Latin Christian, but, in that balmy climate of the south, ruling in half-Byzantine, half-oriental state, with a harem and eunuchs, a true representative of his lovely island, shared then as ever between east and west.

Time has dealt kindly with this dynasty of gifted pirates. Mosaics, the best which Greece could provide, still embellish the walls of the noble cathedral of Monreale, which looks down upon the flowers and orchards of the Conca d'Oro. In that same earthly paradise an exquisite cloister still invites to repose, and the visitor, noting what he there sees of building and sculpture, of jewelry and decoration, must admire the splendour of the Norman princes now sleeping in tombs of dark porphyry, who in the twelfth century brought about so great an assemblage of the arts and crafts of their age.

Very different was the Scandinavian scene from which the Vikings had sallied forth to slay, to burn, and to conquer. No Monreale, or Caen, or Durham rose in the solitary valleys of Norway. There the Viking aristocracy bled to death in civil war. By the thirteenth century Scandinavia was empty of personal eminence. The days of her influence were over. A rude, unlettered peasantry extracted a sorry living from a barren soil.

BOOKS WHICH MAY BE CONSULTED

C. F. Keary: *Vikings in Western Christendom.* 1891.
B. S. Philpotts: *Edda and Saga.* (Home University Library.) 1931.
Axel Olrik: *Viking Civilisation. Ed.* H. Ellekilde. 1930.
Saxo Grammaticus. Tr. O. Elton. 1894.
T. D. Kendrick: *History of the Vikings.* 1930.
Sir Charles Oman: *A History of England before the Norman Conquest.* 1910.
C. Plummer: *The Life and Times of Alfred the Great.* 1902.
G. M. Trevelyan: *History of England.* 1926.
C. H. Haskins: *The Normans in European History.* 1915.
C. H. Haskins: *Norman Institutions.* 1918.
G. Turville-Petre: *The Heroic Age of Scandinavia.* 1951.
E. S. Duckett: *Alfred the Great and his England.* 1957.
Sir Frank Stenton: *Anglo-Saxon England.* 1943.
H. Shetelig and H. Falk: *Scandinavian Archaeology. Tr.* E. V. Gordon. 1957.

CHAPTER XVI

SAXONS AND SALIANS

Europe in 900. Germany and the Huns. Henry the Fowler and Otto I. Foundation of the Holy Roman Empire of the German Nation in 962. Its significance for Germany. Limitations to imperial power. Quarrel with the Church. Revival of the Papacy after 1046. Leo IX. Hildebrand. The War of Investitures and the Concordat of Worms. The Hildebrandine controversy. Its consequence for political thought. German colonizing movements on the northern plain and middle Danube. The Empire fails to profit. The hard Germany and the soft. No Franco-German problems in the middle ages.

WHILE THE Northmen were thus assailing its outer fringes, Europe began to develop those diversified political characteristics which led in modern times to the formation of the separate nationalities of Germany, Italy, and France. At the beginning of the tenth century no one of these countries possessed the organization proper to a state, and still less the conscious personality essential to a nation. There was a king of the western Franks but no France, a king of the eastern Franks but no Germany, a king of the Lombards but of Virgilian Italy only a reminiscence. What is now known as France was a collection of fiefs, one of which, the Ile de France with its capital at Paris, was destined to devour its neighbours until its power was co-extensive with the frontiers of the present state. Germany, bounded on the east by the Elbe, was a loose assemblage of tribal duchies—Saxon, Franconian, Bavarian, Swabian—under the nominal rule of an elective king. The Italians, once the proud and privileged members of a great empire, were parcelled out into a congeries of dissimilar polities, a papal patrimony much diminished by usurpation, a Byzantine province, Lombard fiefs, independent cities. No Gascon or Breton would have pretended to owe allegiance to France. No Venetian or Genoese would have felt bound to follow the banner of a Marquis of Ivrea or a Duke of Benevento. The Germans were more homogeneous. Yet this violent and romantic forest folk, now so submissive to authority, exhibited through the middle ages a surprising appetite for discord and rebellion.

Unlike France and England, Germany suffered little from the Northmen. For her the Magyars, a Mongolian race who had slipped into the empty Pannonian plain, dividing the northern from the southern Slavs, constituted at the beginning of the tenth century a more serious menace. Again and again these formidable horse archers carried their devastations into the heart of Europe, piercing even to the plains of Italy and France and beyond to Andalusia. But as Wessex and Alfred stemmed the onrush of the Danes in England, so Saxony and Henry the Fowler gave a check to the Magyars. The Saxon hero was not, like the West Saxon, a man of comprehensive genius and vivid sympathy, but a good methodical German soldier who, confronted with a novel form of attack, set himself down to devise the best means of defence, and found in the construction of well-garrisoned wooden forts and the use of the cavalry arm the proper reply to the swift-moving levies of his enemy. Henry's victory at the Unstrut in 933 brought glory to his house and put a new heart in his people. He was succeeded by a yet greater son, Otto I, whose victory on the Lech in 955 finally liberated his country from the Magyar pest. What the soldier began, the priest completed. In 1000 the wild Hungarian people followed its royal shepherd into the Christian fold and, after many centuries had elapsed, formed the south-eastern bastion of the Latin faith against the conquering tides of Islam.[1]

In spite of these days of confusion the conception of an organized world state co-extensive with the domain of a world religion still floated vaguely in the minds of men. Even before the victory on the Lech Otto had a claim higher than that of any contemporary to be regarded as the temporal chief of Latin Christianity. The tribal duchies of Germany had been brought, not without fighting, to acknowledge his authority. He had obtained the submission of Bohemia and had strengthened the German powers of defence and offence along the Slavonic frontier. Moreover, finding in 951 a pretext to intervene in Italian affairs, he had assumed the Italian crown and had appointed a deputy, Berengar of Ivrea, to represent him in absence. To these striking achievements the great triumph over the Hungarians furnished an impressive complement. Though he came of a race which had never been included within the Roman Empire and had only recently been admitted within the Christian fold, few would now dispute Otto's claim to be Roman Emperor should he care to advance it, for since Charlemagne no ruler had held a position of such widespread influence and prestige. Accordingly when in 962 Otto marched to Rome at the request of Pope John XII, and was by that unscrupulous pontiff crowned Roman Emperor, the world accepted the fact without a protest. So correspondent was his enterprise with the needs and ideals of society that the Holy Roman Empire of the German nation lasted till the nineteenth century, the embodiment of that aspiration after order and harmony which the reason of man is always pleased to entertain and his perversity as surely to frustrate.

So the Holy Roman Empire was founded; to some German writers a matter of pride, to others of poignant regret. There are those who reflect with sentiments of exultation upon an institution which in its mid-course excited the enthusiasm of Dante, in its decline the amused observation of Goethe. To such it is pleasant to recall how, when western Europe had reached the nadir of disorganization, the scene of the first

[1] Genealogical Table C.

EUROPE IN THE TIME OF OTTO I

concerted defence and political recovery was laid in Saxony by Henry the Fowler, how after that valiant prince had given security to his people, Otto, his still greater son, led all the German races against the Hungarians, redeemed Italy from degradation and helped to restore the Papacy to the respect of the western world. To this school of historical interpretation the revival of the Empire was not only a European but a German necessity. They dispute the notion that Germans were sacrificed to Italian influences. They contend that the imperial title gave to the German king a new prestige with tribes other than his own, that it developed national feeling and strengthened national pride, and that it was a means of securing for the service of the German monarchy the indispensable loyalty of the German Church.

With greater cogency it can be argued that the revival of the western Empire was unfortunate for the Germans. The area of Germany even in the days of Henry the Fowler was greater than that which a mediaeval monarch could conveniently control. The addition of Italy to that area meant that any real government of either country became impossible. The results of framing the permanent policy of the state upon a scheme too ambitious to be realized are what might be expected. Whereas in the tenth century there was no part of the Carolingian Empire which seemed more likely to be united under a single monarchy, three centuries later Germany had become an anarchical federation of principalities and republics.

A contributory cause of this great political calamity was the elective character of the German monarchy. In England and France, where the elective was succeeded by the hereditary principle, the development of the state proceeded more or less upon a continuous plan. In France the monarchy assumed an absolute, in England a constitutional form, but in both countries the kingship remained a fixed centre, and, being identified with the government, exercised a formative influence on the national life. In Germany things took a different turn. It was not convenient either for the Pope or for the tribal dukes and great prelates in Germany that the monarchy should receive the power which the adoption of the hereditary principle would confer. Election, then, was retained. No dynasty was allowed to take deep root. The Saxons were succeeded by the Salians and these by the Hohenstaufens.

Only after many vicissitudes, during which the imperial capital was transferred to points as distant as Palermo and Prague, was a centre found in Vienna and a long-lived dynasty in the Austrian Habsburgs.

The East Roman Emperor ruled over an organized state, a strongly fortified capital and a subject church. No one of these advantages belonged to Otto and his immediate successors. The Holy Roman Emperor was a wanderer. His court moved from farm to farm, from town to town, and as he travelled, administering such justice as he might with the aid of his attendant clergy and nobles, his distant capital on the Tiber was in the hands now of the Pope but more often of a camarilla of turbulent Roman nobles.

In theory the Empire was conceived of as world-wide; but no Holy Roman Emperor exercised authority in France or Spain, in Britain or Scandinavia, in Russia or the widespread dominions of the Byzantine Empire. The influence of Otto's revival was correspondingly circumscribed. For the unity of the German and Italian peoples, for the fortunes of the Papacy, for the growth of political thought in Europe, and for the fate of the Slavs in the Baltic plain, the revival of the Empire as a German institution was of the greatest moment. In central Europe events and political speculations were for many centuries fashioned or capriciously influenced by this singular institution. Elsewhere its light shone with a fainter glow and the Holy Roman Emperor was regarded as but a foreign sovereign whose pretensions were remotely correspondent with his powers.

Grave as these disabilities were, they might but for one circumstance have been surmounted. In the middle of the eleventh century the Empire came into collision with the Papacy over two critical questions affecting the life of the Christian church and the administration of the German state, the celibacy of the clergy and the right of investiture. It had been part of the policy of Charlemagne to endow the German church with a lavish hand and to lean upon its help in the tasks of government. That policy was renewed by Otto and his successors. With a liberality not unmingled with prudence they piled gift on gift upon the German prelates, expecting in return that from these royal and submissive nominees entertainment would be provided for the royal court, subsidies for the royal treasury, and a full complement of men-at-arms whenever the royal host might take the field.

A very mundane Church of fighting archbishops and bishops suited the convenience of a German king, and was indeed the chief pillar upon which his government was based. More securely than upon any tribal duke or feudal lord could he count upon the secular assistance of German prelates for the conduct of his administration upon either side of the Alps.

To this policy the Church, as soon as a clerical spirit revived in Europe, was bound to take violent exception; and to such a revival the Emperors themselves contributed. Secular though these sovereigns might be in their use of ecclesiastical patronage, they were nevertheless devout according to the measure of their age, some, like the Saxon Henry II and the Salian Henry III, attaining to a high level of personal piety. Moreover, they conceived it to be their duty as advocates and defenders of the church to protect the Papacy against violence and indignity, and if necessary to intervene when the pressure of turbulent nobles or the choice of the clergy and people of Rome had raised an unworthy man to the Papal Chair. In the interests of the Holy See Otto I had hanged thirteen Roman nobles, and Otto III, his grandson, a lad in his teens, had made two papal appointments, one of which, though of a young man of twenty-three, was respectable, while the other was Sylvester II, the most distinguished savant of his age. But no Emperor rendered more service to the Papacy than the devout Henry III, who at the Synod of Sutri in 1046 deposed two or perhaps three bad Popes and then proceeded in succession to appoint four good ones.

The affect of these four appointments was to clear the Papacy from the scandals which had attached to it, to restore to it the moral leadership of the Church, and to precipitate a quarrel with the Empire which, lasting with intermissions for two hundred years, consigned Italy and Germany to centuries of political confusion and helplessness. If it be asked how effects so far-reaching could be produced by the appointment of a succession of elderly men to the bishopric of Rome, the answer is to be found in the fact that Leo IX 1048- and his successors brought to the discharge of their office a 54 doctrine of great explosive power, long prevalent in Europe and capable under papal direction of becoming a political force of the first order. They were Cluniacs. They belonged, that is to say, to a movement which, starting in the Burgundian monastery of Cluny more than a century before as a campaign for chastity, piety, and discipline in the monasteries, had widened out, as such movements are apt to do, into a comprehensive programme of church reform. The earlier Cluniacs had been content to preach the sublime virtues of purity, self-discipline, and peace, and to introduce into the mechanism of their order a system of central supervision and control for the protection of these frail flowers of the Christian spirit. The later Cluniacs were more ambitious. For them the teaching of Christ would never be established on earth save through the medium of an independent Church governed by an omnipotent Pope. There were, indeed, differences of opinion. Some were moderate, others extreme, but the general spirit of the movement, which was passionate and unequivocal, was to exalt the papal power and to insist upon a clear-cut professional standard for the clergy. In Lorraine, on the Rhine, in Bavaria, in North Italy, such theocratic ideas of every degree of refinement and crudity fermented in clerical brains, but more particularly among the monks, who, like the miners of modern industry, lived a life apart and were thus peculiarly prone to the acceptance of contracted doctrines in an enthusiastic form.

To this mass of exalted opinion the Papacy under the compulsion of Leo IX now gave the support of its authority. Leo was a Cluniac. To the discharge of his high duties he brought the spirit of the autocrat, the cosmopolitan, and the reformer. He regarded the Papacy, not, as so many of his predecessors had done, in the light of a local and lucrative dignity, but as a great international institution of unlimited authority and complete independence which had been entrusted with the spiritual mission to inspect, to reform, and to inspire. It was a symptom of his wide outlook and active spirit that he made Cardinals of foreigners, that he held synods in France and Germany, that he secured the South Italian Normans for his allies, and that under his rule papal legates were despatched far and wide through Europe on disciplinary missions. His immediate successors trod the same path of high papal doctrine. They supported the *pataria* or popular anti-German movement in Milan. They denounced heresy and lay patronage. In 1059 by a clever stroke of policy advantage was taken of an imperial vacancy to confide to the College of Cardinals the choice of a new Pope. The high clerical proceedings of the Curia were from that date inspired by the genius, at once fervent and subtle, of a squat, ill-favoured Tuscan peasant, first known to history as Cardinal Hildebrand and after his election to the Papacy in 1073 as Gregory VII.

To this stern and implacable idealist we may principally ascribe the spread through Europe of a theocratic philosophy as menacing to the nascent state life of the eleventh century as in our own times is the communism of Lenin to the capitalism of Wall Street. With imperious courage Hildebrand conceived of the world as a single Christian polity governed by an omnipotent and infallible Pope, a Pope bound by no laws, by whom an offending prince might be driven from his throne, cut off from the sacraments of the church, and severed from the allegiance of his subjects. Believing that the time had now come to reconstruct the militia of the Catholic church, he preached the doctrine of a celibate clergy under the undivided control of the Vicar of Christ. At one and the same time he was prepared in the interests of an autonomous clerical profession to break up the family life of the German clergy and to sap the power of the German king. His claims were exorbitant. The church was to retain its temporal possessions, its palaces and farms, its cattle and its money. No fragment of the vast wealth which made it in Germany the indispensable servant of the state was to be surrendered. But it was to be independent, an Empire within an Empire. As the soul was nobler than the body, as the sun outshone the moon, so was the spiritual superior to the temporal power. In a Roman synod held in Lent of 1075 the right of the lay prince to invest a prelate of the Church with the symbols of his office was denounced as an intolerable inversion of the divine law.

It seems certain that Hildebrand, who was perfect in all the parts of the ecclesiastical diplomatist, did not advance without carefully measuring his ground. He must have known that in openly denouncing lay investiture he was challenging the basis of imperial rule in two countries, he must have foreseen that his challenge would be taken up, he must nevertheless have counted on success. Nor was his calculation unnatural. Henry IV had only just succeeded to his father's throne after a long minority, which had fostered all the 1056 elements of disobedience in his kingdom. He was young, 1106 inexperienced, headstrong. At the outset of his reign he was called on to confront a serious rising of the Saxon peasants who could not be brought to see by what right a Swabian prince pretended to establish a capital among their pleasant hills and to hold down a free population with his Swabian garrisons. He had won a victory, but still had many enemies on either side of the Alps, monks, peasants, princes, the anti-German rabble of the Lombard towns, who might under papal leadership be combined into a formidable coalition. In that age of superstition the Church possessed powers over the soul more mighty than armies. If it denied the validity of sacraments administered by married priests, if it threatened excommunication, if it proceeded in the last resort to depose a temporal sovereign, hearts were troubled, loyalties impaired, a great body of opinion was swung from its moorings. On all these harassing circumstances Hildebrand must have counted when he threw his fateful challenge to Henry IV.

The contest began with an exchange of blows which at once revealed the disparity between the moral resources at the disposal of the rival powers. The Emperor deposed the Pope and the Pope replied by deposing and excommunicating the Emperor; but whereas Gregory VII was little the worse for Henry's deposition of him, the consequences of excommunication were serious for a sovereign whom many of his more powerful subjects were already anxious to abase. At a diet of German princes Henry was flatly informed that unless he were absolved in the spring when the Pope was expected in Germany, his throne was forfeit. He knew better than to wait for a Roman judgment delivered in an atmosphere of German mutiny. Swallowing his pride and steeling his courage, he crossed the Alps in the dead of winter, sought out the Pope in the mountain fastness of Canossa, and doing penance there and receiving absolution returned to confound and amaze his enemies.

But the German princes were already too far gone in sedition to retreat. They proceeded to elect Rudolf of Swabia as anti-king, and when Rudolf fell fighting on the Elster (October, 1080), pursued the Emperor with their hatred to the end, replacing Rudolf by Hermann of Luxemburg, and finally, when Hermann was in his grave and Henry was old and grey, stirring up his two sons to unfilial rebellion. A

German civil war contrived for the deposition of such a man
as Henry could not fail to enlist the sympathy and, after no
long interval, the active support of Hildebrand. Rudolf the
anti-king was acknowledged by the Pope. Wibert, an anti-
Pope, was set up by the Emperor. Instantly all Germany and
Italy were ablaze. On the imperialist side were ranged the
peasants and priests of the south-west, the lesser nobles of
Franconia and Swabia, and the main body of the German
townsmen. But Saxony, the most warlike of German provinces, under Otto of Nordheim, the most redoubtable of
German nobles, rose against the Emperor, and only after the
stiff Saxon neck had been again bowed beneath the Swabian
yoke was Henry free to cross the Alps and to place his considerable military talents at the disposition of his Italian
friends.

Little comfort did Italy derive from his intervention. Four
times did he lay siege to Rome and as often was compelled to
acknowledge failure, But neither had Hildebrand cause for
gratification. To save his capital from the Emperor he invoked
the aid of the South Italian Normans. The Saracen levies
of Robert Guiscard were as little famous for clemency as was
the Roman population for the Christian virtues of meekness
and patience. The allies of the Pope met with a furious resistance in the streets of Rome and exacted a terrible revenge.
To Hildebrand, dying in exile at Salerno (May 25, 1085),
the ways of Providence must have seemed strange and bitter,
for no Goth or Vandal had brought such destruction upon
the city of St. Peter as this priest who had devoted a life to
its service.

The war of the Investitures, outlasting Hildebrand and
Henry, was brought to an end in 1122 by a compromise (the
Concordat of Worms) anticipated sixteen years before in the
cooler atmosphere of Britain, under which the secular prince,
while continuing to exact homage for the temporal possessions
of the Church, consented to renounce the investiture by ring
and staff,which were the symbols of spiritual authority. Each
party claimed a victory. It was the cause of civil government
in Germany and Italy which suffered a ruinous defeat from
this protracted struggle.

There was nothing new in the Hildebrandine philosophy.
The virtues of chastity and humility, of love and justice, had

been continually preached to unheeding ears. The theory that the Roman Church, being founded by God, was "the mother and mistress of all Christianity," that it was infallible in doctrine, universal in dominion, and the sole means of salvation for erring and straying men, was no novelty in western Europe. Nor was Hildebrand the first to maintain that the Bishop of Rome was the supreme and autocratic ruler of the Catholic Church. What was novel in this extraordinary man was the ardour, the courage, and the persistence with which he carried on a critical campaign against the deep-rooted corruptions of his age. It was not a battle of clergy against laity. The priests who were enjoined to break up their families, put away their wives, or abjure their concubines, were as much incensed against the Pope as the prelates who were subjected to his minute and harassing supervision. In Germany, where papal interference was at its maximum, the greater part of the clergy were opposed to the passionate crusade of the puritan autocrat. How can we be surprised? Celibacy is a hard virtue, the conquest of the natural love of woman a poignant human sacrifice darkening the sunlight of young manhood. The battle to which Hildebrand summoned his clergy was so long and desperate that victory was not finally won till the later years of the sixteenth century. But it may be asked whether it would have been won even then, if at one of the darkest hours of the Church's history, when the clergy were sunk deep in worldliness and vice, a great moral genius, commanding all the resources of the Papal Chair, had not forced upon his clergy, without fear or favour, and in defiance of the strongest secular power in Europe, the austere ideals of the celibate life.

Out of the Hildebrandine controversy rose a political debate which continues to this day. The clerical party contended that righteousness was set above material power, that temporal sovereignty was founded on contract, and that the unrighteous king might lawfully be deposed. The imperialist advocates argued otherwise. They disputed the social contract, denied the papal supereminence, and claimed for the Emperor an indefeasible, hereditary, and absolute authority. Few now read the rival tracts of Manegold, the papal, and Petrus Crassus, the imperialist, pamphleteer. Yet in these dry pleadings there is still a living core of interest. Is the state all in all? Is material power alone to be worshipped, or does

Christianity divide the allegiance of the citizen? Less coura-
geously than in the eleventh century, but still audibly, these
questions are asked in Germany today (1934).

Meanwhile a great task was awaiting the German people
which under happier auspices might have been turned to the
advantage of the German monarchy. From the Elbe to the
Niemen stretched a long level plain, now gleaming with
thriving tillage and well built towns and villages, but then a
waste of forest, lake, and marsh, sparsely occupied by tribes
speaking a strange Slavonic tongue and worshipping heathen
gods, such as Triglav of the triple head, and Redigast, and
Svantovit, whose shrine at Arcona in Rügen overlooks the
dark waters of the Baltic. To the bishops, the nobles, and the
husbandmen of Saxony these vast mysterious spaces, whose
eastern limit no traveller could fix, were as alluring as the
plateau of the North American continent to the frontiersmen
of Virginia and Massachusetts. Here beyond the Elbe was
rich land to be had for the asking, forests to be cleared,
marshes to be drained, villages to be built, and a heathen
population to be converted, taxed, tithed, and reduced to
bondage. "The Slavs," so runs a proclamation of the leading
bishops and princes of Saxony, "are an abominable people,
but their land is very rich in flesh, honey, grain, birds, and
abounding in all produce of fertility of the earth when cultivated so that none can be compared with it. So say they who
know. Wherefore O Saxons, Franks, Lotharingians, men
of Flanders most famous, here you can both save your souls
and if it please you acquire the best of land to live in."

The colonization of this northern plain was perhaps the
principal achievement of the German people during the
middle ages. Not without rebuffs, husbandry and commerce,
church building and town building followed behind the axe
of the German frontiersmen. By slow degrees at convenient
spots along the bleak sea coast little fishing villages grew
into great trading towns and ultimately into the powerful
Hanseatic League, which covered the Baltic with its shipping
and made of it the second commercial highway of the mediaeval world. Frisians, Flemings, and Walloons, hearing of
the new empty country, in which farmers might live at their
ease, pressed forward to share the advantages of the German
pioneers.

Naer Oostland willen wy riden
Naer Oostland willen wy mêe,
Al over die groene heiden,
Frisch over die heiden,
Daer isser een bettere stêe
Als wy binnen Oostland komen
Al under dat hooger huis,
Daer worden wy binnen gelaten
Frisch over die heiden;
Zy heeten uns willekomen syn.

To the Eastland we will ride,
To the Eastland we'll go too,
All over the green fields,
Gaily over the fields!
There is a better place
When to Eastland we are come
Right under the high wall,
There we shall be let in,
Gaily over the fields!
They will bid us welcome.

It is not to be pretended that this long and exuberant adventure was unattended by serious evils. The Saxon frontiersman of the middle ages, to whom rough nature imparted something of her own asperity, was as little disposed to be tender to the Abodrites and Wends as was the New England settler of the seventeenth century to the Red Indians who from time to time raided his holding. Only in Pomerania, where the native population were peaceably brought over to Christianity by Otto of Bamberg, one of the best of the German missionaries, was the onward march of the German people unaccompanied by the use of force. At no time, however, have great colonizing movements, involving the displacement of a weaker by a stronger population, been accomplished without serious injustice. The struggle between North German Christianity and Slavonic heathendom exhibits many, if not all of the abuses which in a later age characterized the colonization by the white races of the western hemisphere. There was murder and treachery, expropriation and enslavement. The Slavs were not always patient under the hand of the despoiler. From time to time they rose in revolt (as in 983, 1018, and 1066) and overwhelmed the German settlements with fire and sword.

A similar colonizing movement, though more narrowly contracted, went forward in the milder climate of the middle Danube. Here the Bavarian pioneers were confronted by the stubborn strength of the Magyar nation and the hardly less intractable wilderness of forest and hill which on either side flanked their eastern advance. The conditions of the problem governed the mode by which it was attacked. The Bavarian Ostmark, established by Charlemagne against the Avars, renewed by Otto I against the Hungarians, extended by the campaigns of Henry III, was a military colony divided among nobles, bishops, and abbots, who were pledged to defend it, and populated for the most part by their Bavarian serfs. Thus while the vast spaces of the north-east were mainly won by free adventurers of the Saxon race, a greater measure of military organization was necessary for the making of that far smaller German territory which is known as Austria. The modern traveller who pursues his journey from the Dutch to the Russian frontier passes through a country peopled, save for a few Wendish villages, by Germans speaking the German tongue and penetrated by the German spirit. Only the ethnologist and antiquarian can bring to his notice the surviving relics of a different population long submerged or violently exterminated. In the south it is different. Whether the attack was softer or the resistance harder, the enemy was not absorbed. Not all the seductions of Vienna, for so many centuries the centre of German illumination in that backward corner of Europe, not the prestige of the Austrian Empire, nor the intolerance of the Catholic Church, nor the dominion of a German bureaucracy have broken the stubborn heart of the Czech and the Slovak, the Magyar and the Slovene. To this day they cherish a non-German mind and speak a non-German speech. Had the German monarchs of the middle ages been free from the distractions of Italian politics, they might, one would imagine, have secured for themselves an accretion of strength through the direction of these colonizing movements. This opportunity was not taken. No part of the territories wrested from the Slavs was reserved for the domain of the German king. It fell to the Margraves of Brandenburg and the Bavarian Ostmark to reap the advantages which but for a long train of untoward circumstances, the acceptance of the imperial crown by Otto I, the war of the Investitures, the successful resistance of the Saxons to the attempt of Henry III and his son to establish in Saxony the seat of the German monarchy, might have been secured for the German state. In modern times the leadership of Germany has been shared between two great land colonies, Prussia and Austria. The growth of the movement out of which these states arose has little connection with the spectacular Italian and papal wars which form the central theme of mediaeval German history. Yet what in the German past can be more important than this immense and secular migration, this moving frontier of stalwart peasant families steadily advancing eastwards, clearing forests, reclaiming land, draining marshes, bringing in with their heavier ploughs a more intensive method of cultivation, and followed by monk and priest, trader and mason, peddling Jew and ingenious craftsman, the outpouring of a fecund and vigorous people, which has left enduring traces on the history of mankind?

A French historian has pertinently contrasted the eastern and western front of the German Empire during the middle ages—in the east the fighting Margraves on the Elbe, in the west the prelates and priests of the Rhine; in the east the German race at its hardest, its fiercest, its most enterprising, in the west the same people softened by clerical government or municipal affluence. As the tides of Germanism swept forward towards the east they receded in the west. The long intermediate territory which in the division of the Carolingian Empire among the sons of Louis le Débonnaire had been assigned to Lothair, and had from him taken the name of Lotharingia, was an unstable compound, soon dissolved into a number of separate fiefs, principalities, and cities, of which some were Latin, others Teutonic, but all in the middle of the eleventh century included within the Holy Roman Empire. To this Empire belonged Alsace and Lorraine and the territories which are familiar as Switzerland, Franche Comté, and the Low Countries. Moreover, partly by bequest, partly by conquest, the Emperor Conrad II had come into possession of the kingdom of Arles, which comprised Provence, Dauphiné, and Savoy, some of the most classic ground of Latin civilization. But the hold of the German Empire on such part of this western area as was peopled by the Latin race was slight and precarious. As the French monarchy in-

1024-
39

creased in strength, the Empire began by slow degrees to give ground, until by the end of the fifteenth century the valley of the Rhone, save for Avignon, had passed from the German to the French allegiance.

These changes were effected without great shock. A Franco-German war was not in the middle ages a political possibility. The German emperors, when they were not engaged in putting down rebellion in their own dominions, were occupied with Italy or the eastern advance. The eyes of the German people were turned towards the east where land was empty and conquest easy, and not towards the west where these conditions were reversed. Nor was there present that condition of geographical contiguity which is provocative of friction in the modern world. Between France and Germany ran a belt of principalities, duchies, and counties across which the two countries, though little love was lost between them, might shake hands. To these reasons may be added one yet more powerful. France was occupied in the west. For the better part of the middle ages she was involved with England in the greatest civil war of mediaeval history.

BOOKS WHICH MAY BE CONSULTED

C. R. L. Fletcher: *The Making of Western Europe*. 1912-14.

H. H. Milman: *The History of Latin Christianity*. 1867.

J. Bryce: *The Holy Roman Empire*. 1904.

W. von Giesebrecht: *Geschichte der deutschen Kaiserzeit*. 1881.

A. Hauck: *Kirchengeschichte Deutschlands*. 4 vols. 1904-20.

Cambridge Mediaeval History, Vol. V.

Zeller: *Histoire d'Allemagne*. 1890.

G. Barraclough: *The Origins of Modern Germany*. 2nd Ed. 1947.

G. Barraclough: *Medieval Germany*, 911-1250, 1938.

Cambridge Ecomomic History of Europe. Vol. II. 1952.

W. Ullmann: *The Growth of Papal Government in the Middle Ages*. 1955.

CHAPTER XVII

THE FOUNDATIONS
OF ENGLISH GOVERNMENT

Prostration of France in the tenth century. Rise of the Cape-
tians. Sources of their authority. The Norman Conquest of
England. Its completeness. England becomes a province of
the Latin world. England's debt to William the Conqueror.
Preservation of Saxon customs. Consolidation under Henry II.
French interests divert England from its proper tasks.

NOTHING IN the condition of France during the tenth century
indicated the strength or the unity which she was afterwards
to attain. To the northerners who spoke the *langue d'oïl*, the
langue d'oc of Provence and Aquitaine was only one degree
less foreign than the Celtic of Brittany or the Norse of Bayeux.
The country, which had become a chaos of warring fiefs,
was rendered miserable by pillage, turbulence, and insecurity.
Even in the north the Carolingian monarchs, though enjoying
the superstitious prestige of legitimacy, were confronted by
many vassals as powerful as themselves and little disposed to
respect their authority. In Aquitaine and Gascony, or in the
counties of Barcelona and Toulouse, the value of these
phantom kings as guardians of peace or directors of policy
was exactly zero.

From this state of political prostration France was ultimately rescued by a new royal dynasty which possessed,
together with other valuable qualities, the merit of furnishing
for a period of three hundred years a lawful male heir to the
throne. There was among the vassals of the king a certain
family which shone out above others for a remarkable tale of
public service performed on a critical occasion and at a
critical spot. Robert the Strong, Count of Paris, fought for
ten years against the Northmen and died on the field of battle.
The record of Eudes, his son, the hero of the famous defence
885-6 of Paris against a great Scandinavian armada, was equally
illustrious. For this exploit Eudes was rewarded by the duke-
dom of France, a dignity which the saviour of his country

might in such an age of violent ambitions be emboldened to exchange for the monarchy itself. But the Robertonians were as distinguished for caution as for courage. More than a hundred years passed during which the most powerful man in the kingdom was content to serve and wait. Then in 987 it so chanced that Louis V, the last surviving male in the direct line of the royal house, met with a fatal accident in the chase. Hugh Capet, with the encouragement and help of Adalbert, Archbishop of Rheims, seized the occasion and founded a dynasty which lasted eight hundred years. "I promise," he swore, "to grant to the people entrusted to my care justice according to their rights."

From the long duration of this famous house it might be tempting to conclude that its stability was never in serious danger. This was not so. The Capetians, indeed, enjoyed two great advantages over any feudal competitor. They held Paris and Orleans, and were thus stationed on the waters of the Seine and the Loire. No feudal vassal could boast of a domain so central or of a capital so populous, convenient, and easy to defend. The island city of Paris proved to be the key to supremacy, and this key valour and prudence had secured for the Capetians. But the election of Hugh, the most powerful by far of the French nobles and generally favoured by the Church, was not unanimous. The Counts of Flanders and Toulouse and the Duke of Aquitaine refused their recognition, a cloud in the sky foreshadowing the defiant ambitions and jealousies which continued to surround the throne of France.

A second resource, however, the Capetians possessed, the value of which became increasingly evident with the lapse of time. They were kings. By comparison with some of their feudatories they might be poor and weak, subjected to the humiliating defiance of robber barons even within the precincts of their own domain and hard put to it to make a living from their farms, but they had a reservoir of power peculiar to themselves. The King of France was the heir of the Roman tradition of empire, "the eldest son of the church and most Christian king," the head of that new feudal society which was at first so inimical to monarchy but afterwards, as its customs became defined, a source of regal prerogatives unknown to the ancient world. Upon each of these three foundations it was possible for the theorist to erect an imposing fabric of regal prerogative. To the feudal lawyer the king was the suzerain of suzerains, entitled to the homage and allegiance, the aid and counsel of his vassal, and the overlord from whom all land was immediately or mediately held. To the church-man consecration was an eighth sacrament, establishing the religion of royalty. To the Roman lawyer there was no limit to his prerogative. When Philippe de Remi, Sire de Beauvoisis, jurist and poet, wrote his *Coûtumes de Beauvoisis* in the thirteenth century, he echoed the famous maxim of imperial Rome that the princes' pleasure must be taken as law.

Length of life, coupled with the wise practice of their house always to crown the son in the lifetime of the fathers, give to 987- the first four monarchs of the Capetian house the better part 1108 of their claim to be counted among the benefactors of their country. They escaped the tempest of the War of Investitures, for the Pope, having the Germans on his hands, was too wise to force France into the ranks of his enemies by an over-close scrutiny of practices which were undoubtedly simoniacal. If these rulers achieved nothing sensational, at least they held their ground, governing mainly through the bishops, but themselves also active in a succession of miniature campaigns. One unfortunate calculation, to be ascribed to Henry I, had far-reaching consequences. In the struggle between Geoffrey Martel of Anjou and Duke William of Normandy, the King of France took the weaker side and was defeated on the fields of Mortimer and Varaville (1054 and 1058). These were the first exchanges in a duel which lasted nearly four hundred years.

The Church had helped to set up the new French monarchy. It was now to give its blessing to the establishment of a throne in England, which more seriously than any other power threatened the disruption of mediaeval France. William 1027? Duke of Normandy cannot be described as one of nature's -87 clergymen. The rule of priests he refused to tolerate either in Normandy or in England; but, like other statesmen-conquerors, he neglected no influence, however remote, which was likely to advance his ambitions. The Roman Curia was offended with the condition, at once lethargic and independent, of the Anglo-Saxon Church. William, remote as he was from the acceptance of Hildebrandine ideas, saw in the Pope a convenient ally in an enterprise long and profoundly meditated, and the conquest and pillage of

England by the Normans was carried out under the banner
and sanctified by the authority of the Vicar of Christ.

In all particulars of military and political organization our
island during the long reign of the monkish Edward had been
allowed to fall behind the duchy of Normandy. There authority was concentrated in the hands of the duke, here the ambitions of the great earls of Wessex and Mercia, Northumbria
and East Anglia filled the political stage. The Normans were
skilled in the use of cavalry and bowmen. The English, absorbed
in their own affairs and possessed by the sluggish spirit of
conservatism which was then so characteristic of the national
character, had failed to develop proficiency in either of these
arms. The consequences of this disparity in preparation were
astonishing. The force at the disposal of William the Norman
for the subjection of a brave population of a million and a
half can barely have exceeded twelve thousand. Yet after
Harold's army, which was largely drawn from the south-
eastern counties of England, had been defeated in the battle   1066
of Hastings and its commander slain, England, save for a
few local revolts, ill-combined and speedily suppressed, lay
prostrate beneath the heel of the conquerors.

No country has been more completely subjugated. If the
English population expected to receive from William the
measure of indulgence which had characterized the Danish
conquest of the island fifty years before they were grievously
deceived. The volunteer adventurers from Normandy and
Anjou, Brittany and Flanders, who flocked to William's
standard, were not so much on the duke's errand or the Pope's
as on their own. If they donned their mail to put a Norman
bastard on the throne of England it was in the confident hope
that a handsome share of English land and loot would be
available for themselves. They were not disappointed. As the
island was conquered bit by bit, the properties of the Saxon
thanes were dealt out to the hard-headed gentlemen adventurers from abroad. A new French-speaking aristocracy, in
comparison with their Saxon predecessors most formidable,
cruel, and versatile, dragooned the wretched peasants to its
imperious ends, dominated the countryside, and gave from
its imposing castles a new impulsion to the national life.

England became once more a province of the Latin world.
In the palace and castle, in the law court, and on the hunting
field, wherever the ruling class were brought together for

business or amusement, the speech was that of northern France. The chance that this island, which had slipped out of the grasp of Rome in the fifth century, might develop without foreign admixture an Anglo-Saxon life of its own, or play a part as a member of a Scandinavian empire, was now gone. The Norman conquest drew England once more into full communion with the inheritors of Rome, with their theology, their architecture, their poetical literature, their law, their social and political organization, with all that was moving in the Roman Curia or in the law school at Pavia, or among the active monasteries of Normandy, Burgundy, and Lorraine. Two great Italians, Lanfranc of Pavia and Anselm of Aosta, held in succession the see of Canterbury, bringing to England standards of scholarship, discipline, and philosophy to which the country had long been a stranger. The cruelty of the conquest was mitigated by the culture of the conquerors. From the soil of the plundered country vast cathedrals rose to the heavens, erected by the labour of a subject peasantry and in scale as novel to the Saxon ploughman as is the first towering vision of modern New York to a poor lad fresh from a humble cabin in Connemara.

By what may seem to be a paradox the completeness of William's despotism in England was a blessing in disguise. The great evil which affected the life of Europe in the eleventh century and indeed throughout the middle ages was anarchy and private war. The Roman system of government having been broken down and the Carolingian system having also failed, nothing effectual had by the time of the Norman conquest of England been found to replace them. The Church indeed employed such influence as it possessed to relieve the society of Europe from the incubus of perpetual war. It initiated local "pacts of peace" and on a more general scale the Truce of God for the protection of Sunday and the high feasts of the Church. But influence is not government, and until the three cardinal principles of government—a defined system of law administered and enforced, a money revenue ascertained and collected, a loyal force adequate to defence—had been reintroduced into Europe the seeds of liberty would not flourish.

Such a government, harsh, despotic, but in the long run salutary, England owed to William the Conqueror. With an even hand he crushed Saxon rebels and Norman mutineers.

The great English earldoms were broken up, and the estates of the Normans, whether by chance or prevision, were so widely scattered as greatly to reduce the dangers of feudal opposition. If, then, feudalism was promoted in the sphere of tenure, it was deprived of its worst evils in the sphere of government. As in Normandy, the barons held their land of the king and owed him military service in respect of their tenures; yet the main work of governing the country was never allowed to be monopolized by the nobility. The king was supreme. His commissioners travelled the shires. His sheriffs presided over the county courts. The Domesday Survey, compiled in 1086 for the purpose of collecting the Danegeld, shows with what meticulous curiosity every source of revenue was explored by the agents of the Norman fisc. In the local jury the Normans possessed an instrument inherited from Carolingian times, which was soon shown to be serviceable not only in those fiscal enquiries to which it was first applied, but also in the determination of judicial issues. When the royal court in the reign of Henry II began to apply the jury to cases of disputed possession, the most frequent form of legal action in violent and uncertain times, its popularity was assured. Litigants frequent the court which promises them cheap and effectual redress. Such redress the Curia Regis in the twelfth century found and applied, and thus gathering to itself the main part of the legal business of the country, built up that imposing system of the Common Law by which the Anglo-Saxon world on either side of the Atlantic is to this day content to be governed.

The roots of that system lie deep in the soil of Teuton antiquity. It was a part of William's strength that he regarded himself as the lawful heir of Edward the Confessor, that he was crowned by the Witan, and worked through the old popular courts of the hundred and the shire. The primitive ideas of English citizenship, such as that men were bound to attend the courts, to follow the hue and cry after malefactors, to serve in the fyrd or militia, and to help with the bridges, the roads, and the forts were too essential to be discarded. Norman England could no more be governed without the active co-operation of the English people than British India can be administered without a numerous body of Indian officials. As Hindu caste survives under the British raj, the fabric of Anglo-Saxon law and custom has continued, despite some Norman innovations, and all the more effectually by reason of that taut system of centralization which the Normans introduced, to shape the life of the English people.

The task of centralizing the government was rendered easier by the fact that Norman England was a small country. Wales, Scotland, and Ireland lay outside the confines of William's dominion. Northumbria, as a penalty for rebellion, was reduced to a wilderness. In an area so contracted the Norman sheriffs, who were the agents of the king, carried out the royal pleasure.

So, during the century which followed the Norman conquest, the foundations were laid for the construction of a free and well-governed state. Normans and English intermarried. Under the shelter of a government strong enough to keep the baronage in its place a rural middle-class, that valuable feature which most sharply distinguishes mediaeval England from its continental neighbours, maintained itself in rude comfort and respectability and in due course of time became a principal pillar of constitutional government in our island. Progress, indeed, was not continuous. There was tyranny under Rufus, anarchy under Stephen; but the tyranny of Rufus was contested by Anselm, the anarchy under Stephen was terminated by the strong rule of Henry II. Before this sovereign, whose brilliant power of thought and action amounted to genius, had finished his work, royal judges were going on assize as they have ever since continued to do, representing the authority of the king and the majesty of the law, the jury was fast superseding archaic methods of proof, such as the ordeal and the duel, and the king had established his position as fountain of justice and guardian of the public peace. Racialism was dead. In the old national militia, which was now recreated and revived, the King of England possessed a defence force more reliable than the feudal levies, cheaper and more popular than a mercenary force. In the exactitude of its treasury control only the Norman island of Sicily could stand comparison with the England of Henry II. Not a sixpence was allowed to go astray. In comparison with the loose financial methods of Germany and France the English exchequer was a marvel of efficiency.

In becoming King of England William the Bastard did not cease to remain Duke of Normandy. Neither to him nor to his followers or descendants was there any anomaly in the existence of a French-speaking state lying athwart the Channel. If Sicily went with Apulia, England could well go with Normandy. The King of England was in respect of his Norman Duchy a vassal of France. Many of his tenants-in-chief possessed lands, all possessed relatives, on the continent. To no one of them, in search of military adventure, were the hills of Wales, the moors of Scotland, or the bogs of Ireland as attractive as the familiar fields of France. So long, then, as any part of France remained annexed to England it acted more powerfully than even the Electorate of Hanover in the time of George II as a magnet upon English policy. But many years were destined to pass before the ruler of England could regard himself as an island king. Even after Normandy was lost in the reign of John, and together with this great province, Anjou, Touraine, and Maine, England still retained possession of Guienne, Auvergne, and Aquitaine, the important provinces in the south-west of France which Queen Eleanor, the divorced wife of Louis VII, had brought with her hand to Henry Plantagenet.

From this geographical interlocking, as also from the quarrels of seamen and traders, there resulted a chronic state of hostility between the Kings of England and France which lasted with some intermissions until the middle of the fifteenth century. Beginning as a French civil war the struggle developed into a clash between two distinct and self-conscious nations. No great armies were employed, no long campaigns were fought, no new philosophies were developed in this protracted and desultory struggle. Mediaeval warfare was partly a social convention, partly an amusement, partly a financial speculation, when it was not a crusade or the fruit of personal pique or injured pride. But however slight and frivolous this mediaeval fighting may seem measured against the sacrifice and slaughter of modern war, the wars between England and France in the middle ages had far-reaching consequences for both countries. Out of this struggle two nations emerged as sharply distinguished in social structure and personal temperament as they were opposed by a long tradition of envenomed hostility. France was victorious, but failed for many centuries to turn her victory to enduring account. England was defeated. She lost Rouen in 1204, Bordeaux in 1453, Calais in 1552. Every yard of French soil was surrendered, every end for which she had been fighting was sacrificed. The tombs of the Conqueror and Henry II lay in an alien land. Yet only after she had suffered this staggering reverse did she by slow stages find her way to the great tasks which were awaiting her, the union of the British Isles, the conquest of an Empire across the seas. Engaged in her struggle with France she had been blind to the true line of her advance. Opportunities had been neglected. Nothing had been carried through with persistence. Even Wales, conquered by Edward I, was not finally incorporated until the reign of Henry VIII. Not till after Charles Edward had been defeated at Culloden (1745) were the Scottish Highlands made truly subject to the British Crown. The spirit of the Irish Celt, often assailed, remains to this day defiant and insoluble.

BOOKS WHICH MAY BE CONSULTED

H. W. C. Davis: *England under the Normans and Angevins.* 1905.

W. Stubbs: *Constitutional History of England.* 1880.

Mrs. J. R. Green: *Henry II.* 1888.

F. Pollock and F. W. Maitland: *History of English Law before Edward I.* 2 vols. 1898.

Chronicles of Benedictus Abbas. (Rolls Series.) 1867.

F. W. Maitland: *Memoranda de Parliamento.* (Rolls Series.) 1893.

A. F. Pollard: *The Evolution of Parliament.* 1926.

McKechnie: *Magna Carta.* 1905.

T. F. Tout: *Edward I.* 1893.

E. Lavisse: *Histoire de France,* Vol. II. 1903.

Bainville: *Histoire de France.*

C. Petit Du Taillis: *The Feudal Monarchy in France and England.* Tr. E. D. Hunt. 1936.

F. L. Ganshof: *Feudalism.* Tr. P. Grierson. 1952.

A. L. Poole: *From Domesday Book to Magna Carta.* 1087-1216. 1951.

F. Barlow: *The Feudal Kingdom of England,* 1042-1216. 1955.

CHAPTER XVIII

THE EARLY CRUSADES

Struggle of the eastern Empire under the Macedonians, 867-1059. Points of weakness in Byzantine civilization. Rise of the Seljuks. Manzikert, 1071. Alexius Comnenus appeals to the west. Urban II and the Holy Places. Schism between Greek and Roman Churches. Aims of the Sicilian Normans. Effects of Christian disunion. Circumstances in western Europe favouring the First Crusade. Its success. Increasing friction between Greeks and Franks. Role of the Italian cities. Franks and Syrians in Palestine. Fall of Edessa and the Second Crusade. Imperfect concert between Greek Empire and the Kingdom of Jerusalem. Conquests of Saladin and the Third Crusade. Results of Crusading movement.

WHILE THE house of Egbert was struggling to preserve an Anglo-Saxon nation in Britain, a dynasty hardly less remarkable was engaged at the other end of Europe in defending the Byzantine Empire against the ring of enemies who threatened to destroy it. The resources at the disposal of the Macedonian Emperors (867-1056) were far superior to those which were at that time enjoyed by any sovereign in the west. They had a capital superbly fortified and inhabited by a population more numerous than the Paris of Philip Augustus or the London of Charles II, a trained civil service, an organized system of finance and law, an army widely recruited and strengthened by a well-disciplined force of axemen from the north, a navy which could draw upon the inherited maritime skill of the Levant, and a gold coinage (the bezant) which went the round of the world. But perhaps the most important characteristic distinguishing this old civilized government from the newer and ruder states of the west was its skill and experience in diplomacy. No European politicians were so well posted in barbarian psychology, no foreign office so well versed in the art of dealing with half-savage princes and people. In no capital of the world were diplomatic relations so numerous and extended as in the city in which Asia and

Europe unite. And among the diplomatists who even more than the soldiers maintained the Empire must be numbered the missionaries of the Greek Church, exercising a compelling force upon barbarous minds not only by the content of their teaching but by the elaborate splendour of the Greek liturgy, with its appeal to every sense through incense and music, vestments and candles. Some barbarians were kept loyal by gifts and pensions, others by marriages arranged with ladies of the Greek aristocracy, others by high-sounding titles. Upon all such as might be attracted to the capital it was hoped that an elaborate court ceremonial devised to exhibit the Emperor as a divine autocrat raised high above the common clay of humanity would make a suitable impression. Nothing certainly was more remarkable in this old and civilized government than the skill with which it contrived to protect itself by distant and outlying friendships and understandings, the knowledge which it succeeded in acquiring of the wild peoples of the steppes, and the promptitude with which it was able to embarrass its enemies by bringing into the field against them an unsuspected ally.[1]

Moreover, the government, inheriting as it did the imposing tradition of the Roman Empire, could never fail, when it fell into vigorous hands, to cherish exalted ambitions. The four fighting Emperors of the Macedonian house—Basil I, Nicephorus Phocas, John Zimisces, and Basil II—were soldiers whose Spartan temper and inflexible will were well adapted to the necessities of those iron times. Taking the offensive on every front, they gave to the boundaries of the Empire an extension such as it had not known since the days of Justinian. The robber island of Crete was rescued from the Saracens by Nicephorus Phocas. Cilicia, Syria, and Palestine were overrun by the armies of John Zimisces. Antioch and South Italy were recovered, the distant mountain country of Armenia incorporated in the Empire. But of all the triumphs of this strenuous dynasty none was so vital to the continued existence of the Byzantines as the reduction, after thirty years of fierce fighting and adroit diplomacy, of the Bulgarian Empire by Basil II. When Basil the Bulgar-slayer died in 1025, after wisely conceding to his conquered enemies their cherished customs, he left his state stronger, richer, more influential, and better defended than any state in Europe.

867-
1056

[1] Genealogical Table D.

Byzantine history is a tissue of sharp and disappointing contrasts. Spells of high military energy are succeeded by periods of civil turmoil and base intrigue. Learning and culture are often found combined in one and the same person with manifest cruelty or connivance in crime. We read of an Emperor whom we are prepared to admire for his activity, his learning, and his patronage of the arts, and then we are told that this cultivated Byzantine composed scurrilous verses to be branded with red-hot irons on the foreheads of three condemned heretics. We study the works of a learned princess, who was familiar with most of the Greek classics, who idolized her father, and composed an elaborate history in his honour, but was yet concerned in a plot to assassinate her brother. The state whose craftsmen wrought the mosaics of Ravenna and the gorgeous miracle of St. Mark's at Venice, whose politicians were theologians and whose theologians were politicians, whose poets were still haunted by the echoes of Meleager or Callimachus, and whose scholars were still dominated by the shade of Homer, produced the most violent city mob in Europe and descended to the basest mutilations—the blinding of the eyes, the cutting off of the hand, the ear, and the nose—in the punishment of its criminals or political offenders.

The modern critic, then, finds much to reprehend in the Byzantine Empire. Its organization had defects. It lacked the liberal institutions which are alone capable of giving to a population habits of self-reliance and initiative. Despite much well-meant legislation it was unable to protect its agricultural population from the suction of the town or the *latifundia* of the acquisitive landlord. It suffered overmuch from the tempestuous pressure of monks and mobs. But in the ninth and tenth centuries Byzantium was the undisputed queen of European culture. Even in the eleventh century, though the west was then fast drawing level, it could show a society easily superior to that of any western city in art, learning, and civilized habits. Moreover, it performed a great office in policing a vast miscellany of races, most various in quality and many of them vile, savage, and dirty. It was therefore, a calamity that the death of Basil II in 1025 should have been followed by fifty-seven years of feeble government and civil strife during which the army was allowed to dwindle through neglect. The results were serious. The Empire lost all its holdings in south Italy to the Normans. More important still, it was defeated by a new enemy, the Seljukian Turk.

Towards the end of the tenth century a body of Turkish freebooters, under the leadership of the sons of a certain Seljuk, rode out of the steppes of Turkestan with their short bows and curved scimitars to seek their fortunes by war and pillage. Embracing Islam with neophyte intensity and prospering in all their undertakings, the Seljuks grew from a company into a tribe and from a tribe into a people. So swift was their onward march to power that in 1055 Togrul Beg, their leader, having already conquered Khorassan and Persia, was proclaimed Sultan in Bagdad and loaded by the effete Abbasid Caliph with all the titles and honours which are indicative of secular pre-eminence in the Moslem world. The course of Turkish victories so brilliantly inaugurated by Togrul was continued by Alp Arslan, his successor. Syria and Jerusalem were wrested from the weak hands of the Fatimite Caliphs of Egypt, after which the invaders threw themselves upon the one formidable power which was left in Asia and gained an overwhelming victory. On the field of Manzikert (1071), north of Lake Van, in Armenia, the flower of the Byzantine army was mown down by Alp Arslan's horse archers, the Emperor Romanus Diogenes was taken captive, and all Asia Minor was laid prostrate before a pitiless foe.

The Byzantines had suffered many defeats at the hands of barbarous enemies, but none so serious as Manzikert, for the force of the Empire depended upon its control of those Asiatic provinces which a single battle had now delivered into the hands of the infidels. It was from the Anatolian provinces of Asia Minor that the Emperor had obtained his stoutest soldiers and most brilliant generals, from the Asiatic littoral that he had derived the best part of his fighting marine. Nowhere was the spirit of adventure more lively than on the frontiers of the Asiatic themes, nor a prouder tradition of service than among the great barons of Asia Minor, whose well-armed retainers and large resources, when not employed in mutiny, had constituted a powerful element in imperial defence. All these sources of power were now summarily cut off by the Sultans of Rūm,[1] who, establishing themselves first at Nicaea and then at Iconium, spread a belt of desolation across the fairest province of the Greek Empire.

[1] A shortened form of Rumania, or the East Roman Empire.

To this tremendous challenge there was no immediate reply from Byzantium. The battle of Manzikert, which had been preceded by civil strife and unwise military reductions, was followed by a decade of political paralysis. Then, in 1081, a happy revolution brought to the Byzantine throne a man whose qualities were exactly fitted to restore an almost desperate situation. Alexius Comnenus, who belonged to one of the great soldier families of Asia Minor, was as resourceful as he was cultivated and courageous. In him the taste for theological disquisition was blended with the zeal of the educational reformer, the energy of the general, and the craft of the diplomatist. Finding disorganization in every department of the state, menaced by a Norman invasion from the west and by the devastating raids of barbaric tribes from the north, this temperate long-headed young sovereign brought to bear upon all the difficult foreign and domestic problems by which he was confronted the precise measure of skill which was necessary to solve them. Only when these preliminary obstacles had been overcome, when the army and navy had been to some extent re-created, when Robert Guiscard had been manoeuvred out of Dalmatia and the nomad hordes were driven back across the Danube was Alexius free to address himself to the grave menace of the Seljuks. He determined to appeal to the Latin west to come to the succour of the Christian Empire and suffering churches of the east. Jerusalem, Antioch, Edessa were already in the hands of the infidel. Constantinople would be their next objective. So a letter was written to Pope Urban II which had the effect of unloosing the First Crusade.

Twenty-one years earlier, Pope Gregory VII, in response to a similar request from an eastern emperor, had conceived with characteristic energy and passion of such an enterprise. But the plan of a crusade derives not from Byzantium but from Rome. The object of Alexius was to obtain western soldiers for the reconquest of the Asiatic dominions of the Byzantine Empire. The principal interest of Urban If, the theme of the great speech which he delivered at the Council of Clermont, the leading motive of the many orations which he afterwards addressed to his lively French compatriots, was the recovery of Jerusalem and the Holy Places. The two objects were not incompatible, but since each might be separately pursued there was from the first the danger

1095

that the recovery of the Holy Places, appealing as it did more powerfully to the imagination of the Frankish chivalry, might be preferred to the defence of the Byzantine Empire.

The danger was aggravated by the fact that, eighteen years before Manzikert, the eastern and western Churches had formally broken off relations. It is a common characteristic of the great quarrels of history that the deepest causes of variance are not those which are most openly disclosed. The rift between the Greek and the Roman Churches was ostensibly theological. Whilst both Churches accepted the fundamentals of the Christian Faith as laid down in the Ecumenical Councils, the Greeks objected against the Latins that they had added words to the Creed which described the Holy Ghost as proceeding from the Son as well as from the Father, that they used unleavened bread, that they fasted on Saturday, and that they caused their priests to shave their beards. But these grounds of dissension, favourable as they were to the production of interminable treatises, did not stand alone. Other causes rooted in political and ecclesiastical ambition, as well as in circumstances of national temperament and character, tended to envenom the quarrel and to frustrate every one of the thirty separate efforts which were made to compose it. The contempt of the Latin for the Greek, old as the days of Juvenal, had survived the barbaric conquest of the west and was repaid by the scorn of the virtuoso for the philistine, of the legitimist for the upstart. The Byzantines regarded themselves as the heirs not only of ancient Hellas but of imperial Rome. For them the Franks, the Normans, the Germans were members of the barbaric world, and the western empire of Charlemagne an impertinent usurpation to which the Popes of Rome had improperly lent their authority. A certain primacy they might be willing to concede to the See of St. Peter. Roman legates might be received in Constantinople, the judgment of the Roman Curia might occasionally be invoked; but the claim of Rome to exact obedience and to exercise disciplinary jurisdiction over the church was one which no Patriarch of Constantinople would for a moment admit. Nor is this unintelligible. The ninth and tenth centuries, which witnessed the obscuration of the Roman Papacy, were illustrious in the annals of the Greek church. Then it was that two Greek missionaries,

Cyril and Methodius, translated the Scriptures into the Slavonic language and made them available in the Glagolitic script, that the Greek church was organized in Russia, and the Bulgarians rescued from the subtle invasion of the Latin rite. For a hundred and fifty years the Patriarchs of Constantinople profited by the brilliant conquests of the Macedonian emperors. Greek priests and Greek monks followed the victorious march of Greek armies to Apulia, to Cicilia, to the Armenian highlands, to the Danube, and, though the Macedonian dynasty came to an end and was followed by a period of political confusion and disaster, the proud spirit of empire still survived in the Patriarchs of Constantinople. To Leo IX, speaking the autocratic mind of the revived Papacy of the west, the Patriarch Michael Cerularius reaffirmed (1054) the autonomy of his Church and its detestation of the corrupt practices of Rome.

To the Latin world, then, Byzantium naturally appeared in a double aspect. On the one hand it was a Christian power confronted by non-Christian enemies and therefore deserving of Christian support. But on the other hand it was tainted by heresy, contumaciously defiant of Rome, and the foe of every Roman missionary enterprise in south-eastern Europe. That the schism between the two Churches was a misfortune, and that steps should be taken to bring it to an end, was a principle which the Greek and Latin clergy were always willing to salute, but for which they were never disposed to make any hearty sacrifice of prejudice or pride. The Latins, however, held that there were two avenues to theological peace—the way of agreement, difficult, but not under political pressure impossible; and the way of conquest. To the Normans in particular it seemed from the first that the shortest and most satisfactory method of dealing with the Greeks was to dethrone the Emperor, to capture Constantinople, and to subject the Greek Empire by force to Latin rule. That was the theory of Robert Guiscard, of Bohemond his son, of Roger II and William II of Sicily his kinsmen—in fact, of this whole race of northern robbers who had turned the Greeks out of southern Italy and dreaded nothing so much as a war of revenge. It was a doctrine which won recruits in many quarters, among the merchants of Venice, who saw in the Greek Empire incomparable occasions for commerce and loot, among vehement Latin theologians like St. Bernard, among monkish statesmen like Suger. There were even occasions (as for instance in 1108 and 1281) when the Pope was himself prepared to promote the destruction of the Christian Empire of the east.

It is difficult to exaggerate the disastrous effect of this profound estrangement between the two halves of the Christian world. The failure of the Crusaders to retrieve hither Asia from the Moslems needs no other explanation. It was to this inveterate animosity, compounded of racial and religious feelings and quickened by political ambition and economic rapacity, that we must ascribe the most disgraceful act of mediaeval history, the diversion of the Fourth Crusade to the conquest of Constantinople and the mutilation and pillage of the richest and most civilized of the European states. In 1261, after nearly fifty years of Latin rule, the Greeks returned to Constantinople. If they had little love for the Latins before the conquest of their capital, it may be imagined with what sentiments of aggravated passion they viewed the authors of their bitter humiliation. It was in vain that piety and prudence counselled a union of Christian forces before the advancing menace of the Ottoman Turks. What was proposed by high dignitaries in ecclesiastical councils, as at Lyons in 1274 or at Ferrara and Florence in 1438, was violently repudiated by the monks and clergy of Constantinople. Great Latin victories over a common foe might have stifled their inveterate misgivings; but such victories were not forthcoming. The gulf which had been dug in 1054 by the rival challenges of Pope and Patriarch remained unbridged to the end. Thanks to the divisions of the Christian world the Turks established themselves on European soil, carried their arms to the Danube, conquered Greece and its islands, and finally in May, 1453, seized the last prize of political ambition, the unconquered city of Constantinople itself. Here, by grace of these same rivalries, the Turk is still permitted to rule.

These dark shadows, however, were not within the field of vision at the first excited and tumultuous launching of the Crusade. At rare moments of history the feeling of Christian fellowship overmasters the jealousies and hatreds by which the church of Christ is ever liable to be rent asunder. In the

brilliant prospect of common action and common sacrifice
for a cause held to be great and sacred, dividing memories
are laid aside and petty suspicions are discarded. That such
an exalted emotional experience was vouchsafed to the
chivalry of western Europe as it took the Cross in response
to the Pope's appeal is established by evidence and may be
inferred from probabilities. For the time had now come when
Europe, which had so long been exposed to barbarian
attacks, could carry the war into the enemy quarters. The
Saracens had been expelled from Sicily and Crete, the navies
of Venice and Genoa and Pisa ruled the Mediterranean, the
overland route to Constantinople had been opened by the
conversion of the Hungarians to Christianity and by the
incorporation of Bulgaria into the Byzantine state. In Spain
the Christians had conquered Toledo, from Sicily the Normans had assaulted the Saracens of Africa; and while the
massive eastward movement of the Germans was rolling
back the worshippers of Triglav and of Svantovit, Scandinavia,
long the torment of the continent but now emptied of its
unruly sons, had withdrawn into the backwaters of history,
where she lay becalmed till Gustavus Adolphus came forward 1630
to give to the Protestant cause in Germany the glory of his   -2
sword and of his name.

It is also to be remembered that in France, which more than
any other country was the soul of the Crusades, the Church
had already succeeded in giving to the military caste something of its own code of aspiration. The institution of chivalry,
as it was developed at the end of the eleventh century, had
the great merit of laying stress upon the responsibilities
attaching to the possession of force. The young knight was
initiated into his knighthood with all the solemnities which
the pious imagination of those days could devise. He must
take a ritual bath, spend a night of solitary prayer, make
confession of his sins and partake of the sacrament. The
duties of knighthood were rehearsed to him in a sermon.
He must protect the Church, the widows and the orphans,
the desolate and the oppressed. He was already, in all but
name, enlisted as a Crusader.

The first military enterprise of united Europe was distinguished for its absence of organization. The Crusaders
who, in a wild fit of enthusiasm, first left their homes for the
east were empty of all that it most concerned them to know.

They knew nothing of the geography, climate, or population of the countries through which they proposed to travel. They were short of commissariat, cumbered by crowds of non-combatants, ignorant of hygiene, and contemptuous of discipline. These large bodies of enthusiasts, recruited from north-eastern France, Lorraine, and Germany, rushed off without leaders by the land route to Constantinople and suffered a terrible penalty for their violent marauding. Decimated during their passage through Bavaria and Hungary, they were annihilated by the Seljuks soon after they had set foot upon the Asiatic shore.

The great muster of western feudalism which started for Constantinople by four different routes in August, 1096, exhibited, though in a lesser degree, the same deficiencies. There was no unity of command. There was an abounding ignorance of geography. The armies were burdened with long trains of camp followers and disgraced by undisciplined pillaging. But here there was a core of experienced soldiers, horse and foot, serving under chieftains of skill and authority such as Godfrey of Bouillon and his brother Baldwin, who led the men of Lorraine; Bohemond, son of Guiscard, the captain of the Apulian Normans, with his brilliant nephew Tancred; and Raymond of Toulouse, whose Provençal followers were of all that concourse the best equipped. To this circumstance we must attribute the surprising fact that the First Crusade succeeded in attaining its objects, that the four armies, though not without serious wastage, did actually meet before Constantinople, that being conveyed across the Bosphorus they were able with Greek assistance to capture the Moslem capital of Nicaea and to restore to the Greek Empire not only the littoral but much of the interior of Asia Minor, that despite the molestation of the enemy they accomplished in their leather coats and heavy chain armour the long and thirsty march through Iconium to Antioch, that they besieged and took that strongly fortified and famous city and beat off a formidable attempt to recapture it, and that these achievements were ultimately crowned by the capture of Jerusalem itself. No succeeding Crusade rivalled these remarkable exploits. The armies of Godfrey and Bohemond founded the Latin principalities of the east, which, though they have now been extinguished for more than 650 years, are recalled to the reader by the genius of Tasso and

Walter Scott and to the traveller by the superb shell of many a giant fortress, standing proud and lonely among the pink hills of Palestine.

To these successive blows delivered by the Frankish chivalry on the Turks and Saracens, the Byzantine Empire owes its continued existence for a further period of three hundred years. It is seldom, however, that the allies in a coalition for war, even if that war should prove to be successful, are inspired at the conclusion of their operations by feelings of gratitude for the help that has been rendered or of satisfaction for the results that are achieved. The Latins owed much to Alexius. Without the help of Greek convoys, Greek supplies, and Greek guidance they could never have accomplished their difficult journey from the Balkans to Syria. Equally great, if not greater, was the debt of Alexius to the western army, which drove the Turks from a capital (Nicaea) within easy reach of Constantinople, restored many flourishing provinces to his empire, and dispelled the haunting fear of a Seljuk conquest of European Thrace. Yet neither party was satisfied with the other. The Latins complained that the Greek Emperor had made use of the advantage which belonged to him as the head of a wealthy and experienced government to exact from their chiefs an oath of fealty. They accused him of having failed to give them a stipulated measure of military support, and with some reason averred that but for the timely arrival of sea-borne supplies from Europe, their victorious army would have perished ignominiously of famine when encamped before the walls of Antioch. Every victory they ascribed to their own valour, every reverse or miscalculation to the perfidy of the Greeks. A popular idea, widely disseminated in the west and reinforced by every subsequent disaster to crusading armies, was that the Greeks, out of the fear and hatred which they entertained for the Latins, deliberately made their overland passage to the east as difficult and dangerous as possible. Alexius on his side had good grounds for distrust and dissatisfaction. His first campaign as Emperor had been fought against the Apulian Normans who had occupied Durazzo and were openly bent on driving him from the throne. That Bohemond, the fierce Norman leader, had experienced a real change of heart was most improbable. The inference to be drawn from his conduct, as from that of most of his associates, was that they

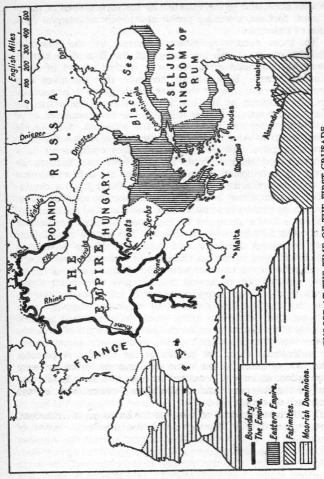

EUROPE AT THE TIME OF THE FIRST CRUSADE

were far more concerned to achieve principalities for themselves than conquests for the Empire. It was natural, then, that Alexius should endeavour to secure, as far as security could be obtained from oath or treaty, that territories once belonging to the Greek Empire and hereafter recovered by the Crusaders should be returned to their former allegiance. The oaths were reluctantly sworn, the treaty (for treaty there appears to have been) was reluctantly signed. Oaths and treaty were alike disregarded, when Bohemond seized Antioch for himself and Godfrey of Lorraine was installed by his followers as the first Defender of the Holy Sepulchre. In the maintenance of states which had been thus created the Latins could not count upon Greek assistance.

The bold experiment of the Crusaders in founding Christian states under a Syrian sky, though it was favoured at the time by the dissensions of the Moslem emirs, must, but for one circumstance, have broken down without delay. The great Italian republics were passionately interested in the extension of their eastern trade. Navies from Venice, Genoa, and Pisa co-operated in the sieges of the coast cities of Syria and were mainly instrumental in effecting their reduction. Yet even so the Christian states were in a precarious position. The Italians had no interest beyond the Syrian ports, the pilgrims from overseas no broader concern than a safe access to the Holy Places. The vital importance of conquering from the Moslem the whole of Syria up to its natural frontiers does not seem to have been apprehended and could not, in view of the slender numbers at the disposal of the Frankish princes, have been accomplished without permanent reinforcements from Europe. Such reinforcements were not forthcoming. For lack of numbers the vigorous Kings of Jerusalem were compelled to leave the eastern frontier in enemy hands and on that undefended and indefensible frontier were always exposed to attack.

The knights-errant who founded the kingdom of Jerusalem, the principality of Antioch, and the smaller counties of Edessa and Tripoli organized their new states upon a system of military feudalism such as they had known in France, but to which they were compelled by the special need of martial vigilance to impart an additional austerity. The Assizes of Jerusalem, a collection of customs compiled by John of Ibelin, a Cypriot lawyer of the thirteenth century,

presents the picture of a society as rigorously dedicated to
war as was ancient Sparta. In no instrument of the middle
ages is the theory of feudal society so elaborately stated or
the duties of military tenure so stringently defined. Institutions, however, depend upon the spirit of the men who
work them. Under the seductive influences of an eastern
climate, the rigidity of the Latin settlers insensibly relaxed.

Seljuk Kingdom of Rum

Armenia

Edessa

Antioch

Land recovered by the Byzantine Empire
Crusaders Lands:—
    Kingdom of Armenia
    County of Edessa
    Principality of Antioch
    County of Tripoli
    Kingdom of Jerusalem

Tripoli

Seljuks of Damascus

Jerusalem

Fatimites

RESULTS OF THE FIRST CRUSADE

Syrian women, Syrian dishes, Syrian ways of life, began to
appeal to these rude adventurers from the west and to temper
their fanaticism. In Syria they found a society strange, to some
extent abhorrent (for the Moslem women went veiled), but
in many respects more refined and dignified than their
own. Friendships were made between Frankish and Arab
chieftains. The fierce religious intolerance of the Christian
was softened by the spectacle of pagan valour and courtesy.
Even the half-military, half-monastic Orders of the Knights
Hospitallers and the Knights Templars, which had been
specially created for the protection of the Holy Land, were

not exempt from the insidious infection of the east. The curious autobiography of Ousama, an Arab prince, whose society was much affected by the Templars, shows how deep by the middle of the twelfth century had become the gulf between the polite and cynical tolerance of the permanent settler and the raw enthusiasm of the newly arrived pilgrim from the west.

So long as the Frankish states were confronted with a ring of small Moslem emirs, each acting independently of the other, they were able, slender as were their resources in men and money, to maintain an existence. But this advantage was not destined to endure. Three capable Moslem rulers, coming one after the other, altered in the course of half a century all the weights and balances of the near east. Zanghi of Mosul conquered Aleppo and Edessa. His son Noureddin made himself master first of Damascus and later of Egypt, and finally, when Noureddin died in 1173, his place was taken by Saladin the Kurd, to whose brilliant and effortless gift of leadership the whole east between the Tigris and the Nile was in time made submissive.

The fall of Edessa in 1144, the first stage in this swift series of accumulating dangers, provoked an immense movement of agitated feeling in Europe. Edessa was a place in the imagination of the Christian world only less sacred than Jerusalem itself. That this home of early Christianity, the first of the new Latin states to be created as a result of the Crusades and the outlying bulwark of the Latin position in Syria, should be taken by the infidel, was regarded as terrible in itself and even more terrible for what it might portend. In an atmosphere of all-pervading excitement which the fiery eloquence of St. Bernard contributed greatly to inflame, Conrad III of Germany and Louis VII of France took the Cross and conducted their respective armies, still much encumbered by non-combatants, by the land route toward the east. A modest reinforcement of capable knights conveyed overseas in Venetian galleys would have been infinitely more effective than these imposing armaments led by the two principal sovereigns of the west.

The German army, save for a small fragment, wasted away in Asia Minor before it reached its destination. Of the French, who unwisely pursued the long and difficult coast route and were severely routed by the Turks in southern Phrygia, only the mounted knights, being transported by sea from Attalia, reached the scene of action. The Second Crusade was an unrelieved failure, marked by the needless wreck of two fine armies and the siege of Damascus, undertaken with half a heart and broken off after a few days by Baldwin II of Jerusalem, to the disgust of the princes from the west and to the infinite detriment of the Christian cause.

The west having thus signally failed to restore the situation in the east, it was natural that in due course the King of Jerusalem should look for aid to Constantinople. The Greeks, should they care to exert themselves, might with their money, their fleet, and their greatly improved army, supply exactly that additional force which was necessary to check the rising power of Nouredd n. But Manuel Comnenus, their new ruler, was not too anxious to place the Latin kingdom of Jerusalem in a position of security. So long as he could recover Antioch, the prime object of his south-eastern policy, he was well content that the King of Jerusalem, to whom he had given a niece in marriage, should be kept quiet by the Arab on his flank. Seldom can there have been a keener sense of disappointment among the Latin residents in the east than when, in the summer of 1159, this showy and ambitious Greek Emperor marched a large army in and out of Syria without so much as a skirmish with the enemy. That Manuel preferred to treat with Noureddin rather than to fight him is probably to be explained by the fact that Antioch had been already surrendered to his rule.

Still, the Byzantine alliance was too valuable to be lightly thrown away. Amaury, who succeeded to the kingdom of Jerusalem in 1163, instead of concentrating his efforts upon the conquest of Aleppo and Damascus, was much taken with the idea of the conquest of Egypt and upon one of his four separate expeditions against that country received the assistance of an imperial fleet. His siege of Damietta in 1169 was a failure, but memorable for two reasons, alike as the last co-operative enterprise of Greek and Latin in the Crusades and as the first triumph of Saladin, the new Vizier of Egypt.

No Greek blood was shed in the battle of Hittin (1187), which sealed the fate of the short-lived Frankish kingdom of Jerusalem. The Greek Empire, to which the dynasty of the Comneni had given a century of prestige, had fallen once more upon evil times. Its main army had been defeated

1143
-80

(1174) with huge losses by the Sultan of Iconium. It had quarrelled with Venice. In a mood of fierce suspicion against Mary of Antioch, the widow of Manuel and the Empress regent, it had disgraced itself by a *pogrom* against the French and Italian colony in Constantinople, and when Saladin's war cloud was ready to burst upon Syria, it was exposed to

RESULTS OF THE THIRD CRUSADE

a deadly attack from the Normans, still faithful to their original thesis, that only a Latin power enthroned in Constantinople could finally settle with the Moslem world. There were no Greeks then on the field of Hittin. Only a force of some 1,300 Frankish knights and some 15,000 foot could be gathered together to oppose the great cavalry army of Saladin. What avail was brilliant courage against overwhelming numbers? The Latins were annihilated, the Holy Cross was captured, and the Holy Sepulchre, the dream of centuries and the first great prize of united Christendom, passed once more into paynim hands (1187) and so for 731 years remained.

At the news of this tremendous disaster a Crusade was organized, no longer by the Pope, but by the three foremost sovereigns of the west, Frederick Barbarossa of Germany, Philip Augustus of France, and Richard Coeur-de-Lion of England. But from these royal preparations, elaborated with all the improved knowledge and technique which a century of contact with the east had now made available, there was no result but the capture of Acre and a truce with Saladin granting to the Christian pilgrims free access to the Holy Sepulchre at Jerusalem. Here, indeed, was a shameful conclusion to an ambitious prelude and a damaging commentary upon the power of the Christian motive to fuse the energies of western Christendom and to direct them to a common end. In extenuation it may be said that the Third Crusade suffered one grave misfortune in the death through drowning in Cilicia of Frederick Barbarossa. Had that great German captain, the foremost soldier of the west, who had conducted his army across Asia Minor with conspicuous skill, and with an absence of casualties contrasting most favourably with the experience of preceding armies, survived to measure swords with Saladin, the result might have been different. As it was the Crusade served but to exhibit the national jealousies of France and England, the ill-will between Genoa and Pisa, and the intrigues and counter-intrigues of Conrad of Montferrat and Guy de Lusignan, the rival claimants for the shadowy throne of Jerusalem. Against this dark background of petty and paralysing spite the military prowess and generous nature of Richard Coeur-de-Lion shine with ineffectual glory.

What remained of the conquest of the First Crusade was a line of Syrian ports of which Acre was the queen. These the strong material interests of Italian commerce were sufficient for a century to preserve. When Marco Polo started on his famous voyage to China the Italian mariner, as he approached the shores of Palestine, could still see the banner of the Cross floating from the citadel of his predestined port and hear across the waters the familiar salutation of the Christian bells.

Had the Crusaders been brought into contact with the best that Asia could give, and had they been able to absorb it, the Persian poetry of Omar Khayyam, the finest mind of the eleventh century, would have passed into the intellectual currency of Europe long before the days of Edward Fitzgerald.

The Crusaders, however, never pierced to the best and most cultured peoples of the east. They saw nothing of the Persians, the Chinese, or the Indians. Their dealings were with the children of the steppes or the deserts, with the Turks or the Saracens, and with those softer peoples of the Levant who had suffered under Turkish or Saracen rule. Yet these limitations notwithstanding, the enlargement through the Crusades of western experience and material wealth was immense. Arts and crafts of the Orient, rich, intricate, and costly, strange lands and peoples were made familiar to a society, limited and largely barbarized by a long series of public calamities and only just emerging from the dominion of anarchy and fear. The new wealth of the east flooding into the Italian cities and thence distributed to northern Europe gave fresh strength and importance to the towns. Gains there were doubtless in the field of the spirit, a sense of the religious unity of Christendom which, once excited, was never wholly lost, a quickening of the romantic motive in vernacular literature, something of Arabic medicine, chemistry and accountancy, a larger and more exact appreciation of the non-Christian world than had hitherto prevailed. Of geographical knowledge, either directly resulting from the Crusades or indirectly from the missionary journeys to the far east to which the Crusades gave rise, there was a notable increment. The task of government, too, was perhaps made easier by the diversion of many turbulent spirits upon this distant quest. What, however, of the Christian religion? Candour compels the admission that the main effect of this vast movement of adventure and piety, curiosity and greed, was not to bring Christ nearer to man but to found the commercial empire of Venice in the Levant.

BOOKS WHICH MAY BE CONSULTED

Sir Charles Oman: *A History of the Art of War in the Middle Ages.* 1924.

W. Heyd: *Histoire du Commerce du Levant au Moyen Age.* 1885.

O. Delarc: *Les Normands en Italie.* 1883.

C. H. Haskins: *The Normans in European History.* 1915.

H. Derenbourg: *Ousâma ibn Mourkidh: Un Emir Syrien au Premier Siècle des Croisades.* 1886.

J. Gay: *L'Italie Méridionale et l'Empire Byzantin (867-1071).* 1904.

G. Finlay: *History of Greece, B.C. 146 to A.D. 1004. Ed.* H. F. Tozer. 1877.

Cambridge Mediaeval History, Vol. IV.

F. Chalandon: *Histoire de la Domination Normande en Italie et en Sicile.* 1907.

Sir Steven Runciman: *History of the Crusades.* 3 vols. 1951-4.

R. Grousset: *Histoire des Croisades et du Royaume franc à Jerusalem.* 3 vols. 1934-6.

Cambridge Economic History of Europe, Vol. II. 1952.

CHAPTER XIX

FREDERICK BARBAROSSA

Blow to German unity through election of Lothair. Origin of feud between Guelph and Ghibelline. Frederick Barbarossa unites the rival factions, but makes no contribution to permanent German consolidation. His struggles with the Lombards and the Pope. His quarrel with Henry the Lion. A German federation based on respect for law alien to ideas of the time. Union of Germany and Sicily in 1186. Large ambitions and early death of Henry VI.

IT WAS no good omen for the stability of the German state when, upon the death of Henry V, Lothair of Supplinburg was placed upon the vacant throne. Four generations of Franconians had succeeded four generations of Saxons, the crown passing from father to son by election during the father's lifetime with the unbroken concurrence of prelates and princes. And then in 1125, when it might have been expected that the principle of hereditary succession would have taken root in the political soil, the opposite principle, which placed the disposal of the crown in the hands of the great chieftains, was emphatically affirmed. So strong did the current now continue to flow in favour of free election that in 1156 the Princes Electors are spoken of as a substantive and important body in the state.

A yet greater misfortune, first manifesting itself under Lothair but growing to most formidable proportions under his successor Conrad III, was the feud between the Welf and

Hohenstaufen families.[1] Of this historic quarrel which convulsed two nations and into which the most far-reaching issues of principle and policy were absorbed, the cause is no more dignified than the disappointed ambition of a south German clan. The Hohenstaufen were a powerful Swabian family who had good grounds for hoping that Henry V would be succeeded by the head of their house. In this hope they were bitterly disappointed. Lothair of Supplinburg, a Saxon united by friendship and afterwards by marriage with the influential family of Welf (or Guelf), was preferred to Frederick of Swabia, the near relative of the late king, the executor of his will, and the heir of his private estates. From such a decision Frederick of Hohenstaufen and his brother Conrad appealed to the arbitrament of arms. In pursuance of their ambition they did not scruple to involve their country in the familiar miseries of a civil war. Eventually, but not before every man, woman, and child in Augsburg had been destroyed, the king prevailed over the Hohenstaufen rebels. An interval of peace was procured, which, upon the death of Lothair, was followed by a renewal of the struggle. But now the parts were reversed. The Hohenstaufen were in power, the Welfs were in opposition, and it might seem that the resources at the disposal of the crown should have been sufficient to decide the issue. But if Conrad III was King of Germany, Henry the Proud was Duke of Saxony and Bavaria. What the king might do to abase the most powerful of his subjects, that Conrad endeavoured to contrive for the humiliation of Henry the Proud. He deprived him of Bavaria; he endeavoured to strip from him his duchy of Saxony. But there was an obstacle which Conrad, for all his Hohenstaufen *bravura*, could never overcome. The Saxon nation, which had little reason to love a Swabian, stood solid and staunch for the Welfs. Even when Henry the Proud suddenly died, leaving a lad of ten as his heir (*Henricus Leo, Dux Saxoniae et Bavariae*, as he afterwards styled himself), the people and princes of Saxony stood together to keep their duchy in the Welfic house. Conrad was compelled to acknowledge the unpalatable fact that his enemy was too strong to be broken and that only by a compromise peace, conceding Saxony but withholding Bavaria, could the country obtain relief from its domestic discords. The peace was struck (1142), but the

[1] Genealogical Table E.

animosities remained, casting a dark shadow over this unfortunate reign and threatening, unless some higher wisdom supervened, the disruption of the kingdom.

It was the great recommendation of Frederick Barbarossa, Conrad's nephew and successor, that his mother Judith was a Welf. With the blood of both factions running in his veins Frederick seemed marked out by destiny to bring the ruinous schism to an end. And this for a time he succeeded in doing, making friends with his cousin Henry the Lion and restoring to him the duchies of Saxony and Bavaria.

A chorus of praise surrounded the red-bearded king during his lifetime and has been echoed in tones of varying enthusiasm by subsequent historians. All the qualities most generally admired in the age of chivalry, courage, energy, good cheer, joy in battle, and love of adventure, the rough justice which goes with hearty common sense, and the geniality which accompanies superb physical health, belonged to Frederick. No German sovereign since Charlemagne possessed qualities so well fitted for the governance of the German people. He could both frighten and charm. Churchmen, nobles, peasants were prepared to regard him as the perfect knight.

To the modern mind it seems incredible that a ruler, succeeding to the government of a great country after a period of grave domestic struggles, should permit himself to be lured into distant enterprises of immense and unmeasured difficulty from which his subjects could not under any circumstances expect to derive a profit. But the German people did not then so reason. They were not disposed to blame a king who left his country to receive the imperial crown in Rome. To them the military expeditions of Frederick into Italy, costly as they were in blood and treasure, were no more reprehensible than the last quixotic crusading voyage undertaken in old age which led to the death of their sovereign in a distant Cilician stream. No German complained of Frederick that he governed too little. If in order to obtain assistance for his Italian wars he made reckless and extravagant concessions to the princes, setting up, for example, a duchy of Austria endowed with exorbitant privileges, no domestic critic raised a protest in the interests of central control. Frederick was the child of his age. If he moved in a mist of archaic romance, musing over Latin classics, fancying that he could revive the Roman Empire without the Roman legions, if he failed to appreciate the triple forces of the Lombard communes, the revived Papacy, and the Sicilian kingdom which were arrayed against him, he was not alone. The Germans, who would not have exchanged their brilliant knight-errant for the best organizer in the world, gave him their admiring confidence to the end.

In Italy the appearance of a German army was at no time regarded as an unmixed blessing. To Frederick it probably seemed a simple part of inherited duty that he should rescue the Pope from the newborn and violent republic of Rome, that he should receive the imperial crown, that he should put down his enemies and encourage his friends, and that he should recover for the Empire such fiscal rights as might have lapsed through the carelessness of his predecessor. But if he expected that these objects could be obtained easily and without resistance he was disillusioned on his first Roman journey. Then he learnt with what faint respect the republicans of Rome were prepared to treat the Emperor who had betrayed and the Pope who had burned Arnold of Brescia, their chosen leader. Hardly had the imperial coronation 1155 taken place when the German army was furiously attacked in the Leonine city and compelled to execute a retreat.

But it was during his second Italian visit that Frederick provoked the great struggle with the Lombard communes which, beginning with the decrees of the Diet of Roncaglia in 1158, lasted until at the Peace of Constance in 1183 the Emperor was in effect compelled to acknowledge defeat. It is the practice of writers zealous for Italian nationality to represent this famous contest as marking the first stage in the growth of Italian liberty. Certainly a fine spirit of heroism and determination was shown in the struggle not only by Milan, which was a populous city, but by many a small Italian town which faced the formidable engines of the imperial army. The mere fact that Frederick at the head of his German chivalry was in 1176 routed by the townsmen of Milan on the field of Legnano was a notification to Europe that a new age was approaching in which statesmen would have to reckon with the military power of a middle class. Moreover, it was a novelty that a large number of Italian cities should combine in a league and enter into relations, as did the Lombards, with the Pope, with Sicily, with Byzantines and Venetians. Such a combination, even had it been unsuccessful, would have furnished a striking illustration of the weight to be attached to urban communities in the politics of Europe. But it is a mistake to suppose that this long-drawn struggle was at the time regarded as a contest between the German and Italian nations. The Italians, many of whom, especially among the northern aristocracy, were still conscious of their German origin, were divided. Some towns stood for the Emperor, others for the Pope. Nor would it have been fair to urge that the claims put forward by Frederick were those of a German usurper. The jurists of Bologna had affirmed that what Frederick demanded of the communes at Roncaglia was due to him as the heir of the Roman Emperors.

Closely mingled with the war of the Lombard League was a quarrel with the Papacy hardly to be avoided so long as Hildebrandine ideas survived in the Roman Curia and a resolute German Emperor was desirous of governing in Italy. At bottom the issue was always the same, "Which was supreme, Pope or Emperor?" or, as it was apt to be put in the feudal language of that time, "Did the Emperor hold his office as a fief from the Pope?" It is the part of wisdom in politics to avoid asking the largest questions, but as soon as this ultimate issue was raised a swarm of minor differences on points of procedure, of administrative convenience, of current Church policy came to life, as flies in the summer heat. Was the Emperor bound to lead the Pope's palfrey and to hold his stirrup? Could he nominate bishops or despoil their sees on vacancies? Could he claim provender for his armies or hospitality for his legates? On the first principle the German princes were of one mind. When at the Council of Besançon in October, 1157, Cardinal Roland, the eminent canon lawyer, acting as legate for Pope Hadrian IV, asked from whom did the Emperor hold his Empire if not from the Pope, the rash ecclesiastic barely escaped with his life.

Two years later this same cardinal, being known for his strong papal views, and having been concerned in bringing about a friendship between the Curia and Sicily, was elected Pope by part of the college, and assumed the name of Alexander III. Other cardinals, either because they had been influenced by Germany or feared Roland and the Sicilians, elected the imperialist Cardinal Octavian, who took the name of Victor IV. Both Popes appealed to Frederick and by him were invited to submit their claims to a synod at Pavia.

And now Alexander III showed the world that the spirit of Hildebrand was still alive. He refused to attend the synod at Pavia. He declined to admit by his presence that the Emperor had any right to preside over a council of the Church or to dispose of the See of St. Peter. To the excommunication of the anti-pope, he replied by excommunicating the Emperor, by releasing his subjects from their allegiance, and by throwing himself upon the sympathy and hospitality of France.

The stars fought in their courses for this staunch and resourceful ecclesiastic. The Lombards rose against the oppressive German administration to which they had been submitted, with Venice, Sicily, Byzantium, and the Pope actively encouraging. The walls of Milan, which Frederick had razed to the ground, were rebuilt, the population which he had dispersed was recalled. Then in the critical summer of 1167 a crowning mercy was vouchsafed to the Church. Frederick had descended into Italy with a large army, determined to strike at the two nerve centres of rebellion, Rome, from which Alexander was now guiding his coalition, and Sicily, which nourished the movement with funds. At first fortune smiled on the imperialists. The Romans were heavily defeated; the German army stormed into St. Peter's; the Pope fled; the Emperor was crowned by his anti-pope. A Pisan fleet appearing in the Tiber announced the impending conquest of Sicily. But in the course of a few hours the August sun gave to Alexander an unexpected revenge. A sudden fever struck the German army. Alone and unarmed Frederick recrossed the Alps, leaving the flower of his chivalry dead and withered on the Roman plain.

From this blow of fate Frederick never recovered. The army which he brought into Italy upon his fourth expedition was too small to re-establish his authority over an enemy which had enjoyed seven years of respite from German attack. A small force of German knights went down before the numerous cavalry and pikemen of Milan upon the field of Legnano, and their leader, reading the omens aright, determined to treat with the Pope and to admit his claim. The meeting of Frederick and Alexander in Venice on July 24, 1177, is commemorated by three slabs of red marble in the porch of the cathedral of St. Mark's indicating the spot where the

Emperor knelt to the Pope and received the kiss of peace. The scene made a deep impression. Not only to the Venetian crowd on the piazza did it seem emblematic of the vanity of material force and of the triumph of the spiritual principle in human affairs. Yet in truth Frederick, while conceding no point of vital substance, had gained the great advantage of peace.

From the decisive field of Legnano there was one important absentee. For twenty-four years Henry the Lion had been permitted to govern his immense territories of Saxony and Bavaria without let or hindrance from the Emperor. But now a cloud of difference had arisen between the two men. Was it that Frederick had bought Welf estates in Tuscany and Bavaria which Henry coveted? Or that Henry was sated with Italian adventures and preferred to be left free to deal with his own difficult tasks in the north, where as a conspicuous tamer of Wendish heathendom he has left a mark on the life of those regions? Whatever the cause may be, Henry refused to help his sovereign, and Frederick in consequence suffered the bitterness of defeat.

From this open variance there followed after an interval of gathering hostility one result big with consequence for German history. There were among the clergy and princes of Saxony those who hated the imperious Lion and were waiting for an occasion to pull him to the ground. A pretext was found, a charge was levelled, but rather than appear before a hostile court, Henry resorted to civil war. Stern punishment followed upon his inevitable defeat and ultimate submission. He was banished the country, and save for the two cities of Brunswick and Luneburg stripped of his possessions. The great tribal duchies were shared among lesser men, one of whom, Otto of Wittelsbach, receiving part of Bavaria, founded a dynasty which lasted till the German Revolution of 1918.

A tear of American learning falls upon the grave of ducal Saxony. The vision of a German federal state, simple, orderly, based upon the great tribal duchies each duly conserving its customary law (*land recht* or state rights) and anticipating in the heart of mediaeval Europe the principles of the American republic, flatters the fancy of the transatlantic student. But such ideas were foreign to the age of the Lion and the Red-beard. The Lion was a great north German figure, honoured in the sunset of his life, when his fighting days were over and he was allowed to return from exile, as a patron of art and letters and as the builder of the great cathedral of St. Blaise which still enchants the visitor to Brunswick; but he was no more careful of the rights of others than were the enemies who combined to pull him down. Nor had Barbarossa, though his hand was heavy on malefactors, and his rule was distinguished for its penal legislation, a gift for creating institutions. When his brilliant figure left the stage it was seen that his long reign of stern repression and lavish gifts was but a disguised approach to feudal chaos.

A wonderful glamour shines upon Frederick's last stage in Europe through the marriage (January 27, 1186) of his son Henry to Constance, the heiress presumptive of the Sicilian kingdom. The rich and powerful island state which it had been the Emperor's dream to conquer by arms was now to pass into the Hohenstaufen family on the easy terms of a marriage contract. Here, unexpectedly emerging from the diplomatic heaven, was the answer to the humiliations which Frederick had endured at the hands of the Romans and the Lombards, the Venetians and the Pope. Master of Germany in the north with its warlike feudal nobility, and of Sicily with its full treasury, its powerful fleet, its well-schooled Saracen army, the next Emperor would be well placed for imposing his will on refractory Popes and communes. But the very considerations which arrayed this conjunction in colours so pleasing to the Hohenstaufen made it a vital concern for the Papacy that their dynasty should be destroyed. The struggle once engaged was long and bitter. The Popes achieved their end. The offending dynasty was uprooted. But the cost of victory was a subservience to France which led through the Avignon captivity to an incalculable decline in papal prestige and so on to the Protestant Reformation.

The union of two countries so distinctive as Germany and Sicily, and divided from one another by the whole length of the Italian peninsula, presented a new range of difficult problems to the statesman. In Sicily the monarchy was hereditary, in Germany it was elective. In Sicily the King had acknowledged the Pope as his feudal superior; in Germany the claim of the Pope to be the feudal superior of the Emperor was hotly repudiated. It was now the established prerogative of the Archbishop of Cologne to crown the King of Germany. The Sicilian King was crowned by the Archbishop of Palermo. If it were deeply distasteful to the Sicilians to submit to a German sovereign, it was equally offensive to German pride to reflect that a time might come when their king might prefer the palms and orange groves at Palermo to the temperate climate of Aachen or Cologne, when the affairs of the Empire might be conducted by Saracens or Greeks, Englishmen or eunuchs, and German interests fatally postponed to those of a distant island.

That many of these difficulties were present to the acute intelligence of Henry VI is clear from some remarkable proposals which he made to the princes of Germany and to Pope Celestine III. His plan was that princes and Pope should agree to confer upon the Hohenstaufen dynasty an hereditary right to the German throne and that the Pope should crown his infant son Frederick King of the Romans. In return for these favours he proffered concessions—to the lay princes of Germany that their fiefs should be hereditary in the female and collateral line; to the prelates the renunciation of the *fas spolii*; and to the Pope, most important of all, an acknowledgment that the Empire was held as a fief from the Vicar of Christ. The rejection of this bold plan by princes and Pope effectually destroyed the project of an indissoluble union of the German and Sicilian crowns.

The historian is at once attracted and repelled by this hard and crafty son of the Red Beard who passed with his contemporaries as a scholar and died in 1197 after only seven years of rule, having already done many things that were wise, as well as others that were base and cruel, and who seems both in the scale of his ambitions and the novelty of his expedients to belong to the rank of creative politicians. But what principally matters in the context of events is not Henry's conquest of Sicily and designed conquest of Constantinople, nor his pacification of the Welfs, nor the meanness with which he exploited the captivity of Richard I to get money and power, nor that he sought the friendship of the Pope and planned a Crusade, but that he died young, leaving an infant to succeed him. During the long minority of Frederick II the political complexion of the world was profoundly altered.

BOOKS WHICH MAY BE CONSULTED

Cambridge Mediaeval History, Vol. V.
E. A. Freeman: *Historical Essays*. (*Frederick Barbarossa*.) 1892.
W. von Giesebrecht: *Geschichte der deutschen Kaiserzeit*. 1881-8.
Gregorovius: *History of Rome in the Middle Ages*. Tr. A. Hamilton. 1894-1900.
F. W. Thompson: *Feudal Germany*. 1928.
T. F. Tout: *The Empire and the Papacy*. 1903.
W. Stubbs: *Germany in the Early Middle Ages*. Ed. A. Hassall. 1908.
A. L. Poole: *Henry the Lion*. *Lothian Historical Essay*. 1912.
G. Tellenbach: *Church, State and Christian Society at the Time of, the Investiture Contest*. Tr. R. F. Bennett. 1948.
F. Kern: *Kingship and Law in the Middle Ages*. Tr. S. B. Chrimes. 1939.
Z. N. Brooke: *A History of Europe, 911-1198*. 1938.

CHAPTER XX

INTELLECTUAL
AND MONASTIC MOVEMENTS

Renaissance in the twelfth century. Medical studies at Salerno. Revival of Roman Law. English Common Law. Universities of Bologna and Paris. Origins of Oxford. Mediaeval university movements. The Monasteries.

WHILE THE Crusades were thus powerfully affecting commerce and policy, another change, more profound in its effects, was coming over the intellectual life of western Europe. The twelfth century witnessed a renaissance of the European mind which, though more contracted in scope, is comparable in energy and creativeness with that great enlargement of custom and taste which divides the modern from the mediaeval world. The study of law and medicine, of logic and theology, received a new and powerful impetus. As conditions became more settled, travelling more secure, and the superfluities of life more easy to obtain, the thirst for knowledge,

which is one of the primal appetites of man, began to assert
itself afresh. Wandering students ranging from boys in their
teens to grey-haired men might be seen on the roads travelling
to such centres as were known to be distinguished by the
presence of attractive teachers. Guilds were formed of
learners as at Bologna, of instructors as at Paris, and after
the manner of their kind evolved a body of rules and regulations for their guidance. From such associations arose the
University, an institution which some mediaeval writers did
not scruple to rank with the Papacy and Empire as an
international force appointed by God for the direction and
improvement of mankind.

It is a paradox that Italy, the seat of the Papacy, has been
of all western countries throughout history the most secular.
In contradistinction to the universities of the north, which
grew up out of cathedral schools and developed their principal
activities in the sphere of philosophical theology, the universities of Italy were founded by secular agencies and were
mainly, though not exclusively, concerned with the prosecution
of secular studies. The ancient University of Salerno was
famous for a body of medical teaching based upon the writings
of Hippocrates and Galen and the later experience of Jewish
medical science. We may smile at this mediaeval medicine.
It was devoid of the faintest knowledge of experimental
anatomy. It was combined with astrology. It was prefaced
by a careful study of the writings of Aristotle. Yet this is the
principal root from which the science of the Renaissance was
destined to grow. Nor can all value be denied to a course
of training which gave to Dante his profound knowledge of
Aristotelian philosophy and to Galileo his epoch-making
interest in the stars.

More important in its immediate results was the revived
study of Roman law (not that in Italy such learning had ever
been allowed to die out) which is traced to the teaching of
Irnerius during the early years of the twelfth century. The
mediaeval expositions of the Digest, though characterized by
learning and subtlety, were hardly more scientific, since they
were devoid of historical background, than the contemporary
science of the human body. Yet of all the intellectual influences affecting the politics and society of that time Roman
jurisprudence was the most powerful, not only by reason of
the infusion of its principles into the developing science of the

canonist, not only by reason of the improvement which it was the means of introducing into the legal customs of Germany and France, but also because it was an arsenal of autocratic maxims. The great jurists of Bologna did not scruple to apply to the office of the Holy Roman Emperor the high prerogative which the lawyers of a long past age had ascribed to Diocletian or Constantine. In the struggle between the Empire and the Papacy the civilian lent the weight of his learning to the support of the imperial cause; nor was there a sovereign in Europe who was not prepared upon occasion to have recourse to those convenient maxims of absolute power which the learned doctors of the civil law were always so ready to supply.

There was, however, one striking limitation to the influence of this imposing system of jurisprudence. In England the teaching of practising lawyers was carried on, not at the universities, where both the Civil and the Canon Law were taught, but at professional schools, known as the Inns of Court, which were first set up in London in the reigns of the Edwards. To this circumstance we may principally ascribe the fact that the Common Law of England not only preserved its substantive existence, but was upon the whole a force making for liberty rather than for absolutism.

The University of Bologna, which in the twelfth century became pre-eminent as a law school, was managed by a guild of students, who hired the teachers, often failing to pay them their wages, and reduced them, in Dr. Rashdall's words, "to a most humiliating degree of servitude." "The professor," continues Dr. Rashdall, "was fined if he was a minute late for lectures, if he went beyond the time for closing, if he skipped a difficult passage or failed to get through in a given time the portions of the law-texts provided by the University. A committee of students — the *denunciatores doctorum*— watched over his conduct and kept the rectors informed of his irregularities. If the doctor wanted to be married a single day of absence was graciously allowed him but no honeymoon." From this iron and niggardly discipline the University was eventually rescued by the intervention of the city. Salaried chairs were established for professors chosen by the city, who being regularly and sufficiently paid came in time to monopolize the teaching. The civic university became popular in the prevailing secular atmosphere of Italy. By the end of the middle ages few considerable Italian states could afford to dispense with it.

Very different was the character and organization of the great University of Paris, which provided a model for the universities of the north. Here the prevailing study was not law but theology, the directing authority a guild not of students but of teachers. Originating from the cathedral school and subsisting under the shadow of the cathedral, the "Universitas" or guild of Paris masters was long treated with suspicion as an unlawful society, conspiring to undermine the authority of the bishop, his chancellor, and the chapter. For this suspicion some warrant may perhaps be found in the wild ferment of opinion which was excited by the free and fiery dialectic of Peter Abelard, the great Breton teacher (1079-1142), who first established the fame and popularity of Paris as a centre of thought and enquiry.

In truth, however, the orthodox Church had little to fear in that age from the speculations of academic philosophers. The voice of an isolated heretic was soon silenced in the lifetime of St. Bernard. Abelard was driven to recantation and a monastery, and when in the middle of the thirteenth century all the works of Aristotle were made available for study in the west, this immense mass of ancient thought and knowledge was by a long process of devout and laborious gymnastic wrought into an exact and authoritative confirmation of the Catholic Faith.

Oxford derives from Paris, Cambridge from Oxford. If we would recall the turbulent life of those early gatherings of students and teachers out of which our universities arose, we must exclude from our field of vision the imposing buildings, the colleges, the libraries, the lecture rooms which now give to a university its fixity in space. The student of the twelfth century was like the Crusader, a pilgrim, travelling light and travelling often in quest of the Holy Grail of knowledge. Since there were no endowments to chain him to a particular place, since teaching was oral, and Latin the common language of the clerk all over the western world, teachers and pupils alike would wander from town to town and country to country. Sometimes they would voyage singly, sometimes in small groups, and sometimes, at the command of a sovereign or in a movement of protest or indignation, just as a modern trades union strikes against an employer, they would transfer themselves in large droves. Not seldom such a migration was the seed of a new university.

Such, at least, appears to have been the case at Oxford, though the evidence is not altogether complete. We know that in 1167-1168 a large body of English teachers and students were brought back from Paris by order of King Henry II as a result of his quarrel with the King of France; and it is clear that when later, in 1185, Giraldus Cambrensis read his *Topographia Hibernica* in Oxford there was already present in the city that organized body of teachers which is the sign of a *studium generale* or university. We have no direct evidence that the teachers and scholars who were brought back to England from Paris settled in Oxford. Yet it is probable that they did so and that the close and remarkable correspondence between the organization of the Universities of Oxford and Paris was due to this cause. Oxford, like Paris, was under the control of a bishop's chancellor, like Paris was originally organized in four nations with four proctors, and in time, like Paris, developed a system of residential colleges. Both universities were pre-eminent in scholastic philosophy and attractive to students from every part of Europe.

Compared with these two giants in the intellectual life of mediaeval Europe, Cambridge, founded by a secession from Oxford in 1209, and even Orleans and Montpellier, the one renowned for law and the other for medicine, were of secondary importance.

In the ancient world culture and high birth went together. It was the grave misfortune of Europe in the middle ages that these two qualities admired of man were sharply dissociated. The business of the knight was to fight and hunt; the duty of the clerk was to pray and learn. The universities of the middle ages were not designed to civilize the fierce aristocracies into whose hands the conduct of European affairs was consigned as a consequence of the barbaric invasions. Rather they were the result of a spontaneous popular movement carried out under the shelter and direction of the Church and partly as a response to the growing need for doctors, lawyers, and an educated clergy. With all this clerkly hum and bustle, this busy talk about the real and the nominal, universal and particular, the fighting and hunting nobleman had little to do. The students who flocked in their thousands to the universities came, as they have always mainly come, from the middle and lower ranges of society. The poor and ambitious saw in the university a free career to talent. But how many endured to the end of the long course of five or six years in the arts and of twelve or thirteen years in theology which were required for graduation? The failed M.A.'s and D.D.'s of mediaeval Europe must have been almost as numerous as the failed B.A.'s of Calcutta University. Yet something was gained. A thin layer of education, a smattering of Latin and logic was widely spread.

Moreover, the university movement had the virtue of a steady growth in recognized importance and volume. It became the theory that it was the special and, indeed, sole privilege of the Pope or the Emperor to grant the *jus ubique docendi* which was asserted to be the hallmark of a *studium generale* or university. The age of apostolic poverty was succeeded by the age of lavish endowments. In 1252 Robert de Sorbon, the chaplain of Louis IX, founded the first of the sixty colleges which in the middle ages were built for the reception of university students in Paris. A few years later his example was followed by Walter de Merton at Oxford. The visitor to Paris may still see on the left bank of the Seine the Rue de Fouarre where Dante may have heard lectures. He may still enter the curious little Church of St. Julien le Pauvre where the first Masters of Arts of the Paris University used to hold their meetings. But only a name attached to an uncouth modern building recalls the memory of the Sorbonne, and of the sixty mediaeval colleges of Paris not a stone remains. England has been more fortunate, and in the splendid collegiate foundations at Oxford and Cambridge preserves a memorial of the munificence and piety of a vanished age.

The European monasteries of the middle ages were often criticized and often reformed. In the west, Order followed upon Order, Chartreux after Cluny, Cîteaux after Chartreux, Prémontré after Cîteaux, but always with the same tale of high initial ardour and enthusiasm giving place to spells of laxity and imperfection. Yet the possible loss to society through the enforced celibacy of many of the best men and women in every generation was never a matter of comment in an age which regarded celibacy as the first and the hardest of the human virtues. Particular monasteries were assailed, now on grounds of moral scandal, now as hard and grasping landlords. To no one since Rutilius Namatianus in the fifth century did it occur to dispute the value of the monastic life or to regard it as squalid and degrading to man.

The reason is clear. Apart from the shelter which they afforded to devout and peace-loving natures against the rough gales of mediaeval life, the monasteries rendered services which we have now either ceased to require or can obtain more efficiently from other sources. In many cases the monastery was a missionary establishment, sometimes a bank of deposit, a hostelry for the refreshment of wayfarers, an improving landlord, a centre of education and scholarship, as well as of these arts and crafts which are enlisted in the conduct of any great establishment, a collector and recorder of current news, a storehouse of manuscripts, a depository of political knowledge, foreign and domestic, an organ for the reclamation of waste land and for the planting of civilization in barbarous and pagan tracts. The services performed by the great German monasteries of Fulda and Corvey or by the Cistercian monks in Spain and northern England were of this pioneering character. They were at once missionaries, educators, and landlords. The expansion of civilized life in these regions is not a little due to the powerful and often ruthless impulsion of these organized bodies of dedicated men.

We owe much of our knowledge of the early middle ages to Latin chronicles compiled by monks. After the beginning of the thirteenth century historical writing escapes from the cloister and laymen begin to describe in the vernacular language the things which they have seen and the persons whom they have met. We have Villehardouin's sparkling history of the Fourth Crusade and Joinville's exquisite Life of St. Louis, and later the flowing chronicles of Froissart the Fleming and of Villani the Florentine. With the fourteenth century, too, we may dip into the English year-books or legal records and there come across a store, unexampled in volume, of the authentic talk of English litigants in the provincial French which was then the language of the law courts. But the chronicling of the age which lies between the barbaric invasions and the rise of the universities in the later half of the twelfth century was left mainly to the monks. Then the *scriptorium* of the abbey was the only secure centre for literary work and the monkish scribe the chief pillar of learning. If much of his work was poor, scanty, and unintelligent, some chronicles were vivacious and well informed, and here and there the monasteries produced a real historian. Posterity must not repudiate its debt to the mediaeval monasteries, to Monte Casino and Bobbio, to Reichenau and St. Gall, to Corvey and Fulda, to Bec and Mont St. Michel, to Jarrow and later to St. Albans. Much of our scholarship, not a little of our historical knowledge, is founded on the diligence of scribes, many of them nameless, who have toiled over crabbed manuscripts by a feeble rushlight in unwarmed cells in the hope that the labour of their pens might be acceptable to the Lord.

And now Europe has passed into a stage of civilization in which abbeys, while they may still live and function, are differently related to the facts of the age. No longer is the endowment of an abbey by prince or noble regarded as a short and simple road to the soul's salvation. No longer do men go to the abbey for news, for they have the daily press and the wireless; no longer for refreshment and shelter, for there is the inn and the casual ward. The task of education is performed by the universities and schools. Gone, too, is the function of the *scriptorium*, for the printing press multiplies books and the libraries store them; and gone the ministration of charitable relief. Long ago the temporal rulers have turned elsewhere for political counsel. It is with difficulty that the traveller, as he surveys the shell of some ancient abbey, standing ruined and forlorn among the sweet English pastures, can recapture in imagination the distant hours of monastic influence when in a society much simpler than our own and for a population less numerous the abbey was a busy centre of social life and its strongest link with the great world beyond.

Modern society is more willing to avail itself of the gratuitous social service rendered by nuns. In Catholic countries religious sisterhoods still perform much of the humanitarian work which was expected of them in mediaeval times. They nurse the sick, tend the poor, teach the young, console the dying. The education of girls is largely in their hands. That which was purest and best in mediaeval monasticism survives in these devoted women.

BOOKS WHICH MAY BE CONSULTED

R. L. Poole: *Illustrations of the History of Mediaeval Thought and Learning*. 1920.

C. Mallet: *History of the University of Oxford*. 1924.

J. B. Mullinger: *The University of Cambridge from the Earliest Times*, 1873-84.

C. H. Haskins: *Studies in Mediaeval Culture*. 1929.

C. H. Haskins: *The Renaissance of the Twelfth Century*. 1927.

Helen Waddell: *The Wandering Scholars*. 1927.

G. G. Coulton: *Monastic Schools in the Middle Ages*. 1913.

G. G. Coulton: *Five Centuries of Religion*. 1923-7.

G. G. Coulton: *Mediaeval Studies*. 1905-21.

G. G. Coulton: *The Mediaeval Scene*. 1930.

H. Rashdall: *Universities of Europe in the Middle Ages*. Ed. Powicke and Emden. 3 vols. 1936.

D. Knowles: *The Monastic Order in England*, 943-1216. 1940.

R. W. Southern: *The Making of the Middle Ages*. 1953.

CHAPTER XXI

MUNICIPAL GROWTH

Growth and emancipation of towns. Civic feuds. Growth of commerce. Differing municipal development in different parts of Europe. The German Hanse and the Scandinavian countries.

BY THE beginning of the twelfth century the trade and industry of western Europe had sufficiently recovered from the interruption caused by the Saracens to permit of a sensible growth in municipal liberties. The great historic cities of the Roman Empire, whose population had been depleted through the destruction of sea-borne commerce, began to recover something of their former numbers and affluence. Villages grew into walled towns. Suburbs of merchants and craftsmen spread themselves round castle or borough. In France we hear of *villeneuves, sauvetés, bastides*, names which denote the movement towards new urban aggregations which was proceeding through the country. From such developments followed two

consequences of great importance. The merchants and craftsmen organized themselves in guilds and began to demand
conditions under which money could be safely made. In
broad outline they claimed to be permitted to compound for
their own farm or taxes (the *firma burgi*), to be permitted to
make their own bye-laws, to be relieved of onerous feudal
servitudes, to have their civil suits tried in their own courts
and within their own walls, to be able to select their own
officers, and that serfs resident for a year and a day within
a town or borough should be regarded as free. Such is a
rough epitome of the liberties and privileges which with
infinite varieties of detail and liberality are to be found inscribed in the town charters of the twelfth century. It is less
important to consider by what means such charters were
obtained, whether as at Laon by a revolutionary struggle or
as in London by a monetary transaction or by a peaceful
process of permitted growth, than to note the point that in
some way or other all the large and most of the small towns
in Europe had by the end of the twelfth century obtained a
position of special privilege. At one end of the scale were
urban republics, such as Venice or Marseilles and to a
slightly lesser degree London: at the other end little country
towns which had obtained no more than the right to compound for their taxes.

Man is an imitative animal. The privileges liberally accorded
to one city were soon demanded by others less plentifully
endowed; and the third estate, once it had arrived and had
begun to organize its forces, steadily grew in power and
influence.

Being small and insecure (London, a Leviathan among our
English cities, can hardly have numbered more than twenty
thousand inhabitants), mediaeval towns were everywhere
fortified and organized for defence. M. Pirenne, writing more
particularly of the Low Countries, tells us that up to the close
of the middle ages a sum never falling short of five-eighths
of the communal budget was expended on purposes connected
with the maintenance of the walls and the provision of instruments of war. In Italy, despite the fact that she was now fast
securing for herself the leadership of the world in craftsmanship and international commerce, the warfare of city with
city was almost perpetual. Cities would fight about diocesan
boundaries and feudal rights, over tolls and markets, for the

extension of their powers over the *contado* or surrounding country, or in pursuance of the long-inherited feuds of the nobles within their walls. Mere contiguity was a potent cause of fiery and enduring hatreds. If Florence took one side in a quarrel, it was sufficient for Pisa, Siena, and Genoa to take the other; if Milan entered into an alliance with other cities, it would not at least be with Cremona and Pavia; and so long as the exploitation of Corsica and Sardinia was an open question between them, Genoa and Pisa were inveterate in rivalry. Accordingly no large principle of policy decided the alignment of the Italian cities in the great quarrel between Empire and Papacy. Since Florence was papal or Guelf, her neighbour Siena was naturally imperialist or Ghibelline; since Cremona was Ghibelline, Crema must be Guelf. The quarrel between the Empire and the Papacy enlisted, but did not create, the civic feuds of Italy. These animosities, the vendetta of the *consorzeria* or Lombard clan, the feud of aggrandisement and commercial jealousy, the feud arising out of personal slights, were active all over Italy before that universal issue was raised. The great political struggle of the middle ages only gave a new colour and intensity to rivalries already so sharp and warlike that in every city the inhabitants were organized as a militia of horse and foot.

Nevertheless trade and industry made steady progress. In the government arsenals of Venice and Genoa fleets were built for military and commercial purposes upon a scale and with a rapidity which would have astounded the generation that preceded the First Crusade. A constant stream of merchants from every corner of western Europe found their way to the six fairs of Champagne which by the middle of the twelfth century had established themselves as the chief northern centres for the exchange of goods and the settlement of international debts. The Charter of St. Omer in 1127, the first of a long series, marks the rising affluence of the Flemish towns. The wool of England, the cloth of Frisia, the fustians of Augsburg, the silks of Paris were beginning to obtain their international renown. Though the science of political economy was still in the far distance, the Counts of Flanders were shrewd enough to discern the value of a fixed coinage and a single standard of weights and measures. Ghent and Bruges, Cologne and Hamburg were rising into prominence. Lübeck was founded in 1143. Even to an Italian visitor the wealth and importance of the city magnates in London seemed in the reign of Stephen to be imposing. The Danube and the Rhine, the Rhone and the Seine were bringing the civilized world into a commercial relationship. The outlines of the European economic system, as it persisted until the discovery of America, were now fixed.

Very various was the ultimate fate of the cities of Europe, which in the twelfth century, thanks to the principles of self-help and free association, were making such progress in the arts of life. It was the destiny of the English boroughs to be incorporated in a national parliamentary system which, while it limited their independence, enlarged their usefulness. In France the communal movement, born of revolution, ended in royal control. But in Germany and Italy a strong central government was lacking. Here there was no monarch to control, no parliament to canalize and direct the manifold energies of urban life. It is accordingly in these two countries that the power and autonomy of the mediaeval city are most conspicuously illustrated, that cities grow into imperial states, form leagues for commerce and war, and are capable of subjecting the Emperor himself to a decisive defeat. And who, when he considers the variety and brilliance of Italian city life or the vigorous contribution of the Hanseatic League to the commerce and architecture of northern Germany, will be prepared to say that the breakdown of central government was in these regions an unmixed misfortune for the human race?

The flowering time of the Hanseatic League lies in the fourteenth century, before the discovery of the New World had revolutionized the commerce of Europe or the English had developed a mercantile marine, and while the dominant merchant guilds in the Baltic cities were as yet unshaken by mutiny from below. Then a golden opportunity to become the common carrier of the north was spread before the German trader. While the Edwards were ruling in England, many a North German merchant throve on the carriage of wool and cloth, of corn and wine, of fabrics and furs for the wealthy or of pickled herring for all the world. Indeed long before the century had begun, the "Easterling" was a well-known figure in London, so affluent and long established in the *Hans* house or Guild Hall and so important as a factor in the foreign trade of the island, that Easterling in its shortened form of sterling came to denote the standard coin of the British realm.

Not that business in those days was a safe and easy matter for the North German trader. There were pirates on the high seas, bandits and toll-exacting nobles on the roads. More particularly there was the windy peninsula of Denmark, always an uncomfortable blot on the German landscape, since it controlled the Sound which is the channel between the North Sea and the Baltic, and was therefore in a position to work much mischief among the fishing fleets or trading vessels of the mainland. How best to handle these troublesome Danes, to secure privileges for German factories in the Scandinavian countries and in England, or to safeguard German fishing and commerce, were problems too difficult for any one city to solve for itself. Self-help and combination were imperative, for the Emperor was distant and powerless, and the Saxon house which had once been great had gone down with Henry the Lion. At last the great mercantile oligarchies listened to the call of circumstance. There was a union between Lübeck and Hamburg which was by degrees so widened out that every important northern town from Novgorod to Bruges was included within its orbit. It was a league of merchants. No noble or craftsman exercised power in these trading republics, nor did any man of high political genius emerge from their parliaments. The merchants of the Hanse were only by accident politicians. There is no reason to think that they ever contemplated the onerous burden of a permanent federation for the political control of the Baltic. It was sufficient if, meeting at irregular times and with varying numbers, they were able to deal with the pressing commercial problems of the moment. Once only did the Hanseatic traders, coming into sharp collision with a tiresome Danish king, threaten to play a decisive part in the politics of the north. The two wars of the League with Waldemar III are famous in Hanseatic annals. The Treaty of Stralsund (1370), which gave to the victorious merchant republics the control of the Sound and the fisheries and a voice in the selection of the Danish King, appeared to point to the establishment of a traders' empire on the Baltic. Lübeck, wrote Aeneas Sylvius, a gifted Italian traveller, in 1458, "possesses such wealth and such power that Denmark, Sweden, and Norway are accustomed to elect and depose kings upon a sign from her."

Bergen

Novgorod

Riga

Drina

Danzig

King's
Lynn

London

Brugges

Amsterdam

Hamburg

Magdeburg

Elbe

Antwerp

Cologne

Visula

Mainz

Troyes

Basle

Nuremberg

Augsburg

Lyons

Rhine

Chur

Innsbruck

Danube

Milan

Venice

Marseilles

Genoa

Constantinople

English Miles.

0   100 200 300 400 500 600

Alexandria

THE TRADE ROUTES OF

THE MIDDLE AGES

Nothing great came of it. The Hanse produced no Robert Clive. The temperature of co-operation in mediaeval Germany could nowhere and at no time be kept at a steady and effective level.

During the later half of the fifteenth century the League began slowly to decline in power and influence. The herrings, turning their dainty noses from the Baltic to the British coast, provided a gainful livelihood for generation after generation to English and Scottish fishermen. The Easterling was ousted from the British carrying trade. As the century advanced political development assumed a shape which was unfavourable to the "general company of Germ an merchants." The prince out-topped the city. Loyalty to the territorial sovereign proved to be more potent than attachment to a league of merchant towns which, while they had several common interests, were always in the last resort rivals in trade. Brandenburg, Burgundy, Sweden, in their separate spheres of territorial influence, overshadowed the League. By the end of the century the cities on the inland seas had had their day.

To all this mediaeval development of North German trade, the Scandinavian kingdoms, had they been linked in a durable union, might have offered a serious counterpoise. But when has there been a real Scandinavia? Even when Denmark, Sweden, and Norway were brought together under the Danish Crown at the Union of Kalmar (1397-1523) Danish rule was never effectual or uncontested in Sweden. At last the yoke was violently thrown off, in circumstances calculated to brand deeply upon the popular mind of Sweden a horror of the Danes. "The blood bath of Stockholm" contrived by King Christian II (of that German house of O denburg which had ruled in Copenhagen since 1448) was the attempt of a hasty tyrant to found by the pitiless massacre of his enemies a government which was lacking in every element of popular confidence and esteem. The crime was speedily avenged. A young Swede came forward to rally the peasants of his native land against the alien. His name was Gustav Eriksson and he was afterwards known as Gustavus Vasa. The war of liberation (1520-1523) led by this Swedish counterpart of William Wallace of Scotland gave to Sweden a national dynasty and ushered in the heroic period of her history.

BOOKS WHICH MAY BE CONSULTED

W. J. Ashley: *Economic Organisation of England.* 1914.
H. Pirenne: *Mediaeval Cities, their Origin and the Revival of Trade.* Tr. H. P. Halsey. 1925.
C. Cross: *The Gild Merchant.* 1890.
H. Zimmern: *The Hansa Towns.* 1889.
R. Lodge: *The Close of the Middle Ages.* 1923.
D. Schaefer: *Die Hanse.* 1903.
H. Pirenne: *Histoire de Belgique.* 1909.
J. C. L. Sismondi: *History of the Italian Republics.* (Everyman's Library.) 1907.
F. L. Ganshof: *Développement des Villes entre Loire et Rhin au Moyen Age.* 1943.

CHAPTER XXII

THE PONTIFICATE OF INNOCENT III

Zenith of the papal power under Innocent III. The evangelical revival. St. Francis. Challenge to the Papacy from the Albigenses. St. Dominic. Franciscans and Dominicans. The heresies of Joachim of Flora and Siger of Brabant. The Church masters its critics.

As WE cross the threshold of the thirteenth century the dream of world dominion, which had died with an Emperor, springs to life again in the policy of a Pope. We come to Innocent III, the proud Roman patrician and trained canonist, who, reaching the Papal Chair at the early age of thirty-seven years and profiting by a temporary eclipse of the Empire, brought the Papacy to the summit of its power. This is the Pope under whose rule the western Church was imposed on Constantinople, who dared to place England and France under interdict, who launched the most successful of the Spanish Crusades, who exacted from the rulers of England, Aragon, and Portugal the surrender of their respective countries as fiefs to be held of the Holy See, and did not scruple first to ex-

communicate King John, and then, when the culprit had
made an abject submission, to set aside the Magna Carta
and to excommunicate the barons by whom it was supported.
It was this energetic ruler who cleared the Germans out of
central Italy and Sicily, made himself master of Rome, preserved against dangerous opposition the Sicilian inheritance
of his ward, the child Frederick, fomented a terrible civil
war in Germany, and then made and unmade Emperors
on terms most favourable to the Roman Church, and lastly
crushed out the formidable Albigensian heresy in southern
France, and with it the civilization of a brilliant people.

The bare catalogue of these wide-ranging temporal activities
suggests a theocracy tyrannically worked and slavishly
accepted. Such an inference, however, would be false to
history. There was indeed no limit to the claims which
Innocent was prepared to make on behalf of his exalted
office. It was his view that the Pope was the Vicar of Christ,
that he was as Melchisedec, prince and king in one, that he
had the "plenitudo potestatis," and that he had the right,
seeing that a Pope had transferred the Empire from the Greeks
to the Franks, to exercise his own discretion in the choice of
emperors. But to the contemporaries of Innocent there was
nothing outrageous or tyrannical in these opinions. It was
common ground that the spiritual was above the temporal
power, that the Pope was supreme Head of the church and
the ultimate authority on all matters of faith and ecclesiastical
discipline. That he could excommunicate a sovereign, that
he could shake the basis of social order in a state by releasing
its citizens from their allegiance, or impose upon it the extreme penalty of the interdict was not denied. The men of
the thirteenth century were agreed on the principle of a seat
of authority in religion, a supreme spiritual arbiter in temporal
affairs, an institution professing the rule of sanctity and justice,
an ultimate tribunal before which they might lay their causes.
The great multiplication of appeals to the Papal Curia under
Innocent III is proof that the Roman Court met the needs of
the time. Against all manner of local tyrannies and oppressions there was in the last resort an appeal to Rome.

Yet under this apparent concord there was much variety
of belief and experience. The middle ages were neither so
virtuous, nor so orthodox, nor so stupid as is often supposed.
There was bestial immorality as well as stern asceticism,

fantastic heresy as well as compliant acceptance of the orthodox faith, and an intellectual ingenuity which, had it been
directed to the cross-examination of nature, would have
anticipated by many centuries the benefits of modern science.

The problem before the Papacy in the thirteenth century was
how best to control a society greatly enriched in its experience
through the Crusades, more travelled, more acquisitive,
more pleasure-loving, but also, partly by reason of this
opening-out of the near eastern world and the tumultuous
development of lay interests which followed in its train, and
partly owing to the revival of intellectual life, more disturbed
in its beliefs.   The pontificate of Innocent III corresponds
with a brilliant development of vernacular poetry in Germany
and France; a poetry owing its impulses no doubt to the
romance of the Crusaders, though its greatest themes are
found in earlier history, and giving ideal expression to the
sentiments of chivalry which then prevailed in the lay world.

It is during these years that the Minnesingers of Germany
and the troubadours of Provence produced some of their best
work, that Wulfram of Eschenbach wrote Parsifal, that
Gottfried of Strasburg wrote Tristan and Isolde, and that the
spirit of far-off German history is recaptured in the great
epic of the Niebelungenlied.

The expression of the lay spirit in vernacular literature was
one aspect of the sense of liberation which was now coming
into Europe. An evangelical revival was another, a strong
development of positive heresy was a third.

The evangelical revival, which starts with St. Francis of
Assisi and St. Dominic the Castilian, was one of those profound and sacrificial movements of the heart, which long
after its original purity of intention and practice has disappeared, continues to affect the lives of men. St. Francis,
the son of a rich cloth merchant in a small Umbrian town,
was born in 1181 or 1182. As a youth he was gay, careless,
open-handed, in love with chivalry and ambitious of a soldier's
career. Then he experienced a conversion. An illness contracted in prison in Perugia (for he was captured by the
forces of that neighbouring town in a skirmish) brought out
the latent powers of an original religious genius, so loving,
naïf, delicate and gay, so swift and instinctive in its response
to suffering, so full of chivalry and poetic symbolism that
it provides the sovereign charm which unites Christians of

all denominations. One day meeting a leper he dismounted from his horse and kissed him. Later a voice ordered him to repair a ruined chapel near Assisi. He became a hermit, broke with his family, and lived on alms, rebuilding with his own hands the deserted chapels in the neighbourhood. Then on February 24, 1208, he heard the lesson of the day in the church of Portiuncula (Matt. x.): "As ye go, preach, saying, The kingdom of heaven is at hand. Heal the sick, cleanse the lepers, raise the dead, cast out devils: freely ye have received, freely give. Provide neither gold, nor silver, nor brass in your purses, nor scrip for your journey, neither two coats, neither shoes, nor yet staves: for the workman is worthy of his hire." The words struck home. Barefoot he went out into the world to preach repentance.

The religious prospect was troubled and uncertain. The great monastic foundations of the twelfth century, Grammont, Clairvaux, Prémontré, once the early fervour had died away, had settled down to the management of their estates, the sale of their wool, and the discharge of the multifarious responsibilities which worldly endowments bring in their train.

The most powerful of the Popes was carrying out a great secular design, not without much effusion of blood. The contrast between primitive Christianity and the Church as it had become, rich, secure, worldly, ambitious, affected many minds. Prophecies floated about that a new age was at hand, an age of love, dominated by the Holy Ghost in succession to the past dispensation of law and of grace. Heresies were springing up among poor, unlearned folk—there were said to be seventeen heretical sects in Milan—by way of protest against sacerdotal claims and even against matter itself, thought to be the creation of the evil principle. Italy, racked by civil war and hatred, was asking for something which the Roman Curia, so learned and wise in Canon Law and so scrupulous in its judgments, but also so remote from the poor and humble, had not yet been able to give.

It was, then, wise of Innocent III to sanction, as after some demur he did, the rule of St. Francis and to submit the saint to the ecclesiastical tonsure. A great religious force which might otherwise have been lost to the Church was now brigaded in its ranks. The poor brothers of St. Francis (Fratres Minores, Minorites, Grey Friars) wandered through Italy, preaching in Italian as simple folk to simple folk,

and going everywhere, as well into remote hamlets as into
the poor quarters of large towns, with their call to poverty
and repentance. The movement was the more effective because the early disciples were neither churchmen nor school-
men. The illiterate multitude could understand a message,
pure of all subtlety or artifice, and delivered in the vulgar
tongue by men and women who practised the doctrines of
poverty and contentment, love and humility, which they
preached to others. By such manifest enthusiasm those who
were merely orthodox before were tempted to become religious now, and those who were heretical discarded their heresies.
That Italy was saved an Albigensian crusade may be ascribed
to the influence of St. Francis and his followers, who gave
in a form acceptable to the Church the satisfaction which
many Italians were disposed to find in open revolt.

Unlike Francis the founder of the Dominican Order was
trained for the Church and already a cathedral dignitary in
Spain, when a sudden turn was given to his life by an accidental
encounter with a heretic in Toulouse. To defend the orthodox
faith against the impassioned votaries of the Catharan or
Albigensian heresy which was sweeping everything before it
in southern France became henceforth the central passion of
his life. During the eleven critical years (1205-1216) when the
Papacy was at grips with this movement, Dominic was in the
centre of the fray, expounding doctrine, disputing heresies,
and gathering round him a band of preachers like-minded
with himself.

At an early stage of these operations the ardent Spaniard
was convinced that the enemy was only to be met by a moral
force equal to his own. The Cathari professed and to a large
degree practised an extreme form of asceticism. In the
consolamentum or rite of initiation, the initiate, who was
invested like a Brahmin with a sacred thread, swore to renounce the works of Satan and the Holy Catholic Church.
Believing that matter was inherently evil, he condemned
marriage, practised vegetarianism, and refused to countenance the shedding of blood either in peace or war. Perfection
in this hard school of mystical self-discipline was not given
to all, but it was attainable by a few who upon death would
assume a spiritual body without the intervening delays of
purgatory; and these elect and purified souls it was the duty
of the whole Church to venerate. Dominic saw that the

austere mystic of southern France would always prevail over
the soft-living legates and abbots who endeavoured to convert him. Accordingly he took upon himself a life of volun-
tary poverty and inculcated it upon his associates, not out
of mystical enthusiasm, but in his hard-headed Castilian way
as a means of influence. Meeting Francis later in Italy, he
was no doubt confirmed in his view that the renunciation of
worldly goods was, not in southern France only, where it
could be employed as an instrument of war against an
heretical Puritanism, but elsewhere, a source of unusual
spiritual influence. He determined to found an Order of
Preachers bound by vows of poverty and owing obedience
only to the head of their Order and to the Pope. To this project, too, Innocent III accorded his assent.

The army which was then enlisted in the service of the
Papacy was an army very different from any which had
previously been enrolled under its banner. The begging Friars
were ready to go everywhere and to do anything. No mission
was too distant or too dangerous for these dedicated men,
who stood outside every diocese and were independent of
every bishop save only the Bishop of Rome. There was no
country in Europe into which the Friar did not penetrate,
bringing with him the stir of a religious revival. For work in
heathen countries no missionary was more available. He
was to be found in Morocco and Tunis. He preached to
the motley crowds in Syrian seaports. He voyaged to Persia
and India and to the distant parts of China. Nor were his
energies wholly expended on the tasks of the missionary and
revivalist. Dominic, rightly seeing that the time had now
come when the faith must be defended against intellectual
antagonists, was resolved that his Order should be studious.
The old obligation of manual labour was replaced by the
unfamiliar call to learning. The Dominican was charged to
equip himself for intellectual combat and posted to the scenes
of intellectual danger and activity. After a brief interval, the
Franciscan, discarding the pious prejudice of his founder,
elected to tread the same path of education and knowledge.
He too frequented universities and made his contribution
to theological science. If the Dominicans can boast of Albert
the Great and Thomas Aquinas, the most original of mediaeval thinkers was a Franciscan from Oxford. So daring
were his speculations and experiments, so forward reaching

and comprehensive his mind, that it is a moot question to which of the two founders the genius of Roger Bacon would have been more disconcerting, to St. Francis, who distrusted the pride of learning, or to St. Dominic, who hated the poison of enquiry.

In theory the Friars were not permitted to own property. In practice bequests of land, houses, and money were made for their use to the Holy See, to the communities of towns, and to private individuals. Some endowment, bitterly as the principle of property was denounced by "the spirituals" of the movement, was probably essential to the effective and steady discharge of apostolic duty, more particularly in the cities; but wealth brought its familiar dangers. Before the end of the thirteenth century the Friars were sometimes accused of luxury and avarice. Nor were these the only charges. Popular preaching, no less than material wealth, has its special dangers. In his desire to impress and amuse, the travelling Friar often took leave of good sense and sound learning. The monks might be lazy, the parish priests might be dull, but in the eyes of the steadier villagers the Friar was a vagabond, an intruder, and a charlatan.

BOOKS WHICH MAY BE CONSULTED

Cambridge Mediaeval History, Vol. VI.
Sabatier: *Vie de St. François d'Assise.* 1931.
J. E. Renan: *Etudes d'histoire Réligieuses.* 1858.
H. C. Lea: *History of the Inquisition of the Middle Ages.* 3 vols. 1906.
E. Gebhart: *L'Italie Mystique.* 1906.
A. Luchaire: *Innocent III.* 6 vols. 1905-8.
Sir Steven Runciman: *The Eastern Schism.* 1955.
G. G. Coulton: *Five Centuries of Religion.* 4 vols. 1923-50.

CHAPTER XXIII

THE FOURTH CRUSADE

Crusading policy of Innocent III. The Venetians divert the Crusade. Latin conquest of Constantinople. Weakness of the Latins. Rivalry between Venice and Genoa. Opportunity for spreading Greek culture squandered. Decline in religious motives and theocratic ideas.

NOTHING SEEMS better to illustrate the limitations of papal power in the thirteenth century than the fate which befell the foreign policy of Innocent III. The object closest to the heart of that great Pope was the recovery of the Holy Land by a Crusade launched and directed by the Vicar of Christ. All quarrels were to be composed, all schisms ended. The joint force of the reunited Greek and Roman Churches was to be gathered together for the general overthrow of the Moslem power.

Of this ambitious programme, pursued throughout the whole course of his pontificate, nothing was accomplished. Europe was never united. The Holy Sepulchre remained in pagan hands, and the great Crusade which was set on foot to recover it was against the Pope's express injunction diverted by the Venetians for the capture of Constantinople. But perhaps the fact which is most striking is not that the strongest of the Popes failed to realize his hopes of the Crusade, but the obvious decline in the power of the religious motive which his failure implied. "You advise me," replied Richard to Fulk de Neuilly, the promoter of the Fourth Crusade, "to dismiss my three daughters, pride, avarice, and incontinence: I bequeath them to the most deserving: my pride to the Knights Templars; my avarice to the monks of Cîteaux; and my incontinence to the prelates." Neither Richard I of England nor Philip Augustus of France, nor the two contending Guelf and Ghibelline champions in Germany could be enticed to exchange their domestic interests for this distant adventure. By a chapter of accidents the task of directing the course of the Crusade lapsed to the Republic of Venice, upon whose good offices the valiant nobles of France and Flanders who had responded to the Pope's appeal were dependent for their conveyance across the sea. The atmosphere of the Rialto was very different from that of the Vatican. The Venetians, as the leading merchants of the Levant, had made too much money out of infidels actively to desire their destruction, and to the religious indifference and avarice of trade united the pride of a republic which had freed itself from Byzantium and was little disposed to accept dictation from Rome. In the necessities of the Crusaders who were short of money for their passage Enrico Dandolo, the aged Doge, descried a prospect of more than ordinary advantage to his fellow-citizens.

The first idea of the Crusaders was to attack Egypt, from the conquest of which, seeing that it was the centre of Moslem power in the near east, the recapture of Palestine could be expected to ensue. The Venetians, however, thought otherwise. With Egypt they were so little disposed to quarrel that they made a treaty with the Sultan under which they were assured a number of valuable privileges in the Egyptian markets. It was desirable then that the Crusaders should at all costs be headed off Egypt. A far more profitable objective from the Venetian angle was an expedition to overthrow Alexius III, the Greek Emperor who had been so unwise as to penalize the Venetian colony in Constantinople while lavishing privileges upon their hated rivals of Pisa. Fortunately the attack upon this Christian monarch, which was, in truth, but an extension of the commercial rivalry between two Italian cities, was capable of being represented in a specious guise to the simple minds of the Crusaders. Alexius III was vulnerable. He had imprisoned and blinded his brother Isaac Angelus, under whose negligent rule the Greek Empire had sunk to the last abyss of decrepitude. The son of Isaac, called, like his usurping uncle, Alexius, was on tour in the west, seeking to obtain support for the restoration of his father. The young Byzantine prince had little difficulty in enlisting the sympathies of Philip of Swabia, the King of the Romans, and of Boniface of Montferrat, the chosen leader of the Crusade. It cost this enterprising youth nothing to make promises flattering at once to the avarice of the traveller and the piety of the pilgrim. He would distribute 200,000 silver marks, would serve on crusade himself, supply 10,000 men for the reconquest of Palestine, and a perpetual force of 500 knights for the protection of the Christian establishments in the east. Buoyed by such glittering expectations, the leaders fell in with the Venetian scheme and resolved to dethrone the offending Emperor.

At first everything prospered for the imposing Venetian armada in the Bosphorus. Constantinople was taken, the cowardly Alexius found safety in flight, and Isaac and his son were solemnly crowned. The first objective of the Crusaders having been thus secured, it might seem that they should now have been free to accomplish the real purpose of their enterprise. But the expectation that the Greeks would rally two princes, the one blind and incompetent, the other the reckless author of his country's recent humiliation, and both elevated to power by a hateful and insolent enemy, was too wild to be realized. A fierce rebellion broke out against the Latins and their protégés. A second siege of Constantinople 1204 was followed by a second capture, and from that moment the foundation of some kind of Latin state on the Bosphorus became inevitable.

Had it been possible to impart to the new polity something of the concentrated vigour which England and Sicily received from their Norman conquerors, the main purpose of the Crusade might still have been achieved.

But the Latin masters of Constantinople were as little capable of promoting the papal policy as the effeminate Greeks whom they had so violently displaced. Weak in numbers, divided among themselves, hard pressed by the Bulgarians and by a Greek despot of Epirus in Europe, and confronted in Asia Minor not only by the Moslem power of the Sultan of Rum, but by the Greek states of Nicaea and Trebizond, the Latins of Constantinople, so far from being able to contribute to the rescue of Palestine, were only with great exertion enabled to maintain a precarious existence in the crumbling shell of the Greek Empire. Forces which might otherwise have been directed to Syria were required for the support of this new and unsteady creation. So perilous was the position that in 1209 Henry of Flanders, the second Latin Emperor of the east, allied himself with the Moslems of Rum against the Greeks of Nicaea.

Slender, too, was the satisfaction to be derived from the

so-called union of the Greek and Latin Churches. That a Venetian nobleman should be Patriarch of Constantinople and that the Latin rite should be celebrated in Santa Sophia ministered to the pride of the Roman Curia. But there was no real reconciliation. The Archbishop of Athens and the principal Greek prelates, rather than acknowledge the Pope, surrendered their sees and fled to the welcoming court of Theodore Lascaris at Nicaea. From that not very distant exile the leaders of the Orthodox Church sustained the courage, the bigotry, and the hatred of their co-religionists.

The substantial profits of the enterprise were reaped by Venice, its chief artificer. In the division of the spoils the Republic of St. Mark received three-eighths of the city of Constantinople and there set up side by side with the much harassed administration a commercial establishment extending its filaments throughout Romania,[1] and governed by a *podesta* who described himself as despot and lord of a fourth and a half of the Empire. All the important maritime points which commanded the route to the Crimea in the north or to Egypt in the south, Zante and Cephalonia, the ports of Modon and Coron in the Morea, the Cyclades, Gallipoli, Crete fell by degrees into the hands of the Republic or of its adventurous nobles. The voyager among the isles of Greece may still admire the imposing fortifications which commemorate the harsh and soulless government of Venice, the first colonial power to establish itself in Europe during the middle ages.

Indeed, the key to the history of the Levant is the contest of rival Italian cities for commercial ascendancy, for as the Latin Empire was made by the Venetians, so nearly fifty years later, for motives of the same strictly commercial character, it was upset by a Greek restoration relying on the 1261 indispensable help of their rivals the Genoese.

Not a single Greek manuscript is known to have been brought to Europe as a consequence of the Latin occupation of Constantinople and Athens, of Corinth and of Thebes. It would never have occurred to a Crusader, any more than it occurs to the modern Turk, that there is something to be learned from the literature of ancient Greece. A wonderful opportunity was therefore lost of opening out for the instruction of the west the splendid remains of Hellenic poetry and

[1] As the Eastern Empire was then commonly called

thought, and though some scattered rays of that great illumination penetrated to Europe during the thirteenth century they came not from Greece, but by the helpful mediation of the Arabs in Spain.

There is nothing so easy to follow as a bad example. The capture of the Fourth Crusade by the Venetians familiarized Europe with the idea that Crusades could be launched against a Christian and European power as well as against an Asiatic infidel. The seductive notion made rapid progress. The Saracens of Palestine and Egypt were not the only enemies who disturbed the peace of Innocent III. That active pontiff had theological enemies like the heathen Prussians, the Spanish Arabs, the heretical Albigenses, and he had also secular enemies like King John of England, who had refused to accept Stephen Langton as Archbishop of Canterbury. Against all these opponents of Roman theocracy Innocent found it convenient to preach a Crusade. Had the laws of currency been familiar to the thirteenth century, so astute a statesman can hardly have refrained from reflecting that indulgences, like bank-notes, may be over-issued and that no paper promise is apt more rapidly to depreciate than that of which there is an unlimited supply.

One thing was plain. Europe was not prepared to accept a theocracy. The trend of events was towards the making of national states, not towards the acceptance of a papal super-state. The great French victory of Bouvines (July 27, 1214) which enabled Innocent to crush Otto IV, the Guelf who had turned Ghibelline, helped to consolidate the national state of France, and since at the same time it foiled John's ingenious plan for the recovery of his lost French dominions, was good for the constitutional progress of England. To outward seeming the Pope had triumphed in his last duel with a hostile Emperor. Otto was down, renounced by Germany, routed by France. On his German throne was now seated that young Frederick of Hohenstaufen, who had been the Pope's ward, and from whom Innocent had lately extracted those large concessions with respect to the government of the German Church and the separate position of Sicily which he was wont to demand from candidates for the imperial throne. Yet beneath this brilliant surface there was muttering, challenge, uncertainty. There were Germans who asked what business the Pope had to interfere in their concerns. There were Englishmen who, despite the Pope's support of the versatile King John, were determined to defend their great charter; and there were Frenchmen who, notwithstanding the recent affair of Bouvines, were prepared to help them. Finally, there was the enigma of Frederick, master of Germany and Sicily, heir to the Norman and Ghibelline tradition. Despite all his paper promises, was it possible to believe that this half-Sicilian prince would act as a Guelf? The answer to this question was prompt, decisive, and important.

BOOKS WHICH MAY BE CONSULTED

Cambridge Mediaeval History, Vol. VI.

G. de Villehardouin: *La Conquête de Constantinople*. *Ed*. Bouchet. 2 vols., 1891.

L. Bréhier: *L'Eglise et l'Orient au Moyen Age*. 1907.

A. Luchaire: *Innocent III*. 1905-8.

W. Miller: *The Latins in the Levant*. 1908.

E. Pears: *The Fall of Constantinople*. 1885.

Sir Steven Runciman: *History of the Crusades*. 3 vols. 1951-4.

R. Grousset: *Histoire des Croisades et du Royaume franc a Jérusalem*. 3 vols. 1934-6.

CHAPTER XXIV

THE FALL OF THE HOHENSTAUFEN

Frederick II. His greatness and influence. Opposed by Gregory IX and Innocent IV. Goes on crusade. His Sicilian government and anti-papal propaganda. Deposed by Innocent IV. His dynasty destroyed. Consequences of the struggle. The interregnum in Germany. Loss of prestige to the Papacy. Boniface VIII challenges France and England. The Papacy destroys the Hohenstaufen only to become the captive of France.

FROM THE cloud of contemporary detraction, the figure of Frederick II, the last of the mediaeval emperors, emerges temperamental and challenging, to a point of dazzling eminence. He was fluent in six languages, a lyric poet in the warm Sicilian manner, a munificent patron of architecture, sculpture, and learning, a skilful soldier, a statesman of infinite subtlety and resource but also of much careless hardihood. A passionate intellectual eagerness carried him into the fields of philosophy and astrology, of geometry and algebra, of medicine and natural history. He wrote a treatise on hawking, which marks the beginning of experimental science in the west, and travelled in the company of an elephant, dromedaries, and other arresting fauna from the tropics. The traditional inhibitions of his age, so strong in St. Louis, were no fetters for a man who had been nurtured amid the clash of race and creed in Sicily and could use and appreciate the Saracen and the Jew, though to gain political support he would burn a heretic as freely as a Dominican friar. The world marvelled at a prince who talked Arabic with his Saracens, supported a numerous harem, and was so detached from popular prejudice as to challenge the common belief in the ritual murder of children by the Jewish community. Had he not, it was rumoured, written a book entitled *De Tribus Impostoribus*, in which Moses, Mohammed, and Christ were branded as impostors? There was something uncanny in the prodigious energy of this realist in politics, this exquisite in art, this half-oriental at once mystical and sceptical, this daring revolutionary in method and opinion. His contemporaries called him the Wonder of the World, and so despite the lapse of centuries he remains.

Yet among the great men of history he is peculiar in this— that he belongs nowhere. Barbarossa means much to Germany, St. Louis and Napoleon to France, Simon de Montfort to England. No nation can rightly claim Frederick as part of its inheritance, neither Germany, though the instrument which founds German power among the heathen Prussians dates from his reign (1229), nor Sicily, though he chased the Moslems from the island. His work was undone, his dynasty uprooted. The greatest single human force in the middle ages passes in and out of history like a comet which shines and is gone. Only perhaps in the sphere of literature was his influence of enduring importance. Provençal troubadours fleeing from religious persecution found welcome in the tolerant court of Palermo and fired the emulation of Sicilian artists. Descending from the poetic circle which surrounded the poet king a rill of delicate Sicilian verse broadens out and deepens, and gaining richness from the Tuscan speech in its northward course, swells into the solemn music of the Divine Comedy.

The source of this comparative failure is to be found in the opposition of two remarkable Popes, Gregory IX and Innocent IV, the first a fiery zealot, the second a Genoese noble, learned in canon law, skilled in finance, and in the fierce excitements of conflict unburdened by scruple. The object of Frederick was to make of Italy and Sicily a united kingdom within the Empire. The settled purpose of the Papacy, supported by a revived and enlarged league of Lombard towns, was to frustrate this design. In the end the Papacy won the battle. The man was defeated by the institution, and with him passed away the last chance of an effective Roman Empire in central Europe or for many centuries of a united Italian kingdom.

The quarrel first broke out over a crusade which Frederick had in the enthusiasm of youth vowed to undertake, but repeatedly postponed. To the modern mind it seems strange that a young ruler, returning after an absence to a state disordered by a long minority, should be expected at once to depart upon a costly expedition overseas. So too it appeared to Frederick. Only after he had organized government in Sicily, brought Saracens, nobles, and cities to heel and founded the State University of Naples did he set sail for Palestine. He had already been excommunicated by Gregory IX for his delays. He was now excommunicated for his departure (1228). A crusade was even preached against the Crusader in his absence. He returned to the black displeasure of the Church. Yet what he accomplished, despite the papal opposition which was carried from Italy into Syria, was remarkable. Without waste of time, treasure, or blood, this most lukewarm but clear-sighted Crusader obtained from his friend, the Sultan, a treaty according to Christian pilgrims free access to the Holy Places for ten years. Such are the fruits of statesmanship when humanity and good sense are allowed for a moment to replace the blind fury of religious and racial hatred.

What Frederick had to offer to Italy was a cultivated and intelligent despotism on the model which he had succeeded in establishing in his Sicilian *regno*. There he had taken full control of criminal justice, had curtailed the liberties of the nobles, the clergy, and the towns, and built up a royal system of government only to be paralleled in Angevin England. In both countries there was the same concentration of power, the same efficient organ for the collection of taxes, the same system of itinerant royal judges, the same salutary intermixture of classes in the tasks of government. Indeed, the parliaments or general courts of Frederick II, with their representation of nobles, clergy, and townsmen, anticipate the later parliamentary development in England. But there was one significant difference between the two best governed states of the thirteenth century. Whereas the power of the English king rested in the last resort upon the support of a native militia, Frederick relied upon a standing army of Saracen and German mercenaries.

But in the passionate atmosphere of the Italian struggle the merits of this higher form of government were never appraised. The Lombard cities saw in Frederick the enemy of their liberties; the Pope viewed him as an apostate bent on undermining the authority of the Church. The Lombards had to be fought with an army. Against the Pope it was necessary to be equipped with a doctrine. The counsels of the Roman lawyer were reinforced by the dreams of the visionary and the astrologer. With true political instinct Frederick divined that to combat the material and worldly pretensions of the Papacy an instrument lay ready to his hand in the Franciscan doctrine of poverty. "It is upon poverty and simplicity," wrote this luxurious and intricate controversialist in 1227, "that the primitive Church was built in those days when she was the fruitful mother of saints. No one may presume to lay other foundations for men than those appointed by the Lord Jesus." As the contest proceeded, becoming fiercer and more bitter, with the Emperor capturing a General Council, and the Pope plotting, as was believed, the Emperor's murder, Frederick threw out dark hints of a new and better imperial Church to replace the corruptions of Rome. Was it nothing that he had been born at a town called Jesi, and was not his chief minister, Pierre de la Vigne, the true rock, fore-figured in Scripture, upon which the Church of the Christ was to be built? The idea of a mendicant Church governed by an autocratic Empire was not one to appeal to the mediaeval mind. From his retreat in Lyons, Innocent deposed his antagonist and offered his crown with a patient and inveterate hatred to Robert of France, to a prince of Denmark, to Hakon of Norway, and ultimately to Henry of Thuringia and William of Holland.

The Hohenstaufen name still counted for much in Germany. Despite the activity of papal agents, the German princes and clergy, sweetened by concessions so lavish as to consort ill with the effective maintenance of royal power, remained loyal to the house and to the two young princes, Henry and Conrad, who were successively called upon to govern for their absent father. When the worthless Henry rebelled, Frederick had the main part of the country behind him in reducing the rebel to order. Even after the Council of Lyons in 1245 had solemnly deposed him, only a section of the German Church was induced to support the papal candidates, Henry of Thuringia and William of Holland, who were in turn put forward and elected kings.

The struggle was still proceeding when Frederick died in 1250, leaving behind him a reputation as great and as controversial as Napoleon's. To the Fraticelli "the hammer of the Roman Church" was a hero. By these ardent and revolutionary disciples of St. Francis, the great Emperor was remembered not as the luxurious half-oriental sovereign whose cause was supported by Saracen mercenaries in the

south and wicked Italian despots in the north, not as the
sceptic, the astrologer, the passionate love poet, but as the
protagonist of a return to primitive Christianity. To the more
orthodox he was Antichrist. Dante consigns him, alone
among the Roman Emperors, to the pit of hell.

Nobody can outstrip his contemporaries at every point.
Frederick, the most modern and wide-ranging of mediaeval
sovereigns, was both in material resources and intellectual
outlook the prisoner of his age. His largest army, which was
smaller than a modern British division, was ill-matched against
any well-defended Lombard town. Faenza, a city of the
second class, defied him for eight months, Milan effectually
spoiled his design for a united Italy. With pretensions which
acknowledged no geographical boundaries, and with interests
so wide that he has been called the first European, he was
nevertheless unable to master even the Lombard plain.
Again, though qualities belonged to him which in any age
are remarkable—an immunity from the prejudices of colour
and race, which puts most moderns to shame, an inexhaustible curiosity as to the operations of nature, and a strong sense
of causality in the affairs of men—he combined with these
rational promptings the superstitions common to his time,
a blind belief in the oracles of astrology, an undue deference
to the voice of sages, and an inability to distinguish between
the type of question which can or can not admit of a precise
scientific answer. Thus while some of Frederick's questions
led to the discovery of truth, others could only be answered
by an imaginative religious poet. "How many Hells are there?
Who are the spirits who dwell in them? And by what names
are they called? Where is Hell, and Purgatory where? Does
one soul know another in the next life? And can a soul
return to this life to speak and show itself to anyone?" To
such questionings Dante was later to offer a confident reply.

Eighteen years elapse between the death of Frederick
"Stupor Mundi" and the extinction of his dynasty through
1268 the cruel murder of his young grandson Conradin after the
field of Tagliacozzo. During this tormented period the
fierce duel between Guelf and Ghibelline continued to rage
through Italy, dividing cities, classes, and families, but always
dominated by the stern purpose of the Papacy to destroy
the Hohenstaufen and to avert for ever the menace which
such a power as theirs presented to the free expansion of the

papal state. It is significant of the strength of Sicily under Manfred, Frederick's bastard son, and of the divided state of Italian feeling, that the Papacy was compelled to rely upon the foreigner for the means of bringing the war to a successful end. After two papal armies, financed by English 1261 money, had failed, Urban IV, the first Frenchman to sit upon the papal throne, offered the Sicilian Crown to Charles of Anjou, the younger brother of Louis IX. To that wealthy and ambitious prince the Sicilian kingdom was attractive not only for itself, but as a stepping-stone to the conquest of the Greek Empire. Under Clement IV, yet another French Pope, the contract was sealed, with the result that a French army, superior in skill, discipline, and leadership to the levies which Manfred and later Conradin were able to bring against 1268 it, secured for the Papacy its final triumph, for the Guelf party a clear ascendancy, and for Charles of Anjou the Sicilian throne.

The effects of this long struggle may now be briefly summarized. Italy was lost to the Empire. The splendid civilization of Norman Sicily, which had been one of the glories of Europe, was destroyed by the French tyranny of Charles of Anjou, by a tyranny so odious and penetrating that it led to the terrible insurrection known as the Sicilian Vespers and 1282 afterwards to the severance of the island from the French (Mar. kingdom of Naples and to its progressive decline in the scale 30) of political influence. The French troops who had been called in by the Papacy to give the final blow to the Hohenstaufen drove the German mercenaries and officials, upon whom the imperial system had been supported in Italy, north of the Alps; but though this was a real service, the cause of popular liberty was not thereby advanced. Out of the incessant warfare which was at once the plague, the amusement, and the occupation of Italy, there arose that peculiar feature of Italian life, the civic despotism, often cruel and oppressive, but often distinguished for an enlightened patronage of literature and art.

Germany unity was gone past recall. The long absences of the Emperor Frederick, the lavish concessions which he had been compelled to make in 1220 and in 1231 to the princes, lay and ecclesiastical, and finally the furious civil war stirred up by the Pope which had darkened the concluding years of his reign, precluded the hope of any effective restoration of imperial authority in Germany. How little concern was now felt by the German princes for the Empire as an instrument of German government was shown after the murder of William of Holland in 1256. By a train of circumstances, which is still not entirely clear, the choice of the King of the Romans had now become vested in a college of seven electors, three ecclesiastics, and four laymen. To these cynical dignitaries no qualities were more desirable in a candidate for the Roman crown than that he should be a rich and negligent foreign absentee, knowing the value of a German vote, and able and willing to pay the price. The electors were divided, the majority deciding for Richard of Cornwall, the wealthiest man in England, the minority for Alfonso of Castile, the grandson, through his mother, of Philip of Swabia, and the favourite of France and the Papacy. Each of these princes was by his supporters declared to be duly elected as King of the Romans. Of the Englishman it may at least be said that his bribes were handsome, that he spent his money like an open-handed prince, of whom much was expected, and that he made himself welcome among the Rhenish cities. The Castilian was wisely persuaded to remain in Castile. What the election proves is the fixed determination of the German princes to have no strong king over them and to treat the greatest piece of secular patronage in Europe as an occasion of private gain and international intrigue.

The terrible anarchy which prevailed in the land under the phantom rule of this English absentee might have been expected to suggest some doubts as to whether the real interests of Germany were served by its costly association with the Holy Roman Empire. When Richard of Cornwall died in 1271 it was open to the Germans to bring the Empire to an end and to attempt to found upon the model of their French and English neighbours a strong German state. The conservatism, the pride, the self-interest of the electors stood in the way. The question of ending the Empire was not even raised. After two kingless years the choice of the electors fell upon Rudolf of Habsburg, a Swiss nobleman from the Aargau, adjudged to be harmless but destined to be the founder of that famous house to whose mistakes in policy the Prussian critic ascribes the severance of Holland and Switzerland from the German Reich, the catastrophe of the Thirty Years' War and the outbreak of the great struggle of our own century which brought the Prussian and Austrian Empires to the ground.

In this dark and distracted period of German history there are only two points of bright light, the town leagues formed on the Rhine for the preservation of peace and on the Baltic for the promotion of trade, and the steady advance of German civilization eastward into Silesia, Bohemia, and at the expense of the rude and primitive Prussian race.

The papal victory had been won at a cost. Forced payments in support of international institutions, however valuable they may be, are always unpopular. If the problem of financing the regular work of the Papacy was grave, far more invidious was the task of procuring the resources necessary to the conduct of a papal war. Innocent IV shrank from no 1243-expedient likely to suggest itself to the rancorous fiscality of 54 a hard-headed Genoese. To purchase influence he filled English benefices with Italian absentees and pluralists. To obtain money he laid crushing burdens on the clergy of England and France. In the pages of Matthew Paris, one of the best and most vigorous of English chroniclers, it is possible to trace the rising tide of indignation which these unprincipled extortions provoked in the land of all others famed for its obedience to the Holy See. Even Louis of France, whose country was more gently treated, reminded the Pope in a grave letter of protest that "he who squeezes too hard draws blood." The English clergy appealed in 1246 to a General Council. Though the plenitude of the papal power was still undisputed, the old spirit of affection and reverence had given place to anger and mistrust.

Hildebrandine thunders no longer worked the old miracle. When they were repeated by Boniface VIII, in whom the pur- 1294-suit of family advantage was so flagrant that he actually 1303 preached a crusade against the Colonna, his private enemies, the Pope met with stern and immediate resistance in England and France. Neither Edward I nor Philip the Fair would for a moment listen to the doctrine that a king was not entitled to levy a tax upon his clergy beyond the feudal aids (*Clericis Laicos*), or that it was necessary for salvation that he should be subject to the Pope. Each sovereign, in the most drastic manner available to him, made it clear that he was resolved to be master in his own house, and in this resolve was supported by his people. Even when Philip the Fair, in a transport of exasperation, sent his agent Nogaret to Rome, to kidnap the fiery old Pope and to bring him a prisoner to France, not a murmur of protest was heard from the subjects of the most Christian King. Six years later (1309) the Gascon Bertrand de Got, better known as Clement V, having through French influence been elected to the Papacy, set up his residence in Avignon and inaugurated the shameful chapter in papal history during which the Popes moved to the order of the King of France.

BOOKS WHICH MAY BE CONSULTED

Kantorowicz: *Frederick the Second. Tr.* E. O. Lorimer. 1931.
Huillard Bréholles: *Historia Diplomatica Frederici Secundi.* 1852-61.
T. S. R. Boase: *Boniface VIII.* 1933.
E. Boutaric: *La France sous Philippe le Bel.* 1861.
G. Masson: *Frederick II of Hohenstaufen.* 1957.

CHAPTER XXV

THE CATHOLIC MIND

St. Augustine. Siger of Brabant. Albert the Great. Aquinas. Dante.

AT THE beginning of the thirteenth century the fabric of Christian belief in the west still retained the mould which it had received from the mind of St. Augustine. The city of God stood out sharply against the city of man, eternity against time, perfection against sin. The priesthood alone, while performing the miracle of their priestly function, participated in the blessedness of the angels, but as the century advanced, new intellectual and spiritual movements made themselves felt. Men of very different temper and intellect began to feel that the sharp contrasts of the great African father might not after all be so absolute, that even to fallen man it might be given to reach perfection on earth, that the spirit was more important than outward institutions, and faith and intellect than the sacraments or formularies of the Church. Had not

Joachim of Flora, the Calabrian visionary (died 1202), proclaimed that the final stage of the world history was soon to open, when the Papal Church, which belonged to the age of the Son, would give way to the Spiritual Church, which belonged to the age of the Holy Ghost, when popes, priests, and sacraments would be unnecessary, and the Holy Spirit would fill every heart? Such dreams, in the enthusiasm created by the Franciscan movement, ran through Italy, inspiring among the Fraticelli the widest and most passionate hopes.

Philosophers, travelling by a different route, were reaching conclusions equally perilous to the sacerdotal order. Aristotle, now for the first time fully known and closely studied in the west, had become the serious concern of the University of Paris — Aristotle, who believed in everlasting time and uncreated mind, and in a divine intelligence working in man— and so we have eager Aristotelians like Siger of Brabant and his school maintaining such bold propositions as that the human intellect is eternal and the source of such perfection as is permitted to man, and that "a man directed to understanding is entirely disposed to eternal bliss."

These doctrines, the one of the self-suffieiency of individual faith, the other of the self-sufficiency of the individual intellect, struck hard at the heart of papal authority and discipline. Both were overcome by the forces of orthodoxy. The spiritualism of the Fraticelli, the metaphysics and psychology of Aristotle, were caught and harnessed to the chariot of the Church. But because the crisis was eventually mastered, because the doctors of Paris (1277) condemned the speculations of Siger, and because theologians were prepared to show that Aristotle was compatible with the Faith, it must not be imagined that the great opening out and agitation of the human mind which marks the thirteenth century was a matter of secondary consequence. The crisis was grave. The intellect of Europe was on the march. The tender conscience of spiritually minded men was stirred. Papal authority had not as yet been so sharply challenged. Many of the antecedents of the Reformation were already visible. If the Hundred Years' War had not supervened, arresting the development of the European mind and throwing back the progress of culture in the most advanced countries of the west, the forces making for freedom in education and politics would have captured new frontiers in the line of their advance.

At the critical moment Albert of Cologne (1193-1280) and his pupil, Thomas of Aquino (1226-1274), threw their massive intellects into the Catholic scale. These two Dominicans, the first a German, the second a South Italian, profited by the intellectual excitement created by the recovery of the physical and metaphysical works of Aristotle to build round the Catholic Church a powerful philosophic defence. The German was a vast encyclopaedia of knowledge, dominating by its mass. The Italian had a keener edge, a closer grip, a clearer method. Both welcomed the new knowledge, both believed that the essentially experimental philosophy of the pagan thinker could be reconciled with the cardinal doctrines of their Church. The weighty learning of the one, the close argumentation of the other, the vigorous orthodoxy and high character of each, impressed their thoughtful contemporaries. The intellect of the west capitulated to their combined attack.

In that age it was not expected of a philosopher that he should approach the accepted doctrines of the Church with an open mind. Aquinas maintained that since faith and reason were both gifts of God, they must necessarily agree. The truths of revelation might transcend reason but could not contradict it. Faith was the assent of the intelligence at the bidding of the will to propositions which were seen to be possible and good to believe. Of the body of truth contained in revelation, truth inaccessible to reason but not incompatible with it, part only had been committed to writing. The remainder had been handed down by the Apostles, at the intimate prompting of the Holy Ghost, for the observance of the Church. By these unwritten apostolic precepts many a practice lacking scriptural authority, such as the worship of images, was justified. Nothing, then, which in the popular beliefs of that day was held to be orthodox awoke the rational misgivings of St. Thomas, neither the doctrine of transubstantiation, since a rational account could be given of the miracle, nor the eternal torments of the damned, for so did God cause the angels and saints to rejoice as they contemplated His justice and realized the evils which they had escaped. The grim doctrine of a fiery and everlasting punishment handed down from the Jews of the first century had lost none of its popular appeal with the lapse of time.

It was cardinal with St. Thomas that the possession of the

true faith was necessary for salvation. *Extra ecclesiam nulla salus*. Salvation was neither for the unbaptized nor yet, save after confession and absolution by a lawfully ordained priest, for mortal sinners. The drunkard out of reach of the ministrations of the Church suffered the anguish of everlasting flame. Yet all was not thus dark and terrible in the religious landscape which presented itself to the mind of this laborious Friar. Visions of radiant beauty, forms of flawless saintliness and virtue, shone out amid the gloom and attested the goodness of the Creator. Prefigured in Aristotle's distinction of form and matter were the angels. On these consoling objects of philosophical speculation "the Angelical doctor" disserted with eager and enjoying prolixity.[1]

The third great figure in the Catholic firmament was a poet. Italy during the lifetime of Aquinas was in the throes of the political convulsion which tore the Hohenstaufen dynasty from its roots and led to the establishment under papal patronage of the Angevin house in Naples and Sicily. In that fierce struggle Florence, then a city of some 30,000 souls, and noted for its craftsmanship and advanced democratic feeling, espoused the papal side, expelled its Ghibelline or imperialist nobles, and after some sharp changes of fortune passed under the control of the Guelfic or papal party. The harmony of the victors was of no long duration. A personal feud imported from Pistoia clove the Guelfs into rival factions. There were White Guelfs and Black Guelfs.

That the Blacks eventually triumphed over the Whites with the help of the Papacy and the French is a matter only to be remembered because among many victims who were driven into exile by reason of that victory was the great figure of Dante Alighieri.

Dante, who was then thirty-six, was already the author of a body of Italian lyrics, which marked him out as a poet of original genius. He had written the Canzoniere and commemorated his burning passion for Beatrice in the Vita Nuova. He had also mingled with characteristic vehemence and seriousness in the political feuds of the city and as one of the Priors of the Arts had borne a part in its government. His neighbours might note a man proud, reserved, studious, patriotic, and, since 1290 when Beatrice died, living under the shadow of a settled grief.

See Appendix, p. 722.

Exile delivered him from the clutch of Florentine politics and liberated his mind for continuous meditation. His reading was voracious and profound. The romances of chivalry and the lyrics of Provence, while they enchanted his imagination, failed to satisfy his deeper needs. He absorbed the philosophy of Aquinas, the history of Orosius, the astronomy of Ptolemy, the epics of Virgil and Statius. On problems of style, language, and metre he wrote more sense than anyone since the days of Horace and Quintilian, making himself the responsible champion of Italian as a literary language superior to Provençal, and deserving the encouragement of all men of patriotic will. In a passage of the De Vulgari Eloquentia, which has often been on the lips of Italian patriots, he urged that because Italy lacked a king she was not necessarily without a court. Her language was a kingdom in itself. Four centuries and more before Dr. Johnson, the bold truth was proclaimed that the greatness of a country depends upon its authors.

The Divina Commedia, the religious epic which Dante called a comedy mainly by reason of its style, but in part also for its happy ending, was perhaps suggested by the lovely passage of the Sixth Book of the Aeneid in which Virgil recounts the appearance of Dido to Aeneas as he moves through the underworld of shades. Dante, too, would see his love again. Beatrice would meet him in Paradise, and there, typifying divine theology, explain the hidden mysteries of God. To reach her he would descend to the nethermost pit of Hell and climb to the summit of Purgatory, guided in these two first stages of his visionary pilgrimage by Virgil, his master in poetry, and the supreme pattern, as it seemed to the men of that age, of earthly understanding.

Dante is not, then, the first, but is the most remarkable in that long list of apocalyptic writers (among whom Bunyan must be mentioned) who through the allegory of an imaginary voyage or vision have attempted to depict the destiny of the soul. The Divine Comedy owes much to the Dream of Scipio and to the Sixth Book of the Aeneid, but the theme of a descent into the nether world was neither original with Virgil nor was it principally confined to writers of pagan antiquity. There was a Κατάβασις of Heracles and a Κατάβασις of Orpheus as well as that Κατάβασις of Odysseus upon which the descent of Aeneas was modelled. On the Christian side the Pastor of Hermas, the Apocalypse of Peter, the Pistis Sophia, all of them belonging to the second century, exhibit, though with very notable differences, the same root of devotional enquiry into the mysteries of the future life which lies at the base of the Divine Comedy. The visions of the later middle age, such as the Visio Wettini in 824, the Vision of Alberic of Monte Cassino in 1107, and of the Monk of Evesham in 1196, are sufficiently numerous and widespread to dispel the notion that there is anything original in the ground idea of the Divine Comedy. The originality of the Divine Comedy does not consist in its apocalyptic character but in its genius, in the beauty of its language, the technique of its metre, the depth of its thought, the range and glow of its imagination. Of the mediaeval apocalyptic writers Dante alone was to any appreciable degree influenced by Virgil, and it is this fusion of the Virgilian spirit with mediaeval apocalyptic which, informing as it does the whole poem with a tenderness and humanity (not to speak of the learning) quite alien to the outpourings of the monkish visionary, gives to the Commedia its unique place in literary history.

Like all writers of the mediaeval period, Dante draws no clear line between ancient mythology and true history. Charon and Achilles, Tiresias and Nimrod, are to him as real as Cavalcanti, Virgil, or St. Francis; the miracles recorded by Livy and Lucan are true evidence that the work of the Roman Empire was divinely assisted. Ancient poetry was not history to be dissected but mystery to be divined. He conceived that allegory was a necessary quality of great poetry, or in Boccaccio's words that "poetical creations are not vain and simple marvels, as many blockheads suppose, but that beneath them are hidden the sweetest fruits of historical and philosophical truth, so that the conceptions of the poets cannot be fully understood without history and moral and natural philosophy."

This allegorizing and uncritical tendency makes much of Dante's epic remote and obscure to us.

The poet was without humour. Part of a famous speech delivered by Beatrice to Dante in the paradisal moon runs thus:

"If you take three mirrors and put two of them at an even distance from the eyes and the third is placed between the two others just at a little greater distance, and you will place a candle behind you, you will see that if the largeness of the light reflected by these three mirrors is not the same, the intensity is."

Now this passage, the versification of which is a wonderful piece of dexterity, is pure prose. No modern poet would dream of introducing a chilly slab of scientific lecturing into the body of a passionate and mystical poem. But all through his poem, and more especially in the Paradiso, Dante does this frequently.

But if there is prose in the Divine Comedy, as there is violence, obscenity, and grotesqueness, there is no feebleness. Dante is never lax and talkative. He may be dry, tedious, difficult; it will never occur to the critic to describe him as pompous or verbose. The dullness of Dante is not due to a spell of intellectual fatigue, a mood of listless inattention, or to decay of interest, but always to the homiletic quality of a mind which sometimes found its lessons in difficult allegory, and sometimes in far-fetched interpretations of acted life. And it is a sufficient proof of this proposition that there is no part of the Commedia which has not for some quality or other attracted the admiration of good judges.

"He was born," says Ruskin (*Stones of Venice*, ix, 175), "both in the country and at the time which furnished the most stern opposition of horror and beauty and permitted it to be written in the clearest lines. And therefore though there are passages in the 'Inferno' which it would be impossible for any poet now to write, I look upon it as all the more perfect for them . . . and therefore I think that the 21st and 22nd book of the 'Inferno' are the most perfect portraitures of the fiendish nature which we possess."

Among mediaeval poets Dante stands closest to Virgil for the delicacy and minuteness of his observation. The storm crashing through the forest, the frogs slipping into the water from the snake, the lizard which crosses the road like a flash of lightning, the fireflies seen by the peasant in the gloaming, the old cobbler narrowly eyeing his needle, the boxers, their bare bodies gleaming with oil as they stand watching one another for their point of vantage, the duck dipping to escape the falcon, the mother who clutches her child on the alarm of fire, the gamesters crowding round the winner—here are pictures painted fresh from the life. And it is to the frogs, cranes, lizards, ducks, and falcons, to the sheen of fish gliding to their food in a tank of pure and still water, to the peasant who rises grumbling in a hoar frost, and then a few hours later, when the world has changed its face, takes his crook and leads his flocks afield, it is to such pictures of the unobtrusive aspects of Italian country life only to be paralleled in Virgil that the poetical posterity of Dante owes its principal debt. He showed that no piece of real nature, if strictly observed, is alien to the making of poetry.

In common with Orosius, his master in history, Dante held the view that the Roman Empire was the divinely appointed instrument of government on earth, and that this was clearly proved by the double fact that Christ was born in the reign of Augustus and that during the same reign the world for the first time enjoyed universal peace. The De Monarchia is a Latin treatise written to prove, first, that a universal monarchy is a god-ordained necessity for man, second, that the Roman Empire was providentially designed to exercise this universal monarchy, and finally that the Roman Emperor held his title directly from God and was in no way subject to the Papacy. To modern eyes the reasons brought forward in support of these propositions may seem too far removed from the realities of political life to weigh with any sensible mind. But when we divest the argument of its scholastic integument and come down to the fundamental thoughts in Dante's mind we shall find that it is capable of being translated into the terms of an ideal which the world has never relinquished. That the highest activity of man is intellectual and that intellectual progress is arrested by war, that universal peace is the supreme end in politics, that it can be made secure only by the reduction of the whole world under a single government, that in every community there must be lodged somewhere a sovereign power, and that great evils have proceeded and will continue to proceed from the temporal ambition of spiritual rulers, these tenets would not be regarded as absurd, though they might be hotly disputed, by modern politicians. The universal monarchy of Dante is no more chimerical than Tennyson's Parliament of Man or than Mazzini's dream of the Republic.

Aspirations, however distant they may be, play their part in the shaping of human affairs, and Dante's treatise was used as a controversial weapon in the next generation (when the quarrel broke out between Louis of Bavaria and John XXII) and received the honour of burning at the hands of a legate of the Pope.

Nevertheless, Dante's theory of the Empire postulated an order of things which every change in European affairs was involving in darker shades of obsolescence. The last faint hope of an Italy united under the imperial power vanished with the death of Frederick II in 1250, fifteen years before Dante's birth; and the lifetime of the poet synchronizes with a series of political changes every one of which was separately injurious to the restoration of imperial control. The downfall of the Hohenstaufen dynasty, the introduction of Charles of Anjou into southern Italy, the transfer of the imperial crown first to an Austrian and then to a Luxemburger, the steady growth in the territorial ambitions of the Papacy, and of the commercial strength of the Italian towns, these among other causes tended to loosen the bond which clasped Italy to the Empire and to confirm the political divisions of the country.

Amid much that is part of the civilized aspiration of every age, and much that was already archaic and obsolete in his own time, there is one characteristic of Dante's political thought and temperament which alternately loses and gains for him the favour of intellectual men. He was by temperament an aristocrat, by conviction an imperialist. It was not the Roman Republic which he idealized but the Roman Empire, not liberty but law. Critics have often noticed that neither in the Commedia nor in any of his scattered writings is there any sign of sympathy for the poor as a class, of such sympathy, for instance, as suffuses the earnest pleading of Piers Plowman or the early literature of the Franciscan movement.

But in claiming Dante for the aristocrats, the student should remember that to the mind principally occupied with the religious ordering of the universe, the competing claims of class and class which form the matter of political rivalry and meditation become specks of infinite insignificance. The arbitrament of God which peoples the circles of the Inferno and the Mount of Purgatory and the stars of Paradise falls with an equal hand on prince and ploughman.

Great office does not screen the offender in that high court (for while there are several Popes in Dante's Hell, there is but one in Paradise), so that to the Italian of that age reading or listening to the Commedia the supreme impression must have been the vanity of all worldly things when measured against the divine graces of the soul. The Catholic Church is a great democracy. To Dante its power for good had been immeasurably injured by its lust for temporal dominion. As the city of Florence had fallen away from its days of early simplicity when ladies sat at the spindle and the flax and their husbands went in a skin jerkin, so the Church had been corrupted by wealth and power. In the beautiful eleventh canto of the Paradiso where St. Thomas recounts the life of St. Francis, the emphasis is laid upon the marriage of the saint with the Lady Poverty, who, reft of her first husband, the Church, had for a thousand years and more stood "despised and obscure, without invitation."

In such passages as these Dante confesses his enthusiasm for poverty as a religious ideal, hard and heroic, and yet never to be lost sight of if the Church was to be kept pure of offence. The great epic of mediaeval Catholicism is the work of a humanist who was also a scholastic, of a mystic who was also a politician, of a churchman orthodox in belief but ardent in the cause of a puritan reformation.

BOOKS WHICH MAY BE CONSULTED

E. H. Gilson: *La Philosophie au Moyen Age.* 1925.

M. C. D'Arcy: *Thomas Aquinas.* 1930.

E. Armstrong: *Italian Studies.* Ed. C. M. Ady. 1934.

Dante: *Divina Commedia.* Ed. H. F. Tozer. 1902.

Dante: *Opere Minore.* Ed. P. J. Fraticelli. 1855.

Dante: *De Monarchia.* Ed. Dr. E. Moore; Introduction by W. H. V. Reade. 1916.

V. Nannucci: *Manuale della litteratura del primo secolo della lingua italiana.* 1883.

D. G. Rossetti: *Dante and his Circle.* 1892.

Mandonnet: *Siger de Brabant et l'averroisme latin au 13me siècle.* 1908.

A. P. d'Entrèves: *The Mediaeval Contribution to Political Thought.* 1939.

W. Ullmann: *Mediaeval Papalism.* 1948.

CHAPTER XXVI

THE GROWTH OF MONARCHY
IN FRANCE AND ENGLAND

*Divergent constitutional developments of France and England.
Growth of centralization in England. Contracted authority of
French Crown. Louis VII and Henry II. Imperfect unifica-
tion of France under Philip Augustus. Importance of the
rural middle class in England. Parliament and States-General.
Legal development in England and France. Louis IX and
Philip le Bel. Absolutist tendencies in France. Constitutional
tendencies in England. Magna Carta. Simon de Montfort.
Edward I.*

How SHARPLY, despite all the unifying forces of civilization,
are France and England now divided! The one a land of
peasant proprietors, of small highly skilled craftsmen, of a
large bourgeoisie, cultured, economical, and self-centred,
with little or no interest beyond the frontiers of their own
beloved country, the other a country of large landowners and
tenant farmers, of big industrialists and crowded factory
workers, of business men having interests all over the world,
and with a population so much given to travel and adventure
that few families cannot claim a relation who is settled beyond
the ocean.

In the twelfth and thirteenth centuries the contrast between
the two countries was less evident and of a different character.
The Norman Conquest had made of England a province of
French civilization. The language of the aristocracy, of the
government, of the law courts, was French. It was from the
Ile de France that England derived its Gothic architecture. A
great part of France, first Normandy, then the Angevin
Empire of Henry Plantagenet, was, until the beginning of the
thirteenth century, ruled by English kings. Feudalism, chivalry, the Crusades, were French. The university movement, so
far at least as England was concerned, originated in Paris.
The general ideas about law and government, about society
and religion, which prevailed on one side of the Channel

were no less familiar on the other. So intermingled were the two countries that many English towns received charters upon a French model, and some of the terms most closely connected with the growth of English municipal liberties, such as mayor and commune, were imported from France. A traveller passing from one country to the other in the reign of King John would have found no very palpable contrast between the French and the English scene. He would see majestic cathedrals rising in either country, and would find upon examination that they were being built by corporations of master masons under the direction of a bishop or an abbot. He would find monasteries in either country obedient to a French rule, farming wide acres, and dispensing lavish hospitality; would meet monks travelling to fair, market, or tourney, or come across a knot of gaping rustics listening to the eloquence of a travelling Friar. England he would probably pronounce to be at once the rougher and richer country. But so indistinct were the spiritual frontiers between these two remarkable peoples that the barons of the charter did not scruple to invite the heir to the French throne, afterwards Louis VIII, to take the English crown, and that Simon de Montfort, the leader of the national revolt against Henry III, and the great popular hero of English liberty, was the son of the French nobleman who crushed the Albigensian Crusade. To the Frenchman of this period the German was a foreigner and almost intolerable. England was different. Though the commonalty spoke an unintelligible tongue, and for lack of vineyards were driven to a disgraceful beverage, the gentry were of a familiar world and could make themselves intelligible in their provincial French.

France, however, was not the only country by whom England was now influenced. The bulk of the English population was throughout the middle ages to be found in London, in Essex, and in East Anglia. It is in this region, as the Doomsday Survey shows, that a free agricultural population managed most easily to maintain itself throughout the economic disturbances consequent upon the Norman Conquest. Here was not only the most populous but the richest, and perhaps for this very reason the most liberty-loving section of the English people; for it was the quarter from which in after times Simon de Montfort and Oliver Cromwell drew their strength. But the bulk of the trade of London and East Anglia was not with France but with the Low Countries and Cologne, Scandinavia and the Baltic. Indeed, the greatest of all English mediaeval trades was done with Flanders. It was in the Flemish towns, in Bruges and Ghent, that wool from our famous English downs and pastures was worked up into cloth, and sent far and wide through Europe. Thus, while our aristocratic and literary connections were with a Latin people, our trading connections were mainly—though the trading connection with Rouen and Bordeaux was always important—with peoples of the same Teutonic stock as ourselves. In this area our English speech must have been always a better commercial language than French, and for that reason well worth keeping up in our trading towns which attracted then, as they continue to attract with even greater potency now, the most vigorous and enterprising sons of the village. It is significant that Chaucer, the father of English poetry, was a Londoner and a Commissioner of Customs.

The fact of the Norman Conquest, while bringing England fully within the zone of French civilization, was one of the causes which ultimately led England and France to pursue different lines of constitutional development. William I made of England a single state. That work was so well done that it was never undone. The period of feudal anarchy under Stephen was repaired under Henry II, to whose great series of administrative and judicial reforms England owes a centralization of justice for which France had to wait for many centuries. By the time of Henry II's death four great lessons had been instilled into the English people. They had been taught to pay taxes, a lesson which the French monarchy never succeeded in teaching the French people, and which even now is not fully learned. They had been taught that crime was an offence against the king's peace of which the king's court desired to have exclusive cognizance, save where benefit of clergy was claimed, in which case the ecclesiastical court tried the offender, but handed him over to the secular arm for punishment in the case of a conviction. They had learned that there was one law for the whole country, administered by one supreme court, the *Curia regis*, with its judges going on circuits through the country, and everywhere, when on these official errands, representing the power of the king. And, finally, they had become habituated to the disagreeable duty of co-operating in the task of government, either as tenants called upon to render knights' service in the wars, or as citizens called upon to follow the hue and cry, or as jurors for the assessment of taxes, the punishment of criminals, or the adjudication of civil suits in the county courts. The system continued to work under an absent king, like Richard, or under a bad king, like John, who in nothing more fully showed his remarkable ingenuity than in his capacity for extracting fleets, men, and money from the national administration which had been bequeathed to him by better men.

Very different was the position of the King of France at the beginning of the twelfth century. All that Louis VI could call his own was a small domain on the middle waters of the Seine and the Loire. Amiens was in Vermandois, Calais and Boulogne in Artois, Lyons was imperial. Whereas in England there was a national government, in France the King was confronted by great fiefs (Flanders, Normandy, Burgundy, Guienne, Gascony, Toulouse, and Barcelona) nominally subject to the French Crown, but in fact independent. It is significant of the political weights and measures of the country that Louis VI wisely concentrated his energies upon the police of that little territory which was directly under his own control. For him feudalism was the enemy. In a modest way this active ruler was the founder of that system of government through officials drawn from the middle class, which, despite all subsequent political changes, has been found congenial to the needs of France. His chief minister was a monk of the name of Suger, a turgid historian, but as a man of affairs, honest, capable, and trusted.

All this progress was put to the hazard in the succeeding reign. Louis VII, pious, charming, chivalrous, ineffectual, was brilliantly married to a lady who brought him as her dower the Duchy of Aquitaine: but their tempers proved to be incompatible, and after fifteen years of married life Eleanor was divorced. There have been few greater political blunders in the history of mediaeval France. Eleanor married Henry Plantagenet, Count of Anjou, and in accordance with the disastrous notions of that feudal age, a vast area of south-western France (Guienne, Auvergne, and Aquitaine) was now transferred from the control of her first to that of her

1100-37

1137-80

second husband. When Henry became King of England and Duke of Normandy, Louis was confronted with a hostile kingdom stretching from the Cheviots to the Pyrenees, and in every point of material strength stronger than his own. "Your Lord, the King," he observed to Walter Map, "wants nothing—men, horses, gold, silk, diamonds, game, fruits: he has all in abundant plenty. We in France have only bread, wine, and gaiety." A war broke out between the two rival powers which was waged in the intermittent feudal manner for a hundred years.[1]

One advantage belonged to Louis VII which could not be claimed for his adversary. All through life the French King lived in the sunshine of clerical favour. In the struggle between Frederick Barbarossa and Alexander III Louis ranged himself on the side of the Pope, received him as guest, allowed him to behave as if he were the ruler of France, and in return for his submissive piety was presented with the gift of a golden rose. His aureole shone the more brightly by contrast with the dark disfavour with which Henry II was regarded by all the priests and monks of Europe. The English King who scribbled or chatted during Divine Service, who laid down that criminous clerks, if convicted, should be handed over to the secular arm to be punished, and that no appeals should go to Rome without the royal assent, who was for many years violently embroiled with Becket, his Archbishop of Canterbury, and commonly suspected of having directed his murder by the altar steps of his own cathedral, was regarded as the embodiment of the lay spirit in statesmanship, and of all that was most dangerous to clerical prerogative. The contrast between the pious and unfortunate Louis and the wicked, clever, prosperous Angevin presented the immortal problem of the equity of fate. Why were such things possible? Afterwards, when the English were driven out of Normandy by Philip II, the legend grew up that the murdered Becket had appeared to an ecclesiastic in his dreams, saying that he had chosen Philip to avenge his death.

1179-1223   Of this Philip, remembered after his death as Augustus, it may be said that he possessed the rarest of all qualities in a mediaeval ruler, concentration on the possible. Living in a world not of dreams, but of réalities, he allowed nothing to divert him from the great object of driving the Plantagenets

[1] Genealogical Table F

out of France, and of extending the boundaries of his kingdom. *Ampliavat fines regni* is the epitaph on this long-headed, unattractive figure who planted French power on the Channel and the Atlantic, gaining Vermandois by diplomacy, Normandy, Anjou, Maine, Touraine by war, and finally destroying on the famous field of Bouvines the army of an Anglo- 1214 German coalition, which would have robbed him of these conquests.

From this point the territorial formation of France proceeded without interruption until in the fourteenth century Edward III challenged the French crown. The English re- 1337 mained firmly planted in Gascony: but Languedoc fell to France as the fruit of the Albigensian Crusade, Champagne, La Marche, and Angoulême a little later, and Lyons in 1312.

The making of France under the Capetian monarchs was wholly unlike the process by which political unity had been imposed on England through the policy of William the Conqueror. Even where the extension of the royal domain involved fighting, as when Philip Augustus evicted John from Normandy, it entailed none of those revolutionary consequences which followed upon the Norman conquest of England, neither transfer of property, nor the intrusion of a new nobility, nor the depression of the rural population. When the towns and castles governed by the troops of the English king had been taken, the province passed from England to France without further change, and, so to speak, with its soul intact. But in general there was no fighting. The King was felt to be the champion of order and justice, the defender of the weak and the poor against the wicked and the strong, the protector of religion from the Channel to the Pyrenees, and in a vague, unanalysed way the suzerain and master of France. Even under Louis VII a sentiment of devotion to the monarchy is clearly apparent. The successful Philip watered the tender plant, and by an adroit exercise of his rights as a feudal suzerain extended the influence of the French Crown in the territories of his feudal vassals.

From this manner of growth by accretion, it followed that France was never in the middle ages so completely unified as England. The great fiefs were too much a part of the common heritage of France to be subjugated or transformed by the pressure of an iron despotism. They retained, therefore, even

when annexed to the French Crown, much of their former
independence, and as appanages created in favour of the
younger members of the royal family, were more than once
sources of peril to the monarchy itself.

A consequence of the greater measure of authority thus
enjoyed by the great feudal nobles in France was the absence
in that country of a rural middle class burdened by public
responsibilities. In England the main tasks of local government
were discharged by knights of the shire or country gentlemen
of moderate fortune, who attended the county courts, presented criminals to the judges, bore the record of the country
to Westminster, where the doings of the shire court were challenged, acted as jurors in civil suits, and ultimately came to represent their respective counties in the national Parliament. In
France there was no such amateur class of local jurors,
justices, and administrators as the knights of the shire, and
no such popular local institutions as the shire courts. The
administration of the French monarchy was carried out by
professionals. It was the achievement of Philip Augustus to
have created in the office of *Bailli* or *Seneschal* an official
of the royal government who, holding his post at the King's
pleasure, might be trusted to do his will.

Here is the explanation of the fundamental difference
between the development of France and England. In both
countries the monarchy manifested itself as the chief con-
structive principle of the state, and in the thirteenth century
developed representative institutions round the central nucleus
of a royal council. In both countries these assemblies owe
their being not to any abstract theory, but rather to the
pressure of financial needs, or because business was thus
most conveniently discharged, or as a means of reinforcing
the crown in times of crisis.

In both countries insistence is laid upon the essential
principle that the representative has full power to bind his
constituents. But here resemblance ceases. In the great
English councils of the thirteenth century, the Parliaments,
1216- as from the reign of Henry III they come to be called, knights
72 of the shire took their place with burgesses and representatives of the lower clergy, and worked side by side with the
prelates and barons, who were summoned by individual
writ. The strength of this English body, the feature which
gave it a permanent and continuous rôle in English govern-

ment, was that it was in the main an assemblage of persons of an intermediate social rank, who were accustomed to the discharge of public business in their separate localities. The French States-General was not thus rooted in local government, nor closely fused by the presence of a class of representatives who, while they shared the country tastes and pursuits of the noble, were, in point of wealth and station, more nearly akin to the burgess. Consisting of three distinct orders, the nobles, the clergy, and the burgesses, the States-General failed to play a decisive and formative part in the moulding of French policy. So far from furnishing any continuous restraint upon the exercise of absolute power, these cumbrous assemblies met at rare and infrequent intervals and then spoke with a divided voice. It is significant that the total number of States-Generals known to have been summoned between 1300 and 1789 exceeds by two only the number of Parliaments summoned in the single reign of Edward III. The size of France was inimical to parliamentary centralization, and suggested the superior convenience of provincial assemblies.

There was no French common law. The great boon of legal unity secured to England through the judicial reforms of Henry II was not achieved in France till the days of Napoleon. Yet the first steps were taken on the road to legal improvement when the Parliament of Paris acquired in the reign of 1226- St. Louis a substantive and continued existence not many 70 years after the foundation of the Inns of Court in London. This was not a political assembly, as the name might seem to imply, but a judicial corporation, the members of which in course of time acquired their positions by purchase or bequest. A great rôle both in law and politics was played by this legal institution, which numbered many illustrious intellects, and endured until, like all other privileged corporations, it was swept away by the French Revolution; but it was not the rôle of the English common lawyers who in the seventeenth century stood for Parliament against the King. The French lawyer of the island city breathed the air of Roman jurisprudence, and on every occasion might be trusted to support the prerogative of the Crown. Under the influence of the Papal Inquisition, the old Teutonic system of public trial which existed in France and continued to survive in England gave place to a secret procedure, better adapted perhaps to the detection and punishment of crime, but offering fewer guarantees to the accused and easily lending itself to the basest purposes of tyranny. Among the circumstances serving to differentiate the history of these two neighbouring peoples none perhaps is more important than the fact that the Papal Inquisition which was created in France never crossed the British channel.

Philip Augustus may perhaps be called the second founder of Paris. He authorized and supported the University, built the Cathedral of Notre Dame, and gave to the city pavements and hospitals, aqueducts and an enlarged circuit of fortifications. After his reign there was no question but that Paris must be the centre of French government. But how was 1226 France to be ruled? Louis IX, who attained to his majority in 1236, was a saint and mystic. No ruler of his time was more fully penetrated with theocratic ideas, more ardent in self-sacrifice, or, in matters where heresy was not concerned, readier to hearken to the voices of equity and mansuetude. It may be added that his personal courage was high and stainless, and that being exempt from many of the passions of his time, he often brought a shrewd and balanced judgment to the affairs of state. But the respect which we feel for St. Louis as a man must not blind us to his faults as a statesman and a strategist. On two critical occasions he left his country to go upon crusade. One good army was lost among the canals of the Egyptian delta, another in the torrid heat of Tunis. Neither sanctity, nor self-sacrifice, nor the administration of patriarchal justice under the oak of Vincennes could replace the advantages of a good and steady administrative routine, nor shield his subjects from extortion and misery. The good King returned from his Egyptian campaign 1251 to learn of the stern repression of the Pastoreaux, poor country folk, maddened with poverty and inflamed with injustice, who wreaked their hatred of the social order upon the prosperous bodies of the priests. The exquisite art of La Sainte Chapelle shone against a background of social wretchedness.

The moral beauties of St. Louis, better suited to a knight-errant than to a statesman, added lustre rather than strength to the Capetian house. It was given to Philip the Fair, his enigmatic grandson, to supply the ruthless and daring qualities which are absent in the composition of a saint. St.

Louis was a feudal, Philip a national, sovereign. The one issued edicts for his domain, the other promulgated ordinances for France. The spirit of the grandfather was profoundly ecclesiastical. The civil order founded by Philip was pre-eminently lay, and even anti-clerical. St. Louis kept two grand objects constantly before his eyes, personal holiness and the happiness of his subjects, imperfectly as he was able to adjust his means to the achievement of that latter end. In Philip the two great problems were always, no matter at what cost, power and wealth.

There is accordingly something violent and revolutionary about the procedure of this energetic ruler, whose reign coincides with the final conquest of Syria by the Mamelukes 1291 and with the eclipse of all the hopes and aspirations which had been connected with the great age of the Papacy, and with the launching of the Crusades. Frederick of Swabia had captured a General Council; Philip the Fair, backed by his civil lawyers, did not scruple to lay hands upon the Pope himself. Nothing is more eloquent of the altered spirit of the time than the fact that when Boniface VIII ventured to interfere with the King's right to tax his clergy, and proceeded, as tempers rose, to claim supremacy over the secular power, Philip was able without affronting his people to have the Pope's person seized by violence, his Bulls publicly burnt, 1303 and to appeal to the States-General for its support against an interfering Bishop of Rome.

The same spirit of ruthless "laicity" characterizes Philip's dealings with the Templars. The King was needy, the Templars were rich. In that single circumstance is the explanation of an act of cruelty which prefigures, it it does not surpass, the robberies of the Reformation and the massacres of the Jews. For wealth was not the only crime of this famous Order, which had so long fought for the Christian cause under the Syrian sky, and was now fulfilling the office of banker to the King. The Templars incurred the even graver charge of general unpopularity. It is the habit of vulgar and excitable minds to find the explanation of great popular calamities in the treason of leading men. Again and again in French history the cowardly cry "Nous sommes trahis" has gone up in the hour of humiliation. It went up now. The Templars, it was said, had betrayed the Christian cause, which it was their special duty to defend. They had conspired with the Saracens. They were heretical, stained with name-less vices, devoted to secret and unmentionable rites. It was rumoured that they spat upon the Cross. Once let loose, the public imagination poured itself out in an unmeasured torrent of innuendo and attack. The Templars were deprived of an opportunity of reply. Many of them were tortured until from agony they made false confessions. Many were sent to the stake. With the disgraceful connivance of the Pope the Order was dissolved, and its vast resources in money 1312 and land were for the most part annexed to the use of the Crown.[1]

The want of money, which led to this, as to many other acts of unjust extortion, and notably to repeated debasements of the coinage, was a sign that the King of France was now attempting to govern his country. A study of the not alto-gether consistent legislation of the reign reveals Philip's underlying purpose: to draw money from the clergy, from the men-at-arms, from the nobles, and to administer the nation with the aid of lawyers of humble birth. Crown officials multiply their numbers, the organs of central govern-ment become differentiated as in England—the Parliament for legal, the *Cour des Comptes* for financial business, and at the end of the reign, the States-General, as an exceptional measure for the association of the three great orders in the state with momentous acts of royal policy. The government of this king was harsh, irregular, odious. The taxes were mostly farmed out with the inevitable result that the treasury received but a small fraction of the sums which were extracted from the taxpayer. The officials were indifferently and inter-mittently supervised. Still, despite all its defects on the side of publicity, and control, and fiscal science, there now emerges into the light of history a government of France, lay, auto-cratic, and, in so far as the conditions of that age permitted, centralized in the person of the King.

While the French monarchy was thus tending towards absolutism, England was set upon an opposite course. The Norman nobles who had conquered and pillaged this wealthy island did not long remain an alien and exclusive caste. They intermarried with the Saxons, merged with a population

---

[1] The Hospitallers, to whom the property was nominally assigned, obtained in France a very small part of it.

too vigorous to be permanently subjected, and came in the course of a century to regard themselves not as Normans but as Englishmen. After the last great feudal revolt had been crushed by Henry II, they were compelled to accept the national government of the crown as an established institution, in the working of which they were called upon equally with the knights of the shire and representatives of the towns to bear a part.

1174

With this transformation in the character of the nobility from the position of an alien caste to that of a native aristocracy, the principal obstacle to the growth of an English nation disappeared. The tyranny of a bad king was sufficient to provoke a national opposition in which churchmen, barons, and townsmen were alike involved. The Magna Carta, extracted from King John, ranks as the first of our English statutes and is rightly regarded as the corner-stone of English liberties. That document, which played so important a rôle in the parliamentary struggles of the seventeenth century, was no revolutionary or philosophical manifesto, but a restatement of the rights and privileges which were already assumed to belong to the Church, the nobles, the townsmen, and "the community of all the land." The barons of the charter were not concerned to make new law, but to prevent the violation by the Crown of existing rights. They had no theory of liberty as such. The liberties which they were concerned to defend were feudal, ecclesiastical, or municipal privileges. Against royal caprice they offered the bulwark of legal custom.

June, 1215

A later age saw in the charter the foundation of parliament and the jury system. The charter does not mention the word parliament, which first came into use in the succeeding reign, but lays down that no extraordinary aids or scutages are to be levied by the Crown save with the consent of the common council of the realm, an assembly of prelates, barons, and tenants in chief. Nor yet does it mention the word jury. What it says, however, in effect is that no free man should be imprisoned, dispossessed, outlawed, or exiled save by the judgment of his peers or by the law of the land. Those were lofty principles, and since the old methods of proof by ordeal and battle had been falling into disrepute, and were banned by the Lateran Council in 1215, they implied recourse to the criminal jury, an institution which may perhaps have its roots in the standing body of jurors sworn to accuse no man falsely, of whom we read in the dooms of an Anglo-Saxon king.

Much of this famous document, so largely concerned with the oppressions of the royal officers and with abstruse points of feudal law and custom, has now only an antiquarian interest. The importance of the charter is due to the fact that it is the first example in our history of a national protest against a bad government. The shape which the protest assumed, the details which it comprised, the manner in which it was drafted, are of less account than the co-operation of Stephen Langton, Archbishop of Canterbury, of the Mayor of London, and of the most politically minded barons of the land in a common effort to bring the King to account, and to force him to obey the laws and to study the interests of his people. The barons were in grim earnest. In the event of an infraction of the charter they were ready to carry their opposition to the point of civil war, and in proof of their resolute intent appointed twenty-five of their number to safeguard its provisions and to constrain the King, if necessary by the utmost use of force, to observe them.

This high example of constitutional obedience lived on in the national memory. The charter, in support of which a section of the baronage was even willing to put the English crown upon the head of a Frenchman, became a watchword. It was three times revised in the first decade of Henry III's reign. Its three forest clauses were amplified into a separate charter for the relief of those abuses of the forest law, which, of all the innovations of the Norman Conquest, were felt by the country folk of England to be the most oppressive. During the minority of the young King his wise counsellors, William Marshall and Hubert de Burgh, ruled in its spirit. But Henry 1216- III, once he had reached man's estate, showed himself 72 strangely insensitive to the workings of the national mind. Devout, refined, artistic, the builder of Westminster Abbey was, like Charles I, in matters of public policy, blind, obstinate, and untrustworthy. The country hated the foreign favourites, Savoyards and Poitevins, upon whom he lavished power and wealth. It resented his subservience to the Pope. It saw no substantial advantage to English interests, but on the contrary a source of intolerable exaction in the King's ambitious project for securing the Sicilian crown for his young son Edmund. As the clergy were bled white to feed the ambitions of Pope and King, the tide of indignation mounted steadily. At last Henry was told plainly that redress must precede supply. At a parliament at Oxford (1258) he was compelled to accept a scheme of government which placed the conduct of affairs in the hands of the baronial party.

Had the Provisions of Oxford been observed in the letter and the spirit, there would have been no Barons' War. Henry never proposed to observe them. He could count upon the Pope obligingly to relieve him of an oath taken under duress in the papal cause. But he was now confronted with an opposition which was both widely supported and ably led. "The community of the bachelory of England," as the smallest landed gentry are called by a chronicler, was as ready to protest against the lukewarmness of the baronage as later to correct the backslidings of the King. The better part of the clergy, the students of Oxford, the burgesses of the chartered towns, joined hands with this section of the landed gentry in the movement to protect the country against arbitrary rule. Franciscans carried the popular message through the towns and villages and acted as missionaries of the cause. When the quarrel ripened into civil war, Simon de Montfort, the alien Earl of Leicester, stood out as the champion of the national interest. On the high down above Lewes he routed the royal army (1264), and captured the King and Prince Edward, his heir. Yet it is characteristic of the moderation of the English civil war that the outcome of this brilliant victory was not the deposition of the sovereign, but an attempt to bind him in the eyes of the nation assembled in parliament to act on the advice of a baronial council.

Nothing is more calculated to strike the public imagination than the political employment of a victory in the field. Simon's Westminster Parliament (January, 1265) marked an epoch. No assembly had been summoned for so grave a purpose. None had been so widely representative, for in addition to the clergy and barons, the first numerously, and the second more sparsely summoned, every shire was invited to send two knights and many boroughs two burgesses. The representation of the towns was apparently an innovation. Upon the receptive mind of Prince Edward, who was constrained in this widely representative gathering of the constitutional party to swear to an unpalatable peace, the lesson of such a gathering and of the strength to be derived from it made an impression of enduring value to the nation. The work of Simon, which seemed to be frustrated by his defeat 1265 and death on the field of Evesham, was carried forward by his conqueror and disciple, the more judiciously, and doubtless the more securely, since the legend of Simon as the hero and sainted martyr of liberty and justice survived in the memory of the English people.

Edward I is the English Justinian. His reign is marked by such legislative activity as this country has only twice witnessed (in the reign of Henry VIII, and again under the Commonwealth) before the Reform Act of 1832 opened wide the floodgates. The Statute de Donis Conditionalibus, which settled our law of entail, the Act of Mortmain, curtailing ecclesiastical endowments, the Statute of Quia Emptores, which forbade subinfeudation, and so limited the importance of tenure in chief, are among the legislative monuments of this clear-headed and industrious ruler. The greatest, however, of Edward's titles to fame is that in his reign parliament assumed its completed form and became an established instrument for the transaction of public business. The grounds of this momentous change are not to be found in any development of political theory, or special distemper of the public mind, but in the practical convenience of dealing upon a national scale with national questions through a gathering representative of the nation. The development of trade and commerce, the expansion of public policy, the growing demands upon government for justice, police, and administration, had now far outrun the slight and dwindling capacity of the feudal revenue. The paltry income to be derived from aids and scutages, marriages and reliefs was an anachronism in an age when a London merchant buying wine in Bordeaux, or selling wool in Ghent, might out-top the rent roll of a baron or an earl. In his need for money Edward could no more afford to neglect the mercantile community than to spare the broad acres of the Church. To obtain a national revenue he found himself increasingly compelled to the expedient of summoning national parliaments.

The form of these conferences was for a long time fluid and uncertain; the word parliament, which means a talk or interchange of views, was originally applied to any meeting of the King's Great Council, and only by degrees confined to such meetings as were reinforced by representatives from the borough and the shire. The "Model Parliament" of 1295 was attended by prelates, earls, barons, and judges, summoned by individual writ, and by two knights from every shire, two citizens from every city, and two burgesses from every borough, summoned through the sheriff, and by representatives of the lower clergy, summoned under the terms of the writs addressed to the two archbishops. By degrees the lower clergy ceased to attend, having other and more pressing duties to perform. It was a lay House of Commons which voted the Reformation Statutes.

But there was no House of Commons in the reign of Edward I, nor yet that familiar procedure by which bills are drafted in the form of statutes, introduced, debated, and voted on in two Houses, and finally receive the royal assent in the House of Lords, as the Clerk looks over his shoulder at Mr. Speaker, humbly standing at the bar with his following from the lower House, and intones the magic formula *Le roy le veult*, at which the red-robed peers, representing the sovereign, simultaneously remove their archaic cocked hats. The division between the two Houses belongs to the fourteenth, the procedure by bills to the fifteenth, century. The main business of an Edwardian parliament was not so much to legislate as to vote supplies and handle petitions.

A vast miscellany of subjects, some important and others trivial, was brought by way of petition to the notice of this great inquest of the nation, which was termed a parliament. The judges were at hand to deal with such petitions as might involve issues of law. Matters of finance were naturally referred to the officials of the exchequer. The meeting of parliament afforded an opportunity of liquidating the current business of the kingdom. Here local grievances were ventilated and private wrongs redressed, arrears of pay settled, quarrels composed, foreign ambassadors received, and treaties drafted. Much of the work done in a parliament was legal, for the King's Council was still the highest court of justice in the land. The consequences were important. It is common knowledge that lawyers in a parliament of amateurs exert more than their fair share of influence. A mediaeval parliament was full of men learned in the law; and our statute book, which is singularly free from idle rhetoric or hysteria, bears the imprint of the most cautious, the most conservative, and the most insular of professions.

In the closing years of this great King's reign an impressive demonstration was given of that respect for law and constitutional usage which was fast becoming an ingrained political tradition of the people. Edward was a strong, straightforward, and, in the main, a popular ruler; but he was exacting and ambitious, and none too scrupulous in his methods. In the year 1297 he found himself at issue with the clergy, who had been told by the Pope that they were to pay no taxes without Rome's consent, with the general body of the nation, who groaned under the lash of his taxgatherers, and with certain pre-eminent members of the baronage who flatly refused to serve in arms beyond the seas. The King then learned that there were limits to his prerogative which he could not transgress without danger. He was compelled to confirm the charters, to permit amendments in his administration, and to admit that he could not increase the established customs on merchandise or raise aid or subsidy without parliamentary assent.

BOOKS WHICH MAY BE CONSULTED

H. W. C. Davis: *England under the Normans and Angevins.* 1905.

W. Stubbs: *Constitutional History of England.* 1880.

E. Lavisse: *Histoire de France.* 1903.

F. W. Maitland: *Memoranda de Parliamento.* (Rolls Series.) 1893.

McKechnie: *Magna Carta.* 1905.

T. F. Tout: *Edward I.* 1893.

W. H. Hutton: *Philip Augustus.* 1896.

F. Perry: *Louis IX.* 1901.

A. Luchaire: *Social France at the Time of Philip Augustus.* Tr. E. Krebhiel. 1912.

C. Petit Du Taillis: *The Feudal Monarchy in France and England.* Tr. E. D. Hunt. 1936.

A. L. Poole: *From Domesday Book to Magna Carta.* 1951.

F. Barlow: *The Feudal Kingdom of England,* 1042-1216. 1955.

Sir Maurice Powicke: *The Thirteenth Century,* 1216-1307, 1953.

S. Painter: *The Reign of King John.* 1949.

F. Thompson: *Magna Carta.* 1948.

CHAPTER XXVII

WALES, SCOTLAND, IRELAND

*Predominance of England in Wales secured by Edward I.
Quarrel composed by Henry Tudor. Forces making for Anglo-
Scottish Union. Policy of Edward I. Growth of national
feeling in Scotland. True greatness of Scotland follows the
union with England. The tragedy of Ireland. Effect of the
Scottish invasion and the French War.*

EDWARD I WAS the first of our English kings to place in the
forefront of his policy the reduction of Wales and Scotland.
For a comparatively brief interval (1259-1338) between two
centuries of profitless fighting in France, the union of the
British peoples under the English crown became an object
worthy of steady attention. In Wales the strategy of Edward
was brilliant and successful. The great mountain fastness of
Snowdonia was surrounded and subdued. An English
principality, created in favour of the heir to the throne, d.
divided into shires on the English plan, and protected by a 1240
system of formidable castles, replaced the north Welsh
principality of Gwynnedd, which ever since the days of
Llewellyn the Great had been the heart of tribal Wales and
the principal sanctuary of the Celtic tradition. A political
predominance of England in this wild land of narrow valleys
and knotted hills was thus secured; but no more than a
predominance. The Celtic tribes continued to fight among
themselves in their mountain fastnesses and from time to
time would carry fire and sword through valleys up which
the Lords Marchers, themselves often married to Welsh
women, were steadily pushing the tillage and the tongue of
the Saxon race. The Welsh uplands remained much as
Giraldus Cambrensis, himself half Welsh and half Norman,
had described them at the end of the twelfth century. "These
people are light and active, hardy rather than strong, and
entirely bred up to the use of arms; for not only the nobles,
but all the people are trained to war, and when the trumpet

sounds the tribesman rushes as eagerly from his plough as the courtier from his court. They live more on flesh, milk, and cheese than bread, pay little attention to commerce, shipping, or manufactures, and devote their leisure to the chase and martial exercises. They earnestly study the defence of their country and their liberty. For these they fight, for these they undergo hardships, and for these they willingly sacrifice their lives. They esteem it a disgrace to die in bed, an honour to die on the field of battle."

The victory of Edward, though it was followed by wise measures for the pacification of the country, was powerless to alter the stubborn spirit of the Welsh people. In all essentials the Welshman remained as Giraldus describes him, warlike and flighty, jealous and eloquent, sensitive on points of family honour, quick to take up a quarrel and avenge an insult, temperate in food and drink, tricky and versatile in intrigue, and passionately devoted to poetry and song. It is true indeed that Anglo-Norman civilization, spreading from the great Welsh monasteries, and from the castles of the Marcher Lords, exercised an influence on this race of quarrelsome nightingales. English and Welsh families on the border mingled their blood. Welsh bowmen fought side by side with the yeoman farmers of England in the French wars of the fourteenth century, and contributed not a little, since the long bow was a Welsh invention, to secure victory for the King of England. Welsh gentlemen attended the University of Oxford, or, like Owen Glendower, learned their law at the Inns of Court. Wales took what England had to give, but yet remained as different from England as mountain is different from plain.

Long after England had adopted an orderly way of life, the little mountain land upon her flank remained a cauldron of seething and primitive passions. Just as the overspill of our modern Irish factions almost brought English politics to the point of civil war, so the fighting spirit of the Welsh Marcher Lords counted for much in the Wars of the Roses. But the quarrel between England and Wales was finally composed 1485 by Henry Tudor's victory on Bosworth field. A Welsh dynasty ruled over England for a century, incorporated Wales in the English parliamentary system, and made of England a Protestant country. It was a Welsh Prime Minister who brought the British Empire in triumph out of the great war.

The problem of Scotland was different in one important particular. All Scotland south and east of the highland line might equally, so far as its racial composition, its mode of government, and its legal customs were concerned, have been accounted part of English Northumbria. Saxons, Danes, Norsemen, with an infusion of Celts, stronger no doubt in the northern than in the southern region, but both north and south of the Cheviots subordinate to these stronger strains, constituted the population alike of Northumbria and of the Scottish kingdom. Anglo-Norman nobles held lands on either side of the border; Anglo-Norman law and Anglo-Norman legal textbooks were as much respected at Edinburgh as in London. It had been part of the policy of David I, one 1124-of the ablest of Scottish kings, and himself the son of an 53 English princess, to imbue his rude subjects with some tincture of the more advanced civilization of the south. In this design he had been successful. The traveller who reached Edinburgh from York in the middle of the thirteenth century would have found little in the speech, appearance, and manners of the people, or in their military and ecclesiastical architecture, to apprise him that in the course of his ride he had crossed a frontier between deadly enemies.

A political union between Scotland and England was therefore in itself a natural arrangement, more natural than the union of England with Wales, Ireland, or Gascony. It was Edward's object to accomplish it. By the Treaty of 1290 Brigham it was arranged that Edward's son and heir should marry Margaret of Norway, the heiress to the Scottish throne, and that the two kingdoms should be brought together in a personal union, each conserving its own rights and customs. Few mediaeval treaties are wiser than this far-sighted transaction, which, could it have been carried into effect, would have saved Britain from centuries of border warfare, and Scotland from the grinding poverty of its proud and desperate isolation. But it was not to be. The Maid of Norway died at sea, the Treaty of Brigham became waste paper, and Edward was driven to achieve his object by other and more questionable means.[1]

What followed afforded a signal instance of the charac-

[1] Genealogical Table G

teristic weakness of every mediaeval government, its inability
to control the rapacity and maladministration of distant
agents. A dispute having arisen as to the claims of thirteen
rival candidates for the Scottish throne, Edward was invited
to the invidious task of arbitration. He decided, apparently
without sinister intent, that John Baliol had a better claim
than Robert Bruce. John Baliol was accordingly crowned
king. But the successful candidate had little cause to bless his
benefactor. He was treated as the puppet of his English
overlord. Indignation drove him to rebellion, and rebellion
brought down upon Scotland the heavy hand of the English
King. The land was conquered and governed as a province
of the English kingdom.

And so, but for the tyranny and oppression of Edward's
agents, Scotland might have remained. To the leading men of
the country, whether lay or ecclesiastical, there was nothing
in itself oppressive in the English connection. There was no
literature of Scottish nationalism. In no respect was the
southerner so alien as the Highlander from Argyll or Inver-
ness. But oppression released new forces in the Scottish
nature. The common people rose against the invaders and
found in William Wallace, a man from nowhere, an inspired
leader of revolt.

The birth of this little Scottish nation is justly accounted
one of the cardinal facts of British history. The two founders,
William Wallace, the guerilla leader, and Robert Bruce, the
royal statesman, are acclaimed by their compatriots to this
day as the architects of Scottish greatness. But to the critic
who asks what use Scotland made of the independence so
bravely won, so triumphantly secured on the field of Bannockburn (1314), the answer is less reassuring. The history
of mediaeval Scotland is a tangle of savage broils and convulsions. Measured by the greatness of its statesmen and
soldiers, its thinkers and divines, its authors and its artists,
the greatness of Scotland belongs not to the era of mediaeval
liberty and isolation, but to that less unhappy and distracted
period which, following the personal union of the two kingdoms under the house of Stuart, witnessed the steady advance
of the Scottish people in all the arts and accomplishments of
peace.

Irish history is a tragedy. Often invaded but never subdued, the Irish have not been permitted either to build up an independent civilization out of their native stock of thought and feeling, nor yet forced to receive the discipline of a power stronger and more cultivated than themselves. Again and again the fatal words half-conquest are inscribed upon the annals of this gifted and unfortunate people. The Romans stopped at Anglesea. It was part of their prudence never to cross St. George's Channel, part of Ireland's misfortune that she lacked the convenience of Roman roads and never tasted of Roman order. Centuries passed. The Irish received Christianity from St. Patrick (432), and from their new religion acquired an impulse which at the darkest hour of European history brought them to the forefront of Christian culture. But Ireland was not long permitted to be a centre of worldwide illumination. Night again descended with the Danish invasions, when all that was brilliant and attractive in the social life of the people was obliterated by a new barbarism; save for the Danish seaport towns, nothing was left but an untamed wilderness. Then came an event which was destined to exert an enduring influence on the fate of the Irish people. England was conquered by a race gifted beyond all others with the power of organizing conquest and of turning it to civilized ends. But the Normans had no eyes for the island across St. George's Channel. Sicily, Normandy, Anjou, distracted their attention; and when at last, with the formal encouragement of Pope Hadrian IV (the only English Pope), it was resolved to conquer the island, the enterprise was not undertaken by King Henry II, who was far too busy with the affairs of his wide Angevin Empire, but left to the courage and appetite of private adventurers. Again the conquest was not complete.

The Anglo-Normans who followed Richard de Clare, the Earl of Pembroke, upon his Irish quest were brilliant soldiers. The native Irish, divided among themselves by tribal jealousies, and unprotected by body armour, were easily mastered by a picked force of mailed knights trained in the best school of contemporary warfare. The Ostman towns passed into English hands. But then the real difficulties began. The conquerors settled down as Irish landlords. Many of them married Irish women. Most of them learned something of the Irish language. Surrounded by the sights and sounds of Ireland, the Butlers and Fitzgeralds, the De Courceys and

1169-71

De Burghs, took colour from their environment and began to acquire Irish characteristics. The old story of the victor taken captive by his victim was now repeated. The ancient Ireland, with its tribal law and customs, its language and literature, its evil leaven of a savage and aboriginal population, but shorn of its ancient pride, continued to exist.

These fundamental things the Anglo-Norman invasion had done little to alter. What it did was to give to Ireland a new aristocracy, which could hardly be described as fully English or as fully Irish, but which partook of the qualities of both nations and occupied an intermediate position between them.

The overlord was an absent-minded absentee. Of our mediaeval kings Richard II alone was even disposed to treat Ireland seriously. The English settlers and traders in the seaport towns, the Anglo-Irish nobility, the native Irish tribes, formed three separate communities, which only the wisest and most consistent statesmanship, and perhaps not even that, could have brought into stable and harmonious relations.

During the reign of Edward I, when England was free from continental entanglements, some progress was made in the development of Irish commerce and the spread of the shire system, the chief political export of the mediaeval Englishman. A century of peaceful penetration might have ended with the establishment of Irish unity. But again Ireland was dogged by misfortune. In the year after Bannockburn, 1315 Edward Bruce, the brother of Robert, seeking to cause the utmost annoyance to the hated Englishman, made a violent irruption into the island. In the next year he was joined by his brother. The invasion of the Bruces let loose upon the unfortunate country a war of savages. The tender plant of Irish prosperity withered away, the English influence was rolled back within the narrow compass of the Pale, and the progress of a century was suddenly arrested. These disasters were not repaired. With the outbreak of the Hundred Years' War the attention of the English government was diverted from the needs and bogs of Ireland to the more attractive and splendid quest of the French crown. Ireland sank back into its western mists, and when, in the sixteenth century, a serious effort was again made to reconquer the country for English civilization, there was added to existing sources of division the new and deadly fact of religious schism. England became Protestant, while Ireland remained true to the Roman Faith.

BOOKS WHICH MAY BE CONSULTED

P. Hume Brown: *History of Scotland.* 1899-1909.
A. Lang: *History of Scotland.* 1900-07.
Owen Edwards: *Wales.* 1901.
A. G. Little: *Mediaeval Wales.* 1902.
G. M. Trevelyan: *History of England.* 1926.
Mrs. J. R. Green: *The Making of Ireland and its Undoing.* 1908.
J. E. Lloyd: *History of Wales.* 2 vols. 1911.
E. Curtis: *History of Mediaeval Ireland.* 2nd Ed. 1938.
W. Alison Phillips (ed.): *History of the Church of Ireland.* 3 vols. 1933-4.

CHAPTER XXVIII

THE HUNDRED YEARS' WAR

The French War and English opinion. The English army. Strength and weakness of France. The campaign of 1346. The Black Death. The terrible decade. The Treaty of Calais. French recovery under Charles V. French relapse. Burgundians and Armagnacs. Richard II. The Lancastrians. Henry V and Agincourt. Treaty of Troyes. Defection of Burgundy. Joan of Arc. End of the war. Spirit and consequences. The Wars of the Roses. March of English genius.

THE HUNDRED YEARS' WAR, which appears to a distant posterity as a tissue of calamitous follies, was regarded with very different eyes by the English subjects of Edward III and Henry V. To our forefathers there was nothing fantastic in the idea that an English King should claim the crown of France, or endeavour to subject that country to his dominion. They made no protests against the initiation of the war, nor demanded, even when success appeared to be hopeless, a pacifist government to bring it to a conclusion. The fountains of their wrath were reserved, as in the popular risings in 1381 and 1450, for ministers who were thought to be responsible for failure abroad or extortion at home. Parliament met frequently, for without parliaments the King could not obtain the taxes wherewith to nourish the war; but no parliament refused the taxes. No critic rose to point out that England was neglecting the tasks which lay to her hand in Wales, Scotland, and Ireland to pursue a desperate and sterile quest in France. A war with the French became part of the national background, and, in the public mind of England, though interspersed with taxes, almost assumed the aspect of an ordinance of fate.

That it was thus popular may be ascribed to the fact that the English, who were the aggressors, pursued their quarrel upon enemy soil. While France sustained all the calamities of invasion, England enjoyed the advantages of successful rapine in a bountiful land beyond the sea. The burden of heavy taxation was offset for the commonalty of our island not only by the glamour of foreign victory, but by the conviction that the war was good for trade, that it enabled England to sell her wool in Bruges and Ghent, to buy her wine from Bordeaux, and to find a continental market for her tin, her iron, and her hides. And this national and middle-class sentiment about the war was reinforced by the character of the English armies. The old feudal forces, based on tenure, were now discarded for a long-service army, raised by commissions of array, and so far as the infantry arm was concerned composed of English yeomen and of Welsh archery. An English army of the fourteenth century, unlike its French counterpart, was the mirror of a nation, not of a class. The cavalry was no longer the sole or even the most important arm. There now appeared for the first time upon the battlefields of the continent that steady British infantry, drawn from the humbler regions of society, which again and again has disconcerted the calculations of brilliant commanders. In the fourteenth century these stalwart countrymen were entrusted with a weapon which in range and hardiness outstripped all competitors, and in the use of which they had attained by devoted practice upon the village green an unequalled skill. The British yeomen who decided the day at Crécy and Agincourt were armed with the long bow, and, as the famous heavy cavalry of France advanced to the charge, aimed at the horses. A cloud of arrows brought the assault to a sudden standstill, and before a blow had been exchanged, the dismounted riders were floundering on the ground in their heavy armour, an easy prey to their assailants.

In the first decades of the fourteenth century France showed all the promise of a great nation. Her soil was rich, her vegetation was varied, her peasants and burgesses were economical and laborious. In no part of Europe, save perhaps in Venice, was the art of civilized life so well understood or so happily practised. The French were more refined than the English, more comfortable than the Germans, more open to world influence than the Spaniards, less afflicted by the violence of domestic discord than the citizens of Italy. For the last two centuries no country had given so many patterns to European thought as the land of Abelard and St. Bernard, of the Crusades and the Troubadours, of chivalry and scholasticism. Much also she owed to good fortune. The Capetian house, which for three hundred years had never failed of a male heir, had spared her the evils of palace revolutions and disputed successions. She had given dynasties to England and Sicily, and later had sent princes of the house of Anjou to reign in Hungary and Naples. The quixotic King of Bohemia thought that no place in the 1310- world was comparable to Paris. Even the Papacy had 46 become French, for a French Pope, surrounded by a college of cardinals in which France exercised a predominant influence, was established at Avignon, and divided only from French territory by the breadth of the Rhone.

From this position of apparent strength there were three important deductions. The convenient shelter of the Capetian dynasty was not destined to be immortal. In 1316 Louis, the son of Philip IV, died, leaving only a daughter, but no male heir. He was followed by his brothers Philip V and Charles the Fair, the French lawyers obligingly discovering that, since females were excluded from the succession to a certain form of property under the law of the Salian Franks, they were incapable of sitting on the French throne. Then, in 1328, Charles died without male issue, and was succeeded by his cousin Philip of Valois. The title of the founder of the Valois dynasty was not accepted without challenge, for Edward III of England was the grandson of Philip the Fair by his mother Isabella, and claimed that a female, if she could not herself reign in France, was entitled to transmit the regal dignity to her male heir. Not for three hundred years had such a doubt been cast upon the legitimacy of a King of France.[1]

The second drawback was even more serious. All through the fourteenth century the nobility of France lived in a kind of feudal honeymoon, learning nothing, forgetting nothing, and foreseeing nothing. They waged private war, as if the state were not in danger. They oppressed their villeins, as if it were not through their labour that the life of the country was sustained. They were blind to the strength which came to their antagonists from the social fusion, which exposed the richest English barons and the poorest English yeomen to the equal perils of a soldier's life. Though the power of plebeian infantry to defeat the most aristocratic cavalry in the world had been demonstrated again and again, at Courtrai in 1302 and later on the moonlit field of Crécy, it was necessary for a French king to be brought as a prisoner to London, and for an English king to receive the crown of France in Paris, before the lesson was taken to heart. It is a curious illustration of the inability of a military caste to receive the teaching of experience that, although the English brought artillery upon the 1346 field of Crécy, it was not until the battle of Formigny 104 1450 years later that the French were able to produce a culverin which outranged the flight of the English arrow.

Another source of weakness was so inveterate that only the convulsion of the French Revolution was able to effect a radical cure. The French people, for all their brilliance, could neither impose a good tax nor pay a bad one. Even under the best of her mediaeval kings the fiscal system of France was deplorable. The taxes were farmed, with the familiar result that more was wrung from the taxpayer than ever found its way into the coffers of the state. The *gabelle*, a salt tax, was crushing for the poor. The traders were oppressed by an impost on sales, by constant tampering with the coinage, and, under Charles V and his successors, by a ruinous system of internal customs duties. The sale of offices, carrying fiscal exemptions, was a vicious expedient invented by Philip the Fair and revived by Charles V; and the poison of favours and exemptions, once sanctioned, spread like a gangrene through the whole system. It is characteristic of the fiscal weakness of the country that the large ransom demanded by England for King John of France, who was captured at the

[1] Genealogical Table H.

battle of Poitiers, could not be otherwise met than by the sale of a French princess to Galeazzo Visconti, the upstart and opulent Duke of Milan.

The struggle between France and England, which might easily have been occasioned by a sailors' quarrel in a Channel port, or by a foray across the border of Aquitaine, or, since French aid was now (1336) openly given to the party of David Bruce and the cause of Scottish independence, by some incident in the course of that northern warfare, did, in fact, arise from an event in Flanders. In 1336 all Englishmen travelling or resident in that country were, by the orders of Count Louis acting upon instructions from Paris, arrested and cast into prison. The outrage produced a reply from England which threatened to bring the flourishing industries of Flanders toppling to the ground. The export of English wool was forbidden, and the English market was closed to the import of Flemish cloth.

At this critical juncture the course of western policy was determined by the vigour and resolution of a Flemish brewer. Jacob van Artevelde of Ghent preferred economic prosperity in free alliance with England to economic ruin in feudal subjection to Philip of France. He forced a rupture, and to quiet the scruples of the Flemings prevailed upon Edward III to claim the crown of France.

The first serious action in the war was an English naval 1340 victory at Sluys, so complete that for a space of thirty years it gave to England the mastery of the Channel. Yet for six years no effort was made to exploit this advantage. Why should England invade France seeing that the danger to the English trade with Flanders had been averted, and the power of the French to land forces in England was, for the time being, effectively broken? But the embers of this quarrel were widely spread, and the flame which died down in one quarter spurted up in another. A disputed succession to the Duchy of Brittany brought England and France into the field in support of rival claimants. Philip stood for Charles of Blois, and Edward for John of Montfort, the champion of that part of the duchy which was Celtic in speech and race, and therefore most strongly opposed to the invasive influences of the French.

The outlines of a great panorama of war were now defined.

In Flanders, in Brittany, in Aquitaine, in Scotland, the power of France and England stood opposed. The idea of an English converging movement from Normandy, Brittany, and Aquitaine outlined itself in the mediaeval manner, not very distinctly or with any close attention to detail, but nevertheless in such a way as to make 1346, the year in which the English sacked Poitiers, won Creçy, besieged Calais, and routed the Scots at Neville's Cross, an *annus mirabilis* in the war. Yet from all these far-flung victories there resulted only one point of permanent advantage to the victors. Calais became an English town in 1347, and so remained until it was lost under Queen Mary in the sixteenth century.

The year of the capture of Calais was marked by the advent of a calamity more destructive than a century of mediaeval warfare. The Black Death, a bubonic plague originating in the far east, swept along the lines of mediaeval traffic into every part of Europe. It was conveyed from Asia Minor into Italy and Spain, entered France by Marseilles, England through Dorsetshire, and swept eastwards through Germany and the Scandinavian countries into Poland, Austria, and Russia. Mediaeval figures, upon the basis of which it has been calculated by a modern writer that one-fourth of the population of Europe perished of this plague, are notoriously untrustworthy. We have no complete means of checking the statement of contemporaries that a hundred thousand lives were lost in Venice, Florence, Paris, and London, sixty thousand in Avignon, fifty-seven thousand in Norwich, or that the death roll of Germany, which admittedly suffered less than Italy and France, reached a figure of one and a quarter million. But there can be no doubt that the mortality was upon such a scale as to produce in its train those grave moral disorders and far-reaching social consequences always to be expected when mankind is overwhelmed by some vast natural calamity which it is unable to forecast, to measure, or to mitigate.

It was observed of the plague that it sought out by preference the young and the strong. Sometimes the enemy was merciful, and slew by a sudden stroke; more often the patient was condemned to a few hours of hopeless agony. In Avignon, where the plague raged for seven months, a creditable but forlorn attempt was made to diagnose the cause of the malady. Bodies were exhumed and examined by order of the Pope. But the disease pursued its deadly course, working havoc among the narrow, unclean mediaeval streets, and upon the decks of ships, so that they drifted over the waters without guidance from their lifeless crews, and stripping the fields of the labour which should drive the plough, reap the harvest, or tend the cattle.

Among the moral results of this disaster the most shameful was a series of attacks upon the Jewish population, who at Mainz and other German-speaking towns were burned in their hundreds or thousands by an infuriated mob in the belief that the plague was a malignant device of the Semitic race for the confusion of the Catholic creed. One consequence of some significance for Europe ensued from this outburst of western barbarism. The Jews who were persecuted in the Rhenish cities found now, as on earlier occasions, an asylum in Poland. Casimir the Great took occasion to renew the protection which a predecessor had accorded to this community in 1260; and the high proportion of Semites to be found in modern Poland is not a little due to his enlightened policy, pursued at a moment when no western Jew was safe from the fury of Catholic mobs. 1333-70

Other reactions to the calamity were less atrocious than these. Some people, as in Boccaccio's famous description of the plague in Florence, surrendered themselves to the pleasures of the moment. Others, like the flagellants, who marched in melancholy penitential processions, flogging themselves with rods of iron, fell into ecstasies of religious emotion. There were those, again, who took to a life of reckless brigandage. But beyond these passing excesses, which disappeared with their exciting cause, the plague exercised certain durable effects, so that when it died down in 1350 (to be renewed at intervals by minor visitations), and men resumed their normal habits of mind, European society was not quite what it had been before.

The change was not catastrophic. Rather it would be true to say that the sudden destruction of life (which was specially evident in the monasteries) had set in motion a series of small shiftings, which, in their accumulated and accumulating effects, amounted to a revolution. In England, perhaps, the changes were more noticeable than elsewhere: in the monasteries a marked decline in literary activity and discipline;

in the impoverished country parishes empty rectories and absentee priests; in the grammar schools the substitution, with a new race of teachers, of English for French; in architecture the spread of the Perpendicular style, simpler than the older forms of Gothic, more easily standardized, and better adapted to the capacity of a diminished band of travelling masons; and finally, in agriculture a marked acceleration of that process of converting labour services into money payments, which led in time to the disappearance of an unfree village population and to the break-up of the mediaeval system of tillage.

The last of these changes, which is not peculiar to England, was due to the fact that owing to the dearth of labour the peasant was able to demand a higher price for his toil, and the lord of the manor was no longer always in a position to secure the working of his demesne land save by the novel expedient of labour hired from outside. The revolutionary possibilities of such a situation gave great alarm to the governing class both in France and England. In France workmen were forbidden to take more than a third of their former wage. In England, Parliament called labourers and artisans to their old rate of wage and forbade them to move from one county to another. Political economy, like nature, may be expelled with a fork, but it always returns. The legislation of the Edwardian parliaments was unavailing to arrest a process grounded in the economic necessities of the time. As the value of labour services to the lord steadily diminished, the convenience of a mobile labour supply, remunerated by money payments, became by sure degrees more clearly apparent. So the old manorial economy was gradually sapped by new forces, and as the villein became detached from his bondage to the soil, and began to sell his labour freely in the market, voices were raised challenging the whole social order and asking the question which in every virile generation is put to society by equalitarian men:

> "When Adam delved, and Eve span,
> Who was then the gentleman?"

The tragedy of the plague neither sobered the frivolity nor mitigated the ardour of the rival aristocracies of France and England. The national quarrel was revived at the earliest

moment and prosecuted at the expense of the miserable peasantry of France with a barbarous and animated zest. The ten years (1350-1360) which follow the
accession of John the Bountiful to the throne of France were
written in flame and blood on the annals of his distracted
kingdom. Petrarch, who travelled through the country four
or five years after the battle of Poitiers, said that it had been
so wrecked and ravaged by the English armies that he could
scarce persuade himself that this was the same flourishing
land which he had previously known. Arson and pillage,
murders and rape, burning crops and mutilated cattle,
marked the progress of the proud island race and their
continental levies. In these methods of barbarism the Black
Prince won a pre-eminence which has secured for him an
abiding place in the popular memory of western France.

The experience of this terrible decade was the first impressive indication to the world that the remote inhabitants
of England, whose defeat at the hands of the yet more savage
Scots upon the field of Bannockburn was no distant memory,
had now become a great military nation. In a series of
unexpected victories, sometimes, as at Poitiers, obtained
against overwhelming odds, these strange people had overthrown the ancient military glory of France. One English
army led by the King had appeared before the walls of
Rheims and Paris. Another, advancing from Bordeaux, had
carried fire and sword through the olive groves and vineyards,
the gardens and the tilth of Languedoc, wasting the highest
revenue-producing areas under the French monarchy and
involving it in the greatest embarrassment and distress.

It is difficult to imagine any form of humiliation to which
this nation, only a generation before esteemed to be the
proudest in Europe, was not now subjected. The King of
France was a prisoner in England. A crushing tribute was
imposed upon his people for a ransom. The disbanded
marauders of the wars, gathered into free companies, pillaged
the countryside, and dared to levy blackmail on the Pope.
Even the patient tillers of the field, upon whose broad
shoulders had fallen the principal burden of these cruel wars,
rose at last against their enemies the nobles in a formidable
revolt. The Jacquerie of 1358, which was characterized, as
every rising of the desperate poor is apt to be, by great
ferocity, was put down with ease; but the country was no

EUROPE IN 1360

stronger for that bitter victory, nor for the terrible social chasm which it left behind it. Save for one circumstance which impeached the completeness of the English triumph, France was prostrate. Paris had escaped the clutch of the enemy, and so long as Paris was French, France was not English. Yet even here a popular revolution, fomented by patriotic fury, public distress and disloyal intrigue, nearly succeeded in displacing the Dauphin by Charles of Navarre, that smooth and perfidious intriguer, who was the tool of England and pledged by a secret instrument to hold the crown of France as a vassal of the English King.

When at last the French had made the discovery that by the avoidance of pitched battles they could tire the patience of their enemy, it became part of British prudence to accept a peace. The Treaty of Calais, 1360, assigned Normandy to France, Aquitaine, Calais, and Ponthieu to England, an arrangement deeply humiliating to French pride, but permitting France to enjoy a few years of necessary breathing space. When the quarrel was renewed the balance was no longer tilted in favour of England. Charles V, now ruler of France, was a very different man from his prodigal and thriftless father. If a bad financier can ever be described as a good king, Charles the Wise merited that description. He had seen too much of mob rule during the evil days which followed the disaster of Poitiers to be enamoured of popular government, and it was not through the States-General, which he summoned once only during his reign, that he proposed to restore the fortunes of France. His main merit was that he divined the essential elements of victory, a navy which could dispute the seas with England, an army which would harass without engaging the enemy, and a people recalled to sentiments of loyalty and hope. First of all the French kings he endeavoured to give his subjects a sense of the sea, visiting himself, and causing others to visit, the ports and dockyards in order that money might be more freely spent on the ships. Privileges for the towns, titles for the townsmen, economy in administration conciliated the general favour. The country was rid of the plague of the free companies or marauding soldiers from the disbanded armies, who were sent over the Pyrenees to die in a Castilian civil war. As for the army, it was placed under the Breton Bertrand du Guesclin, a great master of Fabian tactics, who, in the

1364-
80

campaign of 1369-1375, stripped England of all her overseas possessions save Bayonne, Bordeaux, and Calais. Before the end of the reign of this prudent and successful king, the French sailors were ravaging the English coast, and a Spanish navy had appeared in the Thames. Edward III and the Black Prince were dead. In 1380 Richard II was a lad of thirteen. The good fortune of the French monarchy seemed to be assured. Indeed, but for the fact that King Charles had embarked upon an attempt to conquer Brittany before he had finished with England, the soil of France might have been completely cleared of enemy occupation during his reign.

But then followed one of the most disastrous periods in the history of France, during which all the gains which had marked the later years of Charles V's reign were thrown away and the continued existence of the French nation was again imperilled. The source of this extraordinary relapse is to be found in an accumulation of unexpected evils—a long minority, a mad king, a spirit of fierce rivalry and faction among the princes of the blood and their noble followers, and finally in the formidable circumstance that for sixteen years England could rely upon the active co-operation of the most powerful subject of the French Crown.

It has already been noted that the kings of France had acquired the habit of creating appanages or great territorial domains for the princes of the blood, a method of decentral-

1350-64 ization often convenient but sometimes dangerous. Such an appanage John the Bountiful, in his light-hearted and short-sighted way, had created for his youngest son Philip, who

1363-1404 had earned for himself by his courage on the field of Poitiers the title of Le Hardi. To him was accorded the Duchy of Burgundy, a splendid fief in itself, famous for its wines and cookery, and French to the core, but destined by reason of three fortunate marriages to be joined to territories richer and more populous than itself, and for the most part estranged from France by race and language and by the potent affiliations of trade and politics. In a word, Philip espoused the heiress of Flanders and married two children into the Bavarian house of Wittelsbach, which ruled the greater part of the country now known as the kingdom of Holland. These were fateful alliances. It was doubtless the calculation of Charles V that the Burgundian dukes would bring the rich Flemish cities into the orbit of French influence. What happened was

the opposite. Rich Flanders proved to be a more powerful
magnet than poor Burgundy, Brussels a more attractive
capital than Dijon, the preservation of English goodwill a
more important consideration than a close friendship with
France. As time went on the dukes of Burgundy began to
feel the effects of their new environment. They became less
French and more Flemish, and behaved as the ambitious
masters of an independent and rival state established on the
eastern flank of France.

If Charles V had been succeeded by a strong man no great
evil might have resulted from the rise of this new power; but
his successor, who ascended the throne in 1380, was an un-
balanced and vicious boy, who, soon after reaching his
majority, lapsed into a state of acute mania. The incapacity of
Charles VI ultimately left the government of France to be
disputed between Louis of Orleans, the King's youngest
brother, and John of Burgundy, his powerful cousin. Louis
was young, attractive, and through his Italian wife, Valentina
Visconti, touched by the spirit of the Renaissance. John 1404-
the Fearless was violent and of a rougher mould. The first 19
stood for an energetic course of action against the hereditary
foe, the second prudently recognized the economic inter-
dependence of Flanders and England. On every question
which divided France, and notably on the schism in the
Church which was caused by the election of rival Popes, these
two leaders took opposite sides. Louis stood for Benedict,
the French Pope at Avignon; more wisely, since the support
of the capital was vital, the passionate Burgundian espoused a
policy of neutrality, which brought him the favour of the
doctors, the students, and the rabble of Paris.

Then occurred one of those startling political crimes which
in periods of great tension announce that patience is exhausted. One night in 1407 Orleans was murdered in a Paris
street. There is no mystery about the origin of this crime,
since it was avowed by the Duke, and defended by a don,
nor any doubt of its importance, seeing that it split France
sharply into two halves so furiously estranged that, by reason
of their divisions, northern France, including Paris, passed
into the control of an English king.

It was a sinister fact, which has often been repeated in the
course of French history, that the full violence of the party
contest was nowhere so fully felt as in Paris. The capital,

which should have been the seat of order, was, on the contrary,
the centre of the storm. It was so after the disaster of Poitiers,
when the cause of constitutional reform was ruined by terror
and treason; it was so again after the murder of the Duke of
Orleans, when the intellectual proletariat of the University, in
strange alliance with the powerful corporation of butchers,
and supported by the Duke of Burgundy, besieged the Bastille
and attempted to secure the persons of the royal family, enac-
ting a series of revolutionary scenes which anticipate in many
curious particulars the events of the French and more
recently of the Spanish Revolution.

Neither in England had the course of politics run smoothly
1377- since the death of Edward III. The reign of Richard II, the
99 son of the Black Prince, was happy only by reason of the
fact that in it peace was eventually made and maintained with
France. In other respects it was an uneasy reign, marked by
fierce factions and by abrupt vicissitudes of policy, by widespread social discontent, and by a disquieting growth of
heresy which challenged the whole fabric of the papal Church.
But of all the issues which were calculated to endanger
national peace none was so grave as the danger to the constitutional liberties of the country which disclosed itself in
the last two years of Richard's reign. Whether it was by
reason of his second marriage to Isabella of France and to
the influence of French example, for, as we have seen, the
French States-General met only once during Charles' reign,
or from a strange fit of impatience and exasperation, such
as may seize hold of temperamental natures, Richard in the
last two years of his life showed a plain intention to discontinue parliamentary government. In this he seriously miscal-
culated the temper of his countrymen. All through the
French war, parliament, which had come in the course of the
reign of Edward III to be divided into two houses, had been
accustomed to meet and to vote supplies. The claim of the
baronage and of the prelates, and, in a lesser degree, of the
burgesses and knights, to take a hand in the burden of national
affairs had by this time become established; and it was too
late now to reverse the engines. Edward II had been deposed
because he governed too little, Richard II was deposed because
he attempted to govern too much. Without any serious convulsion in the national life, the last of the Plantagenets was
displaced by Henry of Lancaster and murdered in prison,

a lone, courageous, extravagant figure, more humane and enlightened than the fierce Gallophobe nobles around him, but pledged to a strange and unpopular cause.

The house of Lancaster stood for two principles which appealed to the Englishman of that time, religious orthodoxy and constitutional government. The policy of toleration which had permitted so great a heretic as John Wycliffe to die in his bed was exchanged for a course of persecution, which, in a very short time, frightened learning and respectability away from Lollardy, and reduced the movement to obscurity and ignorance. But while speculative liberty was suppressed, Parliament took full advantage of the new dynasty to press for the control of legislation and finance. The constitutional advance, which is marked under the Lancastrian dynasty, was not indeed maintained, for liberty depends upon the preservation of order, and the main characteristic of English governments in the fifteenth century was their failure to maintain the law. Yet the precedents first established by the Lancastrian parliaments were not forgotten, for it was to them that the common lawyers made their appeal in the great struggle between Crown and Parliament in the seventeenth century.

England has never been an easy country to govern. "A wondrous and fickle land is this," said Richard II as he lay in the Tower, "for it hath exiled, slain, or ruined so many kings, rulers, and great men, and is ever tainted, and toileth with strife, variance, and envy"; and Henry IV, a cheerless, cold-blooded soldier, somewhat worn by his early campaigns in Prussia and Hungary, and soon falling ill of an incurable malady, found that the governance of England was no easy matter, what with the Lollards and the Scots, the Welshmen rebelling under Owen Glendower, and the Percies making such trouble on the north that they had to be beaten in a pitched fight at Shrewsbury. A prudent statesman succeeding to the heritage which Henry IV left behind him might well have concluded that what was truly needed for the establishment of the new dynasty was peace abroad. Henry V, however, was not built for prudent courses, but was all flame and martial ardour, as he lives in Shakespeare's verse. If England were not easy to govern, she presented in contrast to the divisions of France the spectacle of a united people. The baronage and clergy supported the Crown, the schism in the

1399-1413

1413-22

Papacy was no schism in England. Whatever inner dangers existed—and there was a party hungry for the property of the Church—were overcome by the animating prospect of war in France. Henry negotiated simultaneously both with the Burgundian and with the Orleanist or Armagnac factions. He was ready to offer himself to the highest bidder. Encouraged by the divisions of France he never for a moment doubted of victory.

1415   The capture of Harfleur and the battle of Agincourt were the first results of the young King's resolve to renew the glories of Crécy and Poitiers, and to show that in point of military prowess the house of Lancaster was worthy to succeed the Plantagenets. The French had neither army nor navy to resist the invaders. A section of the French nobility, almost entirely drawn from the Armagnac faction, sacrificed themselves vainly on the field of Agincourt, as French nobles had sacrificed themselves at Crécy and Poitiers, and later, fighting against the Turks, at the great slaughter of Nicopolis in 1396. But neither these victories nor Henry's later conquest of Normandy would have led anywhere had it not been for the vendetta between the rival parties in France itself. The Burgundians, who had stood aloof from the Agincourt campaign, and watched with unconcern the fall of Rouen, were swept into the war on the English side by a grave political crime. In 1419 John the Fearless was treacherously murdered on the bridge of Montereau by Tanneguy de Chastel, one of the Dauphin's intimates, and the flames of civil discord burst out afresh. For the Burgundians and also for the city of Paris, the Dauphin was henceforward impossible. They vowed to exclude him from the succession, and secured for Henry V of England (Treaty of Troyes, 1420) the regency of France and the hand of a French princess.

All through the war with France the English had in great measure owed their military successes to French, Breton, and Flemish allies. The famous army of the Black Prince which won the battle of Poitiers was largely recruited from Gascony. One of the best of its captains was a Gascon nobleman. And now when Henry V had revived the association of France and England under a common crown, the governing factor in the situation was again the friendship of a continental faction. Everything depended upon the continued alliance of that party in the French state to whom no Englishman could be so odious as an Armagnac. So long as Philip the Good of Burgundy found it to his interest to support the Lancastrian cause, the small English garrisons which were posted to the towns of northern France were regarded as auxiliaries of a local faction, rather than as alien instruments of a usurper's rule. But when Burgundy changed sides (Treaty of Arras, 1435) the whole complexion of affairs was altered. It was thenceforward no longer a question whether England could maintain her footing in France. Without French support her position was untenable. Only the pace of her reluctant withdrawal remained to be settled.

Behind the great altar of the abbey church at Rheims lay the tomb of St. Remi and within the tomb a dove-shaped reliquary. In that reliquary was a crystal vase containing the sacred oil which a dove from Heaven had brought down for the consecration of Clovis, the first Christian King of the Franks. With this holy fluid, always by a miraculous dispensation maintained at its original volume, St. Charlemagne and St. Louis, and many Kings of France less illustrious than they, had been anointed, and at the solemn ceremony of their consecration had sworn to rule their subjects with justice and mercy. In the eyes of the pious it was a matter of doubt whether a King of France could be regarded as in a complete sense a lawful king if he had not undergone in the cathedral at Rheims this immemorial rite.

Henry V was never consecrated. He died prematurely in the full tide of his manhood (1422), poisoned, as the English soldiers maintained, by the magic verses of the Armagnacs, and leaving an heir of nine months, whose tender years would long preclude him from taking the solemn engagements of a newly consecrated King of France. The way was clear for the Dauphin Charles, chief of the Armagnacs and eleventh child of the mad king, a sickly, timid, pious youth, frightened of the English, still more frightened of the violent passions which raged around him as he held his fugitive court at Bourges, Poitiers, or Chinon, but still the head of the Valois house and the descendant of the Capets.

Joan of Arc divined that Charles must be consecrated at Rheims. Celestial voices spoke to the peasant girl as she plied her household tasks or tended her father's sheep at Domrémy, bidding her ride out of Lorraine into France and there relive the city of Orleans which was besieged by the English, after which she must conduct the Dauphin to his consecration at Rheims. With a sublime simplicity of purpose Joan accomplished these two missions. Nine days after her arrival before its walls, Orleans, which had already endured a siege for more than seven months, was a free city. To the Dauphin, who doubted even his own legitimacy, she brought the warrant of her inspired confidence, and the political credentials which the rite of consecration could alone supply. It is idle to pretend that this girl of eighteen was a military expert. Good soldiers were at her side. Her strategy was spiritual. Ardent herself and clear of hesitations, she gave courage and elation to a disheartened cause.

May, 1429

The fear and hatred which she inspired among her opponents are a measure of her success. While the Armagnacs regarded her as a saint and a heroine, she appeared to the whole Burgundian and English interest to be a very wise sorceress and an unquestioned heretic. How else could they explain the sudden transformation of the whole war, the relief of Orleans, the defeat of Patay, the capture of Troyes, the coronation of Rheims, the threat to Paris, the exchange in the ranks of their enemies of a feeling of dejection for one of confidence and hope? A prophetess could only bring such victories to a bad cause if she were inspired by the Evil One. The University of Paris, which was Burgundian to the core, and had not scrupled to defend its Burgundian opinions by a pretorian band of butchers, was convinced that Joan was a witch.

After the consecration her task was accomplished. The work of national deliverance to which she had given so strong an impulse could proceed without her. Having fallen into the hands of the enemy at Compiègne, she was handed over to the English chieftains, who, with the active and enthusiastic help of Pierre Cauchon, the Bishop of Beauvais, and of the doctors of the Paris University and of other notable French divines, burned her to death as a witch in the market place of Rouen. It is to be remarked that Charles VII, who owed everything to this girl, never raised his finger to help her in her extremity. A young male peasant from the Gévaudan, professing also to be a visionary of pure and saintly life, had promised to bring Charles victory whenever he appeared, and the assistance of Joan was no longer indispensable. To her

May 28, 1431

English enemies, whose views are enshrined in Shakespeare's *Henry VI*, she was a wicked sorceress employed by bad men to make trouble for good, honest, valiant Englishmen who in a fair fight could always beat the "Coué," but were ill matched against the magic of a wizard.

The martyrdom of Joan gave to France a sense of moral unity such as the country had never yet known. One by one England was divested of all those advantages which had belonged to her in the earlier stages of the conflict. The Burgundians made their peace with France in 1435. Paris went over to the enemy in 1436. And meanwhile Charles, growing in prudence as he advanced in age, and being well served by able men of the middle class, such as Jacques Coeur the financier and Jean Bureau the first French expert in artillery, the arm with which Napoleon frightened all Europe, constructed an efficient instrument of government.

Under the Ordonnance sur la Gendarmerie of 1439, the King set up a regular force under royal officers, to be financed by a royal tax, the *taille*, while at the same time he struck hard at the inveterate lawlessness of the nobility, who were forbidden to tallage their demesnes, or to raise troops without royal licence, or to levy private war. It is characteristic of the great nobles of France that they rose in rebellion against a scheme of reform so essential to the strength and security of the French nation. The Praguerie was crushed. The Royal Army of France, cavalry, infantry, artillery, was formed in defiance of the feudal traditions of the Ancien Régime, and in the last campaign of this long war (1449-1453) made its first triumphant appearance on the battlefields of Europe, announcing that the age of artillery was come. Rouen, Bayonne, Bordeaux, fell in turn before the organized patriotism of France. Calais alone of all her French possessions remained to England after the peace was signed in 1453.

1440

A curious feature of this long war was the persistence, despite cruel atrocities, of the spirit of the tournament. War, which was in practice an orgy of arson and pillage, was at the same time conceived of as the sport of kings, the matching of champions, and the ordeal of God. Edward III challenged Philip VI, Henry V challenged Louis the Dauphin to put all to the test of single combat. The display of personal courage and the observance of the conventions of chivalry were deemed to be obligations more binding upon the great Anglo-French military brotherhood than the obscurer virtues of clemency or discipline. On the evening of Poitiers, the Black Prince, who did not scruple to butcher the population of Limoges without regard to sex or age, waited at table upon the captive King John with ostentatious ceremony. The high-bred *camaraderie* between noblemen who spoke the same language, enjoyed the same sports, worshipped according to the same rites, and obeyed the same canons of social behaviour, brought some mitigation to the conflict, save only where it was waged by rough sailors on the unchivalrous sea. It is significant of the spirit of those times that in the year after Creçy the French widow of Earl Aymer of Pembroke founded a college at Cambridge, wherein French students were to receive a preferential claim to appointments, and that when the news came to Paris of Edward III's death, the King of France commanded a solemn service to be held in the Sainte Chapelle to the memory of a great hero, who was also his most dangerous and persistent foe.

A necessary effect of the long war was to end that close interpenetration of France and England which had helped through the Norman Conquest to fashion England and through the Angevin Empire to mould the administration of France, and had brought so much good and evil to both countries. In England the French language had given place to the native tongue in literature and the law courts, in parliament and the pulpit, in the official correspondence of kings and in the private letters of cultivated persons. The great contribution which English writers had made to the common literature of the two peoples was now brought to a standstill. French and English writers went their several ways, the English acknowledging the spell of French models, but also, under Chaucer's leadership, listening for the first time to Dante and the Italians. Between the two nations a steady feeling of bitterness and estrangement replaced the old relations of tolerance, which are reflected in the amusing chronicles of Froissart. The feudal age, leaving in Sir Thomas Malory's prose romance of Morte d'Arthur (1470) an imperishable after-glow, had passed away, and was now replaced by the clash of states.

A great war cannot proceed without far-reaching consequences for human life. There is nothing so efficacious in breaking the hard crust of custom as a sudden enlargement in the scale of state expenditure. The need for state money creates new problems, opens new horizons, establishes new claims, brings new men to the forefront of affairs, disturbs the economic relations of classes. The fiscal necessities of Edward III were the financial opportunities of the Florentine bankers and the constitutional opportunities of the English parliament. Out of the fear of war risks the English took to the manufacture of cloth and so established the first of their capitalistic industries. A fall in the value of money and a corresponding rise in prices were the natural effect of the disastrous currency policy pursued by the French kings under the pressure of war, and produced, not for France only, all the embarrassments which inflation inevitably brings in its train. As the existing taxes became insufficient, new sources of revenue had to be discovered; as price levels rose, the relations between the employer and the employed, the trades-man and the customer, the landlord and the peasant became difficult and embittered. In the decade between 1375 and 1385 a wave of popular discontent passed over western Europe. It was felt in Flanders, in northern France, in Ghent, and most seriously in the English peasant rising of 1381. Everywhere the ruling class was for a moment seriously alarmed. A new force had made itself manifest and given a shake to the obdurate fabric of European caste. The warrior aristocracy could no longer ignore the great underworld of thrusting ambitions which was now helping to shape society. It is significant that the English government which proposed the poll tax of 1381 was under the impression that all the wealth of the kingdom had passed into the hands of the artisans and labourers.

There was a further unexpected effect of these economic disturbances. Monetary inflation presented to the Popes of Avignon a problem of extraordinary difficulty. Whence were they to obtain the revenue necessary to support that imposing establishment which in the thirteenth century had supplied to Europe its active organizing principle, and was still regarded as a necessity of civilized life by Latin Christians? John XXII, the Frenchman from Cahorsin, invented Annates. That ingenious financier and theologian took the first year's revenue from every benefice. Other engines of extortion, notably the habit of papal provisions, were invoked in aid of the apostolic budget, and created, more particularly in

England, deep resentment and formal opposition. The effects were far-reaching. Long before it had occurred to the common man to challenge the faith or impugn the credentials of the Papacy, the moral authority of papal government was gravely impaired throughout northern Europe by its corrupt and demoralizing methods of finance.

The English epilogue to this long French drama was the suicide of the feudal nobility in the Wars of the Roses. The nobles, to whom it had become a second nature to fight in the fields of France or among the hills of Wales, and for whom an affray at arms was little more serious than the pursuit of the deer and the fox, were not easily accommodated to the humdrum ways of peace. Many of them commanded little armies of liveried retainers, who could be entrusted to intimidate a jury, to despatch an enemy, or to help themselves without ceremony to the purse of the travelling merchant or to the goods of neighbours poorer and weaker than themselves. Against this evil of the "overmighty subject" the weak government of Henry VI was entirely unable to cope.

So two aristocratic factions, led by rival pretenders to the Plantagenet inheritance, fought out their public and private quarrels amid a people either heartily indifferent to the issue or honestly perplexed as to whether its interests were likely to be best served under the Red Rose of Lancaster or the White Rose of York. It was fortunate for England that this should be so. It was well that no question worthy to engage the passions of a great people was involved in this blood-letting of the old aristocracy. The two great movements which during the fifteenth century made for the welfare of the English nation, the growth of industrial and mercantile prosperity and the advancing cause of peasant freedom, were unaffected by the vendetta of the country houses. When the storm finally blew itself out it was found to have occasioned little damage. Rather the state profited by the elimination of forces which obstructed the working of government and the observance of law.

Though the loss of the French dominions was the subject of many bitter regrets, the English neither felt nor had reason to feel that they were inferior to their neighbours. They still cherished the belief that some day the glories of Crécy and Agincourt could be revived. They learnt from Sir John

Fortescue to congratulate themselves upon the free constitution which it was their privilege to inherit, and to contrast the wellbeing and plenty of the English cottagers with the harsh lot of the French peasantry under their noble taskmasters. If they lost the long war, they none the less emerged a proud nation, hungry for action and consumed with restlessness within the boundaries of their small island. Nor had their development been confined to the arts of war. The contemporaries of Crécy and Agincourt had shown many forms of excellence more enduring than the prowess of their bowmen. They had developed a language so rich and flexible, and so happily compounded of Latin and Teutonic elements, that none is more fitted to express the thoughts and feelings of a poetic, imaginative, and humorous people. They had discovered in Chaucer and Langland two poets of genius. They had built the beautiful chapels of Winchester and New College. In needlework and the illumination of manuscripts, as also in the arts of the goldsmith and the carver, they had given evidence of possessing in addition to those robust and virile qualities by which they were generally known the rarer attributes of delicacy and taste. Nor had they shrunk from the arduous work of consistent philosophic thinking. John Wycliffe, writing without fear in the reign of Richard II, had drawn in anticipation the whole map of Protestant thought and belief.

BOOKS WHICH MAY BE CONSULTED

A. Luchaire: *Manuel des Institutions Françaises.* 1892.
E. Lavisse: *Histoire de France.* 1903.
W. Stubbs: *Constitutional History of England.* 1880.
Anatole France: *Vie de Jeanne d'Arc.* 1908.
Sir Charles Oman: *The Great Revolt of* 1381. 1906.
Sir Charles Oman: *A History of the Art of War in the Middle Ages.* 1924.
Sir Charles Oman: *Warwick the King Maker.* 1891.
S. A. Armitage Smith: *John of Gaunt.* 1904.
Sir John Fortescue: *The Governance of England. Ed.* C. Plummer. 1885.
Shakespeare: *Richard II.*
Shakespeare: *Henry VI.*
Bernard Shaw: *Saint Joan.* 1923.

N. Valois: *La France et le Grand Schisme d'Occident*. 1896.
Froissart: *Chronicles*. (Everyman's Library.) 1906.
K. H. Vickers: *England in the Later Middle Ages*. 1913.
Bainville: *Histoire de France*.
A. R. Myers: *England in the Later Middle Ages*. 1952.
A. B. Steel: *Richard II*. 1941.
E. Perroy: *The Hundred Years War*. Tr. W. B. Wells. 1951.

CHAPTER XXIX

GERMANS AND SWISS

Foundations of the Habsburg power. Louis of Bavaria. Growth of German towns. Decline of German literature. Emancipation of the Swiss. The Habsburgs lose Switzerland for Germany, but gain the Empire for themselves. Nullity of the Habsburg Emperor when the Turks take Constantinople.

THE ELECTION of Rudolf of Habsburg to be King of the Romans in 1273 marks the opening of a new era in the history of central Europe. The old imperial game of attempting to unite under a single effective sovereignty two countries so large and so dissimilar as Italy and Germany had come to an end with the death of the last scion of the last of the great imperial families, and the upstart Swiss noble who found himself suddenly lifted to the highest dignity in Europe felt no romantic or antiquarian scruples in abandoning to the Pope the Romagna, the Exarchate, the imperial claims in Tuscany, and the suzerainty over Sicily. Rudolf was not interested in Italy. The achievement of his vigorous reign was to wrest Austria from Ottokar of Bohemia (battle of the Marchfield, 1278) and to found the power of the Habsburg house in the valley of the Danube, where it remained an imposing and dominating influence till the world war.[1]

Political disunion nevertheless continued to be a prevailing feature of German life. The vigorous and intelligent Teutonic stock which had overrun the Roman Empire and given dynasties to Italy and Spain, France and England, and even to Russia, was stricken by a palsy at the heart and deprived

[1] Genealogical Table J.

of all weight and initiative in the affairs of Europe. The old principles of racial patriotism which promised in earlier days to supply some measure of moral coherence were now almost wholly effaced. Saxony and Bavaria had been dismembered by Barbarossa, the Duchy of Swabia had foundered during the minority of Frederick II. Germany was not so much a state as a field in which princes, prelates, and imperial cities, and thousands of small nobles claiming to hold immediately of the empire, pursued their separate ambitions with just so much political combination as might furnish the illusion of national greatness, and just too little sacrifice of personal convenience to enable the illusion to become a reality. Everybody fought for his own hand. So faint was the spirit of German patriotism that the crown was even offered to Edward III of England (who was prevented by his parliament from taking it), and that for a space of fifty years after 1346 the German people were content to have their affairs managed from the Bohemian capital of Prague.

The prime source of all these evils is to be found in the selfish policy of the College of Electors. For them every election presented a golden opportunity for rapacity and intrigue. If a candidate was uninfluential, if he was not heir to the last Emperor, if he was acceptable to France and the Papacy, if he had no great territorial position in Germany, and, above all, if he was lavish in his promises, then he was likely to be acceptable to the Electoral College. In these circumstances it is not surprising that the highest secular office in Europe sank steadily during the fourteenth century in dignity and repute.

There was but one exception to the general rule otherwise observed till 1742 against the choice of an Emperor with a great German territorial position. Louis of Bavaria was Emperor from 1314 to 1347. His election was disputed, and his reign embittered by civil war, by a long contest with the Avignon Popes, and by humiliating surrenders to France. Despite some engaging merits and a great territorial position, for the Rhenish palatinate, the counties of Holland and Hainault, the Tyrol and Brandenburg were, in addition to Bavaria, governed by the Wittelsbach house, this unfortunate prince died excommunicated by the Pope and deposed by the electors. Centuries passed by before the imperial dignity was again held by a prince whose territorial possessions were

wholly situated within the confines of Germany. Charles IV
and his son Wenzel were first and foremost Kings of Bohemia.
Sigismund, the younger brother of Wenzel, was primarily
King of Hungary. The long line of Habsburg Emperors from
1438 onwards were only as to the smaller part of their territories rulers of German-speaking people. It suited the convenience of the electors that the Emperor should be pushed
into the uttermost corners of the Reich and closely occupied
with non-German ambitions. For Germany itself they wanted
not a national monarch, but an elective president of a Diet
dependent on their favours.

It follows that the real interest of German history during the
fourteenth and fifteenth centuries lies not so much in the
action of the central royal government, which within the
proper limits of Germany was seldom able to discharge even
the most elementary duties of taxation and police, as in the
rich and varied life of the people, in the growth of territorial
principalities, in the free activities of great cities like Nuremberg and Augsburg, in the vast development of trading
activity on the Rhine and in the cities of the Hanseatic
League, or in the colonization and conquest of Prussia by
the knights of the Teutonic order. The lack of political
discipline, which is characteristic of this age, was consistent
with a steady and indeed remarkable growth of material
wealth. Aeneas Silvius, who visited Germany in 1458,
reported that nothing more magnificent or beautiful could
be found in all Europe than Cologne with its wonderful
churches, city halls, towers, and palaces, that some of the
houses of Strasburg citizens were so proud and costly that
no king would disdain to live in them, that the Kings of
Scotland would be glad if they were as well housed as the
moderately well-to-do burghers of Nuremberg, that Augsburg was not surpassed in riches by any city in the world,
and that Vienna had some palaces and churches which even
Italy might envy.

The picture of the Italian visitor is the more remarkable
when we reflect that in Germany private war was chronic, that
no convoy of merchandise could travel safely without an
armed escort, and that the imperial cities had only been able
to win and maintain their prosperity by the armed vigilance
of their citizens. In such circumstances an intense civic
patriotism was strongly developed. The citizen of Augsburg,

of Cologne, of Lübeck, or Magdeburg cared little for the claims of remote imperialism, but very greatly for the grandeur of his own city. For this his kinsmen had shed their blood, and for this he was prepared, if need be, to repeat the sacrifice. Beside such near and urgent loyalties his sentiment for the German Reich was faint and distant.

As often happens in an age of fierce violence and expanding wealth, the civilization of the German people was in the fourteenth century distinguished by an energetic materialism. It has been remarked by Döllinger that when Louis of Bavaria was engaged in his long-drawn controversy with the Popes, he was compelled, by reason of the lack of native jurists or theologians or of any German university, to call upon Englishmen and Italians to conduct his literary campaigns. No German poet was comparable with Chaucer for sweetness or humour, with Villon for passion, with Petrarch for elegance, or with the Minnesinger of the age of chivalry. The solid German middle-class inaugurated its conquest of a place in the sun by a salvo of inharmonious prose which the world has been content to forget. In a country so broken and disordered a standard or general level of excellence was not to be expected; but the soil of German human nature was nevertheless rich in its capacities, and from its confused but retarded vegetation rare plants emerged—here a mystic, there an inventor, an architect, a craftsman of virtuosity. The beer was excellent, the folk music good, and the people which stood so low in the scale of statesmanship and literature produced the two discoveries which have done most in modern times to revolutionize human society. Gunpowder and the printing press came from Germany.

The crowning proof of Imperial weakness and impolicy in the later middle ages is the emancipation of Switzerland. The idea of secession was never present to the loyal hearts of this mountain people. The Swiss did not rise against the Emperor. On the contrary, they wished to be immediately dependent on him and to sweep away the intervening feudal tyrannies which plagued their lives and obstructed their access to his throne of justice. In all the Swiss leagues, from the first union of the three Forest Cantons in 1291 to the Treaty of Basel, February 22, 1499, which closed the final war of liberation, the rights of the Emperor and the Empire

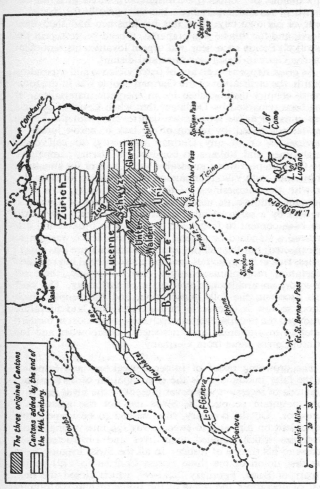

The three original Cantons

Cantons added by the end of the 14th. Century.

English Miles.

0   10   20   30   40

THE GROWTH OF SWITZERLAND

were expressly reserved. But German statesmanship was wholly unable to harness the loyalty of this valiant people. Even when the Swiss pikemen and halberdiers had shown themselves again and again to be the most formidable fighters in Europe, as at Morgarten (1315), Sempach (1386), and Näfels (1388), even when they had fought on even terms with the French and defeated the Burgundians, and had become the one great centre of military energy in the German Reich, so that it might have seemed to be a prime object of policy to assign them a large and important part in the governing confederation, they were treated with studied neglect. The strongest community in the Empire had no voice in its counsels; and, so far as the imperial constitution went, might never have stepped into the sunlight of history. It is a curious commentary upon Imperial unwisdom that when, at the Diet of Worms in 1495, a real and necessary effort was made to improve the imperial constitution by introducing a common system of taxation and an imperial court of justice (Reichs Kammergericht) the Swiss were simply left out of account. The burghers and cowherds of the cantons learnt they would now be expected to pay "the common penny" and to submit to the decrees of a distant court as members of a federation which they had no share in directing. "They want to give us a master" was the natural interpretation placed upon these one-sided proposals coming from an external body, and a master they were resolutely determined to reject. The Swabian war of 1499, marked by an uninterrupted series of Swiss victories, is in effect, though not in name, the Helvetian war of independence. After that the freedom of Switzerland was in substance secured.

Deep-seated social differences explain the antagonism which led to this result. In the first half of the fifteenth century the Swiss inspired something of the fear and contemptuous disgust which is now felt by conservative households in France and England for the Russian communist. The struggles in Switzerland had not merely been directed against the tyrannous agents of the Habsburgs, but also against the local nobility. There had been social as well as political manifestations of the new power of urban and rural democracy against the feudal rights and privilege of an older time. The conservatism of the German nobility was profoundly alarmed by this new and dangerous portent of Swiss democracy

1934

"liquidating" the aristocracy in its area. The contagion might spread. The peasants of Germany might wish to become Swiss, to form leagues, to fight battles, to dispute the long-descended privileges of their lords. Every German noble felt that his order was menaced by this unmannerly rout of cowkeepers and tradesmen who, by sale, mortgage, or force of arms, had made it clear that Switzerland was not safe for aristocracy. Nor did the Emperor Maximilian misrepresent the feelings of his well-born subjects when in a public proclamation he referred to the Swiss as "an ill-conditioned, rough, and bad peasant-folk in whom there is to be found no virtue, no noble blood, and no moderation, but only disloyalty and hatred towards the German nation."

The liberation of the Swiss, which marks the first triumph of the democratic principles in Europe over an area larger than the city state, was the more remarkable by reason of the prevailing drift towards princely power and authority. The Swiss had no superfine ideas to give to the world. Their civilization was infinitely poorer than that of Italy, Germany, or France. They had contributed nothing then, as they have contributed but little since, to the stock of European science or culture. Yet few historical events have been more beneficial than the establishment of Swiss freedom by the valour and energy of a subject race and a divided people.

The Swiss not only gave lessons in the military art to all the armies of Europe: they helped to restore to the continent of Europe the idea of political liberty. This they showed to be a force capable of welding together peoples differing in speech and race and ultimately even in religion. And so through the age of despotism Switzerland remained the pattern of a *parvenu* state, governing its own affairs without the assistance of nobles or kings, and reminding Europe that the catalogue of political experiments was not yet exhausted. Here men could breathe freely and hither resort for the fearless discussion of questionable matters. Long before the loveliness of snowflakes was discovered, and while its mountains were regarded with universal horror and aversion, Switzerland had become a place of refuge for the uneasy, anticipating on a miniature scale the later rôle of the United States, but with a greater influence on religious life.

The enemy in conflict with whom the Swiss cantons won their earliest and latest triumphs was the house of Habsburg.

The cruelty of Albert I, the son of Rudolf of Habsburg, and of his oppressive agents, called into life the original league of the forest cantons. It was Habsburg pride which was abased on the fields of Morgarten, of Sempach, and of Näfels, and a century later in the last and decisive conflict of the Swabian war. All through the formative years of the Confederacy, the Swiss could count upon the steady hostility of this Austrian family, which, having sprung from a Swiss root, regarded the rebels with a peculiar and local malevolence.

If then the Habsburgs are the makers of Austria, they are also the makers, or from the German point of view the losers, of Switzerland. This was the great rebuff experienced by a family whose territorial aggrandizement and fortunate Empire-winning marriages have passed into a proverb. Save for this, everything on a long view turned out well for these steady, rather dull, acquisitive men. Even their failure to obtain the imperial crown between the death of Rudolf of Habsburg in 1291 and the elevation of Albert V to the Empire in 1437 was a blessing in disguise, for during that century and a half, undisturbed by imperial claims and duties, they built up for themselves the position of being the largest territorial holders in Germany. So when the Empire returned to them with Albert they were able to keep it with one brief intermission (1742-1744) until the end.

There was something in the racial and geographical conditions of the Danube valley which seemed to demand such a dynasty, firm, steady, unintellectual. Frederick III, the first 1440-Emperor to show the famous Habsburg lip, and the last 93 Emperor to be crowned in Rome, was as great a nullity as ever played an important part in history. Without any of the engaging gifts of Edward II of England, Frederick was just as little fitted as that unfortunate monarch for the despatch of business. A clever Italian diplomat like Aeneas Sylvius could twist him round his little finger. Yet this dull, obstinate bigot ruled in Vienna for more than fifty years, leaving no print of mind or will upon the conduct of affairs. The Turks conquered Constantinople and overran Hungary. The rôle of Austria as the chief remaining bulwark of Christianity against the Ottoman Turk became charged with a new significance, which could hardly escape the meanest intelligence. But no event, however startling, could ruffle the placidity of Frederick, no problem however grave could excite his sluggish mind, or the most alarming prospect inflame his torpid imagination. Inertia was the principle of his life. The most important station in Europe at one of the most critical moments in her history was occupied by a blockhead.

BOOKS WHICH MAY BE CONSULTED

Coxe: *History of the House of Austria.* 1847.

J. Bryce: *Holy Roman Empire.* 1904.

J. F. Kirk: *History of Charles the Bold.* 3 vols. 1863-8.

Aeneas Sylvius Piccolomini: *De rebus et gestis Frederici III.* Ed. A. F. Koller.

K. Dändliker: *Short History of Switzerland.* Tr. Salisbury. 1899.

W. T. Waugh: *A History of Europe,* 1378-1494. 1932.

E. Bonjour and G. R. Potter: *Short History of Switzerland.* 1952.

G. Barraclough: *Origins of Modern Germany.* 2nd Ed. 1947.

CHAPTER XXX

CRITICS AND REFORMERS

Political ideas of Dante. Growth of scientific interest. The Papacy at Avignon. The Great Schism, 1378-1417. The Conciliar idea launched in the universities. Mystical movements of the fourteenth century. Wycliffe. Survival of Lollardy in England. Influence of Wycliffe on Bohemia. Progress of that country under the house of Luxemburg. Charles IV and the Golden Bull. The University of Prague and John Hus. Bohemian Puritanism. The Hussite Wars, 1417-1431. Compact of Iglau, 1436. Mixture of racial and religious animosities in the Hussite movement. Effort to reform the Church from within. The Conciliar Movement. Its failure. The Papacy triumphant over its critics, 1450.

WITH THE advance of the fourteenth century the idea of a Christian Society organized under the joint authority of Pope and Emperor, though it still continued to haunt the imagination of men as part of the ultimate purpose of God, became increasingly divorced from the realities of European life. The Empire had ceased to command. The Popes in exchanging

Rome for the pleasant retreat of Avignon had incurred the suspicion of every state in Europe which at one time or another was brought into opposition to the government of France. The age of pan-European movements was passing away. A new era of national consolidation had set in. To the sacerdotal pretensions of Boniface VIII England and France replied with a national manifesto, and the Hundred Years' War, the supreme political fact of the century, was the first of the national wars of Europe. Out of it emerged the two leading states of the west, each sharply conscious of its own superiority and of the other's deficiencies, and each inveterate in its rivalry with the other. In this long and cruel contest, the Papacy, ingeminating and enjoining peace, but always suspect of French sympathies, played a useful but mostly ineffectual rôle.

We have already seen how, in his Divine Comedy, as also in his Latin treatise on Monarchy, Dante sums up the regrets of a poet and a moralist upon a world which had swung away from its anchorage in the divine purpose. He saw the Papacy corrupted by wealth, the Empire broken and humiliated, his beloved Italy enslaved by foreigners. The universal monarchy designed for the rightful ordering of human society had been challenged and despoiled by the wickedness of men. Only in an imperial restoration and in the purification of the Church by the Franciscan spirit of evangelical poverty did he discern the hope of improvement. But the principle upon which it had been sought to organize the Christian world in the thirteenth century had now gone beyond recall. New men, new ideas, new forces, were pressing forward. The clergy no longer held the monopoly of learning and culture. The layman was coming into his own. Though European society still remained mainly agricultural, a wealthy middle class had been developed from the commerce of the towns, and was now beginning to patronize art and letters. We have reached the age of Chaucer, Froissart, and Boccaccio.

Even in those regions where thought was icebound in theology we become conscious, as we advance in the fourteenth century, of genial currents setting towards the illimitable ocean of scientific discovery. Led by the original genius of Duns Scotus, the Franciscans of Oxford, no home then of lost causes, but on the contrary conspicuous for its pioneering enterprise, challenged the power of the human mind to accommodate the claims of faith and reason. The mysteries of religion they pronounced to be unintelligible, the laborious travail of theology and philosophy to be an idle exercise of the spirit. Vain was the celebrated fabric of scholastic logic, vain the imposing and ingenious work of St. Thomas, harmonizing the newly found Aristotelian learning with the text of Holy Writ, as at the Cairene University of Al Azhar the Moslem doctor of today finds all science in the words of the Prophet. The human mind must feed on other pastures. The Oxford Franciscans and their French disciples of the University of Paris turned from the pursuit of theological subtleties to the science of observation and experiment. They touched upon psychology and optics; they affirmed that the celestial and terrestrial bodies were composed of the same matter and governed by the same mechanical laws. They made approaches towards a theory of gravity. To Nicholas Oresme, the French pupil of William of Ockham, belongs the credit of suggesting that our earth moved with the planets, and of contributing the first page to the vast body of scientific literature on the subject of currency.

Suddenly the warm current of lively scientific curiosity, after flowing freely for half a century, froze and was lost. The old scholastic logic resumed its sway at Oxford, as the quarrel of the orthodox Church with the Lollard heresy spread through the life of the English people; nor was it until the middle of the seventeenth century that the spirit of Roger Bacon and William of Ockham lived again among the gardens and quadrangles of Oxford, with Boyle and Mayow, Wilkins and Wren, Hooke, Petty, and Evelyn, and that the status of English science was secured by the foundation of the Royal Society.

It would be an exaggeration to say of the seven French Popes who ruled at Avignon from 1309-1378 that they were wholly untrue to the conception of their office. In France at least they worked for peace, in the near east fruitlessly for a Crusade. If they made the machinery of papal government odious by their exactions, they left it a good deal more effective than it had previously been. One of them was learned in theology, two were austere in conduct, a fourth organized an expedition against the Turkish corsairs, and by a rare act of courageous toleration at a time when the Jews were suspected of contriving the Black Death, extended his protection to these innocent but unpopular people.

But it would be idle to deny that the Papacy greatly suffered in public esteem by reason of the Avignonese captivity. All over Italy these French Popes were unpopular, first because they their Frenchmen, who filled the College of Cardinals with their compatriots, and secondly because they had deserted Rome for a city which, though not technically in France, adjoined the dominions and was exposed to the influence of the French king. The splendour and luxury of the papal court, to which the artists and scholars of Italy and France were attracted, the shameless nepotism with which the highest positions in the Church were lavished on the relatives of the Popes, and even upon boys, the grinding exactions of the papal tax collectors for the support of this magnificence, and for the prosecution of the temporal aims of the Papacy in the Italian peninsula, shocked scrupulous minds all over Europe. Even critics not remarkable for austerity commented on the clerical fortune-hunters, who crowded the streets of Avignon, whence all church patronage was dispensed, and where every office, so it was reputed, might be had for a price.

The flight of the Papacy to Avignon had been justified by the turbulence and insecurity of Rome. The return to Rome was prompted by the discovery that Avignon itself was not secure, but exposed to the ravages of the dangerous bands of hungry mercenaries, who, after the Peace of Bretigny in 1360, were loosed on the suffering population of France; and the return was undertaken the more readily since the papal state, which had now been reconquered, was awaiting a master, and might not wait indefinitely if the master failed to come. To the joy of every pious and patriotic Italian heart the move so vehemently advocated by St. Catherine of Siena was undertaken by Gregory XI, a Frenchman and the creator of eighteen French cardinals, in 1377. In the following year Gregory was dead.

Then ensued the Great Schism, which, lasting from 1378-1417, and dividing the Roman Church into two opposing camps, came near to destroying the unity of the Latin west. The real question had nothing to do with religion. The Italians wanted the Papacy for Italy, they wanted its money, its influence, its prestige. The French intended that the

Pope, whether established in Rome or ruling in Avignon, should continue to be, as he had been during three-quarters of a century, the servant of their particular interests. The technical question as to which of the two rivals, Urban VI or Clement VII, was the rightful Pope was never submitted to dispassionate analysis. It was sufficient that Urban VI was the Italian, and Clement VII the French candidate. National passions and political alliances determined in each man's case which of the rivals was in truth the Vicar of Christ. France, Scotland, Savoy, and later Castile and Aragon were Clementine; England, Bohemia, Hungary, and later Portugal were Urbanist. The essentially political character of the struggle was illustrated by the fact that Clement endeavoured to entice the French to conquer Italy, and that with this endeavour in view he arranged the marriage of the Duke of Orleans, the brother of Charles VI, with Valentina Visconti of Milan, and caused Queen Joan of Naples to adopt as her heir Louis of Anjou. In these two transactions were rooted the French claims upon Naples and Milan, which, more than a century later, led to the French invasion of Italy by Charles VIII.

At this crisis Europe for the first time experienced the weight in public affairs of an organized body of academic opinion. The University of Paris, led by two vigorous and broadminded ecclesiastics, Jean Gerson and Pierre D'Ailly, was deeply concerned with the grave scandal which was undermining the discipline and affecting the honour of the Church. In a sermon preached before King Charles VI of France (June, 1391), Gerson urged that if the schism could not be ended by the simultaneous resignation of the two Popes, or by arbitration between them, there was no method open but the summoning of a General Council of the Church. Once put abroad, and with the failure of each successive attempt to accommodate the rival obediences, the idea of a General Council attracted adherents, and as it grew in favour, became in the mind of its protagonists something a great deal bigger than a mere expedient for healing the schism. They saw in the General Council a divine instrument for the reformation of the Church in its head and members, and a means of subjecting the Pope to a permanent system of constitutional control.

The time was ripe for reform, for on this topic of the true

ordering of the Christian Church Europe had long been full of uneasy questions. Was the Church, as the Fraticelli proclaimed, "the Great Babylon," and the Pope in truth Antichrist? Were the Apostles, as the Franciscans affirmed at Perugia (1322), empty of all earthly possessions, and should the Vicar of Christ tread in the same path of saintly piety? One such Pope had sat in the chair of St. Peter. Celestine V was an old, simple, destitute hermit. He had been driven from the throne by Boniface VIII, to whose ambitious secular policies it was customary to trace the abasement of the Papacy at Avignon. To the passionate idealists of Italy Celestine stood for all that was good, as did Avignon for all that was evil, in the Christian Church. It was not apparent to these simple men that institutions have value, and that they need for their support money and wisdom.

The Church has always found room for idealists and mystics; and the fact that in the fourteenth century mystics like John Eckhart and John Tauler conformed to its discipline, while repudiating its methods, has been put down to the credit of Catholic charity. But outside the Church, and in spite of the pitiless working of the Inquisition, the heresies of the puritan and mystical temperament flourished abundantly, taking different forms and colours (Catharists in Corsica and Bosnia, the Vaudois in the Alpine valleys and among the hills of Naples and Sicily, the Beghards in Germany), but united in their challenge to the pomp and ambition of the papal see, to its sacraments and ceremonies, and to the claim of the priesthood to a special measure of divine authority.

More important than these scattered and unlettered movements was English Lollardy. This was a protest against the whole system of mediaeval Church teaching and practice, launched by a great divine, and supported during its formative years by the influence of Oxford, then the most free and powerful University in Europe, yet, despite its unsentimental appeal to the scholarly intellect, carrying a simple message to the hearts of humble folk, and a promise which all might understand of a regenerate society. We know little of the outward history of John Wycliffe, the prophet of this movement for the reform of the English Church. He was born in Yorkshire in 1324, he taught in Oxford, where he became for a time Master of Balliol, and, on being expelled from the University in 1382, returned to Lutterworth, his cure of souls in Leicestershire, where he lived quietly until his death two years later. Within these limits of time, Wycliffe anticipated all the main positions of the Protestant Reformation.

He was one of those high-minded, energetic radicals who owe nothing to the graces but everything to character. As he contemplated the manifold scandals of the Church, his plain, massive Yorkshire brain was stirred by a sombre moral indignation to the issue of a long succession of tracts and sermons in Latin and English, often exaggerated in language, but stamped with a courage and integrity which mark their writer as one of the first English apostles of free thinking and plain speaking. His great academic position in Oxford, won by a complete command of the intricate dialectical art, then much affected by learned men, gave him a prestige which the monks and friars were unable, save with the outside help of king and archbishop, seriously to impair. But his message was not only, or indeed mainly, to the wise. He believed in English preaching and in an English Bible, in preaching based on Scripture, and in Scripture made available for all. An order of poor teachers, schooled by his models, spread the message through the countryside. The English Bible which bears his name was translated in the circle of his disciples.

His first entrance into national politics was as the expert ally of John of Gaunt, who, like many other parliament men at that time wished to see the Church disendowed and its broad acres returned to the nobles and gentry. For this violent course many plausible reasons could be assigned. The country was harassed by taxation for an unsuccessful French War. The Church was reported to possess a third of the land in the country. Many of its best benefices were under the odious system of Provisions, and, in defiance of the law, conferred by the connivance of King and Pope on non-resident Italians. Much of its wealth was drained away from the country by papal taxation. From the remainder it was contended that the state exacted an insufficient toll. The disendowment of the Church, then, was urged as a measure, not only good for clerical ethics, but also calculated to relieve the laity from a crushing burden, and to strengthen the fiscal revenues of the Crown. With these arguments based on national convenience Wycliffe was in accord. His outlook, which was that of a patriotic English Erastian, was strongly opposed to the cosmopolitan theory of the mediaeval Church. In a pamphlet entitled *De Officio Regis* he claimed for the national sovereign powers of ecclesiastical control and discipline in terms which would have satisfied King Henry VIII.

Once embarked upon a criticism of the Church as he saw it at work in the reign of King Edward III, Wycliffe was drawn on further and further until there was hardly a part of the structure which escaped his censure. The bishops, the Caesarean clergy, as he called them, were too much engaged in affairs of state to attend to their proper clerical duties. Monastic life was not so much abominable as useless. The Friars lowered the whole tone of the Church by the sale of indulgences for sin, by their style of empty, sensational preaching. From his denunciations of the secular occupations of the Episcopate he was led on by an easy transition to condemn prelacy and to advocate a form of Church government differing little from what was subsequently known as Presbyterianism. From the authority of the Church he appealed to the authority of Scripture, and finally launched an attack upon the central mystery of the Catholic Faith. In an interesting treatise, *De Civili Dominio*, Wycliffe argues with a logic impregnated with feudal conceptions, that "dominion" or power is founded on grace, or, in plain language, that the claim to exercise any form of authority is grounded on virtue, and disappears where virtue is not. From these premisses it followed that an unworthy priest could not administer the sacraments, that the authority of the Pope belonged to him only in so far as he showed himself possessed of the Grace of God, and that the claims made on behalf of the ecclesiastical hierarchy as an institution possessing independent validity were invalid. By 1380 he had reached the position that Transubstantiation was a false doctrine, and that the priest had no magic whereby he could transform the substance of bread into the body of Christ.

It will be seen that the idea of a Christian Church which Wycliffe had gradually built up for himself was in abrupt contradiction to the world of belief and practice into which he had been born. Protestant in the fullest sense it was not, for Wycliffe retained his faith in purgatory, and did not refuse to the Virgin Mother a special place in the veneration of mankind. But in its repudiation of popery and prelacy, in its appeal to the authority of Scripture, in its denial of the miracle of the Mass, and of the special claim of the clergy to be endowed with spiritual power, as well as in the rationalizing contempt with which he handled such established practices as compulsory confessions and prayers for the dead, pilgrimages and the worship of relics, the doctrine of Wycliffe was indistinguishable from that of the Puritan divines of the seventeenth century. Moreover, in the southern and more civilized parts of England these tenets were popular. Orthodoxy was still supreme, but ever since the Norman Conquest a stubborn vein of anticlericalism had been manifest in the English people. With this feature of the national character Wycliffe's teaching was in harmony.

Thus we may explain the fact that Lollardy survived the condemnation and death of its founder and outlived the persecution of the Lancastrian age. With the loss of Oxford, which was easily recovered for orthodoxy and once recovered was kept under an iron heel, the movement was deprived of the learned character which originally belonged to it, and became a religion of humble unlettered men and women, who met in secret to ponder Holy Writ, or to listen to the voice of a travelling preacher; but as such a religion it persisted until the sixteenth century, when it was merged in the tidal wave of the Protestant Reformation. We find it alive in London and East Anglia, among the poor charcoal burners of the Chiltern beechwoods, and in the country towns and villages of the west. Though there was yet no printing press to multiply copies of the Bible, or the tracts and sermons of Wycliffe, though transcription was a slow process and the possession of transcripts might lead to a fiery death, the English Lollards went on unsubdued, handing down from father to son the tradition of their simple Christian faith, and cherishing the memory of their heroic martyrs. We may conjecture that for every devoted member of this proscribed communion there were hundreds of an easier and more compliant temper who, while making their peace with the established order, had long ceased to render it a real allegiance. The English are a race slow to move. That they moved so far and so fast in the sixteenth century is due to the fact that for the first time since the conversion of the island to Christianity a religious alternative to the faith of Rome had been propounded by Wycliffe, and that, being in essentials congenial to the national temper, it had found adherents in many classes of society. Such is the justification for saying that the

Protestant Reformation in England springs not from a German but from a native root.

The most important consequence of this English movement has now to be recounted. The kingdom of Bohemia was inhabited by a Slavonic people who had first received Christianity from an eastern and Slavonic source, but afterwards, coming under German influence, were compelled to accept the discipline of the Roman Church. Racial characteristics are deeply graven on this stalwart peasantry. The Czech, in becoming a Roman Catholic, retained, with the mysticism and excitability of the Slav, that aversion to the Teutonic temperament which is persistent in men of Slavonic blood. The Roman Church, alien in itself, and for its pomp open to the criticism of simple folk, was not made more acceptable by its association with the Germans. In the thirteenth century Bohemia was noted for its puritan heresies. In the later half of the fourteenth protests against the corruptions of the Church culminated under the quickening impulse of Wycliffe's writings in a great national movement, the first of its kind in Europe, for a new organization of the Christian religion.

In the thirteenth century little general notice wolud have been taken of the inner turmoil of a small obscure country on the confines of Europe. But the native line of the Premyslids came to an end in 1306, and a new era opened for Bohemia with the advent of a foreign dynasty. The monarchs of the house of Luxemburg came from a region on the borders of France and Germany. They were members of that brilliant and adventurous French-speaking aristocracy, which had filled Europe with their fame during the crusades, and in the fourteenth century furnished to Froissart the principal material for his vivacious chronicle.[1]

The first of the family to rise to eminence is the brave and chivalrous Henry, one of the most accomplished knights of his age, who, being elected King of the Romans in 1308 1308 (his brother being Archbishop of Trèves and therefore an 13 elector) and afterwards crowned Emperor in the Lateran palace at Rome, appeared to Dante to be the ideal ruler appointed to bring peace and order to Italy. Only Barbarossa among the mediaeval German Emperors was more passionately loved and bitterly lamented than this valiant prince, who died suddenly, as he was marching against the King of

[1] Genealogical Table K.

1310- Naples, poisoned, it was said, in sacramental wine through
46 the malice of Florentine Guelfs. His son, John of Bohemia
(for he had married the Slavonic heiress of that country),
a blind Don Quixote, ever engaged in forlorn and perilous
1346- adventures, fought with the chivalry of France in the Hundred
78 Years' War, and left his bones on the field of Creçy.

Charles IV, the son of John, though in a different fashion,
was also remarkable. As prudent as his father was reckless,
as concentrated as his father was dispersed, this hard-
headed scholar of the Paris University was perhaps the first
of mediaeval monarchs to see the world through plain glass.
He also was present on the field of Creçy, but resolved that
no vain sacrifice should wreck a promising career. To make
sacrifices was not in his nature. The history of the mediaeval
Empire had been a long tale of sacrifices, of German resources
wasted uselessly in the endeavour to rule Italy from a northern
throne, to compose Italian differences, to checkmate the
remorseless opposition of Italian Popes. For such sacrifices
Charles, becoming King of the Romans and in due course
Emperor through papal favour, was not prepared, It was not
for him to spend his energies upon the senseless feuds of
Guelf and Ghibelline by which Italy was torn to pieces. Nor
did he essay an impossible and heroic operation upon the
complicated texture of the German Reich. A strong German
monarchy was now impossible, and Charles knew it. On the
other hand, a state of irredeemable anarchy in Germany was
possible, and that Charles knew also, and by a wise precaution endeavoured to prevent. The Golden Bull of 1356,
which is Charles' gift to the constitutional development of
Germany, recognized the unhappy fact of German division,
but by defining the College of Electors and securing that the
electorates should be indivisible and should descend by the
rule of primogeniture, minimized the evils incidental to
this situation. Charles then refused to be drawn into heroic
and forlorn adventures by the glamour of his imperial title.
He declined to play the rôle of a mediaeval Emperor, distracted by the confluence of a thousand calls proceeding from
every quarter of his vast dominions. What he attempted was
the more limited but practical task of making his hereditary
kingdom of Bohemia the strongest state of central Europe.
In this he was successful. No matter what test be applied,
Bohemia advanced in power and influence under the fostering

care of Charles IV. Its territories touched the Danube in the south, and a point not far distant from the Baltic Sea in the north. Its expanding trade attracted German immigrants. Its capital became a centre of art, learning, and letters, the seat of an archbishopric, and of an academy which drew students from Poland and from every part of Germany.

The University of Prague, founded in 1348, at a time when there was no comparable institution in any German land, gave to the movement of religious reform in Bohemia a force and consistency which would otherwise have been lacking to it. One of the teachers in this University was a priest of of humble origin, whose memory is the greatest national possession of the Czech race. John Hus was born in 1369. He was a man of rare purity and depth of character, studious, patriotic, of great eloquence as a preacher, who set himself in the first instance to attack the manifold corruptions of the Bohemian Church. The proclivities of his mind and nature drew him to the philosophy of Wycliffe, which for many years had been studied and admired in Prague. "O Wycliffe, Wycliffe," he exclaimed, "you will trouble the hearts of many." Eloquent sermons delivered in the Bohemian language, the character of which he greatly contributed to form, spread abroad the doctrines of the English teacher. The strength of Hus lay in the fact that he had no misgivings. When once he had grasped the idea that the ultimate test of Faith was Scripture, that only so far as he acted in accordance with Scripture was the Pope to be obeyed, everything else seemed to follow, the acceptance of clerical poverty, the doctrine of predestination, the condemnation of indulgences. These truths seemed so patent to him that he could not persuade himself that, once explained, they would not be equally compelling for others. He stoutly denied that he was a heretic. How could one be a heretic who persistently appealed to the very words and authority of Christ? The Council of Constance, to which he had been enticed by the safe conduct of King Sigismund of Hungary, decided to burn him. He went to the stake like a hero, kindling by his 1415 death the first of a long series of religious wars.

Bohemian Puritanism, while full of religious mobility and vigour, was closely bound up with national pride, and with the ambition for political independence. It was a movement partly for the reform of a profligate, idle, and ignorant clergy, but partly, also, for a Bohemian Church on a national basis, and for the expulsion or subordination of the Germans. A light is thrown upon this last aspect of the struggle by a decree of King Wenzel in 1409, which transferred the control of the University of Prague from the Germans to the Bohemians. So passionate was the pride of the German masters and students that, rather than submit to the dominion of the Slavs, they emigrated in a body, founded the University of Leipzig, and spread far and wide through Germany their violent abhorrence of the Bohemian cause. The bitterness of the religious war was deepened by that intense racial animosity which is found when two mutually uncongenial races are intermingled in the same geographical area, and maddened by the jars of daily intercourse.

Even before the martyrdom of Hus, events had been rapidly moving towards a violent breach with Rome. Two scenes in particular which were enacted in Prague marked the rising feeling of the contending factions, the first the public burning, under the authority of a papal Bull, of 200 Wycliffite books, the second the execution of three young men, who, when the papal Commissary had set up a mart for the sale of indulgences in the city, had the audacity to denounce indulgences as an organized lie. That more blood was not then shed may in part be due to the policy of King Wenzel, who shielded the Hussites from the extreme measures of their antagonists.

In condemning Hus to the stake the Fathers of Constance roused the soul of a nation. The Bohemian nobles banded themselves together in defence of the new-found liberty of preaching. The grant of the chalice in the sacrament to the laity became a war-cry rallying every type of Puritan opinion. A fierce feeling that Christians had been deprived of their sacramental rights by the malignant jealousy of the priesthood was mingled with the denunciation of clerical wealth, in some cases prompted by the rapture of the ascetic, in others by the vulgar land hunger of the acquisitive squire. In 1419 the first blow was struck in the terrible twelve years' war which secured for Puritan Bohemia a special place in the Christian commonwealth. John Ziska, "Rhinoceros Ziska," as Carlyle calls him, a nobleman of Wenzel's court, marched to the town hall of the Neustadt in Prague, butchered the burgomaster, and "defenestrated" his Catholic associates.

Ziska was one of nature's generals. Under the rigid discipline of this stern and disinterested commander an army was formed of a type hitherto unknown in Europe. The followers of Ziska were religious and racial enthusiasts. They condemned games and dancing, music and drunkenness. To their fierce and sombre temper the flute, the drum, and the trumpet were as obnoxious as a foul oath, a loose woman, a rich wardrobe, or a German burgess. As they marched into action, with their huge flails and roaring the Ziska psalm behind the sacred chalice, they struck terror into armies whose inner moral principle was weaker than their own. The resourcefulness of their leader lent additional power to the stern enthusiasm of his ragged Puritan following. Ziska was the first European commander to make full use of the artillery arm, or to see the value of a mobile barricade of waggons as a factor contributing to the steadiness of a peasant army. Since Prague was too moderate to be relied on, he established a military capital on the lofty hill of Austi, which in the biblical phraseology of his followers was known as Tabor. So long as Ziska lived to lead them, the Taborites were invincible.

The Bohemians were right in thinking that only by arms and terror would they be able to secure the right to worship God and order His Church to their own liking. No help was forthcoming from the patronage of royal personages. Wenzel, the friendly but incompetent debauchee, died in 1419. His brother Sigismund, King of Hungary and King of the Romans, proved to be no friend but a bitter enemy, who had to be driven out of Bohemia by force of arms. The crown was offered to Poland, but the sovereign of that bleak and barren region refused from cowardice an opportunity, never destined to recur, of forming a great Slavonic confederacy, which might claim, with the help of Bohemian principles, the common allegiance of those who followed the Greek and Roman rites. In reluctant isolation, fighting as a reluctant republic with improvised generals and an improvised army, the Bohemians withstood five crusades, routed one undisciplined imperial army after another, carried fire and sword into the heart of Germany, and eventually compelled the Roman Church for the first time in its long history to sign a capitulation.

Against the Papacy and the German world the Hussites

presented a united front. They asked that the word of God should be freely preached, and that the Communion should be administered in both kinds, that the temporal power of the Pope should be abolished, and priests be made to return to the apostolic life, and that the clergy should be subjected to secular penalties for crimes and misdemeanours (The Four Articles of Prague, 1420). But behind this common programme were violent divergencies of sentiment and opinion. The Utraquists or Calixtines[1] were moderate, the Taborites were extreme. The Utraquists accepted all seven sacraments, the Taborites only Baptism and the Eucharist. For the Utraquists any settlement with Rome would be tolerable under which a Bohemian layman might receive the Communion in both kinds. The Taborite went much further. He condemned prayers to the Virgin and the saints, he allowed laymen, and even women, to occupy the pulpit, he acknowledged no hierarchy in the priesthood. In one respect both parties were alike. Eloquently as they preached the doctrine of liberty, they practised against differing opinions a savage and consistent intolerance.

Two years after the death of Ziska in 1424 Bohemia was paralysed by internal discord. Then from the ranks of the Taborites there emerged a figure hardly less remarkable for native military science and power of organization than Ziska himself. Procopius the Great was a priest, and, as a priest, took no active part in fighting, but, like Carnot, he was an organizer of victory. Moreover, he was clear-sighted enough to realize that the best defensive for Bohemia was an offensive on every front. Peace could be secured only by victory. At the battle of Tauss, August, 1431, the Taborites inflicted on the papal forces of Cesarini a defeat so thorough as to convince that great ecclesiastical statesman that only by the way of peace could the Bohemian question be finally settled. So, on November 26, 1436, after protracted and arduous discussions, a compact was signed at Iglau, and the Church for the time being recognized the Utraquists. At last Rome had been brought to concede a place in her system for an Evangelical Church, founded on the free preaching of the Gospel.

In the course of the struggle the Hussites had neglected no

---

[1] So called because they claimed that the laity should receive the Communion in *both* kinds, the chalice as well as the paten.

means of placing their case before the public eye of Europe. Their pamphlets were read far and wide, they had sympathizers in many lands. The spectacle of Rome defied in a series of savage battles exercised a profound and terrible impression upon Europe; but for the victors themselves the struggle was a great tragedy. In a wild outburst of vandalism the Taborites destroyed the wonderful monasteries and churches with which Bohemia had been endowed by the munificence of preceding ages. Wasted and impoverished, the little country faced an unfriendly future.

Years before the last shot had been fired in this civil war the early enthusiasm of the sectaries had died away. The famous Taborite army, its losses replenished by soldiers of fortune, had ceased some time before the peace with Rome to represent all that was best in the religious thought of Bohemia. In the long and bloody battle of Lipan (1434) it was annihilated by the Calixtines, and with it there passed out of Bohemian life that element of competent and fiery fanaticism which made the Bohemian name terrible and odious throughout Europe.

The Hussite wars, while they should primarily be regarded as the prelude to the Protestant Reformation, are also important as marking the reaction of a Slavonic race against the onward pressure and dominating influence of the Germans. The quarrel of Bohemia will not be understood unless we can enter into the emotions of a small people struggling to preserve its soul against a race more numerous and more advanced than itself. Passionate discipline and willing sacrifice made the Bohemians masters of their destiny; but the fruits of victory were snatched by a greedy nobility, and lost in 1620 at the battle of the White Hill, when the Protestant cause was overwhelmed, and the little country with its girdle of mountains was caught in the Austrian and Catholic net, from which it was only delivered after much fretting and uneasiness by the flashing scimitar of the great war.   1918

The immense difficulty of getting Europe to work together for a common end, which is felt so keenly today at Geneva, was illustrated in a most signal manner during the fifteenth century by the failure of the Conciliar Movement to reform the Church. No reasonable person in that age denied that the Church was in urgent need of reform. Most educated people gravely feared the onward march of heresy. All were agreed that the schism in the Papacy was a scandal which should be ended without delay. To the deeper thinkers the lesson of the age seemed to be that the papal supremacy, which had been so flagrantly abused at Avignon, should henceforth be subjected to some system of regular supervision and control through the Councils of the Church. Accordingly councils met at Pisa, at Constance, at Pavia, and at Basel. The movement which began with divines ended by exciting the interest of statesmen. The questions to be discussed speedily outranged the original difficulty of two rival Popes each supported by a separate "obedience," and neither willing to give way to the other. And as the problems were numerous and grave, the attendance came to be representative and weighty, so that the assemblies of Constance and Basel wore at times the air of being not so much meetings of divines as congresses of statesmen and diplomatists gathered for the settlement of European affairs. Small, however, was the benefit which resulted from the stir and bustle of these famous gatherings. The council of cardinals summoned to Pisa in 1409 was not even able to put an end to the schism. So far from securing a vacancy in the papal office, it left Europe shamed by three competing Popes in place of two. It is to the credit of the larger and more representative

1414   assembly of Constance that it did eventually succeed in deposing two Popes and securing the resignation of a third. The schism was ended. There was at last a vacancy in the papal office. A golden opportunity seemed to have offered itself for the reformation of the Church, and for the imposition of such limitations as it might seem expedient to impose upon the power of the Pope. But the opportunity was not seized. When the council was called upon to decide whether it should reform the Church before it elected a Pope, or elect a Pope before it proceeded to reform the Church, it resolved, England and Germany dissenting, to postpone reform. This decision was just the kind of blunder which an assembly not very profoundly moved by moral issues was likely to make. The reform of the Church through a general council, difficult enough during a papal vacancy, would clearly be rendered far more arduous by the election of a Pope. By its choice

1417-   of Odo Colonna, who took the title of Martin V, the
31   council raised up a formidable rival who, alike as an Italian politician and as heir to the long tradition of papal autocracy,

was bound to work for the frustration of its constitutional aims.

So the plan for a general reform of the Church fell to the ground. The Fathers of Constance burnt Hus and Jerome of Prague, and issued decrees providing for decennial meetings of general councils, for a council in five years' time, and for the convocation of a council always and automatically on the occasion of a schism; but as for reform it had capitulated to the Pope, whose main interest was in the establishment of his Italian principality, and who preferred to make provisional concordats with separate states rather than to work through the machinery of a rival authority.

The Council of Basel which met in 1431 was no more successful. All the main influences which combined to thwart the reforming zeal of the Fathers of Constance were equally powerful at Basel. Martin V, the Roman noble, had been succeeded by the Venetian Eugenius IV. To Eugenius, as to Martin, a general council, endeavouring to set itself above the Pope, to reform his finances and to limit his patronage, was abhorrent. From the first the Council of Basel could count upon the persistent hostility of the Pope. Moreover, though the Fathers of Basel did not, like the earlier council, divide themselves into nations, so that it was easier for the lower clergy to assert their influence and to put forward plans of radical reformation, the national spirit in Europe was as strong in 1431 as it had been in 1417. The French and the Spaniards were as reluctant as ever to countenance the idea of reform, and Eugenius, no less than Martin, saw that his best interest lay in coming to an agreement with national sovereigns rather than with the general council of the Church.

Yet it would not be fair to deny that one considerable achievement may be ascribed to the Council of Basel. It provided a theatre in which the theological differences between the Hussites and Catholics could be, and were, examined and discussed. The theological debate between the leaders of the Hussite cause and the theologians of Basel is one of the most creditable episodes in a violent and intolerant age, and the council may be given the credit of having at last succeeded in securing a compromise-settlement, which, though violently resented by the Taborites, was acceptable to the main body of Bohemian opinion. In no other respect, however, was the Council of Basel able to advance the cause of Church reform or to limit the prerogatives of the Pope. This was through no lack of radical ambition. The council put out comprehensive decrees, such as that a general council should not be dissolved without its own consent, that an appeal from a general council to a pope was heretical; it attacked papal patronage, and by its denial of annates or firstfruits threatened the ruin of papal finances. It even went as far, in 1439, as to depose Eugenius, its enemy, and to elect a wealthy widower with seven children, who was both a duke and a hermit to the papal chair.

In these proceedings the council clearly outstepped the limits of prudence. The public opinion of Europe was not prepared for so grave a reduction in the prerogatives of the papal power, and the prospect of a new schism added to the unpopularity of the council. Eugenius was not a clever man, but rash, headstrong, and limited. Nevertheless, he was clever enough to profit by the mistakes of his adversaries at Basel, and, circumventing the council, to treat with the French and Germans. It is significant of the new tendencies in European politics, of the growing influence of nationalism, and of the declining influence of the mediaeval Church unity, that the foundation of the liberties of the Gallican Church was laid in 1438, while the Council of Basel was sitting and behind its back, by a treaty between the Papacy and the King of France, known as the Pragmatic Sanction of Bourges, and that in the following year a similar treaty was made with the Germans at Mainz. The final and decisive blow to the authority of the council came in 1445, when Frederick III, King of the Romans, sold the liberties of the German Church to the Pope in exchange for a promise of the imperial crown.

The Councils of Constance and Basel had been largely promoted by the Emperor Sigismund. That mercurial and flighty statesman had been anxious to shine in the eyes of the world as a Church reformer, a cosmopolitan ruler, a pacifier of dissensions civil and ecclesiastical. He had espoused the Conciliar Movement in the hopes of arresting the spread of the Bohemian heresies, and of facilitating his assumption of the Bohemian crown, and so long as the Emperor stood by the councils, even though his authority was not undisputed in Germany, the councils were a serious power con-

1419-
37

fronting Rome. Accordingly the treaties made between the Pope and Frederick III were of the utmost importance. The one secular authority from which the council might have expected effective assistance dealt a shattering blow to all its policies. By the final compact of 1448 Frederick restored to the Pope his revenue from annates and most of the rights of patronage of which he had been deprived by the stringent decrees of Basel. It was a crowning victory. The forces of reform were routed. The attempt of the Church to set its house in order through the medium of general councils had been frustrated by the underlying political differences of Europe, and most fundamentally by the opposition of the Pope, by the appetite of an Emperor, and by the determination of Italy never to accept the dominion of the barbarians of the north.

Once more the Italians were restored to their control of the papal office. With Martin V begins the long line of Pontiffs for whom the cares incidental to the management of an Italian state are a primary consideration. Martin V placed the Papacy before the Church, Italy before Europe, his Colonna kinsmen before everybody. His business it was to restore order to the city of Rome, which had been exhausted by civil war, to purge the Campagna of brigands, and to recall the distant provinces of the Church to a sense of obedience to the papal see.

The Papacy did not easily or at once adapt itself to the savage conditions of its old Italian home. If to some the papal restoration was a source of pride and profit, by others it was viewed with feelings of the strongest hostility and distrust. The Roman republicans hated the idea that the proud city of the Scipios should be placed under the humiliating governance of priests. They drove Eugenius IV into exile; they rose in arms against his successor Nicholas V. And the nobles of Rome and the Campagna, in whom generations of anarchy and bloodshed had made of disobedience a second nature, were even more dangerous than the Roman mob. The Restoration Popes did not feel themselves precluded by sentiments of Christian piety from applying to these disorders the harshest treatment which the refined cruelty of their mercenary captains and executioners could supply. They slew, tortured, hanged their opponents. Palestrina, the principal home of the Colonna family, was levelled to the ground by Vitelleschi, whose odious cruelties, exercised in the service of Eugenius IV and branded in the pages of Lorenzo Valla, cast a deep shadow of gloom over the rebirth of the papal state.

Thus sternly delivered from their local troubles the Popes advanced with a sense of triumph to meet the future. The difficulties, which ever since the schism had seemed so menacing to the continued authority of the Papacy, were now overcome. The Council of Basel, long a much reduced and discredited body, was finally dissolved in 1449; Felix V, the elderly antipope, had resigned. The German Empire under the lame and venal guidance of Frederick III had made its peace, renouncing the hard road of reform, accepting papal finance, patronage, and authority. The Bohemians, who had filled Europe with the terror of their name, were now quiet and apparently composed. No one murmured the name of Wycliffe. At the jubilee of 1450, Nicholas V, a scholar Pope, who had made of his court the principal centre of Italian learning and letters, and is famous as the founder of the Vatican Library, looked out, as it appeared, upon a subject world. It was the year in which the Spaniard, Torquemada, published a famous treatise (*Summa contra hostes ecclesiae*) which concentrated the orthodox reply to all the errors which had been afflicting the Christian commonwealth.

The great attack upon the fortress of papal power had been decisively repelled. Few would then have predicted that half a century later the onslaught would be renewed on a wider scale, with added power, and with results fatal to the unity of the Latin Church.

BOOKS WHICH MAY BE CONSULTED

G. M. Trevelyan: *England in the Age of Wycliffe.* 1909.

J. Loserth: *Wycliffe and Hus. Tr.* M. J. Evans. 1884.

M. Creighton: *History of the Papacy during the Reformation.* 1882.

R. L. Poole: *Wycliffe's Tractatus de civili Dominio.* 1885.

Ranke: *History of the Popes. Tr.* S. Austin. 1847.

Gregorovius: *History of Rome in the Middle Ages. Tr.* A. Hamilton. 1894-1900.

W. R. Inge: *Christian Mysticism.* 1899.

Lechler: *John Wycliffe and his English Precursors. Tr.* P. Lorimer. 1884.

A. S. Turberville: *Mediaeval Heresy and the Inquisition.* 1920.

E. Denis: *Huss et la Guerre des Hussites.* 1878.

E. F. Jacob: *Essays in the Conciliar Epoch.* 1943.

K. B. McFarlane: *John Wycliffe and the Beginnings of English Nonconformity.* 1942.

CHAPTER XXXI

MEDIAEVAL SPAIN

Struggle of Christians and Moslems. Splendour of Cordova under the Ummayad Caliphs. The Christian opportunity in the eleventh century. Absence of Christian unity. The Reconquista, 1086-1266. Almoravides and Almohades. Long suspension of religious struggle. Iberian localism. Debt of mediaeval Spain to France.

THE HISTORY of Spain during the middle ages is that of a country in which two sharply contrasted civilizations, one Christian in religion and Celtiberian, Roman, or Visigothic in race, the other Moslem, Arab and Berber, are confronted with one another, and condemned despite much mutual influence and attraction to a long struggle for ascendancy. From this contest, which was closed only when, in 1492, the year of the discovery of America, Ferdinand and Isabella conquered the little state of Granada, the Christians emerged victorious. The Jews, and later the Moriscoes, were driven from Spain. By a singular act of intolerance, to be ascribed as much to the bigotry of the Christian mob as to the dark fanaticism of the queen, the country was rid of that part of its population which was most likely to minister intelligently to the advancement of its material needs, so that the way might be cleared for the undisputed predominance of the Catholic Church. Such was the *praeparatio evangelica* for a great period of conquest and colonization during which the arms of Spain were employed in the old world and the new for the defence and propagation of the Roman Faith. And it is from this close association of royal policy with religious intolerance that some are disposed to derive the decline and fall of the Spanish Empire.

For more than two hundred and fifty years the emirs and
caliphs of the Ummayad house administered, from their
populous capital of Cordova, a state which appreciated the
values and possessed the luxuries of civilized life. The visitor
to Cordova in the tenth century travelled through a land which
bore abundant signs of the supervision of an improving
government concerned to promote the interests of agriculture, trade, and industry. He found peasants tilling rice
and sugar cane in fields which had been irrigated by Arab
engineers, mechanics working delicately in glass, ivory, and
leather, and scribes who had discarded parchment for paper.
Entering the capital, he marvelled at the oriental eccentricity
which required nine hundred public baths for the refreshment
of the body and four hundred mosques for the elevation of
the soul. The streets were paved with stone, fountains
sparkled in arcaded courts, and hundreds of lamps, many of
them of silver, illumined the columns of marble and jasper
which sustained the greatest of the Moslem temples. Nor
were these amenities the jealously guarded monopoly of the
Arabian conquerors. Among the subjects of the Caliph were
numerous Christian communities belonging to the conquered
race who were permitted on payment of a tribute to multiply
and prosper under the Crescent. The Mozarabs (would-be
Arabs) formed an important part of the general community
and together with the Jews constituted the principal channel
through which the culture and knowledge of Arabia and
Greece percolated to the Latin world in that age.

Until the beginning of the eleventh century the small
Christian states which had been formed among the cold,
damp mountains of northern Spain were wholly unable to
cope with their powerful adversary. Their population was
sparse. Their kings, devoid of a regular army or a revenue,
were dependent on the favours of the nobles and the towns,
which they purchased by extravagant concessions. The
Arabs carried all before them. Under Abdur Rahman III
and the famous Almansor, the dissensions of the Moslems
were quelled, their armies organized, and their banners
carried in victory into every part of the peninsula. Barcelona
was conquered in 985, Santiago was despoiled in 997. Save
for Leon and part of Catalonia (like Castile, the land of
castles) all Spain was dependent on the Caliph.

Then ensued one of those revolutions of which the history

of oriental despotisms provides many instances. From the death of Almansor in 1002 (*Mortuus est Almanzor et sepultus est in inferno*) there dates a swift declension in the political virtue of the Cordovian Arabs. Emir fought with emir, tribe with tribe. The caliphate disappeared. Cordova became a republic. The Christian opportunity had come.

At no point in the period of active warfare which now opened out were the Christian powers fully united against the enemy, or themselves secure from ruinous subdivision under the terms of a royal will. Alfonso VI of Castile first conquered Toledo in 1085. Alfonso I of Aragon wrested Saragossa from the enemy in 1118. These were important victories, entailing large extensions of Christian territory and influence, but they were the triumphs of independent sovereigns whose states differed from one another in speech, temper, and organization and found it quite as easy to quarrel as to agree. So inveterate indeed was the localism of Christian Spain that only the most powerful motive would have sufficed to overcome it. Such a motive was wanting. The period of the Reconquista must not be conceived as one of unremitting warfare between the Crescent and the Cross. The Arab in the age of his glory had been tolerant and civilized. The Christian had been amenable to friendliness and culture. There were spells of peace, intermarriages between royal and noble families, campaigns in which Moslems and Christians would be fighting side by side. The great legendary hero of mediaeval Spain, Rodrigo de Bivar, the Castilian nobleman who goes by the name of the Cid Campeador, was for many years before his famous conquest of Valencia in the service 1034-of a Moslem prince. On the Arab side a policy of wise 99 toleration, which was seldom departed from, permitted Christians not only to dwell at peace in the territory of the Caliph, but to serve in his armies and even to hold high office in his adminstration.

It is thus no accident that the great period of the Spanish Reconquista, which begins with the conquest of Toledo in 1085 and ends with the conquest of Murcia in 1266, corresponds with the epoch of the Crusades. The enthusiasm generated by Urban II did not stop short at the Pyrenees. In the warm excitement of a general movement the barometer of Spanish fanaticism, which had often fallen to ruinous levels of indifference, mounted to an altitude of stable fervour.

French, German, and Italian knights fought in the army of
Alfonso VI and helped in the capture of Toledo.   English
and German adventurers on their way to the Second Crusade
sailed up the Tagus, stormed Lisbon, and presented it as a
1147 gift to Alfonso Henriques, the first King of Portugal. The
cult of St. Bernard, the inspired prophet of the Second
Crusade, spread into Aragon, Castile, and Portugal. Monasteries were founded on the Cistercian model as pious outposts
on the disputed frontier; and to these were associated by a
momentous provision three of the four orders (Calatrava,
Alcantara, Evora), half monastic and half military, which
provided, in the campaigns that were to follow, the shock
troops of the Spanish Crusades. The Order of Santiago,
differently affiliated and even more illustrious, springs from
the same motive.

While the Christians of the north were receiving a fresh
impulse from the general stir of crusading enthusiasm, the
position of affairs in southern Spain was completely transformed by two successive waves of immigration from Africa.
If the Arabs of Cordova had lost much of their primal fierceness in the temperate warmth of an earthly paradise, the
Berbers on the other side of the Straits of Gibraltar retained
a full measure of Moslem zeal and barbaric courage. On the
appeal of their Spanish co-religionists a powerful body of
Almoravides from the Sahara swept into Mohammedan
Spain and soon established a complete ascendancy over the
Arab tribes who were disputing for its mastery. At the
battle of Zallaca (October 23, 1086) Alfonso VI, the victor
of Toledo, received a severe check at the hands of Yussuf-ul-
Tashvin, the Almoravid. Much that had recently been
gained for the Cross was now surrendered to the Crescent;
and had the Almoravides been allowed to consolidate their
position these territories would have been safely retained in
Moslem hands. But there followed a second wave of immigration from Africa. The Almohades (Unitarians) of the Atlas
mountains were even fiercer and more intolerant than the
Berber tribes of the desert who had preceded them into the
land of promise. They conquered Morocco, burst into Spain,
subdued the Almoravides, and in the later part of the twelfth
century rolled back the tide of the Christian advance. At the
1195 battle of Alarcos, Alfonso VIII of Castile was routed by an
army of these formidable Berber mountaineers. Equally with

the capture of Jerusalem by Saladin eight years earlier, Alarcos served to remind Christian Europe how imperfect was its organization for the conduct of a sacred war.

The intolerance of the new invaders of Spain had one beneficial but undesigned effect. The more intelligent of the Jewish and Mozarabic communities, who set a value upon

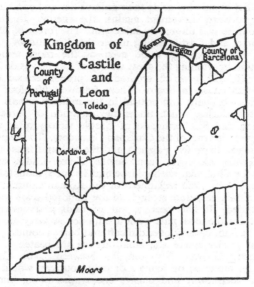

CHRISTIAN KINGDOMS OF SPAIN

intellectual freedom, fled into Christian territory and were welcomed by the enlightened sovereigns of Castile and Aragon. Among the learned fugitives from the puritan bigotry of these Berber wanderers were some, like Averrhoes and Maimonides, who were destined to exercise a worldwide influence as disseminators of philosophical thought. Others were content with performing a more humble, but, at that stage of the world's knowledge, a most important intellectual function. By their translations from the Arabic they made available to the Latin west the science of the ancient world. It is not least among the titles of Alfonso VI that he encouraged the Jews of Toledo, a city which contrived under Christian rule to preserve its oriental character, to address themselves to this valuable task.

It is immensely to the credit of Innocent III that he never ceased to urge upon the little Christian kingdoms of Spain that they should lay aside their animosities and combine in a great forward movement against the enemy. In this endeavour he was ultimately successful. The forces of Aragon, Navarre, and Castile acting under the direction of Alfonso VIII, illustrated the value even of the most temporary coalition by winning the great victory of Las Navas de Tolosa (July 16, 1212) which secured the preponderance of the Christian cause in Spain. There followed fifty-four years, the most brilliant and critical in the military annals of the country, during which under the direction of James I of Aragon and St. Ferdinand of Castile victory after victory crowned the arms of the Christian Crusaders. To the prowess of Aragon there fell Valencia and the Balearic Isles; to that of Castile, Cordova, Jaen, Seville, Xeres, Cadiz, Murcia. Save for Granada, sheltered behind its lofty mountains, all Spain was by 1266 reclaimed for the Roman Church.

The long desperate struggle of five hundred years was now suspended. It had been a war of raids and devastation, waged for the most part without supplies, strategy, or discipline, by light cavalry over difficult and barren country, where "large armies starve and small armies are beaten." Major engagements were few and far between. The Castilian cavalry, mounted on jennets or light coursers, would hover round their swift and elusive enemy, harassing him with darts and javelins, in the hope of breaking his formation and completing his discomfiture by a sudden charge. Loyalty was imperfect, desertion frequent, and unless the prospect of booty was good, the Christian *caballero* would not scruple to ride for home. The consequences of this inconclusive and ill-conducted war, carried on over vast inhospitable distances, were inscribed on the society of Castile. As the fields were insecure from Moorish forays, the population began to swarm into the walled towns, and there developed advanced forms of democratic self-government and self-sufficiency. The shepherd was more important than the ploughman, the townsman than the countryman, the soldier and the priest than the tradesman or the artisan.

The contempt of the Spaniard for agriculture and his calamitous belief in gold as the sole true form of wealth have been traced to the wars of the Reconquista, which intensified the already formidable difficulty of tilling the barren plateau of central Spain.

In the age of crusading zeal it seemed a possibility that Christian Spain might be able to overcome the deep divergencies which separated its several units, that the lesson of Las Navas de Tolosa might be learnt, and that, if unity was out of the question, some loose form of Christian confederation might be possible. The opportunity was not taken. The kingdoms of Portugal and Castile, of Aragon and Navarre, went their several ways, developed divergent interests, and were too busily occupied with internal discords or foreign ambitions to conceive plans for Spanish or Pan-Iberian unity. Navarre, which lay astride the Pyrenees, had its heart in France. The heart of populous Aragon was in Sicily, Naples, and Sardinia, in the Balearic Islands, in the promotion of its Mediterranean trade, in its manifold connections of culture and commerce with Provence, but not in the acquisition of Granada (divided from it by Murcia, now a strip of Castile) nor yet in the politics of its western neighbour. Portugal was an Aragon on the Atlantic, Lisbon a western, but far less flourishing Barcelona. The little country lay behind its mountains, its back turned on central Spain, and, therefore, although often united by family bonds with the Castilian royal family, only slightly by reason of that forbidding frontier associated with the Castilian people.

As for Castile it stood apart, central, isolated, proud, priest-ridden, digesting as best it might its spreading conquests, and those burdensome legacies of its long crusade, the vast estates of the military orders, the preponderant position of the Church, together with the Jews, the Moslems, the Mozarabs, whose presence in a crusading state (now out of business) was to a nation of proud and courageous aristocrats an unwelcome necessity. To the difficult tasks of such a government the Castilian kings of the fourteenth and fifteenth centuries were plainly unequal. So ill-ruled was their country that the only effective force for the maintenance of order was a league or brotherhood (Hermandad) of cities. The student of language, literature, and art finds much to excite his interest and admiration in the manifold energies of the Castilian people during this period, in the gradual perfection of an aristocratic language, in the profusion of ballads and of prose romances, *Libros de Caballeria*, reflecting the manners and feelings of a knightly class, or in the great Gothic cathedrals which rose under the direction of French architects. But what historian can examine the reign of Pedro the Cruel, when French and English were called in to take part in a fratricidal civil war, or study the turbulent reigns of his three successors with any expectation of the renown which was awaiting Castilian statecraft? It is not from these dreary struggles that the greatness of Spain was to proceed, but from the work of obscure cartographers in Catalonia and Majorca (the most illustrious were Jews) who laid the basis of an oceanic empire.

The Moslem civilization of mediaeval Spain can only to an inconsiderable degree be ascribed to the genius of the Arabian people. The small band of bloodthirsty orientals who enabled Turk and Moslem to conquer Spain did not come into a waste or barbarous country, but into a land long settled by the Romans which still, despite the shock of the barbaric conquest, bore abundant signs of ancient opulence. Into this mould of established civilization the invaders injected currents of intellectual influence from Damascus, from Cairo, and from Bagdad. They introduced into Spain the Arab language and literature. They imposed the Koran. They were the means of reconnecting Europe with the eastern centres of art and scholarship at a time when the western channels between east and west were blocked. It was, however, the strength of the Moslems that their civilization was not racial but religious. The invaders of Spain, though they were cruel and licentious, were never so foolish as to attempt an exclusive ascendancy of the Arab race. It was not from Arabia that fresh Moslem immigrations were to be expected, but from the African Berbers who were close at hand; nor was it from Arabia that the Arab emirs furnished their harems, but from the households of Christian Spain, which it was their habit to raid twice a year for treasure and slaves. Purity of race, therefore, was never an object entertained or pursued by the Moslem conquerors of Spain. They married Spanish virgins, employed Jewish doctors, and were not ashamed to go to Byzantium

for the artists and craftsmen who decorated their mosques
and palaces. For the tillage of the soil they relied upon a
native peasantry, whose pedigree, in Andalusia at least, must
have reached back to Roman days.

As for Christian Spain, so rich in noble churches and
monasteries, it was, in most of the arts, a province of France.
In the eleventh century the Spanish religious houses obeyed
the rule of Cluny, later they were subject to the house of
Cîteaux. In all sacred architecture, save where, as in Catalonia, it was influenced by Byzantine or Lombard workmanship, French influence is predominant. The great cathedrals
of Burgos, of Toledo, of Leon, were built by French artists
after French designs. The Spaniards gave the commissions
and paid the bills. Though a vast amount of building was
done in Spain during the middle ages, it was only towards
the end of the fifteenth century that Spanish architects became
prominent. As for the decorative arts, carving and gilding,
glazing and painting, these (without a twinge of self-reproach)
the Spaniard was content to concede to the alien.[1] Later,
when Madrid (which was only a hunting lodge in the middle
ages) became the capital of a great empire, the patronage of
foreign artists was extended upon a lavish scale by the
sovereigns of the Habsburg house. Great models were then
proposed for the imitation of the Spaniards. Titian could be
seen at Madrid. El Greco worked at Toledo. But whether
it was from some native vulgarity, which undervalued paint
and canvas for their cheapness, or because of a certain
strict and sombre religiosity in the Spanish temper, defining
certain subjects only as worthy of the brush, there was no
popular flowering of the painter's art in Spain. Perhaps
there can be no such flowering save when thought and fancy
can play in freedom. Velasquez was an exception, preaching 1599-
no doctrine, constrained by no convention, and daring, a 1660
solitary among Spainiards of his age, to paint only what he
saw.

BOOKS WHICH MAY BE CONSULTED

R. Altamira y Crevea: *Historia de Espana y de la Civilizacion
    Española*. 1902.

Royall Tyler, *Spain, A Study of her Life and Arts.*

S. de Madariaga: *Spain.* (Nations of the Modern World Series. 1930.

Louis Bertrand and Charles Petrie: *The History of Spain.* 1934.

H. Havelock Ellis: *The Soul of Spain.* 1908.

Cambridge Mediaeval History.

R. Tyler: *Spain, A Study of her Life and Arts.* 1909.

Dozy: *Histoire des Musulmans d'Espagne jusqu'à la Conquête de l'Andalousie par les Almoravides.* 1861.

R. B. Merriman: *Rise of the Spanish Empire.* 1918-25.

H. V. Livermore: *A History of Portugal.* 1947.

H. S. Chayter: *A History of Aragan and Catalonia.* 1933.

CHAPTER XXXII

MEDIAEVAL RUSSIA

The aloofness of Russia. The Greek colonies. The Norsemen on the Dnieper. Vladimir and Christianity. Influence of the Greek Church. Work of the Norsemen. Tatar invasion. The rule of the Golden Horde. Its lasting effects. The Grand Dukes of Moscow. Rise of Lithuania. Tatar defeat at Koulikovo, 1380, and birth of a Russian nation. Ivan the Great, 1462-1505, and the Byzantine heritage.

THE BARBAROUS populations of the Russian plain were far withdrawn from the thoughts, ideals, and activities which, during the middle ages and afterwards, moulded the life of the Latin and Teutonic races. In this wild, half-Asiatic country there was no use of Latin or scholastic philosophy, no mediaeval analogue to the University of Paris or the Parliament of Westminster. The great movements which shook the west meant nothing to Russia. Here Popes did not quarrel with Emperors, setting alight in the process a flame of political discussion which laid bare the origins and credentials of the state. Here was no renaissance of classical learning, quickening into new life the intellectual ardour of a cultured people, no Protestant Reformation backed by princes and breaking and transforming the Catholic Church. And as the Russians pursued their way without Latin or scholasticism, without parliament or university, without a literature of political debate or a sustained challenge to religious tradition, so they were spared the wars of religion which for two centuries moulded the life and fashioned the moral being of western Europe. In these decisive spiritual experiences of the west, "Holy Russia," slumbering in oriental seclusion, had no share.

In part geography offers an explanation. The vast inclement country, alternately parched by the summer sun, or buried under a pall of arctic snow, constituted a world sufficient to itself, uninviting to others. Unfriendly nature had here imposed a task so rigorous as to leave little energy over for the refinements of life or the higher types of social organization. In the forest zone there was no corn, in the arable zone no timber, in the zone of the arable steppes a treeless waste of spring pasture. The goal set before the mediaeval Russian was the settlement and colonization of a land so vast that it always seemed empty, and so flat that it offered a perpetual temptation to movement, which only the invention of serfdom was able to arrest. How that goal was reached, we can but conjecture. The valiant labour of innumerable spades and axes goes unchronicled. Generation followed generation to the grave without leaving a mark upon the written page; yet in each generation forests were cleared, villages and towns were built of wood (stone being unobtainable in that unmountainous land), and burned down in some high gale and built again; rough lumbermen plied their trade upon the waterways, village communities tilled the rich black soil, which had been the granary of the ancient world, herdsmen galloped on rough little ponies over the heaving grasses of the southern steppes, war was waged upon the wolf, the bear, and the beaver, and a coarse, violent, emotional race of men lived, bred, toiled, quarrelled, and died.

The dawn of history in Russia broke on the shores of the Euxine. Here was a chain of Greek colonies (Olbia, Cherson, Panticapaeum, etc.), and in these a vivid life of commerce and art which did much for the culture of the rude Scythian tribes of the hinterland. But all this brilliant civilization which had left monuments of its taste extending over 800 years (400 B.C. to A.D. 400) was blotted out by successive tides of barbaric invasion. After the Sarmatians and Avars, the Goths and the Huns had done their worst and passed westward, who would have suspected that Homer had been recited, and Demosthenes declaimed by Greek, and probably also by

Scythian, schoolboys in the ruined cities of the Euxine coast? The contact of the rude north with the literature and art of the classical age was abruptly broken and never renewed.

The Russian of today, then, owes nothing but a treasury of museum pieces to these ancient Greek colonies of the Euxine. The influences which first made a rudimentary state among the Russian Slavs were not Greek but Scandinavian, the sphere of their operation not the sea coast, but the great waterways which connect the Baltic with the Euxine. Here it would seem that German traders as early as the first century had built themselves stations, and here, after circuitous wanderings from south Russia to the Danube, and from the Danube to the Carpathians, the main body of eastern Slavs was by the eighth century collected, and engaged in the marketing of forest produce. The real story of Russia begins from the moment that the city states on the Neva and Dnieper, menaced in their trade by Turkish nomads, but also paralysed by internal dissensions, called in a body of well armed warriors from Sweden to collect their taxes and defend their caravans.

The coming in 862 of Ruric and his Norsemen (or Ruotsi as the Finns called them) was decisive. The rivers and lakes from the Baltic to the Black Sea fell into the keeping of this valiant race of merchant warriors. They established themselves in Novgorod and Kiev, carried on an extensive slave trade, organized fleets, armies, and principalities, and plunging for the highest stakes, launched six attacks on Constantinople, and attempted the conquest of Bulgaria. The passive Slavs of the west were content to be called Russ, after the name of these convenient auxiliaries, who convoyed their cargoes down the seven cataracts of the lower Dnieper, enabled them to market their honey and their furs, and were of the mettle to beard the Emperor in his capital, and to extort commercial concessions from Constantinople at the point of the sword. From the Ruotsi or Varangians, they learnt the elements of state life, and by them were introduced to the sobering discipline of a state religion.

The conversion of Russia to Christianity was effected, it would seem, by a monster of cruelty and lust. That Vladimir (980-1015) was a fratricide, who maintained 3,500 concubines, has not prevented his canonization as a saint. All sins were forgiven to the man who made Kiev a Christian city and of the Russians a people obedient to the Christian rites. It is said that at some point in his violent career it occurred to this capable barbarian to examine the credentials of the leading religions. The Moslem creed, since it condemned strong drink, was rejected offhand. "Drinking," observed Vladimir, "is the joy of the Russes. We cannot exist without that pleasure." A papist who had the misfortune to observe that "whatsoever one eats or drinks is all to the glory of God" was curtly dismissed with "Our fathers accepted no such principle." When the Jewish apologist was compelled to confess that Jerusalem was in alien hands, the Varangian prince pertinently observed, "If God loved you and your fathers, you would not be thus dispersed in foreign lands. Do you expect us to accept that fate also?" There remained the Church of the Byzantine Empire, with its images and mosaics, its solemn music and swinging censers, its resplendent vestments and ordered ritual. A commission of enquiry, thrilled by the brilliance of a service such as only St. Sophia could provide, reported strongly in favour of the Greek religion. "When we journeyed among the Bulgarians, we beheld how they worship in their temple called a mosque, while they stand upright. The Bulgarian bows, sits down, looks hither and thither like one possessed, and there is on happiness among them, but instead only sorrow and a dreadful stench. Their religion is not good. Then we went to the Germans and saw them performing many ceremonies in their temples; but we beheld no glory there. Then we went on to Greece and the Greeks led us to edifices where they worship their God and we knew not whether we were in heaven or on earth".

The objective once determined, the business of conversion was carried through with the high hand of a pirate. Seizing Cherson, a jewel in the Byzantine crown, Vladimir threatened destruction to its inhabitants unless he was given the hand of a Byzantine princess. The blackmail was successful. The reluctance of a woman was overcome by the stern reason of state, and in that old Greek city the pirate from the north was wedded to Anne, the sister of the long descended Emperors Basil and Constantine (988). Returning to Kiev, the zealous neophyte submitted Nerun, the most popular idol of the Slavs, to a handsome flogging at the hands of twelve stalwart men, commanded the collective baptism of his subjects in the waters of the Dnieper, and set himself to make of Kiev a city

of Christian churches and one of the architectural glories of
the Byzantine world.

The acceptance of the Greek instead of the Latin form of
Christianity is an event of capital importance for the history
of Russia. In the Latin west, ecclesiastical was separated from
secular power; in the Greek world, the church was a department of the state. Ideas of liberty were generated by the collision between church and state in the west. A passive subservience to Caesar was the fruit of all Byzantine teaching. The
Greek Church brought with it many undoubted benefits, the
music, literature, and architecture of a civilized people, a more
developed conception of the state, the advanced notions of
criminal law which were to be found in the codes of Justinian
and Basil, as well as those lofty ethical ideas, so sharply
opposed to Russian practice, which are distinctive of Christianity in all its forms. That the uphill battle against Russian
polygamy was waged with a certain measure of success is to
be attributed wholly to the influence of the Greek Church.
There was, too, having regard to the backward civilization of
the inhabitants, an advantage in a church which used the native
language in its liturgy, and was admittedly national and not
worldwide. But for these advantages a heavy price was paid,
in the isolation of Russia, in its severance from the Slavs of
Poland and Bohemia, but above all in the failure of the
Russian Church to educate within the souls of the nation the
power or the desire to resist the despotism of its rulers or to
fight the battle of the downcasts and outcasts of society.

To the piratical rulers of the house of Ruric, princely power
over the new city states was an indivisible family heritage,
distributed on a rota according to seniority. The older the
member the higher and more lucrative his command, so that
at every change in the personnel of the ruling family there
were promotions and occasions of heartburning and dispute.
On such terms it was hopeless to expect the construction of
a stable polity on the Dnieper.

After the death of Jaroslav the legislator in 1054, we enter
upon a period of endless family wars, mainly waged for the
purpose of deciding which among the large number of Ruric's
descendants was at the time the eldest, and consequently
entitled to rule at Kiev as Grand Prince of the local confederacy. In the course of these struggles Kiev itself, the city of
400 churches, was stormed, sacked, and ruined of malice

prepense (1169) by a member of the princely family, who was resolved to remove the seat of power from the turbulent republic of the Dnieper to a town of his own choosing in the heart of his forests. The name of Andrew Bogoliouski of Souzdal is worth recording. He is the founder of Vladimir, the second of the Russian capitals, and was himself the first of a long line of Russian autocrats. With him Russia makes a new start upon the poor clay soil of the remote forests of the central plain, whither the population of the west had been steadily trekking in search of security from nomad raids.

With the fall of Kiev the first period of Russian history comes to a close. The Vikings had achieved much and attempted more. They had founded in the principality of Kiev a great Russian state, waged war against the Greeks and Bulgarians, against the barbarous Polovtsi or Kumans in southern Russia, and most persistently among themselves, and though Greek fire had again and again repulsed them from the Bosphorus, and the sword of John Zimisces, the first captain of his age, had decided once for all that there was to be no Norman conquest of Bulgaria, the fame of their exploits lived on in the ballads of the Russian Slavs. A fragment from the tale of the Armaments of Igor (1185) may be taken as emblematic of the age when the Varangian war bands, buccaneers and boatmen, controlled the western waterways of Russia and Kiev was the queen of Russian cities. "My own brother, my own bright light, thou Igor! We are both sons of Sviatoslav. Brother, saddle thy swift horses, mine are ready for thee saddled at Kursk beforehand. And my men of Kursk are experienced fighters, nursed amid trumpets, rocked in helmets, fed at the spear blades. Well known to them are the paths; familiar are the ravines; their saddle bows are strong; their quivers are open and their sabres are whetted. They themselves gallop like grey wolves on the field, taking honour for themselves and for their prince glory." Unlike the Normans the Varangians of the Dnieper never became landlords, but remained to the end fighters and traders, danegeld collectors and slave-dealers, following their occasions on land and water.

While the strength of the house of Ruric was wasting away in the internal struggles of a series of hostile principalities, Russia was invaded by the Tatars. Few catastrophes so great or so enduring in their effects have overwhelmed a young and struggling country. The Tatars were no undisciplined horde of feckless barbarians, but a force of some half a million trained light horsemen, representing an empire which in the lifetime of Jingis Khan, its creator, had been extended from Manchuria to the Caucasus at a cost of more than eighteen million lives. No empire had ever occupied so large a portion of the earth's surface as that of Jingis, or had been the cause of so much human suffering in the winning. No army had yet invaded Europe which in point of numbers and skill could compare with the cavalry of Batou, the grandson of Jingis and the nephew and lieutenant of the Great Khan Ogotai, who, in 1227, had succeeded to the throne of his father.

The princes of Russia, acting without combination or the support of an armed peasantry, were no match for the hammer blows of these formidable orientals. The Russian chivalry of the south, of the centre and the north-west, was defeated in detail at the battles of Kalka (1224), the Oka, and the Sit (1238), and every important Russian town, Novgorod excepted, was burned or put to the sack. Not until they had ravaged Moravia and Silesia, had taken Cracow and Pesth, and menaced Vienna, was a check administered to these terrible adversaries of the west. The credit for precipitating the Mongol retreat has been variously assigned to the death of the great Khan Ogotai (December 11, 1241), to the valour of the Czechs, the Poles, and the Germans, who, if they did not win victories, at least offered resistance, or to the Russians, who had absorbed the main part of the shock and paid the chief part of the penalty. The real cause was geographical. The deliverance of central Europe from its great peril may be safely ascribed to distance and desolation.

The colossal empire of Jingis was shattered; not so the rule of the Golden Horde, which Batou had founded in the south-eastern steppes of Russia. For a space of two hundred years the Tatars of the Golden Horde, shaking themselves free of the Great Khan who succeeded to the power of Jingis, and embracing the Moslem Faith, continued from their capital of Sarai on the lower Volga to dominate the politics of Russia. The small Russian principalities and city republics were permitted to survive and to retain their customs, but on a footing of debasing subservience to their Asiatic masters. Compelled to seek investiture at the court of the Khan, to pay him a capitation tax in furs and money, and to furnish infantry contingents to his army, the Christian princes of Russia sank to the lowest depths of degradation. Even Alexander Nevski (1252-1263), famous for his victories over the Livonian knights, the Swedes, and the Finns, saw to it that Novgorod and Souzdal paid tribute to the Horde.

This long spell of soul-destroying servitude left a deep mark on the Russian people. It is to this period that we must trace the final estrangement of Russia from western Europe, and a retardation of culture which has never been repaired. It is now that the gloomy and pitiless despotism of the grand princes of Moscow was erected among the pine forests of central Russia, and that the last embers of Russian freedom were stamped out by the joint oppression of church and state. Only the monks and priests, being exempted from the Tatar capitation tax, profited from the general misfortunes of the country and built up for themselves, in that atmosphere of superstition and terror, a position of territorial wealth and power, such as only the shattering convulsions of the latest Russian revolution could destroy.

No episode in the history of this tempestuous people is more shameful than the rise of the Muscovite power. The grand princes of Moscow overcame their neighbours and rivals, not by the vigour with which they attacked the enemy of their race, but by the success with which they courted his favour. If holy Moscow has grown into a great city from the small village in Souzdal, of which we first hear in 1147, it is because its princes in the fourteenth century obtained the assistance of Tatar armies against their Russian rivals, and constituted themselves the tax-gatherers and police agents for the Tatar Khans. It was the acquisition of this last lucra- tive but debasing monopoly which enabled Ivan Kalita (Ivan, 1328- the money bag) to distance all his rivals and neighbours and 41 make a new central Russia in the heart of the great plain after the earlier and apparently more promising western Russia on the Dnieper had fallen into dissolution. The publican or tax farmer is an odious figure in every age, but it was reserved for Ivan Kalita, the first grand prince of Moscow, to distance all tax farmers in infamy by petitioning to discharge this invidious office for the benefit of the heretic oppressors of his race. This Ivan was a realist. He sought power where power lay, in the camp of the Great Khan, and determined that no

other should share his prize. "It shall be for me to know the
Horde." he said, "and not for thee." In the gallery of
melancholy and formidable tyrants who built up the Muscovite power, this plodding, money-chasing man, who steadily
extended his domains by purchase, seizure, colonization, or
treaty, who did not scruple to use Tatar troops against his
enemies, but who kept the peace and put down robbers, is a
typical figure.

We cannot ignore him. By his policy of servile compliance
he secured for his country fifty years of respite from Tatar
raids. Under him Moscow, which was now at the very centre
of the new colonial populace, became the seat of the Metropolitan of the Russian Church and the political capital of the
country. He is one of the makers of the Russian state, dying
after his career of extortions and economies in the habit of a
monk with a tonsured head, like every other prince of his
mediocre but serviceable line.

This Muscovite or colonial Russia was built on an agric-
cultural foundation, and was therefore more enduring than
the commercial confederacy of Kiev. The Viking princes of
the west were military auxiliaries or *condottieri*, engaged by a
chain of river republics, and limited by the appetites and
traditions of an alien race already trained to the arts of civic
government. These conditions did not prevail in central
Russia. When the descendants of St. Vladimir trekked east-
ward into the forest lands of the Volga basin they found no
ready-made cities, but a number of isolated river stations,
freshly established in virgin soil by pioneering colonists and
screened by vast spaces of impenetrable forest from the
terrible nomads of the southern steppes, whose depredations
had been the prime cause leading to the establishment of the
Viking power on the Dnieper. In this environment of industrious and remote tillage the prince threw off his character of
soldier, slave-trader, and bandit and assumed the quality of
a colonizing landlord. The rota system of succession was
abandoned as inapplicable to dispersed holdings and settled
landed interests. The princely power descended in the direct
line, and when it had become the practice of the Muscovites
to assign to the eldest son the lion's share of the inheritance,
the ground was cleared for the creation of a stable and
expanding state.

Meanwhile a vast political change was overtaking all that

western side of Russia, over which the Varangians in earlier days had established their power. Among the forests and marshes of the Niemen a fragment of the ancient and pagan Lithuanian race had contrived to escape the conquering thrust of the military monks of Germany, and to nurse, in solitary independence, the flame of political ambition. Suddenly this small nation sprang into the forefront of history under the impulsion of four capable and enterprising rulers. The conquests of Gudimin (1315-1340) and of Olgerd, his son (1345-1377), brought Lithuania to the Dnieper, made of Kiev a Lithuanian city, and subjected western Russia to the control of a power established in the distant Lithuanian capital of Vilna. A divided and prostrate people, still reeling under the shock of the Tatar invasion, was not in a position to make an effective resistance to these pagan invaders from the west. The Greek Christians bowed the neck to the worshippers of Perkun, the God of Thunder, and preferred the lax finance of the Lithuanian savage to the penetrating extortions of the Tatar.

It may be asked how so small a people was able to sustain the burden of an empire thus widely spread and rapidly acquired. The answer is that the Lithuanians were not long unaided. A personal union of the Grand Duchy of Lithuania with the kingdom of Poland was effected in 1386 under Jagellon I, who at the same time abjured his paganism and was received into the Roman Church. Henceforward the Lithuanian empire rested upon Polish swords and Roman missionaries.

So by the end of the fourteenth century, if we exclude the nomad population of the southern steppes, two Russias stood face to face: the Russia of the west, Lithuanian and Polish in its political direction, Roman, Jewish, and Greek in its creed; and the Russia of the east, all of a piece and Muscovite and Byzantine to the core. The conflict between these two Russias, between the Muscovite or Great Russia and the Lithuanian or Little Russia, is one of the great themes of Russian history. From it was generated that bitter antagonism between the Russian and the Pole, which, surviving into modern times, brought a Polish army within reach of Kiev, 192 and a Russian army of retaliation to the very outskirts of Warsaw, while Pilsudski was at the head of Poland and Lenin still master of the Russian state.

Planted between the Roman heresy of the west and the Tatar heresy of the east, "Holy Moscow" steadily extended its influence. Churches, monasteries, convents, multiplied rapidly. The metropolitan of Moscow stood side by side with the prince, corroborating and exalting his authority, and placing at the disposal of the temporal power the tremendous engine of religious fear. At last the time came when a Muscovite prince, breaking a long tradition of dishonourable subservience to the Tatars, struck a blow for Russian freedom. In 1380 Dimitri Donskoi [of the Don], already renowned for domestic victories and for his repulse of a Polish and Lithuanian invasion, smote a great Tatar army on the field of Koulikovo. The spell was broken. Though the Tatars returned soon afterwards and put the inhabitants of Moscow to the sword, it was shown that the armies of the Horde were not invincible. The field of Koulikovo witnessed the birth of a Russian nation, and of a new patriotism largely founded on the possession of a common religious creed and owing much to the teaching of the Greek Church, which had fused together the Slavs and Finns and all the minor tribes and families of men who lived obscurely in the great dark plain. Animated by this common spirit and equipped for the first time in 1389 with cannon, the Muscovite forces were henceforth a match for their oriental adversaries.

It is, however, to Timur, the great Tatar conqueror, even more than to Dimitri, with his army of a hundred and fifty thousand men, that the emancipation of Muscovy was principally due. Timur was not content with Christian adversaries, but pillaged and disorganized the Golden Horde. After his destructive invasions (1390 and 1394), the task of the Muscovites was easier and their success assured.

The Grand Dukes of Muscovy were the heirs at once of the Tatar Khans and of the Byzantine Caesars. To the Khans they owe an example of tyranny, a method of finance, and opportunities of emolument and power throughout that vital part of the Russias which is drained by the Volga and its tributaries. From Byzantium they derived the support of an ordered Church and that profound doctrine of imperial authority which was the legacy of the Roman Empire to the mediaeval world. So when Constantinople fell into the hands of the Turks and the last of the Palaeologi perished fighting for his throne, Moscow became from the force of circumstance the capital of the Greek Church in Europe, and its prince the heir to the Byzantine Caesars. Was there not, it was asked, a divine dispensation in accordance with which three cities were chosen in turn to be the centres alike of a world empire and a world faith? Rome had been followed by Constantinople. The high privilege and awful responsibility now devolved upon Moscow. Such were the beliefs and aspirations of the monks and priests of the Russian Church, and such the historical logic which led Ivan the Great (1462-1505) to call himself Tzar or Caesar, to take in marriage a Byzantine princess and to blazon the two-headed eagle of the empire on the arms of Muscovy. Here was a romance of history and a dream of empire, running counter to the tumultuous liberties of an earlier Russia, but destined to sustain a long course of ambitious policy, which was shattered only by the disasters of the great war and the well- **1917** knit dogmatism of a Jewish Communist from Germany.

BOOKS WHICH MAY BE CONSULTED

A. Rambaud: *Histoire de la Russie*. 1884.

V. Kluchevsky: *History of Russia*. *Tr.* C. J. Hogarth. 1911-31.

Donald Mackenzie Wallace: *Russia*. 1912.

Makeef and O'Hara: *Russia*. (Nations of the Modern World Series.) 1925.

Sir Bernard Pares: *History of Russia*. 2nd Ed. 1937.

B. H. Sumner: *Survey of Russian History*. 1944.

R. Grousset: *L'Empire des Steppes*. 1939.

A. Eck: *Le Moyen Age russe*. 1933.

CHAPTER XXXIII

RISE OF THE ITALIAN DESPOTS

Italian disunion. Commerce and war. Condottieri. The five states. Milan and the Visconti. Venice. Florence. The Albizzi. Rise of the Medici. Naples. Union of Naples, Florence, and Milan.

WITH THE disappearance of the Hohenstaufen dynasty, Italy lost its last shred of political unity. Henceforward the visits of the Emperor were rare and fleeting, and had as little influence upon the government of the Italian people as the wing of the flying osprey upon the waves below. The country which was now left to find its own salvation was, if we except the kingdom of Naples and the papal domain, a medley of city states, each cherishing with a passionate tenacity its individual life and special commercial and political ambitions, making wars and alliances as the interest of the moment might dictate, and never scrupling to change its allegiance with a shift of the wind. In this scene of ardent rivalries and unstable combinations the fortunes of cities would mount and fall, now riding on the crest of the wave, now sunk into the trough, so that in the course of a single year the Venetians, being besieged by Genoa, were so desperate that they talked of refounding their republic in Crete, and again so exuberant that there was no bound to their ambition. And what was true of each city was true also of the living and turbulent factions within it. The picturesque towers of San Gemignano recall the days when the family feuds of the local nobility were waged within the city with a lordly disregard of vulgar convenience.

This amazing combativeness was the index of a vitality which found its expression in so great an outburst of commercial, artistic, and literary activity as to raise Italy far above any other European country in the scale of civilization. The northern visitor to the Lombard plain was astounded by the network of canals, the busy trade, the highly developed finance and skilled craftsmanship, the number of populous and wealthy cities stationed at so small a distance the one from the other, and by the many signs of public and private splendour. In the first half of the thirteenth century Fra Bonvesin da Riva, one of the early poets who wrote in the vulgar tongue, describes Milan as a city with two hundred thousand inhabitants, with fifty thousand men able to bear arms, with four hundred notaries, two hundred doctors, two hundred jurisconsults or *judices*, eighty schoolmasters, fifty copiers or sellers of books, sixty noblemen's houses, a hundred and fifty castles in the *contado* with dependent villages, with three hundred butchers and as many bakers, and a thousand farmers to cater for the population. The name of Lombard Street in the city of London records the fact that the Lombards were pioneers in banking, and that there was a time when the bankers and money-changers of Europe were called by this name.

The Italian despot was the necessary product of these two incompatible conditions of commerce and combativeness. Sooner or later every city felt the need of a strong hand either to avert some definite danger, or to keep the spirit of faction within bounds, or to maintain and extend its industry and commerce. Sometimes it would invoke the help of a successful soldier, sometimes that of a civilian magistrate from some other city, who, being unconnected with local feuds, might be trusted to act with impartiality. At first, since the spirit of liberty was vivacious and strong, these experiments were made with a tentative caution. The *podesta* was appointed for a year, or for a short term of years; but the convenience of having, more especially in difficult times, an authority capable of taking prompt action, of evading the restrictions of a popular constitution framed for narrow and local needs, and of exercising a vigorous policy, was found to be so great that the institution, once adopted, became rooted in the political morals of the country.

The despot who commands the Italian scene in the fourteenth and fifteenth centuries was the *podesta* made permanent and hereditary. One of the earliest members of his class was Can Grande della Scala of Verona, whose father was elected Capitano del Popolo for life, and who shines in history as the patron of Dante and Giotto, and as the pioneer in that distinctively Italian association of a stern tyranny, a sumptuous court, and a liberal, and indeed munificent, patronage of the arts.

The increasing concentration upon the arts of peace which produced as one of its results the *podesta* and the hereditary despot, also led to the substitution of mercenary for civic armies. The Italian *condottieri* played their appointed part in the progress of civilization. They announced the advent of a new philosophy which regarded war no longer as the pride and privilege of the ruling class, but as butcher's work to be delegated to specialists. The merchant, relieved of his military obligations, was able to attend to the improvement of his fortunes and the government of his city, while the disfranchised noble—for under the constitutions of most Italian city states the nobility were excluded from any part or lot in the government—found in the life of the *condottiere* a congenial field for his tastes and activities. The development, therefore, of these mercenary armies, so far from being a sign of decadence, was an indication that in Italy, at least, a new and truer scale of human values was making itself apparent. It was realized that war was a necessary part of the political conditions of the age, but not so important that it should absorb the energies of men who were better employed in the amassing of fortunes, the building of churches, the painting of pictures, or the governing of states. Later on the system lent itself to abuses, to wars, which the well-paid combatants on either side had no interest in concluding, to expensive but bloodless battles, and to that general relaxation of civic and military fibre censured by the patriotic Machiavelli which, from the end of the fifteenth century, exposed Italy again and again to the insolence of foreign invasion.

There have been many instances in history of a despotism which numbs and abases the spirit of a subject population; but the Italian despotisms, though darkly stained by cruelty, craft, and caprice, do not appear to have stunted the free expression of the human spirit, or to have introduced habits of servility and abasement. The age of the despots in Italy is one of the flowering times of the human genius, during which, quite apart from the wonderful achievements of elect individuals, the energy of the popular will was still unimpaired and formidable, and those despots were most successful who, like the Medici in Florence, stood close to the people and understood their needs.

The process by which a number of independent city states were gradually merged into large units cannot be traced in a general history. It here must suffice to say that by the beginning of the fifteenth century the political affairs of Italy were regulated by the relations of five principal powers—the kingdom of Naples, the papal states, the republic of Venice, the despotism of Milan and Florence, which, though nominally republican, was in truth directed by the power of the Albizzi family. The long duel between Genoa and Venice for the dominion of the seas had been decided in the war of Chioggia (1378-1381) in favour of Venice by one of the most complete and sudden reversals of military fortune. Henceforward Genoa, always rent by internal factions, and narrowly confined between the sea and the mountains, is more important in the Bosphorus than in Italy.

In this complex of powers the central fact was the persistent rivalry of Venice and Milan, the first enriched by the trade of a great overseas Empire, the second by agriculture, by an incomparable breed of horses, by flourishing silks and embroideries, by its frontier at the base of a great commercial route across the Alps, and lastly by an industry in arms and armaments, which equipped fighting men all over the world and irrespective of creed. The master of such a city could easily make himself the richest man in Europe.

This is exactly what happened to the great Ghibelline family (Frankish in origin as was indicated by their ruddy hair and fair complexion) who obtained political control of Milan and absorbed most of northern and much of central Italy into their territory. The Visconti became the richest family in Europe, so rich that a Visconti bride was the most brilliant prize in the marriage market of Europe, and so successful in their royal marriages that they are connected through the female line with the five royal houses of Valois, Habsburg, Tudor, Stuart, and Hanover; though whether it should ever have been a source of pride to point to a Visconti descent may be doubted, for, while some princes of that family were men of integrity, others were cruel, treacherous, cowardly, and profligate.

Gian Galeazzo Visconti, the most conspicuous figure of the dynasty (1378-1402), was one of those fortunate men whose personal ambition, pursued without moral scruple but always with pertinacity, chimed in with the public interest at the moment. It suited well with the needs of a city, whose upper class was divided into the Guelf and Ghibelline factions, that there should be one master hand to compose disputes. It was agreeable to the merchants, the craftsmen, and the peasantry of the *contado* to enjoy the protection of a strong government; and though the cities under Milanese dominion might regret their independence, they were consoled by the solid advantages of a more economical administration and a more prosperous trade. Moreover, since it had become the habit of the Lombard nobles to live in the city, the master of Milan, as Commines observed, was the master of the state.

There was a certain bigness of vision in this fair-haired nobleman, the first hereditary Duke of Milan, which fixes the attention of posterity. He divined the foreign peril, and saw that without a strong and compact state in northern Italy, such as he proposed to found, Italian independence was insecure. Fine sentiments can hardly be attributed to a man whose character is deeply stained by craft and cruelty; but at least it will be conceded that Gian Galeazzo was a shrewd judge of political opportunity, who saw that with the Papacy distracted by schism, and Naples paralysed by internal discords, the field was clear of the two most formidable obstacles which might thwart the expansion of his state. He had also, combined with the mean treacheries of his nature, the not uncommon ideal of a civilized and princely grandeur. He built bridges, castles, palaces. The *Certosa* and the University of Pavia are tokens of his ambition to shine as the patron of religion and learning.

As to his victories, they were due to no military skill of his own, for Gian Galeazzo was not a campaigner, but to Facino Cane, the very skilful leader of his mercenary army. Decisive and most alarming these victories were to the two neighbours who were most concerned to check his progress. Vicenza and Padua were wrested from Venice. The republic of Florence, despite the services of Sir John Hawkwood, a famous English *condottiere* whose monument may be seen in the Duomo, was caught in a noose of cities, Siena, Perugia, Assisi, Pisa, which found the road to safety in the acceptance of Milanese rule.

The half-century of northern Italian history which follows the death of Gian Galeazzo in 1402 is filled with the wars of Milanese ambition and Venetian and Florentine defence. The precious and irredeemable years during which it would have been possible, had there been a concerted Italian effort, to save Europe from the Turks, were consumed by three of the wealthiest and most advanced communities in the world in a contest which had no significance for civilization. The five wars between Milan and Venice, the last of which was protracted for seven years, effectually paralysed concerted effort in the east, and when at last peace was made at Lodi in 1454 it was too late. The Turk was already master of Constantinople.

Neither did the Milanese realize their ambition. Even if there had been no Pope in the background, Venice and Florence were sufficiently wealthy, and therefore sufficiently powerful, to prevent the establishment of a northern Italian kingdom centred in Milan. Despite the skill of Filippo Maria Visconti, who after an intervening period of anarchy restored and enlarged his father's duchy, it was still very far from being the kingdom of his dreams, for Venice and Florence barred the way, and at Filippo's death in 1447 were holding a winning advantage.

The story of Venice, though marked by sharp reverses on sea and land, had been one of so much material prosperity and domestic peace as to give the impression of an almost miraculous sagacity in the management of affairs. No other Italian state seemed to be so contented or so fully assured of a stable and equable life. A blessed immunity from the two great plagues of Italy, exiles plotting ruin to the constitution or family feuds bringing storms and bitterness into politics, marked her out from less fortunate cities. Cheap and efficient justice, taxation bearing lightly on the poor, a brilliant round of spectacles and amusements, and a number of small, self-supporting, and self-sufficient trade guilds to keep the people happy and occupied, and to provide a modest theatre for the display of talent, were other elements making for harmony and content. Nor were these blessings purchased at the expense of national strength. The life appointment of the Doge was a guarantee of continuity, the wide powers accorded to the Council of Ten a pledge of administrative firmness. There was even a note of tyranny in the elaborate system of detection and espionage by which the government felt the pulse of the city and guarded itself against unpleasant surprises; but if a tyranny, the rule of the Doge was of all tyrannies the most paternal and benignant. As an example of the enlightenment of Venetian legislation we may note that children were forbidden to work in dangerous trades, and that there was a compulsory load line for ships, provisions which were not until late in the nineteenth century introduced into the statute book of Great Britain, then the leading industrial and sea-going country of the world.

Nature had placed Venice in a key position between east and west, and, using the favours of nature with skill, she outdistanced Genoa and Aragon, her nearest rivals. The main part of the carrying trade of Europe was done in Venetian bottoms. Her galleys brought sugar and spices to England, supplied Flemish weavers with English wool, and Mediterranean towns with Flemish cloth. The long conflict with Genoa was not, like many mediaeval wars, frivolous and unnecessary, but a deadly, inexorable struggle for markets. Commerce shaped Venetian policy, and empire when it came was not so much an end in itself as an incident of expanding business. The sea was the element upon which the whole fortune of Venice was embarked and the exciting cause of all generous ambitions. The young Venetian noblemen went into the navy as the natural avenue to fame and fortune. Six fleets, each appointed to serve in a different area, but all built on a common pattern, so that the consul in every port could keep and provide spare parts, attested the enterprise and forethought of the Venetian government in everything which pertained to the administration of the marine.

More specifically the foreign policy of Venice had been long shaped by the triple need of securing the Dalmatian coast, of winning for herself a safe agricultural base in Italy, and a control of such alpine passes as were necessary for her convoys of merchandise. In the pursuit of these objects the republic had been brought into contact at different times with 1412-47 the Hungarian monarchy and with the masters of Padua and Verona; but in the first half of the fifteenth century her one dangerous adversary was Filippo Maria Visconti of Milan, who, with the aid of his famous *condottiere* general, Francesco Carmagnola, had by 1421 acquired for himself a dominating position in northern Italy.

Could Venice sit still while this ambitious rival consolidated his power? Could she trust him not to attack Verona at the moment most appropriate to himself? Was not attack the truest form of defence, and the extension of the Venetian rule over the Lombard plain the one sufficient guarantee of security? The case for the preventive war was vehemently urged in 1421 by the young Foscari and countered by the old Doge Mocenigo with arguments such as the wise in every age have brought against this immoral doctrine; and so long as that wise old man lived the preventive war was averted. But in 1423 Mocenigo died and Foscari took his place as Doge. The voice of peace was no longer predominant in the counsels of the Venetian Government; and with Florence pressing for war and Carmagnola deserting to her side, Venice entered the lists against Filippo Maria.

The republic of San Marco had little reason to be satisfied with her decision. There were in the military market other swords besides that of Carmagnola, and notably the sword of one Francesco Sforza, the son of a distinguished *condottiere* from the Romagna, himself a man of immense animal vigour and endurance, who was to prove himself in these long wars a fine and resourceful soldier as well as one of the most adroit politicians of his age. Carmagnola was no match for such an antagonist, and after some initial victories attracted the dangerous suspicions of his paymasters. When the Venetian fleet was destroyed in the Po in 1431, the government wished to know what their turn-coat general was doing, decoyed him to Venice, and there caused him to be secretly tried and publicly executed as a traitor. The iron courage of Venice in thus solemnly destroying a famous and popular *condottiere* chief was widely admired as evidence of an almost inhuman resolve to place the civil above the military power; but it brought neither victories not wisdom in its train. When Filippo Maria died in 1447, leaving no male heir, prudence would have directed overtures of friendship to the new republican government, as yet weak and uncertain, which was set up in Milan. But in an evil hour, and under the impulsion of the same headstrong party which had been the source of all the trouble, Venice decided to strike down her rival. She had reckoned without the crafty *condottiere*, who had taken the precaution to wed the only daughter of the last Visconti, and this mistake was Sforza's opportunity. Coming forward as the defender of the young republic, he first defeated the Venetians on land and sea, and then, when Venice was so humiliated as to crave his alliance, turned against his old friends and employers and made himself master of the Milanese state. At the end of twenty-five years of almost incessant fighting Venice was faced with a Duke of Milan in comparison with whom Filippo Maria Visconti was an infant in subtlety and force.

It may be doubted whether Sforza could have accomplished his *coup d'état* but for the sudden revolution of policy in Florence. The Milanese *condottiere* was assisted by the long purse of his friend Cosimo de' Medici, a Florentine man of business, who in 1434 had been recalled from exile and had then made himself the *de facto* ruler of his state. It was the opinion of this cool observer that Venice, rather than Milan, was the true enemy of Florentine commerce.

Florence, the spiritual capital of Italy, the birthplace of Dante, of Petrarch's family, and of Boccaccio, was upon its material side renowned for banking, commerce, and the manufacture of cloth. In the great quarrel between the Guelfs and the Ghibellines, the Florentines, to whom the conception of imperialism in any form was anathema, embraced the papal, and consequently also the French side. And since Florence did not live on religious and political aspirations only, but had an eye to the main chance, she made money out of her papalism by becoming banker to the Roman Curia. To be a banker on a great scale is to be a diplomatist and a statesman. The banking business of Florence brought her into political relations with many governments in many lands. The great banking family of the Acciaiuoli, who may be described as the Rothschilds of the fourteenth century, provided a prime minister to Naples, a seigneur to Malta, a despot to Corinth, and a dynasty of Florentine dukes to Athens. Yet despite the development of cosmopolitan finance and big business, the spirit of the Florentine people had remained passionately and enviously equalitarian. While no family would admit the superiority of another, every family was ambitious to be first.

These fickle, jealous, and aspiring moods were reflected in a constitution which was entirely incompatible with efficient government. There was a rage for checks and counterchecks, for election and the lot, for short terms of office, and for the restriction of real power to the greater guilds or mercantile communities. If it were not that the nobles and the working class were alike disfranchised, one might describe the old Florentine constitution as a democracy doctrinaire to the point of insanity. The Gonfalonier of Justice, head of the signoria or cabinet, was allowed to hold office for two months only. Nor could any proposal of the signoria pass into law until it had secured a two-thirds majority in each of five separate committees or assemblies. It would be difficult to conceive provisions more calculated to impair the quality and check the momentum of government.

At the first serious test such a constitution inevitably broke down. When Florence began to be sensible of the menace of her neighbours, and as the conception began to prevail that the city itself was not enough, but that the acquisition of the surrounding country was necessary if trade connections were to be secured, the elaborate precautions of the old constitution, which was so popular that no one dared to propose to discard it, had simply to be evaded. The Parte Guelfa, a party organization, was the first body outside the constitution which seriously addressed itself to the task of violating the spirit, while observing the letter, of Florentine democracy. There was not much delicacy about the methods of this organization, which anticipated some of the worst practices of American gangsters. But Florence was never a tame or submissive city. The outrageous practices of the Parte Guelfa, combined with industrial grievances, produced the great popular revolution of the Ciompi (1378), which secured for the Arti Minori or Lesser Guilds a place within the pale of the constitution. But though the Parte Guelfa was henceforward stripped of the influence which it had abused, the constitution still remained popular and impossible, and the need for circumventing it correspondingly urgent.

At this juncture in Florentine history the control of affairs passed through a counter-revolution into the hands of a patriotic Florentine business family, who knew how to maintain and keep an effective measure of authority without manifest injustice or public odium. Maso and Rinaldo Albizzi were uncrowned rulers of Florence from 1382 to 1434. Their powers of efficient decision, their knowledge of trade, their enthusiasm for art and letters, their combination of liberality to the poor with their ruthlessness to dangerous men, their studious care to behave as ordinary citizens, and to conceal the springs of power, made them acceptable to Florence and her subject cities. Moreover, there was public danger. The rule of the Albizzi synchronizes with the development of the Milanese menace, when the *condottieri* of

Gian Galeazzo and Filippo Maria were in the field, and a strong hand was needed at the helm.

Meanwhile another family, less oligarchic, more wealthy, but ever since the revolution of 1378 noted for its attachment to popular causes, was gradually coming to the front. The Medici were bankers. The opulence, the knowledge, the widespread influence in foreign courts and capitals which come to the great cosmopolitan banker, belonged in full measure to this gifted and remarkable Florentine family. So indispensable did their financial services ultimately become, that it was a generally recognised maxim that a failure of the Medici banks would mean a collapse of the whole fabric of European credit. But while banking supplied the economic foundation upon which the Medici built up their rule in Florence, it was only one among many explanations of their success. If the Medici were bankers, they were also farmers, who could talk beasts or crops with the Tuscan husbandmen, connoisseurs in literature and art, and experts alike in the larger and more generous aspects of statesmanship, as in the sordid minutiae of political intrigue. Everything which had been done under the Albizzi was carried forward upon a greater scale and with a higher degree of imagination by a more gifted family. The taxes were still used to help friends and injure enemies. The elections were still jerrymandered. The letter of the constitution was still kept, while its whole drift and spirit were ingeniously frustrated. However frequently elections might be held, the result was invariably the return of the Medicean candidates. To these manifest irregularities the democracy of Florence turned a blind eye. A high capacity for government, a splendid court, a liberal and intelligent patronage of the arts, coupled with simple and popular manners, secured for Cosimo de' Medici and Lorenzo his grandson a brilliant period of substantial power.

Among the Italian states none should have been more powerful, but none was in fact less effective, than the military kingdom of Naples. The destiny of states has little connection with the charm of their climate, the romance of their scenery, or the long descent of their inhabitants. A political tragedy seems to brood over the lovely Italian land, "the favoured home of bandits and brigands," which was first touched by the sunlight of Greek civilization. Nothing has greatly prospered there for any long period of time. The soil is a palimpsest of broken and luxurious civilizations, of great achievements which have no sequel. The Normans were replaced by the Hohenstaufen, under whom Naples became perhaps of all the countries of Europe the most advanced and efficiently governed. But the power of the Hohenstaufen was broken, and the two Sicilies were transferred by the Pope to the alien rule of Charles of Anjou. From that date forward misfortune followed misfortune. Charles was a selfish and worthless tyrant. The Sicilians, with a spirit characteristic of their island, rose against him, massacred his officers, and placed their country under the house of Aragon, which could claim descent through the female line from Manfred, the bastard son of Frederick II.

Thenceforward Aragon was pitted against Anjou. The war was fierce, long, and, from the point of view of the Neapolitan Angevins, a failure. The island remained with Aragon, the third strongest naval power in the Mediterranean. But this was not the end of the troubles which continued to distract southern Italy. The Angevins were an ambitious and shallow race, more interested in show than in government. They were not content with the kingdom of Naples in addition to their French county of Provence. The elder branch of the family went to rule in Hungary, while the younger branch remained in Italy; and since no combination of territories was too fantastic for an Angevin, Lewis of Hungary invaded Naples in the hopes of uniting the kingdoms under his own sceptre. Even when this foolish project had been renounced, ard Naples had been permitted to settle down under a cadet branch of the Angevin family (Charles III of Durazzo and his son Ladislas and his daughter Joanna II, 1382-1435), who, having no French possessions, were able more closely to identify themselves with Neapolitan interests, the monarchy rested upon uncertain foundations. The claims of the Durazzo house were disputed in Sicily and in Provence, and the sovereign was confronted with a baronage which found its interests best served by intrigue with a foreign pretender. In these circumstances the tasks of monarchy, which in England and France had been a source of national power, were gravely obstructed. A foreign dynasty, a succession of indifferent kings and bad queens, a distracting uncertainty and unrest arising from the disputed succession gave to Neapolitan politics under the house of Anjou an air of ruffianly melodrama. At last (1435) in the wise and charming Alfonso V of Aragon Naples found a statesman for its ruler, a true prince of the Renaissance, firm, munificent, cultured, and for the moment powerful. Alfonso saw that only by a close union with Florence and Milan could his house be securely protected against the French. That union he succeeded in effecting. It was the one triumph of Neapolitan statesmanship in the fifteenth century, its one contribution to the political welfare of Italy. After Alfonso's death the combination was broken by the treachery of Milan, and thereupon there was opened up a new chapter of troubles for Italy and for Naples, so vast in its consequences that for some historians it has been held to mark the watershed between the mediaeval and the modern world.

BOOKS WHICH MAY BE CONSULTED

Janet Trevelyan: *History of Italy.* 1928.

J. A. Symonds: *The Renaissance in Italy (The Age of the Despots).* 7 vols. 1875-86.

E. Armstrong: *Lorenzo de' Medici and Florence in the Fifteenth Century.* 1896.

Horatio Brown: *Venice: A Historical Sketch of the Republic.* 1893.

C. M. Ady: *A History of Milan under the Sforzas.* Ed. E. Armstrong. 1907.

P. Villani: *The Two First Centuries of Florentine History.* Tr. L. Villani. 1894-5.

G. Villani: *Chronicles. Selections tr.* R. E. Selfe. 1896.

W. F. T. Butler: *The Lombard Communes.* 1906.

J. C. L. Sismondi: *History of the Italian Republics.* (Everyman's Library.) 1907.

J. Burckhardt: *The Civilisation of Renaissance Italy.* Tr. S. G. C. Middlemore. 1950.

D. M. Bueno de Mesquita: *Giangaleazzo Visconti, Duke of Milan.* 1941.

G. Mattingly: *Renaissance Diplomacy.* 1955.

D. Waley: *Mediaeval Arrieto.* 1952.

J. P. Trevelyan: *A Short History of the Italian People.* 4th Ed. 1956.

M. V. Clarke: *The Mediaeval City State.* 1926.

CHAPTER XXXIV

THE OTTOMAN TURKS

*Weakness of the restored Byzantine Empire. The Catalan
Company. Rise of the Ottoman Turks. The Janissaries. The
Serbs. Kossovo. The intervention of Timur. Angora. The
Hungarians. Early triumphs and final defeat of Hunyades.
Christian disunion and fall of Constantinople.*

THE BYZANTINE EMPIRE, which for centuries had stood as the
bulwark of European civilization against the Orient, was
shaken beyond recovery by the Latin conquest. The Greek
restoration of 1261, though productive of a late flowering of
scholarship and literature, was followed by no revival of
Greek power. The Emperors of the house of Palaeologus
re-entered upon a shrunken and divided heritage, the acknowledged weakness of which was a perpetual invitation to
insolent attack. While the great Anatolian recruiting grounds
of the old Byzantine Empire had long passed under the
control of the Turcoman Sultan of the house of Seljuk, who
ruled at Iconium, the major part of the Balkan peninsula was
in the hands of the Bulgars. Greece, save for a province in
the Peloponnese, was a medley of Frankish fiefs. What
remained to the Empire was a narrow strip of the Asiatic
littoral, Constantinople and western Thrace, Thessalonica
and the Thracian Chalcidice, the despotat of Mistra (in the
Peloponnese), and a few islands in the Aegean. These, even
if they were as valuable as Rhodes, which was taken by the
Knights of St. John in 1310, the Emperor was unable to
defend against serious attack.

There can be no better illustration of the deep-seated weakness of the Byzantine Empire during the early years of the
fourteenth century than the strange story of the great Catalan
Company. Everything relating to this fierce body of mercenaries seems charged with weighty premonitions of the future.
It was recruited from that needy and ambitious nobility of
Spain which was later destined to fill the world with its

military renown. It was schooled in the wars of Sicilian independence (1282-1302) to meet on even terms the chivalry of Italy and France, and on the conclusion of that bitter struggle it embraced the service of the Byzantine Emperor. It was led by Roger de Flor, a pirate (incidentally the son of Frederick II's German falconer by an heiress from Brindisi), who was made a grand duke and even a Caesar, and was married to a Bulgarian princess. But compliments, which were cheap in Constantinople, meant little to these proud and quarrelsome strangers. The Catalans took the measure of their Greek employers, and came to the conclusion that no insolence was too gross for a government so weak and nerveless. Instead of settling down to a laborious campaign against the Seljuks, the Company preferred to quarrel with the Genoese of Galata, who supplied ships to the navy, and to fight the Alans, who were the *corps d'élite* in the army of their employer. Nor did they quit imperial territory until they had seized Gallipoli, the key fortress of the Hellespont, and beaten the Emperor himself in a pitched fight.

Meanwhile (1308) the Duchy of Athens, which had prospered for a century under the mild rule of a Burgundian family, had fallen to Walter of Brienne, the fiery son of a brood famous for its adventures in many lands.

In a moment as calamitous for himself as it was fortunate for the Emperor, the new Duke of Athens called upon the help of the great Company. The Catalans, who, when not quarrelling with others, quarrelled among themselves and were fresh from the butchery of eleven colonels, descended into Greece, fought for a year, and seeing that the land was fair, refused to accept their discharge, save on terms which the duke was unable to concede. As the traveller from Athens descends the hills into the lovely vale of the Cephissus, he beholds on his right the battlefield (1310) which brought death to Walter of Brienne and gave his duchy into the hands of the Aragonese for seventy-four years. The Catalans, six thousand four hundred strong, were stationed among the green March corn some way back from the coast road, a tempting mark for the superior numbers of their adversary. But between the Duke and his enemy lay a marsh, concealed and artificial, and here Brienne and his horsemen were butchered by the long Catalan knives as they lay engulfed and helpless on the sodden ground. The armies of Xerxes and

Darius were civilized in comparison with the new Catholic masters of the Parthenon.

Beyond the Hellespont among the Bithynian hills there were men of a certain Turkish tribe who ruminated on this strange Spanish portent. What marvels could not a small force of resolute men achieve, if only the infantry were disciplined! The Spanish lesson was not lost upon the grave and receptive Ottomans. The time was not far distant when they too would fashion an infantry army, seize Gallipoli, beat the Imperials, and tread the sacred soil of the Acropolis as masters.

The history of the Ottoman Turks is one of a family of simple shepherds and herdsmen, gradually gathering power and influence, and by patience and justice, mingled with a persevering course of cruelty and craft, attracting the most heterogeneous elements to its service until it was in a position to make rapid and gigantic conquests, and to fashion and support a mighty Empire. Othman, the founder from whom the race derives its name, prefigured, albeit upon a small scale, some characteristic features of the future policy of his line. The scene of his life work was the ill-defended frontier province of Bithynia, where he engaged in a guerilla warfare with the Greek Christians, first as an emir under the Seljuk Sultan, and after 1307 as an independent prince. His religion was deep and unaffected, his policy adjusted to the counsels of the holy men of his faith, his administration of justice remarkable in those venal and violent times for impartiality. But passionate as were his Moslem beliefs, he had the vision to discern that while the Moslem religion might be the creed of a great state, a Turkish tribe could not suffice for its foundation. Marriage, enslavement, the attraction of military renown must win adherents. So he chose his wife from Cilicia, seized a Christian damsel for his son, and employed as his *alter ego* in war Michael of the Forked Beard, a Greek apostate from the Christian faith.

The conquest of Bithynia which was begun by Othman was completed by Orchan, his eldest son. The two famous cities 1326 of Nicomedia and Nicaea passed at the cost of one inconsiderable battle against an imperial army into the hands of the Ottomans. So inexpensive were these conquests, so shameful had been the conduct of the imperial campaign that a mere soldier would have been tempted to pursue his military advantage and to attack the European possessions of his feeble enemy. But Orchan was no mere soldier. The twenty years following the victory of Pelekanon, perhaps the most fruitful in the history of the Ottoman people, were spent at the beautiful Bithynian capital of Brusa in the organization of a state. Instead of leading his Ottomans against the emirs of the Asiatic coast, or the populations of the Balkan peninsula, the wise Orchan and his advisers employed themselves in building mosques and colleges, hospitals and caravanseries, in the establishment of a coinage, the prescription of a national headdress (a plain cap of white felt), and, most important of all, in the organization of an army. It is to the period of this momentous halt at Brusa that we must ascribe the foundation of those distinctive military institutions which made the Ottoman Turk for many centuries the terror of eastern Europe—the *akindji* or light skirmishers, the feudatory cavalry, the Sultan's guard, and above all the famous infantry force, which has now to be described.

The "janissaries," or new soldiers, were Christian children, taken by force from their homes, and brought up as Moslems in seminaries designed to efface all trace of their earlier affections and affinities, and to make of them the pliable instruments of the Ottoman state. Some, and these the most unfortunate, were drafted off to serve as pages in the palace, others were employed in the civil service, but the main body passed into an infantry corps, so brave and devoted that no Turkish army with a stiffening of janissaries failed to give an excellent account of itself on the field. The janissary was a slave. The affections which sweeten the character, the interests which expand the mind, the ideals which give elevation to the will, were denied him. An iron discipline effaced the past and impoverished the future. He was made to forget father and mother, brothers and sisters. He could never hope for wife or children. The barrack was his home, fighting his trade, the Koran his religion, and he went forth to slay the enemies of the Sultan and of Allah with the inflamed and contracted fanaticism of a monk.

The suggestion that this force should be recruited by a tribute of Christian children is said to have come from Black Habil, the proud Vizier of Orchan, and it is clear that without such a tribute a regular recruitment could not have been maintained. It followed, as a consequence, that the Ottoman Empire was made and maintained, not only, or even mainly, by men of the Ottoman race, but by the slave children of Christian parents, who had issued through the seminaries of the janissaries, with the appointed stamp of military subservience and the Moslem faith. The most distinguished men of the Ottoman Empire will be found to have passed from Christian homes through these institutions.

While an Ottoman State was thus forming on a new mould in hither Asia, a new power, profiting by the civil wars and corruption of the Greeks, had manifested a raw vehemence in the Balkans. A competent modern writer has described the Serbs as the Celts and the Bulgars as the Lowland Scots of the Balkan peninsula; and everything in Serbian history announces a brave, spirited, but temperamental people. Under Stephen Dushan, one of those great men who give aspirations to a race—a soldier, a legislator, and a statesman 1333-—the dominion of Serbia was extended from the Danube to 55 the Aegean by the seizure of Albania, Epirus, and Thessaly, triumphs which, though they are deeply printed on the national memory of the Serbs, failed to satisfy the impatient leader of an impatient people. With an ambition which expanded with success, Stephen assumed the imperial title, and proposed as the goal of his endeavours the subjection of the Greeks.

A year after Stephen's death, with his last dream unaccomplished—it was the year in which France and England struggled at Poitiers—Suleiman, the heir and successor of 1356 Orchan, crossed the Hellespont under a harvest moon and founded on the Gallipoli peninsula the first Turkish settlement on European soil. A little later, while he was flying his hawks in a field near Bulair, Suleiman died from his horse's stumble, and was buried where he fell. "For a hundred years," says Von Hammer, "he was the only Ottoman prince who lay buried in European earth; and his tomb continually invited the races of Asia to perform their pilgrimage to it with the sword of conquest. Of all the hero-tombs which have been hitherto mentioned in connection with Ottoman history, there is none more renowned or more visited than that of the second Vizier of the Empire, the fortunate Caesar of the Hellespont, who laid the foundation of the Ottoman power in Europe."

1359   With the accession of Suleiman's brother, Murad I, Europe at last discovered, what before it had not even suspected, the mighty force which had been steadily accumulating for more than a generation in the small Ottoman state beyond the Hellespont. Murad crossed to the Gallipoli peninsula and found himself invincible. Thessalonica and Adrianople, next

1361 to the capital the two principal cities of the Greek Empire, passed into his hands with such ease as to suggest that the last day of the Greek Empire was at hand. But as Orchan was cautious so was Murad. A pause was necessary to consolidate the European conquests, to convert Adrianople into a Moslem capital, and to set up that system of military fiefs which was necessary for the supply of the cavalry arm. When these objects had been achieved, and the supremacy of the Sultan had been established in Asia Minor, an advance might be made on Constantinople and Belgrade. The Emperor was pliant. The spirit of the Greeks was low and submissive. It was only in the north-west, on the side of Serbia, that the Christian cause was likely to find an effective champion. Stephen Dushan was dead, but something of his spirit still survived in the breast of King Lazarus, his son, so while the Sultan was engaged in a victorious campaign against his Turkish adversaries in Asia, a great confederacy of the

1387 Christian peoples of south-eastern Europe was organized under the leadership of the Serbian King for the destruction of the Mussulman power. Serbs and Bulgars, Bosnians and Albanians, Poles, Hungarians, and even Mongols from the Dobrudja, but nobody of the older European nations, not a Latin nor a Greek, gathered together in the Christian camp. It may be safely assumed that an improvised army, in which seven languages are spoken, will always, however high be the courage of its individual members, prove inferior to an experienced force which long and arduous discipline has fused into a unit. So it proved on the famous and hard-

1389 fought field of Kossovo, which is commemorated in the heroic poetry of the Serbs. The Turks were victors, but in the hour of victory Murad fell by the hand of a Serbian patriot.

   Twelve years of continuous success followed the abasement of the Christian Slavs, years marked by the transfer of many loyalties, by the annihilation of a great crusading army from the west (Nicopolis, September 28, 1396), and by the extension of the Ottoman borders to the Danube and the Euphrates. The pitiless Bayazid, whose first public act had been the murder of the brother who had shared with him on the previous day the perils of Kossovo, seemed by the opening of the fifteenth century to have reached the climax of human fortune. Wherever the blood-red flag had waved, whether on the European or on the Asiatic front, it had brought victory. As the Sultan surveyed the scene from his voluptuous court at Brusa, as he reflected upon his vast harem, upon his Christian auxiliaries and slaves, upon the subjection of the Seljuks and the pusillanimity of the Greeks, and upon the strong network of his power, now extended over two continents, he felt that the time had come for one last inconsiderable operation, the replacement, whether in peace or war, of the Greek in Constantinople. In 1400 he ordered the Emperor out of the city, and meeting with a noble defiance, was preparing to deliver the lethal blow.

The impending stroke was averted in mid-air. A catastrophe supervened, which for many centuries made of Bayazid the standing example of the mutability of human fortune, and secured fifty years of respite for Constantinople. Timur (or Tamerlane) the Mongol, an old white-haired cripple from the far east, an intellectual specialist in chess, theology, and conquest, and perhaps the greatest artist in destruction known in the savage annals of mankind, was now approaching the confines of the Ottoman dominions at the head of his mammoth army of horsemen. Bayazid was rash enough to provoke the indignation of the master of Delhi and Samarcand, of Bagdad and Damascus, and paid the penalty for his presumption. On the wide plain of Angora the famous Ottoman army, the instrument of so many conquests, was enveloped and destroyed by an overwhelming force of Mongol cavalry. Bayazid was made a prisoner, and as he proceeded in a closed litter upon his melancholy journey to Samarcand, the victors streamed westward to wreck his capital, and to ravage his country to the brink of the Hellespont and the Aegean.

July 20, 1402

The recovery of the Ottoman Empire after this overwhelming disaster is as remarkable as the inability of the Christian powers to turn it to account. When we consider that the Ottomans had lost all their Asiatic possessions, that their Sultan was a captive, and that his sons were fighting one another for his inheritance, the situation might well have

seemed desperate. But what was lost in Asia was saved in
Europe. Adrianople was now a Moslem city, in which were
concentrated the resources of experience, courage, and
perseverance necessary for the restoration of the state. Here
for forty years was the nucleus of an effective government.
Here were civil servants and soldiers, lawyers and dervishes,
jurymen and law courts, seminaries for the education of
janissaries, and leaders imbued with the old spirit of military
pride. It was a good centre for the levying of Christian
slaves; and it was, in fact, from this capital of Adrianople,
which the Greek Emperors neglected to assault, that Mohammed I and Murad II issued forth to restore their Empire.

It is characteristic of the unorganized state of western
Europe that no serious effort was made to deal with the
Ottoman problems until forty years after the battle of Angora.
The golden moments, when the enemy was without soldiers or
Sultan, were allowed to slip by. Nor was it until Murad
II had recruited the army and refashioned the state, and
was making life in Hungary intolerable by his slave-raiding
aggressions, that western Europe woke up once more to
its serious responsibilities in connection with the eastern
danger.

The protagonist in the new Crusade was the nation which
had most reason to fear and resent the revived power of the
Ottomans. The Hungarians are among the bravest and most
stalwart of the fighting races of Europe, exhibiting the steadfast qualities of the Turk, with whom they are racially allied,
as well as others which belong to the more gifted and imaginative peoples. Under the rule of two spirited Angevin monarchs (1309-1382) this valiant but backward nation had advanced in military cohesion and in the arts of peace. Charles
Robert and his successor, Lewis the Great, supplied exactly
that form of stimulus which was best calculated to excite and
regiment the disordered energies of a proud aristocracy.
These princes, part French, part Neapolitan, introduced into
Hungary much of the chivalry of France and something of
the refinement of Italy. They set up a court, held tourna-
ments, created a feudal army, and by the establishment of
military orders, and the lavish bestowal of rewards, attracted
to the service of their persons the wayward loyalties of their
Magyar nobles. But the government of Hungary, which
demanded the undivided energies of a vigorous man, was,

soon after the death of Lewis, transferred to a son-in-law, who, of all the princes of Europe, was the least capable of concentrating his attention upon the necessary task of Hungarian defence.

Sigismund (1387-1437), husband of Mary of Hungary, was far too much distracted by the affairs of Bohemia and the Empire to give to Hungary the attention which a country "so dangerously placed in relation to the advancing power of the Ottoman Turks" imperiously demanded. After the disaster of Nicopolis, his policies in this area were half-hearted, shame-faced, and intermittent. He continued to rule, but ceased to govern, and the forces of Hungary, which, under a vigorous King, would have been deployed against the Turks, when their power had been shaken by the blows of Timur, were left unused.

With the death of Sigismund in 1437 the scene was changed by the appearance of a genius. It so happened that while Murad was engaged in his wars of recovery the Hungarians discovered a great soldier in John Hunyádi, reputed to be the natural son of King Sigismund by a Hungarian mother. The high military qualities of Hunyádi, which were exhibited in many a small affray with the Turks, attracted general atten-tion. He was placed in command of the army of a confed-eracy so wide as to include not only Hungary and Poland, Serbia and Wallachia, but the Duchy of Burgundy, Genoa and Venice, the Pope in Rome, and the Emperor in Constan-tinople. While a fleet of Italian and Flemish galleys was despatched to the Hellespont, Hunyádi, at the head of the army of the league, crossed the Danube, chased the Turks out of Serbia, and routed them so handsomely both south and north of the Haemus, that for the first time in their 1444 history the Ottomans were compelled to sue for peace.

This was the critical moment in the history of the near east. Two smashing victories had been won by the Christian army, which was now south of the Haemus, and within an easy march of the Turkish capital. The mountaineers of Albania were rising in rebellion under George Castriotis, soon to become famous as Scander Beg. Seljuk emirs were causing trouble in Asia Minor. It was the obvious duty of the Hun-garian commander to press forward to Adrianople, and to clinch his triumph before the enemy had recovered from the stunning effect of his unexpected success. No such oppor-

tunity had yet been given to the Christian powers of the west
to turn the Turk out of Europe, and 477 years were fated to
go by before an occasion, equally favourable, was once more
presented and declined.

In spite of his winning advantages, Hunyádi decided to
break off the campaign and treat with his enemy. Whether
he was influenced, as some say, by a Turkish bribe, or was
acting under the impulsion of the Serbs, or whether there were
other personal or military factors of the case, he gave to his
shaken opponent the exact respite which was needed to assist
his fortune. After that unhappy choice, made in the dead of
winter, things went ill for a while with the great Hungarian
commander. He connived at the perfidious breaking of a
treaty, which, though insufficient, had nevertheless been
signed and sworn to by King Ladislas of Hungary, and so
provided the Turk, for this time only, with the rare advantage
of the better cause. Late in the year he advanced again to the
Danube, and before the walls of Varna (November 10, 1444)
experienced a decisive defeat. But though his army was
routed and his sovereign killed, the spirit of Hunyádi was
still undaunted. Four years afterwards he was again in the
field at the head of a small but well-appointed army of
Hungarians and Wallachians: but the curse of Balkan disunion was upon him. At a critical moment in a three days'
1448 battle, the Wallachians went over to the enemy on that very
field of Kossovo which had crushed out the hopes of Serbian
freedom. For a decade Hungary was eliminated from the
ranks of powers capable of taking effective offensive action
against the Porte.

We have now reached the last stage in that long course of
persevering ambition, which, starting in an obscure fastness
among the Bithynian hills, ended in the palace of the Caesars.
Constantinople was still a Greek and an imperial city. Its
fortifications, though less strong than of old, had yet sufficed
to fend off an attack by Murad II, and since the city had never
been taken, a belief prevailed that it could never fall. Cities,
however, are not defended by beliefs, but by will and material
power. Had the Greeks been resolute and united, had the
navies of Genoa and Venice been placed at the disposition of
the imperial government, had there been among the Greek
and Italian peoples a common will to save Constantinople,
saved it would have been. But there was no such will. To

most Greeks the red hat of a Roman cardinal was even more odious than the Turkish fez, to most Latins the heresy of the unmanly Greek was less pardonable and more to be condemned than the false worship of the conquering Ottoman. And while theological animosities were strong, religious zeal was at a low ebb. To the merchants of Ragusa, of Genoa, and of Venice, the rise of this new Ottoman Empire presented itself not as a calamity to the Christian Faith, but as an incomparable occasion for lucrative commercial concessions. How could these astute traders afford to quarrel with a state already so powerful and likely for many years to control the political destiny of Asia Minor and the Balkans?

While Mohammed II was besieging Constantinople the Genoese merchants of the Galata suburb, who had all to lose in the Euxine, were negotiating arrangements for preferential trade in the Ottoman Empire.

Constantine XI, the last of the Caesars, though the nominee of Murad and his vassal, shines out in the final crisis of the Empire as a statesman and hero, prepared alike for compromise and for sacrifice. The Greek population of Constantinople, for whom the quarrels of monks were always more important than the clash of races, were unworthy of such a leader. While Mohammed's artillery was battering at the walls the public opinion of the capital was inflamed by denunciation of the Emperor who, in the desperate hope of winning the west to his side, had dared to recognize the Roman Church and to permit the celebration of Roman rites in the church of St. Sophia. To these wretched theological preoccupations we may perhaps ascribe the fact that the main part of the defence of the city was undertaken, not by the Greeks, but by Spaniards, Germans, and Italians. And as the defending force was not principally Greek, so the attacking army was not wholly Turkish. The levies of Mohammed were largely recruited from men of a Greek and Christian stock. So it happened that on May 29, 1453, by default of the Christians, the great city was breached and stormed, the last of the Byzantine Emperors perishing honourably in the death agony of the Empire.

The conquerors were Asiatic nomads and so remained. Sir Charles Eliot, describing the interior of the house of a Turkish gentleman in the nineteenth century, observes that it contained no more furniture than could be carried off at

1448-53

a moment's notice on a waggon into Asia.[1] A certain dignity of bearing, coupled with a grave exterior polish and a sense of humour and irony, were noted by western observers as favourable traits in the Turkish character, an abstinence in food and drink as a recommendation in their armies. But the culture of the west was not valued. The Turk remained an alien in Europe, having no part or lot in its traditions, and limited in his notions of imperial government to the philosophy of a slave-owning oligarchy in a world of potential slaves.

BOOKS WHICH MAY BE CONSULTED

G. Finlay: *History of Greece*. *Ed.* H. F. Tozer. 7 vols. 1877.

J. Von Hammer-Purgstall: *Histoire de L'Empire Ottoman, Traduit de l'allemand M. Dochez*. 3 vols. 1840-2.

H. W. V. Temperley: *History of Servia*. 1917.

C. G. Macartney: *Hungary*. (Nations of the Modern World Series.) 1934.

Gibbon: *Decline and Fall of the Roman Empire*. *Ed.* Bury. 1896-1900.

Cambridge Medieval History.

"Odysseus" (Sir Charles Eliot): *Turkey in Europe*. 1900.

H. A. Gibbons: *The Foundation of the Ottoman Empire*. 1916.

P. Wittek: *The Rise of the Ottoman Empire*. 1938.

A. S. Atiya: *The Crusade in the Later Middle Ages*. 1938.

D. M. Vaughan: *Europe and the Turk, 1350-1700*. 1954.

[1] "The very aspect of a Turkish house seems to indicate that it is not intended for a permanent residence. The ground floor is generally occupied by stables and stores. From this a staircase, often merely a ladder, leads to an upper storey, usually consisting of a long passage, from which open several rooms, the entrances which are closed by curtains and not by doors. There are probably holes in the planking of the passages and spiders' webs and swallows' nests in the rafters. The rooms themselves, however, are beautifully clean, but bare and unfurnished. . . . The general impression left on a European is that a party of travellers have occupied an old barn and said, 'Let us make the place clean enough to live in; it's no use taking any more trouble about it. We shall probably be off again in a week.' "

CHAPTER XXXV

NEW PERSPECTIVES

General lack of scientific progress in the middle ages. Growth of geographical knowledge. The realization of China. The circumnavigation of Africa.

WE HAVE now reached a point in European history distant by some two thousand six hundred years from the civilization described in the Homeric poems. During that long period the mind of man had produced noble literature, great buildings, imposing systems of philosophy and religion, statues and pictures which have never lost their appeal. It had asked questions of the soul, the heart, the brain, the senses, of everything but nature, or if a question was sometimes put to nature, the challenge was not followed up, but remained as an example of a fruitless and brilliant intuition. Accordingly little progress was made in those arts and discoveries which increase man's power over the blind forces of matter and raise the general standard of well-being. Locomotion remained where it had always been. Three thousand years had not supplemented the speed of a horse or the force of the wind which filled the sail. The vast majority of Europeans continued to live in stifling cabins, their experience circumscribed by narrow boundaries, their lives shortened by malnutrition or disease. For any serious addition to the great prehistoric inventions such as the wheel, the sail, the plough, the world was condemned to wait until the age of steam, petrol, and electricity.

Yet in one important respect the Europeans had made a notable advance in knowledge since the period of the Crusades. They had obtained a fuller and more accurate acquaintance with the earth and the sea. It was now known that the earth was round, and that far away at the other end of Asia a traveller would find China, Japan, and the spice islands. The Genoese had crossed the Sahara to the Sudan and in 1336 had a settlement in southern China. The Portuguese, who had learned their seacraft from Genoa, were feeling their way down the western coast of Africa. The sailors of the Mediterranean, ever since the early years of the fourteenth century, when the Venetians launched their "Flanders galleys," had been taking to the Atlantic in increasing numbers. Seacraft had become a branch of exact knowledge, and in the Italian and Catalan *portolani* of the fourteenth century had provided the mariners with scientific charts.

This expansion of geographical knowledge was due not only, or perhaps chiefly, to the spirit of adventure and curiosity which is characteristic of Europeans, but also to the lure of wealth. The east supplied luxuries, which once tasted were ever afterwards objects of insistent pursuit. From the east came silk and spices, silk which as early as the fourth century had become so popular through the Roman Empire that even the poorest women would not go without it, and spices (cinnamon, pepper, nutmeg), a precious cargo in a small bulk, which raised cookery to an art and gave to appetite a new incentive.

In the middle of the sixth century the silkworm was smuggled into the Roman Empire. What weighty consequences hung upon the transplantation of this trivial animal! A flourishing silk industry was established first in Syria, then in Sicily, and afterwards in Italy and Spain. In respect of this important commodity Europe was rendered independent of China, and deprived of one of the principal motives which otherwise might have impelled her upon a course of far-eastern adventure.

As for the spices, they came indeed to Europe, but at what a price! First the Indians, then the Arabs and Abyssinians, who as early as the third century had closed the Red Sea route to the Roman navigators, and after these the Mamelukes of Egypt, exacted their toll before the precious wares reached the counters of the Venetian merchant. To eliminate the exorbitant profits of these oriental middlemen by the establishment of some direct means of contact with the east became an inevitable object of economic desire.

The overland route across Asia was 7,500 miles long, and for much of the way difficult and dangerous, but it had been opened for European travellers for more than a century by the tolerant wisdom and policy of the Mongol Khans. During the hundred years of the Tatar peace (1264-1368) technicians and missionaries from the west were welcome in China. Then the veil suddenly fell. The Mongol power was broken, the missionary stations were obliterated, and with central Asia once more plunged in chaos, China retreated into impenetrable darkness and the sternest isolation. But the secret was out. The wonderful story, published in 1299, in which Marco Polo recounted his Asiatic voyages and his seventeen years' residence and travel in China, made an intellectual revolution in Europe, quite as important as that great expansion of human knowledge which two centuries later proceeded from the discoveries of Columbus.

It was now realized that the habitable globe was altogether unlike what it had been imagined to be, and that there was at the further end of Asia a country distinguished for its vast population, its imposing opulence, its paper currency, and for a standard of civilization and public order which equalled, if it did not surpass, the culture of Italy.

Such a discovery opened an endless series of suggestions and possibilities. In 1428 Don Pedro of Portugal procured in Venice a copy of Marco Polo's travels, and presented it to his brother Prince Henry the Navigator, under whose intelligent direction (1415-1461) Portugal was fast taking the lead in oceanic exploration.

Meanwhile the idea of the circumnavigation of Africa was beginning to claim increasing attention. It was no new project. The feat had been achieved by the Phoenicians, if we may trust Herodotus, in the sixth century before Christ; and achieved it would have been again, we can hardly doubt, under the Roman Empire, but for the fact that the Romans, having the command of Egypt and the Red Sea route, had no compelling economic motive to attempt it. But from the turn of the thirteenth century there was one city in the Mediterranean which experienced the force of such motives to the fullest extent. Genoa was the rival of Venice for the eastern trade. Venice was in league with Egypt, and by her compact with the Mamelukes possessed a monopoly in the distribution of such oriental wares as were conveyed to Europe by the Red Sea route. Of that monopoly she could be dispossessed only by one of two ways. Either her power might be destroyed in battle, or her wealth might be sapped at the source. The first method had been tried, and in the war of Chioggia had met with signal failure. There remained the second. A ship

might sail round Africa and without let or hindrance from
Arab or Turk fetch the spices overseas to Europe. This plan
was first attempted from Genoa. In May, 1291, Ugolino di
Vivaldo, a citizen of the republic, set out with two galleys to
find his way to India by the ocean route.

Vivaldo was lost at sea off the African coast. The fourteenth
century came and went without an attempt to repeat his
gallant enterprise, but meanwhile the Portuguese, placing
themselves under the naval tuition of Genoa, had learnt to
build and to sail ocean-going ships, and by visits to the
Canaries and voyages in search of Guinea, were steadily
equipping themselves for the great achievement which, after
a break of twelve hundred years, again let Europe into the
Indian Ocean and so opened a new chapter in the affairs of
the world.

The modern historian sees in the capture of Constantinople
by the Turks, and in the almost contemporary discovery of
the Guinea coast by the Portuguese, two events of profound
significance, the first as firmly closing Europe's principal gate-
ways to the east, the second as opening out the great period
of oceanic discovery and exploration which has spread
European domination through the planet and altered the
economic weights and balances of the world. Of these events
the first alone was regarded by contemporaries as marking
an epoch; for who could contemplate without emotion the
conquest of the great Christian capital by a Moslem power?
By comparison how trivial and inconspicuous was this new
Guinea trade in gold, ivory, and slaves opened out by the
enterprise of the King of Portugal! Even Zurara, the official
biographer of Henry the Navigator, is careful that the renown
of his hero should not rest upon activities so novel and in-
glorious as the organization of maritime trade and discovery.
Such is the way of the world. The future passes under our
eyes and we do not see it. As for the English, who of all the
peoples of the west were destined to reap the greatest profit
from the ocean-faring habit, they were at this time still
fiercely growling over the loss of their French possessions
and blind to the fact that, working from these obscure
voyages of the Portuguese, a good fairy was preparing to
place their remote island right in the centre of the habitable
globe.

BOOKS WHICH MAY BE CONSULTED

H. Pirenne and A. Renaudet: *La Fin du Moyen Age.* 1931.
C. R. Beazley: *The Dawn of Modern Geography.* 3 vols. 1897-1906.
G. F. Hudson: *Europe and China.* 1931.
H. M. Stephens: *History of Portugal.* 1891.
Horatio Brown: *Venice: A Historical Sketch of the Republic.* 1893.
Voyages and Travels of Marco Polo. (Everyman's Library.) 1908.
J. Huizinga: *The Waning of the Middle Ages.* Tr. F. Hopman. 1924.
E. Prestage: *Portugese Pioneers.* 1933.
G. H. T. Kimble: *Geography in the Middle Ages.* 1938.

CHAPTER XXXVI

THE NEW EUROPE

Mediaeval and modern times. The wider world. Nationalism. Capitalism. Artillery. The Protestant Reformation. Catholic rivalries. Rapid spread of the Reformation. The age of religious wars. Their effect on France and Germany compared. French diplomacy and German Protestantism. Absence of religious war in England. Dying down of the religious motive in politics during the eighteenth century.

No SINGLE date can be chosen to divide the mediaeval from the modern world. The change was gradual and uneven, swifter and more complete in one place than in another, and never so complete over the whole field as not to leave behind it mediaeval patches, just as in the middle ages themselves we may find here and there flashes of the human mind which appear to be strangely unmediaeval, and to anticipate in ways which are almost uncanny the spacious outlook and complex sentiments of the modern world.

Mankind is slower to move than city dwellers in the western countries are always willing to allow. Modes of life and thought rooted in deep antiquity still exercise their empire in certain places and on certain minds. The belief in magical charms and necromancy, in astrology and witchcraft is not yet extinct. Some superstitions perpetuate themselves by a native and ineradicable vitality in peasant homes; others are specially embalmed in religious rites. The elementary mysteries of nature, the waxing and waning of the moon, the procession of the heavens, the secret forces of reproduction and growth from time immemorial shaped the mythology of the European peasant. In Catholic Churches swinging censers still wave their incense round the coffin, as once they did, to chase away the demons who would waft the soul of the dead to eternal fires. Still as in the middle ages wonder-working miracles invite the pilgrim to be healed of his rheumatism, his gout, or his broken limb. If the present age has new shrines and other modes of locomotion, and Lourdes has replaced Compostella and Canterbury, if the pilgrim no longer trudges staff in hand, or rides at ease upon a palfrey, but is whirled in excursion trains or motor-cars to his pious destination, the mentality of the votary remains unchanged. The mechanical conveniences of modern science convey a survivor from the mediaeval world.

In matters social, political and economic vestiges of this earlier period are hardly less notable. There is perhaps no part of Europe which has moved further from the middle ages than Great Britain, yet it was not until 1835 that the mediaeval constitutions of the English towns were reformed out of existence with all their picturesque and convivial abuses and made to give place to the common democratic pattern which suits an industrial and levelling age. Nor is the face of our rural landscape altogether cleared of mediaeval features. Here and there the traveller may still come across the open fields and scattered strips which were characteristic of mediaeval tillage, but which in England, earlier and more completely than elsewhere, gave place to the enclosures of improving landlords. And if such traces of mediaeval usage can be found in Britain, how much more numerous are they in the backward eastern parts of Europe where the priesthood has been long sunk in ignorance and sloth. Nor until the nineteenth century did the downtrodden peasantry of Galicia begin to experience any sensible change or improvement in their condition or mode of life. Within living memory the Prince of Montenegro would dispense a patriarchal justice to his subjects, sitting under a tree like St. Louis of old. Still the Albanian goes armed like the Afghan and lives the life depicted in the *Iliad*. Still do the Bulgarian villagers practise rites and superstitions which may have brought a smile to the lips of Euripides. A fine observer of modern Greece reports that the real spiritual equipment of the Greek people today consists in a number of ideas and superstitions, some of which are "disguised under a thin veil of Christian assimilation," while others may "still wear the classic garb unaltered." Gifts of money and salt and bread still propitiate the three Fates. Charon's obol is still placed on the lips of the dead. Nereids and vampires, goblins and demons still haunt the streams and mountains or send the mariner to a watery grave.[1]

In the fabric of peasant society in Europe there is thus even yet many an antique pattern which has been little altered by the lapse of time. But if the modern scene is not all rational illumination, neither was the mediaeval wholly black with superstition. There was Roger Bacon, the Oxford Franciscan, who laid down the axiom that nothing could be fully known without experiment, and first insisted upon a knowledge of chemistry as necessary to the training of a physician. There was Chaucer, whose close and whimsical observation of human eccentricities of character seems to prefigure the genius of Charles Dickens, and Villon, robber, murderer, and poet, in whose poignant lyrics, more than in Victor Hugo's 143 *Notre Dame de Paris*, mediaeval Paris lives again with its irony and laughter, its sentiment and sensuality, its brooding melancholy and mingled moods of crime and penitence, wildness and culture, cruelty and romance. Life was uncomfortable for men of original genius in the middle ages. Bacon spent ten years in prison, Petrarch was prosecuted as a wizard at the instance of a cardinal for his undue addiction to Virgilian studies, but the spirit of modern science lived in Bacon as the spirit of modern humanism may be found in Petrarch. Even in the fourteenth century there were men so brave as in secret to dissect the human body. The great Vesalius, acknowledged parent of modern anatomy, had more 1514- than one obscure precursor in the age of Faith. 64

Yet, despite the inevitable gradualness of change, the broad contrast between the mediaeval and the modern emerges with sufficient plainness. A society divided between lay and cleric gave place to a society divided into rich and poor, an atmo-

[1] Rennell Rodd, *The Customs and Lore of Modern Greece*.

sphere hostile to free enquiry to one in which science could live and mature. During the early middle ages the Church was the sole depository of culture, the one supreme agency by which the barbaric tribes could be inducted into the great tradition of Christian and Roman civilization, the real inheritor of the political tradition of the shattered Empire of the West. Language, literature, politics, law, were all conditioned by the common educational mould which had survived the wreckage of the secular power. The use of Latin was universal among the literate class, and Latin was the *lingua franca* of western Europe. The spirit of the ancient Roman jurists lived on in the canon law, which was enforced by ecclesiastical courts in every quarter of Latin Christianity. The thinking of Europe, whether in the schools and universities or outside them, was carried on by tonsured clerks over a field of experience which was strictly confined by the sacred texts and their ancillary literature. Old knowledge was lost, and new knowledge was not acquired. Without the ballast of natural science, the human intellect fell a prey to extremes of rashness or timidity. To write in a vernacular language was felt to be a condescension which needed an apology. 1304- Even Petrarch preferred the *Africa*, a dull epic written in 74 Latin, to the charming Italian sonnets which are his chief claim to immortality.

The political theory of the middle ages was shaped by the surviving prestige of the Roman Empire and the overpowering authority of the Roman Church. It is true that the original unity of the Roman Empire had been broken by the shock of the barbaric invasion of the west. There was a western Empire which was Latin and an eastern Empire which was Greek. But the idea of an Imperial and Christian unity continued to survive. If the Greek and Latin churches could not be reconciled—and the hope that they might be reconciled was never wholly abandoned—the Latin church of the west was at least regarded as one indissoluble and immortal whole. The Pope was the supreme guardian upon earth of faith and morality. Above the chaos and violence of the temporal world his was the final oracle calling rulers and subjects alike to practise justice, to ensue peace, and to abide by the truths of revealed religion. In a poor and ignorant society mainly composed of soldiers, priests, and peasants, such a view of human governance found acceptance, the more readily since Christians

lived for the most part in the shell of the ancient Roman
Empire and were almost unconscious of the existence of wide
tracts of the globe into which the name of Rome had never
penetrated.

To this Roman and clerical outlook upon the world, the
sixteenth century, the first age which may be regarded as distinctively modern, offers the sharpest contrast. The lay mind,
fortified by the free use of the vernacular languages and by the
full recovery of Greek and Hebrew, had come into its own.
The close interrogation of nature, which was to lead to the
development of modern science, had begun. Painters examined the human frame, surgeons dissected it. Verrocchio, the
sculptor, was also an anatomist. The discovery made by
Copernicus, a Polish astronomer, that the earth revolved
round the sun, steadily secured adherents. A new lay culture,
aristocratic in origin, for it had chiefly grown up in the luxurious courts of the Italian despots, was made a general possession through the invention of printing. Strong and continuous
as were the theological interests, they were now balanced by
an exciting body of new knowledge, having no connection
with theology, and the fruit of mental processes which
theology was unable to turn to account. With a sharp gesture
of impatience Europe turned away from the vast literature of
commentaries and glosses, which the pedants of the later
middle ages had inscribed "in letters of opium on tablets of
lead."

1473-
1543

An important part of this new knowledge was geographical.
The Portuguese conquest of Ceuta on the African coast in
1415 had been the first step in that long and wonderful series
of marine adventures which led to the circumnavigation of
Africa by Vasco da Gama, to the foundation of the Portuguese Empire in the east, and to the discovery by Christopher
Columbus, the Genoese sailor, of the new world beyond the
Atlantic. The Mediterranean ceased henceforth to be the
centre of the civilized world. The sceptre of commerce passed
from the cities of Italy to the nations having easy access to the
Atlantic Ocean, first to Portugal, then in succession to Spain,
the Netherlands, France and England. A civilization which
had sprung up in the river basins of the Euphrates and the
Nile, and had spread round the littoral of the Mediterranean,
was now carried far and wide on ocean-going ships to distant

1492

lands. Europe began to enter into that new phase of its existence, which is marked by the foundation of colonies and empires beyond the ocean, and by the gradual spread of European influences throughout the habitable globe.

The discovery of the new world, coinciding with the swift diffusion of printed books, taught the Europeans that "Truth" in Bacon's noble phrase "is the daughter not of authority but of time." The inhabitants of this continent had long known that the earth was round, and that if they sailed far enough to the west they would find the Indies. Nothing, however, had prepared them for the emergence of an intermediate land-mass of incalculable vastness and resources. If their expectations of the shape of the planet were confirmed, their estimate of its size was rudely overthrown. The world was far bigger than they had thought. The old notions of geography, taught for centuries by learned clerks and believed in all the universities, were suddenly shown to be in sharp contradiction to established facts.

The consequences were farther reaching than the additions to positive knowledge resulting from the geographical discoveries. Insensibly mankind acquired a new attitude towards knowledge itself. Authority no longer went unchallenged. The past was no longer supreme. As the planet unfolded its unending wonders, generations grew up for whom truth was not a complete thing already given in ancient books, but a secret yet to be retrieved from the womb of time.

Not that among the many visions of the future which were excited by the first impact of America there was present the thought that some day this new continent would become the receptacle for the overspill of Europe. America would have many uses. It would bring a new spiritual Empire to the Catholic Church and new temporal dominions to the masters of Spain and Portugal. The mariner, the treasure hunter, the trader, and the missionary would be drawn across the Atlantic. Dignified Spanish noblemen would administer law and justice among the native Indians, and represent the majesty of the Spanish Crown in its overseas provinces. But nothing either in the travel tales of returned sailors or in the economic state of Europe during the early half of the sixteenth century encouraged the expectation that great blocks of European settlers would find new homes in America. Even after a century of Atlantic voyaging Francis Bacon, who was the prophet of scientific method and the father of physical geography, warned his compatriots against American colonization. If English emigrants there must be, Ireland, that little neglected island across St. George's Channel, had the prior claim upon their attentions.

Meanwhile the political framework of the mediaeval Empire had given way before the growth of national states. A universal monarchy, supported by a universal church, though it corresponded to the aspirations of Europe during many centuries, was never closely adjusted to its needs or respected by its observance. The Empire had never secured a general allegiance. The claims of the Papacy had often been countered by the will of princes. By slow and painful steps, as feudal licence was brought under the control of central power, national states were formed, first of all in England, where the conditions were favourable, then in the Christian states of the Iberian peninsula, in France, and in the larger principalities of the German federation. By the end of the fifteenth century national governments had been established, not without the assistance of the new invention of gunpowder, in England, France, and Spain. In England the suicide of the old feudal nobility in the Wars of the Roses was the prelude to the establishment of Tudor rule.

Framed against the background of mediaeval licence, the type of government which was now coming into vogue was remarkable for strength; judged by modern standards it was pitiably weak. The resources, moral, intellectual, and material, at the disposal of the most powerful monarchs of the sixteenth century were indeed paltry when we measure them against the disciplined social conscience, the organized national education, the powerful instruments for the accumulation and concentration of knowledge, the great military and naval establishments and vast revenues which support the fabric of a modern state. The papers which nourished the machine of English government during the whole reign of Queen Elizabeth would probably be outweighed in a month by the accumulations of the least important of our modern government offices. The strongest army put into the field by Francis I would have withered away before a single division of the army of Pétain or Foch. Even in the most advanced states of the sixteenth century the government lived from hand to mouth, improvising armies and navies to suit parti-

cular occasions, and driven to the most desperate expedients
for finance. To recruit, to pay, to feed a national army were
feats not only beyond the power of any government to
execute, but beyond the scope of any statesman to conceive.
Charles VII of France had asked of every parish in France
that it should maintain an archer for the wars. The scheme
broke down at once. His successor, Louis XI, fell back on a
force of foreign mercenaries. The chronic insolvency of
Charles V, judged to be the most powerful monarch of his
time, is symptomatic of a weakness which afflicted all governments alike.

Nevertheless it is to this age, which witnessed the disruption
of Latin Christianity, that we may ascribe the clear emergence
of that more efficient form of social and political communion
which claims the free yet disciplined loyalties of a nation. In
the sixteenth century Europeans began, in larger measure
than before, to think in nations, to act in national groups,
and to render to the head of the national state some part of
the loyalty which had previously been paid to the undivided
Church. Roger Ascham, the schoolmaster and educational
reformer who taught Queen Elizabeth, is a typical figure in the
new lay educational movements which gave support to vernacular literature and national pride.

The formation of the strong continental monarchies ushers
in a period of acute diplomatic rivalry which was governed
by the conception of the balance of power. While the
mediaeval sense of a common European interest had faded
away, no country had acquired a measured estimate of its
own strength and resources. Romantic ambitions, the legacy
of the Roman and Carolingian ages, filled the minds of rulers
who would have been better occupied in attending to the
welfare of their subjects. Statecraft was still immature,
political economy had not been invented, and the art of
domestic comfort was neither understood nor intelligently
pursued. In the absence of exact statistics the vaguest notions
prevailed as to the wealth and population of the European
States. It was a common belief that dazzling conquests might
still be made and held within the old framework of European
society.

Whether international states had international obligations
was a question which no one at the opening of the sixteenth
century was much concerned to ask or answer. Travel was

difficult, the relations between governments were rare and intermittent. Every state tried to overreach its neighbour and to extend its borders. The greatest opportunity offered to Europe to undertake a grand work of co-operative civilization was thrown away. The discovery of the New World, which under wise direction and a happier temper of the public mind might have led to a harmonious subdivision of the new continent between the interested powers was, on the contrary, made the signal for an outburst of cruel war and piracy on the high seas which lasted for generations. All this was taken for granted. No political thinkers rose to the size of the vast events which were changing the face of the world. Sir Thomas More surrendered himself to the pleasant fancies of Utopia, while Machiavelli, the great Florentine publicist, had eyes for no bigger thing than an Italy liberated from barbarians.

Money, which has always been a power in human affairs, had become more plentiful in the later middle ages, and was destined to become more abundant still through the importation of Peruvian silver before the sixteenth century had run its course. In all the progressive countries of the west the growth of trade and commerce, which had received its first important stimulus during the Crusades, had created an influential middle class whose material interests were opposed to the continuance of feudal disorder. Capital was coming into its own. Great merchants and bankers, a Jacques Coeur of Bourges, a Fugger of Augsburg, a Dick Whittington of London, a Roberto Strozzi of Florence, out-topped many a great feudal noble in their command of free capital, and rose to positions of political influence. For many years the Empire was financed from Augsburg, while the Italian enterprises of France depended upon the support of the Strozzi Bank of Florence, with its branches in Lyons, Venice, and Rome. Capital then must be counted as a force in aid of those monarchical nation states whose consolidated power is one of the new facts distinguishing the Europe of the sixteenth century from the conditions of the feudal age.

Upon such a Europe, kindled by new knowledge and new horizons, and charged with the spirit of national pride and independence, fell the spark of the Protestant Reformation. A challenge to Roman doctrine was no new thing. It had been made by Wycliffe in England and by Hus in Bohemia. The problem how best to reform the manifest abuses of the Church

1324
84

1373-
1415

had ever since the first schism engaged the attention of serious minds throughout Christendom. Councils had met, deliberated, and dispersed, without effecting any serious improvement. The Pope, for whose sovereign authority no menace seemed to be more formidable than the recognition of a General Council as a regular and established organ of Church government, had been able to circumvent the conciliar movement by entering into separate and direct concordats with national governments. The ill-organized and tumultuous deliberations of an international assembly, whose members were divided from one another by race, language, and allegiance, were no match for the experienced diplomacy of the Roman Curia. A combination of the Papacy on the one hand, and the temporal powers on the other, might always be relied on to frustrate the endeavours of an ecumenical council. The Protestant Reformation, however, was neither initiated nor assisted by councils of the Church. It arose out of a passionate sense of the contrast between the simplicity of the Apostolic age and the wealth and fiscal exactions of the Roman Church; it was sheltered by the help and assisted by the appetites of certain temporal princes. And finally, in those regions of northern Europe in which it succeeded in securing a foothold, it was protected against the forces of Catholic reaction by a widespread confiscation of abbey lands and the creation of a vested interest in the spoils of the plundered church, which was in certain regions so deeply rooted that neither war nor revolution was able to disturb it.

This great religious convulsion divided Christian Europe at a time when the Ottoman Turks had completed their conquest of the Balkan peninsula, acquired Egypt, and created a formidable navy. Yet so faint was the Christian motive as a shaping power in politics, during the first half of the sixteenth century, that Francis I and his son Henry II of France did not scruple to ally themselves with the Ottomans against Charles V at the very time when the head of the Habsburg house stood out as the protagonist of Catholic orthodoxy against the heresy of Luther. Indeed, it is to these national and dynastic rivalries, more acute and powerful in the early part of the sixteenth century than in any previous age, that we must ascribe the victory of Protestantism over a large part of northern Europe. It is a mistake to suppose that persecution never succeeds. Persecution crushed the Albigenses and

Lollards, and stamped out the seeds of Protestantism in Spain, Italy, and Bohemia. If the temporal powers of Europe had been united to put down the Lutherans of Germany or the Calvinists of Geneva there is no reason to think that they would have failed in their work. But they were not united. The great duel between the house of Valois and the house of Habsburg was the dominating issue of the age. The heresies of Germany were far too embarrassing to Charles V to be otherwise than welcome to Francis I, under whom was first established that long French tradition of fostering heretics abroad and suppressing them at home, without which all Germany might have been reclaimed for the Roman Church.

The course of the Reformation in England was similarly governed by the great continental rivalry of the age. In the critical year, 1527, when the continued allegiance of England to the Papal See depended upon the Pope's acquiescence in Henry VIII's repudiation of Catharine of Aragon, the Pope was in consequence of the Franco-Imperial war a prisoner in the hands of Charles V, who was Catharine's nephew. Even had he wished to be compliant, and there were papal precedents for the action which was urged upon him by the English Court, Clement VII was no free agent. He could not give his consent. The same Habsburg and Valois rivalry, which ultimately helped to make north Germany Protestant, precipitated the breach between England and Rome during the reign of Henry VIII, and again sheltered the young Anglican Church from overthrow during the perilous days of Queen Elizabeth.

The religious disruption of western Europe was not effected without a terrible struggle. During the first half of the sixteenth century the great Habsburg-Valois rivalry absorbed the energies of the two leading Catholic powers on the continent. Protestant beliefs spread far and fast. They conquered the greater part of Germany and Switzerland; they were received into the Scandinavian kingdoms, penetrated into Italy and Spain, carried all before them in Scotland and Bohemia. According to the Cardinal of Lorraine, two-thirds of the inhabitants of France were infected with the new heresy in the reign of Henry II. For the space of a century the movement continued to gather force, and as happens when religious movements become popular and appeal to 1547-59 the plain man's jealousy of ostentatious power and ill-used wealth, the original core of true religious ardour was surrounded by a wide penumbra of selfishness, carelessness, and greed.

Then came a reaction. In 1559 Henry II of France, renouncing his dream of Italian conquests, and sobered, no doubt, by the defeat of his army on the field of St. Quentin, signed the Treaty of Cateau Cambrésis with the Imperialists, and resolved to devote himself to the extirpation of heresy at home. A new era opens. The dynastic struggle is suspended. The religious wars begin. Could the Lutherans hold Germany? Could the Calvinists win France? The Papacy, aided by the recently established order of Jesuits, embarked upon a systematic endeavour to reconquer the territory which had been lost to the Roman Faith.

The religious war in France lasted, with intermissions, from 1560 until the Edict of Nantes in 1598 secured for the Protestant Huguenots toleration and a privileged position, an *imperium in imperio*, within the French kingdom. It was fought with great bitterness and marked by many acts of mob violence and military atrocity; but it left no deep scar upon the social well-being of the French nation. At the end of her religious wars, France emerged more powerful than she had ever been before. Her army was the strongest in Europe, her diplomacy the best informed, her court the most resplendent. The seventeenth century marks the zenith of the French monarchy. It was under Richelieu and Mazarin that the foundations were laid for the long, imposing dominion of Louis XIV.

1643-
1715

Far otherwise was the effect of thirty years of religious war upon the disjointed federation of Germany. When the Peace of Westphalia in 1648 put a term to the quarrel, settling frontiers for the rival confessions which have ever since been substantially maintained, Germany was a ruin. Her population was depleted, her treasuries were drained, her establishments of education and learning were grievously injured, and her pride and confidence sapped and impaired by a long succession of ruinous reverses and humiliations. It is no fantastic conjecture that the Thirty Years' War put the civilization of Germany back by two hundred years, or that the ease with which a people so virile was subjected to the yoke of Napoleon in the first decade of the nineteenth

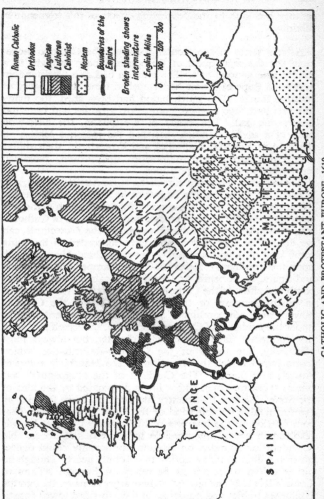

CATHOLIC AND PROTESTANT EUROPE, 1610

century was due to the depressing effects of this tremendous calamity.

After a series of spectacular successes the Catholic movement for the reconquest of Europe had been brought to a sudden and general halt. The reunion of Latin Christendom under the Pope of Rome had vanished from the category of possible things. Too much blood had been shed, too many interests had been created, competing loyalties had been too deeply engaged. The Peace of Westphalia, the hard-won prize of a savage conflict, inscribed the religious schism on the map of Europe. Catholics and Protestants, their differences unbridged, their animosities unappeased, remained entrenched in their war positions.

The result is the more surprising since Austria, Spain, and France, the three leading countries in Europe, were true to the ancient faith. Had these powerful States, each orthodox, each anxious for the maintenance and promotion of Catholicism, chosen to act in combination against the Protestants, can we doubt but that they would have succeeded in imposing some kind of religious unity, however mechanical and unreal, upon the Continent? Heresy had been stamped out in Austria and Spain, in Bohemia and Poland. Against a resolute and combined effort of the Catholic powers, could it have survived in north Germany or the Netherlands? But the Catholic powers were not combined. At the critical moment France, under the guidance of Cardinal Richelieu, set herself to thwart first indirectly, later (after 1635) directly, but always most effectually, the forces of the Counter-Reformation which manoeuvred under the direction of the Habsburg rulers of Austria and Spain. "The Cardinal of the Huguenots" was one of those rare men whose life is dominated by the idea of the State. He saw his country menaced on every frontier by the formidable combination of the Habsburg powers. That combination in the interests of his sovereign master he was resolved in every way possible to weaken and abase. No consideration founded on religion or morality could deflect his iron will or arouse emotion in his chilly heart. Though on his accession to power as Secretary of Foreign Affairs to Louis XIII (1624) he had no regular army or navy, though the Huguenot nobles and burgesses in their fortified towns constituted a State within a State, though his life was menaced by domestic intrigue, he never relaxed in his sleepless opposition to the great secular agencies of the Catholic priesthood. At home he crushed the political strength of the Huguenots, while according them religious freedom. Abroad he financed the Protestant cause, fought its battles and ensured its success. Now he was at work obstructing the Valtelline, the corridor between the Spanish Milanese and Austria. Now he was supporting by force of arms a French candidate for the Duchy of Mantua. At a dark hour in the Protestant fortunes the Swedish army of Gustavus Adolphus was set in motion by French subsidies. If the continent of Europe is partly Protestant today, the cause is possibly to be found in the persistent diplomacy of a Roman cardinal.

The final episode in the long and tragical conflict between the Protestant and Catholic principles in Europe was destined to exercise a far-reaching influence upon the balance of power in the world. The Huguenots were among the most industrious and deserving subjects of Louis XIV. In commerce and marine adventure, as in all branches of industry such as the weaving of silk, which in that age demanded a high measure of technical skill, these Protestant Frenchmen distanced their Catholic fellow-citizens. But in the eyes of Louis XIV and Madame de Maintenon, his fanatical wife, these people, by reason of their religious views, had no place in a Catholic state. No technical skill, no contribution to the material well-being of the community, atoned for the deadly fact of religious heresy. The Huguenots were first persecuted and then expelled. The protection which had been assured them under the Edict of Nantes was withdrawn in 1685, and a community, which, if it had prevailed, might have given to France the lead in colonial development, transferred its knowledge and skill to the more congenial soil of her Protestant rivals.

The fortunate island of Britain was spared the religious convulsions which tormented the continent. In the southern part of the island a national Church, Erastian in government, Roman in ritual, Calvinist in theology, was set up and firmly secured by the end of the sixteenth century, not indeed without some bloodshed and local disturbance, but upon the whole with an astonishing measure of tranquil acquiescence on the part of an essentially untheological people. The chance of a

successful Catholic reaction, which was never very great after
the nobles and squires of England had been glutted with the
1588 abbey lands, vanished altogether with the ruin of the Spanish
Armada. The Civil War of the seventeenth century was
fought, not over the issue of Catholic and Protestant, though
the fears of Rome, as a dark, malignant, unscrupulous power,
haunted the imagination of the Roundheads, and gave a
sinister meaning to every ritualistic practice, but over parliamentary liberties and Anglican ceremonial. It is only in the
later part of the seventeenth century, when Louis XIV was
beginning his persecuting career, that the danger of a Catholic
reconquest of the island became once more an important
factor in politics. Charles II was a secret, James II an open,
Papist. Both kings worked, the first with subtlety and reserve,
the second with gross and blatant unwisdom, for a Catholic
restoration in England to be established with the assistance
of an army from France. But the plot was defeated. It is
permissible to doubt whether, even with the assistance of
French bayonets, the Catholics of England could have prevailed against the strong Protestantism of the City of London,
of the eastern counties, and of the fleet. When the final
test came, not a man was found to risk his skin for King
James.

The revolution of 1688 which brought William of Orange
to the English throne was glorious because it was bloodless,
and bloodless because the country stood so solid for the
Protestant cause that it could afford to be clement.

The defeat of the Counter-Reformation in England ushered
in a new period of European history. In the eighteenth
century the rivalry of England and France continued, but
tended to be fought across the ocean, in Canada and India,
rather than upon the continent of Europe. Colonies and
commerce became more important as motives of public
policy than religious affiliations and dynastic alliances. The
Puritan of the second generation was apt to be a shrewd,
money-making man of business. Conservatism—or, as it was
then called, Whiggism—in politics, rationalism in philosophy,
an easy-going comfort in social life, were the mottoes of the
Hanoverian age. The wealth, the prosperity, and the liberty
of England began to attract the attention of foreigners.
Though the genius of Shakespeare was still a mystery, the
idea began to get abroad that much could be learned from the

country which had been the spearhead of the Protestant resistance to Louis XIV. Voltaire was the pupil of Bolingbroke. To Montesquieu it appeared that the English had discovered the secret of political freedom. The philosophy of Newton and Locke passed as a formative element into the guiding minds of eighteenth-century France. The small island became once more for a few decades what it had been during the flowering time of mediaeval Oxford, the preceptress of Europe.

Such is the general trend of the story which has now to be recounted. A religion widely held and strongly entrenched in the social and political tradition of western Europe is roughly challenged by new spiritual forces and over a large part of Europe compelled to accept defeat. A "totalitarian" conception of the social order loses colour and actuality as the Christian community of the West dissolves into fragments which it is unable to re-absorb. Views of life based upon freedom of thought, upon the rights of the individual conscience, upon the self-determination of states and even of small religious sects, corrode the ancient fabric of the all-embracing church and give rise to trains of revolutionary thought which in the end transform the institutions of Europe and shape the life of the modern world. The more vigorous north falls away from Rome. The less vigorous south, though only after inner convulsions, stands firm in the ancient ways. In the long dispute which bathes Europe in blood, the basest and noblest motives are ineradicably blended. Cranmer's Prayer-book and Milton's *Paradise Lost*, Loyola's *Spiritual Exercises* and Pascal's *Pensées*, the Catholic music of Palestrina and the Protestant music of Bach, may be taken as illustrations of the depth of emotion aroused in religious men of genius on either side of this great controversy. But the great mass of the European people has never been in any true sense religious. The dominant figure in the period of Europe's religious wars are the statesmen, soldiers, and adventurers, who make use of the raw enthusiasm of the masses to achieve their secular ends. A Wallenstein in Bohemia, a Marlborough in England, rises above the storm, shapes policies, directs armies, amasses wealth, and fills Europe with the fame and fear of his prowess. A Chinaman of the period, had he been in a position to survey the turbulent

European scene during the sixteenth and seventeenth centuries, might well have asked himself whether the art of living was not better understood by a people which had no religious quarrels because they had no religion but only an ethical code of deportment, whether the vast liberation of human forces brought about by the Protestant Reformation with all its infinite consequences for art and music, science and letters, was worth the price of long and savage wars, and whether an attitude of mind towards the ultimate mysteries less aspiring, less heroic and less confident than that which prevailed among western Christians was not in effect more conducive to human comfort.

BOOKS WHICH MAY BE CONSULTED

Excellent short bibliographies for the greater part of the ground covered may be found in A. J. Grant, *A History of Europe from 1494 to 1610* (1931), and in D. Ogg, *Europe in the Seventeenth Century* (1925). For more extended bibliographies see *the Cambridge Modern History* and the standard national Histories—*e.g.*, Lavisse for France, and for England Froude, Gardiner, Macaulay, G. M. Trevelyan, and the composite Histories published respectively by Messrs. Longmans and Methuen.

CHAPTER XXXVII

THE ITALIAN RENAISSANCE

Reasons why the Renaissance began in Italy. The place of Florence. Versatility of the great artists. Religious and lay motives in Italian art. Humanism. Lorenzo Valla. Niccolo de' Niccoli. Vittorino da Feltre. The Renaissance Popes. Venice. The aristocratic character of Italian humanism. Sharp contrasts in Italian life. Spread of Italian Influence. The Prince *and* The Courtier. *Limitations of Italian influence.*

THE FIFTEENTH century, which is intellectually so barren in England, witnessed the effulgence of the Italian Renaissance. During two hundred years (1340-1540) the cities of Italy produced an output of art, scholarship, and literature such as the world had not seen since the glory of ancient Athens. But when Italy passed under the political domination of Spain, and was subjected to the religious rigours of the Catholic reaction, with its Jesuits' Order, its Holy Inquisition, and its Index of prohibited books, the broad and prodigal stream of Italian imagination, which had flowed so powerfully and so long, shrank into a feeble channel. A sickly mystical sentiment replaced the robust virility of the creative age. The great painters, who at Venice longer than elsewhere continued to sustain the highest traditions of their art, were not replaced as they passed away, and Italy, after having to an incalculable degree enriched the intellectual life of Europe, and earned for herself the permanent gratitude of mankind, descended from her place of pre-eminence. The prose of France, the poetry and drama of England, the music of Germany, henceforth meant more to the world than all the studios and academies of Florence and Venice.

It is natural that the rebirth of European art and letters should have taken place in a land where the marbles of antiquity still gleamed among the cypresses and olives, and the tradition of humane learning, descending from classical times, had never been wholly interrupted. Here too was the eager rivalry of competing cities and luxurious courts, and many a patron who would pay high for a picture, or a manuscript, a secretary, or a tutor. Here finally were ruins, inscriptions, coins, and medals, inviting, and since the days of Petrarch attracting, the enquiry of the scholar.

The humanist movement, which had been gathering strength ever since the middle of the fourteenth century, acquired an astounding and brilliant velocity during the period of almost unbroken peace which divides the Treaty of Lodi in 1454 from the French invasion of Italy under Charles VIII forty years afterwards. While Lorenzo de' Medici was master of Florence, and an effective if uneasy accord between the four leading Italian states preserved Italy from foreign aggression, art and letters advanced with great strides. More particularly was this true of Lorenzo's own capital on the Arno, which was already famous for the names of Dante, Petrarch, and Boccaccio. Here was gathered together a constellation of illustrious men who made Florence the artistic and intellectual capital of Europe. When we consider that a catalogue of great Florentines born and working during these forty years would include the names of Michael Angelo, Donatello, Fra Filippo Lippi, and Sandro Botticelli, that to these great artists must be added Machiavelli the publicist, Guicciardini the historian, Ficino the Platonist, and Politian the Latin scholar, that Luca della Robbia and Domenico Ghirlandaio were Florentines, as well as Verrocchio, Perugino, and Leonardo da Vinci, and that Lorenzo himself showed genius alike as a poet, a statesman, and a virtuoso, we can form some faint impression of the blinding splendour of a society so led and quickened. It was a source of strength that the artists of the Italian Renaissance were not too highly specialized. In Florence, for instance, painters and sculptors belonged to the same corporation as the doctors and apothecaries, and were often instructed by jewellers, who combined science with trade and a wide acquaintance with the arts and crafts. Prodigies of versatility were not infrequent. Men passed and repassed from painting to sculpture, from sculpture to architecture and metalwork, and from these forms of energy to poetry, philosophy, and natural science. The classical examples of this omnicompetence are Michael Angelo, Leonardo da Vinci, and Alberti. The first is not only to be remembered for his statues and frescoes, but as a man whose skill in fortification defended Florence during a famous siege, as a man who took captive the heart of his host in Bologna through his readings of Dante, Petrarch, and Boccaccio, and finally as one who, having passed the age of 70, composed a series of sonnets, whose note of rare and exalted passion had not been heard in Italy since the death of Dante. Leonardo, again, was not only the painter of Mona Lisa and the Last Supper, but architect, mechanician, and man of science as well. His notebooks reveal a mind eager to grapple with all knowledge and experience, curious as to the orbit of the sun and moon, theorizing on marine fossils found among the crags of the Apennines, concerned with problems of linear perspective and anatomy, and investigating the ultimate truths of mechanics. The same wide competence and curiosity were characteristic of Alberti, the first athlete and horseman of his age, who composed melodies, painted pictures, built churches, wrote a comedy, and expounded the science of architecture in ten books, written in a prose so pure and elegant that it may be read with pleasure to this day. No branch of applied science seemed to be alien to Alberti, who devised machinery for raising sunken ships, and is said to have anticipated some modern discoveries in optics. Alberti's gifts are his own, but a spacious curiosity was a note common to the creative artists of his time.

The art of the Italian Renaissance, in its earliest Florentine as well as in its later Venetian manifestations, continued, since the Church was the greatest of patrons, to conform to a Christian tradition. For one subject taken from the classics, twenty were chosen from the Bible. Some distinguished painters, Fra Angelico, Fra Filippo Lippi, Fra Bartolomeo, were friars. But as time went on the painting of religious subjects lost much of the spiritual character which had originally belonged to it. The figures became less ascetic, less conventionally hieratic, and closer to the flesh and blood of human life. The Madonna of Titian was a handsome model, not an idealized vision of holy motherhood. On this, as in other branches of Italian activity, the lay and sceptical spirit of the age, nowhere stronger than in Rome itself, left its decisive imprint.

A love of personal glory was a feature of the age. Rich men commissioned portraits and statues and called upon painters and sculptors to give them an immortality in art. How magnificent and how swiftly renowned was Florentine sculpture, Englishmen who have never seen a statue of Donatello or Michael Angelo under an Italian sky may learn by a visit to Westminster Abbey, where the tomb of Henry VII carved by the chisel of Torregiano invites their admiration. And as the patron sought immortality from the artist, so the artist desired immortality for himself. The days of anonymous architecture, of Gothic cathedrals built by generation after generation of nameless craftsmen, were past. The architect of the Renaissance, basing his craft on the doctrines of Vitruvius, expected within his own lifetime to reap a harvest of fame from his completed work.

It is characteristic of the force and individuality of the Italians of the Renaissance that their architecture, though profoundly influenced by the writings of Vitruvius, was never a pedantic or servile imitation of ancient models. The Italians, while respecting the rules of their Roman master, were sensitive to the promptings of personal taste. The forms of the antique were adapted to modern usage, its rigours tempered to a new softness and luxuriance. A garden would enter into an architectural design, and complete, with its level parterres, its straight terraces, its rectangular lakes, and solemn lines of cypress or yew the imposing façade of the country house. Even Palladio of Vicenza, whose four books on architecture obtained a great authority through Europe, was not able to constrain to his severe classical proportions and measurements the profuse imagination of his compatriots. The Italian passion for decoration struggled with the stern canons of classical construction, and ultimately, in the baroque churches of the seventeenth century, obtained a mastery.

The architecture of the Renaissance, spreading outward from Rome, which was its centre, and claiming in the new St. Peter's its chief ecclesiastical triumph, covered Europe in the course of the sixteenth century with palaces and houses no longer built for defence but for the convenience and enjoyment of their owners. Azay le Rideau and Fontainebleau, Hatfield and Knole, announce the advent of a more luxurious age, when the fortified castle gave place to the country house, when town building began to sprawl at ease beyond the city walls, and the architecture of fear, which sprang from the barbarian invasions of the third century, yielded before the new social possibilities of composure, magnificence, and delight.

In the field of literature the main feature of the Italian Renaissance was a falling away from the scholastic and theological interests of the middle ages, and a compensating development of a passionate concern in the life and letters of pagan antiquity. Not all of this great movement of the human spirit was of equal value. Some who might have written passably in their native Tuscan thought it necessary to express themselves in frigid and pretentious imitations of Cicero. Others threw ethics and religion to the wind. In general an excessive value was placed upon an easy command of Latin eloquence. Aeneas Sylvius, whose *Artis rhetoricae precepta* was written in 1456, rose to the Papacy on the strength of his Latin oratory. The humanist of the fifteenth century, like the Greek sophist or the mediaeval friar, was exposed and often succumbed to the temptations which in every age beset the popular preacher. So long as the classics existed in manuscript, only the humanist in possession of a codex held the key to knowledge, and could open or close the casket of marvels at his will. The travelling scholar, who lectured on Plato or Homer, read out the text and supplied the comment. It was through his brain and voice alone that his audience obtained access to the ancient mysteries. And when have audiences been more emotional, more ready to learn, or easy to lead? The humanist was orator, poet, scholar, teacher. The general would take him to the camp that he might deliver Ciceronian addresses to the troops; the government would employ him on solemn embassies, or to write despatches, or to make public orations upon occasions of state; the prince would receive him into his castle as wit, instructor, librarian, companion; men and women of every rank crowded to his lectures, wept at his eloquence, and lived upon his ideas. In such conditions profound and thorough scholarship was not to be expected.

Yet the achievement of the Italian humanists, despite the shallowness and artificiality of their Latin writings, was of great value. They led the way to the rediscovery of the true meaning and beauty of the ancient world, first of the Latin classics, and then of Greek literature itself. To them western Europe owes the recovery of Plato and a vast addition to its knowledge of classical texts. Having discovered that the past is as real as the present, and that the future will view the present as the present views the past, they began to think about posterity, and to imagine how their own age would look in the centuries to come. The great school of Florentine publicists and historians is distinguished by this new sense of historical continuity, leading backward to the past and forward to the future.

1403-72 So fast was the influx of new manuscripts (Cardinal Bessarion brought over 800 Greek codices from Constantinople) that there seemed no bounds to the possibilities of the future. Anything might come to light: the lost books of Tacitus, the lost plays of Sophocles, the lost decades of Livy; and the excitement was intensified by the difficulties of interpretation. A whole *apparatus criticus* had to be constructed from the beginning in the case of Greek, and nearly from the beginning in the case of Latin. Grammars, dictionaries, treatises on ancient art and archaeology, disquisitions on the meaning of terms, all the technical aids to culture were combined with the exposition of the rhetorical beauties of the new literature.

In this sudden crowding in of new tastes and fresh points of view, a place was found for scientific historical criticism. Its

1405-57 parent was Lorenzo Valla, whose bold treatise criticising the authenticity of the Donation of Constantine opened a new epoch in European scholarship. Valla first of all argued on general grounds that neither would Constantine have made, nor Pope Sylvester have accepted, the Donation. He then proceeded to point out that if the Empire of the Western World had really been surrendered to the Pope, the gift would have been evidenced by the existence of papal coins. He observed that Eutropius, writing early after the alleged event, made no mention of this momentous transaction, that the original text had never been produced, and finally that the document was of a barbarous Latinity, betraying so clearly the system of the papal chancery as to bear upon its outer surface all the signs of an interested forgery. It is a remarkable evidence of the toleration which then prevailed in Italy that the author of this audacious attack upon one of the cherished privileges of the Papacy himself became the secretary of Pope Nicholas V.

In such an atmosphere of leisure and freedom the lives of scholars became interesting to others. The world, which has always been attracted by the doings of kings and captains, was now invited to read the biographies of men whose sole title to the regard of posterity was that they loved books and manuscripts and lived the life of disinterested culture. Here is a picture from Vespasiano of Niccolo de' Niccoli, whose private library of eight hundred manuscripts was one of the glories of Florence.

"First of all he was of a most fair presence, lively, for a smile was ever on his lips, and very pleasant in his talk; he wore clothes of the fairest crimson cloth, reaching to the ground; he never married in order that he might not be impeded in his studies; a housekeeper provided for his daily needs; he was, above all men, the most cleanly in eating and also in all other things. When he sat at table he ate from fair antique vases, and in like manner all his table was covered with porcelain and other vessels of great beauty. The cup from which he drank was of crystal or of some other precious stone. To see him at table, a perfect model of the men of old, was in truth a charming sight. He always willed that the napkin set before him should be of the whitest, as well as all the linen. Some might wonder at the many vases that he possessed, to whom I answer that things of that sort were neither so highly valued then nor so much regarded as they have since become, and Niccoli having friends everywhere, anyone who wished to do him a pleasure would send him marble statues, or antique vases, carvings, inscriptions, pictures from the hands of distinguished masters, and mosaic tablets. He had a most beautiful map on which all the parts and cities of the world were marked, others of Italy and Spain, all painted. Florence could not show a house more full of ornaments than his, or one that had in it a greater number of graceful objects, so that all who went there found innumerable things of worth to please varieties of taste."

It is now too that we begin to hear the praise of the best abused and most deserving servant of society. Vespasiano, who has painted for us the rounded culture of the scrupulous, old-world Florentine bachelor, has bequeathed to us also the portrait of a schoolmaster. Vittorino da Feltre stands as the pioneer of the educational movement which has resulted in the foundation of our English training in the humanities. He was a small, spare, gay man of a nature that seemed to be always laughing, a good horseman and gymnast, an inde-

1396-
1446

fatigable and devoted trainer of body, mind, and character. His school became famous through Italy, and among his posthumous disciples we may include Colet and Wolsey, John Milton and Charles Kingsley, and all our modern headmasters, so far as they seek to train mind and character through the instrument of fine literature, music, and art, and combine with this generous curriculum a care for the development of the body.

The rulers of Rome could hardly be indifferent to the lustre which shone upon the secular courts of Italy through the patronage of art and letters. The papal office, which had lost much of its spiritual prestige during the schism and the Avignonese captivity, was now usefully employed on the promotion of learning, the collection of artistic treasures, and the embellishment and restoration of a famous but long-neglected capital. Nicholas V, the scholarly son of a poor bell-ringer, founded the Vatican library, and gave commissions to Fra Angelico, Benozzo Gozzoli, and Piero della Francesca. The brilliant Aeneas Sylvius, who built the Piccolomini Palace at Siena, brought to the Holy See the engaging gifts of a traveller, a man of letters, a diplomatist, and a virtuoso, and even recovered as Pope Pius II much of the antique zeal of a crusader.

To Paul II his successor, who collected gems and bronzes with the ardour and knowledge of a Venetian connoisseur, is due the restoration of the arches of Septimius Severus and Titus. And so the Popes of the Renaissance continued, building, restoring, decorating, collecting, and in pursuit of these cultivated tastes, spending and taxing, until with the accession of Leo X of the house of Medici in 1513 the papal patronage of the arts soared to a climax of munificence and splendour, and with the crushing cost of the new St. Peter's staggered the loyalty of half Christendom.

The visitor to Rome who enjoys the collections and buildings of that age will find it difficult to condemn the Popes of the Renaissance for such enlightened, if expensive, activities. What is open to censure is the naked and unscrupulous ambition by which some of the Renaissance Popes endeavoured to extend their temporal dominions at the expense of their Italian neighbours. When we consider the gravity and imminence of the Turkish peril, and the urgent need for the political

1447-55

1458-64

1464-71

combination of the Italian States, the policy of a Pope like Sixtus IV, who in his ambition to found a temporal monarchy built up a scientific system of nepotism, and twice embarked upon war, stands high in the scale of political iniquity. Not least among the causes of the revolt from Rome was the widespread feeling in northern Europe that the Popes were Italian princes, to whom the advancement of their temporal power was a more important interest than the furtherance of the spiritual welfare of Christendom.

For meanwhile the republic of Venice was confronted with the new and formidable fact of the Turkish conquest of Constantinople. A short-lived peace (1454-63), more expeditious than glorious, was followed by the outbreak of a difficult war from which Venice emerged shorn of Dalmatia, Lemnos, and Morea, and condemned to pay an annual tribute to the Sultan. The proud and adventurous aristocracy of Venice was not prepared tamely to acquiesce in so humiliating a conclusion. What had been lost in the east might be regained in the west. The disaster which had befallen Venetian arms in the Aegean might be repaired at the expense of Milan, Ferrara, or Naples. In a restless search for compensations Venice ultimately decided to inflame the appetites and invoke the ambitions of France.

Yet despite these political agitations the last half of the fifteenth century is memorable in the history of the Venetian renaissance. The Basilica of St. Mark, begun in 830 and completed in 1484, preserves more perfectly than any existing building in the territories once belonging to the eastern Empire the quintessential spirit of Byzantine art. It was a noble reply to the barbarous devastations of the Turk to complete upon the free soil of Venice a building which might serve as a perpetual memorial of the splendour and taste of the vanished Christian Empire of the east. But there was another side to the artistic and intellectual life of Venice which was not represented by Byzantine mosaics or by jewels recalling the designs of the Scythian goldsmith of antiquity. Venice was on the frontier of two worlds, Greek and Latin. St. Mark's is Greek. The exquisite art of John Bellini, one of the pioneers of Venetian painting, is wholly associated with the Italian schools.

The invention of printing, which in the north was destined to spread Luther's fiery prose through the length and breadth of Germany, was characteristically employed by the Italian race to further classical studies. The hero of Italian printing was Aldus Manutius (1449-1514), critic, grammarian, literary historian, moralist, the founder of the Aldine Press at Venice. In the annals of Italian humanism there is no finer or nobler figure. Aldus had suffered from one of the worst plagues of youth, a thoroughly bad school book. A platonist and educationalist, he came to see that the improvement of Italian education principally depended upon a supply of good and cheap literature. So he settled in Venice, a city which was secure from war alarms, where he could find a cultured society and count on the assistance of Greek immigrants, and there set up a printing press, which issued in swift succession classic after classic, in editions so cheaply and beautifully executed, so trim and handy, that they are still a pleasure to consult. The doom of the vast and cumbrous folio was pronounced. The Venetian gentleman slipping down the Grand Canal in his graceful gondola could drink in the beauties of Homer from a tiny volume of the clearest print.

The humanism of the Renaissance, unlike those mediaeval types of piety or heroism which are embodied in the Gothic cathedrals or the Chansons de Geste, was not popular but aristocratic. The message of the humanist was to the elect. The soul of a people will never be greatly stirred by the religion of the artist or the savant. Philosophy, erudition, the critical examination of texts, the passionate pursuit of art for art's sake, these activities will always be confined to a small intellectual minority of the human race. So it is now, so it was then. If the humanist of the Renaissance elevated taste, he also enlarged the distance between man and man.

The Italian Renaissance, like most great movements of the human spirit, was the achievement of a comparatively small minority of gifted and creative men working in a sensitive and intelligent society. What they accomplished would have been impossible without the vivid Court life of Italy, the patronage of the Church, or the widespread Italian appetite for the enjoyments of the eye and the ear. In no other European country would the shops have been shut when a popular poet was reciting his verses or an artist's virtuosity have been permitted to condone a murder. Only in Italy was it expected of a nobleman that he should turn out a sonnet, appraise a picture, or read the classics. By comparison the French aristocracy, till Francis I showed a better way, were barbarians, dedicated to the camp, the tourney, and the chase. Not that Italian life, for all its civility, was either comfortable or secure. The country was unpoliced. Every man went armed against the sudden animal hatreds of his neighbours. Every palace, however resplendent with marbles and pictures, was a fortress, cold as the tomb in winter, and with few of those comforts which even the most modest householder in Islington or Putney now demands as his due. The autobiography of Benvenuto Cellini depicts a society in which 1500-crimes of violence and acts of atrocious cruelty and treachery 71 were almost too common to be seriously regarded. Such was the Italian temperament, as swift to anger and cruel revenge as it was sensitive to the subtlest enchantments of form and sound.

From this flowering of talent in Italy the fighting aristocracies beyond the Alps derived a new range of interests. Transalpine noblemen, their rusticity tempered by Italian travel, took to the encouragement of art and letters. The gulf which divided mediaeval society into lettered clerk and illiterate fighting man began to close up. Even for noblemen it became a fashion before the end of the fifteenth century to frequent universities, to open books, and, in the adornment of their homes, to study magnificence.

There was, for instance, in the England of the Wars of the Roses no figure more generally detested for his ruthless cruelties than John Tiptoft, Earl of Worcester (1427-1470), the instrument (for he held the office of Constable) of King Edward IV's sharp revenges. He was known as "the butcher of England" and "the fierce executioner and beheader of men." Yet his cruelty, after the Italian fashion, was blended with a high degree of cultivation. Few Latinists in the island were more accomplished than this ruthless aristocrat who had been educated at Balliol and had afterwards mingled with the humanists of Padua and rifled the bookshops of Florence. Tiptoft was a precursor. A long line of Italianate Englishmen followed in his steps, "devils incarnate" as it was the fashion in the days of Queen Elizabeth to describe them, but having derived from their Italian discipleship, together with many moral poisons, a range of taste, knowledge, and experience which permanently enriched the culture of their country.

Two ideas, destined to exert an enduring influence in the sphere of politics and education, were bequeathed to Europe by the Italy of the Renaissance. The first, that of the pure politician, was contained in *The Prince* of Machiavelli, written in 1513, and the second, that of the scholar-gentleman, in Castiglione's *Courtier*, which was composed three years later. Machiavelli was a Florentine diplomatist and an Italian patriot who employed an exile's involuntary leisure in depicting the kind of ruler best suited to liberate the soil of Italy from the profane presence of barbarian invaders and to restore the glories of Ancient Rome. What was startling in this brilliant treatise was its objectivity. The Prince is an artist in "power politics," using without scruple and remorse such measure of force or fraud as may enable him to extend and secure his conquests. A realist who sees life through plain glass, a close student of contemporary forces expecting nothing better of life than life can give, the Prince of Machiavelli was far removed from the saintly ghosts who figured in the manuals of mediaeval churchmen. The naked doctrine of power politics stated without concealment or reserve, but representing what was in fact the practice of the age, came as a shock to public opinion. The world was not accustomed to a political treatise in which there was nothing either of morality or religion. That its hero was Cesare Borgia, the "nephew" of Alexander VI, an assassin Pope, and himself, despite brilliant personal accomplishments, widely known for successful assassinations and treacheries, added to the challenge a further note of audacity.

Equally characteristic of the Italian spirit of that age was Count Baldassare Castiglione's *Cortegiano* or *Courtier*. The author, who had received his impressions of a highly cultivated Italian court under Duke Guidobaldo of Urbino, drew a picture of the ideal courtier which obtained a wide popularity through Europe. The courtier must be trained in the school not only of the court, but of the camp. He must be a man-at-arms and a sportsman, an athlete and an intellectual, a virtuoso in the arts and a citizen in the world, well read in Greek, Latin, and Italian, with some practical knowledge of drawing and music and a superficial and apparently effortless mastery of all the fashionable graces and accomplishments of his time. Such a conception of education chimed in with the mode of the age. The *Cortegiano* was rendered into many languages.

To Sir Thomas Hoby's charming English version (1561) Milton's view of a generous education as that which "fits a man to perform justly, skilfully, and magnanimously all the offices both private and public of peace and war," is plainly indebted.

To the Greek orthodox world, whether living under the Sultan or the Tsar, all this prodigal outpouring of Italian genius was of no significance. The Italian Renaissance meant nothing either to the Russians or to the Turks. Save for a few scattered borrowings, a Venetian portrait in the Seraglio at Constantinople, the Kremlin in Moscow (taken from Milan), and some skilful touches in Agra and Delhi, the operation of Italian taste and intellect was confined within the limits of Latin Christianity. Russia was a world apart and not until the eighteenth century a factor to be reckoned with in European politics.

BOOKS WHICH MAY BE CONSULTED

Trenchard Cox: *The Renaissance in Europe* (1400-1600). 1933. Examples taken from the works of art in London Museums and Galleries.

M. Creighton: *History of the Papacy during the Period of the Reformation.* 1882-94.

Janet Trevelyan: *A Short History of the Italian People.* 1929.

E. Armstrong: *Lorenzo de' Medici and Florence in the Fifteenth Century.* 1896.

P. Villari: *Life and Times of Girolamo Savonarola. Tr.* L. Villari. 2 vols. 1897-8.

G. Vasari: *Lives of Italian Painters, Sculptors and Architects.* 8 vols. 1900.

B. Berenson: *Central Italian Painters of the Renaissance.* 1897.

B. Berenson: *North Italian Painters of the Renaissance.* 1907.

B. Berenson: *Venetian Painters of the Renaissance.* 1894.

M. von Wolff: *Lorenzo Valla.* 1893.

L. B. Alberti: *Opere volgari. Ed.* A. Bonucci. 1843-9.

L. von Ranke: *History of the Popes. Tr.* S. Austin. 1847.

H. A. Taine: *Philosophie de l'Art en Italie.* 1865.

Machiavelli: *Principe. Ed.* L. A. Burd. 1891.

Vespesiano Da Bisticci: *Vite de uomini illustri del secolo XV. Ed.* L. Frati. 1892.

Cambridge Modern History, Vol. I.

J. Morley: *Machiavelli.* Romanes Lecture. 1897.

J. Zeller: *Italie et Renaissance*. 1883.

H. Brown: *The Venetian Printing Press*. 1891.

J. A. Symonds: *The Renaissance in Italy*, Vols. IV and V. 1875-86.

A. F. Didot: *Alde Manuce et l'héllenisme Venise*. 1875.

The Book of the Courtier. Tr. Sir T. Hoby. *Ed.* W. R. Raleigh. 1900.

W. Ormsby-Gore: *Florentine Sculptors of the Fifteenth Century*. 1930.

J. Burckhardt: *The Civilisation of Renaissance Italy. Tr.* S. G. C. Middlemore. 1950.

G. Mattingly: *Renaissance Diplomacy*. 1955.

H. Butterfield: *The Statecraft of Machiavelli*. 1940.

J. Pope-Hennessy: *Italian Renaissance Sculpture*. 1958.

CHAPTER XXXVIII

FRANCE AND BURGUNDY

Louis XI. He defeats the Nobles and buys off the English. His good fortune. Contrasted with Charles of Burgundy. Services of the Burgundian Dukes to Flanders. The Flemish art of the fifteenth century.

WHILE ITALY was in a ferment of artistic creation, France was experiencing the arrest of cultural progress which is the natural result of great political calamities. The most splendid period in the artistic history of Florence coincides with the long and painful convalescence of France from the havoc of the English wars, with the sharp rivalry between the Burgundian duchy and the French kingdom, and with the stages by which a weak and harassed government in Paris staggered back through its own skill and the follies of its adversary to a sound and national foundation. During these anxious years there was no French patronage of Italian genius and little sign of native artistic talent. The great sculptors of the thirteenth century whose statues adorn the cathedrals of Chartres and Rheims had left no successors. Jean Fouquet, the painter, was from Brussels. It was not until their invasion of Italy in 1494 that the French became aware of the splendours of the Italian scene, and were prepared for a reception of the Italian renaissance. Verrocchio, silversmith, engineer, painter, lapidary, musician, and sculptor, and perhaps the central figure in the artistic development of the Quattrocento, had already been six years in his grave.

Charles VII, the king who had led France out of the miseries of the long English war and given to his country a government and an army, died in 1461. His son Louis XI, 1461- who had been a rebel and exile, continued the valuable but 83 pedestrian work. In his shabby old hat and clothes this eavesdropping, cheeseparing, cautious monarch, who believed that everyone had his price, but was quick to strike off the head of an offending nobleman, and even to shut up a treacherous cardinal in an iron cage, seemed to be an enigmatic compound of craft, cruelty, and vice. Yet those who, like Philippe de Commines, the Burgundian, knew the man and understood the difficulties of the time, recognized in Louis an assemblage of gifts which, though they brought him no popularity with the foolish, illiterate, madcap nobles who were the pest of society, saved the monarchy of France from the worst humiliations. His native wit taught him that a statesman should be a good listener and greedy for information, that, so far as possible, everybody of real political importance, both in his own country and in neighbouring lands, should be known to him personally, that he should spare no pains to win over an enemy, harbour no grudges, exercise a long-sighted patience, always be willing to learn from his own mistakes, and, putting away pride, to retrace his steps. After a first ebullition of impolitic anger, natural in a returned exile, against the prominent supporters of the old régime, Louis thought better of it, and made it an object to win back the men whom he had wronged.

At a difficult crisis he showed more than once great resources of courage and skill. Soon after his accession he was confronted by a formidable coalition of malcontent 1465 nobles (the so-called League of the Public Good) led by Charles, Count of Charolais ("The Bold"), heir to the Burgundian Duchy, and supported by the Duc de Berri, his own brother, and by the Duke of Brittany. The enemy forces were on the outskirts of Paris. The loyalty of the capital was wavering. Any mistake might be sufficient to ruin the unpopular young man (so long a stranger) who had ejected from their places his father's counsellors and surrounded himself by a camarilla of his own choosing. But Louis never even stumbled. Throwing himself into Paris with a powerful force, he won over his opponents in the city by a wise clemency. With Paris at his back he could play with ill-disciplined enemies, avoiding a general engagement, but so harassing them with skirmishes that they were brought to the point of desiring peace. If, in order to obtain a breathing-space, within which to sow dissensions among his foes, Louis granted them terms (Treaty of Conflans) which were far too generous to be permanently consistent with French welfare, that too was part of his serpent's wisdom.

Had the Duchy of Burgundy been in strong hands, or if England had been able and willing to take an effective share in the conflict, the horrors of the Hundred Years' War might easily have been repeated. It is fortunate, perhaps, for Europe, and certainly for France, that Charles, by his headstrong attack upon the Swiss, threw away the great position which four prudent rulers had secured for the Burgundian house, and that the wars between the Yorkists and the Lancastrians on the other side of the Channel precluded any effective interference of England in the affairs of the continent. An English expedition against the old enemy was still possible and still popular, but its object was no longer conquest but barefaced blackmail. Twice in twenty years English armies 1475 were transplanted to the soil of France, and withdrawn for substantial cash payments. Immunity from the still formid-1492 able English archers was adjudged by Louis and his heir to be cheap at the price.

In other ways Louis was helped by fortune. It was good fortune that Charles the Bold had no male heir, so that on his death in 1477 Burgundy, Picardy, and Artois reverted to the French crown; good fortune again that René, the last King of Aix, died with a similar lack of male issue, so that Maine and Anjou and the Imperial fief of Provence became part of Royal France in 1480; and finally a crowning act of Providence that Francis, Duke of Brittany, that old Celtic province which was so proud of its independence and so rich in sea craft, had no son to whom he could bequeath the ancient quarrel of his race. To these successive strokes of fortune is principally due the fact that France, which after the accession of Louis XI seemed to be on the point of disruption, was at his death compact, powerful, and well guarded on every front.

In the brilliant narrative of Commines, Louis and Charles stand out in clear relief as contrasted embodiments of wisdom and folly. Louis by patient intrigue and with the least possible waste of blood and treasure overcomes all his enemies, and leaves his kingdom stronger than he found it. Charles from a restless and costly military ambition throws away a great inheritance. It is specially noted of Louis that he preferred to work with men of the middle station. In his aversion from bloodshed, in his distrust of the nobility, in his preferences for mercenaries (he brought the Swiss into the service of the French crown), and in his encouragement of trade and commerce he typifies a new type of statesmanship. Like his contemporary Edward IV, though to a more conspicuous degree, he is a business king.

Taken as a whole, the work of the Burgundian dukes, though it bears the stamp of coarse ostentation, is also significant as an index of that deeper change from mediaeval feudalism to the national state, which began in the fifteenth century to transform the political complexion of western Europe. The Burgundians were lavish, vulgar, flamboyant, cherishing as their ultimate ideal the status of monarchy and the construction of a compact polity in the valley of the Rhine and its affluents which should comprise some of the wealthiest commercial communities in Europe. Old traditions and loyalties meant little to them. Their state was carved out, with little regard to the antecedents or the affinities of its component parts, by the rude surgery of conquest. A steady policy of aggrandisement, pursued for four generations, brought this vigorous and pertinacious family within sight of its goal.

With the death of Charles the Bold before the walls of Nancy the whole artificial structure fell to pieces. Yet the 1477 work of the Burgundian dukes was not wholly in vain. They are the makers of Belgium. To the county of Flanders, which is the kernel of the modern Belgian kingdom, they gave a novel sense of independence and unity. Their ambitious policies, their meteoric triumphs, their happy mixture of the popular with the grandiose, educated a school of publicists and historians of more than average merit. They made of Brussels, where they kept their court, one of the most showy capitals of Europe. The commercial greatness of Antwerp owes much to their encouragement, and to the restraint which they imposed upon the rival pretensions of Bruges and Ghent.

In the conflict of economic interests, of which in that time of rapid growth Flanders was the scene, the dukes could always rely upon the rising commercial interest against the force of old-fashioned industry, with its fettering monopolies and outworn technique. It was their policy to make of Flanders, so far as this was possible, an economic unity, to foster the fine arts as well as the interests of trade and commerce, and to remove the internal obstacles to the transit and exchange of commodities. French in origin, in language, in tastes, they nevertheless set themselves to learn the Flemish language, and were too wise to attempt what indeed was impossible—the suppression of the Teutonic tongue in which so much of the business of Flanders was transacted.

But if, having an eye to the main chance, they made Flanders, where the memory of the old war comradeship with England was still living, the centre of their dominion, the dukes never forgot their original home. Brussels was the capital, but old-fashioned Dijon was the family burial-place. The art of the Flemish painters and sculptors spread westward through Burgundy into France, and there exercised a profound influence. And, as Flanders influenced France, so France, through the Burgundian dukes, influenced Flanders. The predominantly French character of Belgium today may be traced back to the period when Flanders under a French dynasty was for the only time in its history the heart and centre of an ambitious and conquering state.

Though it was encouraged by ducal patronage, the art of the Flemings, as of the Burgundians, grew naturally out of mediaeval soil. Whereas the renaissance in Italy was marked by an abrupt aversion from the mediaeval and the Gothic, and a clear-cut and vehement preference for the models of pagan antiquity, there was no such sense of conscious innovation among the artists of the Burgundian duchy. Quietly, insensibly, they glided out of the mediaeval into the modern world. The development of their painting owed more to close observation than to literary theory or intellectual preferences and aversions. Delicacy of feeling, fidelity to fact, scrupulous technique, were the distinguishing features of the Flemish art in the fifteenth century. From the Flemings who were its inventors the Italians borrowed the use of oils. And it is to the painting of this gifted people that the young, crude, and bustling principality owes the greatest part of its renown.

The art of the Netherlands, equally with that of Italy, springs from a vivid city life reposing on the base of material affluence. In the activity of their guilds, in their prizes for craftsmanship, as also in their public encouragement of literary and dramatic enterprises, the burgesses of the Low Countries vied with the inhabitants of Florence and Venice. The two great town systems of mediaeval Europe, that of Italy and that of the Netherlands, by the eclipse of which the civilization of the western world would have been fatally impoverished, grew up in substantial independence. The Flemish painters of the fifteenth century required no lessons from Giotto or his school in the art of painting the human form as they saw it. A native force of realism diverted them from Byzantine conventions. They painted from the life, but with a brilliance of colouring as if to challenge the gloom of northern skies and with a preference shaped by rich and secular patrons for domestic themes so portrayed as to exhibit every familiar detail with cameo-like distinctness. Their influence, like that of the Italians, was widespread. By the end of the fifteenth century northern Germany from end to end was an artistic colony of Flanders.

BOOKS WHICH MAY BE CONSULTED

A. W. Ward in *Cambridge Modern History*, Vol. I, chap. xiii.

C. de Cherrier: *Histoire de Charles VIII.* 1868.

J. F. Kirk: *History of Charles the Bold.* 3 vols. 1863-8.

C. Legeay: *Histoire de Louis XI.* 1874.

Sir W. Scott: *Quentin Durward.*

L. E. de Laborde: *Les Ducs de Bourgogne.* 1849-52.

C. Petit Du Taillis in Lavisse: *Histoire de France*, Vol. IV.

P. Fredericq: *Essai sur le rôle politique et social des Ducs de Bourgogne dans les Pays-Bas.* 1875.

E. A. Freeman: *Historical Essays, First Series (Charles the Bold).* 1892.

L. Battifol: *The Century of the Renaissance.* 1916.

J. Huizinga: *The Waning of the Middle Ages.* Tr. F. Hopman 1924.

CHAPTER XXXIX

THE GERMAN RENAISSANCE, 1450-1500

Intellectual progress of Germany in the later half of the fifteenth century. The spread of printing. Its effect in diffusing a popular interest in religion. Failure of Maximilian's attempts to reform the Empire. The real greatness of Germany at this time. The arts and crafts. Albrecht Dürer and Peter Vischer. Cusanus.

THE LATER half of the fifteenth century is marked in the history of Germany by a notable enlargement of culture, learning, and education, and also, as in Italy, by the development of the power of the territorial princes. The present reputation of the Germans as the leaders of the world in book learning may be traced back to this age, which witnessed the foundation of eight German academies, and the epoch-making invention in part due to John Gutenberg of Mainz of the art of typography. The immense revolution in the intellectual opportunities of mankind which followed upon this last discovery may be inferred from the speed with which, in an age unhampered by patents, it spread throughout Europe. Printing from metal types reached Italy in 1465, Paris in 1470, London in 1477, Stockholm in 1483, and Madrid in 1499. It has been calculated, but on an estimate which is probably too conservative, that by the close of the century some nine million printed books must have been in existence as against a few score thousand manuscripts which, up to that time, had contained the inherited wisdom and poetry of the world.

The credit of spreading the printing press through Europe must be principally ascribed to the Germans. Printing was known as the German art. The German printers and book-sellers went everywhere in search of custom. By the end of 1500 they had more than a hundred presses in Italy and at least thirty presses in Spain. An immense missionary enthusiasm for the new art, and an intelligent appreciation of its significance for life, spread through the country. "As the apostles of Christ," wrote Wimpheling, a contemporary, "formerly went through the world announcing the good news, so in our days the disciples of the new art spread themselves through all countries, and their books are as the heralds of the Gospel and the preachers of truth and of science." It is a remarkable illustration of the keen eye of the German trader for these apostolic opportunities that in 1494, only two years after the expulsion of the Moors from Granada, three German printers were already established in that town.

The work of her early printers and bookbinders is one of the glories of Germany. Europe owes much to these inspired tradesmen, who were scholars and artists, as well as business organizers on an international scale, and even in a general history the names of the first great booksellers, of a Koberger of Nuremberg, or a Froben of Basel, may be recalled without impropriety. Some early German folios have, indeed, rarely been surpassed for beauty and magnificence. And if the main part of the literature which then issued from the German presses was theological, if during the first fifty years there were more than a hundred editions of the Bible and fifty-nine of the *Imitatio Christi*, this was due to the fact that here, as elsewhere, the clergy constituted the bulk of the lettered class, and were the chief patrons of the book trade. In the sixteenth century the printed book acted as a powerful inducement to liberating and critical movements of thought: but the first consequences of typography were otherwise, and are to be found in an awakening of popular religion and in a diffused interest in the reading and discussion of religious books.

It would not, therefore, be fair to urge that the period of German history which immediately precedes the Reformation was characterized by symptoms of degeneration and decay. There were, indeed, many grave faults in the political and social structure of the country. The Church, which is computed to have held a third of the landed property, was far too wealthy to be wholesome; the upper clergy too much given to idle ostentation or profligate expenditure. Private war was common, and, until the Diet of Worms in 1495, not seriously checked. The country, therefore, suffered from the irregular depredations of one of the idlest and most selfish aristocracies in Europe. Nor was there in the political framework of the German Empire any force capable of educating a firm body of patriotic and disinterested opinion, which might countervail the evils of class selfishness or petty localism. In this regard

1493-
1519 no episode is more instructive than the career of the Emperor Maximilian, the founder of Austrian unity, the darling of the Tyrolese, the first of chamois hunters and "the last of the knights." Few German rulers have been more deservedly popular than this handsome, chivalrous, and most generous sovereign. None have been more energetic, more eloquent, more seductive, or more desirous of maintaining what he believed to be the true tradition of his high office and the honour of the German name. Yet despite all these admirable qualities Maximilian was unable to stir up the lethargic body of the German Reich to take effective action against the Turks in the east or the French in Italy. His attempts to provide an adequate reformation of the German Constitution at the Diet of Worms in 1495, and again at Augsburg in 1500, broke down against the solid opposition of the selfish interests. He could secure neither a standing imperial army nor a regular system of imperial taxation. His lieges refused to serve with the forces, or to pay the "common penny" (a graduated property tax), or to co-operate in the setting up of machinery for the enforcement of the decision of an imperial tribunal. Save for the fact that some slight improvement in the sphere of justice and police was secured by the proclamation of a perpetual land peace, by the establishment of a stationary imperial court, and by the division of the Empire into ten circles, the feverish attempts of this well-meaning and high-minded Emperor to make of the German Federation an effective power in the world were entirely frustrated. The Emperor had become a pathetic shadow. The real centre of political strength lay in the electors and princes.

There is, however, no necessary connection between political good sense and the spiritual and artistic progress of a people. The essential virtue of Germany lay, not in its empire or its great prelates and princes, and still less in its grasp of the essentials of public policy, but in the thousands of gifted and ingenious town workers, who built Gothic churches and cathedrals, developed the organ, wrought as carvers and sculptors in stone and wood and bronze, and by their engravings, paintings, and metal work secured a brilliant repute throughout the world for the craftsmanship of the German race. The drawings and engravings of Albert

1477-
1527 Dürer, and the noble array of bronzes which for a space of fifty years were cast in the foundry of the Vischer family at

Nuremberg are monuments of the virtuosity by which in the last epoch before the Reformation Germany partially atoned for the prevailing corruption of the Church and the violent confusion of her public life.

The development of the plastic arts in Germany, which with Peter Vischer the younger had reached a high point of virtuosity, experienced a sudden check in the third decade of the sixteenth century. The rich old vein of German craftsmanship seems to have worked itself out. Conventional patterns and ideas borrowed from the Italians replace the early German work which, though it missed the simple beauty of the Italian masterpieces, was sincere, strong and true to the native character. Nuremberg, which in the fifteenth century was the Florence of Germany, ceased to be a living centre of decorative art. With the coming of the Reformation an ill wind began to blow upon the sculptors and painters. It was not only that the country was poorer by reason of the discovery of the new oceanic routes, but that the swift onrush of religious and social anarchy turned the minds of the German people into other channels. Religion, not art, was the governing interest. It is significant that Holbein, finding Basel too uncomfortable for a German painter, fled to the shelter of the English court. It was not, then, in painting or sculpture, nor even in the gentle art of woodcarving, once, as is natural among woodland peoples, a universal pursuit, that the Germans found satisfaction for their artistic cravings. Luther's hymns pointed a new way. The Germans gave themselves to music. By the end of the eighteenth century they led Europe in this the most universal of the arts and the one common language of all religions.

This, however, is to anticipate. The person in whom, before the storms of the Reformation, the intellectual life of Germany is most fully represented, is Nicholas Krebs, later known as the Cardinal Cusanus from his birthplace at Cues 1401- in the Moselle valley. A strong vein of mystical religion, rooted 64 perhaps in his early education with the Brethren of the Common Life at Deventer, was combined in Cusanus with the passion of a humanist, the eloquence of a statesman, and the laborious curiosity of a Teutonic scholar. As a young man he had studied mathematics and canon law in the university of Padua, and there mixed with a brilliant circle of Italian savants who were at that time skirmishing on the frontier of mathematical, astronomical, and geographical knowledge. Thereafter a timely piece of preferment opened many doors on either side of the Alps to the ambitious youth. Becoming secretary to Canon Orsini, an Italian intellectual and the Apostolic Legate in Germany, he found the chief stars in the Italian literary firmament shining on his path. Toscanelli, the geographer, Valla, the scholar historian, Poggio, the discoverer of Tacitus, became his friends. With the true grammarian's ardour he threw himself upon the monastic libraries of his native Rhineland, and before long was rewarded by the reappearance of twelve lost plays of Plautus. Thenceforward the name of Treviranus (for Krebs was from the diocese of Tréves) became famous in the learned world. A Deanery, a Tyrolese Bishopric, a cardinal's hat, rewarded the happy discoverer of a dozen salacious Latin comedies. In turn the oracle of the Council of Basel and the henchman of Pope Eugenius IV, Cusanus earned golden opinions by his substantial good sense, his omnivorous reading, and his high character. Whether he was transcribing Latin manuscripts in Germany, or bringing back Greek texts from Mount Athos, or commenting on the Koran, or composing an atlas of central Europe, this indefatigable student was inspired by the sentiments of a good Christian, a good European, and a good German. It is noteworthy that in a treatise on Catholic concord, written at the age of thirty, he attacked the abuses of the Church with severity, and advocated as a remedy against the terrible disorders of Germany the establishment of an Imperial army. It was not until after Germany had suffered the humiliation of Napoleon's conquest that the brilliant Goerres, another German publicist from the Rhineland, advocated, but again without success, the same plain remedy for the same obvious evil of German anarchy and helplessness.

As an ecclesiastic Cusanus is honourably distinguished for the vigour with which he assailed the immorality of the German clergy and the pagan superstitions still rife among 1450 the German peasants, as well as for his disbelief in the use of military force against paganism, and for his faith in the powers of knowledge, reason, and eloquence as binding forces in human affairs. It is not, however, either as humanist or as ecclesiastic that he is now chiefly remembered, but as the author of a book, De Docta Ignorantia, in which it is claimed that several guiding principles of modern philosophy and science may be plausibly discerned. To many a patriotic German Cusanus appears as the precursor of Copernicus, Descartes, and Hegel. It is not, however, to a corpus of mystical theology written by a busy ecclesiastical statesman that the world must look for pioneering work in the sciences. If the cloudy folios of Cusanus are here and there lit by a brilliant flash of intuition into the nature of the physical universe, if his vision of an Absolute in which the contradictions of the intellect are finally harmonized wears a modern air, the method of the author was always mediaeval. Conclusions confirmed by modern science are reached by arguments which every man of science would now repudiate as fanciful and foolish. The real interest attaching to the work of this learned and laborious Teuton is that in him we see a powerful intellect moving on mediaeval and thoroughly German lines, but played upon by the first enlivening aspersions of Italian science.

BOOKS WHICH MAY BE CONSULTED

J. Janssen: *Geschichte des deutschen Volkes seit dem Ausgang des Mittelalters. Tr.* M. A. Mitchell and A. M. Christie. 1896-1925.

C. Ullmann: *Reformatooren vor der Reformation. Tr.* R. Menzies. 2 vols. 1855.

F. A. Gasquet: *The Eve of the Reformation.* 1905.

F. Paulsen: *Geschichte des gelehrten Unterrichts auf den deutschen Schulen und Universitäten.* 1885-96.

E. Müntz: *Histoire de l'Art pendant la Renaissance.* 1889-95.

W. B. Scott: *Albrecht Dürer, his Life and Works.* 1869.

L. Geiger: *Renaissance und Humanismus in Italien und Deutschland.* 1882.

A. D. Vandam; *Social Germany in Luther's Time, being the Memoirs of Bartholomew Sastrow.* 1902 (abridged). With preface by H. A. L. Fisher.

W. Bode: *Geschichte der deutschen Plastik.* 1885.

Cecil Headlam: *Peter Vischer.* 1901.

Sprenger: *Albrecht Dürer.*

B. A. Daun: *Ada, Krafft und seine zeit.* 1896.

W. Waetzoldt: *Dürer and His Times.* 1950.

E. Panofsky: *The Life and Art of Albrecht Dürer.* 1955.

CHAPTER XL

NEW MONARCHY IN ENGLAND

The Wars of the Roses. Their origin. Henry VI and Edward IV. Social and economic effects. The significance of Henry Tudor. The first English colony.

THE EXPULSION of the English from France in 1453 was followed two years later by the outbreak of the Wars of the Roses. It is difficult to imagine a combination of public calamities more complete than a long civil struggle supervening on the miscarriage of a foreign campaign. But the defeat and the civil war were blessings in disguise. Once the forlorn attempt to conquer France was definitely abandoned, England was able to find her true line of development in the enlargement of her influence over the British Isles, in the expansion of her commerce and industry, and in the foundation of colonies beyond the ocean. That she was able to play an effective part in such tasks as these was due to the fortunate and unparalleled thoroughness with which the feudal virus was eliminated from the body politic by the Wars of the Roses.

The contest between the rival houses of York and Lancaster is distinguished from the feudal insurrections upon the continent during the same period by one notable characteristic. Both English parties accepted the unity of the kingdom and the system of government by King, Council, and Parliament, which had been handed down from earlier times. The object of the Yorkists in the earlier stages of the war was not to shear away great provinces, as the League of the Public Good attempted to do in France, nor to reduce the kingship to a cypher as it was in Germany, nor to carry out any defined scheme of constitutional reform, but to storm their way into the Council, and through the Council to govern the country. Neither party can lay claim to a policy founded upon a disinterested concern for the public advantage. Private family feuds, and more especially the feuds of the Welsh marcher lords, war-restlessness, the need for occupying great bands of armed retainers, whom the cessation of the French wars had thrown out of work, were important factors in the Wars of the Roses. Yet it would be unjust to deny to the leaders in this fierce contest any concern for the national interest. The war between York and Lancaster was not wholly frivolous, but arose out of the greatest of all public issues, that of peace and war. Henry VI and his minister Suffolk were resolved to wind up the miserable French war, which Gloucester and Richard of York were ardent to continue. The Treaty of Tours (1444), negotiated by Suffolk, was felt to be doubly ignominious when it became known that it provided for the cession of Calais to France, and for the marriage of the English king to Margaret of Anjou, a woman of the enemy race. A fierce atmosphere of hatred and suspicion was generated by a quarrel which in every castle of the land raised the burning issue of employment or idleness, adventure or war weariness, appetite or common sense, the forlorn endeavour to revive old glories, or the ungrateful acceptance of inevitable defeat. Gloucester, the special enemy of the French queen, and Suffolk, the popular scapegoat for the pusillanimous peace, inaugurated by their sudden and violent ends the hideous period of assassination, judicial murder, and battle which disgraces the last age of Catholic England.

If the Yorkists were the first to resort to arms, they could urge in excuse humiliations abroad and mismanagement at home. The Lancastrians were blamed for the loss of the French conquests, nor could the conspicuous piety of Henry VI, or his noble educational foundations at Eton and Cambridge, atone in the eyes of his contemporaries for an ignominious foreign policy, a feeble character, a mind occasionally overclouded by insanity, or for the acute unpopularity of his masterful French wife. After his defeat at Towton (1461) the career of this blameless prince lacked no element in tragedy. A bitter exile was succeeded by a harsh imprisonment, and this by a cruel and violent death.

In contradistinction to the mild and ineffectual Lancastrian saint, his murderer, the Yorkist leader, belonged to that more modern and efficient type of statesmanship which was now coming to the front in the progressive states of Europe owing 1461- to the growing importance of industry and commerce. 83

Edward IV was not a virtuoso like Lorenzo de'Medici, nor a genius in diplomacy like Louis XI, but a good soldier with a handsome presence, affable manners, and the sound, middle-class instinct which led the wiser heads of that time to appreciate the importance of promoting the interests and enlisting the support of the money-making part of the community. Being intent on raising supplies with as little trouble to himself or others as possible, he was sparing in the summoning of Parliaments and preferred the direct method of a benevolence extracted from the wealthy to taxes collected by a cumbrous method and more widely diffused in their incidence. But with some attractive merits Edward combined certain grave faults. His morals, even judged by the standards of that age, were shamelessly loose, his industry irregular, his avarice inordinate, and to the crime of political murder (including fratricide) he added the supreme error, in a people dominated by social conventions, of finding a wife outside his class. The nobles of England, who never forgave Edward II for his addiction to the pursuits of a locksmith, a builder, and a waterman, took it ill that Edward IV should have secretly married into a family of thrusting upstarts. The beauty of Elizabeth Woodville was no compensation for the fact that her father, though the husband of a duchess, started life from the lowly grade of a knight. The Yorkist dynasty sank under the burden of the misalliance. When Edward died of his debaucheries at the age of forty, the children of the unpopular match evoked no protective sentiment of loyalty or enthusiasm. Their uncle Richard, who seized the throne, was well advised in thinking that the country was unprepared to make any serious sacrifice on behalf of Edward V and his young brother. Yet the heart of the English people was not so entirely hardened by the atrocities of the civil war as to acquiesce without a protest in the murder of the children in the Tower. Courage and ability did not save the unnatural uncle and the usurping king. His deposition was desired and plotted, not only by the Lancastrians, but by a large section of the Yorkist Party as well. 1485 On Bosworth Field, Henry Tudor, the son of a Welsh country gentleman, but descended through Margaret Beaufort, his mother, from John of Gaunt, and the sole surviving representative of the Lancastrian claim, made an end of Richard and his Yorkist following, and founded the strong dynasty which was destined to carry England through the religious and political troubles of the next age.[1]

The Wars of the Roses were ended. The English aristocracy had almost bled itself to death. But though the violent struggle was fought over a wide area of the country, and has been computed to have cost a hundred thousand lives, its social and economic effects were strictly circumscribed. No English town was sufficiently interested in the rival factions to stand a siege. The armies which hacked at each other with bills, or shot at each other with arrows, or less effectually and more expensively exchanged salvoes from their newfangled and professionally manned cannon, were not drawn from the townsmen or the peasantry, but from the class of the great nobles and their liveried retainers. The social progress of the country suffered less from these disorders than might have been supposed. The quarrels of Mortimers and Percies, of Nevilles and Mowbrays, meant little to the villein, the craftsman, or the merchant. Trade pursued its even course. Fortunes were made. Wealthy men built houses of brick or stone for their personal use, or founded almshouses and colleges for the salvation of their souls. To Sir John Fortescue the position of the English peasantry appeared to be sharply distinguished from that of the peasantry of France by its prosperity. Villeinage was steadily dying out under the pressure of economic forces. Yet this long civil war was accompanied by one of the greatest evils which can afflict an organized society. It paralysed the working, though it could not destroy the mechanism, of British justice. The royal judges still went on assize, the King's Courts still sat at Westminster, the Sheriff still held his tourn, and the Justices of the Peace still sat in their Petty and Quarter Sessions. Reluctant jurors were still summoned to serve on juries and punished for non-attendance. But wherever the interest of an influential landowner and his retinue were involved, the course of justice was deflected by intimidation. The statutes against "livery and maintenance" were powerless to check an acknowledged evil but a popular practice. If two great families were involved in litigation at the Assizes, rival bodies of armed men, bearing the liveries of the lords by whom they were maintained, would ride into the county town and browbeat the jury and the judge. There was no rascal in the country so

[1] Genealogical Table L.

flagrant or notorious that he could not, if maintained and supported by a powerful noble, escape the merited retribution of the law.

Nevertheless, it is significant that, despite the anarchy and turbulence of the age, a writer like Fortescue finds it possible to exult in the laws and constitution of his country. The English were then, as they have continued to be, a litigious people. Their lawyers were then, as they remain to this day, an influential and conservative profession, proud of their recondite science, and zealous for the honour and dignity of their calling. The violence of the civil war, and the frequency of judicial murders during that tempestuous epoch, did not efface the memory of the early Lancastrian days when Parliaments met frequently, and the law was administered, and constitutional precedents were stored up for future use. The tradition of parliamentary government survived, though the Parliaments under Edward IV did little but pass acts of attainder or connive at murder and confiscation; but local justice had broken down through local terrorism.

The restoration of the rule of law demanded the establishment of some new system of criminal equity, which should enable the great offender to be brought to his account, without the paralysing incubus of those unhappy gentlemen of the jury whose verdicts were dictated by panic or by greed.

The significance of the reign of Henry Tudor consists in 1485- this, that he reasserted the power of the national state over 1509 feudal indiscipline, and through his marriage with Elizabeth of York, the daughter of Edward IV, gave a signal to the country that the bitter feud between the two rival houses was henceforth to be composed. Save for an irreconcilable Yorkist remnant supported from Ireland and Flanders, and formidable only by reason of its foreign friends, the country welcomed the new omen of peace. The risings of the impostors Lambert Simnel and Perkin Warbeck were successfully frustrated, and perhaps the more easily for the reason assigned by Bacon that "it was an odious thing for the people of England to have a king brought in upon them on the shoulders of the Irish and the Dutch." Henry Tudor had no standing army. Though he would have liked, as a Spanish ambassador observed, to govern England in the French fasion, he knew that he could not do it. From the first he was shrewd enough to see that without the good humour of the English people his dynasty could not survive.

To the student of politics nothing is more interesting than the process by which a nation, demoralized by a long course of rancorous strife, is gradually recalled to peace and sanity. To do this was the function of Henry VII. Many kings have been more spectacular, but none more valuable than this laborious and frugal monarch under whose wise and vigilant treatment the poisons of the last feudal war were finally drained away from the national system. If his rule was autocratic, it was free from some of the worst autocratic vices, for there was no jealousy of able men, no megalomania, no camarilla of court favourites. The king's advisers were either the tried companions of his youthful exile, or able lawyers, or men like Morton, Fox, or Warham, who had risen by force of brains and character through the democratic avenues of the Church. It was better frankly to commission Empson and Dudley to plunder the nobles than to follow the French practice of giving to the whole aristocratic class a privileged exemption from royal taxes. No contemporary reproached Henry for his sparing use of Parliaments. In that age common justice was much to be preferred to the arduous exercise of political liberty; and common justice was improved. At last there was in Henry's "Star Chamber" a court so powerful that it could strike fear into the heart of the greatest noble in the land.

The advent of the Tudors did not and could not mean the isolation of England. In self-protection Henry was obliged to seek foreign alliances and to attend to English interests in Ireland and Scotland, from each of which countries, as the story of the Yorkist risings showed, an enemy attack might conveniently be launched. So the heir to the throne was married to Catharine of Aragon, and Margaret, the King's daughter, to James IV of Scotland, while the long process of restoring English authority among the Irish, which culminated in the Parliamentary Union of 1800, was launched in 1494 by a measure (Poyning's Act) subjecting the Parliament of the Irish Pale to the Privy Council in London.

Before the end of the century a certain Genoese mariner, by name John Cabot, had sailed from Bristol under the king's patent (1496) in a west country ship with a west country crew, and had returned with the exciting news that he had struck land on the other side of the Atlantic. Newfoundland, the oldest of the British Dominions, dates from the reign of Henry VII, when it is first perhaps possible to discern the outline of England's future rôle in the world as a country exercising a predominant influence in the British Isles, closely knit to the continent of Europe, but also impelled by the spirit of commercial and maritime adventure to vast enterprises beyond the ocean.

BOOKS WHICH MAY BE CONSULTED

James Gairdner in *Cambridge Modern History*, Vol. I, chap. xiv.
Vickers: *England in the Later Middle Ages*. 1913.
Sir John Fortescue: *Governance of England*. Ed. C. Plummer. 1885.
Paston Letters Ed. J. Gairdner. 4 vols. 1900-1.
J. A. Froude: *Life and Letters of Erasmus*. 1894.
P. S. Allen; *The Age of Erasmus*. 1914.
Erasmi Epistolæ. Ed. P. S. Allen. 1906-1938.
H. A. L. Fisher: *History of England*, 1509-47 (Longmans). 1910.
Francis Bacon: *History of the Reign of King Henry VII*. Ed. J. R. Lumby. 1876.
C. L. Kingsford: *Prejudice and Promise in Fifteenth-Century England*. 1925.
G. R. Elton: *England under the Tudors*. 1955.
S. T. Bindoff: *Tudor England*. 1950.
K. Pickthorn: *Early Tudor Government*. 2 vols. 1934.

CHAPTER XLI

FRANCO-SPANISH RIVALRY IN ITALY

Charles VIII and Italy. The risk from Spain. Union of Aragon and Castile. Religious concentration and political expansion of Spain. The relations of Spain and Portugal. The treaty of Tordesillas. Spain linked by marriage with Flanders. Vast consequences for Europe and the world. The French invasions of Italy, 1494-1559. Alexander VI and the scandals of Rome. The new spirit of rationalism and Erasmus.

WE HAVE now reached an episode in European history which proves how feeble are the affinities of religion, of race, and of culture, when weighed in the balance against the cupidity and war-lust of mankind. Spain and France were, at the end of the fifteenth century, the leading Latin and Catholic countries of the West, allied in race, in religion, in their common possession of a Romance language and literature, and having reached a general standard of cultivation which, though sensibly below the Italian, was far higher than that prevailing in eastern Europe. Of this Latin and Christian civilization the Turk was declared the inveterate foe, and since he was master of the eastern Mediterranean, and threatened the shores of Italy and Spain, it might have been expected that the formation of a Latin League to oppose him would have been the dominating concern of western diplomacy. It was not so. Instead of combining against Islam, the Latin powers broke out into violent quarrels among themselves. Italy was the prize of victory and the scene of contention. It is one of the cruel ironies of history that this country, which had enjoyed a rare and almost unbroken spell of peaceful civilization, during which it had shown mankind new summits of artistic excellence, was now destined, for more than sixty years, to serve as the battlefield of French and Spanish armies.

For this the Italians were in part to blame, for the prime cause of the tragedy was Italian discord. The long peace, while effacing the memory of the savage realities of war, for the local struggles sustained by *condottieri* were almost bloodless, had brought the Italians no nearer to a common mind. Still as in the days of Dante, State plotted against State, and still there survived that pleasant Italian notion, proper to artistic studios, that battles might best be delegated to competing bands of mercenary troops. Whether the mercenary force was small or large, native or foreign, was hardly, in the low temperature of Italian patriotism, a matter of principle. Yet it was a grave thing for Italy and the seed of much future trouble when Ludovico Sforza, the powerful Regent of Milan, associated himself with the discontented subjects of Ferrante of Naples and appealed to Charles VIII of France to revive the old Angevin claim in the Neapolitan kingdom. Nothing could be said for Ferrante. He was a despicable and dangerous lout. But a French army, unlike the *condottieri*, would fight to kill, and since Ferrante was of the royal line of Aragon, though of a bastard branch, the fall of his house would not pass unnoted by the King of Spain.

At more than one juncture in her history the dangerous cry has gone up, "La France s'ennuie." It was so in 1494. The reign of Louis XI, so full of solid benefits, was not sufficiently spectacular to please an idle and adventurous nobility. A madcap rising, "La Guerre Folle," disturbed the wise regency of his daughter, Anne of Beaujeu, and warned her young brother Charles, the heir to the throne, that if he was to govern he must show the sport which a mettlesome aristocracy demanded of its king.

Of all adventures an Italian war was the most attractive. What could be more alluring to youthful ambition than the prospect of a cavalcade in glittering armour under the blue Italian sky, riding across a beautiful land which, by reason of its internal political divisions, seemed likely, failing the intervention of the chivalry of France, to fall a prey to the Turk or the Spaniard?

Expeditions of pleasure are never at a loss for a solemn excuse. The Turk had actually for a time flown his flag in 1283-Otranto. The Aragonese ruled in Naples, which had once 1442 been Angevin, while the Emperor Maximilian, whose second wife was Bianca Sforza, was suspected of harbouring designs on the rich Duchy of Milan, which the princes of the house of Orleans had long regarded as their eventual prize.

Charles VIII of France, a young and licentious hunchback of doubtful sanity, was the master of the strongest artillery in

Europe. Though every wise head in Paris was opposed to the Italian adventure, for the kingdom was ill-compacted, its finances uncertain, and the marine available for Mediterranean service of little account, the King yielded to the tempters, who flowed in upon him from Milan and Florence, from Rome and Calabria with their griefs, their aspirations and their bribes. He would descend on Italy, not merely as a conqueror, not merely as the claimant of his Neapolitan heritage, but with the star of freedom flaming on his banners. Italians suffering from oppression would flock to his camp and fill his treasury with ducats. He would restore a republic to Florence, drive the Aragonese from Naples, and then, perhaps, when a grateful Italy lay prostrate at his feet, eject the Turk from Europe and place the Imperial Crown upon his victorious brow. His mounted gendarmerie, drawn from the nobility and gentry of France, his formidable body of halberdiers and pikemen from Switzerland and Germany, his Gascon cross-bow men, and the light, quick-firing artillery, which was the latest triumph of French mechanical ingenuity, would give Europe a sensation which it would not soon forget.

Diplomatic precautions were not neglected. Having through the good management of his sister, the Regent, espoused Anne, the heiress of Brittany (1491), he was secure against attack from the north-west. That he might cross the Alps with an easier mind he bought the acquiescence of Spain by the cession of Cerdagne and Roussillon (two provinces on the brink of the Pyrenees which had been pawned to Louis XI by John II of Aragon) and purchased quiet upon his eastern frontier by giving away Franche Comté to the Emperor. But despite these lavish concessions of territory, there was one eventuality against which Charles could not provide. Whatever treaties a Spanish king might sign, he would never tolerate the French in Naples. It was not merely a question of honour. The granaries of Sicily furnished a welcome supplement to the meagre harvests of Spain.

The risk of the Italian adventure, which was in any case great, for no populous and civilized country readily submits to the invasion of thirty thousand licentious foreign soldiers, was much increased by a momentous change which not long before had come over the political complexion of Spain. The maritime state of Aragon, whose sailors and merchants were known in every port of the Mediterranean, had been united with the kingdom of Castile by the marriage of Ferdinand and Isabella in 1469. A political union, founded on a marriage, cannot be expected to change the psychology of differing peoples. The inhabitants of Catalonia, the richest and most important part of the kingdom of Aragon, have never been assimilated with the Castilians, from whom they are divided by speech and by all those profound differences which distinguish landsmen from seafarers, merchants from farmers, nobles from bourgeois, and a community stationed on a great world thoroughfare from one mainly living in secluded pride on a high inland plateau. But while Catalonia has always chafed under the Castilian yoke, the marriage of Ferdinand of Aragon with Isabella of Castile offered benefits of such a quality that they have never been renounced. In virtue of that union Spain became at once a great European power, strong by land and sea, and rose to a position, which was maintained until the close of the sixteenth century, of commanding pre-eminence in the world.

The restless ambitions of Aragon, whose navies had won kingdoms in the Balearic Islands, in Sicily, and in Naples, were now to be supported by footmen drawn from the upland farms and cities of Castile. The advantages which ensued from the unity of Spain were inestimable. A mutinous and disorderly people was reduced to some sense of discipline by the joint force of a strong monarchy and a subservient church. By degrees the spirit of a narrow and jealous localism was mitigated by a larger outlook upon Spanish needs and world-wide opportunities. But there was a reverse side to the medal. By inheriting the Italian policies of Aragon, Spain was committed to a long series of Italian wars, as deleterious to herself as they were mischievous to Italy.

For Isabella, one of the narrowest and most influential women in history, was a bigoted Catholic. The first exploit of the united Spanish kingdom was the conquest of that little state of Granada, which, under the enlightened rule of its Moslem sovereigns, offered a spectacle of civilized luxury to be matched in no other part of the Iberian peninsula, and in few even of the most favoured regions of France and Italy. Whether the destruction of this Moorish polity was a blessing or a bane may be variously debated; but it is at least reasonable to remember that the Spanish Moslems, unlike the Ottoman Turks, were susceptible to the call of art, science, and philosophy, that their rule was tolerant, their state weak and harmless, and that their expulsion from European territory, under the driving impulse of Queen Isabella, was the first step in a steady course of religious persecution which permanently impaired the strength and vitality of Spain.

Hateful as this policy may appear to a tolerant age, it aroused no antagonism among the Christian subjects of Ferdinand and Isabella. The doctrines of the Catholic Church were everywhere accepted. The principle that it was the duty of the Christian State to suppress heresy within its borders was nowhere denied. While local liberties were hotly defended, the sacred cause of intellectual freedom went by default.

A deep instinctive sense of political need helped to strengthen the forces of orthodoxy in a country whose foreign policy had for long worn the colours of a religious crusade. The union of Aragon and Castile had done so little to abate the inveterate localism of the Spanish provinces, the municipal and provincial privileges and institutions were still so jealously preserved and defended, that the assistance of the Church, as the one institution common to all Spain and held in universal veneration by its inhabitants, became of supreme importance to the government.

So successful were the sovereigns of Spain in securing the entire obedience of their clergy that no Protestant Church was ever brought into a more complete subjection to the temporal Prince than was the Catholic Church of Spain during the great epoch of the Spanish Empire. King and Church, Church and King constituted one indissoluble instrument for the propagation and defence of the orthodox Faith.

In sharp contrast to this austere religious concentration, which made Spanish rule everywhere synonymous with the persecution of differing beliefs, was a vast and sudden enlargement of the political and economic horizon of the country. France became an enemy, Italy a battle-ground, England an ally, the Holy Roman Empire and the Netherlands an annexe through marriage, the Atlantic Ocean a pathway to the Spanish dominions, illimitable and mysterious in the distant west. The harbours of Biscay and Santander, of Vigo and Ferrol, of Cadiz and Seville, woke to a new life with the expansion of oceanic enterprise. New adventures crowded in, new rivalries revealed themselves, new combina-

tions were formed for attack and defence. Spanish diplomacy
was compelled to work upon a large canvas. Nobody could
say of Spanish politics, in the age which was now opening out,
that they suffered from an undue concentration of purpose or
an ignoble restriction of outlook. The danger rather was one
of excessive distraction between ends as various as domestic
reorganization and Italian conquest, the duel with France and
the colonization and settlement of the American continent.

Among the many policies of the Spanish monarchy a
developed naval imagination might have included the conquest
or incorporation of Portugal. This unneighbourly neighbour
was now leading the western world in marine enterprise. The
sailors of Portugal had tapped the wealth of Guinea, touched
at the Cape, were about to coast round Africa, and to open
a new way to opulence and empire in the Indies. The growing
power of the little state, its fine Atlantic seaboard, its noble
harbourage in the Tagus, might have tempted a keen rival in
colonial enterprise to aggression. It might have been argued
then, as it was contended by a Portuguese writer in 1624
(when Portugal was in fact united with Spain), that the true
capital of the Iberian peninsula was Lisbon, its nerve centre
the Atlantic seaboard, and the first of its political objectives
to destroy an enemy navy wherever it might be found. Had
such counsels prevailed at the close of the fifteenth century,
the beginnings of Atlantic exploration might have been
stained by a bitter civil war between the two Christian powers
of the Iberian peninsula.

Nothing of this occurred. Ferdinand and Isabella, who
were not greatly disturbed by sea-dreams, resolved to have
Portugal bound to them by ties of family alliance, strong
enough to resist the strain of colonial rivalry. So when Spain
followed in the wake of Portugal and claimed her share of the
New World, conflict was precluded by the arbitration of the
Pope. The award of Alexander VI, under which all the lands
and islands already discovered or hereafter to be discovered
"in the West, towards the Indies or the Ocean Seas" were
partitioned between Spain and Portugal, has been assailed as
a presumptuous infringement of human liberty. It was one
of those political arrangements which, however useful as a
temporary adjustment of the divergent interests, inevitably
break down under the stress of facts. Neither in France, nor
in Holland, nor in England was this papal arbitrament re-

garded as tolerable. What right, it was asked, had a Pope, and least of all a Spanish Pope, to reserve the new world for the Spaniards and Portuguese? And how could it serve the Papacy that it should at this early date commit itself to the doctrine that India and America were for ever closed to the mariners of the north? Yet an instrument, however imperfect, which effects for a time a *modus vivendi* between rival states by defining their respective spheres of influence, cannot wholly be condemned. The five bulls of Alexander VI served a useful though momentary purpose. They became the basis of the Treaty of Tordesillas (June 7, 1494), by which everything east of a line drawn across the Atlantic at a point 370 miles west of the Cape Verde Islands was assigned to Portugal, while everything west of it was accorded to Spain. The line so drawn just enabled Portugal to claim Brazil.

It was the merest accident that Christopher Columbus made his famous discovering voyage under the Spanish flag. Portugal, England, and France had the offer of his cherished secret and burning ardour. A Spanish Commission sat upon his project for five years, and then rejected it, and it was only by the narrowest margin, and through the influence of a priest and a woman high in the Queen's favour, that this unfavourable verdict was finally reversed. Columbus was a brilliant sailor, raised to the point of greatness by the glowing resolution with which, despite rebuffs and difficulties, calculated to daunt men of average courage, he pursued his dream victoriously to the end. Crossing the Atlantic in three small caravels, he struck Watling Island, one of the Bahamas, on October 12, 1492, and named it San Salvador. He had sailed for five weeks over a lonely, unknown sea, stilling the mutinous misgivings of his crew by his unconquerable faith, until he had reached what until the end of his life he believed to be the eastern fringe of Asia. The discovery of the West Indies is his title of fame, the first voyage across the Atlantic his great contribution, for he had no gifts for the difficult problems of colonization or government on land, which embittered his later visits, and thought that nothing better could be done with the native Indians than to enslave them. To the commercial speculators who buzzed round the Court of Barcelona a few unintelligible slaves and a handful of gold seemed to be a poor reward for a sequence of expensive voyages, and a derisory substitute for the promised spices of the east. The great navigator was suspended from his command and sent back to Spain in chains, there to be confronted by the deep grudge of disappointed investors and the fiercer anger of returned colonists. In Spain, the country of his adoption, he died in 1506 a disgraced and humiliated man, but the discoverer of America and to be remembered till the end of time.

The discovery of the new world cannot rightly be regarded as originating in no higher purpose than the quest for spices and gold. Religious aspirations were blended with economic appetite. At the Vatican, and more particularly among the Franciscans, whose missionary enterprise was world-wide, the oceanic enterprises of Portugal and Spain aroused the strongest interest as likely to lead not only to the evangelization of heathen people, but also to an attack on the Moslems to be delivered from the east. It was known that the Negus of Abyssinia was a Christian, and it was believed that there still survived in India, as a result of the mission of St. Thomas, a Christian state ruled by a monarch known as the great Khan. From these distant oriental potentates it was fondly hoped that Catholic Europe would receive effective assistance in one last grand crusade against the infidel. Such was "the plan of the Indies" sketched out as early as 1454 by Nicholas V in a bull despatched to the King of Portugal. And it was in such an atmosphere of exalted expectation that Columbus himself set out to discover the Indies in the west.

Meanwhile the suction of remote events was drawing into one unnatural amalgamation three sharply distinguished States, Spain, the Netherlands, and the imperial federation of Germany. Two fateful marriages and five unexpected deaths changed the face of European politics. In 1477 Maximilian, son and heir of the Emperor Frederick III, married Mary, the heiress of Charles the Bold of Burgundy. Years passed. Mary died, Maximilian became Regent of the Netherlands, and then (1493), in succession to his father, Holy Roman Emperor. Philip, the son of his Burgundian marriage, a fine, handsome youth, grew to manhood, and, being heir to great wealth, was eagerly sought in wedlock. As early as 1491 there was talk of a union between the Flemish Archduke and Joanna, the third daughter of the King and Queen of Spain. The children were young, the negotiations leisurely, but in 1496 the match was made. Joanna of Spain became the wife of Philip of Flanders. Who could then have foreseen the violently contrasted fates of the happy couple, or the far-reaching consequences of their marriage, the early death of the handsome Philip, the madness of his wife, the long list of tragic funerals which brought her most unexpectedly to the throne of Spain, or the vast perspective of power and pride which opened out before her little child, heir to the government of Spain and the Netherlands, and destined to follow in the footsteps of Maximilian, his grandfather, as the wearer of the Imperial Crown? While events were thus preparing for the empire of Charles V, the main preoccupations of Spanish statecraft were naturally with the old world rather than with the new.

The contemporaries of Charles VIII can hardly be blamed for thinking that Italy, so far gone in political decomposition, and yet so famous, opulent, and cultured, was a prize much to be preferred to the freshly discovered islands on the other side of the Atlantic, of which bronzed seamen were talking on the quays of Barcelona and Lisbon. If a field for conquest was necessary, here was the field in which the harvest could most swiftly be reaped. Yet it is deplorable that despite the needs of their own subjects and the call of the new world, the rulers of France and Spain should for a period of sixty years have wasted their strength in a struggle for predominance in Italy, to their own grave mutual injury, and to the abasement of a cultured and relatively peaceful country, which was forced to become the theatre of a savage war.

It has been urged in extenuation that but for the French and Spanish armies Italy would have been conquered by the Turks. It might as well be argued that these purposeless wars are justified by the heroism of Bayard or by the brilliant verse of Ariosto's *Orlando Furioso*. Such shadowy conjectures may afford consolation, but do not constitute a defence.

Like all subsequent French invasions of Italy, the Italian 149. enterprise of Charles VIII is the story of an early triumph followed by a sudden and complete reverse. At first fortune smiled on the glittering army with its mediaeval accoutrements and imposing train of artillery. Ludovico Sforza, the ruler of Milan, who had himself invited the expedition, was not the man to obstruct its progress. Savonarola, the Dominican, one of those great Puritan preachers who from time to time arise in the Latin and Catholic south, welcomed the French as liberators to Florence, his adopted city. Rome opened her gates. Without a blow struck Charles was master of the Neapolitan kingdom. But then, when the main objective of the campaign had been reached, the real difficulties disclosed themselves. The invading army, which was partly German and Swiss, was not, as Savonarola's vision had painted it, a flight of purifying angels commissioned to put an end to luxury and lust and the abuses of the Papal Church, but was as ill-behaved, as licentious, and as brutal (though with some shining exceptions) as French and German levies of this period were wont to be. As the army passed southwards it left behind it a trail of burning indignation. An Italian league was swiftly formed to eject the invaders and 1495 bar their retreat. On the field of Fornovo Charles cut his way through the enemy, and with this victory to his credit, but with the loss of every yard of Italian soil, regained his native land.

Partly because of Fornovo, but still more because the French army lived on the enemy country and returned home laden with booty, the idea of an Italian war retained its lustre 1498- in France. When Charles died (1498), Louis XII, his cousin 1513 and successor, was drawn southwards by the same flattering mirage of Italian glory. The old story repeated itself. Facile successes were followed by grave complications, by defeats in Italy, at last even by the invasion of France. Milan was conquered and lost, Naples was shared with Spain and then lost, Venice was driven from her mainland possessions by a league of France, Papacy and Empire, and then restored by a papal confederation against France. In the unstable atmosphere of Italian diplomacy the friend of today became the enemy of tomorrow. Julius II, the warrior Pope, who assisted France against Venice, was soon afterwards the contriver of the Holy League to expel the French from Italy. Louis could count on no firm Italian friendships. His armies were beaten at Novara (1513), and, stripped of all his Italian conquests, he returned to France to deal with the English who had captured Tournai, and with the Burgundians who were besieging Dijon. Such were the final humiliations inflicted upon "the father of his country" by the lure of Italy. Milan, Naples, Venetia, were won and lost, and the soil of France invaded at two points. Still the lesson went unheeded.

Frances I, the nephew of Louis XII, young, artistic, high-spirited, and self-indulgent, was not the man to forget that his uncle had been turned out of Milan by an army of base-born Swiss peasants. He crossed the Alps, confronted the Swiss mercenaries who guarded Milan, and by the brilliant victory at Marignano (1515) secured Lombardy once more for France, on a fleeting tenure. 1515-47

Meanwhile conditions were becoming steadily more adverse to the prospects of an enduring French success in Italy. Spain was the rival, with an advantage at sea, with a stronger corps of infantry, with the wealth of the new world beginning to find its way into her coffers. Under Ferdinand the Catholic Spain was strong enough to eject the French from Naples. 1479-1516 Under Charles, Ferdinand's Flemish grandson, the power of Spain was made yet more redoubtable by the tribute of the Netherlands and (after 1519) by the man power of the Empire. As time proceeded the opposition to France gathered force and was recruited from every quarter. In the course of a generation the Pope, Milan, Venice, the Swiss, Spain, Flanders, the Empire, drew the sword to prevent hegemony in Italy. Yet Francis I persevered in his Italian designs, and though he was defeated and taken at Pavia in 1525, his countrymen did not desist from their forlorn enterprise, or surrender their Italian claims until Henry II signed the Treaty of Cateau Cambrésis in 1559. It was a Spanish victory. The far-off result of Charles VIII's lighthearted cavalcade was the deliverance of Lombardy and Naples to the strict and solemn rule of the orthodox Spaniard, the eclipse of the Italian Renaissance, and the obscuration under a cloud of Spanish and clerical tyranny of that free play of the Italian imagination, which is capable of spells of incomparable brilliance, but equally of a cynical and patient acceptance of the discipline of tyranny and defeat.

Italy had long exercised, if only through Rome, an influence on northern Europe. In the fifteenth century scholars from England, Germany, and France visited the country, studied in its universities, and came back with cargoes of medical and classical knowledge. Even if Charles VIII had never crossed the Alps, the Italian Renaissance would in due course of time have affected the life currents of northern peoples. But the wheels of history run rapidly in war. Processes which otherwise might be slow and gradual then become swift and vehement. Every campaign is a voyage of discovery, every diplomatic interchange a revelation of foreign human nature. It was so with these Italian wars. They accelerated, if they did not occasion, the spread of the Italian Renaissance among the peoples of the north.

Among the figures on the Italian stage revealed to the general eye of Europe as the curtain went up in 1494 was 1492- that of Rodrigo Borgia, a wealthy Spaniard, who two years 1503 earlier had bribed the Sacred College to make him Pope, and had assumed the name of Alexander VI. Apologists can be found for anything. The indulgent eye of modern criticism has withdrawn the gravest charges which were levelled against this Pontiff by his contemporaries. It is content to leave only as established sensuality and simony, worldliness, perfidy, and secret poisoning. There are periods in the life of any institution in which a rough bestial nature may have its uses. The stalwart Spaniard was not rougher, more licentious, or more cruel than the fierce families of Rome and central Italy with whom it was his business to cope. If he was a murderer and conspirator, he lived in an atmosphere of murder and conspiracy. A submissive papal state in central Italy, such as it was Alexander's object to create, could not be made by soft words and spiritual exercises, but by force and treachery, administration and finance. Here Alexander was in his element, working in part for the Holy See, but more obviously for the advancement of the Borgia family. How Cesare Borgia, the Pope's brilliant son, endeavoured to aid his father in the Romagna, and what resources of force and fraud he employed to this end, is recorded in *The Prince* of Machiavelli, who saw, as we have already noted, in the career of this unscrupulous adventurer the model of the new statecraft, unweakened by pity and uninfluenced by ethics or religious faith.

The spectacle of depravity presented by the Rome of the Borgias was deeply disturbing to spiritual natures. "The scandal," wrote Savonarola, "begins in Rome and runs through the whole clergy; they are worse than Turks and Moors. In Rome you will find that they have one and all obtained their benefices by simony. They buy preferments and bestow them on their children or brothers, who take possession of them by violence and all sorts of sinful means. Their greed is insatiable, they do all things for gold. They only ring their bells for coin and candles; only attend Vespers and Choir and Office when something is to be got by it. They sell their benefices, sell the sacraments, traffic in masses. . . . If a priest or a canon leads an ordinary life he is mocked and called a hyprocrite. It has come to pass that all are warned against Rome, and people say, 'If you want to ruin your son make him a priest.' " In such language as this there may be some exaggeration, but in essentials the indictment was true. Though there was much genuine religious life in Catholic Europe at the end of the fifteenth and beginning of the sixteenth century and though a genuine effort was made by good and able men, such as Hegius at Deventer in the Netherlands, or Nicholas of Cusa in Germany, or Dean Colet in England, to improve education and knowledge and to reform the abuses of·the Church, Rome had definitely lost the moral leadership of Europe. No court had a worse reputation for avarice, corruption, and vice. In 1499 the probability that Germany and Spain would renounce their allegiance was freely discussed.

The spiritual declension of Rome was the more important by reason of the new spirit of rationalism which was springing up in northern Europe. Of this spirit, so far as it did not 1467. transcend the limits of Catholic orthodoxy, the herald and 1536 prophet was Erasmus of Rotterdam. Few men have exercised a wider or more salutary influence upon his generation than this delicate, impecunious little Dutch scholar, who after a passionate course of self-education in the Netherlands and England, in France and in Italy, became to a degree unequalled until the days of Voltaire the acknowledged chief of European enlightenment. Erasmus, like every lettered man of his age, was influenced by the classics of Greece and Rome, which it was the glory of Italy to have recovered. Yet, differing from many Italian scholars, he was neither pagan, nor aesthete, nor metaphysician, but a plain, orthodox Christian, somewhat poor on the side of imagination, since Terence was his favourite poet, but abounding in those gifts of clarity and grace, good sense, moderation, and wit which were best calculated to commend his message to the world. For he was a man with a message, a prophet as well as a savant. His enemies were pedantry and superstition, ignorance and stupidity, violence and vice. Against these evils his long course of incessant literary activity offered a continuous and brilliant protest. Though he visited universities, and even for a time (1500-1513) held a Chair of Divinity at Cambridge, he was no college pedant, but a citizen of the world, interested in conduct above all things, and quite as much concerned with popularizing knowledge as with extending it. In particular he wished to see the Scriptures translated into every language. "I long," he writes, "that the husbandman should say them to himself as he follows the plough, that the weaver should hum them to the tune of his shuttle, that the traveller should beguile with them the weariness of his journey." Even his more technical works, such as his editions of the Greek Testament and of the early Fathers, illustrate his concern for the needs of the general reader. He resolved to get behind the Latin Vulgate to its Greek original, to turn from the subtle disputations of the scholastic theologians to the teaching of the Early Fathers, where he was disposed to find the spirit of the early Church pure and undefiled. That the true and primitive Christianity had been obscured by the intellectual detritus of succeeding ages and might be recovered by a great feat of careful and imaginative scholarship was the core of his grammarian's faith.

Apart from the new and fruitful direction which he gave to biblical studies, Erasmus stood out as the prophet of a humane, tolerant, and enlightened Catholicism. He did not scruple to pour scorn on the ignorant, idle, and vicious monks, on the superstitious worship of relics, on the evils connected with pilgrimages and the sale of indulgences, and on other notorious abuses of the Church; and his raillery, conveyed in vivid popular Latin, went the round of the republic of letters. Yet his critical spirit was never sharpened to the point of 1501 heresy or revolt. In the *Enchiridion Militis Christiani* he expounded the eternal gospel of that inner religion of the heart, which dispenses with the support of outward observance and ceremonials, and finds its nourishment in meditation on the holy texts. It is clear that he was not interested in the subtleties of theological doctrine.

The popularity of his writings was immense and unprecedented. His *Colloquies*, his *Praise of Folly*, his *Adagia*, were the earliest "best-sellers" in secular printed literature. The gift for persiflage was never more effectively employed. The priestly caste, once so formidable and dominant, was held up by this light and engaging satirist as an object of amusement and contempt. The wickedness of war, the ineptitude of the old educational methods, the prevailing hollowness of religious life, were denounced with an earnestness which was all the more impressive by its immunity from any suspicion of the ponderous, the fanatical, or the insincere. For a time he marched abreast with Luther. Then the two men diverged. Luther broke away from Rome. Erasmus believed that the Roman Church could be reformed from within. The violent and intolerant spirit of the Protestant Reformation was abhorrent to the humane and pacific temper of the Dutch scholar. While Germany was convulsed with religious strife, Erasmus from his quiet retreat at Basel (1514-35) was attempting through an elaborate series of editions and translations from the Fathers to revive for the direction of the Roman Church the thought and spirit of early Christianity.

The importance of Erasmus for the history of Europe consists in the fact that, in the age of the Reformation, he embodied, with a surpassing attractiveness and brilliance, that tradition of Christian and classical culture which was and remains the common possession of all Europe. In any list of good Europeans the name of Erasmus would rank high. He had the idea of a Europe organized for rational ends, true to its past, but purified of its abuses, and bound together in a perpetual bond of peace and fellowship. Such an inspiration is still cherished by the small band of humanists who in every country endeavour to sweeten the bitter waters of political life.

BOOKS WHICH MAY BE CONSULTED

J. S. C. Bridge: *A History of France from the Death of Louis XI.* 1921.

H. Lemonnier in Lavisse: *Histoire de France, Vol. V.*

R. B. Merriman: *The Rise of the Spanish Empire.* 1918-25

J. Fiske: *The Discovery of America.* 1892.

C. R. Markham: *Life of Christopher Columbus.* 1892.

E. J. Payne: *History of the New World called America.* 1892-9.

S. E. Morison: *Admiral of the Ocean Sea: A Life of Christopher Columbus.* 1942.

S. E. Morison: *Christopher Columbus, Mariner.* 1956.

B. Penrose: *Travel and Discovery in the Renaissance, 1420-1620.* 1952.

CHAPTER XLII

THE TURKISH PERIL

*Selim I and Suleyman the Magnificent. The capture of Rhodes.
George Podiebrad and Matthias Corvinus. The field of Mohacs.
Consequences for Austria.*

FOR MOHAMMED the Conqueror the fall of Constantinople
was not an end but a beginning. This able and ambitious
ruler regarded himself as commissioned to conquer the
world for Islam, just as Lenin, long afterwards, and by other
and less warlike processes, aspired to convert mankind to the
Communist faith. An obedient people trained to every hardship but that of independent thought, a skilled professional
army, and a fine train of artillery gave Mohammed a commanding advantage against divided opponents. The roar of
the Turkish guns was heard on the Euphrates, on the Danube,
and on the Albanian coast. When the Sultan died in 1481,
Asia Minor, Greece, and the main part of the Balkan peninsula had been subjected to his yoke, and the Turk was astride
the Adriatic, holding the Ionian islands, Scutari, and Otranto,
and menacing the security of Italy and Rome.

After the brief rule of the nerveless Bayazet the course of
Turkish conquest was renewed by two of the most remarkable
figures of the Ottoman house. Selim I, who dethroned his
father Bayazet in 1512, is, next to Mohammed his grandfather, the principal architect of that wide Turkish Empire
which endured the strain and stress of many centuries and
was broken only by the tremendous shock of the last great
war. It was Selim who conquered Syria, Egypt, and Arabia,
and upon the resignation of the last Kaliph of the Abbassid
line brought the Kaliphate into the Ottoman house. To him
were solemnly tendered the keys of the Kaaba at Mecca, a
symbol of supremacy over the Moslem world. From the days
of Selim Stambul became the undisputed centre of Islamic
power in three continents. Bagdad, which was the capital of
the Abbassids and the principal scene of a civilization far

beyond the reach of the Turkish mind, now sank to the position of a distant provincial city.

Three great victories specially distinguish the military record of Selim's strenuous successor, Suleyman the Magnificent: the capture of Belgrade from the Hungarians, the forced capitulation of the Knights Hospitallers in Rhodes, and the bloodstained field of Mohacs (1526), which sealed the doom of Hungary as an independent kingdom. Belgrade was the gateway into Hungary, Rhodes the half-way house between Constantinople and Egypt, and Hungary the last effective barrier between the Turks and the Austrians.

The effect of these triumphs was the more impressive by reason of the high military reputation of the Magyar nation, and the confidence which was generally reposed in the skill and valour of the Christian garrison in Rhodes. Under John Hunyades and his son, Mathias Corvinus (1458), the frontiers of the Hungarian kingdom had been triumphantly defended and the Turks more than once compelled to accept defeat. The reputation of the Knights Hospitallers of Rhodes was of a different order, for while the Magyars had only recently won their way into the forefront of European history as the main defenders of the Christian cause on land, the Knights of Rhodes had ever since the Crusades been the easternmost spearpoint of Christendom against Asia and Islam. Rhodes was a small island. The Hospitallers in number and equipment were far inferior to their assailants. But they had survived so long that it was natural to think that they would survive for ever. That they were permitted to go down before the Turks, with the passive acquiescence of Genoa and to the unconcealed satisfaction of Venice, was a sharp advertisement to the west that the Turkish navy was mistress of the Aegean, and that the two great Italian cities which had conveyed the Crusaders to Palestine had now turned round and joined the enemy.

The collapse of Hungary was equally spectacular and for the history of Europe far more momentous. It has been one of the standing misfortunes of Europe that the Poles, the Czechs, and the Magyars have never been able to devise any durable form of political co-operation. An incompatibility of temper based upon differences of language, race, and religion has always proved stronger than the compulsion of political convenience or necessity. From Bohemia, the richest and

most civilized of these three monarchies, Poland was estranged
by religion, Hungary by religion, race, and language alike;
and since the nobles of Poland, Bohemia, and Hungary knew
how to extract a full measure of selfish indulgence from a
weak and elective kingship, it followed that at the very time
when the princes of the west were consolidating their power,
the states on the eastern border were undergoing the opposite
process of feudal dissolution.

The last act of Bohemian and Hungarian independence was
marked by one of those rare opportunities which, once
missed, never return. In the spring of 1458 two remarkable
men were elected to the thrones of Bohemia and Hungary.
1458- George Podiebrad was a Czech noble who had won the
71 confidence of the Bohemian nation by his successful defence
of the Hussite faith against a strong Catholic and German-
izing minority. His firmness, his moderation, his willingness
to treat religion as a question upon which the State might
tolerate differing opinions, as well as his success in putting
down rebellion, gave him a position of national authority
such as no Bohemian ruler had enjoyed since the days of
Charles IV and no Bohemian ruler was destined to enjoy again
till the days of Mazaryk. The youth who almost simultaneously mounted the Hungarian throne enjoyed a comparable
1459- advantage. Like Podiebrad, Matthias Corvinus was of
90 national stock. He was the son of that illustrious soldier John
Hunyades, who had driven the Turks from before the walls of
Belgrade, and he inherited much of his father's vigour and
activity. To the qualities of a soldier he added a perception
of the arts of peace. The conqueror of Vienna was also the
founder of Pressburg University, and the first to introduce
among the backward nobles of Hungary many of the accomplishments and arts of Italy. A close alliance between two
men, each in his ways so remarkable, and each in his own
country so popular as Matthias Corvinus and George Podiebrad, would have been of the greatest value. The conjunction
of Hungary and Bohemia under such rulers might have imposed a final limit upon the incursions of the Turk and
averted from the two Christian monarchies of south-eastern
Europe the destiny which was awaiting them of absorption
in the Austrian Empire. But the two men, though united by
marriage, drifted into a fatal antagonism which proved to be
ruinous to both kingdoms. Bohemia was attacked by

Hungary, and Hungary in its turn, unfriended and alone, was allowed to go down before the Turk. The cause of the sudden downfall of two kingdoms apparently on the high road to stability and power was religion. George of Bohemia stood by the Compacts of the Council of Basel, which accorded to the Hussite Church in Bohemia the use of the cup by the laity in the sacrament. But to the papal Curia, which had never accepted the Compacts, the policy of the Hussite chief was impermissible. Podiebrad was excommunicated. It was 1466 determined in Rome to depose the heretic and to replace him by the Catholic Matthias. The Hungarian king yielded to temptation and joined forces with the Catholic malcontents 1468 of Bohemia. In the terrible civil war which ensued the Bohemian patriot held his own, but in self-defence was compelled to name as his successor a Catholic prince from the Polish royal family. In 1471, on the death of Podiebrad, Vladislav Jagellon succeeded to his throne.

The advent to power of this insufficient Polish alien who was in turn called to govern Bohemia and Hungary was a signal in each country for an outburst of aristocratic pretensions. Among the turbulent landowners of the eastern kingdoms the Pole was as helpless as a French master in a class of rebellious English schoolboys. He had neither army nor treasury, could do nothing without the Diet, and was expressly debarred from introducing any novelties into Hungary. Against the serried discipline of a Turkish army the feudal levies of such a monarchy were bound to fail.

The issue was tried upon the field of Mohacs (1526), a battle big with consequences for Europe, for after the Hungarian army had been defeated and Louis the last Jagellon king was killed, and the whole country up to the gates of Vienna had been overrun by the Turks, there was no life left in the proud Magyar aristocracy. The greater part of Hungary was seized and held by the Turks until late in the seventeenth century; the remainder fell to Ferdinand of Austria, the brother-in-law of Louis and the heir to his pretensions. The long subjection of Bohemia and Hungary to the Habsburg house, lasting until the Treaty of St. Germain after the recent war, was the direct result of that fatal day. Not until the Italian victory of Vittorio Veneto (1918) had sent the Austrian Empire toppling to the ground were the effects of the field of Mohacs finally undone.

For indeed there was born upon the field of Mohacs a new spell of life for the Holy Roman Empire and for the Habsburg house. The defence of Christian Europe against the Turks, which might otherwise have been conducted by the Hungarian nation, now devolved of necessity upon the Archdukes of Austria. Their "ramshackle Empire," built up by a succession of happy marriages, received a justification in the eyes of Christian Europe by reason of the fact that through the eclipse of Hungary it had become the necessary and only valid bulwark against a great and aggressive Moslem Empire. That it reposed on a multi-national basis was no matter of reproach in the sixteenth and seventeenth centuries. But as the Empire of the Habsburgs was made by the Turkish peril, so at each stage in the decline of Ottoman power it lost something of its original prestige and authority. In the end Turk and Austrian succumbed to the same enemy. The spirit of nationality born of the French Revolution first set aflame the Christian nations of the Balkans and then, spreading among the Croatians, the Czechs and the Poles, involved the Austrian Empire in ruin.

BOOKS WHICH MAY BE CONSULTED

Cambridge Modern History, Vol. I, chap. iii; Vol. III, chap. x.

J. Von Hammer-Purgstall: *Histoire de l'Empire Ottoman*. Traduit de l'allemand par M. Dochez. 3 vols. 1840-2.

S. Lane Poole: *Turkey*. 1908.

L. von Ranke: *The Ottoman and Spanish Empires in the Sixteenth and Seventeenth Centuries*. Tr. W. K. Kelly. 1843.

F. Downey: *The Grande Turke Suleyman the Magnificent*. 1929.

La Jonquière: *Histoire de l'Empire Ottoman*. 1881.

G. E. Hubbard: *The Day of the Crescent*. 1920.

G. Finlay: *History of Greece*. Ed. H. F. Tozer. 7 vols. 1877.

G. G. Macartney: *Hungary* (Nations of the Modern World). 1934.

Sir P. Rycaut: *The Present State of the Ottoman Empire*. 1668.

F. Palacky: *Geschicte von Böhmen*. 1844-67.

E. Denis: *Fin de l'Indépendance Bohème*. 2 vols. 1890.

H. F. Brown: *Venice: A Historical Sketch of the Republic*. 1893.

Zinkeisen: *Geschichte des Osmanischen Reiches*. 1840-63.

New Cambridge Modern History, Vol II. 1958.

D. M. Vaughan: *Europe and the Turk*. 1350-1700. 1954.

CHAPTER XLIII

THE GERMAN REFORMATION

*Causes of the Reformation. The new learning. The attractions
of Protestantism. Literary power of Protestant leaders. Martin
Luther. Indulgences. The ninety-five theses. The breach with
Rome. Charles V and the Edict of Worms. Luther's auxiliaries.
His partial success He denounces the peasants. Zwingli and
Luther. Lutheran successes in Scandinavia and Prussia. The
rift beyond repair by 1541.*

THE PROTESTANT REFORMATION was a revolt against papal theocracy, clerical privilege, and the hereditary paganism of the
Mediterranean races. On the one side it took the aspect of an
insurgence of the lay spirit against clerical claims and immunities, on the other of a religious revival and an attempt
to retrieve the original ways of the Christian Church. It
occurred when it did partly because the abuses connected
with the papal government and the Church were then felt to
be specially grave and partly because the desire for a simpler
and more spiritual form of Christianity, which at that time
possessed many ardent minds, coincided with the appetites of
secular princes, who, finding their traditional revenues inadequate for the growing needs of the state, cast covetous
eyes on the wealth of the Church. It corresponded with the
rising tide of nationalism, and was quickened by the conversion of the Papacy into an Italian state. A great movement
of intellectual emancipation preceded its advent and accompanied its course. Thousands of separate little rills of doubt,
criticism, and protest which had been gathering volume for a
generation suddenly flowed together into a brawling river of
revolt. The public mind recoiled from the discipline of the
past. Old limitations upon thought and learning fell away.
Reuchlin in Germany went back to Hebrew, Valla in Italy
and Budé in France to the real Latin and Greek of antiquity.
A spirit of brilliant forward-reaching enlightenment came into
Europe, challenging traditional knowledge and shaming old

abuses or superstitions by its scorn and mockery. Of the soldiers of light no country had a monopoly. Machiavelli and Valla were Italians, Von Hutten was German, Zwingli Swiss, Rabelais French, More English, Erasmus Dutch. Of these some were sceptics; others remained faithful to the Roman Church; others when the rift came went into revolt.

The enlightenment of the sixteenth century, though quite distinct from the Protestant movement, was one of the causes which helped it to succeed. The new learning weakened the traditional sentiment of reverence by which many of the beliefs, traditions, and customs of the Roman Church had long been supported. The layman could now read for himself. He could learn Greek and even Hebrew, getting behind the official Latin of the Roman priest to the original languages of Holy Writ. The Vulgate was no longer sacrosanct. There were texts older than the Vulgate, more sacred, at once unknown to the main part of the Latin priesthood, and accessible to the scholar who cared to learn. The thought inevitably sprang up that the virtuous layman could reach his God without the intermediacy of a priest. The movement appealed at once to that which was most lax and that which was most rigorous in the moral temper of Europe. There were those who, like the Anabaptists of Münster, threw off all the moral restraints of the old order. At the opposite extreme was that indwelling spirit of Christian stoicism which animated Calvin's polity at Geneva and Oliver Cromwell's New Model army, and out of which was fashioned the austere, money-making civilization of the New England colonies and their daughter states.

Against the aesthetic beauty of the Roman Church and the Roman ritual the reformers could offer two great popular attractions. The first was the delight of congregational singing, the second the interest of a service conducted in a language intelligible to the unlearned. Nor was there in this attempt to reach the common man any necessary vulgarity. Music often touched a high, language a sublime, level. Luther's Bible, Tyndale's Bible, and Cranmer's Prayer-book, Calvin's French version of his own *Christianae religionis institutio* are in their respective languages masterpieces of prose writing. Of Luther it may be said that a passion for music and prodigal gifts as a writer were almost as important a part of his equipment as deep learning and spiritual force.

He counts as one of the makers of the German language, rich, copious, animated, but inferior in refinement to Tyndale and Cranmer. It is a fact of great importance for the history of the Protestant Reformation that among its earliest professors were certain writers of temperament and genius, whose words have still power to stir the heart. Few passages in our English Bible are more familiar than the wonderful thirteenth chapter of the first Epistle to the Corinthians. In substance the translation is the work of William Tyndale, who was burned as a heretic in 1537. The leaden literature of the Lollards and the Hussites may be searched in vain for so great an artist.

Martin Luther, the Saxon peasant to whom the German 1843-Reformation owes its origin and character, was one of those 1546 men who achieve a commanding position in the world not because they are original, but because they are representative. Luther was not a profound theologian; nor was he a philosopher. He did not believe in free enquiry or toleration, and so far from acknowledging the possibility of development in religious thought, held firmly to the belief that all truth as to the ultimate problems of life and mind was to be found in Holy Writ. It is not therefore from Luther, a savage anti-Semite, that the liberal and rationalizing movements of European thought derive their origin. Though he promoted a rebellion, he was not a revolutionary, but a self-experiencing religious genius who in his search for personal salvation was led by degrees to take up an attitude which made him the champion of the German nation against the claims of the Roman Church.

A great part of his power lay in the fact that he was German to the marrow. All the strength, all the weakness of the German character was reflected and magnified in his passionate temperament, its tenderness and violence, its coarseness in vituperation and old-fashioned Biblical piety, its music and learning, its conviviality and asceticism, its homely common sense and morbid self-scrutiny, its paroxysms of contrition and heady self-confidence. Not since Barbarossa had there been a German so typical of his age and race as this emaciated but very typical Saxon friar, with his rough combatant ways, his clear ringing voice, and unending command of words, jests, images, and arguments.

Let it not, however, be imagined that the German people,

among whom Luther was brought up, were prepared for a Protestant theology or an heretical church. Had Luther in the first instance come forward with any such proposals he would have been the mark of almost universal animosity; but he did nothing of the kind. He denounced the sale of indulgences. The source of his extraordinary influence was due to the fact that he, an Augustinian monk, launched an attack upon those practical abuses of the Roman Church which every right-minded German, however much attached he might be to the Roman connection, regarded as morally and theologically indefensible. In so doing Luther spoke not only the mind of Germany but the better mind of the Church itself.

The idea that the Pope could issue indulgences for the re-mission of sins of every kind was rooted in the theory that there had been accorded to St. Peter and his successors the privilege of dispensing to the faithful an inexhaustible treasury of merit. Originally due to the sacrifices of Christ, the treasury of the Church was continually augmented by the merits of successive generations of believing Christians. The concep-tion of merit, not as something ephemeral and personal, but as a store of spiritual wealth which could be accumulated for the benefit of the living and the dead, appealed alike to the religious imagination of the pious and to the pecuniary needs of the Popes. What could be more convenient to an embar-rassed exchequer than the possession of a fund filled without effort, maintained without anxiety, and always capable of being employed to pecuniary advantage? As the financial attraction of the spiritual treasury disclosed itself, the moral judgments which had originally accompanied its admini-stration were thrown to the winds. Confession and repentance were no longer insisted on. From Pope Julius II a plenary indulgence could be earned merely by a contribution to the rebuilding of St. Peter's. Pope Leo X went further still. To all who set out upon a crusade against the Turks he promised the everlasting bliss of heaven. *Claudo tibi portas inferni et januas aperio Paradisi.* Usurping the prerogatives assumed only to belong to the Almighty, the banker Pope (for Leo was a Medici) claimed not only to remit the temporal penalties for sin but even to expunge the sin itself.

The scandal worked to a climax in a great money-raising campaign for the new St. Peter's which was conducted, so far as the provinces of Mainz and Magdeburg were concerned, by the Dominican preacher John Tetzel.

"It is incredible," wrote a contemporary, "what this ignorant and impudent friar gave out. He said that if they contributed readily and bought grace and indulgence, all the hills of St. Annaburg would become pure massive silver, that so soon as the coin rang in the chest, the soul for whom the money was paid would go straightway to heaven." It was such effrontery which provoked Luther to post upon the door of the castle church of Wittenberg (October 31, 1517) those ninety-five theses which, being swiftly circulated by a friendly press, lit the fires of the German Reformation.

By this time Luther had reached the fundamental convictions which inspired his course of future action. Prayer, fasting, scourgings had brought him no peace nor lightened by one featherweight his agonizing burden of imputed sin. On the one hand he saw the abject wickedness of man, on the other the dazzling and unapproachable goodness of God. Where could he find a bridge across the dark chasm? By degrees, first on a visit to Rome, whose patent corruptions caused him to recoil, later at Erfurt, through the teaching of Staupitz, he received a vision of hope. Faith was the bridge. Man if he had faith could be saved, despite his inherent and desperate wickedness. Works were of no avail. Pilgrimages and ceremonies, the telling of beads, the lighting of candles, the worship of relics, were only obstructions on the pathway to salvation. Faith, the condition of Grace, Grace, the reward of Faith, were all that mattered in the dark history of predestined man. It was a graft from the tree of his master St. Augustine, once unperceived, but, now that it was recovered ever afterwards held with fanatical tenacity.

Once embarked upon the ship of grace, Luther drifted far and fast into tumultuous waters. If works were of no avail, of what value was the monk's vow or the priest's unction? By 1520 he had come to the conclusion that every baptized Christian was a priest, that Rome was Babylon, that the Pope was Antichrist, that priests should be allowed to marry, and that divorce was lawful. In three famous treatises, the first an appeal in German directed to the laity and urging them to take in hand the reformation of the Church (To the Christian Nobility of the German Nation respecting the Reformation of the Christian Estate), the second a Latin treatise addressed to the theologians (*De Captivitate Babylonica Ecclesiae Praeludium*), and the third a curious letter "concerning Christian Liberty," directed to Leo X, professedly as an eirenicon, Luther completed and made irreparable his breach with Rome. "For your see," he observed to the Pope, "which is called the Roman Curia, which neither you nor any man can deny to be more corrupt than Babylon and Sodom, I have indeed shown my detestation, and have been indignant that the Christian people should be deluded under your name and under cover of the Roman Church; and so I have resisted and will continue to resist so long as the spirit of faith lives in me." An Italian humanist may be excused for failing to discover any note of conciliation in such an utterance. Leo issued a bull excommunicating the rebel, and the rebel replied (December 10, 1520) by publicly burning the bull.

Meanwhile a grave Flemish lad of nineteen, having been chosen Emperor after a vast expenditure of money and intrigue, addressed himself to the novel and troublesome problem of dealing with a heretic who was also a national hero. Napoleon long afterwards charged Charles V with missing one of the great opportunities of history by refusing Luther's invitation that he should put himself at the head of the reforming movement in Germany. But how was it possible for Charles, a Habsburg, a Holy Roman Emperor, and a king of orthodox and Catholic Spain, to lead a national German rebellion against the papal see? The traditions of his house and of the imperial office, his own creed and upbringing, the conservative bent of his mind, the prevailing sentiments of his Flemish and Spanish subjects, made such a course impossible. Of necessity Charles was brought to view himself as the personal champion of the Papacy and as a shield and buckler of the established order.

So, amid a great commotion of the public mind and with a strong current of popular feeling running against the papal court, Luther was summoned to Worms to attend upon the young Emperor and his first Diet. He was charged to retract his writings. With a pride which must have been fortified by the sense of outside support he replied that, since Popes and Councils had often erred and contradicted themselves, he would withdraw nothing unless it were disproved by Scripture

or evident reason. He lost nothing by his steadfast bearing.
Though the Pope and Emperor entered into a league (May 8,
1521) to seize his person and to stamp out his opinions, he
remained for a few more years the favourite of a great part
of the German people, and more particularly of the middle
class who plied their industries in the towns. The Edict of
Worms, which made of him an outlaw, was, from the first,
a dead letter.

Political conditions favoured the reformers. The Emperor,
distracted between a thousand claims and drawn away from
Germany in part by the war with France and by the necessity
of suppressing the serious revolt of the Spanish Comuneros,
was never in a position to apply the steady adverse pressure
by which alone a middle class movement which had captured
the printers could be brought into subjection. His brother,
Ferdinand of Austria, having the Turks upon his hands, was
in no better position to deal with the German heresy; and as
for the French, for whom Charles was the most formidable
of rivals and enemies, the Lutherans appeared to this orthodox
but very political nation to be deserving of every encouragement as a standing source of annoyance to the imperial
government.

One prophet does not make a church. Lutheranism owes
much to a statesman, a scholar, and a university. Frederick
the Wise, Elector of Saxony, was one of those men who,
without being either powerful or in any way brilliant, influence history from the respect which they inspire, and by the
opportune exercise of a kindly and paternal moderation. A
mild, prudent, peace-loving ruler, proud of his chapel choir,
his pictures and his castles, and of the University of Wittenberg of which he was the founder, and much occupied with
pious Biblical exercises, Frederick gave to the new movement
just that encouragement which was most necessary to carry
it through the critical early stages of its growth. When Luther
was proscribed both by the Emperor and the Pope, the old
Elector saw to it that he was hidden away and sheltered from
his enemies, and it was in Frederick's state, and with
Frederick's support, that the fiery thoughts and hot passions
of the great heretic were moulded into the fabric of the
Lutheran Church.

The scholar was Philip Melanchthon. "I am rough,
boisterous, stormy, and altogether warlike, I am born to

fight innumerable monsters and devils, to remove stems and stones, cut away thistles and thorns, and clear away wild forests: but Master Philip comes along softly and gently with joy, according to the gifts which God has abundantly bestowed upon him." In these words Luther defined his relation to Philip Melanchthon, the gentle Greek scholar, who, in December, 1521, provided the new religion with its first elementary work on theology, the *Loci Communes*, the first book which, as Ranke observes, had appeared for several centuries in the Latin Church containing a system constructed out of the Bible only.

The University was that of Wittenberg, which became at once the principal seminary of Lutheran doctrines and a standing challenge to the traditional learning of the Sorbonne. Hither learners flocked from every part of Germany. Here was the great factory of Lutheran literature. It was in this little centre that the national mind of Germany, as it was affected by the passions and events of that tumultuous age, was first expressed in language which all Germans could understand. Hence, too, certain divines in the East Anglian University of Cambridge derived the evangelical doctrines which helped to make England a Protestant country, and gave to an obscure fenland seminary a new and sudden pre-eminence in the intellectual life of the English people.

Yet despite the initial tide of a boisterous popularity the reformers failed to make of Germany a Protestant country. The inveterate political divisions which had paralysed this tempestuous people for centuries proved to be stronger than the widely spread indignation against papal abuses.

Some states accepted the new order, others remained faithful to the old. There was a League of Catholic States stitched together at Ratisbon (1524) and a counter-League of Protestant States set up at Torgau (1526) and enlarged at Smalkalden (1531). In the end, after a religious war which retarded the development of the country for two hundred years, Germany found peace, the newer civilizations of Saxony and Hesse, Prussia and Brandenburg embracing the Lutheran faith, while, broadly speaking, those parts of Germany which had been incorporated in the Roman Empire, notably Bavaria, Austria, and the Rhineland, remained faithful to Rome.

Thus the Lutheran movement, which had originally been

national and popular, became in the course of a very few years neither the one thing nor the other. The new confession was restricted to certain principalities and free cities and everywhere was closely dependent upon princely and governmental favour. Great bodies of opinion, whole classes of society, were alienated and denounced. While the humanists, who had found much to admire in the denunciation of papal obscurantism, were estranged by the ascending scale of Luther's violence, Luther himself recoiled from the revolting peasantry (1525), and in a treatise which marks his breach with German democracy invoked upon the suffering toilers in the fields, from whom he was himself sprung, the condign vengeance of the princes.

From that moment the Lutheran Church ranged itself definitely on the side of civil order and authority. In principle the decision was wise. The ship of reform would have foundered in an ocean of anarchy. It speaks much for Luther's common sense that he stood out against every form of irresponsible lawlessness, whether of raving prophets or evangelical *condottieri* or anarchical Anabaptists. But the manner in which he dissociated his movement from the peasant rebellion, his failure to suggest points of accommodation and compromise, and the encouragement which he gave to a course of repression so savage that it left the German peasantry more defenceless and abased than any social class in central or western Europe, are serious blots upon his good name. The German peasants were rough men and rough fighters; but their grievances were genuine and their original demands were just and reasonable. That Lutheranism should have been associated with the reprisals of a hard and merciless landowning aristocracy, and with the degradation of the most deserving class in the community, proved to be a serious deduction from its vitalizing energies.

Of hardly less importance for the future of German protestantism was its emphatic breach with the Swiss Reformation. The Swiss were still the most famous mercenaries in Europe. Physically robust, but backward in all the arts and refinements of life, and separated by their mountains from the general movements of Europe, the Swiss were now (1522) for the first time swept into the reforming current and roused to a scrutiny of creeds and customs. The movement began in Zürich. It was partly moral, partly humanistic and patriotic, partly religious, and not a little, as all movements of religious revolt are wont to be, an impatient chafing at ancient and respectable restrictions. The Zürichers led by Ulrich Zwingli, a democrat, a republican, and a humanist, began to realize that it was not a very creditable thing for a self-respecting Züricher to receive a pension or retaining fee from a foreign power. The fibre of latent nationalism began to vibrate among the burghers of this quiet lake city. "They would be neither French nor Imperial, but good Zürichers and Confederates." And with this determination to be at all costs Swiss there was combined a resolve to be on no account Roman. Zwingli denounced fasting in Lent, the celibacy of the clergy, monastic vows, the use of Latin in the church services, and the doctrine of the real presence. More radical, more enlightened, less mediaeval than Luther, the Swiss reformer drove forward without misgiving towards a complete breach with Rome. By 1529 six of the thirteen cantons and some few towns in southern Germany were captured for Zwinglian reform.

Philip the Landgrave of Hesse, the ablest German prince who had embraced the Lutheran cause, saw how much advantage would accrue from a junction of the Swiss and German forces, and had politicians been in command of the two movements such a junction would have been effected. Unfortunately Luther and Zwingli were not statesmen but theologians, each resolute to maintain every inch of the ground which he had taken up in advance. It was in vain that the Landgrave prevailed upon the contending divines to meet **1529** in conference at Marburg. Despite many minor points of agreement, on the central problem of the eucharistic presence in the sacrament there was a gulf between the disputants which no argument could bridge. For Zwingli the sacrament was a symbolical ceremony. Luther, while rejecting the orthodox view that the body and blood of Christ replaced the elements, held that they coexisted with them as fire is present in molten lead. "*Hoc est corpus meum*," he wrote upon the conference table as he took his seat, and from the compulsion of that plain text could see no escape. The dream of a wide Protestant confederation, comprising Swiss cantons, south German cities, and north German principalities, was shattered on the obstinate rock of those four words.

Lutheranism, then, made no conquests in Switzerland, and

was compelled to cede much of its original advantage in Germany. But in revenge it conquered and still retains the three Scandinavian kingdoms; a low-temperature religion, agreeable to Erastian kings, and adapted to the long winters of the rigorous north.

The twenty years which followed the Edict of Worms are among the most uncertain and critical in German history. Serious men confronted with that welter of confused and conflicting ideas must often have asked themselves whether the fabric of the German Reich would survive so great a shock, and whether even civilization itself would not be submerged in chaos. A hope persisted that the gulf could be bridged, and that if only a Council were summoned the acknowledged scandals in the Church could be put down and a basis provided upon which all true Christians might be content to unite. To no one did the restoration of religious peace seem more necessary than to the good and conscientious Charles V.

But the Emperor could do little that was helpful. Affairs in Spain, in Africa, in Italy, and in the Netherlands were for him more pressing than the composition of religious differences in Germany. Only once (1530) in that critical period of twenty years did this care-laden monarch show himself among his German subjects. Then, presiding over a Diet of the Empire at Augsburg, he was brought to reject a certain *Confessio*, or statement of belief, drawn up by the conciliatory Melanchthon, which, under its appellation of the Confession of Augsburg, has been ever since accepted as the classical exposition of the Lutheran Faith.

So without serious interference from the high powers the Lutheran Faith spread through northern Germany, and was even adopted in Prussia, where Albert of Brandenburg, the Grand Master of the German Order, decided (1525) to secularize his duchy and to hold it as a fief of the Polish crown, introducing at the same time the Saxon order of ritual and Church government. The consequences may easily be imagined. With every year the new system struck fresh roots in the soil, created new attachments, and became more difficult to dislodge. It followed that, when Charles returned to Germany in 1541, after nine years' absence, and again addressed himself to the task of reconciliation, the problem was, by reason of those vested interests, more difficult than ever. The last serious attempt at accommodation broke down at Ratisbon. By this time the differences between the Lutheran and Roman Churches were too wide, too deep, too numerous to be bridged.

BOOKS WHICH MAY BE CONSULTED

T. M. Lindsay: *History of the Reformation: Vol. I, in Germany; Vol. II, in lands beyond Germany.* 1905.

B. J. Kidd: *Documents illustrative of the Continental Reformation.* 1911.

T. M. Lindsay: *Luther and the German Reformation.* 1900.

The Table Talk of Martin Luther. Tr. and ed. William Hazlitt. 1848.

Luther's Primary Works. Tr. and ed. H. Wace and C. Buchheim. 1896.

L. von Ranke: *Deutsche Geschichte im Zeitalter der Reformation.* Tr. Sarah Austin, *History of the Reformation in Germany.* 1905.

L. Pastor: *History of the Popes.* Ed. F. I. Antrobus and R. F. Kerr. 1894-1933.

S. M. Jackson: *Huldreich Zwingli 1484-1531.* 1903.

W. Oechsli: *History of Switzerland, 1499-1914.* Tr. E. and C. Paul.

E. Belfort Bax: *The Peasant War in Germany.* 1899.

E. Belfort Bax: *Rise and Fall of the Anabaptists.* 1903.

New Cambridge Modern History, Vol. II. 1958.

CHAPTER XLIV

ENGLAND'S BREACH WITH ROME

Henry VIII in youth. Humanism and orthodoxy. The temper of England. The social problem. Prestige of the monarchy. Absence of concerted opposition. Thomas Wolsey. The divorce. The Reformation Parliament. Thomas Cromwell. The Dissolution of the Monasteries. The Act of Supremacy. Henry's middle way. Thomas Cranmer. His two services to the Reformation. Edward VI and Mary. Reasons for her unpopularity. The Marian martyrs. The enemies of England.

A LAD of eighteen, tall, ruddy, handsome like Edward IV his grandfather, bursting with animal vigour, and skilled in all manly exercises, Henry VIII seemed in 1509 to be an accomplished specimen of the young Renaissance prince. With a passionate appetite for hunting, gambling, love-making, and jousting there was mingled a taste for the society of the learned and a fancy, not too seriously entertained, for a province in France and the Imperial crown. Soon after his accession he was married to a grave and gentle lady, Catharine of Aragon, six years his senior and the widow of his elder brother Arthur, who had died suddenly at Ludlow after four months of marriage, in his sixteenth year. A dispensation from Pope Julius II (1503) had sanctioned, despite the formal text of Leviticus, this union with the widow of a deceased brother.

Apart from the pleasures of the court and the chase, the young king was noted for two interests, hitherto not greatly observed in English monarchs. He was fond of the sea. He built the royal dockyards at Woolwich and Deptford, founded Trinity House, a school for pilots, supervised with the minutest attention the construction of a royal fleet, and laid the foundations of English naval power. He was the first English king to have a navy in any real sense or to make it fashionable. When the *Princess Mary* was launched in 1519 the whole court attended the ceremony, and Henry, as we learn from the French envoy who was present, "acted as pilot and wore a sailor's coat and trousers made of cloth of gold, and a gold chain with the inscription *Dieu et mon droit*, to which was suspended a whistle, which he blew nearly as loud as a trumpet." In this as in many other matters the young king divined the moods and marched with the spirit of the English people.

His second interest was theology, then becoming, as economics in our age, a basic study for politics. He read and discussed the Thomists. He even wrote a treatise in refutation of Luther, which was published in 1521 and earned him the title of Fidei Defensor from Pope Leo X. And as he advanced in age and egotism his sense of theological security so developed that he seemed to himself on all high matters of theological doctrine to be a sole and sufficient judge, on intimate terms with the purposes of God and His special confidant. His views were papalist, and upon such fundamental subjects as the Mass or the celibacy of the clergy profoundly orthodox. It was as a champion of Pope Julius II against Louis XII of France that he first drew his sword in a foreign quarrel and won that victory of the Spurs and that other more famous victory of Flodden Field, which, though they were of no lasting importance, gave England the name once more of being a formidable power in Europe.

The English people, unlike their monarch and unlike the Scots, were untheological. Few countries had been so little touched by heresy or so widely noted for their devotion to Rome. Lollardy was a recent exception; but Lollardy had, at the time of the accession of Henry VIII, lost its hold upon the universities and country houses, and was now the faith of a scattered handful of obscure and humble men, plying a modest craft in some London alley or burning charcoal among the beech forests in the Chilterns. In the great doctrinal controversies over Predestination or Justification by Faith which rent the continent the manor houses and country houses of England were little interested. In the main the Englishman paid an uninstructed loyalty to the familiar things, and in particular to the Mass and the Roman liturgy. But in the universities, where the servants of the State received their education, and more particularly in the University of Cambridge, a certain doctrinal ferment had been created by contact with Lutherans and their writings. In the early days of Henry VIII such innovating opinions were confined to an elect academic circle.

But if the English people were prevailingly orthodox, they were also very generally anti-clerical. More particularly was this true of the laity in London and the trading cities. The new commercial class had begun to challenge the credentials of the old, wealthy, and domineering Church. The English Ghibellines grudged the privileges and envied the possessions of the priests. They were indignant that the clergy should be immune from the criminal jurisdiction of laymen and that laymen should be subjected to the criminal jurisdiction of the Church. Why, they asked, should a murderer virtually go unpunished if he could recite a verse of the Psalms and so claim benefit of clergy, and what right had a bishop's court to condemn a layman to be burned for heresy without let or hindrance from the secular authority? These and other complaints, which had received some legislative interference in 1512, were passionately ventilated in the Parliament of 1515.

A *cause célèbre*, the mystery of which has never been wholly cleared up, inflamed the controversy to a white heat. Richard Hunne, a wealthy and charitable merchant tailor, was found dead by hanging in the palace of the Bishop of London. Laymen believed that Hunne had refused to pay the mortuary dues exacted by some avaricious priest for the burial of his infant son, that having lost his suit in the ecclesiastical court he had complained to the King's Bench, and that he had for this reason been foully slain by the officials of the bishop. The clergy took another view. While lay London was willing to believe anything evil of the priests, the bishop's court sitting over the corpse decided that the merchant tailor was an unrepentant heretic who had committed *felo-de-se*. His body was accordingly burned and his property declared forfeit to the Crown. The great issue was joined. In the atmosphere of angry recriminations roused by the death of Hunne all the ultimate issues of Church and State were canvassed and discussed. Only a prompt dissolution of Parliament saved an ugly and menacing quarrel.

But if opinion was for the most part lay and anti-clerical, it was not revolutionary. The course of the English Reformation was inflamed by no such widespread social bitterness as that which inspired the Peasants' Revolt in Germany. There were certain things which the English people could not stand. Over-taxation was one, a war with the Netherlands, which would ruin the wool trade, was another. The dangerous disturbance over the "Amicable Loan" in 1523, and the menacing tone of public opinion in 1528 when Henry projected war with Charles V, were the red lights of warning which showed the observant sovereign the limits of his power. But if the pockets of the landowners, the graziers and the cloth-dealers were respected the government had no great cause to fear. There was indeed a grave social problem which is at the bottom of all the popular risings of the century. Land was coming in an increasing degree to be treated from a commercial standpoint. Owing to the steady development of the cloth trade, which was England's premier industry, sheep became more profitable than corn, pasture fifty per cent. more remunerative than arable. The appetites of landowners and land speculators from the town were quickened. Big profits were to be made out of land and they might be made in many ways, by concentrating holdings, by enclosing common lands for arable or pasture, or by turning plough lands into sheep runs. These expedients had been practised in the fifteenth century. They were in no sense novel; but in the sixteenth century they were carried out upon a scale which occasioned widespread distress, alarm, and commentary. What was to happen to the yeoman who was deprived of his holding, to the many ploughmen on a farm who were replaced by a single shepherd, to the poorer commoners whose living was taken from them by enclosure? The problem of a dispossessed rural class, of homes broken up and villages dispeopled, of vagabonds tramping the roads and flocking into the towns, was serious in itself. It was rendered still graver by its association with a course of Church policy which turned every zealous Catholic priest into a potential leader of revolt, which threw the monks upon the labour market, and dislocated the mediaeval machinery by which relief was given to the poor.

It is possible that the evil was more serious in imagination than in fact and that the economic results of the enclosures have been over-estimated by contemporary writers. But that the immemorial tranquillity of English village life was now newly disturbed, and that a new sense of insecurity was very generally created among the rural poor, is beyond question.

As generally happens in periods of economic disturbance, the rich were becoming richer and the poor becoming poorer. The power of the vested interests was sufficiently strong to frustrate the attempts of the government to apply a remedy.

It is remarkable that despite all these materials for discontent, to which may be added a steady rise in the price of the necessaries of life, the Tudor government was never seriously shaken by popular disorders. Without a standing army or a regular police, it was able on each occasion and with no great difficulty (using, however, in 1549, a chance force of foreign mercenaries who happened to be in the country) to master rebellion. For this there were three main reasons. The risings were local and disjointed. The nobles and gentry stood aloof from the poor. Of all the political sentiments of the people, respect for the crown and the dynasty ranked first. The spirit of political obedience was the more deeply implanted in the nation by reason of the freshly remembered dynastic war which had been brought to an end on Bosworth Field.

The Tudor monarchy stood between the country and a renewal of civil strife. The maintenance of peace and order, the enforcement of justice, the repression of aristocratic insolence, the protection of the poor, the encouragement to commerce were its attendant blessings. The dynasty survived the perils of a minority. The attempt to upset the rightful order of succession by calling Lady Jane Grey to the throne was defeated by one of the most instantaneous and spontaneous movements of English history. Though no woman had sat upon the English throne since Matilda, it was sufficient for Mary, as it was for her sister Elizabeth, that they were the children of a Tudor king. To the English people of this age, the exercise of constitutional rights did not present itself as an ideal. Their dominant anxiety was that the Tudor dynasty should rule and endure. So strong was the monarchical sentiment that Shakespeare could write of King John without mention of Magna Carta, and so strong in point of fact was the monarchy that, despite the crimes and cruelties of Henry VIII, it carried the country through this critical period of its annals without the convulsion of religious war.

For a period of fourteen years (1515-29) Henry was content to leave the real government of the country to Thomas Wolsey.

The irony of this extraordinary man's career is that while all his ambitions were bound up with the Papacy, nobody did more to prepare the way for an Erastian state. By himself replacing the Pope in England as *Legatus a Latere* and by gathering up into his hands all the reins of ecclesiastical power, Wolsey superseded the mediaeval constitution of the native Church and taught Henry to be master in his own house. To the end he aspired to be Pope; yet even the Lutherans did not instil into the public mind so great an aversion from the foreign jurisdiction of the Papacy as did this cardinal, who in virtue of the bulls which he obtained from successive pontiffs established for himself a novel and odious form of ecclesiastical tyranny in England.

It has been argued that Wolsey was a great conservative reformer who, but for a fatal accident, would have saved the Catholic Church in England. Some reforms he partially carried out, such as the dissolution of the smaller monasteries, and the application of their endowments to the foundation of colleges in Oxford and Ipswich. Others, notably the establishment of thirteen new sees, he appears to have envisaged.

But it may be permitted to doubt whether a man who embodied in his own person almost every abuse which may be charged against the Catholic Church in the sixteenth century, who was a pluralist on a vast scale, who was loose in his private morals and notoriously neglectful of pastoral duty, had in him the heart of a reformer. Power, not reform, was the master passion in the breast of this son of the grazier of Ipswich, who combined in his own person the functions of Lord Chancellor, Archbishop of York, Bishop in succession of Bath and Wells, Durham and Winchester, Abbot of St. Albans, *Legatus a Latere*, and, in addition, farmed three bishoprics for non-resident aliens. But that such a man should have initiated reform was an omen of future changes.

He was the last of the great ecclesiastical statesmen to govern England. After Wolsey the laymen began to come into their own. But during his fourteen years of power he was, by permission of the king, autocrat of England, unchecked by colleagues, by Parliaments, or by Convocations. In the Star Chamber he bridled the nobles. As Chancellor he curbed the ecclesiastical courts. Presiding over the Court of Requests, he brought cheap legal remedies within reach of the poor.

The king was content to delegate the hard work of government to a servant who was so able, industrious and submissive to himself.

As a prince of the Church he was not insular but European. It was from Rome that his ecclesiastical powers were derived; it was upon Rome that his supreme ambition was fixed. The fate of the Pope could not be indifferent to him. Alike as an English statesman and as a Roman cardinal, he was determined that the French should not enslave the Pope. If England's old enemy were once rooted in the *castello* of Milan, there would in time be a French Pope, a French College of Cardinals, a French orientation of papal policy— a second Avignonese captivity no less grievous than the first— and the Papacy would be as far from his reach as the moon in heaven.

So it was resolved that England should take a full, showy, and commanding part in the great European duel between Charles and France, extracting profit from each rival, but when it came to serious business siding with the Emperor against the French king. The name of the great English king should reverberate through Europe. The foreigners should realize that the island government was a force to be reckoned with, conciliated, bribed. Wolsey spared no pains to advertise the splendour and power of his master. An immense expenditure of money and labour was put into the great international game. It may be asked to what public advantage. The two continental powers were already well balanced, and the idea that England, which could not keep an army on the continent for more than three months together, could seriously affect the European balance, or disrupt the compact monarchy of France, was chimerical. Moreover, events were destined to prove that the real danger to papal freedom came not from France but from Spain. After the capture of Francis at Pavia came the sack of Rome, and two years after that (1529) the Treaty of Barcelona, which bound Clement hand and foot to Charles. And meanwhile two papal elections had been held and, despite the Emperor's express promise, Wolsey was not Pope. By 1529 the diplomatic education of the cardinal was complete. The wool-dealers would not allow him, for he had tried, to defy the Emperor, and the Emperor was master of papal policy. As a prelate aspiring to fill the Holy See he had backed the wrong horse. As an English Prime Minister concerned for trade he could have backed no other. But there was no compelling reason why he should have backed either. When the great cardinal fell, his shrewder master turned away from the continent and addressed himself to the more immediate and feasible task of extending his authority through the British Isles. Only in Wales was he completely successful. Meanwhile, out of that Spanish triumph in Italy, which was sealed at Barcelona, came the fall of Wolsey and the foundation of the Anglican Church.

Catharine had given Henry a daughter, who was christened Mary, but no son. Again and again she had borne children, but either they were stillborn or they died soon after birth, so that the king, who was passionately desirous for a lawful male heir, on good political grounds began to conceive that there must be some curse upon his marriage. Perhaps the dispensation of Julius II was technically invalid? Perhaps the Pope had no power to dispense in such a matter? The more the king reflected, the more he was persuaded that he was a bachelor, a Christian and ill-used bachelor, and that the familiar papal machinery should be put into operation to admit of the setting aside of Catharine. He had no doubt that the thing could be done. Indeed, it had been twice recently done within the circle of his own family. His brother-in-law Suffolk had repudiated a wife, his sister Margaret had repudiated a husband, and both had married again under a dispensation from the compliant Clement VII. He was the more anxious after 1527 that the Pope should grant him this favour, having fallen in love with Anne Boleyn, and being determined, since such was her will, to make this young and wayward beauty his lawful wife.*

Spain was the obstacle. If the Pope had not been a weak Italian prince overshadowed by Spain, the marriage of Catharine might safely have been annulled. But Clement was helpless. Though Wolsey warned him that the whole Roman obedience of England was at stake, he could not affront the man whose troops had desecrated the shrines of St. Peter and stabled their horses in the Vatican palace. Under the contending pressure of King and Emperor, the wretched Pontiff turned this way and that, spinning out delays, suggesting expedients (even bigamy), but at last consenting to the establishment of a Legatine Court in London under Cardinals

---

* As early as 1514 Henry desired to repudiate Catharine.

Wolsey and Campeggio, from which it appeared that a final decision might at last be obtained. Here Henry and Catharine appeared and pleaded. Here the vulgar but not unjust or inhuman populace of London was permitted to witness part of the great tragic drama which caught the imagination of Shakespeare. But nothing which was felt or pleaded in London mattered: not even the ardent popular feeling for the injured queen, nor the vehement hatred for the young woman who was destined to supplant her. Spain was all-powerful in Italy, and suddenly, under Spanish pressure, the king's case was revoked to Rome.

What followed is very significant. With a great flash of political insight, Henry summoned Parliament to assist him in his conflict with the papal see. Having managed to rule England without Parliaments (save for one brief exception) for fourteen years, he now called Lords and Commons to Westminster, kept them sitting for seven years and passed through Parliament the statutes which were required to secure the independence of the English Church from Rome and its subjection to the Crown. It has often been said that the House of Commons of 1529 was packed; but there is no evidence that this was so. Henry might safely reckon that an assembly of English squires and burgesses would not be unwilling to help him break the financial and legal ties which bound England to a foreign spiritual power. Had he asked them to renounce the Mass they would not have been so compliant. Had he been a Lutheran, as Anne Boleyn was commonly reported to be, his difficulties would have been insuperable. But in dogma he was a pillar of the old church, and Henry's orthodoxy was just as important as the revolutionary audacity with which in the sphere of constitutional relations he challenged Pope and Emperor to do their worst. The Protestant Reformation in England succeeded because it was carried through by stages and because the first or constitutional change was represented as being a reversion to the good old (mythical) times when kings were really masters of the English Church. Herein, too, Henry showed his shrewd sense, for nothing commends a radical change to an Englishman more effectually than the belief that it is really conservative.

The place left vacant by Wolsey's fall was in part filled by a layman who had been trained in the cardinal's service and had there learnt that the way to the king's favour was despatch, assiduity, and subservience. Thomas Cromwell looked at the world with the eye of a hard-headed adventurer who had campaigned in Italy and read *The Prince* of Machiavelli. He felt that the trend of events was making towards the secularization of politics. No man, prominent in England at that time, was less clerical or more remote from those appeals of sentiment and history, doctrine and piety which stir the hearts of religious men. He undertook the task of dispossessing the priests and uprooting the monks in the spirit in which an unemotional, unscrupulous solicitor handles a hard and intricate matter of business for a shady but important client.

Next to the management of the Reformation Parliament Cromwell's great task was the dissolution of the monasteries. He had promised the king that he would make him the richest sovereign in Europe, and though many religious houses were gravely burdened with debt, there was still a noble harvest ready for the reaper. There were other reasons for including an assault upon the religious houses in the strategy of an anti-papal campaign. The monks and nuns constituted the papal garrison. They were for the most part exempt from episcopal supervision. They were subject to a foreign superior. So long as they were tolerated it might be expected that every abbey or nunnery in the land would be a seminary of Catholic ardour and propaganda. Moreover, there was no better means of associating the propertied classes of the country with the great religious change than by a lavish distribution among them of the broad acres of the monasteries. We cannot say whether such a distribution was part of a preconceived plan. Neighbourly appetite made it inevitable. The wealth of the monasteries was no sooner garnered for the State than it was lavished upon the fortune-hunting squires and nobles of the country. Henceforth the strongest class in England had a vested interest in the Protestant Reformation. It was, designedly or undesignedly, the master-stroke of Henry's anti-papal campaign.

An air of spurious respectability was thrown over what would otherwise have appeared a naked act of spoliation by the evidence of immorality reported by Cromwell's Commissioners.

Immorality was, indeed, prevalent, as we know from less suspect sources; but the real grievance against the monastic institution was not vice which was perennial, but uselessness which was new. The abbeys had outlived their function. They had ceased to learn, to teach, to record, to illumine. Inspiration and initiative appear to have deserted them. At best they could pretend to an innocent and meditative repose. At worst they were the repair of the ne'er-do-well and the criminal. If their wealth had been applied to education, the general intellectual and moral tone of the country would have been greatly raised, but the Reformation would have been less secure, the Cecils, the Russells, and the Cavendishes would not have entered upon their princely fortunes, nor Thomas Cromwell have gone to the scaffold a millionaire.

These immense changes, which were felt in every village, were carried through with a ruthless expedition. An English government has never been more determined as to its course or more tyrannical in its methods. At the very opening of the Seven Years' Parliament clergy and laity were cowed by learning that having connived at Wolsey's legatine Commission they had exposed themselves to the dire penalties of Praemunire. The Act of Supremacy of 1534, which made the king supreme head of the Church, and more than the Annates Act or the Appeals Act or any other act of the Reformation Parliament embodied the central principle of the controversy, was taken as a test. To swear to it, as the king required, was to abjure the Pope. To refuse was death by the executioner's axe. Sir Thomas More and Bishop Fisher, the two greatest figures in that last age of Catholic England, went to the block rather than swear that oath; but their example was not followed. The terror, the admiration, and the loyalty inspired by the tremendous figure of the passionate king carried all before it.

Even D'Arcy, the leader of the Pilgrimage of Grace, the great northern revolt arising out of the dissolution of the monasteries, avowed that he would never have dreamt of drawing sword against the king. Nothing seemed to affect Henry's popularity, neither the repudiation of Catharine, nor the execution of Anne Boleyn, nor the death upon the scaffold of the best prelate and the most gifted humanist of the age.

The English Church was severed from Rome, the royal supremacy was affirmed, but there still remained the unsettled problem of the doctrine and the ritual. In the general fermentation of spirit which then prevailed these high and difficult matters might, but for one extraordinary circumstance, have led to a protracted period of confusion and chaos. That circumstance was the king. Henry was firmly resolved and to his own satisfaction adequately equipped to step into the place of the Pope and to prescribe to his people, under the most terrible penalties which an obedient Parliament could contrive, what they should and should not believe. It was the king who drew up in 1536 the first doctrinal formulary of the Church of England (Articles devised by the King's Highness to establish Christian quietness). It is owing to the king's influence that, despite Thomas Cromwell's desire for a religious and political union with the Protestant powers of Germany, England never accepted the Augsburg Confession nor was allowed to drift into the general orbit of German theology. It is to the king that we must ascribe the special colour and deliberate pace of the Protestant movement in its early stages. The royal theologian was neither cosmopolitan, nor philosopher, nor idealist. He was resolved that the theology of the Church should be English, not German, and framed not by Philip Melanchthon, but by himself. Men of a finer temper in quest of a theology might have asked themselves what was true, or primitive, or best suited to advance the higher needs of man. Henry sought the settlement which at the moment appeared to divide his people least. In 1536 he advanced towards Reform. In 1539, warned by the Pilgrimage of Grace, he stepped sharply backward and enacted the Six Articles. At the end of his life, under the influence perhaps of Catharine Parr, he moved forward again. A general revision of service books was ordered and the Litany sanctioned in 1545. The "Great Bible," largely based upon the melodious translation of William Tyndale, was already by royal order placed in the churches and made accessible to all. To the end of his days, pursuing the *via media* which is dear to statesmen, he burned Lutherans for heresy and hanged Catholics for treason.

In the last fourteen years of his reign he was assisted by a man who has printed an enduring mark on the English Reformation. Thomas Cranmer was a Cambridge divine, married to a German wife, and already far advanced in his hostility to Rome when he rendered to Henry those services in connection with the divorce which laid the foundation of his future eminence and peril. In quiet times this refined and learned theologian would have passed a blameless and honourable career. His morals were pure, his religious feeling was deep and tender, and he was animated by a sincere desire to restore the Church to its pristine beauty. But he had no courage. In the sordid business of annulling a marriage the king could always rely upon the timid compliance of the Archbishop of Canterbury.

But despite this grave weakness Cranmer conferred upon the English Church two immortal services. He is the main author of the Anglican Prayer-book, to which he contributed the Litany and the Collects. A Catholic writer, who loves good English better than he loves Thomas Cranmer, thus eloquently acknowledges the quality which has given to the Prayer-book an enduring appeal: "Through the Litany, which is from his hand, through the Collects, through the Prefaces, through the admirable music of the special prayers, mainly due to his invention, he gave a strength to the newly established religion which it could never have drawn from any other source. He provided a substitute for the noble Latin on which the soul of Europe had been formed for more than a thousand years, and he gave to the Church of England a treasure, by the aesthetic effect of which more than by anything else, her spirit has remained alive, and she has attached herself to the hearts of men."[1]

His second service was the manner of his end. After a life of time-serving Cranmer died a hero and a martyr. He had been compelled by the order of Queen Mary to sign six recantations, and he knew that his recantations were published. As he went to the stake he threw them into the fire, reaffirmed his beliefs, and "finally stretching forth his arm and right hand, he said, 'This which hath sinned, having signed the writing, must be the first to suffer punishment'; and thus did he place it in the fire and burned it himself."

The interval which elapses between the death of Henry VIII and the martyrdom of Cranmer is marked by a continuation, though in a more violent form, of those oscillations of Protestant and Catholic influence which had been kept within limits by Henry's masterful will. During the reign of Edward VI the reformers gained control of the government, advancing by cautious stages under the enlightened rule of

[1] Hilaire Belloc, *Thomas Cranmer.*

the Protector Somerset, but at a swifter and more angerous pace under his successor Northumberland. But then ensued a sharp reaction. In 1553 the boy king died. Under his father's will the next heir to the throne was the Princess Mary, a woman of thirty-seven years, well set and well proven in her loyalty to the Roman faith. The accession of so staunch a Catholic was received by the extreme reforming party with eyes of dismay. They foresaw the undoing of all their work. The English liturgy would go, the Bible would go, the English Church would be reconciled to Rome, the Protestant bishops would lose their sees, the whole reforming connection would be exposed to grave personal risks. To avert these evils and also to secure his continued power Northumberland determined to alter the succession. His plot failed. The people of England preferred Mary Tudor to Lady Jane Grey, the granddaughter of that other Mary who was sister to Henry VIII and married to the Duke of Suffolk. And then what was anticipated happened. The old worship was restored, the Church was solemnly reunited to Rome, and, save for the fact that not even a Marian Parliament ventured to disturb the great vested interests created by the dispersal of monastic wealth, the work of the Reformation was formally demolished.

But though Parliament-men were very generally indifferent about religion, voting one way under Edward and the reverse way under Mary, there were in England two deep sentiments which were either unsatisfied or affronted by the government of this high-principled, unfortunate, and bigoted lady. The first was the sentiment of nationality. Mary by her own desire was married to Philip of Spain. Though the marriage contract was drawn up by Bishop Gardiner with the utmost skill and with the special view of safeguarding English independence, the match was unpopular. The Spanish king was not liked, nor his attendants, nor the thought that England was now an adjunct to a foreign country. There was even a rebellion against the marriage, led by Thomas Wyatt, and frustrated by the courage of the queen herself. And when it was known that the marriage would bring no heir, the thoughts of th people turned to the Princess Elizabeth, who was not th daughter of a Spaniard nor married to a Spaniard, but English or Welsh on both sides, the child of Anne Boleyn and Henry, and the fruit of that marriage which had brought about the disruption of the bond between England and Rome and let loose the great tide of the reforming movement.

The other was the sentiment of humanity. In moments of excitement the English were capable of great savagery, but they could recognize the face of virtue when they saw it. Their sympathies had been enlisted by the misfortunes of Queen Catharine. They were now excited by the still greater tragedy occasioned by the Marian persecutions. The number of Protestants condemned to the stake for their beliefs under Queen Mary did not probably exceed three hundred; but in this number, small as it was in comparison with continental standards, were included the chieftains of the reforming party and the men most eminent for virtue and talent in the country. The fires that kindled round Cranmer and Latimer and Ridley were not soon extinguished. In the Martyrology of John Foxe, in which the lives and deaths of the victims of Marian zeal are vividly recounted, the Protestant world obtained a record, deemed only less sacred than the Bible itself, of the high spirit which animated the fathers of their faith, and of the courage with which, rather than betray their convictions, they faced the fiery torments of the stake. Nothing so greatly served to purify and deepen the Protestant religion in England or to implant in the minds of the common people a horror of Rome as these ill-judged severities, undertaken against the prudent judgment of Charles V, on the initiative of a solitary and miserable woman. The memories of the divorce with all its sordid impurities were washed away in a clarifying stream of heroism and sacrifice.

The independence of England during this unsettled period was by no means secure. It was an open question whether the country would become a satellite of France or of Spain, or whether it would have the force to strike out on a course of its own. The master-key to national security lay in the union of England and Scotland. This truth was realized by Henry VII, who laid the foundations of concord in a royal marriage, realized again by Henry VIII, who planned the marriage of Edward VI with the infant Mary Queen of Scots, and again by the Protector Somerset, whose schemes for Anglo-Scottish union prefigured in many minor details the ultimate settlement. But the obstacles were formidable. The Scottish aristocracy, who controlled the course of policy in the northern kingdom, were as corrupt a body of robbers as any in Europe, and would in smooth weather as lief sell themselves for a pension to London as to Paris. But they could not wholly unlearn the lessons of their national history, the centuries of raiding on the border, the haughty claims of the English kings, the long alliance with France, the traditional devotion to the papal see. Nor was their appetite for an English understanding improved when in the dark days after the defeat of Solway Moss (1542) Henry VIII revived the ancient claims of suzerainty which their ancestors had rejected, or when the same headstrong policy was continued under Protector Somerset, when their country was invaded, when Edinburgh was burnt, when a Scottish army was defeated at Pinkie. The elevated arguments addressed by the Protector to the Scottish people on the advantages of Union were not rendered the more persuasive by these operations. It is little wonder that the French party gained the ascendant. The child Mary, who was affianced to the young Prince Edward in 1543, was married in 1548 to Francis, the heir to the French throne.

This then was the cloud which overhung the political future of England. Scotland and France might eventually be united under the French husband of Mary Queen of Scots. In that event the Spanish alliance might be an essential condition of English security. But Spain was Catholic and the drift of English opinion was towards reform. A Spanish alliance might not always be obtainable, or might be forthcoming only at a price which England would not be prepared to pay. With a Catholic Ireland in the west and a Catholic Scotland in the north, with Spain doubtful and France hostile, a Protestant England would be in a position of dangerous isolation. That was the anxious prospect which led Somerset to press for the spread of reforming opinions among the people in Scotland; and that was the situation, modified only by the advance of the Scottish reformation, that the government of Elizabeth was called on to face.

BOOKS WHICH MAY BE CONSULTED

Histories of England: G. M. Trevelyan, 1926. C. R. L. Fletcher, 1905-23. J. A. Froude, 1856-1870. H. A. L. Fisher, 1906. A. F. Pollard: *Henry VIII.* 1913.

A. F. Pollard *Wolsey.* 1929.

A. F. Pollard:: *A Life of Thomas Cranmer.* 1926.

F. A. Gasquet: *Henry VIII and the English Monasteries.* 1906.

H. Belloc: *Cranmer.* 1931.

G. Cavendish: *Life of Thomas Wolsey.* 1930.

W. Roper: *The Life and Death of Sir Thomas More.* 1822.

Sir Thomas More: *Utopia.*

R. B. Merriman: *Life and Letters of Thomas Cromwell.* 1902.

R. W. Chambers: *The Saga and Myth of Sir Thomas More.* 1926.

J. S. Brewer: *The Reign of Henry VIII.* Ed. J. Gairdner. 1884.

R. W. Dixon: *History of the Church of England.* 1893.

W. Stubbs: *Seventeen Lectures on the Study of Mediaeval and Modern History.* 1900.

F. Seebohm: *The Oxford Reformers of 1498.* 1867.

J. B. Mullinger: *The University of Cambridge from the Earliest Times.* 1873-84.

A. F. Pollard: *English under Protector Somerset.* 1900.

A. F. Leach: *English Schools at the Reformation.* 1896.

J. M. Stone: *History of Mary I, Queen of England.* 1901.

H. Forneron: *Histoire de Philippe II.* 4 vols. 1881-2.

New Cambridge Modern History, Vol. II, 1958.

G. Constant: *The Reformation in England. Tr.* R. E. Scantlebury and E. I. Watkin. 2 vols. 1934.

P. Hughes: *The Reformation in England.* 3 vols. 1950.

G. C. Morris : *Political Thought in England. Tyndale to Hooker.* 1953.

M. M. Knappen: *Tudor Puritanism.* 1939.

R. W. Chambers: *Thomas More.* 1935.

G. R. Elton: *The Tudor Revolution in Government.* 1953.

THE EMPIRE OF CHARLES V

Its significance. Centres of opposition. Main objectives of Imperial policy. Charles popular in Spain. Financial difficulties. The Netherlands. Their financial importance. The Inquisition in the Netherlands. The circumnavigation of the globe. Mexico. Peru, and Greater Spain. Spain's treatment of subject races. Spanish victories in Italy. Clement VII and the sack of Rome. Doria brings Genoa over to the Imperial side. Charles at his zenith, 1530. The Spanish dominion in Italy.

THE Empire of Charles V constituted a political transformation of Europe which in the order of importance does not fall far short of Caesar's conquest of Gaul, or Charlemagne's inclusion of Germany within the realm of the Franks.[1] It was an empire which came to comprise countries so widely different in every particular of temperament and tradition as Spain and the Netherlands, Germany and Naples, the old civilization of the Lombard plain and the newly-conquered realms of Mexico and Peru. It was the occasion of wars, so wide in their scope that they may almost be called Pan-European, and of that direct rivalry between France and Germany for the hegemony of Europe, which ever since, in one form or another, has tormented the repose of statesmen. It gave to Spain, than which no country was more rigid in its conservatism, a passing supremacy in the modern world, which first in France and then in England was viewed as an international peril. It led to the extermination of Italian liberties and by a clear chain of cause and effect to the rejection of papal authority by the insular monarchy of England. To it we may trace the first stage in that gradual severance between the Netherlands (then closely united to Spain) and the German *Reich*, out of which, in due course of time, were developed the Protestant Dutch republic and the Catholic kingdom of Belgium. Equally well we may regard this widespread empire as marking the beginning of modern history

[1] Genealogical Table M.

or as the last grand attempt to recapture for the Roman Church the old mediaeval unity of faith and government. On every front, against the Lutherans in Germany and the Netherlands, against the Turks in Hungary and Tunis and Algiers, and in every quarter of the Mediterranean Charles was the appointed champion of the Catholic Faith, the secular arm of the spiritual power. The Spanish galleon, the Spanish pikeman, the Spanish military governor, the Spanish priest announced the assumption by the newly-soldered Spanish State of a missionary and imperial rôle.

But the heart of Europe was no longer one. France, which might have agreed with Charles the Catholic, was bitterly opposed to Charles the Emperor. Italy perforce (save for the faintest Lutheran sprinkle) accepted the control of a Latin power which might at least serve to shield the Italian coast towns against the Turks. But in the Teuton north the stiff, unintelligible Spaniard was an object of fear and aversion. Here the Lutheran states, supported by German pride and French hatred for the Imperialists, maintained their footing; and here, too, in the Netherlands an opposition was generated against Spanish control so fierce and persistent that among all the reasons which have been assigned for the decline of Spain, the revolt of the Flemings and the Dutch ranks as the foremost.

The head of this vast empire was a man wholly devoid of charm, magnetism, or chivalry. He was no soldier. He had no imagination. He was incapable of original thought on any subject. In appearance and manner he was ungainly, with a protruding Habsburg lip and a stutter in his speech. When, at the age of eighteen, he became a king he could speak French and Flemish, but knew nothing of Spanish, his mother's speech, or of Spain, his mother's land. But he was teachable, courageous, persevering. After the first ebullience of youthful indiscretion was over he grew old rapidly and developed a tough, persistent sagacity which enabled him to surmount difficulties that would have overwhelmed a baser nature. A Fleming by birth and heredity, he ended, having abdicated the throne, in a Spanish monastery. By insensible degrees finding that Spain was the real centre of his power, he became a Spaniard. Yet, however much he might endeavour to do justice to the different parts of his realm. he was never anywhere the complete master, never rich or powerful or . ble

THE EMPIRE OF CHARLES V, 1525

to fuse the incompatible peoples who owned his sway. To the end of the chapter Spain and Flanders, Wittenberg and Rome remained wide as the poles asunder.

As against other Christian sovereigns, his policy was purely defensive. He proposed to keep what he had inherited or considered that he had a right to inherit. But the defence of an empire so new and formidable could not be accomplished without fighting. France was a necessary opponent, a rival over Burgundy, over Navarre (the little Pyrenean state which Charles had in 1516 promised to restore to its old French ruling family, the d'Albrets), over the Imperial election, over Milan. The prospect of a French state in the Lombard plain, or in the gulf of Genoa, intercepting the marine communications between Spain and Germany, was a menace which Charles felt bound to resist. Milan and Genoa must be imperialists if German *Landsknechts* were to be passed easily into Spain or Spanish pikemen to figure on German battlefields.

To wrest Milan from the French was not in Charles' eye an act of wanton aggression, but the restoration of an essential link in the chain of Imperial defence. The Turk was different. It was a sacred duty imposed on the Emperor by his historic office and by the common voice of Spain to assail the infidel on every front. Castile cared much for Navarre and nothing for Italy, Aragon cared much for Italy but nothing for Navarre. Neither Aragon nor Castile was interested in the Netherlands. But all Spain hated and feared the Turk, and with redoubled vehemence ever since Khaireddin Barbarossa the corsair went into the Turkish service, and from his lair in Algiers began to prey upon the Spanish coast. The Spaniard was schooled by history to the idea of a Crusade. So long as his Emperor was fighting the Lutheran or the Turk he was well content; for other parts of the far-flung imperial policy he showed a fainter concern.

The crown was popular. The revolt of the Comuneros which disturbed northern Spain after Charles first went to the country was so little republican that the chief treasure of the rebels was the person of the mad Queen Joanna. Their grievance was not that a young king had descended upon Spain from Flanders, but that he had come with a cortège of greedy Flemish attendants, had squeezed the country for money, and then had returned to the north leaving Spain to the tender mercies of Adrian, Bishop of Utrecht, an unpalatable Dutch prelate who knew nothing of the country or its speech. Even so, part of the Castilian aristocracy rallied round the king and defeated the rebels on the field of Vilagos (April 23, 1521), so that when Charles returned to Spain in

1522, his renown enhanced by the Imperial title, his orthodoxy proved by the Edict of Worms, with a good train of artillery and 3,000 German *Landsknechts*, he found a people prepared to obey, and, within limits, to vote him supplies. That he refused to shed blood brought him the admiring gratitude of his subjects, who (1522-9) were soon taught that he was prepared to learn their ways and to give them the kind of government which they wanted. Though the temper of Castile permitted of autocracy, Charles was scrupulous to respect the constitutional rights which were so dear to the Aragonese. He was quick also to see and acknowledge the power of the Spanish Church. The Moriscos of Valencia were told that they must accept Christianity or leave the country, an act of intolerant folly in the eyes of a modern economist, but of politic concession to the prevailing prejudice of that age. Welcome also as a defence against possible trouble in the west was his marriage to Isabella of Portugal, and a certain Burgundian magnificence, foreign to the frugal habits of the country but not thought unbecoming in a king who was also an emperor and the foremost sovereign in Europe.

The finance of a world-wide imperial polity presented a problem new to Europe, which Charles could not wholly solve even with the help of the Fuggers and Welsers, the two German banking firms whose loans were indispensable. At the end of his reign, despite the fact that the taxation of Spain had been roughly trebled and little had been spent on the country itself, there was a deficit of some thirteen to twenty million sterling and, what was a specially ominous feature of the Spanish budget, a steady increase in the *juros* or annuities granted out of the State revenues in return for ready money, than which there was no more unsound method of raising an internal loan. Worst of all, the nobles of Castile refused to be taxed (1538), and thereafter were excluded from the Cortes. Thus the difficulty of financing the empire, instead of developing parliamentary liberties in Castile, hastened their extinction. The Cortes, deprived of any representation of the landed interest, became a shadow, a Parliament of thirty-six town members.

Nevertheless the vast disjointed empire was kept together in a loose personal union under the Habsburg house. The provinces of the Netherlands were ruled first (1507-30) by Margaret, Duchess of Savoy, daughter of Maximilian and consequently aunt of Charles V, and afterwards (1531-35) by Mary of Austria, sister of Charles and widow of King Louis of Hungary. But Charles was always in the background. When the populous city of Ghent refused to pay its share of the tax which had been voted by the States of Flanders towards the war with France, and drifted so far into rebellion **1539** as to arrest the imperial officers and even to traffic with Francis I, Charles collected an army and inflicted condign punishment on the rebels. Thirty-two of the leading citizens were put to death, the constitution was abrogated, and the proudest republic of the Netherlands was degraded to the status of a town on the demesne and compelled to support an imperial garrison.

If an empire of any kind was to be kept together it was clearly necessary to resist the pretensions of a city like Ghent to determine whether it should contribute or not to the Imperial wars. But in truth neither Ghent nor any other Flemish or Dutch city was interested in the wide ambitions of the Emperor. They were proud of Charles. They were on a long view benefited by the policy which resulted in the addition of Tournai and Frisia, Utrecht and Overyssel, Gröningen, Deventer, and Gelderland to their loose formation. But what interest had they in Navarre or Milan or in the recovery of the lost duchy of Burgundy? The commerce of the Netherlands cried out for peace. The policy of Charles involved them in continual war. The burghers of the north were compelled to bear the main financial burden of the empire and were entitled to say that they got little in return, save a savage persecution of heretical opinion.

It is this religious persecution which is the chief blot upon the fame of Charles V. That he was himself a Fleming made him the more resolute to cleanse his native land from the taint of heresy. It was a sacred debt to God and country to stamp out unbelief. Finding, on his return from the Diet of Worms, that Lutheran opinions were spreading fast through the Netherlands, he introduced the Inquisition (1522) in the plausible belief that an instrument which had been so successful against the Moriscos in Spain would be equally efficacious against the Dutch and the Flemings. But the courage of the northerners was of the finest and most obdurate. When Henry de Voes and John Esch, the protomartyrs of the Protestant religion, were burned at Antwerp (July 31, 1523) they gave a foretaste of that indomitable spirit which, fifty-eight years later, triumphed in the establishment of the Protestant Dutch Republic. "As they were led to the stake they cried with a loud voice that they were Christians; and when they were fastened to it, and the fire was kindled, they rehearsed the twelve articles of the Creed, and after that the *Te Deum laudamus*, which each of them sang verse by verse alternately until the flames deprived them of voice and life."

It is claimed that some thirty thousand men and women perished for their beliefs in the seventeen provinces during the reign of Charles V. Of these, some were Anabaptists, rebels against the whole order of society as well as declared foes of the Roman Church, but others were Lutherans and Calvinists, whose sole crime was that they would meet together to read the Scriptures in their native tongue and were resolved to worship God after their own fashion. For the Anabaptists no penalties were esteemed too terrible. These poor sectaries, whose revolutionary beliefs were for the most part the fruit of social misery, were drowned, roasted by slow fire, burned alive, or put to other forms of exquisite torture. The scaffold or stake which sufficed for the Lutherans was held to be an inadequate reward for desperadoes who dared to denounce property as well as priesthood. Nevertheless, heresy persisted. The spirit of Lutheranism was too deeply implanted in the land of Thomas à Kempis and of the Brethren of the Common Life to be subdued by persecution, however severe. Persecuted, imprisoned, their conventicles banned, their Bibles burned, their preachers slaughtered, the Protestants of the Netherlands continued to offer a passive resistance to the government. When Charles resigned his throne in Brussels in 1555, his successor found in the northern provinces a people so fiercely settled in their Protestant convictions that with all the might of the Spanish empire he was unable to bring them to account.

In the year in which the Inquisition was introduced into the Netherlands, and while Luther was still hiding in the Wartburg, and it was reasonable for all good Catholics to hope that "the quarrel of monks," as the Lutheran nuisance appeared to be, would yield to a few years of firm government, the *Victoria*, a galleon of eighty-five tons flying the Spanish flag, under John Sebastian del Cano, cast anchor in the

Guadalquivir after an absence of three years. This little ship had circumnavigated the globe. Starting as one of a fleet of five under the general command of Ferdinand Magellan, the *Victoria* had rounded Patagonia, crossed the Pacific, and, after Magellan's death among the Spice Islands, had fought her way across the long wastes of the Indian Ocean to the southern tip of Africa, and so home.

The young Emperor was exalted by this new proof of the manifold favours of Providence to the Habsburg house. Was it not clear that Austria was destined to rule the universe? *Austriae est imperare orbi universo.* The vision of a Catholic Austria governing a Catholic world rose before his eyes. Already Cuba was Spanish and already Hernando Cortes, starting from Cuba, had won Mexico for Spain. With a mere handful of Spaniards, but with the invaluable aid of horses and guns, this resolute and resourceful commander had overpowered the Aztecs, a race of bloodthirsty cannibals who here maintained a curious and mutilated civilization, knowing nothing of coinage, of beasts of burden, of cows or of goats, had kidnapped their king Montezuma and made himself master of their capital city. There have been few clearer examples in history of the power of prestige in war. The Aztecs were as innocent as they were cruel. They found in the Spaniard a source of bewildered amazement. His fierce animal energy, his horses, his guns were things outside the orb of their experience. They were ready to believe the fable industriously circulated by Cortes that the mysterious strangers who had suddenly dropped from nowhere with their uncanny attendant animals were demi-gods whom it was idle to vex or to resist.

The subjugation of Mexico or New Spain was only one among many manifestations of the exploring enterprise of the Spanish conquistador. He was to be met among the swamps of Florida and on the banks of the Mississippi and the Colorado. He founded Panama, entered Nicaragua, drew German financiers after him into Venezuela. But among the many great achievements of these daring pioneers none was so important as Pizarro's conquest of Peru. Here were to be found in abundance the gold, the silver and the precious stones which in the eyes of all materially minded Spaniards constituted the main object of colonial adventure. Here was Eldorado so long sought, so painfully secured; but so compelling in its attractions that it at once became the standard against which all other conquests and colonies were necessarily measured. Compared with the precious metals and jewels of Peru, Argentina, the greatest potential granary in the new world, was a country not worth the exploitation. Indeed if the Plate River which waters that fertile country had the power to tempt the Spanish explorer, it was only because it appeared to be a waterway leading straight to the coveted treasures of New Castile.

Pizarro was an illiterate foundling who like many a poor Spaniard in those days took to the sea for a livelihood, having already tried other avocations. The autumn of 1522 found him in Panama, a needy fortune-hunter greedy for enterprise and lucre. Here he learnt from one Pascual de Andagaya, a Spanish mariner, of a rich land on the Pacific coast of South America inhabited by a people known as Incas. Pizarro was one of those men who are devoured by greed as dipsomaniacs are consumed by thirst. The vision of great wealth easily got and easily handled filled his dreams and shaped his career. Gold was his religion. In search of gold he felt no fear and respected no scruple. He set off at once for the fortunate land with one ship and a hundred men. His expectations ended in failure. Two years later he renewed the attempt (1526) and was rewarded by the sight of well-cultivated fields and of natives wearing jewels and ornaments of gold. His purpose was thenceforth inexorably fixed. When his followers wished to take advantage of a relief ship and to return to Panama he drew a line on the sand with his sword, saying, "Friends and comrades, on that side are toil, hunger, nakedness, the drenching storm, desertion and death, on this side ease and pleasure. There lies Peru with its riches; here Panama with its poverty. Choose each man what best becomes a brave Castilian. For my part I go to the south." With these words he stepped south of the line and was followed by sixteen of his shipmates.

What he then discovered was a state the like of which has never exactly been repeated in any part of the globe. The vast empire of the Incas was remarkable for its application on a great scale of a system of despotic communism. Nobody was allowed to be idle. Nobody was allowed to overwork. Everyone was liable to transplantation, on evidence of overcrowding. The temples and palaces, the roads, aqueducts, canals and tillage of these opulent and ingenious sun-worshippers excited the admiration of the conquistadors. The gold and silver fired their greed. After a careful exploration of this wonderful land Pizarro returned to Spain and there obtained a commission from the Emperor (July 26, 1529), which entrusted him with viceregal powers over the country which he had still to conquer. In treachery and violence no conquistador surpassed Francisco Pizarro. Atahualpa, the unfortunate ruler of the country, was wickedly kidnapped, mulcted of his treasure, and after a mock trial burned to death in the great square of Casamanca (August 29, 1533). It was a sinister feature of this hideous crime that it was carried out with the applause and connivance of the missionary friars.

The conquest of Peru, the last and richest of the great colonial prizes which fell to Spain during the reign of Charles V, was not an unmixed blessing. No community has ever been ethically advantaged by participation in a gold rush. The Spaniards of the sixteenth century, who caught the gold and silver fever before philanthropic ideals had been properly organized and brought to bear upon the problems of industry, were no exceptions to this rule. They quarrelled among themselves and submitted the miserable and helpless natives of the country to a most grinding oppression. Money was mistaken for wealth and the true foundations of economic prosperity were ignored. Demoralized themselves, the treasure-hunters of Peru spread the taint of their merciless avarice through the body politic of Spain.

"Before the abdication of Charles, Mexico and Central America, Venezuela and New Granada, Peru, Bolivia, and Western Chile were organized possessions of the Castilian Crown. Argentina and Paraguay were still in the early stages of settlement, California and Florida in that of discovery." When it is considered that this great extension of Spanish empire and discovery were undertaken at a time when Spain was almost continuously involved in a war with the greatest of European powers, and often with the Turks, the achievement is astonishing.

That hideous oppressions were practised by the Spanish colonists is the dark blot upon this record. But it is due to Europe to point out that the weight of the Emperor was cast on the side of clemency, that when an issue arose, as it often did, between philanthropic missionaries and exploiting colonists, he was on the side of the missionaries, that largely as a consequence of the intervention of the home government the native populations of the American mainland were for the most part preserved from destruction, and that in the list of missionary heroes who have dedicated their lives to the relief of the subject races there is no nobler figure than Las Casas, the first priest to realize and denounce the iniquities practised by his compatriots in the Spanish colonies and the pioneer of all those later humanitarian movements by which men have endeavoured to mitigate the exploitation of the new world by the old.

The Italian wars of Charles V are commemorated by the genius of Titian and Ariosto, but are of less enduring importance for the world than those distant conquests beyond the Atlantic Ocean. Yet to contemporaries few events seemed to be more big with the future than the overthrow of the French military power in Italy. It had been so sudden. It appeared to be so complete, The French were beaten at Bicocca in 1522; they were again defeated at Pavia in 1525 when their king Francis was taken captive and shipped off to Spain. Milan, wrested from the French, was handed over to Francesco Sforza as an Imperial fief, and became thenceforth under the thinnest mantle of disguise a Spanish dependency; and as through Milan Spain held the keys of the north, so through Naples and Sicily she was mistress of the south. To the poetic mind of Ariosto the Italian victories of Charles seemed to portend the world empire which was destined eventually to bring peace to mankind.

Such a demonstration of Spanish power was alarming to all those Italians who for one reason or another were concerned to prevent any one foreign state from obtaining a mastery over the peninsula. In particular it shot tremors of apprehension through the intelligent and well-informed statesmen who ruled in the Vatican. By birth, office and experience (for as Cardinal Giuliano de'Medici he had long been in the forefront of politics), Clement VII might have seemed to be well fitted to lead a great Italian movement against the Imperialists. Unfortunately, with all his skill in negotiation, his quickness and penetration, his subtlety and culture, he was devoid of those moral and intellectual qualites which are essential to leadership. He was one of those men who sweep so many small things into the field of vision that the big things are crowded out. When a clear decision was needed. Clement would hover between competing courses. When it was essential to enlist every Italian prince in a campaign against the Spaniards, he would throw away the aid of a powerful auxiliary by insisting upon the restoration of two paltry towns which the Duke of Ferrara had filched from the papal state. In a situation which required a world outlook and a resolute will this charming and cultivated Tuscan gentleman exhibited the parochial perspective of an Italian princelet and the nervous indecision of a fussy invalid.

Under such a leader no great scheme could come to fruition. Charles was aware of the Pope's intrigues with the Regent of France, with Venice, with Morone the Chancellor of Milan, he was aware of the Holy League of Cognac which was formed against him and of the army of the League which was gathering in Italy, and, being forewarned, saw to it that the imperial troops were so reinforced as to be able to deal with the situation.

The Pope was helpless and isolated in Rome. Even in the Vatican he was not safe from the Colonnas, that fierce Ghibelline clan, who never lost an opportunity of paying off old scores against a Pope. But there was a worse enemy to face than the Colonnas, under whose local and humiliating pressure Clement had been forced to withdraw his contingent from the army of the League. Twelve thousand Lutheran *Landsknechts*, marching without pay and living on the country-side (as was the manner of the Imperial forces), descended into Italy to chastise the Pope who had dared to affront their Imperial master. "The Pope," said George von Frundsberg, their leader, "is the Emperor's worst enemy and has begun the war. For the honour of God he must be hanged, though I have to do it with my own hand." In such a mood the formidable army of hungry Germans, joining hands with the imperial forces under the Constable of Bourbon, moved southward without molestation upon Rome. What then happened, though it was wholly undesigned, and in no sense the result of instructions from Spain, was a startling lesson to the priests of the danger of running counter to the Emperor's will. On the night of May 6, 1527, forty thousand wild and mutinous men, as fierce a body of troops as any in Europe, were collected outside the walls of the papal city. They forced an entry, drove the Pope into the Castle of St. Angelo and then for eight terrible days gave full vent to their cruelty, rapacity, and lust. All the churches and the monasteries were sacked. Friars and priests were beheaded; "many old nuns beaten with sticks, many young nuns raped and taken prisoner." The Church of St. Peter and the Holy Palace were turned into stables for horses. Two-thirds of Rome was left in ruins. To some it seemed that this terrible punishment was a divine revelation. "In Rome," says a grave contemporary, "all sins were committed—sodomy, simony, idolatry, hypocrisy, fraud, Surely then what has come to pass has not been by chance but by the Judgment of God." In Florence the lesson to be derived was that the Medici might now be safely expelled and a republic established in their place. To the world it was clear that more than ever before the Imperial yoke was fastened on Italy.

Again, the menace of the Empire had become so great as to provoke a coalition of powers against it. France and England joined with Venice to reduce the Imperial pride and to free the Papacy from the Spanish yoke. A French army under Lautrec recovered most of the Milanese and passed uncontested through Italy to the siege of Naples. The city, closely invested by the French on land and by a Genoese squadron in the harbour, seemed in June, 1528, like to fall. Was all Italy to pass from Spanish into French control? But then followed one of those sudden changes of fortune which are specially liable to affect small armies operating at a distance from their home. In the south the army of Lautrec, decimated by casualties from disease which it was unable to replace and demoralized by the death of its commander, was compelled to abandon the siege of Naples and to capitulate at Aversa. In the north the French went down before a reinforced Imperial army at Landriano. But more important still as affecting the permanent balance of power in the Mediterranean was the defection of Andrea Doria, the great Genoese seaman, from the French to the Imperialists. A sailor of fortune, but also a Genoese patriot, Doria harboured many grudges public and private against the French. It angered him to see a French garrison in his native city. He viewed with disfavour the commerce, growing too rapidly under

French encouragement, of Savona, the neighbour and the rival. In the very middle of the siege of Naples, when his defection would be most injurious to the French and most helpful to their enemies, Doria swung the whole influence of Genoa into the Imperialist cause. The strongest Italian navy in the western Mediterranean was henceforth enlisted on the side of Spain. For Charles the alliance of Genoa brought three decisive advantages. It denied the Italian coast to the French, it opened the gateway between Spain and Germany, and it gave to Italy a keen sense of pride in the Imperial victories. In Ariosto's great epic, Doria is singled out from among the paladins of Charles as the friend who had brought him victory in every war.

Neither in this nor in any other Italian campaign did the Emperor take a personal part. The Spanish victories in the field were won by Spanish captains commanding disciplined Spanish footmen who had been schooled not only to handle the pike but in a skilful use of fire-arms. To Charles, however, belongs the credit of securing the fruits of victory by a wise exercise of diplomatic temperance. After Landriano he broke the hostile coalition by a separate peace with France. He had something to give and much to receive. Under the Treaty which was concluded at Cambrai (August, 1529) the Emperor surrendered his claims to the Burgundian inheritance of his grandmother Mary, while Francis renounced his claims in Italy and his feudal rights in Flanders and Artois. Eleanor the sister of Charles was married to Francis.

The Emperor was at the zenith of his power. He was master of Italy. He had made a family compact with Clement VII, by whom he was crowned at Bologna with the iron crown of Lombardy and the golden crown of the Empire. Ferdinand his brother would succeed him as emperor, Philip his son as King of Spain. And he had now received what was the prime condition for any successful operations against the Turks, a peace with France. When in 1535 he led an army to Africa and took Tunis, he shone out before Europe, despite the evil memory of the sack of Rome, as the champion of the Christian Faith.

He had not finally settled his account with Francis I. That accomplished but worthless monarch, who carried statesmanship to such a point of cynicism that he encouraged heretics abroad while he persecuted them at home and even offered the shelter of Toulon harbour to the Turkish corsair Barbarossa, had not yet, despite all that was written in the Treaty of Cambrai, relinquished his dreams of Italian conquest. The marriage of his eldest son Henry to Catharine de'Medici, a kinswoman of the Pope, was a signal that the French claims in Italy were still alive. In effect war broke out over Milan in 1536, was stayed two years later (Treaty of Nice, 1538), was resumed in 1542, and was finally composed so far as Charles and Francis were concerned by the Peace of Crespi in 1544. Nothing important was changed by these two short struggles. Spain still remained mistress of Milan and Naples. France, save for the loss of Boulogne to England, maintained her frontiers. The diplomatic honours rested with Charles, who showed much skill in decoying Francis with hopes of the Milanese succession, and in his last war secured the assistance of England. But what was principally illustrated by this long duel for Italy was the sharp decline in the old conception of the Christian Commonwealth of Europe. Though the infidel was knocking hard at the gates, the army of the Holy Roman Emperor had sacked the churches of Rome, and the most Christian King was the declared friend and ally of the Turk.

The Spanish dominion in Italy, which was finally established in 1539, lasted until the end of the wars of Louis XIV. The brilliant intellectual agitation of the Renaissance was exchanged for a period of profound repose, during which the Jesuits, the Inquisition, and the Index combined to stifle the free movement of the mind and to mould it to the Catholic pattern. Life became more sedate and decorous. Hypocrisy replaced effrontery. The open parade of vice or atheism became dangerous and therefore unfashionable. There was a rally of all the virtuous elements in Italian society towards a reformed Church of Rome. Only among a small circle of Neapolitan intellectuals and in the Republic of Venice, which maintained its independence of Spain and kept the Pope at arm's length, was there any survival of that earlier liberty of thought and speech which had made Italy the preceptress of Europe in the previous age. The nimble-witted Italians laughed at their strong and solemn rulers, shrugged their shoulders, and, being relieved by these useful aliens of the burden of government and war, not unthankfully obeyed.

Among the terms of the family compact made between

Charles and Clement in 1529 was the restoration of the Medici to Florence. The undertaking was carried out in the following year. The city was besieged by a large Imperial army under the command of the Prince of Orange, captured after a brilliant defence, robbed of its republic, and compelled to submit to Alessandro de'Medici, the bastard son of a mulatto slave woman. In the long annals of Europe the downfall of a short-lived Italian Republic may be of little moment; but circumstance gave to the eclipse of republican liberties in Florence a special significance. The city was the capital of Italian genius. The republic, which was the creature of a prophet's enthusiasm, had enlisted the hopes of a series of native historians whose grave pages still burn with classic ardour. Its walls were defended by Michael Angelo, its countryside by a patriotic militia realizing the dream of Machiavelli, and if it had survived it might have taught the Italian people that lesson of military self-help which alone could bring them safety, unity, and self-respect. But the city fell, and it is noteworthy that one of the causes of its surrender was the treachery of an Italian *condottiere* from Perugia, whose assistance had been unwisely invoked.

BOOKS WHICH MAY BE CONSULTED

E. Armstrong: *The Emperor Charles V.* 1902.

F. A. Mignet: *Rivalité de François I et de Charles V.* 2 vols. 1876.

H. C. Lea: *The Moriscos of Spain.* 1901.

Helps: *The Spanish Conquest of America.* 1900-4.

J. S. C. Bridge: *A History of France from the Death of Louis XI.* 1921.

Henri Lemonnier in Lavisse: *Histoire de France*, Vol. V, i; V, ii.

R. B. Merriman: *The Rise of the Spanish Empire*, 1918-25.

R. Altamira y Crevea: *Historia d'España y de la civilizacion española.* 1902.

J. Fiske: *The Discovery of America.* 1892.

W. H. Prescott: *History of the Conquest of Mexico.* Everyman's Library. 2 vols. 1929.

W. H. Prescott: *History of the Conquest of Peru.* Everyman's Library. 1908.

H. M. Stephens: *Portugal.* 1891.

Janet Trevelyan: *A Short History of the Italian People.* 1929.

New Cambridge Modern History, Vol. II. 1958.

K. Brandi: *The Emperor Charles V.* Tr. C. V. Wedgwood. 1939.
J. H. Parry: *The Spanish History of Empire in the 16th Century.* 1940.
F. A. Kirkpatrick: *The Spanish Conquistadores.* 2nd Ed. 1946.

CHAPTER XLVI

CALVINISM

*The clarion of reform. The Evangel in Zürich. The field of
Cappel. Geneva. John Calvin. His stoicism and belief in
predestination. Founds a theocratic state. The democratic
character of Calvinism. Geneva becomes the training ground
for the reformed ministry. Far-reaching influence of Calvinism.*

THE influence of Luther upon mankind was not restricted to
that German and Scandinavian area which was permanently
won for the Lutheran Church, but penetrated everywhere.
His bold challenge rang through Europe. Was it true that
the world had been treading a false road for more than a
thousand years, that the Papacy was an imposture, the special
sanctity of the priesthood a fiction, and that rites, ceremonies,
and institutions interwoven with the familiar life of Europe
were unnecessary and even harmful? Only the dullest indifference could fail to be startled by such a message. Opinions
might differ as to its value. Some might think it very good,
others very wicked. But no one could deny that it was
exciting. Poles, Czechs, and Magyars caught at it in snatches.
Spanish merchants carried it in little printed quartos over
upland roads to be rendered into Castilian prose. Cambridge
divines discussed it over their tankards; Oxford booksellers
sold it across the counter. In Paris it was hawked about under
the noses of the doctors of the Sorbonne. If Erasmus more
than any other man aroused the great curiosity, it was Luther
who initiated the great revolt. In Switzerland and France,
Scotland and England, countries in which reform assumed a
shape differing from the Lutheran model, it was he who
sowed the seed and prepared the ground.

Ulrich Zwingli went too fast. He tried by means of a trade
embargo to compel the five Catholic cantons of eastern
Switzerland to admit the evangelical teaching which found

favour in Zürich and Bern, and paid for his temerity on the bloodstained field of Cappel (October 11, 1531). With his soldier's death Zürich lost its pre-eminence in the Swiss reforming movement. In the eastern part of Switzerland which was mainly German in race and language the old religion recovered its ascendancy. The results of that short six weeks' war have never been reversed. What was Catholic at the close of that struggle is Catholic now. The dream of Zwingli that the evangelic faith might spread through the whole Confederation, that democracy might everywhere replace oligarchy, and that Bern and Zürich might acquire that weight in the affairs of the Confederation which their numbers demanded, was dissolved. The most gifted and attractive of the reformers, though in private morals far from flawless, failed from an impetuous under-estimate of the ardent peasant champions of the Virgin and the Saints, whose log cabins were strewn high among the Alpine pastures and forests and far removed from the heresies of town-bred men.

The direction of the Swiss reforming movement passed to Bern and then to a city lying outside the Swiss Confederation and containing no more than thirteen thousand inhabitants, but destined, partly through its geographical position—for it was placed on the confines of four nations—and still more through its association with one of the great religious leaders of the world, to become the capital of western Protestantism and for centuries a chief city of refuge for the persecuted minorities of that faith: it passed to Geneva.

For thirty years Geneva had been struggling to rid itself of the control of the Duke of Savoy and of its Prince Bishop. The struggle partook of the bitterness of a civil war. The Episcopal party were styled by their adversaries the Mamelukes. The party of liberty were known as the Eidgenossen (sworn companions), a name which, in its French form of Hugenot, was soon destined to be heard throughout Europe. But in the end (October, 1536), with the help of Protestant Bern, Geneva achieved its liberty and was prepared to give heed to certain French missionaries who with Bernese encouragement were spreading evangelical teaching through the Pays de Vaud. Of these none was so effective as the vehement William Farel, at whose instance a young French scholar travelling through Geneva on his private occasions

in 1536 was prevailed on to stop and permanently to exchange
a life of study for one of active ministration.

The young scholar was John Cauvin (Calvin), the son of a
notary public, born at Noyon in Picardy in 1509, and already
famous, though he was only twenty-seven years of age, for
three remarkable publications—a learned commentary on
Seneca's *De Clementia*, an academic discourse, so full of
evangelical enthusiasm as to necessitate his hurried departure
from Paris, and an introduction to Biblical study entitled
Christianae Religionis Institutio, which was published at Basel
and dedicated to King Francis I.

Nobody could less resemble Martin Luther than this
studious and polite young Frenchman, of the upper middle
class, and never more at his ease than among men and women
of noble birth, who had absorbed whatever Paris could give
him of the humanities or Orleans and Bourges of law. Of
Luther's vast animal power, of his gaiety and wit, his coarseness and humour, his wild vein of romance and crabbed
scholasticism, his naïve peasant superstitions and morbid
self-criticism there was nothing in Calvin. The Frenchman
was quiet and reserved, lucid in thought and expression,
always superior by reason of his ready store of patristic and
Biblical learning to those with whom he was brought into
controversy, and possessing the great advantage which comes
to a man who has won his way to settled convictions with no
visible scars of an inner conflict. A stern simplicity in the
processes·of his thought gave him a searching power over lax
and uncertain minds. We may call him an intellectual athlete,
or a saint without sentimentality, or simply a born director
of the conscience. His work was to make of Geneva an
evangelical republic and to lead the reforming or Huguenot
party in France.

In accounting for his influence in France, Renan says that
Calvin succeeded in an age and in a country which called for
a reaction towards Christianity simply because he was the
most Christian man of his generation. This is largely true,
but not the whole truth. Calvin was a Christian. His private
life was simple and austere; his passions controlled, his ends
lofty. All his physical and intellectual powers were employed
in the endeavour to bring back into the world the Christianity
of the first three centuries, of which in his quiet, ardent,
intellectual way he had constructed a convincing image. His

correspondence was enormous. From his adopted home in Geneva he dispensed spiritual counsel to all the Huguenot congregations of France. Now he would strengthen the doubter, now prick on the slothful, now encourage the down-hearted or rebuke the backslider. But neither his Christian piety nor the unflagging energy of his pen would have made him a power in France had it not been for the fact that he possessed in a very high degree the logical structure, the clarity and grace of phrase, the conciseness of statement and sense of measure which alone give to a French intellectual the ear of France.

"Your Serenity," writes the Venetian Ambassador to the Doge in 1561, "will hardly believe the influence and the power which the principal minister of Geneva, by name Calvin, a Frenchman and a native of Picardy, possesses in this kingdom. He is a man of extraordinary authority, who by his mode of life, his doctrines, and his writing rises superior to all the rest." And the influence of Calvin the man was supported by the singular prestige attaching to Geneva, a city in which the magistrates were chosen by the people, the ministers by their flock, in which there was no privileged church or aristocracy, but all were equal before the law as they were equal in the eye of God.

The editor of Seneca was, like his master, a stoic, believing that virtue should be practised for its own sake and without regard to future rewards and punishments. That stoical ideal, transformed by the teaching of the Gospels, lies at the heart of the Calvinist religion. Nor has its moral influence been weakened by that other doctrine of predestination, that some are pre-ordained to eternal life and others to eternal damnation, which Calvin could not have found in the Gospels, but deduced from the teaching of Paul and Augustine.

Indeed, among the European peoples none have been sterner in the practice of religion or more ruthless in the pursuit of wealth than the professors of a doctrine which seems to make all human effort unavailing and to invite to a life of apathy and ease.

Save for a period of three years (1538-41), Calvin lived in Geneva from 1536 to his death in 1564. Here he framed a new type of theocratic state which exercised an influence over the spirit and structure of the "reformed" churches through-out the world. The key to his organization was the discovery that during the first three centuries of the Christian era the unworthy were excluded from the Communion table. Calvin determined to revive that ancient discipline, and to confine the supreme privilege of the Church to worshippers of a proved and tested godliness. That such an end could not be achieved without a minute and irksome supervision into private life did not deter him. He welcomed conditions under which pastors and laymen alike would be subjected to a rigorous control, and though it was against his principles to invoke the lay power in aid of spiritual discipline, he was content that in Geneva the strong arm of the magistrate should assist the Church. What sacrifice was not justified to bring godliness back to earth? So a supreme Council, part lay, part clerical, was set up in Geneva to enforce a code of penalties on laxities of private conduct and belief. Adultery, blasphemy, and heresy were punished by death. It was a sombre, fault-finding, inquisitorial government which, being taken as a pattern in other lands, was a source of much cruelty and suffering in the New World as well as in the Old. In Geneva itself it led to the burning of Servetus, the Unitarian, with the concurrence and approval of Calvin himself.

Against this undoubted evil must be set the value to Europe of a new type of religious society, which, unlike the Lutheran Church, was independent of princely favour. Under the democratic system set up by Calvin each church was governed by an elective body of lay elders and deacons. Two important results followed. The first was the close association between Calvinism and a universal theological education, the second that Calvinism, unlike the Lutheran Church, never dried up when the original creative impulse was exhausted. How vital this creed still is, and how closely connected with a popular training in the Bible, may be realized by the visitor who enters any Welsh Sunday school today.

It was part of Calvin's greatness that he was not only the central figure in a wide European movement, but that, working intensively within the narrow circumference of Geneva, and against every description of obstruction, he made of it the high school of the reformed religion. During his long course of Biblical teaching he boasted in a valedictory letter addressed to the ministers of Geneva that he had never perverted a text of Scripture; and it is due to his exertions that Geneva became not only a well-educated city, but in a more specific sense, and particularly after the formation of the University in 1559, a training-ground for the Protestant or Huguenot ministry. Calvin found Geneva turbulent, divided, uneasy, immoral. He left it a Protestant Sparta, the soul of all that was valiant, devoted, and, it may be added, fiercely intolerant, in the evangelical movement of that age.

Of all the forms assumed by the Protestant Reformation, Calvinism has been the most far-reaching in its scope and the most profound in its influence. It made the Protestant Church in France, it fashioned the Dutch Republic, it was accepted as the national religion of Scotland. Before Calvin's death his creed had been received in the Protestant cantons of eastern Switzerland, in the Palatinate, and by the majority of those Hungarians who had broken with Rome. Even in England, where it was confronted with an overwhelming body of conservative sentiment, it exercised an influence over the Thirty-Nine Articles, which constitute the declared creed of the National Church, so palpable that Queen Elizabeth, little as she sympathized with the spirit of Geneva, was excommunicated as a Calvinist. Afterwards, but only for a time under the Long Parliament, and through force of arms rather than a change in national sentiment, Calvinism became a predominant force in English politics. With the Restoration it receded into the background, a minor but never a negligible element in the religious consciousness of the country. But if Geneva agreed ill with the merry court of Charles II, it was just the thing for the north American littoral. Here ever since the voyage of the *Mayflower* in 1621, and more particularly in the New England colonies, it has exercised a profound influence on church and state, reaching into the middle decades of the nineteenth century. From its harsh and gloomy teaching the reasoned optimism of the pragmatist, who exalts positive achievement, and the extreme idealism of the Christian Scientist, who negates the reality of pain and evil, are varying and characteristic reactions.

BOOKS WHICH MAY BE CONSULTED

Mark Pattison: *Collected Essays.* *Ed.* H. Nettleship. 1889.
T. H. Dyer: *The Life of John Calvin.* 1850.
H. F. Henderson: *Calvin in his Letters.* 1909.

A. Bossert: *Calvin (Grands Écrivains Français)*.

Ch. Borgeaud: *The Rise of Modern Democracy in Old and New England*. *Tr*. Mrs. Birkbeck Hill. 1894.

Ch. Borgeaud: *Histoire de l'Université de Genève*. I, l'Académie de Calvin, 1559-1798. 1900.

L. Häusser: *The Period of the Reformation*. *Tr*. Mrs. G. Sturge. *Ed*. W. Oncken. 2 vols. 1873.

New Cambridge Modern History, Vol. II. 1958.

CHAPTER XLVII

GERMANY AGREES TO DIFFER

Balance of Catholic and Protestant forces in Germany. The first serious set-back to the Lutheran movement. Philip of Hesse. Charles V attacks the Lutherans. The inconclusive character of the war. France invoked by the Lutherans. The Peace of Augsburg, 1555. The Treaty of Cateau Cambrésis, 1559. France loses Italy but gains Metz, Toul, and Verdun. The new figures on the stage.

IF the Lutherans could not be peaceably recalled to the Catholic faith, could they be suppressed by force? In 1540 the big battalions were with the Catholic powers. The Lutheran religion was professed by a number of small German states, by Saxony, both electoral and ducal, by Hesse and Brunswick, by Brandenburg (since 1539) and Prussia and by a number of important cities in north and south. These Protestants, as they were called in virtue of a protest against Catholic claims drawn up in 1531, were organized, could put an army in the field, and had even won a military triumph against the Habsburg house by restoring to Würtemberg its banished Lutheran duke. But compared with the might of the Catholic states, had these been united or able to mobilize their resources, compared with Spain and France, Italy, Austria, and the Netherlands, not to speak of the Catholic half of Germany, the military and financial resources of the Smalkaldic League were inconsiderable. Against an army even approximately representing the potential resources of Catholic Europe, any force which the German Protestants could have put into the field would have been inevitably destroyed. These conditions were never realized. Neither then nor at any other time has religion been an exclusive motive in European politics. Other motives, other elements have always been present. Charles was a sincere Catholic, but even Charles was often at variance with the Pope. Had the Catholic princes in the German Diet been asked to choose whether they would prefer a Germany united in the Catholic creed under a strong emperor or divided under a weak one, they would have chosen the second alternative. There was not a prince, Catholic or Protestant, who would vote for any scheme to mobilize the resources of the Empire easily and effectively for the pursuit of a strong policy whether Catholic or Lutheran. The princes were content that the Holy Roman Empire should continue, because it was ancient, elective, interwoven with their own privileges, so long as the Holy Roman Emperor did not presume to interfere with their internal affairs. So Diets met, and feasted and dissolved with nothing done except to recognize or ineffectually not to recognize the accomplished fact of religious disunion. The knowledge that the League of Smalkalden was organized for resistance and had friends abroad acted as a deterrent against a precipitate recourse to force.

The reformers had also, in all the earlier stages of their movement, the advantages which belong to an energetic body of earnest men carrying out a campaign against generally recognized abuses and for purposes of dialectical dispute better equipped than their opponents. The intellectual and moral attack was strong. The intellectual and moral defence, until the Jesuits came into the field, was weak. The ordinary forces of blind conservatism which might have been organized against the new movement were disarmed by its emphatic repudiation of the peasants and Anabaptists. Thanks to the regulative influence of Luther, who lived to 1546, the German reformers did not create the kind of panic which leads opponents to think that they are confronted with one of those perils to the ultimate decencies of life which at all costs and before everything else must be averted. Of all the forms assumed by continental dissent the Lutheran was the most conservative. Its church services were based on the Roman model. Its doctrine of Consubstantiation was not far distant from the Roman thesis of a change in the elements. Its original professors were not men standing outside the Church, but for the most part monks and priests of exceptional piety, who believed that they could bring the Church to its true and original ways. The line between Catholic and Protestant is now sharply and deeply graven. In the first generation of the reforming movements the outlines were more fluid, and intermediate possibilities more easily entertained. An Arch-bishop of Cologne was drawn towards the new doctrine, and at one time there was even an expectation that all three Rhenish Archbishoprics might go over to the Lutheran camp.

In all religious movements there is a period of danger. It comes when the first passionate enthusiasm begins to die down, and the statesmen are called in to regulate and organize. The princes who succeeded the preachers in the control of the Lutheran movement were in point of morality little, if any better than the average of their age and country. One was apparently worse.

The first serious set-back to the Lutheran movement, the first incident which gave to its opponents a formidable handle of attack, was the divorce of Philip of Hesse in 1540. To those who had been fiercely assailed for their low moral standard, it was gratifying to know that the great Lutheran chieftain was no better than anyone else, that he was pre-pared to reject a lawful wife in order to marry another woman who had captured his fancy, and that in this profligate course he had been encouraged by Lutheran divines like Bucer and Melanchthon, and by the opinion of the great Dr. Martin himself that polygamy had the sanction of Holy Writ. Nor was the scandal lessened by advice of the divines that the second marriage should be concealed. Philip of Hesse had no intention of concealing his second marriage. He was not prepared, as Luther recommended, to tell "a great bold lie for the good of the Christian Church." But the fact that such advice was tendered cooled his enthusiasm for his Lutheran associates, drove him for a time into the Emperor's camp and apvertised a rift in the Protestant ranks.

While the two German parties were watching one another with eyes of anxious hate, Charles made peace with France (September, 1544), and was thereafter free, should conciliation fail, to try the expedient of force against the Lutherans. There were many coherent arguments which might be used in favour of such a course, notably the recent triumphs of the Protestant faith in the Palatinate and in Cologne, and one influential firebrand, his father confessor, to advise it. But the Emperor was no great believer in a religious peace thus violently promoted, and only after long hesitation and with a significant attempt to conceal his true purpose, determined to gather an army, enlist allies, and to strike.

In launching an attack upon John Frederick of Saxony and Philip of Hesse, the two foremost leaders of the Lutheran cause, the Emperor was careful to found his action on considerations of politics only. The princes were to be punished not for heresy but for disobedience. Though the Pope was providing men and money, Charles knew that an open crusade against heresy would have little chance among the Germans. He was himself relying upon heretical aid, and notably upon the military talents of the wicked and aspiring Maurice of Saxony, to whom he had secretly promised John Frederick's electoral hat.

The war which ensued was marked by the inability of the Protestant generals to make use of a great initial advantage, by the paralysing defection of Prince Maurice and by a crowning Imperial victory at Mühlberg on the Elbe (April 24, 1547). But the religious problem was no nearer solution for Charles' military success. The defeat of the Lutheran army, the capture of John Frederick and the unconditional surrender of Philip of Hesse made no alteration in the general balance of the opposing creeds. Nor were the Germans any whit the more disposed to help the Emperor to solve that evil of political anarchy which continued to be the curse of German public life. When Charles proposed a German league with permanent officers, a permanent revenue and a regular army, his suggestions fell stone dead upon the Diet. When he divulged a plan for making the Empire hereditary in the Habsburg house, it was at once rejected by the electors. Apparently the most resplendent figure in Europe, he was in Germany subject to every rebuff and humiliation. The princes distrusted him because he wanted power; the Catholics because he wished to reform abuses; the Lutherans because he believed in the Pope. A well-meant scheme for a religious *modus vivendi* known as the Interim (May 13, 1548) was everywhere denounced and nowhere observed.

Then followed an episode bringing immediate humiliation to Charles, still greater humiliation to Germany and leading through a long and connected chain of events to those two great Franco-German wars which have devastated Europe in the nineteenth and twentieth centuries. The leading actors in the drama were Maurice of Saxony and Henry II, the new King of France. Maurice had in 1546 sold himself to Charles for place and power. He wanted to rob John Frederick of the electorate and to transfer to his own (the Albertine) branch of the Wettin family the possessions which belonged to the Ernestine line. He wanted other things as well, for he was a highly appetitive adventurer, and some of these, though in the main his reward was rich, he had not received. He had won the electoral hat but not Magdeburg. Other grievances, of a less personal nature, may have weighed with him, such as the continued imprisonment of his father-in-law, Philip of Hesse, and the violation by the Emperor of the municipal liberties of certain Protestant towns. Slipping swiftly from disappointment to distrust, from distrust to anger, he began secretly to weave a coalition against the Emperor, and being in search of a powerful ally turned to Henry II of France. There is little favourable to be said of this monarch save that he was brought to see that the true interests of France lay not in Italy but on the Rhine. The proposals of Maurice and his camarilla of Lutheran generals chimed in with this intelligent appreciation of French needs. By the Treaty of Chambord, 1552, it was arranged that Metz, Toul, and Verdun, together with the city of Cambrai, should be handed over to Henry as Vicar-General of the Empire in return for his assistance to the German rebels. The entry of France into Lorraine and Alsace dates from this memorable transaction.

While the French were occupied in seizing their prize, the army of Maurice advancing on Innsbruck caused the Emperor to flee suddenly for his life over the Brenner pass. From that moment Charles exercised no further influence over the fate of Germany.

Accordingly it was not by Charles but by his brother Ferdinand, one of the wisest rulers of the Habsburg house, that religious peace was given to Germany. Charles had worked for comprehension based on compromise. Ferdinand accepted the necessary fact of division. The guiding principle of the Peace of Augsburg (September 25, 1555) was *cujus regio, ejus religio*. The princes, without interference from the Emperor or the Diet, were to be allowed each in his own territory to settle the form and character of the Church. The idea, always cherished by Charles, that the forces of a reunited Germany might be launched against France was now recognized as an idle dream. Catholic would not yield to Lutheran, nor Lutheran to Catholic. On the most difficult question of all, Ferdinand decreed a compromise. Catholic archbishops, bishops, or priests embracing Protestantism should forfeit their sees or benefices; but no spiritual prince should be entitled to impose the Catholic religion by force upon his subjects.

The Peace of Augsburg cannot be reckoned among the great liberating documents of history. It did not even assign a place to those types of Protestant belief which flourished in Zürich or Geneva. Still less did it enunciate the principle of religious toleration. But as a rough, serviceable solution of a grave controversy, it deserves to be honourably thought of, for, if it did not bring religious harmony, it kept war out of Germany for fifty years.

Four years after the religious settlement (April, 1559) there followed that other treaty signed at Cateau Cambrésis which closes the long struggle between France and Spain for hegemony in Italy. Proud and sensitive states do not lightly relinquish high ambitions. It may readily be imagined that it was not without pain and a certain humiliation that France renounced those dreams of Italian power upon which she had lavished blood and treasure for sixty years. But in the last stage of the struggle she had received two serious warnings. A French army led by the Duke of Guise, the most accomplished of her generals, and encouraged by Paul IV, the most ill-balanced of the Popes, had been defeated by the Spaniards in Naples and rolled back towards the Alps; and much nearer home, within a few days' march of Paris, another army composed of the flower of the French nobility and commanded by the Constable of Montmorency, the premier noble of France and the leading adviser of the king, was overwhelmed before the walls of St. Quentin by an Imperial army under Emmanuel Philibert the Duke of Savoy. Not since the days of Agincourt was such destruction wrought upon the chivalry of France. Never were so many distinguished noblemen made captives. The voice of the prisoners of war, among whom Montmorency was included, was raised for peace.

So the French, withdrawing from Piedmont and Savoy, left Italy to the Spaniards. But in the north they had their compensations. No one asked them to return the three bishoprics in Lorraine to which they were now able to add Calais, taken for good or evil in 1558 from the English. Henceforward the continental ambitions of France were drawn towards the Rhine.

The stage was set for new actors. The gallant Charles V had retired from his infinite labours, broken in health and broken in hope, to a Spanish monastery. The treacherous Maurice had fallen in action. Henry VIII, Edward VI, and Mary of England were also dead. Of the great figures of the past, one only, Ferdinand of Austria, now Emperor, was already well proven in war and peace. The new men were Philip, the exact, laborious, and very Catholic son of the retired Emperor, and Emmanuel Philibert of Savoy, the young victor of St. Quentin and the real founder of Turin and of that little sub-Alpine state in the north-west corner of Italy which in the nineteenth century united the Italian peoples under its rule. There was also in England a young woman named Elizabeth, as yet unknown but likely to count in the weights and balances of Europe, and at the Court of France a girl called Mary, daughter of James V of Scotland by Mary of Guise, and perhaps destined to wear upon her head the crowns of Scotland, of England, and of France. As for King Henry of France, he was killed in a tournament, soon after the great treaty was struck, leaving an Italian widow behind him whom the French called Catherine de' Médicis. She, too, was cast for a conspicuous part upon the crowded stage.

BOOKS WHICH MAY BE CONSULTED

B. Zeller: *Histoire d'Allemagne*, Vol V. 1885.

O. Engelhaaf: *Deutsche Geschichte im Zeitalter der Reformation.*

P. Voigt: *Moritz von Sachsen.*

W. Stubbs: *Lectures on European History*, 1519-1648. 1904.

L. Häusser: *The Period of the Reformation.* 1873.

L. von Ranke: *History of the Reformation in Germany.* Tr. S. Austin. 1905.

New Cambridge Modern History, Vol. II. 1958.

G. Barraclough: *Origins of Modern Germany.* 2nd Ed. 1947.

CHAPTER XLVIII

THE COUNTER-REFORMATION

Ignatius Loyola. The Jesuit Order. The Council of Trent. The reforming spirit reaches Rome. Pius IV. Protestant strongholds. Bohemia and the Palatinate. Weakness of the Protestant movement. Occasions of conflict under the Peace of Augsburg. The ineffectiveness of German government. Maximilian II. Disastrous reign of Rudolf II. Jesuit education. Jesuit conquests in Austria and Poland.

ON AUGUST 15, 1534, the year in which Henry VIII broke with Rome, driving Thomas More to shed his blood for the old faith, and Jacques Cartier of St. Malo planted the cross by the gulf of the St. Lawrence, seven obscure students met together in the Church of St. Mary on Montmartre in Paris, and there swore oaths of chastity and poverty, pledging themselves to pass their lives in Jerusalem in the pursuit of those occupations which were regarded as most holy, the care of Christians and the conversion of the Saracens. The leader of the band was a lame Basque in middle life named Inigo Lopez de Recalde, but known to history as Ignatius Loyola. Another was Francisco Xavier. A third was Lainez.

Spain is a land of mystics and monks, of pilgrims and of soldiers. Loyola was a soldier and a visionary. In his sombre, fantastic, indomitable way he represents the religious and crusading genius of his countrymen, just as Luther embodies the old-world Biblical piety of the Saxon peasantry. Fighting in Navarre (1521), he received the wound from which he went lame for life, and thereafter during his slow and agonizing convalescence turned his thoughts to a new form of service, equally heroic, equally romantic, equally sacrificial, and offering to the schooled and dedicated heart opportunities of sublime distinction. He determined to be the soldier of Christ. No mortification of the flesh was too rigorous for this fiery zealot. He abjured his family, lived on bread and water, scourged himself several times a day, and by a rigorous course of prayer and physical repression educated his powers of communion with the Divine. Then, after a voyage to Jerusalem, there occurred to him an experience not often combined with the ecstatic temperament. He became self-convicted of ignorance and hungered for knowledge. In that quest he put himself to school, and eventually in 1528 was brought to Paris, the Queen of Universities. There he studied for seven years, there imposed his domineering will on a body of companions, and there conceived the idea of an enterprise of holy chivalry to be carried out by a company of elect and tested souls.

It was fortunate for the Roman Church that a war between Venice and Turkey frustrated the plan for a missionary life in Palestine to which Loyola and his companions were solemnly committed. In Italy their passion for the advancement of religion found a more practical field. They took vows of obedience, were ordained priests, called themselves the Company of Jesus, and eventually, September 27, 1540, obtained from Pope Paul III the Bull *Regimini Militantis Ecclesiae*, which establishes the constitution of the Jesuit Order.

The significance of Loyola's invention is that he provided the Papacy with a *corps d'élite* scrupulously trained to carry out its behests. The privileges of the Jesuits were large as their responsibilities were strict. They paid no taxes, they acknowledged no princely superior, they were exempt from the jurisdiction of all prelates not of their Order. Their organization was military and autocratic, for they were governed by a general elected for life, who was in all things subject to the Pope. Equally essential were those other characteristics of spiritual self-discipline and respect for education and learning which marked the riper years of Loyola's own life. The novitiate of the Jesuit was severe. The spiritual exercises devised by the founder were calculated to empty the mind of distracting images and to school the will to the dedicated life. But this wise discipline was not intended to be employed upon the perfecting of a race of anchorites. The aims of Loyola were as practical as they were visionary. It was the office of the Jesuit to preach, to hear confession, to educate. "Consummate prudence, allied with moderate saintliness, is better than greater saintliness and mere prudence"; and again, "If the Church preaches that a thing which appears to us as white is black, we must proclaim it black immediately."

Such maxims illustrate the spirit of worldly compliance and absolute submission which gave to the Order its peculiar character. Wherever there was a policy to be shaped the Jesuit confessor was at hand with his counsel. Wherever there was educational work to be done, whether in Europe or in China, the Jesuit school and the Jesuit college, competent, well administered, and strictly controlled, were for more than a century important instruments of Catholic influence and propaganda.

To all intelligent Catholics it had been long plain that the Church had become a mountain of abuses. The need for reform had been acknowledged by Pope Adrian VI, who wrote of the many abominations practised in the Curia itself and of an inveterate and complex malady infecting the whole body of the Church, which it was idle to conceal; and the same theme was restated with greater fullness in a remarkable document (*Consilium quorundam cardinalium de emendenda ecclesia*) which was presented to Pope Paul III in 1538. Nowhere were these flagrant evils more evident than in the papal court and the city of Rome.

The Pope was an autocrat. To any proposal that church reform should be undertaken by national councils, or that an ecumenical council of the Church should have a free hand in making terms with heretics or in defining or limiting the prerogatives of the Holy See, Rome was, by reason of a long tradition of supreme authority, unalterably opposed. The Papacy had had experience of councils in the fifteenth century, and regarded them as evils much to be apprehended and only tolerable if they took their orders from Rome.

Nevertheless, after many delays and obstructions a Council was summoned to Trent, which, although it was sparsely attended and broken by adjournments, one of which was protracted for ten years, marks an epoch in the history of the Roman Church. Out of that Council the Church emerged with its doctrine defined, its discipline strengthened, and its services enriched by the exquisite music of Palestrina. The Papacy entered the Council exposed to many hazards. It issued victorious at every point. So far from being compelled to make concessions to the Lutherans, it had insisted upon putting dogma in the forefront of the discussion, and with its obedient majority of Italian bishops had secured during the early sessions clear-cut decisions upon the three fundamental questions—the authority of the Scriptures, the doctrine of justification by faith only, and the nature of the Sacrament —which divided the Lutheran from the Roman world. By these decisions it finally shattered the Emperor's hope of a scheme so contrived as to soothe the rebel temper of his Lutheran subjects. It drew the line sharp, deep and clear between the Catholic and the Protestant Confessions, ending the search for doctrinal compromise and beginning the period of open conflict. In the words of Lord Acton, a great Catholic historian, "it impressed on the Church the stamp of an intolerant age and perpetuated by its decrees the spirit of an austere immorality." What was then enacted by an ill-attended Council mainly consisting of Italian bishops dependent on the Curia has never been revised, and remains to this day the faith of the Catholic Church.

In the second period of its activity, which opened in 1562 after an intermission of ten years, the Council addressed itself to the problem of discipline and ecclesiastical education. It passed decrees against non-residence and for the establishment of seminaries for the training of priests, but evaded any proposal for meeting heresy half-way or for the abridgment of the papal prerogative. The critical spirit of the Venetian Paolo Sarpi has preserved for us a record of this extraordinary assembly, so unrepresentative of Europe as a whole, so disappointing to the believers in conciliar government, but so true to the tradition of Roman autocracy. The leading figure in the later debates and the man who again carried the papal cause to victory was Lainez, the second general of the Jesuit Order. In that scene of subtle intrigue, furious national Jatreds, and open profligacy the stern, eloquent, and invincible Jesuit stood out like a giant.

Almost as important as the Council, and certainly of more immediate effect, was a notable improvement in the character of the occupants of the papal see, which begins to show itself with the accession of Paul III in 1534, and reaches a culminating point with the Pontificate of Pius V in 1563. The great Popes of the Renaissance were often splendid mundane figures, vigorous, nobly born, cultivated, munificent patrons of art and letters, who took a full and animated share in the political passions and rivalries as well as in the baser appeties of their age. They had "nephews" and "nieces," the offspring of their illegitimate unions, for whom it was one of their principal ambitions to provide establishments corresponding to their rank and position. They often promoted wars. They were patient of flagrant scandals. Their court was founded upon simony, plurality, and non-residence. In the long struggle between France and Spain for hegemony in Italy they could not avoid taking an active part. Paul III, of the great house of Farnese, who may be counted as the last of the Renaissance dynasty, was an irresolute supporter of France. Julius III was an imperialist; Paul IV, of the Neapolitan house of Caraffa, carried his insane hatred of Spain to such a point as to invoke the aid of the Turk against it. But meanwhile a change was coming. The reforming movement which had invaded France and Germany and England had begun to reach Rome itself. There was a feeling in the air that something should be done, and that while the whole world was crying out for change and reformation the Curia could not persist in its old ways. The intelligent and worldly Paul III responded to this new spirit, summoned a Council, and established the Order of Jesuits. The fiery and devout Paul IV felt it yet more strongly, and though he was a man consumed with the political passion of a Neapolitan aristocrat, the artificer of a wicked war to put France in control of his native land, and not above the vice of nepotism, he addressed himself seriously, being the first of the Roman Pontiffs to do this, to the detailed task of practical reform. But the most striking change comes with the Pontificate of Pius IV in 1559. This jovial, worthy Milanese was conspicuous for the absence of the special attributes which had for so long given a mundane quality to the Papacy. He was not well-born. He was neither politician not war-monger nor nepotist. Indeed, he condemned the criminal nephews of his predecessor to death, his own nephew, Carlo Borromeo, being one of the saintliest figures of his age. As for the Council of Trent, he was agreeable that it should be recalled. "We wish for a Council," he said. "We certainly desire that it should be held and be universal. . . . It shall reform what wants to be reformed, even in our own person and even our own affairs."

But perhaps the Pontiff who more than any other typifies the new spirit of austere fanaticism which had come into the religious life of Italy in this age is the humble Michele Ghislieri, who ascended the papal throne as Pius V in 1565.

The Roman populace admired the unusual spectacle of an ascetic Pontiff who walked barefoot through the streets, took no siesta, rose with the dawn, and cut down the expenditure of the Curia to the bone. A figure, he must have seemed, drawn from some mediaeval tomb as he called out that no quarter should be given to the Huguenots, gloated over the cruelties of Alva in the Netherlands or launched those Spanish and Venetian galleys which destroyed the Turkish navy at Lepanto.

Nothing counts like personal example. "It has contributed infinitely to the advantage of the Church," said Paolo Tiepolo in 1576, "that several Popes in succession have been men of irreproachable lives; hence all others are become better, or have at least assumed the appearance of being so. Cardinals and prelates attend mass punctually; their households are studious to avoid anything that can give scandal; the whole city has put off its old recklessness and is become much more Christian-like in life and manners than formerly." Yet the Popes were not yet perfect. The vigorous Sixtus V, under whose Pontificate these words were written, was not only a Philistine, from whose vandal hands no ancient monument, however beautiful, was safe, but also deficient in that gift of charity which is recommended by St. Paul. Learning that some banditti in the Campagna had died of the poisoned food which had been set out for them, this Vicar of Christ and editor of St. Ambrose showed notable satisfaction.

In a campaign for the reclamation of the Protestants to the Roman faith, Germany, where the schism had first arisen and whence it had spread far and wide through Europe, held the prerogative place. It was here that the new heresy appeared to be most firmly established. It was here that it was making most conspicuous progress. It was here that for lack of a strong central Catholic government it was most difficult to temper or repress. The north of Germany, which during the mediaeval struggles between Empire and Papacy had been noted for the ardour with which it espoused the papal cause had become by 1570 an almost unbroken Protestant block. In the ecclesiastical territories of the lower Rhine, heresy, spreading south from Holland, spreading west from Saxony, spreading north from Switzerland, had gathered so great a measure of strength as to engender the apprehension that the great Rhenish Archbishoprics might, despite the ecclesiastical reservation in the Treaty of Augsburg, pass over to the Protestant camp. Calvinism had been established in the Palatinate, Lutheranism in Würtemberg and Baden. Ministers of the Lutheran religion were at work in the castles of the Bavarian nobility and in the towns on the Danube. While the Tyrol remained firmly Catholic, Styria, Carinthia, and the two provinces of the Austrian duchy were largely given over to Protestant rites.

The real strength of Protestantism in central Europe, though this was not clear in 1570, lay in two regions divided from one another by the whole breadth of the country. It lay in that ancient kingdom and electorate of Bohemia, where first the Hussites, then the Bohemian Brethren, and finally preachers from Lutheran Saxony had created among the Czech peasants, and to a large extent among the Czech nobility, a strong revulsion from Rome; and it lay also in the Palatinate, that beautiful region watered by the Neckar and the Rhine, where a succession of Calvinist electors, keeping in touch with their co-religionists in Switzerland and in France, and trading mercenary armies to the Huguenots, made a centre of Calvinist thought and teaching in their capital of Heidelberg and served as a binding link between the militant forces of the Protestant revolt in these countries.

But there were two weaknesses in the Protestant movement deeper than the geographical distance between Bohemia and the Palatinate. The more the Lutheran theologians examined their beliefs and dissertated upon them, the more necessary did it appear to these unpolitical pedants that Calvinism should be held at arm's length, as in many vital particulars clearly erroneous.

A formula drawn up to compose Lutheran differences (*Formula Concordiae*, 1580) traced the line between the two competing faiths in clear and unmistakable terms. Calvinists and Lutherans agreed to differ in theology; and so, when by exercising a joint political pressure upon the Emperor on the occasion of his demand for assistance towards the Turkish war, they might have extracted guarantees for the protection of their co-religionists, Lutheran Saxony took one road and the Elector Palatine another.

The second weakness was still more serious, for it was that lowering of spiritual tone which occurs in all revolutionary movements when the original fervour has ebbed. Luther left no successor. A hundred and thirty-four years barren of Lutheran genius divide his death from the birth of John Sebastian Bach. The age of the prophets and moralists was succeeded by a period of theological pedantry, servile abasement, and, in literature, of revolting and ignoble wantonness. No great thinker or scholar rose from the ranks of Lutheranism. No policies were swayed by this religion, acting as a public influence upon the imaginations and the hearts of men. Yet, in the pious family life of humble people and in its association with Church music, Lutheranism contained sources of inner strength which not even its Erastian organization and the widespread profligacy of German morals were able wholly to destroy.

The religious situation in Germany was still governed by that hard-gotten, ill-drafted Treaty of Augsburg, which nevertheless, since it provided a kind of peace for more than fifty years, ranks among the more successful achievements of German statesmen. Yet neither Lutheran nor Catholic was cordially prepared to operate this compromise of exhaustion. The Lutherans had never accepted the principle of "the ecclesiastical reservation" in accordance with which an ecclesiastic, if he renounced the old religion, was also compelled to abandon the income and revenues which he had so far possessed. The Catholics contended, and the Lutherans disputed the contention, that the Roman Church was entitled to recover all ecclesiastical foundations confiscated since 1552. The Catholic princes claimed the right to expel Protestants from their territory and otherwise to persecute them. In the eyes of the Protestants, who were hardly less intolerant, this was a clear breach of the Edict of Toleration, which they regarded as an integral part of the settlement. It will be readily imagined that at a time when the foundations of belief were fluid, when a prince, a city, a cathedral chapter, or a prelate of the Church might swing over from the Catholic to the Protestant side, raising in each case the thorny question of the disposition of ecclesiastical endowments, the occasions of conflict arising out of the administration of this Peace of Augsburg were numerous and formidable.

Yet the evil was not irremediable. Though there was never that intolerable inflammation of the public mind which is excited when good men are burned for their beliefs, Protestant ministers were expelled from Catholic territory, Protestant preaching was forbidden, it was sufficient to be a Protestant to find every avenue to public employment or to profitable livelihood bolted and barred. But to the credit of the Catholic rulers of Germany it should be remembered that they refrained from imitating the methods of the Spanish Inquisition. In this they were acting prudently. Had a Lutheran gone to the stake, German princes, with armies at their back, would have been compelled by the clamour of their subjects to ask for redress.

The secret of this German collapse was lack of government. There was no strong authority capable of determining the controversies which arose out of the interpretation of the religious treaty or of punishing the infraction of its provisions. The Diets were slow, cumbrous, drunken, ineffective. The princes were far more concerned with the pursuit of their several dynastic and territorial aims than with a comprehensive and well-laid plan for the solution of the religious problem in Germany. But there remained the Emperor. He was a Habsburg, closely connected by family ties with the powerful monarchy of Spain. He was King of Bohemia, titular King of Hungary, though in effect, by reason of the Turkish conquest, *de facto* ruler of only a small stretch of that country, and ruler of the five duchies of Upper and Lower Austria, Styria, Carinthia, and Carniola. No German prince could vie with him in prestige or territorial power. Though his constitutional powers in the Empire had been greatly attenuated, there was still latent in the German people a fund of imperial sentiment to which a great man, had he been able to strike the public imagination, to handle the princes, and to grapple manfully with the pan-Germanic problem, might have been able to appeal. But the Habsburg Emperors of the later half of the sixteenth century were not men of this heroic stature. Ferdinand I (1556-64) was a good and prudent Catholic, who, though he introduced the Jesuits into Vienna, succeeded during his lifetime in securing reasonable conditions for his Protestant subjects. His successor, Maximilian II, who has been praised by Stubbs as "the first European prince of any religion who refused to persecute," who declined the invitation of Pope Pius to attack the Protestants and the request of the Protestants that he should expel the Jesuits, was none the less deficient in the qualities needed for the situation. This attractive and amiable figure, who in youth listened to the teaching of Lutheran preachers, who in middle age married his daughter to Philip II, who in his latest message to the Diet declared that he was neutral in the religious question, and refused the sacraments of the Church upon his deathbed, made no positive contribution to the adjustment of the religious quarrel in Germany. Tolerant himself, he acquiesced in the persecutions enacted by his neighbours. Officially a Catholic, spiritually a Lutheran, he lived balanced between the opposing creeds in a state of ineffective indecision which precluded energetic and uncomfortable resolves.

There followed that critical and disastrous reign of Rudolf II (1576-1602) which brought Germany to the brink of war. The kind of man needed in 1576 for the conduct of the Empire was one of large, genial, energetic temperament, fond of Germany and able to lay that foundation of easy friendship with the political leaders of the German people which was then the only road by which an emperor might recover a position of influence and authority. Rudolf was the opposite of all this. He had nothing in him of the boisterous, hard-drinking, affable German. Brought up in the formal atmosphere of the Spanish court, he had even as a youth, and before melancholia marked him for its own, evinced the fastidious temper of the student, the grandee, and the recluse. The passion for remoteness from the vulgar crowd grew into a deadly malady of the mind. While the Turks were harrying the Hungarian border and Germany was rushing onward to chaos and disaster, this eccentric and irresponsible celibate lived a life apart, far from the madding crowd of Germany, in the high castle which towers over Prague, consorting with astronomers, grooms, and chemists, and content so long as he might be free to enjoy his stables, his books, his mathematical instruments, and his mistresses, to delegate the dull business of conducting the Empire to a succession of incompetent valets. It was not by such a sovereign that the growing tumult among the German people could be composed.

Meanwhile the Counter-Reformation was slowly extending its conquests under the special encouragement of the Dukes of Bavaria and with the notable assistance of the Jesuit Order.

Ignatius Loyola, like all statesmen of the profounder sort, realized the truth that long-range changes in the spiritual direction of mankind must be based on the school. Seeing that the profligacy and ignorance of the Catholic clergy were a mainstay of the Protestant cause, he determined to mend this evil by education. He saw also that under the direction of the humanists a new scale of values had been insinuated into the teaching of the young, culture overshadowing theology, dogma giving place to freedom, and that society had lost that firm grasp of the dialectical defences of the Catholic Faith, which had been built up by the great scholastics of the middle ages.

For his immediate purpose it was more profitable to train the elect than to scatter his gifts to the multitude. The wheels of history are seldom moved by the poor. In the main the world is ruled by station, wealth, and intellect. The educational arrows of the Jesuits were directed, not at the rank and file, but at the pivotal persons whose gifts or position were likely to give them an influence upon their fellows. Being gratuitous and conservative, their system was widely acceptable. They were far too wise to discard the humanities, the teaching in the Greek, Latin, and Hebrew languages which had now established themselves as cardinal requisites of the highest culture, and were careful, which was also popular, to attend to the health and the manners of their pupils. But even more distinctive than the technical excellence of a method which trained the young to learn, to compose, and to discuss was an iron routine of spiritual discipline. The disciple of the Jesuits bore the print of their influence to the grave.

In the fifties of the century the "Spanish priests," as they were called, began to filter into Germany and there to found schools and colleges for the restoration of the Catholic Faith. We find them in Vienna, where they were given control of the University in 1551, in Cologne and Ingolstadt in 1556, in Munich in 1559. All along the Rhine and the Main, at Bonn, Mainz, and Speier, as well as Würzburg, they established centres for teaching and propaganda. With their high but narrow competence the Lutheran schools in the middle of the sixteenth century were ill qualified to vie.

Vienna was the key position. Ignatius Loyola could hardly fail to see that if the Austrian provinces were not soon recaptured for the Roman faith the heart of the Empire would be won by the enemy. Accordingly to Vienna there was despatched one of the greatest Catholic figures of that age, the strenuous and learned Dutchman, Petrus Canisius, who as a mere youth had by his ardour and eloquence saved Cologne for the Roman faith. Canisius became the confidant of the emperor. It is to him that the Counter-Reformation in Austria owes its strongest impulse. He it was who procured for the Jesuits that ascendancy over Austrian education which for many centuries was unbroken. Nor was there among the German victories of the Order any more notable than this, that Ferdinand of Styria, a cadet of the Habsburg house, having been saturated in youth with Jesuit principles, first drove the Protestants out of Styria, and then, as Holy Roman Emperor, headed the forces of the Catholic reaction in the Thirty Years' War.

But the greatest of the Jesuits' conquests has still to be mentioned. The kingdom of Poland was, after its union with the duchy of Lithuania in 1389, larger than any state in western Europe. In this desolate and empty land, where every pair of arms was welcome, the religious credentials of an immigrant had never been closely examined. Jews had fled to Poland in the middle ages from the bitter persecution of the Catholic west and had there been accorded the rights of hospitality, leaving behind them a progeny ever multiplying in numbers and supplying the main part of such urban arts as Poland possessed. More than half the population had always professed the Greek faith. Hussites had filtered in during the fifteenth century and been later followed by exponents of every variety of Protestant belief. Lutherans and Calvinists, Bohemian Brethren and Unitarians spread their propaganda with the greater ease since the power of the Catholic king was confined within narrow limits by the exorbitant privileges of the nobles. But the very fullness of religious liberty accorded to the Poles proved to be the ruin of the Protestant cause. There was no authority in the country to curb the luxuriance or to direct the flow of the differing religious opinions which had spread abroad as a consequence of Lutheran teaching. Compacts, indeed, were made. The Bohemian Brethren brought themselves to join with the Genevans in 1553, and these again to combine with the Lutherans in 1570, but these associations were too long delayed and too weakly compacted; for five years before the Lutherans and Calvinists had patched up their differences the Jesuits were in the field, and with the favouring authority of the Crown had been placed in control of the higher education of the country.

Then ensured a Catholic campaign, slow, sure, methodical, and eventually triumphant. By the end of the seventeenth century the Jesuits had made of Poland one of the most Catholic countries in Europe, a Latin outpost placed between Teuton Protestantism and the Greco-Russian civilization of the east. The voyager who today crosses the Polish frontier into the territory of the Soviet Republic forgets that the populations on either side of the line are united by a community of race. The Counter-Reformation has obscured whatever affinities may formerly have bound the Pole to the Russian. On the one side of the line are Roman churches bright with lights and rustling with the genuflexions of crowds of worshippers; on the other side the organized gospel of atheism by which the new Communist government of the Soviet Republic hopes to replace the age-long Byzantine image-worship of a superstitious and illiterate peasantry.

BOOKS WHICH MAY BE CONSULTED

L. Pastor: *History of the Popes. Ed.* F. I. Antrobus and R. F. Kerr. 1894-1933.

A. W. Ward: *The Counter-Reformation.* 1889.

L. von Ranke: *History of the Reformation in Germany. Tr.* S. Austin. 1905.

J. A. Froude: *Lecture on the Council of Trent.* 1896.

M. Philippson: *La Contre-révolution religieuse du seizième siècle.* 1884.

J. A. Symonds: *Renaissance in Italy: The Catholic Reaction.* 1886.

H. C. Lea: *History of the Inquisition in Spain.* 4 vols. 1907.

H. D. Sedgwick: *Life of Ignatius Loyola.* 1923.

W. Stubbs: *Lectures on European History*, 1519-1648. 1904.

W. E. Collins: *The Catholic South* (in *Cambridge Modern History*, Vol. II, chap. xii).

A. Gindely: *Rudolf II und seine Zeit.* 1863.

G. Droysen: *Geschichte der Gegenreformation.* 1893.

A. Huber: *Geschichte Oesterreichs.* 1885.

B. J. Kidd: *The Counter Reformation.* 1550-1600. 1933.

CHAPTER XLIX

THE FRENCH WARS OF RELIGION

Grave evil of this civil war. The situation in 1559. Catherine de' Medici. The Guises. The Huguenots. The Politiques. The initial compromise. The massacre of Vassy. The use of foreign mercenaries, and the appeal to foreign powers. Catholic victories at Dreux, Jarnac, Moncontour. Coligny restores the Huguenot fortunes, 1569. The Peace of St. Germain, 1570. Coligny's ambitious anti-Spanish policy. The Queen takes fright. The Massacre of St. Bartholomew. Henry of Navarre becomes in 1564 the next heir. Catholic apprehensions. Murder of the Guises. The last of the Valois. The resistance of the League. Triumph of Henry of Navarre. The Edict of Nantes, 1598. Henry's war policy and sudden death.

THE French wars of religion which occupy the later half of the sixteenth century were far more disastrous to the country than the Italian campaigns by which they had been preceded. The Italian policy had been unwise; among other reasons because it sacrificed the pioneering work of the Breton and Norman sailors in the New World, so that after much expenditure of blood and treasure this phase of French ambition ended in frustration. But the wars of religion very nearly broke up the hard-won unity of France, inflicting evils which cannot be measured by battle losses alone. Town was divided against town, village against village, family against family. Armed affrays and assassinations became incidents of ordinary life. Some murders were committed out of religious fanaticism, others in pursuit of private vengeance, others, as in all times when the hideous taint of espionage infects the body politic, out of senseless terror. The morality of the Huguenot saint was embarked upon a struggle which was largely carried on by the methods of the Irish gunmen. The wise French humanist stood aloof, like Montaigne, whose essays, published during the savage tyranny of the Catholic League, express the gospel of an enlightened Epicurean and charitable scepticism.

The position of France when Henry II died in 1559 was roughly as follows: the Genevan or Huguenot propaganda had made great progress. It had found friends in the army and in the Parliament of Paris, and in many country towns had secured a large following of devout adherents. Several persecutions had not checked the movement. Though the price of heresy was burning at the stake and eighty-eight humble Protestants had paid that price under Henry II, the new faith continued to make converts. Little French Bibles and psalm-books circulated surreptitiously and were read in the privacy of household gatherings. Teachers, trained in the fortifying school of Geneva, travelled about with their incitements to heroism and endurance. Nor were the French Huguenots kept in ignorance of the fate of their co-religionists in other lands. They learnt how Protestant women were buried alive in the Netherlands, how Queen Mary sent Protestant bishops to the stake in England, and how John Knox had raised his Genevan flag among the Scots. The congregations of the faithful were knit together in a confraternity of martyrdom. A body of heretical opinion, still imperfectly organized, but anxious, and inflamed, and strengthened by a sense of solidarity with Protestant communities in other countries, confronted the weak and impecunious government of France.

Against this gathering challenge to the ancient faith were ranged the long Catholic traditions of the French monarchy, the disciplined force of the Roman Church, the superstitious furies of the Paris rabble, and always in the background the power of Spain, great at sea, supreme in Italy and the Netherlands, and allied by the closest family ties with the house of Austria.

Had the French throne been occupied at this juncture by a strong, wise, and tolerant king, able and willing to take advantage of those strong feelings in favour of Gallican independence, which prevailed among so many prelates of the French Church, and prepared, like Henry VIII, to be undisputed master in his own house, the country might have been spared a long chapter of misery. But at this critical juncture the government of France devolved in succession upon three of the feeblest sovereigns who have ever sat upon a European throne. Of the sons of Henry II and Catherine de'Medici, the eldest, Francis II, was an invalid; the second

Charles IX, a nervous wreck, if not a madman; the third, Henry III, a degenerate. The real power lay with their mother, who suffered under the double disadvantage of being a woman and an alien.[1]

The position of this cultured and cynical Italian lady of the middle class, suddenly called upon to govern France amid the fierce rivalries which divided the court and country, was one of singular difficulty. A bold policy, which might have attracted a native king, was beyond the reach of a foreigner. An enthusiastic policy, which would have elicited the cordial support of either Catholic or Huguenot, was alien to her indifferent and essentially lay temperament. Encompassed by perils, and in a situation which required the utmost watchfulness, she resolved to preserve the enjoyment of the monarchy for her sons and for herself the substance of power, by the method which seemed to her to be most apt to secure that end, a religious peace based on compromise. The most divergent views have been entertained of her character. To one historian she is "specially distinguished for her genius for maternal love." To others she is the supreme embodiment of human craft and wickedness. Perhaps among her less charitable critics her youngest son is nearest the mark when he described his mother as *Madame La Serpente*. In her contempt for veracity, in her gluttony, and in the remorseless pursuit of private revenge she was an Italian of her age. Her great political virtue was the cool persistence with which she strove to secure a peaceful balancing between two fanatical parties. But though toleration was agreeable to her mind and temper, it was never with her an iron principle. A moment came when this fat, agreeable, industrious woman, whose taste in art was so delicate and true, who liked pictures and jewels and good books, who never forgave or forgot an injury, and was first of all the rulers of France to organize immorality as an instrument of political power, discarded her policy of indulgence and helped to engineer the Massacre of St. Bartholomew.

Overshadowing the Italian queen and her wretched sequence of sons were certain great aristocratic groups, for whom the control of the king's person and therefore of the government was a matter of ambition. Of these groups one was clearly Catholic and the other clearly Protestant, while

[1] Genealogical Table N.

the third occupied an intermediate position, being opposed to the Catholic leaders on the point of policy, and to Protestants in the matter of religious faith. The Catholic group was the party of the Guises. It was led by Francis, Duke of Guise, who was the idol of France by reason of his defence of Metz and his capture of Calais, and upon the ecclesiastical side by his brother Charles of Lorraine, the Cardinal Archbishop of Rheims, who would not have minded being the first patriarch of an independent Gallican Church, but since this was proved to be impossible, constituted himself, at the Council of Trent, a most vehement and skilful advocate of extreme papal claims. The Guises, then, could boast of the first soldier and the leading churchman of the kingdom: but this was not the limit of their influence. A sister of Francis of Guise had been married to the King of Scotland. A niece sat upon the throne of France. With this close association with two crowned heads, with fifteen bishoprics in the family, and with properties widely scattered along the eastern border of the kingdom, the Guises represented the most powerful body of Catholic interests in the country. Spain and Rome, with whom they were in association, looked to this brilliant family to sustain the chief burden of Catholic defence in France.

The chieftains of the Huguenot party were the Bourbon princes, Anthony, King of Navarre, and his brother Louis, Duke of Condé, who was Governor of Picardy and had accepted the position of Protector-General of the Church of France. It cannot be said of either of these great noblemen that they were very deeply rooted in the Huguenot faith; but their influence in the west and south-west of France, as also in Normandy, was considerable, and drew many of the lesser nobility and gentry of these regions into the conflict.

A third group, originally led by the veteran statesman Anne, Duke of Montmorency, and specially strong in central France, were the Politiques. These were men who while adhering to the old faith had little love for the queen mother or for the Guises and therefore occupied an intermediate position between the extreme groups. Montmorency was a strong Catholic, but his three nephews, the Châtillon brothers, took another line. They joined the Huguenots, and one of them, Gaspard de Coligny, Admiral of France, a man of unquenchable courage and deep religious convictions, became the leading Protestant General, and therefore the principal mark for Catholic vengeance.

In the passionate fermentation of these times the slightest incident might provoke a war. The execution in Paris of a Calvinist lawyer provoked in the Protestant underworld, but probably not without countenance from Condé, and even from Elizabeth of England, a plot to seize the king and the Guises at Amboise. The plot was discovered, the conspirators were cruelly punished, and the Guises, advancing from strength to strength, ventured to arrest Condé and to sentence him to death. But then came a sudden reversal of fortune. On December 5, 1560, the young king died. In the midst of their success the Guises found themselves stripped of influence at court, and their enemies established in their place. The queen mother became Regent for her son Charles, who was a minor, and with the help of the Chancellor L'Hôpital, one of the few great statesmen produced in that age, inaugurated a policy of amnesty and conciliation. Condé was released from prison, the Calvinists were amnestied, and the King of Navarre was brought into the Council as Lieutenant-General of the kingdom. An experiment was now tried by Catherine and her wise Chancellor which, in a cooler state of the public mind, might have laid the foundations for a provisional peace. After a colloquy between the leading divines of the contending churches had broken down, as such discussions invariably did, an edict was issued in January, 1562, which legalized, under certain not unfair conditions, the public celebration of Huguenot rites. But by this time tempers had risen high. Images were destroyed, churches defaced, priests were attacked on one side, preachers on the other; and eventually, after a barnful of worshipping Huguenots had been massacred by Guise's troops at Vassy, the civil war, which had been so long held down, blazed into sudden eruption.

It was a property of this quarrel not only that it was largely waged by foreign mercenaries, but that after a short spell of fighting peace would come, not because a settlement really tolerable to both parties was in sight, but either because money had run short, or because a leader had been killed, or from sudden dejection or weakness, or because, mingled with the fierce religious and personal rancours of the time, there was still the underlying sense of French unity as a treasure not

FRANCE DURING THE WARS OF RELIGION

H.E. I—19

lightly to be squandered. To these reasons is to be ascribed the fact that seven wars were found to be necessary before the quarrel between the Catholics and the Huguenots was composed in France.

Neither party scrupled to appeal for foreign aid. The Catholics turned to Spain, the Huguenots to England, even going so far as in the first war to put the English in possession of Havre and to promise them Calais. But one Protestant alliance was never made. Between the German Lutherans and the French Huguenots the gulf was insuperable. German Lutherans fought in the French wars, but they were to be found enlisted, for the most part, not in the Huguenot, but in the Catholic, ranks.

In the first war all the auguries appeared to point to a Catholic triumph, the possession of the persons of the king and queen, the support of Paris, the assistance of an efficient body of Spanish and German mercenaries, the capture of Rouen, and, finally, a Catholic victory at Dreux in Normandy over the forces of Coligny and Condé. But these advantages suddenly melted away when François de Guise fell by the hand of an assassin before the walls of Orleans.

Little good, however, did the Huguenots reap from this crime, for the murder was attributed to Coligny and supplied to the family of the murdered man a motive for revenge far more powerful than the strength of their religious convictions.

There followed four years of uneasy peace, during which Catherine and her sons toured the provinces. The suspicion of the Huguenot party was awakened by a meeting at Bayonne (May, 1565) between Catherine and her sister Queen Isabella of Spain, who was accompanied by the Duke of Alva. That Catherine's main object was to arrange a marriage between her daughter Margaret and Don Carlos, the son of Philip II of Spain, is clear; but other matters were also discussed, and notably the co-operation of France and Spain against the Netherlands. There was enough here to arouse the fears of Coligny, the most active spirit in the Huguenot party, and when Alva was found marching towards the Low Countries along the eastern border of France with a fine Spanish army accompanied by a French corps of observation, the Admiral felt that the time had come to emancipate the court from its Spanish toils. A plan was made to capture Charles IX, and, failing of success, precipitated a fresh outburst of fighting.

The next two wars, which, since they were divided by the short peace of Longjumeau, 1568, may almost be regarded as a single series of operations, are memorable on three accounts. It is now that La Rochelle first emerges as a great marine Protestant fortress, capable of successfully standing a siege. It is now that Henry of Navarre, the son of King Anthony, and afterwards destined to be Henry IV of France, is brought forward as a Protestant leader. But the most striking peculiarity of this period is that after an almost uniform sequence of Catholic victories, after Condé had been taken and killed at Jarnac, and some 6,000 Huguenot bodies had strewn the bloodstained field of Moncontour, the ultimate victory lay with Coligny. Executing a brilliant retreat from the Loire to the south, and then raising a fresh army, the amazing veteran marched upon Paris, and finding the court empty of resources, confounded his enemies, dominated the king, and took control of the policy of France. Charles IX, Aug., who had had a Protestant nurse, was ready to treat. The 1570 Peace of St. Germain recognizes more fully than had been done so far the importance of the Huguenot party as a substantive and separate interest in France. The great nobles, as before, were allowed to hold their Huguenot services in their castles for all who liked to attend them. The Protestant form of worship was to be maintained for all towns where it was actually practised, and in two towns in each administrative district in France. Safeguards were provided against judicial oppression. Four places of great military importance, La Rochelle, Montauban, Cognac, and La Charité, were guaranteed to the party for two years as a security for the fulfilment of the treaty.

And now a new prospect opened out before the Huguenots. Hitherto, largely owing to Guise influence, the French monarchy had been disposed to look to Spain for support in its defence of the Catholic cause. Coligny prepared a complete diplomatic revolution. His idea was to gain protection for his co-religionists in France by setting afoot a national war against Spain in the Netherlands. To this end he worked for a great confederation led by France, but helped by England, by the Dutch, by Venice and Tuscany, and possibly by the Turks, which would bring peace at home and add Flanders and Artois to the dominions of the French Crown. A defensive treaty with England, signed at Blois on April 19, 1572, was the first stone in the new diplomatic building.

Among the dealings of this period of Huguenot influence was a project destined to have a great effect upon the internal situation in France. A marriage was arranged and actually took place (August 18, 1572) between Margaret of Valois, the king's sister, and Henry of Navarre. The Béarnais, the little hook-nosed rustic son of a Pyrenean knight by a fanatically Huguenot mother, was fished out of his remote province, and married into the royal and Catholic family of France. It was a mixed marriage, the first of its kind, and by all good Catholics heartily detested. Whither, it was asked, was France drifting under her light-headed king and Huguenot general? Into a war with the greatest Catholic power in Europe? Into a course which might place France under a Protestant king? Catherine was swift to read changes of temperature. She knew that though a third of the nobility might be Huguenot, the vast majority of the French people remained loyal to the old faith. She feared war, feared the might of Spain, feared Coligny's influence over her son, feared that if she remained inactive, the Guises would strike, and so obtain the mastery of France for themselves, and she was shrewd enough to see that no war waged to give France an inch of territory in Flanders would long be popular with the English government. She therefore resolved to have Coligny killed. The attack failed. The Admiral was wounded by a Catholic gunman, but not seriously (August 22, 1572). The position of the queen mother thus became critical. Paris was full of Huguenot gentlemen, drawn to the capital by the royal marriage, and furious at the dastardly attack upon their great and venerated chief. Lest worse befall, the queen determined to strike again, and this time not at Coligny alone, but in the secrecy of night at all the Protestant leaders. The weak king, fobbed off with the tale of a Huguenot plot, was persuaded to give his assent.

The Guises were eager for revenge, and behind the Guises and their bravos were the sleeping furies of Catholic Paris. At dawn on August 24 (St. Bartholomew's Day) the bell of the Palace of Justice rang out the signal for the slaughter to begin.

Such a carnival of butchery as then ensued, not in Paris

only, where some three or four thousand Huguenots were killed, but throughout the provinces, outran the fiercest anticipations of the court. The Parisians, whose trade suffered from the religious troubles, needed no incitement to massacre the Huguenots or to mutilate their corpses. They killed not the leaders only, but the rank and file, and their example was gleefully followed in the provinces. The head of Coligny was sent to the Pope, the golden rose was sent by the Pope to the king. At the news of the happy extermination of so many heretics the Pope ordered a medal to be struck and Philip of Spain commanded a Te Deum. So great a Catholic triumph had hardly been dreamed of. Coligny was dead. Condé and Henry of Navarre were in the king's hands, and thousands of Huguenot corpses attested the Catholic orthodoxy of France.

The conspirators who contrived the Massacre of St. Bartholomew acted in a panic, but may nevertheless have feared that a king who compromised himself too far with the Huguenots might be overthrown by a fanatical Catholic party controlled by the Guises and based on the Paris mob. Under Henry III, who succeeded his brother in 1574, that danger was very nearly realized. So far from extinguishing the Huguenots, the Massacre of St. Bartholomew had merely been the first act of a fourth war. From their western capital of La Rochelle the Huguenots, now helped by many Politiques, including for a time Monsieur, the younger brother of the king, defied the royalist forces and offered a menace to the unity of France. To the Catholics, and more particularly to the Catholic democracy of Paris, this fierce and continued obstinacy, so bad for business, so unpatriotic (for the Huguenots were in touch with England), was intolerable. The fanatics wanted war to the knife, and they found the king and queen mother still pursuing their familiar policy of offering a peace or a truce to the rebels on every occasion, still governed by the detestable idea that a place might be found for the free public worship of Huguenots in a Catholic state. The treaty of May 14, 1576, seemed to them little better than a capitulation. A Catholic Union was formed, commonly known as the League, with the Pope and the King of Spain as patrons, to stiffen the spine of Roman orthodoxy in France.

In 1584 Monsieur died. He was Catherine's youngest son

and Henry's sole surviving brother, and since the king was childless, the next heir to the throne would be Henry of Navarre. "Better a Republic than a Huguenot King" was the principle of the Leaguers of Paris. Against the Guises, now supported by such an outburst of passionate feeling, Henry III was for many years very helpless. He hung on, protected by assassins, surrounded by a web of plots, while the real authority over Catholic France was wielded by the League. How weak he had become was shown on the Day of Barricades (May 12, 1588) when Paris, obedient to Henry, Duke of Guise, denied the royal troops an entry into the city, and again when the States-General, meeting at Blois under Jesuit influence, passed a series of enactments which, if carried through, would have drained the treasury of its resources and robbed the government of its last vestige of authority. From these humiliations the wretched king, "the worst ruler of the worst dynasty that has ever governed," sought relief by murder. On the approach of Christmas, 1588, the Duke of Guise and his brother the Cardinal of Lorraine were cut down in the Castle of Blois by the king's Gascon bravos.

The old queen mother was lying on her deathbed when her favourite son brought her the news. "Now I am King of France," he is reported to have said, "I have killed the King of Paris." "God grant it may be so," was the answer; "but have you made sure of the other towns?"

The last act of the long drama now opened. While the Catholic League declared Henry deposed from his throne and endeavoured to govern the capital and the country, the thoughts of an increasing number of Frenchmen, neither Huguenots nor Leaguers, were turning to Henry of Navarre, to whom the succession in law belonged. The young southerner had revealed remarkable military qualities. At Coutras he had shown that a Huguenot army, well led, could beat the Catholic levies of the Crown in a set battle. His good humour, his rustic shrewdness, his numerous gallantries, commended him to the common man. He was a Protestant, but a man, whereas his cousin the king, who wore a pearl necklace and ear-rings, though a Catholic, was a fop. The cousins found it in their common interest to attack the Catholic League, which had deposed the one and declared the other incapable of succession. But while their armies lay outside Paris, the hand of Jacques Clément, a crazy Jacobin, struck down the king (August 1, 1589), so ending the long Valois dynasty in France, and opening the way to the direct struggle between Navarre and the League.

The Committee of sixteen who governed Paris for the League under the supervision of the Duke of Mayenne, the younger brother of Henry Guise, ruled like the Committee of Public Safety in 1794, by a system of terror. Its apologists plead that it saved France for Catholicism, which suited the people better than Protestantism, and that its crimes were such as to disgust the country with republicanism for two hundred years. During its violent and unpopular rule France was brought round to the view that the restoration of the hereditary monarchy would divide it least. It would not accept an Infanta from Spain, or a French nobleman elected by the States-General. The main body of the French aristocracy rallied round the Bourbon prince. But so persistent was fanaticism, that even after Henry had abjured his Protestant faith in the Church of St. Denis (July 25, 1593) he was compelled to wait eight months outside the walls of Paris before the resistance of the city was overcome.

The new sovereign brought with him one gift more precious than all the elegant accomplishments of the Valois. He cared for the common people of France and wished to see them prosperous and happy. The memoirs of his able Huguenot minister Sully, though on many points untrustworthy, are at least good evidence of the fact that the government of France under Henry IV was inspired by the idea of the public good. To put down anarchy, to promote agriculture and commerce, to restore peace to a country brought to the lowest point of misery by thirty years of civil war, were some of the aims which the French monarchy now resolutely set itself to pursue. Much was accomplished, as by great public works for the reclamation of marshes and the improvement of roads. The revenue was increased, the debt reduced. Finding the country burdened with a great deficit, Sully left its finance solvent.

But before these remedial measures could be applied in any fullness Henry was compelled to deal with two urgent problems, the Spaniards and the Huguenots. With some assistance from Queen Elizabeth he drove a Spanish army out of Amiens and compelled Spain (Treaty of Vervins, 1598) to relinquish

the positions—Calais, and Blavet in Brittany—which she had
been able to acquire upon French territory as ally to the
Catholic League. The Huguenots presented a far more
serious difficulty. These men of iron, who for more than thirty
years had defied the French crown, and were at any time able
to put an army of 25,000 into the field, were not easily to be
subdued and were in a position to treat with the sovereign
on level terms. The famous settlement known as the Edict of
Nantes was no royal act of grace, still less a philosophic
declaration of tolerance, but a treaty only reached after
arduous and protracted negotiations and accepted with
reluctance as a necessity, imposed by disagreeable, ineluctable
facts. It gave the Huguenots freedom of worship in the
castles of the nobility and in certain specified places, equality
of civil rights, judicial protection, and for their better security
the right of garrisoning more than a hundred fortified towns,
including such great national centres as La Rochelle, Saumur,
and Montpellier, at the cost of the French treasury. In effect
a little Huguenot state, with its army, its fortresses, its civil
government, was authorized to function in the heart of France.

The Edict of Nantes is notable in the history of civilization
as the first public recognition of the fact that more than one
religious communion can be maintained in the same polity.
Long before religious toleration was recognized in England
or Germany, it was, in virtue of this famous instrument,
made part of the constitutional law of France. The strong
arm of the Huguenot had extracted from his Catholic adversary concessions which no Roman would have conceded to
argument.

The foundations were now laid for the most brilliant period
of French history, during which the monarchy was exalted
and revived, the field of industry and commerce notably
enlarged, and the life of the Catholic Church stimulated and
enriched by the challenge and juxtaposition of the Huguenot
faith. These advantages narrow intolerance and martial
ambition were destined to sacrifice. Scaliger, the great
classical scholar, said of Henry that, despite his wit and
shrewd knowledge of human character, he was incapable for
a quarter of an hour of fixing his mind on the future. A more
provident statesman would have endeavoured to govern with
the assistance of the States-General, would have refused to
recall the Jesuits, who in 1594 had been banished from France

as corrupters of the young, disturbers of public order, and enemies of the king and the state, and would have put away from his thoughts the idea of an ambitious foreign war. Henry IV, who was the perpetual mark for the dagger of the assassin, lived on the improvisations of his ready talent. Despite his express promise, and confident in the wisdom of his advisers, he refused to summon the States-General, or to share with his subjects the educative burden of government. In religion he was tolerant and the inheritor from Catherine de'Medici of a system of toleration; yet he recalled the Jesuits, whose intolerant influence at the court and over French education was destined to lead to the expulsion of the Huguenots, and to the undoing of the Edict of Nantes, his greatest achievement.

In foreign policy he, for a time—after the peace of Vervins, 1598—vacillated between the idea of a sustained peace with Spain, to be cemented by royal marriages, and of an attack upon the Habsburgs; but eventually his thoughts turned to war and to a policy, such as that which Coligny had encouraged some fifty years before, of a grand onslaught on the Catholic Habsburgs to be assisted by Protestants from Germany and the Low Countries, and to end in the conquest of the Spanish Netherlands and the advance of the French frontier to the Rhine. The question whether the duchy of Cleves-Jülich, which was on the eastern frontier of France, should become part of the Catholic or Protestant block, afforded a pretext for action. Without adequate diplomatic preparation, and being chiefly decided in his choice of the moment by his passion for the Duchess of Condé, who had been withdrawn by her husband to the shelter of the Austrian court in Brussels, he was on the brink of opening his enormous anti-Catholic enterprise when he fell by the knife of Ravaillac, a Catholic fanatic. The recall of the Jesuits had not disarmed the spirit of the League.

BOOKS WHICH MAY BE CONSULTED

L. von Ranke: *Civil Wars and Monarchy in France in the Sixteenth and Seventeenth Centuries. Tr.* M. A. Garvey. 2 vols. 1852.
L. Romier: *Les Origines politiques des guerres de religion.* 2 vols. 1913-14.

E. Armstrong: *The French Wars of Religion.* 1892.
P. F. Willert: *Henry of Navarre and the Huguenots of France.* 1893
A. J. Grant: *The Huguenots.* 1934.
J. H. Mariéjol: *Catherine de Médicis.* 1920.
E. Faguet: *Seizième siècle. Études Littéraires.* 1894.
L. Batiffol: *The Century of the Renaissance.* 1916.
J. Delaborde: *Gaspard de Coligny, Amiral de France.* 1879-82.
A. J. Butler: *Wars of Religion in France (Cambridge Modern History,* Vol. II, chap. i).
Lord Acton: *Lectures on Modern History (Saint Bartholomew)* 1906.
H. Forneron: *Les Ducs de Guise et leur époque.* 2 vols. 1878.
A. Tilley: *The Literature of the French Renaissance.* 2 vols. 1904
L. Romier: *History of France.* Tr. A. L. Rowse. 1953.
L. Romier: *Le Royaume de Catherine de Médicis.* 1922.
Sir John Neale: *The Age of Catherine de Medici.* 1943.

CHAPTER L

THE RISE OF THE DUTCH REPUBLIC

Orthodoxy in Spain. Philip II. The Spanish army and navy. Spanish finance and economics. Importance of the Netherlands for Spain. Elizabeth elects for Protestantism. The queen's success in Scotland. "Mere English." Maintenance of national unity. The Church compromise. Philip and England. Granvelle in the Netherlands. William of Orange. Egmont and Alva. Orange and Alva. The Pacification of Ghent. Don John of Austria. The rift between north and south. Foundation of the Dutch Republic. The power of Amsterdam. The house of Orange. Causes of Dutch success. The distractions of Parma. The military skill of Maurice of Nassau. The Dutch make a truce with Spain (1609).

IN the great European conflict occasioned by the Protestant Reformation, Spain was marked out to be the foremost champion of the Catholic cause. While one species of Protestantism had established itself in northern Germany, and another was battling in a not uneven contest for its life in France, Spain behind her stiff, mountainous barrier was Catholic to the marrow. Here, as nowhere else in Europe, the defence and expansion of the Catholic Faith were identified with the growth and glory of the nation. The monks, nuns, and priests constituted a large fraction of the population. The Inquisition, which was controlled by the Crown, was regarded as a necessary safeguard. A great auto-da-fé at Valladolid (October 18, 1559) was the opening stroke in a repressive campaign, evoking only sparse and ineffectual protests, against the new beliefs which had come into Spain from Germany. The work which the Spanish Inquisition then did under the impulsion of Philip II was so thoroughly performed that heresy, in Spain a new and unfamiliar plant, was stamped out before it had begun to acquire strength. The Roman Church was henceforth secure. Not until the revolution of 1931 was its control of education successfully challenged by a movement originating in Spain itself and supported, as it would appear, by a majority of the Spanish people.

Philip II was a devout and dutiful Catholic ruler, who conceived it to be his principal mission in life to uproot heresy from his dominions and to support the faith of his fathers throughout the world. A grave, laborious, narrow man, unable to distinguish small things from big, and consequently incapable of delegating work to others, he allowed himself to be so much encumbered by minute duties that he was blind to the large aspects of state policy. Some dark stains rest upon his memory, the murder of an insane eldest son, the secret assassination of an ambassador from the Netherlands. There are few more pathetic pages in history than the life of this melancholy, conscience-stricken, dimly-lit autocrat toiling at his desk over the task, exceeding all human strength, of saving the Catholic empire of Spain from the new, unsettling thoughts and rapacious powers which were abroad in the world.

The strength of Spain consisted in its standing army. There were no infantry troops in Europe better drilled or better disciplined or more experienced in war than the famous Spanish *tercios*, for whom Italy was the appointed training ground. The gentry of Spain flocked to the standards, thinking it no penance to follow a military career under the pleasant Italian skies. During the second half of the sixteenth century the best officers in Europe were probably to be found serving under the Spanish king. Some, like Alva, were Spanish noblemen. But others were Italians, including the greatest general of the century, Alessandro Farnese, Duke of Parma. It is a tribute to Spanish statesmanship that it was thus able to attract to the service of the Spanish crown some of the best talent from the proudest families of Italy.

On the sea Spain was, for several reasons, less formidable. She was partly a Mediterranean, partly an Atlantic, power. In the Mediterranean she was confronted with the task of clearing the sea of Turkish corsairs, and of assisting Venice and the Knights of Malta in arresting the onward progress of the military navy of the Sultan. These were onerous and exacting duties. A mobile and enterprising enemy, based on Algiers and Tunis, raided the Balearic Islands and the Valencian coast. An ambitious monarchy, served by Greek seamen and established in Constantinople, offered a standing threat to the safety of Italy. Now, by the use of centuries, a form of warfare had grown up in these smooth Mediterranean waters which was wholly unsuited to Atlantic weather. The galley impelled by oars, the classic galley of the Roman republic and of the Roman empire, still survived. The tradition of rowing towards your enemy, of grappling with him, and of deciding the issue by a hand to hand infantry fight conducted on sea was as living in the days of Philip II as it was in the times of Xerxes and Pompey. The biggest naval battle in the Mediterranean fought during the century, the battle of Lepanto (1571), when Don John of Austria, King Philip's brother, inflicted a crushing defeat on the Turkish army, was a galley battle, a clash of military row-boats. Yet it did not follow that men trained to fight in galleys would gain any experience likely to help them in the ocean-going sailing ships or galleons which were now becoming an indispensable part of the Spanish naval equipment. On the contrary, the tradition of the galley, surviving into times when the galley was an anachronism, was positively harmful. In the ocean and in the Channel a fleet manoeuvred by fine seamen could always be trusted to beat an adversary whose plans were dominated by the ramrod tactics of a galley fight.

Spain then was hampered by the fact that being compelled to fight on two fronts, she was driven to employ at one and the same time two different types of warship, one extremely ancient and the other very modern, and that many of her seamen were trained in the ancient school. But these disadvantages might have been overcome had there been at the centre of Spanish affairs an intelligent appreciation of the value of sea power in warfare. It is a curious circumstance that in spite of the enormous stake which Spain had acquired in the new world, she made no sustained effort to gain a mastery of the western ocean. The emancipation of the Dutch republic from Spanish control was certainly greatly assisted by the fact that the rebels were left in undisputed command of the sea.

But the root of Spanish weakness lay in finance. No European government in the sixteenth century was financially strong: but Spain is a conspicuous instance of a country owning a vast surface of the globe, both in the old world and in the new, and having immediate access to the richest mineral resources then known to exist, which was nevertheless in perpetual straits for money, and often unable by reason of sheer penury to perform the most elementary tasks of government. The reasons for this paradox are to be found partly in an unintelligent general policy, partly in an ignorance of economic laws and a vicious system of taxation, and not least in the absence of any effective check on peculation and extravagance. The king could raise but little money from Spain itself. Despite their vast wealth, the clergy were immune from taxation. In Castile the nobles, though often subjected to irregular acts of spoliation, were by long custom exempted from contributing to the regular revenues of the crown. In Aragon the Cortes voted a fixed and wholly insufficient sum. Of the immense wealth of Mexico and Peru, only a small fraction found its way into the royal coffers, for in the Spanish colonies peculation was universal. But what was even more serious, since fraud can always be remedied by a stricter method of control, the fiscal system of the Spanish empire was based upon a false theory of trade. What was necessary to its welfare was the greatest possible international exchange of goods. The policy which was, in fact, pursued was protection in its blindest and most extravagant form. Spain had no science and no manufactures. While she could not send her colonies what they needed, she forbade their trade with any power but herself. From such a policy only two consequences were to be apprehended, either a retardation in the material progress of the colonies, or the encouragement of smuggling on a large scale. Both consequences, in fact, ensued. And meanwhile the agriculture and commerce of Spain were hampered by innumerable internal tolls, and by the *alcabala*, a tax of ten per cent. on sales, than which it would be difficult to conceive an instrument more exactly calculated to paralyse the economic prosperity of a people.

If little money could be wrung from Spain, nothing could be expected from Italy. It followed that the most elastic source of material revenue was to be found in the Netherlands. Antwerp was now one of the wealthiest trading cities in the world. She was unhampered by guild restrictions. She had become a great centre of international dealings, easily distancing Bruges and Ghent in the wealth and freedom of her communications, and, owing to the development of oceanic trade, possessing an advantage over Flanders as a banking centre. And fast rising into prominence was the Hanseatic city of Amsterdam, whose prosperity, originally founded on the herring fishing, was now augmented by the growing wealth of all those European states which were situated near the Atlantic littoral. There was opulence in the Netherlands. Here was the fiscal heart of the Spanish empire.

Intimately bound with this Spanish Eldorado by long ties of commercial intercourse was the island in which Philip II had for a time ruled as the consort of its native queen Mary. Philip, like his father before him, was well aware of the value of England as a friend and ally. He knew the worth of English trade to his Flemings and the evils resulting from any interruption of that intercourse; how a hostile England could molest the marine communications between Spain and the Low Countries, and a friendly England most effectually protect them. But he was a devout Catholic. Religion came before everything. The preservation of the friendship of England would in the long run depend upon the faith of the islanders.

Elizabeth determined to be a Protestant. It was a bold decision, for the north of England was Catholic and the Highlands of Scotland and the Irish, while in the Scottish Lowlands a French army under the Regent Mary of Guise was upholding the Catholic cause. But Elizabeth made it, with the concurrence of her great adviser William Cecil, Lord Burghley, and never receded from it. We may suspect that she may have been influenced by her early training and upbringing, which had been Protestant, and by the humiliations which she had endured under her Catholic sister's reign.

The statesmanship of the English government during the first few years of Elizabeth's reign was of an order of excellence higher than that which had yet been attained by any European government. A European war was happily avoided. The Church of England was placed upon a settled national foundation, without civil disorders and with a minimum of interference with liberty of thought. By a timely exercise of courage, for which the credit belongs to Cecil, an armed force was sent to Scotland, which liberated the country from the Regent Mary's French soldiers, who had there been upholding the Catholic cause, and cleared the Lowlands for John Knox and the Protestant religion. No English military exploit, not even Waterloo, has had results so far-reaching as the ill-conducted siege of Leith by an ill-disciplined English army, which resulted in the Treaty of Edinburgh. For the first time for centuries an English army had entered Scotland, not to put a humiliation on Scottish pride, but to advance a Scottish interest. In making secure the Protestant reformation in southern Scotland the government of Elizabeth, as some wise men then foresaw, took the first essential step to the union of the two countries. Foolish courses, which might have prejudiced the success of this great act of statesmanship, such as the revival of the old claim of suzerainty, or the marriage of Queen Elizabeth to a Scottish nobleman, were happily avoided. Skilful courses were pursued. The stroke was effected while England was quiet and France, with some surreptitious assistance to the rebels from the queen of England, distracted with the Amboise conspiracy.

The new queen prided herself upon being "mere English." She knew the prejudice of her island subjects against foreigners, and had seen it exemplified in the storm of disapproval which greeted her sister's engagement to the Spaniard. She did not propose to repeat her sister's error. But flirtation was second nature, and the grave entertainment of proposals of marriage a diplomatic duty, which she owed to her country. In order to keep the Huguenot party in good heart she was prepared over a period of ten years to receive the suit of Alençon, nearly twenty years her junior and, had his character been less contemptible, a mere figure of fun. But in her heart she shrank from sharing her throne with a foreigner. She would die as she had lived, a virgin queen and "mere English." At the end of her long life she said to her last Parliament: "Though you have had and may have many mightier and wiser princes sitting on this throne, yet you never had nor shall have any that loved you better." Englishmen knew that this was so. Vanities and caprices which would have made any lesser woman ridiculous, acts of meanness which would have tarnished any other reputation, never stood between Elizabeth and the romantic devotion of her subjects. They felt that she was a great woman, proud, mettlesome, and preternaturally wise, and that her life was dedicated to the service and honour of her country.

It was generally recognized abroad that a country so rich and powerful as England could never be conquered if it remained united. The hopes of the Guises and afterwards of Philip II and the Jesuits were founded upon the prospect of English disunion. But save for the rising of the northern earls in 1569, when Elizabeth had been on her throne for eleven years, there was no grave menace to national unity; and the call of the Catholic north came too late. The Lowlands of Scotland were already given over to the reformed church, and the main part of the population in central and southern England was satisfied with the Anglican settlement. When war eventually broke out with Spain there was no English party like the French League willing to give support to the foreign invader. London was Protestant to the core. A Spanish garrison, such as that which held Paris for the League, would have been unthinkable in the capital of England.

Foremost among the causes which produced this unusual composure of the public mind was the skill with which the Church was settled upon its new foundations. There were no burnings. The dispossessed Roman bishops were treated with consideration, and though Parliament passed an Act of Uniformity, it was not so administered as to make the profession of differing religious beliefs a dangerous occupation. A convenient and calculated haze shrouded the religious convictions of the queen and made it seem possible that she might after all incline to Rome. If she objected to the sacrifice of the Mass, she did not conceal her dislike of married clergy. Candles should sometimes shine upon her altar and give to the Catholics a delusive glimmer of hope.

Those who were disquieted by the fear that she would proclaim herself Head of the Church, like her father, were consoled by a new vague title, which might mean less, but might also mean quite as much. What was there in this Church settlement that could stir reasonable men to a revolt? The Liturgy, which was Cranmer's Prayer-book of 1552 with some slight variations, was avowedly based on Roman models. The government of the Church was episcopal, the articles of belief very largely Calvinistic. To no one section of theological opinion was the settlement entirely satisfactory. The English divines who had acquired their theology in Switzerland thought it too conservative; the Catholics regarded it as too revolutionary. To those who disliked surplices or Communion tables, or found little warrant for bishops in the Holy Writ, the Elizabethan Church fell far short of perfection. But to the great body of the people, who were not theological, there was nothing intolerable in this settlement founded on compromise. It was not until 1570, when the queen was excommunicated and deposed by the Pope, that the average Catholic was compelled to ask himself the question to whom his ultimate allegiance was really due.

To the King of Spain, England at the accession of Queen Elizabeth appeared not in the guise of an enemy, but as a country to be won over and conciliated. A pious Catholic, determined to root out heresy from his dominions, Philip was never so much of a crusader as to sacrifice the solid political interests of his country to religious propaganda. England was heretical, a grave misfortune, a terrible taint; but England's heresy would never have provoked Philip to attack her. On the contrary, he was well pleased to see an English army abate the pride of the Guises, Catholic though they were, in Scotland. As a Catholic he might be expected to welcome the prospect of a possible union of England, Scotland, and France under Mary Queen of Scots. As a Spanish king he could not but regard such a contingency as a catastrophe at all costs to be averted. And the politician in him was in the last analysis stronger than the priest. So it happened that at the great crisis which established the Protestant Reformation in Scotland and paved the way to the Anglo-Scottish Union Philip was friendly, not inimical, to his heretical sister-in-law. In 1560 Spain helped English Protestantism by her friendship, in 1588 by her enmity.

And now, as an additional reason for keeping well with England, Philip was confronted by serious trouble in the Netherlands. The government of the seventeen provinces had been delegated by the king upon his departure for Spain to Margaret, Duchess of Parma, the natural daughter of Charles V by a Flemish mistress. Margaret had character, intellect, and sympathy. She was a native of the country and could speak its languages, and had she been left to govern the seventeen provinces without interference from Spain and with the help of the native nobility, there is little reason to doubt that her reign would have been successful and popular. But the regent was not a free agent. Secret instructions bound her to execute the decrees against the heretics, and a *consulta* of three advisers was imposed upon her by the absentee sovereign, to whom all questions of policy and administration, great and small, were regularly referred. Of this Camarilla the Cardinal Granvelle, son of the great statesman who for thirty years had been chief adviser to Charles V, was by his industry, his accomplishments, and his vast capacity the acknowledged and all-powerful chief.

The real gravamen against the Granvelle government (for so it was then regarded) was not that it lacked ability or statesmanship, but that it was required against its own better judgment to carry out an odious policy dictated from Spain. The people of the Netherlands were proud of their chartered rights and provincial privileges. They detested the presence of Spanish troops and the cruelties of Spanish religious persecution, and were more particularly apprehensive as to the effects of a new scheme for the creation of fourteen bishoprics, which was thought to portend the introduction of the Spainish Inquisition and yet sharper measures against reformed beliefs. Proud and wealthy native noblemen who had served the state under Charles V asked themselves how long these outrages were to be endured and when they were to be admitted to a legitimate share in the influence and spoils of government, from which they were excluded by the unpopular cardinal and his associates.

The two men who worked together to unhorse the cardinal from his high Spanish saddle were curiously different in temperament and character. Egmont was a generous, vain, somewhat unstable soldier, raised by his victories at St. Quentin and Gravelines to a pinnacle of popular eminence and smarting under the sense of ill-requited desert. William of Nassau, Prince of Orange, was made of tougher, if less showy, materials. The foundations of his character were pride, constancy, and compassion. The great aristocrat resented the pressure of Spanish troops upon Flemish soil, and was filled with pity for the suffering victims of Spanish tyranny. With few military qualities, save an unreadiness to acknowledge defeat, but with great tenacity of purpose and an infinite command of diplomatic resource, William found himself drawn by the course of events to lead a popular movement for severance from Spain. He is exposed to the charge of having been first a loyalist and then a rebel, first a Catholic, then a Lutheran, and finally a Calvinist. In truth he was an opportunist living on a thread of principle, and since he cared for liberty and hated fanaticism, and for these beliefs suffered like his friend Egmont a violent death, he is accounted among the principal champions of European freedom.

In face of the forthcoming signs of storm Philip resolved to drop the pilot. But the withdrawal of Granvelle under the pressure of Egmont and his friends (1564) only steeled the king in his resolve to stamp out the northern heretics. To the terror of the Spanish Inquisition and the rigorous enforcements of the "placards," or anti-heresy edicts, there was now added (August 18, 1564) the requirement that the population of the Netherlands should accept the doctrines of the Council of Trent. A solemn protest against these and other evils was drawn up in the Regent's Council under the influence of the Prince of Orange and taken in person by Egmont to the king (January, 1565).

When it was found that Egmont's mission was all in vain and that the edicts and decrees against the heretics were to be strictly enforced, the temperature swiftly rose. Young nobles, some like Marnix unbending Calvinists, others like Brederode humane Catholics, banded themselves together to resist the Inquisition. This was the body who drew up the uncompromising document known to history as the Compromise, and took to themselves with pride from the lips of a despiteful enemy the appellation of "Beggars" (Gueux), just as certain British soldiers at a later date have not been averse to being known as the Contemptibles. To all this protest and effervescence, which Orange and Egmont endeavoured to moderate,

as well as to a savage outburst of Calvinist iconoclasm,
Philip was quietly preparing a deadly reply.

The reproach against this Spanish king is that he was neither
open, nor intelligent, nor humane. The three men who in the
recent troubles had most helped in the maintenance of order
were Orange, Egmont, and Count Hoorn. But they had been
acclaimed by the "Gueux" and secretly denounced by the
regent. Accordingly their destruction was resolved on.
Without so much as coming to the Netherlands for a fort-
night to study the problem on the spot, the king sent Alva,
his best and most intemperate soldier, with a strong army of
Italian and Spanish mercenaries, to crush the heretics, and
with a special charge to trap and execute the three men in
whom a wiser monarch would have found the principal
pillars of his rule.

The prudent Orange withdrew to the safety of his German
home before the advancing storm, but in an hour fatal to
Spain Egmont and Hoorn were taken by treachery and after
a mock trial beheaded in the public square of Brussels. The
murder of these two influential and courageous men was one
of those political crimes from which governments do not
recover (June, 1568).

During six terrible years Alva tried his doctrine of thorough
destruction upon the stunned population of the Netherlands.
But there were four factors upon which he had not counted,
which taken into combination turned his early success into a
ruinous failure. The first was Orange. The prince was an outlaw,
and having therefore everything to fear and nothing to hope
from the Spaniards, embarked upon the bold course of
raising armies against them. His campaigns were a failure.
He was no general. His troops were ill paid and ill disciplined,
and in a pitched fight unequally matched against the seasoned
veterans of Alva. But if he could not beat the enemy in the
field, Orange could put him to an intolerable expense. To
pay his troops Alva was compelled to resort to a scheme of
taxation exactly calculated to arouse a commercial community to a white fury of indignation. Catholic merchants
who had not raised a finger to save a heretic from the stake
or to protest against the wholesale butcheries of "the Chamber
of Troubles" were furious when they were asked to pay a
ten per cent. duty upon every sale. The argument that
the tax was a feature in a Spanish budget did not appeal

THE REVOLT OF THE NETHERLANDS

to them. The whole country, without distinction of class or creed, was united as one man against a government which levelled such a deadly blow against the trade which was its heart.

A third factor was the sea. The ships were in Protestant

and pirate hands. A new brood of Low German or Dutch Vikings infested the narrow seas, intercepting treasure and supplies, plundering churches, murdering priests and monks, in exchange for barbarities which no land army raised under Protestant banners was yet able adequately to avenge. If the beggars on land were for the moment powerless, the "beggars of the sea" put a new heart into the struggle. With an open encouragement from English heretics like-minded with themselves and with the active countenance of Queen Elizabeth, the Dutch pirates seized the town of Brill and thus unconsciously laid the foundations of a new and famous European state.

April, 1572

Yet the Dutch Republic could never have been created from the sea alone. The Sea-Beggars imparted the original impetus which stirred the northern provinces to throw off the yoke of Spain and to invite William of Orange to lead them to victory. The seizure of Brill led immediately to the capture of Flushing in the north and of Mons and Valenciennes in the south; but, far more important, it opened out the campaign of sieges which has given to the history of Haarlem, of Alkmaar, and of Leyden an imperishable renown. If the Dutch were as yet unable to measure themselves with Alva's veterans in the open field, behind their city walls they fought with the desperate valour of men contending against an enemy who had proved again and again that in the heat of combat he spared neither age nor sex.

It was the cruelty and indiscipline of the ill-paid Spanish army which, in the autumn of 1571 and the spring and summer of the succeeding year, brought the Prince of Orange from the nadir to the zenith of his fortunes. Alva had been withdrawn, Requesens, his successor, had suddenly died, and a Spanish interregnum was a Flemish opportunity which so astute a diplomatist as the Prince of Orange was not likely to neglect. The lights of Dutch Protestantism had been burning low. The prince had lost an army and two brothers on the disastrous field of Mookerheede (1574), his forces had been driven out of the islands of Duiveland and Shouwen, his treasury was empty, he had been rebuffed by Queen Elizabeth, to whom he had offered the sovereignty of his northern provinces, and he knew well that without strong internal support his little Calvinist state, hardly yet in being, would be helpless before the might of the Spanish empire. Suddenly

an unexpected beacon of help flared up in the Catholic south.
The Spanish army, breaking out into mutiny for lack of pay,
seized Alost, and from their bandits' lair carried fire and
sword to the brink of Brussels. In the general state of public
indignation and alarm William saw a golden opportunity to
restore and enlarge the fortunes of his cause. Acting on behalf of Holland and Zealand, he entered into negotiations
with the states of Flanders and Brabant for the exclusion of
the foreigner and the settlement of religion. The terrible sack
of Antwerp, known as the Spanish Fury, swept away the last
cobwebs of indecision which obstructed the Pacification of Nov.,
Ghent. The Catholic south and the Protestant north, the 1576
Low Dutchmen and the Walloons banded themselves together
in a political union to deal with a common danger. When
Don John of Austria, the new Spanish governor, entered
upon his governorship, with all the lustre of his royal blood,
and with the laurels of Lepanto not yet withered on his brow,
he found it necessary to concede to a united demand that the
country should be rid immediately and for ever of the fore n
troops, and that the charters and liberties of the provinces
should be maintained. Even more bitter to this proud and
impetuous dreamer was the predominance of Orange. "The
Prince of Orange," he wrote to the king, "has bewitched the
minds of all men. They love him, and fear him, and wish to
have him as their lord."

But the triumph of the prince was not sustained. The bonds
of union forged in the flames of the Spanish Fury were too
brittle to stand a serious strain. On the vital and unsettled
point of religion the United Provinces were not at one. The
Calvinists at Ghent, not without some unstatesmanlike encouragement from the Prince of Orange, rose in revolt against
their government, imprisoned the Duke of Aerschot, who was
the Catholic leader of the south, and aroused once more the
seething passions of religious hate which had been composed
under the sense of a common danger. It was upon a country
thus inflamed and divided that there now descended at the
head of a choice army of twenty thousand men the most
accomplished diplomatist and soldier of the Spanish empire.
The Duke of Parma was no bloodthirsty blunderer, like Alva;
no chimerical dreamer, like Don John. He could soothe,
cajole, conciliate; but while he disarmed suspicions, he
could also strike. By his crushing victory of Gembloux he

June, finally assured the return of the southern provinces to their
1578 Spanish allegiance.

By this battle it was decided that Holland and Belgium
should lead a separate political existence, which, save for their
brief and uneasy union between 1815 and 1830, has remained
unbroken to this day. That Brussels and The Hague should
now be so remote in spirit, though so near in space, is a
circumstance chiefly to be ascribed to Alva, who crushed the
southern Protestants in the sixteenth century, and to Parma
who prevented their return and revival. These two foreign
officers, the first of execrable, the second of most honourable,
memory, are among the architects of modern Belgium.

It was with deep reluctance that Orange surrendered the
dream of a united Netherlands and assented to the Union of
Utrecht (1579), which his Protestant supporters in the north
had framed as a counterblast to the Catholic Union of Arras.
No choice was now open to him but to concentrate upon the
defence of those hard-bitten northern Calvinists who, in
Holland and Zealand, had placed their destinies in his hand
and were willing to sacrifice everything for their beliefs. To
this end he resolved, much to the grief of his best supporters,
to invoke the aid of the Duke of Anjou, who, as heir to the
French throne and an acknowledged suitor for the hand of
the English queen, seemed likely to offer the best guarantees
of effectual help. It was a bad speculation. Anjou was
treacherous, his army mutinous, his protectorate hateful.
Nothing useful was gained by his shortlived intervention.
But a more powerful auxiliary in the fight against Spain was
destined before long to disclose surprising resources.

The doctrine of political assassination was at this time so
widely held, being specially, though not exclusively, commended by some Spanish members of the Jesuit Order, that
it is no matter for surprise if the government of Spain resolved
to remove its obstinate and formidable antagonist by murder.
The prince was put to the ban of the empire (March 15, 1581),
declared to be an outlaw and an enemy of the human race,
and money, land, or a title were offered for his head. But
there is a nemesis which attends the policy of political
assassination. The victim may fall, but the cause survives,
strengthened by the martyr's blood. On July 10, 1584, Orange
was shot in the Prinzenhof at Delft by a young Burgundian
fanatic named Balthazar Gérard: but though he was only

fifty-one his murder had come too late. Three years before (July 26, 1581), the representatives of Brabant and Flanders, of Utrecht, Guelderland, Holland and Zealand, meeting at The Hague, had signed an Act of Abjuration, renouncing their allegiance to the king of Spain. So though William of Orange was now dead, out of the turmoil and tempest a state of his creating had already emerged, which was destined to cover the seas with its shipping, to build up an opulent empire in the east, to challenge the navies of England and the armies of France, and to earn the gratitude of mankind as an asylum of intellectual freedom, and as the home of a school of painters whose minute and delicate observation of the quiet beauties of life has permanently enriched the culture of Europe.

The new state possessed a constitution to all appearance most unfitted for the rough weather of European politics. It was a federation of seven tiny sovereign republics, each with its own estates or local parliament, and its own elective stadtholder or executive officer, and each claiming to exercise a direct share in the control of finance and foreign policy of the confederation. An assembly of delegates from the provincial estates, with the assistance of a council of twelve, dealt with matters common to the whole Union, and appointed the captain-general of the army, and the admiral-general of the navy; but since the real seat of sovereignty lay not with these central delegations but with the seven local estates, there was no constitutional security either for the coherence of the republic or for continuity and vigour in the conduct of its policy. At any moment, did they so choose, the peasants of Frisia, the canons of Utrecht, or the nobles of Guelders might frustrate by an adverse vote the well-laid plans of the burgher aristocracy of the trading cities.

From the ill consequences of these defects in its polity the republic was saved by three circumstances, the substantial homogeneity of the Dutch population, the pre-eminence of Holland among the provinces, and, most of all, by the special position, which during the first critical half-century of Dutch independence was freely accorded to the head of the house of Orange.

The bulk of the Dutch population, being concerned with trade, industry, and seafaring, shared a common outlook upon foreign affairs and a common understanding of Dutch needs and interests. Feudalism was dead. Noble and priest had given way to the urban middle class. A burgher aristocracy ruled the cities and the cities ruled the commonwealth. By a piece of good fortune, which greatly contributed to the stability and strength of the country, the chief centres of trade, learning, and politics were to be found within the ambit of a single province. Amsterdam and Rotterdam, Delft and Dordrecht, Leyden (the seat of the Dutch university) and The Hague, the political capital of the state, were all situated in Holland. Nowhere in Europe was there in the same area such a concentration of population and commercial power. Nowhere was trade more skilfully managed, or the art of city life so well understood. And as Holland was supreme among the seven provinces, Amsterdam was pre-eminent among its cities. In banking and commerce, in the size of its navy and the span of its colonial enterprise, this vigorous city distanced all competitors. The centralization which was lacking to the constitution was supplied by the force of economic preponderance. In theory local liberties remained unimpaired. In practice the course which found favour with the opulent rulers of Amsterdam was apt to commend itself to the weaker members of the federation.

To a policy thus divided and balanced the princes of the house of Orange supplied an indispensable unity of direction. In nothing was this dynasty more remarkable than in its wise regard for the jealous republicanism of the Dutch. Amid unending perils William the Silent made, and Maurice and Frederick Henry afterwards defended, the liberties of this people. Yet neither their success nor their wonderful record of service tempted them to overthrow the cumbrous forms of the federal constitution. The head of the house of Orange was content with the position of an elected magistrate. Stadtholder in five provinces, captain-general and admiral-general of the republic, he concentrated in his own hands by the free voice of the community the effective powers of the state. For seventy years an accumulation of elective offices gave to the chiefs of this remarkable family as large a measure of authority as was enjoyed by any hereditary sovereign in Europe during that aristocratic age. Then, after the death of William II (1650), came a long minority during which the conduct of the republic was vested in the hands of the principal civil official of its leading province, the Grand Pensionary of

Holland. But the memory of the house of Orange was still alive in the hearts of the Dutch people; and in the hours of their greatest danger, when their small republic was menaced with destruction by the vast military power of Louis XIV, they called upon the great-grandson of William the Silent to save them, and did not call in vain.

Twenty-five years of warfare divide the death of William of Orange from the twelve years' truce signed in 1609, which advertised to the whole world Spain's final confession that she could not conquer the Dutch republic. What saved the Dutch was, firstly, the diversion of Spanish military effort against Elizabeth and Henry IV, and, secondly, the discovery by the United Provinces of a great statesman and a great general. When William fell by the hand of an assassin, the Duke of Parma was on the high tide of his triumphant career. One by one the cities of Flanders and Brabant fell before his victorious skill. He took Brussels, stormed Antwerp, threatened, unless help were speedily forthcoming, to overwhelm those last bulwarks of the Protestant cause, Holland and Zealand.

It is improbable that the small English army under the Earl of Leicester, which Queen Elizabeth threw into Flushing to restore the situation, would have permanently withstood the forces which the Spanish commander was so well able to assemble and inspire. But Parma's efforts were dispersed. He was commanded first to collect an army for the invasion of England, and, when this hope died away with the dispersion of the Armada, to forward his master's interests in the civil war in France. While he should have been mastering Amsterdam, he was directed to relieve Paris. While his troops should have been conquering Holland they were required for a futile occupation of Rouen, and so, charged with miscellaneous and distracting military duties, this great soldier died with his 1592 task unaccomplished.

The Dutch constitution, like the American constitution today, was ill suited to bear the stress and strain of war. Every province was sovereign, and each province was tenacious of its accustomed ways. Fortunately, however, for the future of the republic, the province of Holland was, by reason of its wealth, its population, its energy, and the lion's share which it bore in the charges of the Union, the predominant power in the States-General. And for thirty-two years (1586-1618) the influence of Holland was wielded by its advocate John van Oldenbarnveldt.

To this wise, experienced, and liberally-minded man, who was for so long a period the real civilian head of the new republic, fortune supplied an admirable pendant in Maurice of Nassau, the soldier son of William of Orange.

It was the object of that accomplished officer and of his cousin, William of Nassau, to forge an army which could beat the Spaniards in the open field. This they did. In four brilliant campaigns Maurice liberated the soil of the federated provinces, and showed himself to be the first soldier of his age. There was no department of war in which he was not proficient. His siege dispositions were regarded as a masterpiece of caution and science. His handling of cavalry in action showed the eye of a master. His capture of Gertruidenburg, his cavalry pursuit of Varax during a winter night at Turnhout (1597), the daring and opportune charge which turned defeat into victory on the hard-fought field of Dunkirk, were regarded as supreme examples of the military art. And meanwhile on the sea the Spaniards were mastered. A great naval victory at Gibraltar in 1607 announced the definite superiority of the Dutch and impelled the enemy to think of peace.

There were three great difficulties obstructing agreement, independence, religion, trade. It was intolerable to Spanish pride that these Dutch rebels should be acknowledged as an independent state, that they should be permitted to prohibit the public celebration of Catholic rites, or that they should trade with that vast area in the new world which had been reserved to Spain by the Pope. A peace was found to be impossible: but eventually a twelve years' truce was signed at Antwerp (April 9, 1609). The delicate subject of religion was left unmentioned, but the Netherlands wrung from their reluctant antagonists the acknowledgment of their independence and of their right to trade in Spanish waters.

For during these five and twenty years the better part of the Dutch population had taken to the sea, leaving their land armies to be mainly composed of Germans, English, or Scots. A Dutch captain had wintered in the Arctic ice. A Dutch fleet had visited China and Siam. Dutch factories had been established in the Spice Islands. A Dutch East India Company, the first of the great chartered companies, had been established in 1601. The new-gotten wealth of an expanding world commerce nourished the war effort of this small and vigorous community, and now, after a generation of desperate struggle, enabled it to negotiate a victorious truce with the first military power in Europe.

BOOKS WHICH MAY BE CONSULTED

Motley: Rise of the Dutch Republic. 3 vols. Everyman's Library. 1906.

H. Pirenne: *Histoire de Belgique.* 1907.

F. Harrison: *William the Silent.* 1897.

W. H. Prescott: *History of the Reign of Philip II.* 1855.

Martin A. S. Hume: *Philip II of Spain.* 1902.

P. J. Blok: *History of the People of the Netherlands.* 1892-6.

J. E. Neale: *Queen Elizabeth.* 1934.

R. Altamira y Crevea: *Historia d'España y de la civilizacion española.* 1902.

R. B. Merriman: *The Rise of the Spanish Empire.* 1918-25.

A. F. Pollard: *History of England.* 1912.

F. W. Maitland: *The Anglican Settlement and the Scottish Reformation (Cambridge Modern History,* Vol II, chap. xvi).

J. A. Froude: *History of England.* 1856-70.

A. Lang: *History of Scotland.* 1900-7.

J. Skelton: *Maitland of Lethington and the Scotland of Mary Stuart.* 2 vols. 1894.

P. Hume Brown: *John Knox.* 2 vols. 1895.

P. Geyl: *The Revolt of the Netherlands, 1555-1609.* 1932.

P. Geyl: *The Netherlands Divided, 1609-1648. Tr.* S. T. Bindoff. 1936.

G. N. Clark: *The Birth of the Dutch Republic* (Raleigh Lecture). 1946.

CHAPTER LI

ENGLAND AND SPAIN

Commercial rivalry between England and Spain. Private enterprise and public caution. The Puritan sailors of England. The lure of the East. The first blow. Francis Drake. The Catholic rising in the north. Mary of Scotland. Union of Portugal and Spain. The Armada and its sequel. The passing of Spanish prestige. The expulsion of the Moriscoes. Beginnings of English colonization.

THE rivalry between England and Spain, which developed into open war in the reign of Elizabeth, while it undoubtedly helped to deepen the Protestant sentiments of the English people and had from the first some tinge of religious animosity, was, at the bottom, economic. The seafaring people of England were drawn by their appetite for adventure, for money, and for commerce, to challenge the closely guarded Spanish monopoly in the new world and in the Indies. The war did not arise out of religion. It did not come because the Spanish government was determined to force the Roman faith upon England, still less because Elizabeth was anxious to precipitate a quarrel with Catholic Spain. It came because English seamen, acting on their own initiative, but often not without the sympathy and connivance of the queen, were determined to make good their claim to share in the commerce of the new world.

1560-88   During the twenty-eight years succeeding the Treaty of Edinburgh, nothing is more remarkable than the contrast between the caution of the English government and the venturesome audacity of the military and seafaring section of the nation. While the official history of the government is singularly devoid of event, the unofficial and unauthorized activities of the people open up a new chapter in the history of the world. The object of the queen was to prevent religious disruption and to stave off a foreign war until such time as loyalty to her person had become a settled habit among all her lieges. Her policy, therefore, was to deprecate excessive vigour, and to disclaim responsibility for compromising adventures. To ardent Puritans like Sir Francis Walsingham such a course appeared to be a humiliating betrayal of the Protestant cause. They would have fought the enemy, not surreptitiously and on a system of limited liability, but openly and on every front, in France, in the Netherlands, and on the high seas. The queen's unheroic but statesmanlike avoidance of precipitate risk was little to their liking. For England had now become the first naval power in the world. She had the best shipwrights, the best ships, the best sailors. She had learnt the lesson of naval gunnery and the value of the broadside. Her ships, which were smaller than the Spaniards', could sail closer to the wind, and were easier to handle. Though the Royal Navy was small, amounting only to twenty-two ships of 100 tons and over in 1559, and to twenty-nine ships in 1603, there was always a large pirate and commercial navy in reserve which could be relied upon to co-operate with the queen's ships at a crisis. The growth of the nation's sea-power owed little to official encouragement. It was the result of the strong natural appetite of an enterprising marine population, who suddenly found themselves in the surprising position of being able to compete for the dominion of the world.

The mariners of England in the Elizabethan age, though all were not cut to the same pattern, were apt to possess certain common qualities. Sailorwise, they believed in an overruling Providence, governing the waves and winds and the fate of men. They were proud of England and their queen. They despised foreigners. They hated the Pope, the Turk, and the Devil, but perhaps most of all the Pope, who had allotted the East Indies to Portugal and the West Indies to Spain. Of international law, either as a need or as a fact, they had not the slightest suspicion. They regarded the high seas as a kind of no man's land upon which they might pillage and murder to their hearts' content. Only to a few more curious spirits did marine enterprise suggest the possibility of missionary work. No Protestant chaplain in an Elizabethan galleon was conscious of the noble rôle of the Catholic Las Casas.

Yet mingled with the baser appetites of the buccaneers was a certain largeness and simplicity of imagination which gave nobility to the seafaring movements of this age. The expansion of geographical knowledge and the discovery of Cathay,

or the Earthly Paradise, were motives commonly felt, and not
confined only to men of science or poetic dreamers. Audacity
was bred of success. "There is no land unhabitable or sea
unnavigable," wrote Master Robert Thorne of Bristol (1527)
recommending the northern passage to the Spice Islands to
his sovereign with a *bravura* characteristic of that time.

For still those distant Spice Islands in the East Indies re-
1553 mained the primary quest. Willoughby and Chancellor tried
to reach them by the north-eastern passage and opened up the
trade with Russia. Gilbert, Frobisher, and Davis hoped to
1610 find the north-western passage and rediscovered Hudson
Straits. But both passages were fatally barred by the ice and
snow of the Arctic regions.

There remained no other course, if the wealth of the Orient
were to be reached, than a direct invasion of the trade
monopoly of Spain and Portugal in the South Seas. English
d.   sailors, like John Hawkins, who opened up a traffic in negro
1595 slaves between Guinea and the West Indies, knew that they
could not so trade without the use of force. They armed
their ships, were prepared to fight, and looked forward without
misgivings to a breach with Spain. Only if a violent attack on
an indefensible monopoly is itself indefensible, do these
English sailors stand condemned. The question at issue was
the trade of the world.

It was in 1567 in the Mexican port of San Juan de Ulloa that
the first shot was exchanged in this great controversy. Here
John Hawkins and his young cousin, Francis Drake, were
sheltering from the hurricane after a successful course of trade
and piracy on the Spanish Main, when a fleet of thirteen
Spanish galleons, carrying on board the new Governor of
Mexico, appeared in the offing. Hawkins, who had five ships
only, but was in a position to deny an entry to the Spaniards,
elected to treat. As the two little fleets lay side by side, and
as their crews were fraternizing ashore, a treacherous attack
was suddenly launched against the unsuspecting Englishmen.
Many were slaughtered, three ships were lost, and it was only
after a hard and gallant fight that Hawkins and Drake
managed to extricate themselves from the mêlée. The story
of Spanish treachery and English valour made a deep impression when it was known at home. "Military and seafaring
men all over England," says Camden, "fretted and desired
war with Spain. But the queen shut her ears against them."

For the next twenty-eight years the formidable figure of Francis Drake dominates the seas. There are some who think that his methods of buccaneering were not the best, and that he would have done well to establish a base for his piracies at Cartagena, or at some other spot on the Spanish Main. But he reached his object, which was by incessant and ubiquitous plunderings to drive Spain into war. Nothing was safe from him, neither the towns on the Spanish Main, nor the route taken by the Peruvian treasure across the Isthmus of Panama, nor the Pacific coast, nor the Spice Islands. In the year before the Armada sailed, he burned the shipping in Cadiz harbour. Before that, on his return from circumnavigating the globe, his compatriots called him "The Master Thief of the Unknown World," and his queen, who had gone shares in the loot, went down expressly to Deptford to knight the great discoverer, and the head of the pirates' profession.

Meanwhile, events had been moving forward to the outbreak of that open struggle which Philip and Elizabeth were so anxious to avoid.

The strength of England was now sufficiently manifest to convince its enemies that the country could be conquered only with the assistance of an English party desirous of overthrowing the queen and of establishing once more the Roman Faith. Such a party existed. Adherents of the Catholic Church were to be found scattered through the country, sparse in the south and east, numerous in the north, dominant in the Celtic regions of the British Isles. More particularly was their power to be apprehended in the poor and backward northern counties of England, where the feudal nobles were still strong, and where Scottish priests fleeing from the wrath of John Knox, and Catholic propaganda put about by English exiles in Louvain, combined to sustain the ardour of the ancient faith. In the politics of northern England, whether past or present, aristocratic pride has always played a part. To men like the Earl of Northumberland and Lord Dacre of the western marches, Protestantism was an odious innovation fastened on to the country by the middle class counsellors who had unfortunately gained the ear of the queen. Relying on Spanish and Scottish help, which never came, they rose in revolt in 1569, destroyed the Bibles and Prayer-books in Durham Cathedral, and then, failing to find substantial support, were easily and ruthlessly crushed. The suppression of this premature and disjointed enterprise gave to Elizabeth a decisive advantage of which her enemies would have been wise to take note. The lesson was disregarded. The plots against the queen continued till the end.

For these Catholic discontents Mary of Scotland provided a steady and dangerous rallying point. The story of this unfortunate princess, had it been abruptly terminated during the summer of 1567, would have read somewhat as follows: Daughter of James V and Mary of Guise, Mary had been brought up in the profligate court of Catherine de'Medici, where she was married to Francis, heir to the French throne and subsequently king. Her husband, a mere boy, died in Paris, her mother, Mary of Guise, in Leith. Being lawful queen of Scotland, she was invited into her kingdom by those members of the Scottish aristocracy who were principally concerned to defend the independence of their country from its southern neighbour. Here she was wedded to the young and profligate Earl of Darnley, who, thanks to his mother, had a claim to succeed to the English throne. But though the marriage resulted in the birth of the boy who became James VI of Scotland and James I of England, it was a tragedy deeply stained with blood. The queen had a favourite secretary. He was an Italian of the name of Rizzio, cultivated and agreeable, a pleasant contrast to the brutal Darnley and to the grim Protestant nobles who controlled the policy of the country. Darnley murdered him in Mary's presence. A year later Darnley was himself destroyed, as many thought with the complicity of his wife, who proceeded without delay to marry Bothwell, his assassin. The Scottish nobles, who were not squeamish, recoiled from the national disgrace of these transactions. They imprisoned Mary in Lochleven, intending to bring her to trial for her offence; but Mary escaped. With a reputation deeply tarnished in the eyes of her contemporaries, Catholic and Protestant alike, she crossed the border and threw herself upon the mercy of Elizabeth.

Had Elizabeth returned Mary to meet her accusers in Scotland, England would have been saved from many anxieties. But the Queen was outraged by the idea of rebellion, and had no sympathy with rebels, even when rebellion was helpful to the interests of her country. She hated John Knox, she scolded the Scottish nobles for the indignity which they put on their lawful sovereign, and she could never bring herself cordially to co-operate either with the Dutch or the Huguenots. So she kept Mary in prison in England, and endeavoured to treat with her, suggesting terms of peace that were not unreasonable, as that she should resign her throne to James VI, and allow him to be educated in England; but Mary, who was set on revenge and flattered by ambition, preferred to play for higher stakes. In December, 1568, she was encouraged to hope that she might aspire to the hand of King Philip of Spain.

Accordingly, for nineteen years the captive queen was the 1568-pivot round which revolved the whirlpool of Catholic con- 87 spiracy and intrigue. Plot followed upon plot, encouraged by the King of Spain, by the Pope, who excommunicated the heretic queen and released her subjects from their allegiance, and by the English Catholic exiles abroad. A Protestant Association was formed to protect the life, so often menaced, of the great sovereign, who persistently refused, to the dismay and bewilderment of her Protestant subjects, to protect herself by bringing Mary to judgment. Eventually clear proof was forthcoming of the Scottish queen's complicity in a design to do away with her rival. When Babington's plot was divulged, both Houses unanimously petitioned for the execution of "the monstrous and huge dragon the Queen of Scots." On February 1, 1587, after long and painful hesitation, Elizabeth signed the death warrant, than which there could have been no clearer defiance of the Pope, of Spain, and of all their works. Mary had long outlived the dark shadows of her passionate youth. She had become a heroine of romance, the champion of a faith, and was viewed by the whole Catholic world as a saint and a martyr. Elizabeth, greatly misdoubting, had given a precedent for the execution of a crowned and anointed queen.

Spain was in a position to take up the challenge. A disaster in Morocco, the death of King Sebastian of Portugal, and the 1580 failure of his line, had brought the Portuguese kingdom under the Spanish Crown. The fine Atlantic seaboard, the mines of Brazil, the rich Portuguese possessions on both sides of Africa, the factories and posts in the Spice Islands, the Azores, a halfway house across the Atlantic, and the East Indies, passed by an unexpected stroke of fortune into the hands of Philip II. Forty years later, when the nature of the contest between Spain and Britain was more clearly understood, a Portuguese publicist argued that the King of Spain should transfer his capital from Madrid to Lisbon, and thence launch a navy which should defend India and South America in the British Channel, where alone the great world issue could be decided. The advice was never taken. The Spaniard was never welcome in Portugal. The two countries were never brought to coalesce, and their uneasy marriage was dissolved after sixty years. By a singular irony of fate, the period of Pan-Iberian union witnessed at once the flowering time of Spanish literature and the gradual decline of Spanish and Portuguese power. But in 1580, when the union occurred, it promised to Philip of Spain a vast accession of strength which in England and France was viewed with eyes of acute apprehension and distrust.

Still Philip hesitated. Though England gave support to Portuguese discontent and to Dutch rebellion, the king shrank from the expense and danger of a direct attack on that island of formidable heretics. Eventually, while France was paralysed by the War of the Three Henries,[1] and after Mary Stuart had formally recognized him as her heir to the English throne, he yielded his judgment to the sailors and the exiles and the priests, and, in the mood of Don Quixote pursuing a holy but impossible quest, commissioned his subjects to prepare the conquest of England.

The Spanish Armada, conceived in the spirit of a religious crusade, and prepared at an alarming cost, set sail from Lisbon on May 30, 1588, under the Duke of Medina Sidonia, a foolish and cowardly landsman, who was selected on the ground of his rank alone. The plan was that the fleet should proceed up the Channel to Dunkirk and Nieuport, and thence convoy the army of the Duke of Parma to England, where Elizabeth was to be deposed, and the Infanta of Spain set up in her place. A more chimerical or fantastic scheme it would have been difficult to devise. Exiles are always bad counsellors, and the English Catholics on the continent, who had the ear of the Pope and the King of Spain, had not reckoned upon the change which had come over the temper of the English people during the last two decades. The Puritan spirit had grown strong: the Catholic spirit had proportionately diminished. A generation of peace and prosperity had

---

[1] Henry III and Henry of Navarre against Henry, Duke of Mayenne, the leader of the League or ultra-Catholic party.

consolidated the loyalty of the nation to the crown. Persecution there had been, but not before the Pope's Bull of deposition in 1570, and then upon a scale which contrasted favourably with the burnings of the previous reign, and was far removed from the terrible holocaust of victims exacted by Catholicism in the Netherlands, in France, and in Spain. There was no party in the country which would have favoured a Spanish landing or tolerated a Spanish queen. Even if Parma's army had been disembarked in England with the military reinforcements brought overseas from Spain, they would have found themselves opposed by the united force of a high-mettled and valiant people. But the whole scheme foundered on the incompetence of the Spanish navy. The vast galleons, crowded with soldiers, and obsessed by the antiquated tradition of galley tactics, were outmanoeuvred and outsailed in the Channel by their nimbler opponents, beaten in a great sea battle off Gravelines, and finally ruined by the blustering gales of the North Sea and the Atlantic. A Dutch fleet, hovering off Dunkirk, kept Parma pinned to the shore, while Drake, Hawkins, and Frobisher destroyed and dispersed the galleons of Spain.

The Spanish Armada was not the final but the first act of a long war which outlasted Philip II and Elizabeth, and was only concluded in 1604. On the side of Spain the continuance of the struggle was marked by a great improvement in naval technique, without which it would have been impossible for that country to have preserved, as it succeeded in doing, its essential connection with the new world; on the side of England by a number of daring enterprises, of which the sack of Cadiz in 1597 is the most memorable. On either side the struggle was carried on over a wide field. England trafficked with the Moriscoes in Valencia, with the adherents of Don Antonio, the Pretender to Portugal, while Spain was in league with English Jesuits and Irish rebels, and landed troops in Ireland to co-operate with O'Donnell and Tyrone. The plantation of Munster under Queen Elizabeth, effected at a fearful cost of Irish lives, was an incidental and melancholy consequence of this phase of the struggle between the Protestant and Catholic faction in Europe.

The fate of the Spanish Armada was the first notification to the world that the Spanish empire was not invincible. The preparations for the invasion were well known to have been

made upon a scale which strained to the utmost the resources
of the country. The enterprise had the support of the Pope,
the blessing of the clergy, the prayers of the people. Yet by
some Providence, difficult to reconcile with religious pride,
the great Armada had been brought to nothing by the heroic
seamen of the north and the wild blasts of heaven.

So, though the Spaniard was not ready to accept defeat
and continued the struggle in France, in Ireland, in the
Netherlands, and on the high seas, the haunting fear of
Spanish tyranny passed out of Europe. The victories of
Henry IV showed that Spain could not maintain a foothold
in France. The battle of Kinsale dashed her hopes in Ireland.
In 1609 she was brought to the bitter point of acknowledging
the independence of the Dutch. The anti-Spanish powers
each made peace at the time most convenient to itself, the
French deserting the English, and the English deserting the
Dutch. When the English peace was made by James I in
1604 it contained concessions odious to the veterans of the
Elizabethan age, for it was agreed that Spain might keep
Englishmen out of the Indies and try them by the Inquisition:
but in effect the Spanish offensive had been foiled. The
Armada had completed the process which the Marian
persecution had begun of making England a Protestant
country.

A long succession of reverses experienced by a religious
people may either shake or confirm them in the faith. In the
agony of the great Channel fight the Spanish sailors exclaimed, "God has deserted us." Later the nation was brought
to believe that it was punished because it had deserted God.
The losses at sea, the miscarriage in Ireland, the failure of
the plan to convert England or subdue the Dutch, were
ascribed by the priests to a dark taint of heresy wickedly
tolerated in Spain itself. In their view the first step to the
revival of the country was no plan for fiscal or naval reformation, but the propitiation of an angry and jealous God. The
Moriscoes must confess or leave the country. The advice was
taken. The Moriscoes were disliked on many grounds: because they were dark in skin, because they were skilled and
industrious, because they were thought to be at heart heretical
and to sympathize with the African corsairs who raided the
Spanish coast. Accordingly no act of Philip III was so
popular with the Spanish nation as his expulsion of this

deserving community, numbering half a million of the most skilled agriculturalists and artificers of the country, whereby Spain was rendered so much the less able to sustain the burden of her far-reaching empire.

By the end of the sixteenth century no serious effort had been made by England to colonize the new world. The sailors and gentlemen adventurers who singed the King of Spain's beard were not the stuff out of which colonists are made. Rather than face the hard and steady work of founding communities on the north American shore, the Elizabethan voyagers abandoned themselves to the excitement of discovery, pillage, and war. But the idea of colonization was in the air. It attracted men like Richard Eden and Sir Humphrey Gilbert, Sir Walter Raleigh and Richard Hakluyt, 1553- preacher and sometime student of Christ Church in Oxford, 1616 whose *Principal Navigations, Voyages, Traffiiques, and Discoveries of the English Nation* is the prose epic of this age of adventurers; and it led to the foundation in 1584 of a colony on the north American coast named, after the queen, Virginia, which for lack of adequate support was allowed to fade away and had to be founded anew in the succeeding reign. How colonies should be peopled, governed, or related to the mother country were questions which in the heat and excitement of the war with Spain were left unexamined; but it is plain that the idea of repeating in the new world the polity, privileges, and civilization of the colonizing state was foreign to that age. Even Gilbert and Hakluyt regarded a colony mainly as a means of promoting trade and of ridding the commonwealth of its unprofitable members. Nor had the Elizabethan fighting seamen any notion how to handle the gentle Indians of the North American continent. Sir Philip Sidney, who might have shone out before the world as the ideal colonial governor, setting a standard for others to follow, was stopped by Queen Elizabeth from taking charge of Virginia. Only by slow degrees in the eighteenth and nineteenth centuries did the English begin to learn those lessons of tact and clemency which have made their government of subject races tolerable to the world.

BOOKS WHICH MAY BE CONSULTED

Histories of England: Froude, 1856-70. Pollard, 1912. Fletcher, 1905-23. Trevelyan, 1926.

J. E. Neale: *Queen Elizabeth.* 1934.

G. W. Prothero: *Select Statutes and Other Constitutional Documents.* 1898.

M. Creighton: *The Life of Elizabeth,* 1896.

M. A. S. Hume: *The great Lord Burghley.* 1898.

P. Hume Brown: *John Knox.* 1895.

G. Lytton Strachey: *Elizabeth and Essex.* 1928.

Conyers Read: *Mr. Secretary Walsingham.* 1925.

A. Lang: *The Mystery of Mary Stuart.* 1904.

J. Skelton: *The Scotland of Mary Stuart.* 1894.

R. Simpson: *Edmund Campion:* A Biography. 1896.

J. S. Corbett: *Drake and the Tudor Navy.* 2 vols. 1898.

J. A. Froude: *English Seamen in the Sixteenth Century.* 1895.

M. A. S. Hume: *The Year after the Armada.* 1896.

William Harrison: *Description of England.* Ed. F. J. Furnivall. 1877.

Daniel Neal: *History of the Puritans.* 5 vols. 1822.

W. B. Rye: *England as seen by Foreigners in the Days of Elizabeth and James I.* 1865.

W. A. Raleigh: *Shakespeare.* 1907.

G. Saintsbury: *History of Elizabethan Literature.* 1887.

For chief editions of leading Elizabethan authors, *cf. Cambridge Modern History,* Vol. III, chap. xi.

J. A. Williamson: *The Tudor Age.* 1957.

Sir John Neale: *Elizabeth and Her Parliaments,* 1559-1601. 2 vols. 1953-7.

G. R. Elton: *England Under the Tudors.* 1955.

A. L. Rowse: *The England of Elizabeth.* 1950.

A. L. Rowse: *The Expansion of Elizabethan England.* 1955.

CHAPTER LII

THE THIRTY YEARS' WAR

The main tragedy of German history. Ferdinand II. General character of the war. The rôle of Sweden. Protestant rebellion in Bohemia. The Defenestration of Prague. The Palsgrave and the Bohemian Crown. The responsibility of James of England. The fight on the White Hill. Catholic reaction in Bohemia. The punishment of the Palsgrave. The intervention of Denmark. Wallenstein. The Catholic menace in the north. Gustavus Adolphus restores the balance. His death at Lützen. Oxenstierna makes the Alliance of Heilbronn. The murder of Wallenstein, 1634, and the Peace of Prague, 1635. Religion goes out of the war. The triumph of Richelieu. The reverses of Spain. The Peace of Westphalia.

THE brilliant flowering of European genius which we associate with the names of Shakespeare and Cervantes was immediately succeeded by a catastrophe which plunged a large area of central Europe into an abysm of barbarism and misery. The Thirty Years' War arose out of a religious revolt in Bohemia which might have been isolated, but was allowed to spread until most European states were in varying degrees involved in the struggle. But though Denmark and Sweden, France and England, Savoy and the Netherlands, played a part in the tragedy, the main theatre of the war was always the German empire, and the chief sufferers the German and Bohemian peoples. Nature had already imposed a heavy penalty upon the Germans. By reason of their geographical position they were cut off from the colonizing enterprises which in the seventeenth century enriched the life of the oceanic powers. But to this geographical handicap there was now added the social depression consequent upon the devastations of a war waged with a ferocity to which history offers few parallels. It is indeed impossible to exaggerate the miseries which the helpless peasants of the German empire were compelled to endure in these iron times. There was marauding, there was starvation, there was even cannibalism.

whole villages died out, and, as is always the case in times of extreme and desperate calamity, moral restraints broke down and ceded to wild bursts of profligacy.

At the beginning of the sixteenth century Germany stood
1648 in the forefront of European civilization. By the end of the Thirty Years' War the country was barren of literature and art, burdened by an almost unmanageable language, and in its social manners and customs sunk to a Muscovite barbarity.

The *primum movens* was a crowned Jesuit. Judged by the extent of the changes brought about by his personal initiative,
1619- Ferdinand of Styria, afterwards the Emperor Ferdinand II,
37 must be regarded as one of the great men of action of the century. He was the first pupil of a Jesuit college to mount the imperial throne; and his intelligence, narrowed, embittered and directed by Jesuit teaching, was governed by a single passion and a single purpose. He hated Protestants and determined to uproot them from his dominions. By a resolute course of persecution begun in Styria (1598), continued in Bohemia, and carried throughout the length and breadth of his Austrian dominions he succeeded in his object of "liquidating" the heretics and of bringing all the religious and intellectual life of his realm under the iron rule of the Jesuit Order. But the price was terrific; the violent subversion of the whole fabric of Bohemian society and incidentally the outbreak of the Thirty Years' War. Few men so honest, pious, and consistent have brought upon the world so great an avalanche of misery or have ensured for the intellect of a people so long a period of theological constraint.

Yet the long and wasteful struggle was fought for no trivial ends. It decided the issue whether Germany was to be reconquered from the Counter-Reformation, administering a sharp check to the Jesuit advance, and saving for the Lutheran and Calvinist Churches great tracts of central Europe. But religion, though the most prominent and embittering element in the quarrel, was not here, and perhaps has never been, the sole motive operating in the minds of statesmen.

The Thirty Years' War negatived in the most emphatic manner the idea that Germany could ever again be united under a strong imperial constitution. It showed that even those princes of Germany who cared most for the Roman Church cared more for their own territorial position, and rather than abet a restoration of the Catholic Empire to a position of real authority in Germany were prepared to be neutral or even to ally themselves with the French, so that while the war perpetuated the religious divisions of Germany, it also confirmed its political anarchy. There was yet another political issue, entering largely into the motives of that time and counting for much in the final settlement at the Peace of Westphalia (1648). To whom was the dominion of the Baltic to belong? The great days of the Hanseatic League were now passed. Lisbon and Antwerp, Amsterdam and London had, with the opening out of the new oceanic routes, long out-stripped Lübeck and Rostock, Stralsund and Danzig. The serious competitors for supremacy in the Baltic were no longer the German republics of the League, but the rival kingdoms of Denmark, Sweden, and Poland, the first formid-able by reason of its control of the Sound and by its occupa-tion of the three southern Swedish provinces, the second for the energy and intellect of its remarkable kings, while Poland, which was ruled by a Catholic prince of the house of Vasa, appeared to portend that some day Sweden might be sub-jected to the alien bondage of the Jesuit and the Slav.

It is accordingly one of the characteristic features of the Thirty Years' War that the Swedes, while battling for the Protestant cause and making a decisive contribution to its ultimate victory, were also vitally concerned in securing the political and commercial control of the southern Baltic coast and the freedom of the Sound for their trade, that they made use of the religious struggle in Germany to reach their ends, and that at the close of the war they emerged masters of the Baltic and were endowed in virtue of their German conquests with a seat in the Diet and a large controlling interest in its concerns. The day of Russia was yet to come. Its Baltic provinces were wrested from it by the Swedes. As for the Hohenzollerns of Brandenburg, to whom the prize was ultimately to fall, they were cut off from the sea by Pomerania and held East Prussia as a Polish fief. It was Sweden's hour. For the first time since the Gothic migrations Sweden, a poor barren country numbering a million and a half inhabi-tants, stepped on to the stage of world politics and exercised an influence on the shaping of history. A great king, belong-ing to a dynasty exceptional for talent and energy and deeply rooted in the loyal affections of the peasantry, came forward as the champion of the Protestant religion, made Sweden a first-class power, and by a series of brilliant conquests, largely financed by France, converted the Baltic into a Swedish lake.

There are moments in the history of peoples when a variety of causes combine to produce a dangerous inflammation of the public mind. The centenary year of the Protestant Reformation (1617) was such a moment. For a long time past the quarrel of the creeds in central Europe had threatened a general explosion. There had been grave incidents, even little spurts of open war, happily localized, as at Cologne in 1580, and a state of apprehension so serious as to justify the formation of an armed defensive Protestant Union (1608) balanced by a Catholic League in alliance with Spain. Only the murder of Henry IV of France prevented the outbreak of a general war in 1610 over the succession to the duchies of Cleves-Jülich. And then, in the centenary year, when the pamphlet warfare was at its height, and the air was hot with the recriminations of rival theologians, came the news that Ferdinand, the persecutor of the Styrian Protestants, was advanced to the thrones of Hungary and Bohemia, and designed to succeed his elderly cousin Matthias in the Empire.

The Protestants of Bohemia, though they were sufficiently numerous and influential to extract from the Emperor Rudolf a Charter of Toleration (the Letter of Majesty of July, 1609), were not in command of the levers of government. They were condemned to see their cherished charter administered in a sense adverse to their interests by the body of regents or royal ministers who had been appointed by the Emperor Matthias to conduct the government of the country. The Letter of Majesty had permitted the nobles and royal towns of Bohemia, Silesia, and Lusatia the right of building temples and of practising the Bohemian form of Lutheranism. That right, so it was contended, had been denied at two places, Braunau and Klostergrab, by the intolerance of the Catholic clergy, backed by the imperial authority. The Protestant church at Klostergrab had been pulled down, the Protestant agitators against Catholic persecution at Braunau had been imprisoned. If these things were done under Matthias, what hope had the Protestants of fairer weather under Ferdinand? The announcement that the persecutor of the Styrian Protestants was now king and was shortly to be emperor had heartened every Jesuit in the country. Under the leadership of a Calvinist noble, Henry Matthias of Thurn, the Bohemian Protestants resolved on rebellion.

To a royal decree forbidding Protestants to hold assemblies the answer of the Bohemian nobles was that famous "Defenestration of Prague" which lit the flames of the long war. There were two Catholic ministers, Martinitz and Slawata, who bore the odium of the royal policy and were specially connected with the late unpopular government. At a violent interview in the Hradshin, the great fortress-palace which frowns above the city, these two men and a private secretary were thrown from a window into the castle ditch, an act of premeditated passion designed to notify to all whom the affair might concern that the patience of Bohemian Protestantism was exhausted and that the Calvinists at last were prepared to strike.

A great opportunity was now open to the Lutheran Elector of Saxony and to the Protestant Union. If they had made it clear on behalf of this influential block of German princes that the Letter of Majesty must be respected, and had prevailed on the Electoral College to insist upon this as a condition precedent to the election of Ferdinand as Emperor, it is possible that Bohemia might have been tranquillized and the war averted. But the Protestant Union was not a brave or clear-sighted body. It neither discouraged the rebellion nor gave it active assistance, and Ferdinand mounted to the Empire with a free hand (1619).

Bohemian Protestantism was never a strong or united thing. It must seek allies or perish. In the east it looked to the Turk, to the Hungarian Protestants, and to the dubious help of a weird, barbarous Calvinist prince from Transylvania named Bethlen Gabor; in the south to the Protestants of Austria; in the west, since Saxony was inert and helpless, to that strong fortress of Calvinism, the Palatinate. Deposing Ferdinand, the Bohemians offered their crown to Frederick V, the Elector Palatine, or, as he was known in England, the Palsgrave.

For the Palsgrave was destined to become in the eyes of the now dominant English Puritans at Westminster the paladin of the Protestant cause on the continent. His mother was the daughter of William the Silent; his wife, the lovely Elizabeth, was the daughter of James I, the reigning English king. Every

English Protestant of mettle was prepared to draw his sword for the English princess whose young German husband seemed marked out to lead the revolt against Austria and Spain. The popular idea in London was that Englishmen should be sent to help defend the Palatinate while the Palsgrave went to the rescue of Bohemia.

From this natural, heady, but essentially unwise, enthusiasm James I dissented. In some ways the royal pedant was more enlightened than his subjects. He believed in a thorough union between England and Scotland, and thought that after the long and bloody religious struggles it was high time that a little peace and toleration should be brought into Europe. So he made an unpopular peace with Spain in 1604, and was negotiating a no less unpopular Spanish marriage for his son, being under the spell of a finished and seductive ambassador, when he was suddenly confronted with the Bohemian offer, and the unmistakable sentiment of his subjects.

A wise and far-seeing statesman would have used every effort to dissuade the Palsgrave from embarking upon a desperate enterprise which would involve Europe in war from the Carpathians to the Rhine. But James refused to exercise the influence over his son-in-law which he undoubtedly possessed, and accordingly bears a heavy share of responsibility for the evils which ensued.

For the consequences were these. The Palsgrave, who was no Paladin, but an inexperienced and somewhat timid youth, yielded to the pressure of Calvinist hot-heads, and without counting the cost, allowed himself to be crowned Bohemian king. One sharp battle on the White Hill a few miles outside Prague (November, 1620) was sufficient to settle his fate. A brave man might have attempted to rally the fugitives. The young Calvinist only fled with his lovely wife, leaving the Bohemian Protestants to the tender mercies of Ferdinand. That monarch, who was now supported not only by the Catholics of the League but by the Lutherans of Saxony, saw no reason why he should be gentle with rebels who had intrigued with Turks, menaced Vienna, and placed a heretic haled from the other end of Germany on his throne. He determined to extirpate the Protestant religion from Bohemia, and in this resolution obtained a success which has rarely been equalled in the history of persecution. By a system of widespread confiscation and ruthless repression the country was brought under the Austrian heel. A German ascendancy as intolerant as that of the English settlers in Ireland was imposed upon the Czechs, and not seriously shaken till the nineteenth century. German officials ruled in the Hradshin, Jesuit priests controlled education from the Clementinum. In the wake of the German nobles, fortune hunters, and officials, of the Jesuit priests and the Capucin monks, came the German lawyer expounding the autocratic principles of Roman law. Under his rigid doctrine the Bohemian peasantry was trodden down into serfdom. The first consequence, then, of the Palsgrave's enterprise was the manufacture of a servile state in Europe.

The second consequence was this. The emperor put the Palsgrave to the ban of the empire, and on his own authority transferred the Palatine territory and Electorate to Maximilian of Bavaria, the head of the Catholic League and the commander of the army which had won the battle of the White Hill. From such an act it necessarily followed that the quarrel was carried from Bohemia to the Rhine, and that it was given an entirely new lease of life. The Palatinate was the chief stronghold of Calvinism in western Germany. From the Palatinate armies had supported the revolt of the Huguenots in France and the efforts of the Dutch to throw off the Spanish yoke. Little as the Palsgrave deserved of his co-religionists, they were not prepared to see him ejected from his state in favour of a Catholic ruler, or his Electorate permanently transferred to the younger branch of the Wittelsbach house. The Diet of Ratisbon, sharing their feelings with regard to the Electorate, extracted from the Emperor by way of compromise, that the gift of the Electorate to Maximilian should be limited to his life only: but the territories were otherwise viewed. These had been conquered for Rome, the Upper Palatinate (north of Ratisbon) by Maximilian, and the Lower Palatinate by Tilly, the skilful Walloon general of the army of the League, and these the Diet was content to have permanently subjected to Catholic rule. Such was the measure of the Roman triumph. First Bohemia, then the Palatine Electorate, had been successfully wrested from Protestant hands.

It was the more necessary that the Calvinists, if they were to recover these vital territories, should seek for allies, since a third consequence of the Palsgrave's adventure had been to throw Saxony and the Lutherans upon the Imperial side, and indeed to produce the dissolution of the Protestant Union. That Lutheran Saxony should have joined with Catholic Bohemia in fighting the Catholic battle for Ferdinand in Bohemia is a notable illustration of that deep antagonism between the Lutheran and Calvinist creeds which had prevailed from the first and was more than once fatal to the efficient conduct of the Protestant cause. But it is also significant of another important political fact, the strong conservatism of the Saxon Elector, his disinclination to give countenance to violent novelties, and his desire to work with the Emperor so long as it was possible for him to do so.

In their dark hour the fighting Protestants of Germany asked and obtained the assistance of Christian of Denmark. The motives which animated this Lutheran monarch to intervene in the German quarrel were not so much an anxious concern for the Protestant religion as a keen appetite for Catholic plunder. Among the objects of his desire was a handsome provision for his sons to be obtained from the revenues of certain bishoprics in northern Germany, and since the appetite for ecclesiastical property was by no means a Danish speciality but widely shared by the Protestant princes of Lower Saxony, it was not difficult, with some royal encouragement in England, to patch up an alliance, to provide an army, and to plan a campaign.

While all this was brewing in the north an important change came over the military direction of the Catholic forces. The early triumphs of the Counter-Reformation in Bohemia and the Palatinate had been won not by an Imperial army under Ferdinand, but by the German contingents of Maximilian of Bavaria. That the emperor should be thus dependent for his protection upon a neighbour who might develop into a rival was a situation which could not long be regarded as tolerable in Vienna. An imperial policy demanded an imperial army and an imperial commander. Out of this necessity arose the powerful and enigmatic figure of Albert Wenceslas von Waldstein, Prince of Friedland, commonly known as Wallenstein. The man was a Bohemian noble, born and bred a Utraquist,[1] whose quality had been proved in the Turkish wars. Of religion, unless astrology may be so re-

---

[1] Such was the name given to the Hussites of Bohemia, who had been accorded use of the cup in the Communion Service.

garded, he had little or nothing; but of appetitive desires a supply sufficient to make or mar an empire. His wealth was enormous, for he made profit out of war, out of land speculation, out of everything he touched, and his ambition was equal to his destiny. The vast palace in Prague, with its Italian statues and portico, its long halls hung with showy candelabras, its tapestries, pictures, and curiosities, survives as a memorial to the taste, the splendour, and the success of Wallenstein. This man now came forward with an offer to raise an army at his own charges for Ferdinand, stipulating only that while artillery and munitions captured in war should be handed over to the emperor, the booty should be reserved to the troops.

The Protestant campaign of 1626 comprised two separate enterprises, each of which ended in disaster: an attack to be launched in conjunction with the Prince of Transylvania against the Imperialists in the east, and an advance southward from Denmark against the army of the Catholic League. Nothing came of the eastern project, save the death, in a distant Bosnian village, of Mansfield, the best of the Protestant *condottieri*. As for the Dane, one smashing blow administered at Lutter in Thuringia (August 27) was sufficient to establish the predominance of Tilly and Wallenstein, to open Schleswig-Holstein to the advance of the Catholics, and to eliminate the Danes as a serious factor in the contest.

Once more the Protestant cause was sunk to its lowest depths, but once more the very completeness of the imperial triumph set in motion counteracting forces which were destined to give them check. In the elation born of victory the Catholic Electors conceived a natural but nevertheless unwise idea which was pursued with effects most injurious to the emperor's interests. A considerable body of ecclesiastical wealth, including in northern Germany two archbishoprics and twelve bishoprics, had, since 1552, passed from Catholic into Protestant hands. Of this imposing corpus of property part was honourably expended in maintaining the Lutheran church; part less honourably in the support of the necessaries and luxuries of the secular princes. All this spoil was now in virtue of an edict of March 6, 1629, to revert to its Catholic owners. It may be imagined how disturbing was this upheaval to Protestant administrators who were required under the tyrannical pressure of Wallenstein's troops to surrender property which they had for many years been accustomed to regard as their own. And even Catholics began to murmur when they learnt that Jesuit Fathers were filtering into abbeys where no Jesuits had been before, and that it was proposed on Wallenstein's advice to create out of four opulent north German sees a principality for a hereditary prince. What, it was asked by German Catholics and Protestants alike, was portended by the position and proceedings of Wallenstein? He was admiral of the Baltic, and Duke of Mecklenburg. His large army, recruited from every creed and country, pillaged Catholic and Protestant alike. Did he propose to make his master despot of Germany? Did he design to carve out a kingdom for himself? Was this furious zeal for the Roman religion only a cloak for a plot to subvert the liberties of Germany in the Austrian interest? These doubts passed through many a Protestant and Catholic mind in Germany. Maximilian of Bavaria was an honest Papist, but he had not fought Ferdinand's battle at the White Hill for the purpose of enabling a Bohemian *condottiere* to ride rough-shod over the German princes. At the Diet of Ratisbon (July, 1630) he pressed for Wallenstein's dismissal, and to the surprise of Germany obtained it.

Of this incipient revolt against the alarming predominance of Austria, France, under the guidance of Cardinal Richelieu, took prompt and skilful advantage. Disarming Bavaria by a secret treaty, she arranged to finance (Treaty of Bärwalde, January 23, 1631) a Swedish invasion of Germany to restore the fortunes of the Protestant cause.

In any computation of human excellence Gustavus Adolphus of Sweden should stand high. A brilliant linguist, for he spoke eight languages, a great soldier and trainer of soldiers, a statesman with wide but not impracticable ambitions, a sincere, passionate, and single-minded believer in the faith which he had inherited from his fathers, Gustavus outtops the statesmen of his age in energy, simplicity, and integrity of character. Broadly speaking, he was governed throughout his career by the two great interests of country and creed. For Sweden he desired a safe, unmolested, and predominant share in the commerce of the Baltic, and to that end, as also for a shield against Poland and Russia, a long strip of south Baltic coast: for German Protestantism victory against the Catholics and a wider territory secure against attack.

His early manhood was consumed in warfare. He fought the Danes, the Russians, and later Sigismund Vasa, the Catholic King of Poland, a man of his own family, who dreamt of ruling in Sweden and of there spreading the Roman faith. In these hard wars under the inclement Polish skies Gustavus fashioned the military instrument which has made him famous in the annals of the military art.

The Swedish army, in which there was always a strong infusion of stalwart Scots, was chiefly notable for five characteristics. The men wore uniform. The regiments were small and equipped for speed. A light, mobile field artillery, easy to handle and brilliantly manoeuvred, reinforced the infantry arm. The muskets were of a type superior to that in general use. The cavalry, instead of galloping up to the enemy, discharging their pistols in the Dutch manner, and then turning round and galloping back to reload, charged home with naked steel. To these advantages the quality of the commander supplied an invaluable supplement. Mastering every detail, sharing every hardship, taking every risk, seizing every opportunity, Gustavus inspired his swift and mettlesome followers to endure, to obey, and, if need be, to die.

Before the momentous treaty with the French, Gustavus was already south of the Baltic, and established in East Prussia and West Poland. If ever he had entertained doubts as to a campaign in Germany for the curtailment of the imperial power they were dissipated by certain manifest signs of Ferdinand's hostility. Holding that the throne of Sweden belonged by rights to that Catholic member of the house of Vasa who was ruling in Poland, the Emperor refused to acknowledge Gustavus by his royal title. It required no great discernment to detect that behind this refusal was a plan for engineering a Catholic restoration in Sweden through the person of Sigismund, the Polish king.

So when Wallenstein had made himself master of North Germany, and further proceeded to lay siege to Stralsund, Gustavus made up his mind that the time had come to strike hard for Sweden and the faith. Ferdinand was an enemy on three separate accounts, as the friend of Poland, as the protagonist of the Roman Church, and as a direct competitor

for power on the Baltic—and all Germany seemed to be at
Ferdinand's feet. But, despite his generous and wide-ranging
views for the formation of a Protestant Federation in Germany, "that invincible monarch, the bulwark of the Protestant
faith, the Lion of the North, the terror of Austria, Gustavus
Adolphus," came no nearer than the Dane to solving the
vexed problem of bringing religious peace to the Germans.

To students of the military art all over Europe, and not
least in England and Scotland, as the Civil Wars were destined
to show, the method of Gustavus served as a model. The
quick, victorious campaign in northern Germany, the crushing victory over the overwhelming numbers of Tilly at
Breitenfeld (September 17, 1631), the advance of the Protestant arms to Prague in the east and to Mainz and Worms in
the west, the final defeat of Tilly on the Lech, and Gustavus'
entry into Munich, constituted a dazzling achievement
which long fixed the admiration of Europe. In less than two
years the fortunes of the rival creeds had been violently
reversed.

But there was more show than substance in the Swedish
victory. An ill-paid foreign army subsisting on the country
can never expect to be popular. The Protestants of Germany
were backward in supporting a power of whom it was suspected on good grounds that one of its main objects was the
acquisition of German territory. The Catholics, despite the
hopes of Richelieu, were alienated by the systematic plundering of the blue and yellow brigades, and regarded them not
as friends but as enemies, so that instead of throwing themselves against Ferdinand, Sweden and Bavaria attacked one
another. From that conflict Gustavus emerged victorious.
But there was an imperial army, now once more levied and
led by Wallenstein, with whom a difficult account had yet to
be settled, an army strong enough to drive the Saxons out of
Bohemia, and after it had effected a junction with Maximilian's forces, reaching a figure of 60,000. At Nuremberg,
Gustavus, pitted against the great Bohemian, experienced his
first defeat; and though the honours were easy in the bloodstained field of Lützen (November 16, 1632), the courage of
the Swedes was of little avail, for the king, without their knowledge, had fallen in the fight. "I am the King of Sweden,"
he is reported to have said to the cuirassiers who demanded
his name as he lay on the ground mortally wounded, "who do

seal the religion and liberty of the German nation with my blood."

The war continued, bereft of the last remnant of Protestant idealism through the death of Gustavus. Sweden was not prepared to discontinue a struggle which had given her the valuable bulwark of Pomerania, the sack of many wealthy cities, and a commanding voice in the councils of Europe. If Gustavus had disappeared, there still remained as regent of the Swedish kingdom during the minority of his infant daughter, the sagacious statesman, who, as the partner of his cares and dreams, had long borne the burden of civil government, and had gathered all the reins of foreign diplomacy into his hands. Oxenstierna was resolved to maintain for Sweden the leadership of Protestant Germany. The marshals of Gustavus, for whom campaigning was the salt of life, were at his call; and with their aid, supplemented by the efforts of the Franconian, the Swabian, and the two Rhenish circles (Alliance of Heilbronn, April 23, 1633), the Swedish Chancellor still hoped to be in a position to secure a peace of victory for the Swedish and Protestant cause.

With far less consistency of purpose Wallenstein also meditated a plan for settling the German question.

To the Jesuit Camarilla in Vienna, the conduct of the great Bohemian general after the battle of Lützen gave rise to the darkest suspicions. Wallenstein was inert in war, active in diplomacy. When it was expected that he would exploit to the full the consequences of Lützen, he remained idly stationed in Bohemia negotiating with the Saxons. Neither the capture of Ratisbon by the Swedes nor the alarm of Vienna provoked him to effective action. His thoughts, shaped by the weariness of ill-health and also by a treasonable ambition, turned to a general pacification of Germany to be accomplished through the operation of his unique prestige. The peace of Wallenstein would not have been a Jesuit peace. It would have been too Bohemian, too tolerant to please the Fathers. Perhaps, also, though this is not certain, it would have comprised as one of its conditions a Bohemian crown for himself. But nothing came of these imaginations. It was judged in Vienna that the man was too dangerous to live, and Irish dragoons were ready in the camp at Eger to do the 1634 butchery.

The first effective overtures of peace came from that quarter of Germany which ever since the beginning of the war had shown least appetite for the fight. Lutheran belligerency was a tender plant thriving only in the sunshine of Swedish victories. So when Bernard of Saxe Weimar and Horn, the two generals upon whom the mantle of Gustavus had devolved, were routed on the decisive field of Nördlingen, and all south-western Germany passed at one blow from Swedish into Imperial control, the Elector of Saxony led the Lutherans straight over into the Imperial Camp. The Peace of Prague (1635) was not a chivalrous transaction, for the Lutherans not only threw over their Swedish allies, but pledged themselves to help Austria to evict them from Germany; but peace is always wiser than war, and the Peace of Prague, which by the end of 1635 had been accepted by nearly all the important princes and free cities in the land, was as wise and good a settlement as the situation permitted. The Protestant signatories obtained a guarantee for their form of worship and for the retention for a period of fifty years of the lands and revenues which they had taken from the Roman Church.

But at this juncture, when it seemed that a general peace was in sight, the war entered upon a new and wholly secular phase, losing the religious character which had originally belonged to it, and becoming submerged in the struggle between the Bourbons and the Habsburgs for ascendancy in Europe. There was little indeed of the old theologians' spirit in a struggle in which Catholic France and Protestant Sweden were allied (Treaty of Compiègne, April 28, 1635) with the Protestant Dutch Republic against Lutheran Germany, Catholic Austria and Catholic Spain, in which Savoy sold its friendship now to one side, now to another, and when the stakes at issue were no point of doctrine or ritual, but whether Sweden should be permitted to keep Pomerania or France allowed to retain possession of Alsace. There was little of religion, but there was an intolerable amount of marching and countermarching, of sieges and sacks, arson, murder, and of all the horrors which savage and starving mercenary troops are able to inflict upon a helpless population. The chief contriver of this long spell of agony and chaos was, as has been seen, a cardinal of the Roman Church. For a period of eighteen years (1624–42) the political genius of Richelieu, the Prime Minister of Louis XIII, dominated the European scene. Many qualities essential to statesmanship were lacking to this imperious prelate. He knew nothing of economics or public finance. Despite his long spell of absolute power he never lifted a finger to remedy the confusions, the irregularity, and the oppressions of the French fiscal system which eventually brought that monarchy to the ground. To the whole humanitarian side of politics he was profoundly indifferent. But there was one cause and only one to which his lucid, ruthless, and logical intellect was persistently devoted. He worked with a single mind for the greatness of France as that phrase has been understood by a long line of French statesmen, by Mazarin and Louis XIV, by Danton and Napoleon, by Delcassé and Clemenceau, by Poincaré or his pupil Tardieu. From the outset he formed three projects, to destroy the political power of the Huguenots, to abase the nobility, and to make the king's name feared and respected through Europe. The first object he accomplished entirely, the second in part. To the third, which involved the unmaking of Germany and the downfall of Spain, he made an important contribution.

It is significant of his detachment from religious prejudice that in his great enterprise against the Huguenots he did not scruple to invoke Protestant aid. As a condition of receiving financial assistance from the French treasury the Dutch were compelled to help to reduce La Rochelle, the famous capital of French Calvinism. Odious as this task was felt to be in Amsterdam, there can be no doubt that on a large view of Protestant interests it was well that the Huguenots should be deprived of their power to molest the government of France. An armed minority holding a hundred fortified towns is a block of granite strewn in the path of national development. So long as the Huguenots were a state within a state, Richelieu was unable to marshal the Protestant princes of the continent against the Habsburg house. Only after he was rid of this domestic embarrassment (1629) did France step forward to take that commanding part in the direction of the Thirty Years' War which secured and perpetuated the religious schism in Europe. The nobles did not abash him. He had Montmorency, the first nobleman in France, executed for conspiracy. To balance the power of the aristocracy, he gradually built up the nucleus of a centralized civil service (the intendants) as well as an army and navy in the permanent service of the crown.

The student of diplomacy, if he may avert his eyes from human suffering, will admire the skill with which a Christian prelate prolonged a barbarous and unnecessary war, the apposite liberality with which the flagging enthusiasm of the indispensable Swede was refreshed with supplies of men and money, the subtlety with which the mirage of an impending peace was dangled before his eyes and the address with which his most to be apprehended rivals, the Danes and the Poles, were lulled into a neutral repose. If he notes that some schemes miscarried, such as that Rhenish Confederacy under French protection, which, again and again, under Mazarin, under Napoleon, under Poincaré, has been set up or attempted, he will applaud the span of a design which included the conquest of Roussillon, the invasion of Catalonia, the combination of Mantua, Parma, and Savoy against the Spanish power in Italy, a marriage alliance with England, and the acquisition of Alsace and Lorraine for the French monarchy. It has been pointed out that as a War Minister Richelieu had many defects, that he could neither create an army nor plan a campaign, that he was too jealous of superiority to place eminent men in command, and that it was not until 1643, when he was already in his grave, that Condé's victory at Rocroi announced that France was once more a great military power. All the more to be admired is the cardinal's diplomacy. The French armies made little out of their seven years' campaigning under Richelieu, but at the end of it France was mistress of Alsace, Lorraine and Roussillon, and had set a term to the conquests of the Counter-Reformation in Germany.

1621-
65   In this last section of the war, Spain, ruled by Philip IV and Olivarez, a nerveless king and a headstrong minister, suffered four staggering reverses, the destruction of her fleet, the revolt of Catalonia, the loss of Portugal, and an insurrection in Naples. The common root of all these disasters was the ambition of Spain, a poor, exhausted, ill-administered country, split by geography and history into distinct and opposing compartments, to play a commanding rôle in the theatre of European politics. A statesman unbewitched by the glamour of foreign war would have realized that for a

state sunk so low as Spain at the accession of Philip IV, a long course of peace, retrenchment, and civil reform was imperatively needed. With her finances in utter disorder, her fleet of ocean-going ships reduced to a skeleton, with the Indies lost, with the American colonies held by the slenderest thread, with Portugal and Naples seething with discontent, with her coinage debased and the Netherlands practically gone beyond recall, Spain was no longer in a position to lead the Catholic forces of Europe against the Protestant enemy. Olivarez was able, vigorous, ill-tempered; but he was also a courtier with no foundation of political knowledge. His idle master was flattered by the suggestion that a great foreign war, managed by a capable minister, would restore the ancient lustre to the crown. But the policy inevitably foundered on the rock of finance. To conduct a war to a successful conclusion Olivarez required far more money than the people of Spain, acting through the five Spanish Cortes, were accustomed to supply. Everywhere, but more particularly in Catalonia, the richest but also the most independent province of the Spanish Empire, he met with resistance. In an ill-judged moment Olivarez determined to break the Catalans, to abolish their privileges and to quarter a mercenary army upon them. But Barcelona was not like La Rochelle. It was, next to Seville, the richest port in Spain, and the capital of a population speaking a separate language, having ancient customs, which found it easier to fraternize with a Provençal than with a Castilian, and was in no circumstances prepared to be regarded as a province of Castile. In 1640 the Catalans rose in revolt, and the next year elected Louis XIII to be Count of Barcelona, and formally placed themselves under the protection of the French.

The Catalan rebellion had at once a serious reaction on the position in Portugal. Sixty years of union, so far from improving, had only embittered the relations between Portugal and Spain. The Portuguese chafed under uncomprehending Spanish viceroys, and complained that Cadiz had robbed Lisbon of its commerce. But a yet more deep-seated and legitimate grudge had made the whole connection in the highest degree detestable. Spain had lost Portugal her Empire in the east. The union had involved Portugal in all the enmities which the high-flying Catholic ambitions of the Spanish monarchy had attracted to itself. With these ambitions the sympathy of Portugal was restricted. A thousand times she would have preferred to be quit of a partnership which had led to the wastage of her most precious assets. To these acute discontents the centralizing policy of Olivarez, enforced by the odious Vasconcellos, added a grievance not to be borne. Learning that they were to be treated as a province of Castile, threatened with Castilian taxes, and fired by the example of the Catalans, the Portuguese rose in revolt, and called to the throne a noble of the house of Braganza.

The affair was a matter of three hours. The union was broken, and to this day the breach, widened by twenty-eight years of futile warfare (1640-68) has never been mended.

Olivarex and Richelieu were both right in thinking that a higher degree of centralization was necessary to the more efficient working of their respective states. The reason why Olivarez failed and Richelieu succeeded is that in France conditions were favourable to centralization whereas in Spain they were adverse. All ways in France led to Paris. No ways in Spain led to Madrid. Iberian mountains and Iberian men are obstinate things. Olivarez ignored the mountains and attempted to drive the men. Against such an affront to its cherished quiet and seclusion no race in the world can be trusted to react with a higher degree of mulish obstinacy than the Iberian. The Spaniard dreamt imperially, but refused to pay for his dreams. Nothing would persuade a Catalan that mediaeval standards of finance went ill with the responsibilities of modern Empire.

The renewal of the war with the Dutch after the expiration in 1621 of the twelve years' truce was another speculation which came off ill for Spain. On the death of Maurice of Nassau, the Dutch found in his younger brother Frederick Henry a statesman and a soldier well able to direct the work of national defence. Under this admirable commander, and with the aid of the subsidies of Richelieu and a gallant corps of English adventurers, the Dutch republic opposed a successful resistance to the land armies of Spain.

The sieges of Hertogenbosch, of Maestricht, and of Breda showed that in the art of poliorcetics the Dutch had lost none of their ancient cunning. They could take cities and defend them. In a war of position, as distinct from a war of movement, no troops were more competent: but the swift marches, the sweeping victories, and large scale operations of a Gustavus Adolphus were alien to the genius of this slow and methodical race. The Dutch maintained their positions. Even with French aid, the task of crushing the Austro-Spanish defence in the southern provinces was wholly beyond their strength.

The real genius of the Dutch people was shown not in this land warfare, but on the waters. With the greatest intrepidity they penetrated into the most remote and desolate portions of the globe, exploring the Amazon, bringing tea into Europe from Formosa, founding in Batavia the centre of an Eastern Empire, and carving a Dutch State out of the vast bulk of Portuguese Brazil. In estimating the causes which led to the downfall of the united kingdom of Spain and Portugal, the attacks of the Dutch upon the Portuguese settlements in Brazil and Ceylon must be reckoned as substantial factors.

Against this steady accumulation of colonial activity the united Iberian kingdom made on the eve of its dissolution one last gallant and forlorn effort. A strong fleet under Oquendo, one of the best of the Spanish sailors, was despatched to the Channel to dispute with the Dutch in their native waters; another Armada, partly Spanish and partly Portuguese, crossed the Atlantic to retrieve Brazil. Both these fleets were destroyed by the superior seacraft of their Dutch adversaries. The battle of the Downs (1639), in which Van Tromp defeated Oquendo, is famous in the naval annals of Europe; but the four days' fight of Itamarca, off the coast of Pernambuco (1640), was equally decisive. In combination these two Dutch victories, the first won in European, the second in South American, waters, sealed the doom of the Iberian empire.

The peace of Westphalia, which closed this long war, was the result, not of any inclination of the rival armies in Germany to force a military decision, for of such inclination—war being a most profitable calling—they had none, but of the common sense and humanity of Christina of Sweden, the fatigue of Spain, and the impatience of a congress, which had been sitting three years in two dull little Westphalian towns (Münster and Osnabrück), to bring its tedious and complicated work to a definite conclusion. But there must be no mistake about the undiminished gusto with which the soldiers, Swedish, French, and Imperial, carried on their trade

to the end. Fighting and pillaging was the breath of their
nostrils; and if the diplomatists had not come to an accord,
being shaken out of their leisurely ways by the separate peace
between Spain and the Netherlands in January, 1648, Wrangel
and Königsmark, Condé and Turenne, Collorado and
Piccolomini, might have fought on until the time came for
them to bequeath their war game to yet another generation
of redoubtable captains.

The peace of Westphalia, corresponding as it did to the
balance of religious and political forces of the time, settled for
many generations the public law of Europe. Each of the protagonists obtained some form of mundane satisfaction, the
emperor in the Bohemian crown, acknowledged to be hereditary in his family, France in the Landgraviates of Alsace,
Sweden in western Pomerania and the bishoprics of Bremen
and Verden, and Bavaria in the Upper Palatinate. For the
future history of Europe by far the most important of these
arrangements was the acquisition by France, as a reward for
her intervention in the war of the Landgraviate, of Upper and
Lower Alsace in full sovereignty. As one of her diplomats
then saw and as Mazarin realized afterwards, it would have
been safer for France, and less provocative to Germany, had
Alsace been accepted as an imperial fief carrying with it a
seat in the German Diet. But the error once made could not
be retrieved. A challenge was thrown out to the German
people, which at a later stage, when the sentiment of nationality had become strong, was taken up.

It was not to be expected that out of the passions of this
exhausting war there would emerge the will to religious toleration. Neither side was prepared to tolerate: but at least a
modus vivendi was found in the reaffirmation of that principle
of *Cujus regio ejus religio* which had been the basis of the
peace of Augsburg, and in its formal extension to the Calvinist
faith. The northern bishoprics were saved for Protestantism.
The Lower Palatinate gilded by an eighth electorate was conferred upon Charles Lewis, the son of the "Winter King,"
whose unwise assumption of the Bohemian crown had been
the origin of so many ills; but Bohemia itself, and all the
hereditary dominions of the Austrian house were surrendered
to the Jesuits, and over this wide region the dream of Ferdinand was realized that no heretic should be allowed to worship
or to preach.

A wide difference separates the Germany of Frederick Barbarossa from the weak federation of some three hundred and fifty states (each empowered to pursue its own foreign policy so long as it was not directed against the emperor) which emerged from the Westphalian congress. Then the emperor exercised a real though irregular authority in Germany. Now his power, though confirmed in Austria, Bohemia, and Hungary, was a shadow among the Germans. Then the Swiss and the Netherlands were imperial. Now the independence of the Swiss republic was formally recognized, and the Netherlands, though still nominally part of the Burgundian circle, had in effect broken into a Spanish province and a Dutch republic. Then Germany was a dominating influence in the world. Now it was little better than a cypher. Then there was one religious Faith, now there were three. Out of the distractions of Germany and the prostration of Spain there arose that opportunity for the development of French military ambition of which Louis XIV and Napoleon took full advantage

BOOKS WHICH MAY BE CONSULTED

S. R. Gardiner: *The Thirty Years' War.* 1874. (A short masterly sketch.)

C. R. L. Fletcher: *Gustavus Adolphus, King of Sweden.* 1890.

A. Gindely: *Thirty Years' War.* 1882-3.

Hanotaux: *Histoire du Cardinal de Richelieu.* 2 vols. 1893.

G. D'Avenel: *Richelieu et la monarchie absolue.* 1884.

W. Coxe: *House of Austria.* 1847.

Lavisse: *Histoire de France.* 1900-11.

H. Belloc: *Richelieu.* 1930.

Hallandorf and Schuck: *History of Sweden.* 1929.

A. Gindely: *Waldstein wahrend seines ersten Generalats im Lichte der gleichzeitigen Quellen.* 1886.

C. V. Wedgwood: *The Thirty Years' War.* 1938.

CHAPTER LIII

THE TRIUMPHS OF MAZARIN

*Ascendancy of France in Europe. Anne of Austria and Mazarin.
The First Fronde. The revolutionary movements of France and
England compared. The second Fronde. The depopularization
of Condé. The influence of the Frondes. Diplomatic triumphs
of Mazarin. Hugo Grotius and the Rhenish League.*

THE Treaty of Westphalia, to a greater extent even than the
Treaty of Versailles, might have been dictated by the ghost of
Richelieu. Never has French diplomacy secured a greater
triumph. Never before had the political map of Europe worn
an aspect more favourable to French ambitions. As a military
force capable of giving a serious check to French policies,
Germany, a clumsy federation of powerless, impoverished,
and mutually inimical states, was eliminated. So far from
being a danger to France, she was, on the contrary, a prime
factor in French security, a reservoir of political allies, a
sphere of influence, a buffer against Austria, a prime condition
of European equilibrium. To keep Germany thus powerless
and divided was henceforth and until the French Revolution
a prime object of French diplomacy.

In such an attitude there was nothing malignant. The
French, having no fear of Germany, which was then prostrate
and never likely to be strong, took pleasure in regarding
themselves as the guardian angels and tutelary guides of an
interesting, inoffensive, and much retarded people. They
noted with pride the spread of French literature, French
acting, and French fashions among the awkward and submissive Teutons, and regarded it as a wise dispensation of
Providence that France was now able to resume, under the
most favourable conditions, the civilizing mission of Charlemagne to the barbarians of the east.

But at the time the diplomatic triumph with its manifest
opportunities went unperceived. While the diplomatists were
signing the treaty at Münster, France was in revolution, and
its government barely able to maintain a footing in Paris.

For at the head of affairs in France there were two foreigners, Anne of Austria and Cardinal Mazarin. Louis XIII, dying in 1643, had left an infant of five, whose Spanish mother, cleverly shaking herself free from the Council which had been appointed to guide her path, had assumed the Regency, and called her Italian husband to share the burden. Everything about this arrangement was odious to the princes of the blood, to the nobles, to the Parliament of Paris, and to the mob. They disliked Anne, the Spanish regent. They hated the principle of an omnipotent Prince Minister. There was no evil which they would not believe of Mazarin, that he was a thief, a cardsharper, a perverted libertine, a low-born upstart, a pillager of the public purse. The great diplomatic ability by which this undoubtedly rapacious minister sustained the tradition of Richelieu was lost in a cloud of detraction.

The unpopularity of the government was augmented by the taxes required to finance first the German and then the Spanish war, which, even after the Peace of Westphalia had been signed, dragged on for eleven years. Mazarin was as ignorant as his master Richelieu of the first principles of finance. All his fiscal expedients were bad; but two, since they injured Paris, were dangerous, a tax upon the houses in the suburbs of the capital, and a violent interference with the Parisians' favourite investment, the *rentes* of the municipal Hôtel de Ville.

Revolution was in the air. There was, in that year 1648, revolution in Naples, in Catalonia, in Portugal, in England, and how could Paris fail to experience the general tremor? The market women cried for Maseniello, the Neapolitan fisherman who had dared to defy the King of Spain, while the greybeards of the Parliament meditated the more substantial precedents set by an assembly of like name to their own, which sat at Westminster and had just brought the English monarchy toppling to the ground.

Out of these general conditions arose the two curious rebellions which are known as the First and Second Fronde, rebellions which exposed the monarchy to the gravest humiliations and spreading far and wide through the country at one time (1652) threatened to shake the fabric of the State to its foundations. Michelet says that all the honest people in France were opposed to Mazarin and that all the rogues were upon his side. This is too absolute. Mazarin stood for the continuity of French foreign policy and for the unity of the French state. His opponents in many instances cared neither for the one cause nor for the other. What is true is that whatever sound and serious thinking there was in France either about financial reform, or about constitutional checks on autocracy, or about "the condition of the people" question, was to be found in the ranks of the *frondeurs*, and particularly among the magistrates of the Paris Parliament, who took the lead in the First Fronde and gave it a dignity to which the second rising cannot pretend.

But in the quality and range of its appeal, as also in the character of the organ through which it was expressed, this body of valuable political thought was singularly bare of inspiration and power when we compare it with the passionate and enlightened intelligence, at once enriched and narrowed by religious emotion, which carried the Parliamentary cause to victory in England. A revolution, if it is to have durable results, demands some intellectual preparation; but in France there had been no considered movement for the reconstruction of the monarchy on constitutional lines. The States-General, which had met in 1614, after an appalling manifestation of aristocratic selfishness, dispersed without a message to the country. The Parliament of Paris, a hereditary corporation of magistrates, serious and honourable and able, through the right which it possessed to refuse the registration of royal edicts, to exercise a certain check upon the autocratic power of the Crown, was devoid of any general representative character. A privileged body, it spoke for a privileged class, and only on rare occasions, for brief periods, and by some accidental conjuncture of circumstances, voiced the general will of France. Such an occasion presented itself in August, 1648. The nobles, people, and Parliament were united in protesting against Mazarin's war taxation and in asking for civil liberty and constitutional guarantees. So hot was the feeling that when Mazarin imprisoned Broussel, the venerable protagonist of the Parliamentary claims, twelve hundred barricades rose in Paris and the government was brought to its knees.

Yet even in the First Fronde, when the constitutional issue was clearly defined and hotly felt, there was outside the Parliament no sustained interest in reform or organized attempt to secure it. The leader of the Paris mob, Paul de Gondi, was a born conspirator, fishing in revolutionary waters for a cardinal's hat. The fashionable ladies who played so active a part in this serio-comedy were actuated by motives as far removed as possible from the reform of the State or the improvement of the popular lot. Between the nobles, who wished for the States-General to confirm or extend their privileges, and the Parliament, which regarded that body as a dangerous rival, there was no bond but a common hatred of the cardinal. These differences among the *frondeurs* deprived the movement of all dignity or force.

The First Fronde was mischievous and discreditable enough. A situation, which might have been dealt with by a few timely concessions honestly meant and steadily maintained, was allowed through ill-will and ill-faith so far to deteriorate that Paris was lost to the Court, and only recovered by a formal siege (Treaty of Rueil, March 11, 1649). But at least there was in the First Fronde a definite issue of real constitutional importance. Though the magistrates of Paris prejudiced their cause by their association with the mutinous nobility who stirred up the passions of the mob, they had a cause to which no wise ruler should have refused a hearing, for they stood for civil liberty and the introduction of a system of control over public finance. It is the great blot upon Mazarin's statesmanship that the concessions, which he was twice forced to make to the Parliament, were made in bad faith and withdrawn at the earliest moment.

There was less of principle and more of danger and disgrace in the Second Fronde. It began with the imprisonment of Condé, the victor of Rocroi and of Lens, and the commander of the Regent's army in the first rebellion. No man or woman could long endure the insufferable pretensions of this arrogant soldier. But it was a bold step on the part of Mazarin to imprison a man so wealthy, so formidable, and so famous. A violent spasm of indignation shook the country, bringing Turenne at the head of a Spanish army into Picardy, causing rebellion in Bordeaux, and ultimately leading to the libera- Jan. tion of Condé and the flight of Mazarin. But Condé, though 1651 he could count upon the support of a mutinous faction among the nobles, was the last man, by reason of his infirmities of temper, to compose the differences of a political coalition.

The combination of the nobility of the Sword and the nobility of the Robe was hardly formed ere it broke up. The wise Regent, inspired by Mazarin, set herself to the easy task of raising up against the vainglorious general, from the inner circles of the Fronde, an opponent as vainglorious and ambitious as himself. Paul de Gondi,[1] the leader of the priests and the rabble, went over to the Court for the promise of the cardinal's hat, and Turenne soon after surrendered to a bribe. Each of these recruits was in a position to make a contribution to the royalist cause, for Gondi was the uncrowned King of the Paris *canaille*, and Turenne, the son of a Dutch mother, was the most methodical soldier in Europe. In January, 1652, the situation was so far restored that Mazarin was able to rejoin the Regent at Orleans.

But there was still a formidable obstacle to be overcome before peace could be restored to France. Condé was in the field with friends among the rank and fashion in Paris, with a mutinous rout of nobles at his heels and the private fortune of a monarch, and Condé, though in technical skill inferior to Turenne, was the most fortunate of the French generals who had won their laurels in the Thirty Years' War. But Mazarin knew his Condé, and though the experiment was costly to France, realized that in due course of time that insufferable man could be relied on to forfeit his cheap popularity. As the prince, with some aid from Mademoiselle de Montpensier, a young lady of fashion in desperate need of an exalted husband, entered Paris (July 2, 1652) at the head of an army half recruited from Spain, the cardinal prudently withdrew beyond the frontier. At that, since Mazarinades were of no value without Mazarin, the fun and purpose of the insurrection seemed to evaporate.

Plain men began to ask why this disgraceful turmoil, so bad for trade, so dangerous for France, was kept on foot. They condemned Condé's treacherous treaty with Spain. They resented the presence of his Spanish troops and the outrages of his cut-throats. They asked themselves why Paris should be dragooned by this fantastic rout of idle nobles, smart ladies, street ruffians, and enemy soldiers. The game had been carried too far. It was unpatriotic; worse, it was ridiculous. Sensible that the tide of popular favour was ebbing from him, the prince abandoned his post and withdrew to

[1] Afterwards Cardinal de Retz.

Spain. On October 21, 1652, Louis XIV was once more in Paris and the Second Fronde was at an end.

The lesson of this fantastic rebellion was deeply graven on the mind of the young king. That is the chief importance of the Fronde for general history. Louis XIV never forgot the humiliations of his boyhood, when his mother was hunted from Paris, when the royal army was fired at from the Bastille, and the monarchy nearly destroyed by a rebellious nobility in league with an enemy power. From this experience he drew the moral that France needed the strong hand of an autocratic king, who would trust no grand viziers to transact his business, but would look into everything himself and put a curb upon the nobles. Thus the disorders of the Fronde led straight to the personal government of Louis XIV.

Mazarin lived on till 1661, supported by the victories of Turenne, and achieving in the later part of his life diplomatic triumphs hardly less distinguished than those which had marked his début as Prime Minister. The main business which now confronted him was that of bringing to a successful termination the dragging war with Spain. In a matter of such importance the cardinal allowed no consideration based on religion or ethics to affect his political action. He nourished rebellion in Naples, Catalonia, and Portugal, and did not scruple, in order that he might constrain his adversary to peace, to make alliance with the regicide English republic.

From that union (March 3, 1657) came the battle of the Dunes, when an English Puritan army, appearing for the first time on a continental battlefield, and fighting under Turenne, administered a last punishing blow in the duel between England and Spain, which ninety years before had been opened in the sunny waters of a Mexican port.

The Peace of the Pyrenees, following hard on the heels of the Anglo-French successes in Flanders, completed the terri- Nov., 1659 torial security of France. Catalonia, indeed, was abandoned to Spain, but not before she had shown an obstinate will to break off her precipitate federation with the French. But other conquests made at the expense of Spain—Roussillon and Cerdagne in the south, part of Artois, and a string of towns on the north-east frontier, in Flanders, Hainault, and Luxembourg—were retained under this instrument. That the English were installed in Dunkirk was from the French point of view the only drawback to a welcome peace.

A royal marriage crowned Mazarin's work. The Spanish Netherlands, roughly corresponding to modern Belgium, had long been an object of French ambition. But how could they be won? The way of conquest was expensive and doubtful, the way of marriage cheap and secure. And since it seemed certain to Mazarin that Philip IV's little son by his second wife was too feeble to live, the way of marriage was open. It was the last of the cardinal's achievements that he effected a union between Maria Theresa, the eldest daughter of Philip IV, and Louis XIV. What brilliant results might be expected from this marriage! Perhaps a deal for the partition of the Spanish Empire with Leopold of Austria, who had to content himself with the hand of the younger Infanta, or perhaps even, and still better, the union of Spain and France under a single crown. For Mazarin may have anticipated what proved to be the fact, that the dowry in respect of which Maria Theresa renounced her inheritance would never cross the Pyrenees.

How little can the wisest statesman forecast the future! The marriage, which gave rise to such flattering hopes, was the cause of an exhausting war out of which France and Spain, pitted against the Empire and the maritime powers of the north, emerged sensibly reduced in power and influence.

The terrible lesson of the religious wars did not fall altogether unheeded on the ear of humanity. It produced a great book and an interesting experiment. The book was that famous treatise the *De Jure Pacis et Belli*, in which Hugo Grotius, a citizen of the Dutch republic, first envisaged in its full compass the modern Science of International Law. The experiment was a miniature League of Nations (set up in 1658 on the Rhine by Philip von Schönberg, an enlightened Archbishop of Mainz), the member states of which bound themselves to settle their quarrels by the method of conciliation. The classical work of the humane Grotius has had a lasting influence on the thoughts of peace-loving men. If it has been no more successful than the teaching of the Christian churches in preventing war, it has drawn distinctions which have affected the current moral judgments of states between just and unjust wars, between the position of combatants and non-combatants and between those modes of waging war which fall within or outside the limits of tolerated and conventional barbarity.

A far more restricted measure of success attended the Rhenish Federation. By admitting France into their union the Rhinelanders transformed a pacifist society into a confederacy coloured by the aims of a military and aggressive state.

BOOKS WHICH MAY BE CONSULTED

J. B. Perkins: *France under Mazarin*. 1886.
C. de Cherrier: *Histoire de France sous Mazarin*. 1868.
D. Ogg: *Europe in the Seventeenth Century*. 1925.
V. Cousin: *La Jeunesse de Mazarin*. 1865.
Lavisse: *Histoire de France*, Vol. VI.
G. N. Clark: *The Seventeenth Century*. 2nd Ed. 1947.

CHAPTER LIV

THE GREAT REBELLION IN ENGLAND

Defeat of the Counter-Reformation. Humanism. The Bible. The sea. The scientific spirit. Comparative unimportance of England in Europe. Prevailing intolerance. The Divine Right of Kings. Anti-Catholic feeling. The question of sovereignty. James I. Impeachment of Buckingham. The parsimony of Parliament. Quality of the Parliamentary opposition. Charles I neglects the danger signals. Eleven years of personal rule. Strafford and Laud. The Puritan emigrations. The Scottish rebellion and the survival of Parliamentary government in England. The Long Parliament. John Pym. The Civil War. Oliver Cromwell. Intolerance of Parliament. Struggle between Parliament and Army. The second Civil War and the execution of Charles. Military and naval strength of the Commonwealth. Cromwell's Irish, Scottish, and foreign policy. Character and consequence of the Protectorate.

WHILE the continent was racked with religious wars England passed through the crisis of the Reformation undisturbed by foreign invasion or grave internal tumults. By the end of Elizabeth's reign the main body of the English people were content to accept the state-made Church, neither Roman nor Presbyterian, which it was the achievement of Elizabeth to have sustained against the pressure of contending forces. The attack of the Counter-Reformation had been repelled. The Bull of Deposition, so unwisely issued by Pius V, by confronting the English Catholics with a cruel conflict of loyalties, had alienated from the papal cause that large body of Catholic opinion which was English first and Roman afterwards. Being identified with the enemy power of Spain, the popularity of the ancient Faith suffered an eclipse. The Jesuit plots to kill the queen had been foiled. So strong was the state that it could afford to be sparing in its penalties. Compared with the Protestants burned for heresy under Mary, the number of Catholics executed for high treason by Elizabeth was inconsiderable. Persecution is always deplorable, but these high-minded men were allied with a foreign power to upset the state.

Thus favoured by fortune, the English people received its education from Humanism, the Bible, and the sea. What was lost in the mechanical dislocation of schools throughout the Reformation was regained by the fresh tides of inspiration which passed into the life of the people through these three very different sources. In the Elizabethan age the English, though still rustic, had become a poetry-loving, music-loving Bible-loving, and sea-loving people. The schools preserved that new discipline in the humanities the original impetus to which was found in the teaching of Erasmus and Colet. The nobles and squires sent their sons to Oxford and Cambridge, which now began to acquire their modern office of giving higher education to the laity. Ladies and gentlemen learnt Greek and Latin, Italian and French. The classics of Spain, France, and Italy were rendered into English. To travel in Italy, to write sonnets or blank verse after the Italian manner was fast becoming an object of educational ambition to the fortunate. Stories taken from all the world, from Boccaccio and Bandello and Saxo Grammaticus, as well as from remote Celtic antiquity, passed into the popular drama and furnished part of the new material for Shakespeare's genius.

This free artistic cultivation, spreading right through society, and owing more to the stir and vivacity of the court, the castle, the hostelry, and the playhouse than to the cloistered discipline of school and college, was prevented from degenerating into an Italian licence and triviality by the second great ingredient in the national education, the newly discovered wealth and majesty of the English Bible. For two centuries and a half before the advent of the cheap newspaper and the novel, the sacred books of the Jews furnished the staple intellectual and spiritual food of the poor and middle class of the English people. The authority of this austere and melodious literature was unique and universal. In every parish church the Bible lay free and open to all to read. Here was a people's university. Plunging into this vast miscellany, where all that is most solemn and sublime from the distant east is mingled with the records of a savage antiquity, the peoples of England wandered at their own sweet will, unshepherded and unfettered, and finding always by the way lessons for the conduct of life, some of infinite depth and beauty, but others prompting to gloom, pride, and self-sufficiency.

The third element in the English education of this time was the sea. The romance of geography seized hold of the people as if anything were possible to an age which had thus enlarged the boundaries of hope and knowledge. "Which of the kings of this land before Her Majesty," asks Hakluyt, "had their banners ever seen in the Caspian Sea? Which of them had ever dealt with the Emperor of Persia as Her Majesty hath done, and attained for her merchants large and loving privileges? Who ever saw before this regiment an English Ligier in the stately porch of the grand Signor at Constantinople? Who ever found English consuls and agents at Tripolis in Syria, at Aleppo, at Babylon, at Balsava, and, which is more, who ever heard of an Englishman at Goa before now? What English ships did heretofore ever anchor in the mighty river of Plate?" That in many ways, some clearly to be caught and noted, as in Marlowe's *Tamburlane* and Daniel's *Musophilus*, but others elusive, the sanguine spirit of the sailor-adventurer affects the mood of the Elizabethan poets with something of his own feeling of hopefulness, may be conceded. What is more important than any direct influence upon culture is, first, the discipline which the sea provided for all its votaries, and, secondly, the glamour which this age of adventure and discovery and maritime war cast over the sailor's life. Instead of being looked upon as a thing of horror, as it was by Horace, the sea was henceforward regarded as England's opportunity.

And who in time, knows whither we may vent
The treasure of our tongue, to what strange shores
This gain of our best glory shall be sent,
T' enrich unknowing nations with our stores?
What worlds in th' yet unforméd occident
May come refin'd with th' accents that are ours?

The forward reaching spirit of Daniel's *Musophilus* (1601) may be taken as a symbol of that new formation of the English mind which resulted from the combined action of the Renaissance and the Reformation. The Catholic had provided a coherent philosophy of life, moulded by the Latin genius and perfected in the thirteenth century. From this closed body of doctrine all the forces of humanism, of free Biblical study, and of maritime adventure were now withdrawing the better part of the nation. The centre of intellectual interest had changed. The prophetic genius of Francis Bacon was inviting the student to abandon Aristotle and the Scholastics and to turn to the obedient study of nature. Not by *a priori* reason but by induction were the secrets of the world to be unlocked.

The seventeenth century, which opens with the glowing dreams of Francis Bacon, closes with Isaac Newton's precise demonstration that the whole universe is one vast mechanism. Between these two names lies a long and splendid chapter of English scientific work, beginning with Harvey's discovery of the circulation of the blood in 1624 (reached only because he tested all his theories by experiment), carried on by Robert Boyle's epoch-making work in chemical science, illustrated by the foundation of the Royal Society, and giving to England a place in the intellectual life of Europe, which the insular reputation of a Shakespeare or a Milton could not have secured. For at the death of Queen Elizabeth and right down to the days of Oliver Cromwell England counted for little in Europe. The great school of English drama and poetry which flourished under Elizabeth and her successor James passed almost unnoticed on the continent until Schlegel's translation of Shakespeare into German at the end of the eighteenth century, and even in England it suffered an eclipse under the thickening clouds of the Puritan religion. Nor was England, save under the Commonwealth, of serious account in the weights and measures of continental politics. The navy was neglected under James, and despite Charles' greater interest in naval development was never, through the parsimony of Parliament, brought up to a strength in his reign such as even adequately to protect the British seas from piracy. Valiant English soldiers fought for the Protestant cause in the Palatinate, in the Low Countries, and in the armies of Gustavus. But there was no standing army; nor at any point was the course of continental politics powerfully affected by English interference until Cromwell converted England for the first time in her history into a military state.

During this period of isolation and comparative obscurity the English people were wrestling with two great and inter-related problems, the first religious, the second constitutional and political.

The State Church of Queen Elizabeth was far from content-ing the forward religious spirits who drew their inspiration from the advanced Protestant churches of Switzerland. To some the principle of a State Church in itself was obnoxious, to others the institution of episcopacy, to a large section the use of the surplice, the eastern position of the altar, and a liturgy too closely correspondent to Roman usage. The question therefore arose whether the Church could be so enlarged as to comprehend these widely ranging movements of Protestant thought and feeling, and, if not, what should be the position of the Protestants who should be left outside. Could there be toleration for Puritan scruples within the Church? Could there be toleration of any form of Protestant community recognized to be outside the Church? The first question was swiftly answered in the negative. Comprehen-sion was rejected by James I, by Laud, by the Anglican divines of the Restoration. We may regret that this was so. We may be disposed to think that with a little more elasticity and allowance for the workings of the Puritan conscience in the matter of Church ceremonies during the reign of the first two Stuarts much trouble might have been avoided. But history took the other turning. When three hundred Puritan ministers resigned their livings in 1604 rather than conform to the Prayer-book, as they were required to do, the Stuart dynasty was confronted with the problem which brought Charles I to his grave.

For the idea of toleration, which was the true answer to

the second question and the only solution of the whole problem, was foreign to the mentality of that age, and only at the end of the century, and at the cost of a civil war and a change of dynasty, in part established in an Act of Parliament. Under the long reign of the Roman Church, Europe had received no lesson in religious toleration, and amid the fierce passions released by the great disruption was slow to learn them. John Knox and William Laud were no more liberal than Ignatius Loyola and the Duke of Alva. So long as the great queen lived, the middle way of the Anglican Church was successfully defended, thanks to the firm administration of Archbishop Whitgift, against the Romanist on the one side and the Protestant sectaries on the other. But there could be no mistaking the drift of opinion within the Church: with ever-increasing volume it moved away from Rome and in the direction of Puritanism.

To this set of opinion James I, the strange offspring of Mary Stuart and Henry Darnley, and Charles, his son, were firmly opposed. Not that these two sovereigns desired to return to the Roman fold. The position of Supreme Governor of the Church of England satisfied all the claims of conscience and pride. But they were Episcopalians, and in varying degrees—for Charles was more pronounced than his father—sacerdotalists. "No Bishop, no King," said James to the leading Puritan ministers at the Hampton Court Conference in 1604, and this association of prelacy and monarchy, which became the corner-stone of the Stuart System, was given a kind of sanctification by a new doctrine vigorously preached by courtier prelates that the king held his crown by right divine. The theory was indefensible but convenient. The ministers of an Erastian Church hastened to applaud a philosophy which attenuated the mundane character of their establishment: and King James, whose claims to the succession were assailable, was well pleased to hear that the Stuart Monarchy was established by the will of God.

There is one great objection to making politics hang upon theology. A theocrat may not bend. Concessions and accommodations, which might otherwise ease the march of politics, are difficult for a king who believes that he is the mouthpiece of the unalterable will of God. If the doctrine of the Divine Right of Kings had been merely an amiable flourish, it would have done no harm. But when James told the leading Puritan

ministers in 1604 that if they and their friends did not conform "he would harry them out of the land" it was no mere
flourish. Rather than conform, three hundred ministers
resigned their livings.

The inwardness of the battle thus early engaged between
the Puritans and the Stuart monarchy can be understood only
if we realize the strength of the anti-Roman feeling which then
prevailed, not only among the main part of the clergy, but in
London, in the seaports, and in the fighting class of the community. In these regions of public opinion fear and hatred of
Rome were for many generations predominant emotions. The
Marian Martyrdoms, the Spanish Armada, the machinations
against the life of the great queen were recent memories when
James I came to the throne; and before these recollections had
time to fade came the Guy Fawkes plot (engineered by certain
Catholic gentlemen) to blow up the Houses of Parliament, a
crime the horror of which was so deeply printed on the public
mind that the memory of it is still annually revived in a few
English towns and villages by communal burnings of the
Pope.

To these occasions of rancour and apprehension there was
added the anxiety with which the wavering and uncertain fortunes of the Protestants upon the continent were viewed by
their English co-religionists. The wars of the Huguenots, the
long and desperate struggle of the Dutch, the catastrophe to
the Protestant cause in Bohemia and in the Palatinate aroused
the liveliest feelings of sympathy in England. In the war
mentality which was thus generated little points of ritual and
observance, which to a cooler and more indulgent age would
seem to be trifles, acquired the most solemn and tremendous
significance, so that many would leave hearth and home and
face the storms of the Atlantic rather than see the Communion table in their village church moved to the east
end, where it savoured of the abomination of the Catholic
Mass.

The constitutional issue was whether the true seat of
sovereign authority lay with the Crown or Parliament. It was
perhaps well that this profound question of the adjustment of
forces within the state was never viewed as a matter of philosophical theory, but fought out by practical men in reference
to the day-to-day concerns of practical life and in the light of
historical precedents. For this reason, being inspired by the

stress of experience, the ultimate solution, a Cabinet of Ministers, at once advising the Crown and responsible to Parliament in all its actions, has stood the wear and tear of every kind of political weather, and has proved to be one of the chief contributions which the sagacity of man has been able to make to the science of free government. But the solution was complicated, obscure, unsupported by precedent. Even at the end of the eighteenth century the framers of the American constitution failed to understand the nature and function of the Cabinet system. That it should have been so long missed by the politicians of the Stuart age is no matter for surprise.

The paramount importance of this constitutional issue proceeds from the fact that the gentlemen of the House of Commons had now developed a strong and, indeed, passionate interest in many questions of public policy, and notably in religion, in foreign politics as a branch of religion, and in finance, as to which they found themselves placed in the strongest opposition to the Crown.

The old tradition of England was parliamentary. The Tudor despotism was a novelty, acceptable as the alternative to civil war and invasion, and commended by the prestige, the ability, and the skilful parliamentary management of the Tudor sovereigns. Until the danger of the Armada was overpast there was little disposition to challenge in Parliament the actions of the Crown. But at the end of Elizabeth's reign murmurs were heard which were premonitory of the rising storm. Once even, on the question of Monopolies (1601), when she deemed that the protests of the House of Commons represented the sense of the people, Elizabeth wisely saw that timely concession was the path of prudence. With a grand air, which unlocks the secret of her magic, she made her atonement. "Though God," she said to her faithful Commons, "hath raised me high, yet this I count the glory of my crown: that I have reigned with your love. This makes me that I do not so much rejoice that God hath made me to be a Queen as to be a Queen over so thankful a people."

With none of these captivating graces, and with a point of view sharply contrasted from that of the gentry and common lawyers, who sat in St. Stephen's Chapel at Westminster, James I soon succeeded in fanning the flame of a serious parliamentary opposition. The king was clever, learned, humorous, in many ways more enlightened and humane than the bulk of his people, but intractable through conceit and as bad a judge of a political situation as any man who has ever sat on the English throne. Everything which he touched went amiss. He raised a storm by his philo-Spanish foreign policy. He chose favourites—first Robert Carr and then George Villiers, Duke of Buckingham—who excited general animosity. He alienated the merchants of the city and affronted the fiscal creed of Westminster by endeavouring to raise indirect taxes ("impositions") by prerogative. He had the wrong theory of Parliament and the unwisdom to express it. He told Lords and Commons that their privileges were not of right, but dependent on the royal grace. He said that the House of Commons had "merely a private and local wisdom," and made it clear that while it was their business to vote supplies and to express the views of their constituents, the shaping of the national policy and the ordering of the national Church were high matters of state reserved for the sole consideration of the king. To this the Parliament of 1621 rejoined in a famous protest covering the essential ground of the great controversy that "the liberties, franchises, privileges, and jurisdictions of Parliament are the ancient and undoubted birthright and inheritance of the subjects of England: and that the arduous and urgent affairs concerning the King, State, and defence of the realm and of the Church of England, and the making and maintenance of laws and redress of grievances . . . are proper subjects and matters of counsel and debate in Parliament." These doctrines were so violently opposed to the king's view of the constitution that he tore the offending page from the journals of the House, dissolved Parliament, and impeached seven of its members. Among those who suffered was John Pym, the first leader of the Puritan revolution.

From the premiss that Parliament was free to shape and challenge the whole course of public policy it followed as a consequence that it should also be free to dismiss ministers whose counsels were regarded as dangerous to the common weal. But how was this to be done? No better way suggested itself than the ancient and violent expedient, known as an impeachment, of a judicial trial in the House of Lords on charges preferred by the popular chamber. It was a clumsy, irregular, inappropriate method. The failures of statesmen are not ordinarily due to treason, felony, or misdemeanour, or to other faults which are the proper subject for judicial enquiry, but to errors of judgment, of temper, and of calculation. An impeachment, then, however useful in its political results, was almost always unjust in its procedure and its penalty. Yet during the seventeenth century the Commons resorted again and again to this expedient to obtain what seemed otherwise out of reach—the removal of unpopular or oppressive ministers. With the aid of this clumsy bludgeon the parliamentary leaders of that age levelled the path which led to the smoother and more regular methods of our modern parliamentary practice.

George Villiers, Duke of Buckingham, brave, lavish, affable, was a good companion, but in statesmanship a rash and wayward guide. He had been the favourite counsellor of James I during his declining years, and was the intimate friend and trusted adviser of his son Charles, who succeeded in 1625. Parliament distrusted him, criticized him, and in the end endeavoured to remove him by impeachment. So long as this showy and pretentious favourite stood near to the throne the leaders of the House of Commons could believe nothing good of the government. The quarrels of Charles with his first three Parliaments were, at bottom, due to the fact that the king was resolute to sustain a minister whom the Commons were determined to unhorse. No unwise act on the part of the young king was necessary to create an atmosphere of bitterness over and above his continuing friendship for Buckingham. The bitterness was bequeathed from the old reign to the new. At once Parliament broke with the traditional custom of granting to a new king tonnage and poundage (some £300,000) for life, and proposed this grant for one year only. Frugal to the point of parsimony and suspicious to the point of injustice, they would not trust Buckingham a yard with public money.

It is a fair criticism upon the early Stuart Parliaments, not only that they failed to take account of the shrinkage of the traditional revenues of the crown through the fall in the value of the currency, but that they were unwilling to pay the price of their own policies. They wished to fight the Spaniards, to save the Palatinate, to help the Huguenots against Richelieu, but were wholly indisposed to provide the supplies without which enterprises of this scale and character could not be maintained. Could they have controlled expenditure and administration, they would, no doubt, have been educated to a wiser generosity. As it was they grudged every penny. Their parsimony drove Charles to unconstitutional expedients for raising funds—to ship money, to forced loans, and eventually to a quarrel so hot that it led to a suspension of parliamentary government for ten years.

The quality of the English politicians who were fighting for constitutional liberty during this period was not to be paralleled in any country in Europe. They were for the most part country gentlemen, graced with a tincture of the humanities, who farmed, shot, and hunted, but at the same time took an active part as justices of the peace in the local administration of the shire. The main principles of the English Common Law were familiar to them, and though no body of men could be less doctrinaire, they were tenacious of legal principle. With something of that high religious seriousness which distinguished the Jansenist lawyers of the Parliament of Paris, they had a wider experience of life and a greater aptitude for the rough and tumble of politics. In the main they were grave, passionate men by whom deep issues were deeply felt, and though it had now become, through its system of committees, an instrument excellently adapted for the efficient despatch of difficult business, there were occasions when in the stress of its emotions the House of Commons would break down in a tempest of tears.

Charles was unable to handle these serious, energetic, and difficult men. Virtue and refinement are no substitutes for that buoyant and pliable common sense which alone keeps the statesman's craft above the stormy waters. A troublesome Parliament he would at once dissolve. A specially troublesome member he would commit to prison without trial. He had no conception of an honest deal with an honest opponent, nor any scruple in using his great influence with the judiciary in obtaining verdicts agreeable to the wishes of the Crown. Yet the danger signals were numerous. There were the fifteen peers who refused to pay the forced loan in 1626; there were the five knights who, equally refusing to pay that loan, were imprisoned "by special mandate of the king," and then pleaded in a famous case that even so they were entitled to a release under a writ of habeas corpus; there were the London merchants refusing to pay customs; and finally in the Parliament of 1628 the Petition of Right, drawn up on the pressure of no less a person than Sir Edward Coke, the Chief Justice of the Court of Common Pleas, which declared four practices of the government to be unlawful: commissions of martial law, the billeting of soldiers and sailors on private houses, loans and taxes without consent of Parliament, and arbitrary imprisonment. To no one of these signals would Charles attend. On March 2, 1629, passion exploded.

In the second session of the third Parliament the House refused to adjourn at the king's command. The Speaker was held down in the chair, and at the instigation of Sir John Eliot a resolution was read out to the house that whoever brings in Arminian or Popish innovations in religion, whoever advises the levy of customs before a parliamentary grant, and whoever pays the same, is an enemy to the kingdom and the commonwealth. At that the king dissolved Parliament and initiated a spell extended over eleven years of personal rule.

Chief among the political leaders who were concerned with the passing of the Petition of Right was Thomas Wentworth, afterwards Earl of Strafford. The motives which led this powerful and imaginative statesman first to side with the Parliament and then to transfer his energies to the support of the crown were less clear to his contemporaries than they have since become. Wentworth was accused of political apostasy; but in a war of movement he only can be called an apostate who renounces the better part of himself. This Wentworth never did. Royalism was in his blood, but also the passion for strong, just, and efficient administration. If in 1628 he was found leading the opposition to the Crown, it was because he distrusted Buckingham's policies, thought that the prerogative had been stretched too far, and believed that Parliament was "the great physician to effect a true consent between king and people." If he afterwards, first as President of the North and then during his Irish administration, appears as a forerunner of our long line of English proconsuls, it was because in the passionate stress of the parliamentary conflict he had come to the conclusion that the government of the country could be more safely entrusted to the king than to Parliament. "The joint wellbeing of sovereignty and subjection" remained throughout the grand object to be attained: but he had come to the conclusion that a firm hand or, as he phrased it, a policy of "Thorough" was the medicine for the distempers of the age.

In this enterprise Wentworth could count upon the zealous co-operation of the one second-rate Englishman who has exercised a wide influence upon the history of the world. The ecclesiastical policy of William Laud led to the foundation of the New England colonies and to the armed rising of Presbyterian Scotland against the Anglican Prayer-book, which precipitated the Great Rebellion. To have been the means of launching two movements of such magnitude on either side of the Atlantic as the foundation of New England and the overthrow of Charles I is a measure not of the statesmanship of Laud, but of the extraordinary resentment aroused by his policy. Yet his merits, though far less influential than his blunders, were undeniable. A strong but narrow intellect was in him combined with a deep and unaffected vein of piety, with a morbid sensibility of conscience and with a passion for minute and interfering activities. At Oxford, where he reformed the University and Colleges, he was in his true place. His attempt to harry the English people into the acceptance of ceremonies which at that time were believed to have a Romanizing tendency met with signal and inevitable disaster.

Light indeed as compared with the fierce persecutions in Spain, in the Netherlands, and in Bohemia were the penalties inflicted by this active and efficient Oxford don upon the recalcitrant spirits who refused to accept the uniform high church pattern which he was determined to impose upon the English Church. The Laudian martyrs were deprived of their livings and in some extreme cases sentenced to whipping and the loss of an ear; but they were neither burned at the stake, nor beheaded, nor tortured on the rack, nor condemned to work as slaves in the galleys. Yet the policy of the archbishop was sufficiently detestable to a large section of his countrymen to promote a stream of emigration to the shores of North America. Every year from 1629 to 1640 hundreds of English gentlemen and yeomen, farm servants, and ministers of religion, not dissenting from the Church of England, but desiring within the ambit of that Church to worship God after their own fashion, left their native land and settled upon the shores of Massachusetts. It is a curious result of the innovating policy of a pedantic Oxford prelate that from it sprang the New England states, the source, so it has been stated, of one-fourth of the population of the United States today. The greatest event in the English history of the Caroline age was the undesigned effect of a bad policy. The fugitives from Laud's repression carried with them to New England the institutions and character of their race. The New England colonies, which were closely settled, were always to be distinguished for three features: the Congregational church, the town council, and the village school. These aspects of our old English life were so firmly planted in American soil that when the age of steam erupted upon the American continent millions of emigrants from other parts of Europe they found a land where the inhabitants obeyed the English common law, spoke the English language, and maintained many essential characteristics of English government.

The Great Rebellion arose from the fact that the Lowland Scots, who were at once a military and a Presbyterian people, refused to accept the Anglican Prayer-book which Charles I and his unwise adviser Archbishop Laud attempted to impose upon them. To Charles, who knew nothing of Scotland, it was a complete surprise that the Scots, rather than accept the Anglican liturgy, would put an army in the field, to which the peaceful squires of England could make no immediate reply. The workings of the Presbyterian conscience were as mysterious to him as the readiness of the Scots to face ordeal by battle. While the English gentry had been farming, hunting, and administering the shires the military ardour of the Lowlands had been sustained by feudal broils, by the propinquity of the wild Highlanders, and by the professional zeal and knowledge of many a returned adventurer from the German wars. That the Scots, led by the Earl of Argyll, should presume at their Church Assembly at Glasgow to reject a prayer-book which was good enough for the English was amazing enough: it was still more disconcerting that this impoverished little country should be able at once to throw an army across the border which the King of England could not hope, without a special appeal to Parliament, to repel.

The experience of the Short Parliament, summoned to vote supplies for a Scottish war, but dissolved almost as soon as summoned (April 13-May 5, 1640) was sufficient to show the king that only if he were prepared to redress grievances could he expect to obtain supplies. Yet supplies he must have. The

Scottish army under Alexander Leslie, a veteran of the German wars, crossed the Tweed, occupied Durham and Northumberland, and demanded as part consideration for its retirement a sum of money which could be obtained by Charles in no other way than by resort to a fresh Parliament. A remarkable group of country gentlemen, headed by John Pym and John Hampden, were determined that to this assembly at least members should be returned who should compel the king to redress the grievances of the nation.

The Long Parliament is famous not only in English but in general history as having put a final limit upon the autocracy of the English crown with the far-reaching consequences for the development of political liberties throughout the world which have flowed from that event. In its first session this assembly of earnest and angry men abolished the prerogative courts (the Star Chamber, the High Commission Court, the prerogative jurisdiction of the Councils of Wales and of the North), and solemnly affirmed the illegality of raising money, either by way of tonnage and poundage or of ship money, without parliamentary consent. The boundaries which were then set have never been disturbed. Irrevocably Parliament had then secured its right to control the finance and, through finance, the policy of the nation. Irrevocably also the civil rights of the subject were protected henceforth from the arbitrary interference of the crown.

But at the time nothing seemed less certain than that these essential principles should be fixed and embodied in the constitution. The air was full of alarming rumours, and the spectre of Strafford leading a savage Irish army upon London to restore the power of the Crown haunted the imagination of parliamentary leaders. So long as Strafford was abroad and free, Pym, the driving force of the parliamentary movement, could not reckon on English liberty. An impeachment was launched, and midway in the solemn trial, since a conviction seemed uncertain, was exchanged for the deadly process of attainder. Strafford was too formidable to expect justice from his opponents. The Parliamentarians who voted for death, the mob who howled round the royal palace of Whitehall or flocked to the execution of "Black Tom the Tyrant" on Tower Hill were not thinking of justice, but of safety. The execution of this valiant and intelligent man was an act of war, a stern and deliberate measure of precaution against a great political evil vividly apprehended as menacing the welfare of the state.

After that events moved swiftly towards open strife. Wringing the king's consent to a statute that it should be dissolved only with its own-consent, Parliament, under Pym's leadership, and with the support of the City of London, where the tide of Puritan feeling was running strong, drove forward with a series of measures and proposals calculated to transform the character of the state. Since there was no class of man more unpopular with Pym and his friends than the bishops, it was proposed, with the novel support of a petition numerously signed in the city, that episcopacy should be abolished root and branch. A Puritan Church, managed by parliamentary lay commissioners, seemed to Pym much to be preferred to an Arminian Church controlled by royal nominees who favoured autocracy in politics and leant to ritualism in religion. But Parliament under the same strenuous leadership was not content with arrogating to itself the right to reform the Church. A terrible rising of the Irish Catholics, resulting in a great massacre of Protestants, brought the problem of army control into the forefront of English politics.

Despite all precedents, Pym was resolved that the army for Ireland should be officered, not by the king, but by Parliament. He was also determined that the king's ministers shall be "such as henceforth the Parliament may have cause to confide in." But if Parliament controlled finance, the Church, the army, and the Council, it ruled the nation. To this Charles was by no means prepared to assent. In an access of folly he determined first to impeach and then to arrest (January 4, 1642) the five members (Pym, Hampden, Hazlerigg, Holles, and Strode) who had led the parliamentary attack. But when, on January 4, he came down to the Commons "the birds were flown"; and six days afterwards Charles found it prudent to flee also from the tumultuous and hostile crowds of London.

In the course of these anxious and passionate debates the unity of the Long Parliament, which had been preserved so long as the question at issue was the restoration of the old balance between Crown and Parliament, was broken beyond repair. The moderate Episcopalians were drawn into the royalist ranks by the Root and Branch Bill attacking Episcopacy. Parties were formed, and party differences hardened as it became clear that Pym was no longer claiming what Parliament had claimed before, but was in effect aiming at ultimate sovereignty. It has been calculated that when the civil war broke out thirty members of the Lords and three hundred of the Commons espoused the parliamentary cause.

The English people, among whom there was a long and happy tradition of social harmony, only slowly and with painful reluctance ranged themselves in the opposing camps of Cavalier and Roundhead. The circumstances which generally lend bitterness to civil strife, or unduly protract its duration, were absent here. Class was not ranged against class, nor hunger against affluence, nor yet was the country sacrificed to the vested interests of marauding bands of mercenary troops. From beginning to end the flag of constitutional principle flew high above the combat, visible to all. The country gentry supplied leaders to both sides. The Earls of Essex and Manchester, Lord Fairfax and Oliver Cromwell, the principal generals on the Parliamentarian side, all belonged to the territorial class. A humane and enlightened aristocracy of sportsmen, slow to anger and quick to forgive, drained war of its more malignant poisons, and robbed it of some of its barbarity. The generous terms given to Oxford on its capitulation at the end of the war (June 20, 1646) were a fitting climax to such a controversy.

The war, which lasted five years, was in the end won by the Parliamentarians, who having behind them the fleet, the capital, the clothing towns, and the eastern counties, possessed a decisive preponderance of financial strength. Yet money, though it made ultimate victory secure, seeing that there was no failure of the Puritan morale, was slow to exert its full effect. In the campaign of 1643 the Cavaliers, being better prepared than their adversaries in the cavalry arm, and having in Prince Rupert, the king's nephew, an inspiring leader of horse, established an advantage so menacing to their opponents that Pym invoked the Scots to redress the balance. War ministers must take war risks. Rather than lose the war, Pym was prepared to face the possibility of a Scottish army dominating the political scene at Westminster. On the field of Marston Moor, the biggest battle of the war, his decision July 2 was justified, for a mixed army of Scots, Yorkshiremen, and 1644 East Anglians routed Prince Rupert's royalists, won the north

for the Roundheads, and at one blow saved the parliamentary
cause from the risk of disaster.

1599-
1658   It was on that Yorkshire battlefield that Oliver Cromwell
first exhibited in a great action his outstanding capacity as a
leader of horse. To the controlled momentum of his Iron-
sides, always impulsive but always in hand, the victory was
due. Parliament recognized the genius of its new general.
Though Cromwell was an Independent in religion, and on
that score at issue with the intolerant Erastianism of Westminster, the parliamentary leaders cleared the way for his
promotion and listened to his counsels. Once more, religious
differences were ignored to achieve a military victory. The
war, which under a lax direction, might have dragged on for
many a year, poisoning the life of the country, was brought
to a sharp and rapid end by the resolute and efficient men who
succeeded Pym in the control of the parliamentary machine.
The credit of victory is shared between Cromwell, who created,
and the Parliamentarians who financed, that well-paid and
well-fed professional force of zealous fighters known as the
New Model Army, which won the fight of Naseby in 1645
and delivered the last hammer blows at the dismembered
fragments of the royalist party. True to the maxim that the
first duty of a war government is to win the war, the Puritan
legislators threw their religious predilections to the winds,
and helped Cromwell to forge the instrument which brought
the king to the scaffold and the Long Parliament to a sorry
and shameful end.

For this Parliament which won the war showed itself incapable of making peace. It persecuted the royalists by
crippling fines, ejected the Anglican clergy from their livings,
proscribed the use of the Anglican Prayer-book, and so threw
away the chance of conciliating its beaten enemies. With an
even more surprising measure of unwise intolerance the
Puritan pedants of the victorious House of Commons alienated their friends. The triumph of the Roundheads in the
Civil War had been due to the New Model Army, a body
largely drawn from the small freeholders of the eastern
counties, and distinguished from other parliamentary forces
by its hospitality to every type of Protestant sectarian opinion.
By persecuting the sectaries and refusing the army their just
claims for pay, the Long Parliament prepared its own doom.
An assembly which showed itself hostile to all that was most

free and living in English Protestant opinion, and indifferent to the services of the army which had secured its triumph, was no longer fit to govern England. Oliver Cromwell and John Milton, the two greatest living Englishmen, were outraged by its narrow intolerance.

In the struggle between the Parliament and the army which now ensued, there is one circumstance highly illustrative of the English character. Neither party was prepared to dispense with the monarchy, but each strove to obtain possession of the person of the king, that it might strike a bargain and carry on the business of the country under the familiar old royal firm. In the triangular negotiations between Charles, the army, and the Parliament, each party stood for certain principles which the country needed and which, in their ultimate and necessary combination, furnished the pattern of a stable English peace: the King for monarchy and the English Prayer-book, the Parliament for Common Law and responsible government, the army for religious toleration to be extended to the non-conformists of the Protestant sects. But there was destined to be no restoration for Charles, neither by the army, whose fair terms he refused (not being disposed for the rôle of *roi-fainéant* over bishops without power and sectaries without rein), nor yet by the Scots, whose Presbyterian aid he did not scruple to invoke.

Playing Parliament against army, Scotland against England, and always hoping that by some happy turn of fortune he might master his opponents, Charles, "part woman, part priest, and part the bewildered delicate boy who had never quite grown up,"[1] let every chance slip by. The Second Civil War was the proximate cause of his end. The army could not pardon the king's engagement with the Scots, which brought the Duke of Hamilton's army raiding into Lancashire and threatened England with a Presbyterian monarchy to be introduced and supported by Scottish pikes. When Cromwell returned from the north, after the battle of Preston, his mind was attuning itself to the deliberate resolve of the army that "the man of blood" must be removed, and sweeping parliamentary obstacles from his path by the brusque method of Pride's Purge, he brought the king to that final scene before the Palace at Whitehall, which recalled the English people to their royal faith, and gave to Charles the Martyr, dying like a

[1] John Buchan. *Oliver Cromwell*, p. 120.

great English gentleman and a saint, a final absolution from his many faults.

The prophets who augured a short life for the regicides' republic failed to take a true measure of the energy released or of the organization promoted by the mere fact of a well-conducted war. The whole scale of English government had been enlarged by the ordeal through which the country had passed. To the surprise of Europe the new Commonwealth, so far from being enfeebled or exhausted by five years of domestic strife, was not only in every particular of financial resource and military power stronger than England had ever been, but was also aflame with a militant and aggressive ardour, foreign to its habitual mood. The age of the Commonwealth is filled with battle and bloodshed. Ireland and Scotland were subjugated by Cromwell. An aggressive war was waged first against the Dutch, and then against the Spaniards. Jamaica and Dunkirk were conquered and annexed. For the first and only time in her history England became the chief among military states of Europe. "I have seen the English," wrote Turenne to Mazarin, on the eve of the battle of the Dunes, which gave Dunkirk to Cromwell; "they are the finest troops possible" (June 21, 1657). In tone, discipline, and experience no continental army could vie with Oliver's redcoats. His Irish and Scottish campaigns were part of a general design to secure the predominance of the Puritan Commonwealth throughout the British islands, so that neither Papist nor Stuart could hope to overset it. In a brief and cruel campaign (August to October, 1649) Cromwell wrote his name in blood in the annals of Ireland. Like Strafford, like James I, like Elizabeth, he desired to make of Ireland an English and Protestant people. Similar, but in proportion to his greater energy of conception more notably mischievous, was the measure of his failure. The Cromwellian settlement only aggravated the evils of Ireland. The native Irish, driven from their homes to make way for soldiers and land speculators from England, found a refuge among the desolate bogs of Connaught, where their descendants continue to this day, despite all that has been done for the congested districts, to afford a spectacle of material wretchedness nowhere else to be paralleled in the British Isles. So far from promoting the Protestant religion, the Cromwellian settlement deepened the aversion of the native Irish from a faith which had inspired the massacres of Drogheda and Wexford, and displaced thousands of humble Celtic families to make way for an alien territorial aristocracy. A short-lived legislative union, which brought thirty Protestant Irishmen to Westminster, was no compensation for these evils.

The military subjection of Scotland, which was accomplished in 1652, arose equally from the circumstances of the English civil war. The Scots, though they had resisted the Laudian Prayer-book, had no sympathy with the English sectaries who had executed a Scottish king. They welcomed Charles II, crowned him King of Scotland at Scone, and compelled that festive, intelligent youth, the most reluctant and evasive of converts, to swear to their solemn league and covenant. The hopes of a Stuart restoration to be accomplished through the incongruous help of these grim Presbyterians were effectively shattered by Cromwell at Dunbar and Worcester. *Sept 3, 1650 Sept. 3, 1651*

Then Scotland received its dose of Cromwellian medicine, which, though less drastic than the prescription made out for Ireland, left nevertheless a bitter taste. Cromwell was a great unionist. For the first time, under his Protectorate, England, Scotland, and Ireland were brought under a single Parliament. It was a new portent when the Protector stood out before the world as the master not of England only but of Great Britain. But a union baptized in the wine of violence cannot endure. The work of Cromwell was undone before the harshness of military conquest could be assuaged by the mitigations of civil policy. At the Restoration the old Parliaments reappeared in Dublin and Edinburgh, and the old animosities continued to pursue their unpromising train. Even where religion was no barrier, real union tarried. Where Catholic faced Protestant the black gulf remained unbridged. Forty-seven years rolled by before Scotland and England agreed to agree. Only in 1921, and after the convulsion of a world war, were England and Catholic Ireland painfully brought to the point when they could, at least for the time being, agree to differ.

Across the North Sea lay the Dutch republic, bound to the English regicides by the similarity of its democratic polity and by a common interest in Protestant defence. The idea that English and Dutch might coalesce in some form of political union was so natural that it was actually the subject of negotiation. But the Dutch were rivals at sea, and rivals in trade, and since they had married William of Orange, their late Stadtholder (d. 1650), to Mary, the Princess Royal of England, they were on the whole favourable to the family from whom the English regicides had most to fear. Like ships struck by a rising gale, the two peoples, so nearly united, shot apart. With glowering rage the merchants of Amsterdam learnt that Westminster, aiming straight at the Dutch carrying trade, had decreed (Navigation Act, 1651) that no English goods were to be carried in foreign bottoms; and at Westminster, where the Netherlands were regarded as a nest of plotting and dangerous cavaliers, the feeling was no sweeter. To these occasions of ill-will the jealousies and jostlings of two equal navies in the Narrow Seas added a formidable item, producing a state of feeling in which a small incident might light the flame of war. The refusal of the Dutch to salute the British flag was the signal for a tremendous marine contest between great fleets commanded by brilliant seamen, in which Tromp and Blake enjoyed alternating fortunes, while the far-spread foreign trade of the Netherlands experienced a disproportionate loss. It was the first of three Anglo-Dutch wars which led to the decline of the Netherlands as a world power. Closing it by the treaty of 1654, Cromwell gradually felt his way to diplomatic combinations, which were more in accordance with the Protestant conscience. In the end, allied with Sweden and France, he resumed the classic conflict with Catholic Spain.

Critics have blamed the Protector for throwing the weight of English military and naval power into the scales against Spain. He should have seen, it is urged, the impending predominance of France, and endeavoured to check it. This he did not do. At the one moment when England was really strong, her strength was employed upon the wrong side. Wisdom is easy after the event. At the time there was much to be said for an alliance with a power, which, if hostile, could make mischief by its support of the exiled king, and was traditionally Protestant in its foreign policy. Moreover, the dangerous ambitions of Louis XIV were not yet deployed. Perhaps, had Cromwell lived for another decade, he might have stood out as the champion of Protestant liberties in Europe (anticipating the rôle of William III) against the aggressive intolerance of Catholic France.

One feature of the Cromwellian foreign policy was, however, in accord with the permanent interests of Great Britain. The Anglo-Portuguese alliance, offering to the English fleet the splendid harbour of Lisbon, dates from 1654. Lisbon is the key to the Mediterranean. English fleets, repaired and revictualled in Lisbon, ensured the defence of Gibraltar, and enabled England in the days before steam to figure as a Mediterranean power. With what prodigious *bravura* did she not make her début in this new rôle, when Blake's fleet, chasing Prince Rupert's privateers, called upon Tuscany and the Pope for indemnities, bombarded Tunis, and showed the flag at Malta and Venice, Toulon and Marseilles! Long before the need for a chain of naval ports along the sea route to India had made itself apparent, Blake, the soldier-sailor of the Commonwealth, whose portrait hangs in the Hall of Wadham College in Oxford, had shown with what ease such a feat might be accomplished.

The period of the Commonwealth and Protectorate, though rich in political debate and constitutional experiment, must be regarded rather as an interlude in the domestic history of the British people than as a contribution to its progress. What was attempted or achieved under the kingless government did not survive. Oliver, as had been well said, could neither rule with Parliaments nor without them. He was in the impossible position of being by nature a liberty-loving, constitutional ruler, compelled by the force of revolutionary events to carry on a military government, which had no roots in national assent. A free vote of the people, taken at any time after the execution of Charles I, would have restored the monarchy. But Oliver could not afford to permit such freedom. There were certain fundamentals, his own position, for instance, and toleration for the Protestant sectaries upon whom his power depended, which he could not, without risking the whole fabric of the state, open out for discussion; but it was just such questions which every Parliament desired to discuss. Had the Protector assumed the Crown, as most civilian members of his Council and many London Presbyterians desired, he would, from the point of view of the lawyers, have regularized a situation full of anomaly and embarrassment. A protectorate, even glorified by victories on sea and land, was a more dubious and uncomfortable thing in the eyes of a sentimental and conservative people than the old monarchy.

1657 But Oliver, though he recreated a phantasmal House of Lords, shrank, perhaps out of pride, perhaps out of prudence, or a critical sense of the fitness of things, from the traditional rite of a coronation. A Protector, then, this great man died, bequeathing, as perhaps the most durable memorial of his Puritan rule, that hatred of standing armies as inimical to civilian liberty, which long distinguished the English people, and is still enshrined in the constitutional practice by which the army is maintained on a yearly tenure.

The last years of Oliver's rule were bitterly unpopular. England was divided into eleven areas, each subjected to an officer with the local rank of major-general who was charged with the duty not only of keeping order, but of suppressing vice and encouraging virtue. The country did not soon forget or forgive the petty tyranny of these Puritan tyrants (many of them low-born and ill-bred) who put down the people's sports and harried the gentry with new exactions. Long before the breath was out of Oliver's body, a pleasure-loving nation was yearning for release from the grim constraint of compulsory godliness.

BOOKS WHICH MAY BE CONSULTED

S. R. Gardiner: *History of England.* 1875.

G. M. Trevelyan: *England under the Stuarts.* 1904.

W. H. Hutton: *William Laud.* 1895.

Lady Burghclere: *Earl of Strafford.*

Lives of Oliver Cromwell: C. H. Firth, 1900. John Morley, 1900. John Buchan, 1934. M. Ashley, 1937.

T. Carlyle: *Oliver Cromwell.* 1845-6.

T. Carlyle: *Historical Sketches. Ed.* Alexander Carlyle. 1898.

C. E. Wade: *John Pym.* 1912.

W. Notestein: *The Winning of the Initiative by the House of Commons* (Proc. Brit. Ac., 1918).

C. V. Wedgwood: *The Great Rebellion.* I. *The King's Peace.* 1955.
                                                    II. *The King's War.* 1958.

J. H. Hexter. *The Reign of King Pym.* 1941.

H. R. Trevor-Roper. *Laud.* 1939.

W. C. Abbot: *Oliver Cromwell: Writings and Speeches.* 4 vols. 1937-47.

CHAPTER LV

THE ASCENSION OF FRANCE

Louis XIV. Character of his Empire. Policy of Colbert.
France little attracted by marine enterprise. Partial codifica-
tion in France. Suppression of liberty. The Anglo-French
alliance. The eastern frontier of France. The War of Devolu-
tion. The Triple Alliance. The Treaty of Dover. The Treaty of
Nimweguen, 1678. Louis at his zenith. Charles II and Louis.
Accession of James II to the English throne. Revocation of the
Edict of Nantes. The English revolution of 1688. The success
of William III and the miscalculation of Louis. The advantages
of England. The War of the League of Augsburg.

THE autocracy of Louis XIV, reflecting the mounting ardour
of French national feeling, is the dominant fact in the history
of Europe from that king's assumption of power in 1661 until
his death in 1715. As the Tudor dynasty brought peace to
England after the distractions of a long civil war, and was
the more welcome for that reason, so the long reign of
Louis XIV inaugurated for France a period of security from
foreign attack, and of exemption from the most dangerous
type of civil disorder, which lasted till the revolution of 1789.
No longer, as in the days of the League and of the Fronde,
was the power of the crown confronted by a rebellious nobility
headed by the king of Spain. The nobles of France still
retained the fiscal immunities which divided them from the
roturiers and the peasants: but their teeth were drawn. A
splendid court attracted and held them within its glittering
orbit. In the Byzantine climate of Versailles the proudest
nobles put off their independence, lost contact with local
affairs, and sank to the courtiers' level of intrigue, pettiness,
and servility.

Louis was the first French sovereign to make of monarchy
a serious profession. From the beginning he was resolved
that no minister should exercise, and no favourite influence,
the supreme direction of affairs. "The great, noble, and
delightful trade" of royalty was too precious to be parcelled

out; it was a divine office, entrusted by the providence of God to a divine agent, whose qualifications, as embodied in himself, merited, so he believed, the exalted trust. A dominating eye, a dignified bearing, an assured grace in social commerce were combined in Louis with a fixed habit of sustained industry, a strong memory, and a capacity for using the brains of able men. Though the tide of his animal passions was strong, he worked six hours a day, and never allowed lovemaking to interfere with the discharge of public business. Duty always came first, duty conceived in the grand manner, as labour for great and spectacular ends ministering to the splendour of France and the renown of its sovereign; for the two were identical. "When the state is in view," he observed to his son, "one works for oneself." And so, if a smile was rarely seen to play on the grave, pock-marked face beneath the long peruke, and if St. Simon, the hostile witness of his declining years, speaks of "the heart which never loved anyone and which no one loved," it was because he was the professional king, without a gleam of humour or a touch of mystery, composed, laconic, reserved, egotistical, sustaining upon his sturdy and self-sufficient shoulders the main burden of the state.

Counterbalancing this resolute sense of public duty were certain costly infirmities of temper. The best laid schemes were often swept away by a fit of hot impatience and overweening pride. The monarch, who at one moment seemed to be a miracle of cool and long-headed calculation, at another was found to be acting on a violent impulse proceeding from envy, ambition, or contempt. Commenting for the benefit of his son upon his early military campaigns, he wrote, "My natural authority, my hot youth, and my violent desire to augment my reputation, imparted to me a strong feeling of impatience." He burned to emulate the achievements of the great soldiers of his age and "perhaps to surpass some undertakings which they had deemed impracticable. Luxemburg, Namur, Mons, Ghent, and Brussels were ever before me." Advancing years did not greatly abate his vehemence. To the end he loved glory and hated Protestants; passions which, however widely honoured by his fellow-countrymen, were nevertheless, since they involved France in forty years of exhausting warfare, ruinous to his country and expensive to mankind.

The scale, splendour, and organized power of the monarchy of Louis XIV was something new in Europe. The empire of Charles V, though wider in extent, was less compact, less efficient, less well calculated to strike the imagination of the world. Nationalism, untempered by cosmopolitan association, and unperplexed by racial strains, now found in France its fullest expression; monarchy, as an art, its most brilliant exemplar; administration, as an educative and controlling force, its first real, large-scale illustration. For this result the king was principally indebted to the work of ministers who had received their training under an earlier régime. The first part of his reign is an era of great public servants. In diplomacy Hugues de Lionne (1663-71), in industry, commerce, and naval organization J. B. Colbert (1669-83), in war Le Tellier and his son Louvois (1677-91), were not merely able and efficient workers, but men of initiative and improving zeal, who left the mark of their intelligence upon the methods of the state. Louis himself, the willing victim of unceasing adulation, was no judge of men. After the first race of giants had died away, they were replaced by officials of smaller stature and inferior metal. It is the nemesis of all autocracies that, sooner or later, for lack of the vivifying breath of freedom, they cease to command the best services of the highest and the best men.

Of the statesmen who adorned the early years of the reign, the most unusual in range and distinction was Colbert. In his comprehensive and devouring energy, in his grasp of detail, in his power of surmounting obstacles and getting things through, this cold, resolute, water-drinking nationalist was worth a whole cabinet of ordinary men. "No one," says M. Jusserand, "had before Colbert so clear an idea of the importance of the navy, commerce, the colonies, of sound finance, of the improvement of communications by roads, rivers, and canals." To the idle, pleasure-loving nobles of Versailles he proclaimed the doctrine that the greatness of a country depends upon wealth, and that wealth depends upon work. It is one of his chief titles to fame that during the long course of his active life he preached with a pertinacious courage the unpopular truth that national strength is to be measured, not by the showy uniforms of the household troops, but by industry, commerce, and agriculture, by the service precisely of these classes of the community who were then commonly regarded with condescension and contempt.

Unfortunately he laboured under the false theory common to his age that the wealth of one country can be obtained only by the impoverishment of another. He viewed international trade, not as an exchange of goods and services from which both parties profited, but as a money warfare, in which one country's gain was another's loss. Calculating that twenty thousand ships were sufficient to carry the commerce of western Europe, and that these were supplied in varying proportions by France, England, and Holland, he proceeded to the conclusion that French commerce could expand only through the reduction of the navies of her two commercial rivals. It is amazing that a man of commanding ability should have succumbed to so childish a delusion as to suppose either that the wealth of Europe was limited, or that it consisted of gold. It was also a disaster that from this erroneous philosophy of trade, Colbert was led to give his support to the Dutch war, which, provoking other quarrels, ruined the edifice of commercial prosperity which it was the main object of his life to erect.

It is to the credit of Louis XIV that he should have sustained until his death in 1683 this stern, managing administrator, whom Madame de Sévigné compared for his chill fixity of purpose to the north star. But the fervour of Colbert's nationalism was unmistakable. It was his aim to make the whole world minister to the glory of France and its king.

The methods by which Colbert endeavoured to carry out his spacious policy made a great impression upon his age, and stamped themselves deeply on the life of France. He had the superman's mania for regulation. Nothing escaped his watchful and supervising eye, neither art nor letters, neither industry nor commerce. His tariffs were drawn so high as eventually to stifle trade. His regulations were so minute as to take the spring out of industry. His vigorous arm stretched so far as to clasp the most distant settlements of the crown. It was in vain that the French colonist crossed the Atlantic to Canada, or beat his stormy way past the Cape to the tropical forests of Madagascar. He could not escape Colbert. A forest of regulations, devised on the banks of the Seine, disciplined the life of the royal colonies, and repeated in a wilderness the inequalities of feudal France. While the New Englander breathed the air of liberty, the society of colonial France was cabined and confined by the control of an ultramontane Church and an absolute monarchy. So little did Colbert understand the value of liberty in colonial development, that, even in Madagascar, natives and colonists alike were compelled to settle their disputes by the custom of Paris.

These drawbacks notwithstanding, a great impulse was given to colonization by Colbert. It is largely due to his energy and initiative that France, at the opening of the eighteenth century, found herself possessed of colonies in North America, of fisheries in Newfoundland, of plantations in the West Indies and in Madagascar, and of factories in India. It was a noble legacy imperfectly appreciated and defended. Had the spirit of Colbert continued to inform the shipyards of France, the tricolour might now be waving over the citadel of Quebec, and some part at least of India be numbered among the possessions of the French republic.

The evils of the French fiscal system were too deeply entrenched to be removed even by this capable minister. Colbert was forced to acquiesce in the customs lines which divided province from province, in the exemption of the nobility from taxation, and in that bad and inveterate practice of farming taxes and selling offices, which put a premium on speculation. Thus, while the revenues of the crown were greatly augmented by good management, they were collected in a manner most wasteful to the state and so assessed that the incidence of taxation fell most heavily on the class least able to bear it. The history of Colbert's efforts to raise money for his master's wars is, therefore, a dark chapter of misery and oppression, offering a sinister contrast to the glitter and frivolity of Versailles. While the nobles were hunting, dancing, and gambling, bloodhounds were tracking down the miserable creatures who smuggled salt, and hundreds of helpless tax collectors were suffering imprisonment for their failure to wring from an impoverished peasantry the appointed quota of the *taille*. Against the prime source of these evils Colbert was powerless to contend. Nothing less than a revolution was availing to introduce the principle of equity into French finances.

The moral of Colbert's rule is that no nation can be driven

into paths which it does not wish to pursue. Because the Frenchman was content with a modest competence at home, because he hated and feared the sea, and did not care to risk his fortune on doubtful enterprises at the ends of the earth, Colbert's dream of a great marine empire and of a world trade promoted by joint stock companies was doomed to disappointment. He had hoped for a French Egypt, for a Suez Canal, for a line of naval posts on the sea route to India and the far east, anticipating, in fact, the exact policy which Britain afterwards pursued with success, and for colonies both populous and popular. His countrymen did not share his enthusiasms. The call to marine adventure fell on listless ears. The needs of the eastern frontier, so uncomfortably near to Paris, and so inadequately protected, and the lure of summer campaigning in the familiar European war theatre, where great captains had fought through the ages, and where real glory was always to be won, these were the things which fixed and absorbed the attention of the capital.

Another phase of Colbert's innovating courage is illustrated by his attempt to systematize French law. The "Code Louis," a series of elaborate ordinances dealing with Civil and Criminal Procedure, with Commerce and Marine, and with the negro population of the colonies (Code Noir) cannot, seeing that it maintains torture and excludes Jews and Protestants from the colonies, be reckoned among the humanitarian manifestations of the world. But the jurisprudence of this age is notable, not only as marking the first important step towards the legal unity of France which was afterwards realized under Napoleon, but as laying down the main lines in accordance with which French law courts still conduct their proceedings. Colbert did not succeed in codifying French law. A thick jungle of local customs throve with a kind of cumulative persistence until the revolution. But he bequeathed as part of his legacy to France the idea of a code and some important fragments from which such a code could in time be constructed.

The fierce military and clerical nationalism which dominated France in the reign of Louis XIV found no place for personal liberty. A stern censorship muzzled the press, and sealed the country against the perilous contagion of Dutch and English publications. Pamphleteering was made dangerous to life and limb. No impertinent Mazarinades, or organized protests, emanating, as in the days of the Fronde, from the Parliament of Paris, were permitted to impair the peace of the ruler. The comedies of Molière escaped censure, the wit of the dramatist atoning for the unchristian quality of his mind; but whatever was critical of the monarchy or suspect to the Church was rigorously suppressed. It is a grave detraction from the glory of Louis XIV that, despite his much advertised patronage of literary men, he did nothing to relax the rigours of a system which had made it impossible for Descartes, the greatest thinker of his age, to publish in his native country any one of the writings which announce a new epoch in European philosophy.

The power of France stood out on an eminence all the clearer by reason of the political dismemberment of Germany and Italy, the decline of Spain and the attitude of the Restoration Government in England. From 1661 to 1685 Louis was able in the main to rely upon English friendship. The Stuarts were partly French, for Charles was the grandson of Henry IV, and his sister Henriette (Madame) was married to the Duke of Orleans, who was brother to Louis XIV. Everything attracted them to France, French blood, French hospitality during exile, French splendour, French autocracy, French money, and, perhaps even more strongly than all these circumstances, the spell of the Roman religion of the French monarch, to which Charles was a secret, and his brother James an open, convert. To Charles, therefore, and still more to James, his successor, the friendship of the French was of great moment. With French help they might hope to secure toleration, perhaps ultimately ascendancy, for the old faith. With French supplies they might circumvent the niggardly spirit of English Parliaments. With French troops they might, in the last resort, should the crown again be seriously challenged, defend the prerogatives of the royal house. Save for one brief interval, England was, during the reigns of the last two Stuarts, a client of France.

In any appreciation of the causes which led to the overpowering ascendancy of Louis XIV, the Anglo-French entente which prevailed during the first half of his reign is of great importance. To the very Protestant, but also very commercial, cities of England it was more urgent at this time

to reduce the Dutch than to challenge a power, which, though
it was equally unpopular, was weaker at sea and as yet no
serious rival in the marts of the new world. In the city of
London the Dutch were regarded with feelings compounded
of admiration, envy, and dislike. By their energy and thrift,
by their practice of religious toleration and hospitality, as
well as by the high average standard of their education and
the low average standard of their tariffs, the Dutch had built
up for themselves the largest carrying trade and the strongest
commercial system in Europe. Nowhere was capital so cheap
and abundant, banking so fully developed, shipbuilding so
easy and inexpensive, or mercantile law so well adapted to
the needs of a business community as in the Dutch Republic.
These advantages, clearly apprehended by the English officials
in Whitehall, were not as yet (1660) possessed by the England
of Charles II. In the race for colonies and commerce the
Dutch led, and on the assumption (at variance with the facts)
that the world was not big enough for the Dutch and English
to go their several ways and prosper, a sharp reduction in
Dutch power was instantly demanded by their English rivals.
To the jealously guarded Dutch monopoly in the Spice
Islands and in West Africa, the Restoration Government
replied (1660) by a comprehensive statute fencing off the
English colonial trade from the foreigner. A quarrel ensued
with important consequences. The two wars fought by
Charles II against the Dutch Republic assisted the rise of the
French monarchy, as the later wars fought in alliance with
the Dutch under William III and Anne powerfully contri-
buted to its decline.

Whoever deserved to rule the waves in Charles II's first
Dutch wars, it was not Britannia. That slow-moving lady
was still entangled with the notion that a titled landsman
might command at sea, and that any ne'er-do-well swept up
by the press gangs was ripe for service in the king's ships.
After the four days' battle of June, 1666, when De Ruyter
inflicted some eight thousand casualties on the English fleet,
English sailors were found floating in the water dressed in
their Sunday black just as they had been caught after church
by the press gang. Pay was in arrears, food was short. So
bad were the conditions of the lower decks that three thousand English and Scottish sailors actually preferred service
with the Dutch. Stout and well-built as were the English

ships, valiant and experienced as were many English mariners, that was not the way to rule the waves. Nor yet was it wise to leave an empty fleet lying in an undefended harbour as was done in June, 1667, when the enemy sailed into the Medway, bombarded Chatham, and with little loss to themselves delivered a smashing blow at the English navy. The shock was salutary. London, already scourged by plague and fire, did not soon forget the roar of the Dutch guns in the Thames. Clarendon, the chief minister, was driven out of the country. The Commons actually began to examine naval accounts. By the end of the reign the "tarpaulins" or old salts had come into their own, and an examination had been started for lieutenants at sea. From the rough schooling of the Dutch wars the Royal Navy emerged, a recognized profession.

The problem of the eastern frontier of France, which the 1925 Treaty of Locarno has attempted finally to settle, was opened, in its modern form in 1667, when Louis XIV, on the death of Philip IV of Spain, invaded the Spanish Low Countries on the plea that the rights of Spain in those territories had, by the Law of Brabant, devolved upon his own wife, the eldest daughter of the late king. The flimsiness of the pretexts which led to the so-called War of Devolution have often been exposed. Rarely has the peace of Europe been more wantonly disturbed. Yet there is some truth in the modern French contention that the Low Countries and Franche Comté, though politically annexed to Spain, were for the most part French in speech and culture, and that so long as they remained in enemy hands France was open to attack from the east. The term "a scientific frontier" belongs to the vocabulary of the nineteenth century, but the idea which it connotes inspired the policy of Louis and the work of Vauban, the great military engineer who perfected the defences of France on every front, and combined with the technical mastery of his craft the generous heart and wide vision of a patriot, a liberal, and a reformer. The War of Devolution, then, though aggressive, was not devoid of a purpose connected with the real interest of France. Turenne's campaign of 1667 gave his country a string of Flemish towns (Charleroi, Armentières, Tournai, Douai, Lille) which France retains to this day.

The French invasion of the Spanish Low Countries had one momentous consequence upon which Louis had not reckoned.

It alarmed the Dutch. Swiftly composing its differences with
England, the Dutch republic, under the leadership of John de
Witt, a great civilian statesman, formed with England and
Sweden a Triple Alliance (May, 1668), which, though short-
lived, was sufficient to give a check to France and to induce
Louis to evacuate Franche Comté (Treaty of Aix-la-Chapelle,
1668). To a vainglorious prince there was something particularly wounding in the reflection that a paltry republic of
heretical merchants, which France had raised into life as a
make-weight against a common enemy, should have the
insolence to enter into a coalition against her. With England
and Sweden Louis knew how to deal. They wanted money
and could be bought. The Dutch were reserved for another
fate. In an excess of folly the French king determined to
destroy the republicans of Amsterdam, who had given the
first check to his military ambitions.

In this design Louis was now able to count upon the assistance of Charles II. As early as 1669 it was strongly held by
a small and intimate circle in France and England that the
king had been received into the Roman Church. The secret,
being communicated to Madame, the king's sister, and
consequently to Louis XIV, her brother-in-law, opened out
large horizons of political and religious profit. A plot was
hatched in which Madame, young, pretty, intelligent, and
ardent, was assigned, or perhaps assumed, the leading rôle.
The advantages of the French as opposed to the Dutch alliance
were skilfully dangled before Charles. The elimination of
the Dutch competition in commerce, the destruction of the
Dutch military navy, the partition of Holland between
England and France, the prospect of a royal army of foreign
mercenaries to be stationed in the Netherlands, but to be
available, if need be, for the protection of the crown against
the Commons in England, and finally the restoration of the
Catholic Church to its old place of authority on the island—
these arguments, reinforced by the gift of a witty mistress,
were instilled into the mind of the most recent royal convert
by his enthusiastic sister. The plot succeeded. In 1670 two
treaties were signed at Dover for a great Anglo-French attack
upon the Dutch. Of these one (the Treaty of Madame) was
secret, for it contained the religious compact. To ease his
finances, to secure his monarchy, and to promote the Roman
faith, Charles, the most charming and enlightened of men, was

prepared to betray and ruin his Protestant ally and to endanger the parliamentary liberties of his country.

War is a series of surprises. By all the laws of probability the navies of England and the armies of France should have made short work of the small Dutch republic. But the expected did not happen. At sea the Dutch proved themselves a match for their English antagonists. On land they repelled the French from Amsterdam by flooding the country. The war which promised to be so short and so brilliant dragged on for six years (1672-8), widening out as wars are apt to do and revealing the sturdy spirit of resistance which the ambitions of France had evoked in the Teuton world. At the end of it the French obtained some part of their object, for they gained Franche Comté and a chain of towns on their north-eastern frontier (Treaty of Nimweguen, 1678-9), but the Dutch were unsubdued and more formidable than ever, for a revolution had overturned the republic and given power to a young prince of the house of Orange who, being married in 1677 to Mary, daughter of James, Duke of York, was afterwards destined, as William III of England, to be the soul of the European opposition to France.

Despite the favourable terms of the Peace of Nimweguen, that "French Peace" which the modern French historian finds good reason to applaud, the war presented many features which to a statesman more prudent than Louis XIV would have recommended a policy of moderation and restraint. The appearance of a French army on the Rhine had stirred up a great anti-French coalition in which the emperor and all Germany, save Bavaria, were leagued with Spain, Denmark, and the Dutch. Sweden, in whose famous valour Louis had placed the fullest confidence, was defeated in that decisive battle of Fehrbellin (1675), which first announced to Europe the tough metal in the Prussian soldier, and at once gave to the Great Elector of Brandenburg and to the Hohenzollern house of which he was the chief a position of pre-eminence in northern Germany. These were clear omens of coming trouble to France.

Louis, however, was not a man to take note of these gathering symptoms of European opposition. The military reforms of Louvois had given him a regular army of two hundred thousand strong, equipped with a regular commissariat, armed with the bayonet, and officered on the modern plan by professional soldiers. His navy, under the vigorous administration of Colbert, had grown from a squadron of fifteen to a fleet of two hundred, and though still having much to learn, had startled Europe, and more particularly England, by its full participation in the Dutch war. The work of expanding and consolidating the eastern frontier was therefore continued. Local courts, known as "Chambers of Reunion," were set up to decide upon the extent of the king's rights under the Treaty of Münster in Alsace, the three bishoprics, the Franche Comté, and, since the language of the guns was always ready to repair the silence of the law, the results of the antiquarian enquiry were satisfactory to Louis. The full sovereignty of Alsace was awarded to France and was completed by the military occupation of Strasburg (September, 1681). From the brief war provoked by these high-handed proceedings Louis emerged with conspicuous success. The emperor, distracted by a Turkish invasion which pushed its way to the gates of Vienna, was in no position to add momentum to the operations of the Third Coalition; and the Truce of Regensburg (1684) left Louis in possession for twenty years of all the fruits (the Flanders forts, Luxemburg, Franche Comté, Alsace, Strasburg) of his long and connected endeavour to improve the eastern frontier of France. Here he should have stopped, for he had reached the climax of his fortune.

By this time the ambitions of Louis had given a serious shock to the public law of Europe as it had been fixed by the Treaty of Westphalia. Of that treaty France was a guarantor. By that treaty France was to an extraordinary extent a beneficiary. Nevertheless, to Louis the Treaty of Westphalia was altogether insufficient. He did not scruple to violate it, and with every fresh demonstration of his ambition alienated a friend and increased the muster of his enemies. First he alarmed Holland, then Germany, then Sweden. Finally he lost the friendship of England.

Ever since 1668 it had been one of the primary objects of French diplomacy to retain, if not the friendship, at least the neutrality, of the British. To that end money had been lavished on the crown, the court, the parliament, and even upon Presbyterian ministers. The policy was successful.

Despite the national jealousy inspired by the spectacle of the amazing development of French naval and military power, England, led by Charles, remained at peace with France. The French ambassadors in London were, indeed, under no delusion as to the real feelings of the English people. From the first moment of Louis' invasion of the Spanish Netherlands the country was seized with panic, divined an enemy, and feared an invasion. Later, in August, 1677, Louis was informed by Barillon from London that the only friends of France in England were Charles II and his brother James, Duke of York. The earlier rivalry of Spain, the later rivalry of Holland, now seemed less formidable to the English people than the new military and commercial power of France. Yet with the help of French supplies, an expanding revenue from customs, and his own dexterity, Charles was able to surmount the formidable difficulties which the Whigs, led by the brilliant Earl of Shaftesbury, raised about his path. He saved his crown, avoided war, and, defeating the movement to exclude his Catholic brother from the succession, dissolved Parliament and broke the Whigs. For the last four years of his reign he was able, thanks in part to the continued assistance of Louis, to govern England without recourse to Parliament.

In a country still boiling with sectarian fury it was a great thing to have a king who brought so little heat and so much light to the handling of affairs as Charles II. His wit and charm, his easy manners and pleasant ways, his complete immunity from all kinds of fanaticism, coupled with the play of his scientific curiosity, came like a cooling draught administered to a fevered patient. The open dissipations of his court were not incompatible with spells of well-directed work. In many respects his supple intelligence placed him far above the common standards of his time. Though he was compelled to acquiesce in the persecuting measures of the Cavalier Parliament (1660-7), he was in favour of religious toleration and excited the hostility of his Parliaments by his endeavours to secure it by the use of his power to dispense with laws. Like Oliver Cromwell, he saw the growing importance of overseas colonies and marine strength. The Navigation Laws passed under the Protectorate for the purpose of securing to the mother country a monopoly of the trade with her colonies were during his reign worked up into a system of laws and regulations covering the whole field of colonial intercourse with the mother country.

A delicate sense of the drifts and eddies of public opinion, so delicate as to be incompatible with true civil courage, kept him safe on his throne when a disclosure of his inner thoughts would have brought serious trouble. The country did not know, however much it might suspect, that its constitutional king was at heart an autocrat in politics and a Roman Catholic in belief. It did not know that he was a pensionary of the French Crown. Charles kept silence. Even when Titus Oates was spreading murderous calumnies against his Catholic co-religionists he dined with the villain and spoke no open word of reproach. It was not in his self-indulgent and circumspect character to take a chivalrous risk.

It would have required a stronger man than Charles II to stem the tide of public interest in government which had been released by the passions of the civil war. The nation was on its feet, talking, disputing, reading news-letters, and watching the Parliament men at their work. Marvell's letters to his constituents at Hull are symptomatic of a new age. So, too, was the development of the two party system, Whig and Tory, which first took a defined shape over the proposal to exclude the Duke of York (afterwards James II) from the throne on the ground of his religious faith. The country was strongly Protestant and parliamentary. Only the violent errors of Whig leadership, culminating in the support given to the mendacities of Titus Oates, gave to Charles the opportunity which he took with such brilliant address in 1681 of sending the Parliament about its business.

Charles died in 1685. James, an avowed and zealous Catholic, succeeded to the throne. His plan of action was to secure legal toleration for his co-religionists by packing Parliament with his supporters and by dispensing Catholics from the penalties to which they were subject by the law of the land. No policy either on its religious or on its constitutional side could be more repugnant to a Protestant and parliamentary country, more particularly since it became evident that its successful execution depended upon the support of France, of Ireland, and of a standing army, auxiliaries capable in the temper which then prevailed of ruining any cause with the English people.

James was almost as necessary to Louis as Louis to James,

for the real alternative to James in England was not the Protestant Duke of Monmouth, whose ill-starred rising was crushed on Sedgemoor, but William of Orange, who had been married in 1677 to the Princess Mary, the Protestant daughter of the English king. To Louis, then, it was all-important that this Catholic king should be maintained upon the English throne and that his difficult and incalculable subjects should learn to bear his yoke with equanimity. So long as James was king of England there was no reason to fear that the English fleet would molest the West Indian colonies, which it had been the achievement of Colbert to develop, or an English army take part in continental operations against France. But William of Orange was of all France's enemies the most deadly and persistent, and the conjunction of England and Holland under his leadership was the contingency most likely to spell serious trouble for Louis XIV.

And it now happened that just when it was most important for the general success of French policy in Europe that France should show indulgence to her Protestant citizens, Louis revoked the Edict of Nantes (1685). Though he desired to secure toleration for English Catholics, he withdrew the wise toleration which his grandfather had accorded to French Protestants, prohibiting their worship, proscribing their ministers, destroying their churches, closing their schools, and so driving some two hundred thousand of the best artificers of his kingdom into foreign lands, there to create industries in competition with his own, and to foment sentiments of enduring rancour against France. The best excuse which can be made for this act of gratuitous folly is not that it was counselled by Madame de Maintenon, the discreet, elderly, and very pious lady to whom the king was secretly married in 1683, but that it was popular with the clergy and laity of France. The average Frenchman of the seventeenth century was apt to be at once orthodox in belief and anti-clerical in policy. He was Gallican not Papal, Catholic not Protestant. There was nothing which he feared so much as the renewal of the religious wars, which had broken so many homes, embittered so many families, and left behind them a long train of poignant and dividing memories. To the cool reasoner it must have been apparent that "the so-called Reformed Church" had, ever since the days of Richelieu, ceased to present political dangers. It possessed neither fortresses nor troops. It had been quiet during the agitation of the Fronde. Its members served the state in the army, the navy, and the magistrature, and had won for themselves an eminent place in the world of finance, commerce, and industry. Yet so long as a million Huguenots lived in France with their church councils and schools, their black-robed ministers and peculiar rites, the country felt uneasy. The sect was unpopular, had been dangerous once, and might, through the attraction of clerical marriage, be dangerous again. Some envied the Huguenot his money, others grudged his industry, others were affronted by his rigour, and by the intolerance which he showed to his Catholic neighbour in those regions in which the reformed church had the upper hand. Why, it was asked, should this obstinate and unreasonable sect, which repudiated a religion which was good enough for the king of France, and belonged to a Church which was shaped like a republic, be permitted to sustain its separate and unwelcome being in a Catholic and monarchical country? Year after year the Assembly of the Church of France petitioned for the destruction of this foreign body. Louis, who was not by nature intolerant, yielded to the pressure. By a hundred differing forms of calculated cruelty and oppression it was sought to make the position of a Huguenot so intolerable as to drive him into the Roman Communion. The hateful policy was in a large measure successful. Huguenots, who had preserved their religion through twenty years of harassing but minor acts of persecution, went over in thousands when (1681-85) Louvois' dragoons were quartered in their homes, and pillage, murder, and rape became the price of continued loyalty to the faith of their fathers. When it was believed that the terror had done its work, that the resistance of these obstinate sectaries was broken, and that the conversion of a miserable remnant would be an easy undertaking, Louis revoked the Edict of Nantes. A paean of praise saluted the Christian hero who had at last, after so many vagaries, showed a true concern for the salvation of his soul and emulated the work of Constantine, Theodosius, and Charlemagne. "This," said Bossuet, the court preacher, "is the worthy achievement of your reign and its true character. Through you heresy is no more. God above has made this marvel." But however pleasing to French Catholics, the revocation of the Edict of Nantes was not the way to make J.. ..s II popular in Puritan London.

The "glorious revolution" of 1688, which placed William III on the throne of England, was precipitated by the folly of James in attempting to force the Catholic religion upon his countrymen by unconstitutional methods. The revolution was glorious in that it was clement, and entailed no proscription of the vanquished party. Of land fighting the main part **June** was in Ireland, and here the signal victory of the Boyne, **30,** followed up a year later by the surrender of Limerick, **1690** fastened the political dominion of Protestant England upon the Catholic Irish for two hundred and forty-two years, during which the long duel between France and England for colonial dominion was fought to an issue.

That England should have been able not only to effect this bloodless revolution, but to emerge all the stronger by reason of the triumph of parliamentary principles, was a result absolutely unexpected by Louis, and sharply opposed to the dominant political philosophy of the continent. France, had she exerted herself to do so, could have prevented William from landing at Torbay. But Louis, instead of using his army to make trouble for William in the Netherlands, sent it into the Palatinate, where it was effectually prevented from influencing the course of events. The explanation of this is that Louis counted upon the paralysis of England through a long drawn civil war, and looked with equanimity upon the prospect of his two principal antagonists, the Dutch and the English, being thus embroiled.

We need not be surprised that he was mistaken. The credentials of the Whig party in England, which made the revolution settlement, were not such as to inspire confidence in their moderation and restraint. In their struggle to exclude James from the Crown, the Whigs had stopped short of no extreme of factious violence. They had backed up the baseless and wicked calumnies of Titus Oates against the Catholics. They had given support to Monmouth's armed rebellion against James. Some of them had taken French money; but at the crisis of 1688, under the leadership of Halifax, the Trimmer, one of the great benefactors of the country, they listened to the voice of moderation. Louis could not have foreseen this, nor yet that the cold Dutch soldier-statesman, whom the Whigs had called in to save the state, would stamp

upon the fires of party vengeance and succeed in the extraordinary task of making England a united, albeit a parliamentary, country.

On any comparison of man power the two countries which
had now become combined under William III were immeasurably inferior to France. The population of England
may have been five and a half million, of the Dutch Republic
two and a half million, while the population of France was
of the order of nineteen or twenty million. But in two respects
an advantage lay with England. After the naval victory of
La Hogue (1692) the English sailors established a definite
superiority over the French marine, which had now lost the
incomparable direction of the great Colbert. The second
advantage was perhaps still more important. The form of
government which England had secured at the Whig revolution
was better adapted to stand financial stress and social change
than the autocracy of France. Louis had discarded every
constitutional check upon the royal power. He declined to
summon the States-General. He confined the Parliaments to
the exercise of their judicial functions. The government of
the country was carried on by ministers and committees
working with the king at the centre and in most provinces by
intendants prefiguring the modern prefect. The fiscal privileges of the nobility, who were for the most part occupied at
the front or attached to the court, were left unassailed, and
despite the drain of incessant wars, and the vast authority
enjoyed by the crown, nothing was done to remedy a system
under which the main financial burdens of the state were
borne by the poorest members of the community, while the
contributions of the nobles and the clergy, who were by
comparison wealthy, were wholly inadequate. An autocracy
working in secret can endure only if it redresses social injustice. Failing to do this, and losing its initial momentum
and efficiency with the death of the king's ablest minister and
his own declining strength, the monarchy of Louis XIV left
France as miserable as if victory had been exchanged for
defeat.

But in 1689 the fabric of French government was the most
imposing spectacle in Europe. Of English Parliaments it was
mainly known that they were factious, capricious, venal,
incapable, as it would appear, of steady direction. The fact
that the revolution had transferred power from the crown into

the hands of Parliament was interpreted as a sure sign of weakness by those who failed to perceive that Parliament would be governed for the next century and a half by a territorial and commercial aristocracy, which was neither inexperienced in affairs, nor careless of public interests, nor without the courage and sagacity which go to the making of statesmen. A parliamentary government was a new and untried thing. The Duke of Marlborough at Blenheim and Ramillies showed the world that such a government could conduct a European war, and put armies into the field which could rout the French in a fair fight. The admiration for English institutions which was so widely felt on the continent during the eighteenth century dates from the advertisement of these brilliant victories. The nation of civilians, which affirmed in the Bill of Rights that standing armies were illegal in time of peace, proved itself equal to all the demands of an exhausting war. In finance, banking, commerce, and the science and art of treasury control it stood far above its antagonists.

It was then with England no longer as a friendly rival but as an active enemy that Louis waged his next war for the expansion of France. It was a remarkable struggle, fought against great odds, continued for ten years (1688-97), marked by many victories, and yet ending in a serious check for France. It showed that Louis had taught Europe the art of progressive coalition, for the Triple Alliance had been succeeded by the League of Augsburg (1685), an imposing combination secretly supported by the Pope and comprising the Emperor and the Empire, Holland and Spain, Savoy, England, and Sweden. But it illustrated also the familiar truth that coalitions are rarely as effective in action as they are impressive on paper. The forces of the League experienced a humiliating series of defeats at the hands of the best armies led by the best generals then available in Europe. Catinat won Nice and overran Savoy. Luxemburg scored success after success over William III in the Netherlands. The Palatinate was twice subjected to a ruthless devastation, the memory of which is still among the causes of eangement between French and German peoples. Nevertheless the Treaty of Ryswick, which closed the struggle, was a defeat for Louis. To win peace from his obstinate and unexhausted antagonists the French king was compelled to renounce his conquests, to accord to the Dutch the right of garrisoning the

Sept., 1697

frontier towns of the Spanish Netherlands, to acknowledge the heretic king of England, and to consent that he should be succeeded by a heretic princess. In war, pitched battles do not decide everything. Ultimate success lies with that party to the controversy which can last the longest. That advantage, thanks to the steadfast Protestant mind of William III, lay with the first of the great European coalitions.

BOOKS WHICH MAY BE CONSULTED

Macaulay: *History of England.* 1858-62.

Voltaire: *Le Siècle de Louis XIV.* 1753.

G. Hanotaux: *Études historiques sur le XVIe et le XVIIe siécle en France.* 1886.

D. Ogg: *Europe in the Seventeenth Century.* 1925.

D. Ogg: *Louis XIV.* Home University Library. 1933.

D. Ogg: *England in the Reign of Charles II.* 2 vols. 1934.

E. Lavisse: *Histoire de France*, Vol. VII.

P. Clement: *Histoire de la Vie et de l'Administration de Colbert.* 1846.

J. J. Jusserand: *Instructions données aux ambassadeurs de France depuis les Traités de Westphalia. Angleterre.*

P. Gaxotte: *La France de Louis XIV.* 1953.

M. Ashley: *Louis XIV and the greatness of France.* 1955.

D. Ogg: *England in the Reign of James II and William III.* 1956.

C. W. Cole: *Colbert and a century of French Mercantilism.* 2 vols. 1939.

CHAPTER LVI

THE SPANISH SUCCESSION

The Spanish Succession. The Partition Treaties. Opposition to the Partition in Austria and Spain. Louis accepts the undivided inheritance. The Grand Alliance. The English spirit. War of the Spanish Succession. Its character and duration. The Spanish "side-show." The Treaty of Utrecht. Marine supremacy passes to Britain. Jansenists and Jesuits in France. Pascal. The Bull Unigenitus. Continuance of the struggle in the eighteenth century. Decline of religious and dynastic motives. The seventeenth century. Spiritual hegemony of France.

MEANWHILE a question of vast general importance and affecting in particular the interests of the Dutch and English was hastening to a crisis. What was to become of the Spanish Empire on the death, so long expected and so long delayed, of Charles II, the imbecile invalid without hope of posterity, who ever since 1665 had been King of Spain? The idea that this was a question with respect to which the Spanish people might have a right to be consulted was foreign to the political philosophy of that age. A monarchy was still regarded as a family property, which could be devised by will or shared by agreement among the next of kin. And what a family property was this! The European possessions of the Spanish Habsburgs alone constituted a formidable empire, including, as they did, Milan, Naples, and Sicily, Sardinia, and the Balearic Islands, as well as the Spanish Netherlands and Spain itself. But the non-European dominions were even more imposing, the Philippines and the Canaries, Cuba, Mexico, Florida, California, and Panama, and save for the Guianas and Portuguese Brazil, the vast bulk of South America. Such an empire was too large for the peace of the world, too large for effective government. Its partition either under the will of the sovereign or by an amicable agreement concluded in advance by the interested parties was on all grounds to be desired as the only method of preserving Europe from a world war.

The possible claimants to the Spanish inheritance were in 1698 three young men, Philip, Duke of Anjou, the grandson of Louis XIV, Charles, the second son of Leopold II of Austria, and Joseph Ferdinand, the electoral prince of Bavaria, who was nephew to the King of Spain. Of these three the Bavarian, being the least formidable, was likely to be most acceptable to the interested powers and to offer the best guarantees for the preservation of the European balance.[1] Accordingly a Treaty of Partition was struck between France, England, and the Netherlands, which accorded to the young Prince of Bavaria the lion's share of the Spanish empire (Spain and the Indies) while providing for Austria and France substantial satisfaction from the remainder. These prudent arrangements were, however, frustrated in the following year by the unexpected death of the Bavarian. The problem had to be taken up anew and under far less favourable conditions.

So long as the Bavarian, a comparatively weak and un-controversial figure, was alive it was possible that all the interested parties might be brought to accept a common plan; but with his death the problem became almost insoluble. An arrangement was, indeed, made satisfactory alike to Louis and the maritime powers. By the Second Treaty of Partition it was settled that the Netherlands should go to Austria (a capital point with the maritime powers), as well as Spain and the Indies, while France was to have Naples, Sicily, and Milan to be exchanged for Lorraine; and that Louis should have assented to such an arrangement is a singular illustration of his moderation at this period.

But unfortunately there were two powers, Spain and Austria, to whom the idea of partition on any condition was wholly inacceptable. It was natural that the king and the grandees of Spain should resent the idea of t he dismember-ment of the Spanish empire, but that Leopold of Austria, out of his desire for Milan, should reject the splendid terms offered him by the Second Treaty of Partition was a blunder only surpassed in the catalogue of costly Austrian follies by the ultimatum to Serbia of July, 1914. In face of these obstacles the wise policy of partition upon which William III and Louis XIV had expended great diplomatic ability was doomed to failure. When the Spanish king died in November, 1700, it was found that he had left a will bequeathing his

Genealogical Table O

undivided empire to Philip of France, with the provision that
if the bequest was not accepted in its entirety the prize should
be transferred to the Austrian Charles.

Louis could hardly have refused to take up the inheritance.
It is true that he had only just signed the Second Treaty of
Partition, which had awarded the heart of the Spanish empire
to Austria; but Austria had not accepted that treaty, and
England and Holland could not confidently be counted on to
help France to enforce it. Had Louis refused the bequest to
his grandson everything would have gone to Charles, and
nobody can blame Louis if he shrank from acquiescing in the
transference of the whole Spanish Succession to his Austrian
rival. Had Austria been reasonable she could have had a
magnificent accretion of power without a world war. Had
Spain been prudent she could have escaped a foreign invasion
at the cost of some outlying possessions. But since Austria
and Spain would have nothing less than all, and since Spain
rightly calculated that France would be more formidable as
an enemy and more helpful as a friend than distant Austria,
Louis found himself compelled, for fear of worse consequences, to accept the will. A Spanish cardinal controlling
the death-bed of a royal half-wit had converted the French
protagonist of partition into the shield and buckler of indivisible Spain.

Peace, henceforth, was difficult to preserve. Yet what made
war inevitable was not so much the acceptance of the will by
Louis as the new spirit of arrogant intemperance which the
will created in his mind. At once he broke out into a series of
wanton acts of aggression, exactly calculated to inflame the
hostility of the maritime powers. He poured troops into the
Spanish Netherlands, occupied the Dutch barrier towns, and
compelled the Spaniards to make over to the French the
Asiento, or right of trading in African slaves with the Spanish
Indies. In face of such acts as these, English and Dutch felt
that they must fight for their commercial existence. Even a
Tory Parliament (February, 1701) invited King William to
enter into negotiations with the Emperor and other powers
to put a curb upon the French. In 1701, as again in 1793 and
in 1914, the invasion of Belgium by a great power lit the
flames of war in the spirit of the English peoples.

The foundations of the Grand Alliance, which fought the
War of the Spanish Succession against France, were laid by

the Duke of Marlborough, whom William wisely sent to The Hague to treat with Heinsius, the Grand Pensionary of Holland.

So practical were the aims of the Alliance, as originally defined, that after twelve years of costly strife they were substantially secured in the Treaty of Utrecht (1713). William was content that Philip should rule in Spain and the Indies so long as the Netherlands, Italy, and the Mediterranean islands passed from Spanish into Austrian hands. For this there were reasons grounded upon the maritime needs of the English and Dutch peoples. Unlike France, Austria was neither a naval danger nor a commercial rival. The merchants of London and Amsterdam could therefore safely trust her with possessions which lay along the great trade routes to the Baltic and the Levant.

The death of William III, who for hard upon a generation had been the soul of every European enterprise against France, made no difference to English policy. All his large designs—the Grand Alliance, the war against France, the capture of naval bases in the Mediterranean, the Protestant succession—were, as Professor Trevelyan reminds us, taken up by Queen Anne, the dull, devout, high church daughter of James II, who by a freak of fortune has given her name to a brilliant age. Though the Press had been freed in 1695 and party spirit ran fierce and high, there was enough of the mediatorial spirit in English politics to work parliamentary institutions. By a happy innovation, the germ of a great Civil Service, the Treasury experts continued from ministry to ministry. Whigs and Tories in turn advanced the welfare of the country. The Whigs carried through the Union with Scotland. The Tories passed the Act of Settlement which eventually brought the Protestant Electors of Hanover to the throne. The Whigs financed the victorious war, the Tories coming into full power in 1710 made the welcome peace. Fundamentally, for the worst sore was healed by a grant of toleration to the dissenters in 1689, the country was at one. The popularity of Marlborough with the queen, the skill of his diplomacy, the brilliance of his victories, coupled with the exasperation caused in every English Protestant heart when Louis recognized the Old Pretender as King James III, were causes sufficient to maintain the warlike spirit of the country. Security, commerce, the Protestant succession, were felt to be at stake. If the squires winced at the four shilling land-tax, which was the spine of Godolphin's war finance, they paid up to the end notwithstanding. Such was the English spirit. For the Dutch, robbed of their cherished barrier towns in the Spanish Netherlands, the war was a matter of life and death.

War in the later part of the seventeenth century was not the devastating curse which science and conscription have now combined to make it. It was waged by small mercenary armies, hibernating for half the year, and during the short campaigning season, no longer as in the Thirty Years' War living upon the country, but supplied by a regular commissariat service. Military movements were apt to be slow and deliberate, as befitted an age when even admirals wore full-bottomed wigs and methodical siege warfare constituted the most important part of military science. Commanders, heedful of the difficulty of replenishing their armies with fresh recruits, sought rather to avoid than to invite decisive encounters. Marlborough was exceptional. The English Prince Charming, who, but for the obstructions of the Dutch, could have driven the French from Flanders in the first two years of the war, was as anxious to manoeuvre his opponent into action as his opponent was in general desirous of avoiding it.

His hammer blows were decisive. After Blenheim and Ramillies the allies could have made a peace with Louis securing to them all the original war aims of the Grand Alliance. Blenheim had swept the French out of Bavaria; Ramillies had placed most of Flanders at Marlborough's feet. The brilliant Eugène, with some assistance from Victor Amadeus of Savoy, had established the supremacy of Austrian arms in northern Italy. Yet peace was delayed for seven years.

The cause of this needless prolongation of the war is ultimately to be traced to the beauty and convenience of Lisbon harbour as a port of call and repair for English vessels bound upon Mediterranean errands. England in quest of Mediterranean ports had need of the Portuguese alliance, but how could Portugal, a small power, be expected to enter the lists against France unless the Austrian candidate would come to Spain, rally his supporters, and with Dutch, English, and Portuguese support evict the Frenchman and establish him-

1704
1706

self in Madrid? In the Methuen Treaties of 1703, Peter II of Portugal insisted, as a condition of his alliance with England, that Charles, suitably supported by the allies, should make a bid for the Spanish throne. The bargain was struck. The war aims of the allies were enlarged to include the conquest of Spain for Charles, and an unsuccessful Peninsular War, extending over the best part of a decade, was the price by which England obtained the use of Lisbon harbour, without which the Rock of Gibraltar could not have been held or Port Mahon (in Minorca) wrested from Spain.

It was only by slow and reluctant stages that English politicians were brought to see that the Spanish "side-show" was a forlorn adventure, and that the proudest nation in Europe would never accept an Austrian sovereign imposed on them by odious northern heretics and even more repulsive Portuguese. The Catalans, indeed, inflamed by hatred of Castile, and encouraged by Peterborough's brilliant capture of Barcelona, declared for the Austrian Archduke, but Catalonia has never been an integral part of Spain. In language, in customs, in temper, this maritime province of Aragon had little in common with the inhabitants of the interior plateau. It was no passport to the affections of the Spanish people that Charles should have won the mercurial sympathies of the Catalans. The great bulk of the Spanish people was from the first, and throughout, favourable to the claims of Philip V.

The Austrian hegemony in Italy, which was not finally shaken until the days of Cavour and Garibaldi, dates from the Treaty of Utrecht (1713), which closed the war of the Spanish Succession. The Emperor, foiled of his designs in Spain, then received compensation in Lombardy, Sardinia, and Naples. The predominance in Italian affairs, which had belonged to Spain ever since the days of Charles V, now passed to a Teutonic government whose solid gifts of order and efficiency were unsweetened by qualities likely to engage the sympathies of a Latin people. It is curious to think of the extent to which the fate of Italy depended upon the brains of two Englishmen, Godolphin the financier and Marlborough the soldier, without whom the allied cause, despite all the military science of Prince Eugène, could never have prevailed.

For the greater convenience of the maritime powers the

Emperor was required to rule in the Spanish Netherlands, in which the Dutch were accorded a line of barrier fortresses, a pledge that this valuable province would be defended against France, not by the Dutch alone, but also by one of the great continental monarchies.

Spain, the first prize of the competition, went to Louis. Philip V, who during the war had been twice ejected from Madrid and twice restored, lived to found a dynasty of Spanish Bourbons who survived the French Revolution and the empire, and, though now in exile, still carry the hopes of 1935 a royalist Spain. Though the crowns of Spain and France were finally separated, the close political association of the two Bourbon powers was a feature of the political life of the next century, which came into special prominence when Spain and France assisted the American colonies to throw off the British yoke. The capitulation of the British at York- 1781 town was the answer to Blenheim and Ramillies and the sequence of those victories of Almanza and Brihuega by 1707 which Berwick and Vendôme planted French rule south of 1710 the Pyrenees.

The long reign of Louis XIV did not, therefore, despite the distress of the population during its concluding years, end in failure. The medal "*clausa Germanis Gallia*" was justified; so, too, though in a less literal sense, was that other saying of the Sun King, "Henceforth there are no Pyrenees." That France was free of invasion until the days of Napoleon may in part be ascribed to the improvements in her eastern defences which were effected in the king's early manhood and successfully retained in the end.

England emerged from the struggle having secured not only the original war aims of William III, but one advantage which could not have been predicted. In her long war partnership with the Dutch she had made the sea her special province, while the bulk of the land armies who fought under Marlborough were provided by her allies. As the war proceeded the English navy grew and the Dutch navy, by comparison, declined. The marine supremacy, which had been evenly divided between the two nations in the middle of the seventeenth century, was by the end of the war of the Spanish Succession definitely secured by England. Meanwhile Britain had acquired new stations and centres of power and colonization in the old world and in the new, Gibraltar and Port

Mahon, Newfoundland and Nova Scotia. It was idle for the French, the balance of naval power being what it was in 1713, to contest these acquisitions. They passed to England under the Treaty of Utrecht, together with the treasured right, known as the *Asiento*, of trading African slaves (and incidentally other goods as well) to the Spanish Indies.

Though the four shilling land-tax was bitterly grudged by the squires, England stood the strain of the war better than any other belligerent. Expanding overseas commerce provided the atmosphere of confidence in which individuals may lend and governments may borrow. The Bank of England, the National Debt, the exact practice of the Treasury, enabled England to finance her allies. A European coalition, as in two other more recent war periods, was sustained by the might of British finance.

It was a further note of power that England was able to obtain from Louis XIV an acknowledgment of the Protestant Succession in the Hanoverian House.[1] In his last hours the aged persecutor of the Huguenots was compelled thus to salute the heretic city of London, where nothing was so greatly apprehended for its effect upon the Funds as a violent reopening of the old quarrel between Catholic and Protestant in England.

The suppression of the Protestants in 1685, while greatly impoverishing the religious life of France, failed to reduce it to a dead uniformity. Though the Jesuit had gained a victory and exercised a complete mastery over the court, he was not alone in the field. Within the Catholic Church itself, a movement drawing its nutriment from the same moral roots and, in part, from the same theological authority as Puritanism, challenged the fashionable theology of Versailles and powerfully helped in the first half of the eighteenth century to educate a political opposition to the crown. The Jansenists drew their name from Jansen, Bishop of Ypres (1583-1638), the author of three folio volumes on St. Augustine, which were condemned by the Pope in 1642. Few have read the learned work of this Catholic Dutchman; fewer still could have predicted that from such an unlikely source a stream of spiritual energy would descend upon France and there fertilize and refresh some of the finest religious natures of the age.

[1] Genealogical Table P.

It appears to be a long road from the pedantry of Jansen to the eloquence of Arnauld, the exquisite irony of Pascal, and the finished and contemplative beauty of Racine. Yet Arnauld, Pascal, and Racine were flowers from the same Augustinian stem, nourished upon the doctrine of Grace, which Martin Luther had found in Augustine, and by the light of which many had been brought to a belief in predestination, to an intimate personal piety, and to a repudiation of all easy and superficial ways of attaining salvation.

The bridge between the Dutch bishop and religious people in France was supplied by the appearance in 1643 of a moral treatise written by a young French priest against the notion that frequent Communion could atone for persistent ill living. Sincere natures were charmed by Antoine Arnauld's *De la Fréquente Communion*. Appearing in an age of widespread compliance with profligacy, this burning outburst of devotional eloquence represented the recoil of the Christian conscience from the mundane teaching of Jesuit confessors, who, in their endeavour to reclaim all sorts and conditions of men for the faith, sweetened the taste of religion to the palate of the worldling. An austere form of Catholic piety had long flourished in certain religious communities, notably in the nunnery of Port Royal, near Versailles, and was common among the grave magisterial families of the capital. To such *De la Fréquente* rang like a call to battle against the forces of laxity and vice.

The Jansenists, then, were the Puritans of the French Catholic Church. In beauty and integrity of character, as well as in a stern ardour of principle, perceptible in the rarest manifestations of the Latin genius from Lucretius to Condorcet, the Jansenists offered in their lives, as well as in their writings, an eloquent rebuke to a profligate age. Some went to great extremes. They condemned poetry and art, and preferred the melancholy decay of autumn to the vital exuberance of spring. All desired to return to the conditions of the primitive Church and feared the onward march of science. To the pliant Jesuit, conscious that the Church could live only by adapting its teaching to the changing conditions of a changing world, the rigorous Jansenist appeared to represent a dangerous and impracticable sectarianism. The Jansenist thought the Jesuit too lax; the Jesuit thought the Jansenist too narrow. The one held that mankind would never be led up to the throne of God by a fierce and inhospitable virtue; the other that God would never accept a politic compact with vice. The one strove to make the way to heaven easy and accessible to the many; the other maintained that it must always be difficult and confined to the few.

The clash of opinion gave rise to Pascal's *Provincial Letters* (1656-7). In this famous controversial pamphlet every resource of light irony and passionate dialectic was deployed against the system of casuistry by which the Jesuits were said to obscure the plain distinction between right and wrong. The manifesto was the more important by reason of the fact that the author was not a professed theologian, but a mathematical genius, of amazing precocity and fertility of invention, who united the clarity and force of a first-class scientific mind with the exquisite scruples and sensibilities of a saintly and enthusiastic invalid. Feeling deeply (for he had experienced two conversions) and writing with an ease and simplicity which cleansed French prose of its affectations, Pascal drew a great issue of moral theology out of its hiding place among the folios and confessionals into the open light of day, and exposed it with a merciless clarity to the view of all.

The Jesuit has never quite outlived the force of his assault, and if the epithet Jesuitical still survives in common speech, as denoting a subtlety fringing on fraud, the fact is largely to be attributed to the *Provincial Letters*, which, while they gave to Jansenism a fuller sweep and influence among the moral and intellectual movements of the age, fixed upon the Jesuit Order the stigma of debasing the moral currency of Christendom.

It was the Jesuit, however, and not the Jansenist, who during the long reign of Louis XIV stood upon the steps of the throne, and helped to mould the policy of the state. The Jesuits were the king's friends. The Jansenists, from an early and unfortunate association with some prominent members of the Fronde, were marked out for his distrust. It was a Jesuit victory when, in 1653, five propositions doubtfully alleged to be contained in Jansen's *Augustinus* were condemned by Pope Innocent X, and, again, a Jesuit victory when, in 1661, the *Provincial Letters* were burnt by the common hangman. Later on, in 1669, the Jansenists made their peace with the Pope, and enjoyed a period of relative immunity from persecution. But they were still without popularity or political influence. In the stiffly fought quarrel between Louis XIV and Innocent XI, which developed out of the king's claim to the temporalities of vacant bishoprics, the Jansenists to their honour sided with the Roman Curia in its resistance to an inexcusable abuse of the royal prerogative. This was the unpopular side. The tide of national feeling in France ran strongly with the king in his defence of the liberties of the Gallican Church against ultramontane interference.

The importance of Jansenism as a political influence was yet to come. The concluding years of the king's life were marked by a deep shadow of disaster abroad and gloomy piety at home. Ever since Colbert's death the finances had been in disorder. The short-term loans which had been issued to finance the war gave way to a system of indirect borrowing, and this in turn to the rise of a new class of middlemen, who defrauded the state, and introduced a fresh poison into the atmosphere of the Court. Louis was not a religious man, but he was deeply superstitious. To appease the wrath of the Deity, and to reverse the ill-fortune of his arms, he resolved upon a fresh attack on heretical opinion. He had already broken the Protestants. He was now prepared to listen to the advice of his Jesuit confessor, and to take steps against the Jansenists. The extraordinary brutality with which the campaign was conducted forms a bad page in the history of religious intolerance. The nuns of Port Royal des Champs were expelled, their convent pulled down, their cemetery violated. A French version of the New Testament, published in 1671, with an elaborate commentary by Pasquier Quesnel, a prominent member of the Jansenist party, was singled out to be the object of a combined attack, and since nothing was easier for a Jesuit than to find heresies in the book of an enemy, or to procure their condemnation in Rome, the work of the Jansenist leader was made to incur the censure of the Pope. Against the protest of fifteen bishops and with the lively opposition of the Parliament of Paris, the Bull *Unigenitus* found 101 heresies in a book which most readers regarded as a monument of evangelical piety laboriously erected by a Christian saint.

It was now the turn of the Jansenists to march with the Gallicans against ultramontane pretensions, an alliance which brought legal self-sufficiency and patriotic pride to the assistance of angular virtue. For one Frenchman whose religious beliefs were affected by the Jansenists, there were ten who resented the interference of the Pope, or were jealous of the power of the Company of Jesus. A struggle developed after the death of Louis XIV in which a great body of feeling and opinion, part Jansenist, but more largely Gallican, was arrayed under the leadership of the Parliament of Paris and with the support of twelve Provincial Parliaments, against the alliance of the Crown and the Jesuit Order. The struggle was protracted and violent, raising during its progress almost every political idea which afterwards led to the establishment of democratic government in France. Long before the appearance of Rousseau's *Social Contract* in 1762, the contest between the Crown and the Parliament of Paris, which had for its origin the papal condemnation of a Jansenist treatise, had familiarized the French people with a conception of constitutional government and of popular sovereignty. When the Jesuits were expelled from France in 1764 the stage was cleared for the movements which led to the French Revolution, and to that marked eclipse of papal authority and prestige which is one of the special notes of the revolutionary age.

In history everything is continuous. Yet the Peace of Utrecht may conveniently be taken as marking a point after which the religious and dynastic motives, which had previously played so large a part in the moulding of policy, sensibly declined in importance, while their place is taken by the struggle for colonies and markets. The long duel between England and France for colonial power which distinguishes the eighteenth century had not in it a particle either of religious or of dynastic interest. A new class had come to the front, which cared for none of these things, and was now sufficiently powerful to influence the policy of States.

By this time, too, science was swiftly coming into its own, largely in response to the material needs of a developing civilization. The mediaeval university, being the intellectual organ of the Catholic Church, was confined within the rigid limits of ecclesiastical orthodoxy. Reverence for authority excluded free investigation. The sacred texts of the Bible, the works hardly less dominant of Aristotle, were held to contain all that it was necessary to know, and all that it was safe to believe. What was present in these canonical writings was true, what was absent was unimportant, what conflicted was false. When at the beginning of the seventeenth century Kircher invited a brother Jesuit to look through his telescope at the newly discovered spots on the sun, the professor replied, "My son, it is useless. I have read Aristotle through twice, and have not found anything about spots on the sun. There are no spots on the sun." It was therefore heresy to maintain the Copernican theory of the planets, heresy to deny the creation of the Universe some four thousand years before Christ, heresy to frustrate the bodily resurrection by the destruction of a corpse. Such were the leaden inhibitions which shackled the learning of the mediaeval Faculties.

The world was wider than the universities. Sailors steering by the stars or marking the deviations of the compass, marine engineers reckoning with the tides, miners grappling with asphyxiation from gas or water below the ground, gunsmiths concerned for the durability of their muskets or culverins, built up by degrees a body of knowledge, part technical, part scientific, which lay far outside the university curriculum and was quite unaffected by university prepossessions. Navigation called for astronomy, led on to optics, and through the compass invited the study of magnetism. To frame tables of longitude it was necessary to ascertain the laws of the moon's movement; the determination of latitude implied a chart of the heavenly bodies. In view of the secular struggle between land and sea in the Netherlands it was natural that the first scientific chronology of the tides (1590) should be the work of Stevin, the Dutch engineer. As the art of warfare came increasingly to depend upon artillery, the mining of iron and copper received a fresh impetus with consequences of ever widening importance.

Mining is the prolific parent of science and technology. As early as the seventeenth century it was realized that an educated mining engineer must know triangulation and Euclidian geometry, the use of the compass, and the construction of apparatus for ventilation and pumping. Problems of aerostatics, of hydro-dynamics, of mechanics, imposed themselves upon him. Alike the safety of the miner and the yield of the mine depended upon the laws of physical science.

Hardly less important was the train of scientific thought and discovery, which was opened out by the new developments in the art of war. As early as 1537 Tartaglia was at work upon the trajectory of the flight of a bullet. The most profound problems of physics were suggested by ballistics, the resistance of the air to a ball passing through it, the trajectory of a ball through a vacuum, the free fall of bodies under the influence of gravity. It is significant that Galileo opens his mathematical demonstrations with a compliment to the arsenal of Florence, the scene of so much activity and the storehouse of so much material for the scientific mind.

Meanwhile the strength of the ancient buttresses against the new knowledge had been weakened by the religious and political convulsions of the age. Europe was no longer undivided in faith. Monarchy was no longer unchallenged. The revolutionary and exciting discovery of the true nature of the earth's crust had created a temper favourable to intellectual innovations and contemptuous of the scholastic tradition. Intellectual life of the higher sort was no longer confined to the universities, but found organs appropriate to its needs in bodies like the Accademia del Cimente in Florence or the Royal Society in England, both founded in the middle of the seventeenth century and pledged to discovery and experiment. "Provare e reprovare," the motto of the Florentines, "Nullius in verba," the motto of the Englishmen, showed that the true spirit of science, which had been lost to Europe since the decline of the Greek city republics, was now again coming into its own among the Latin and Teutonic nations.

The seventeenth century witnessed the production of *Hamlet* and *Tartuffe*, of *Paradise Lost* and of Newton's *Principia*. It was the age of Rembrandt and Rubens, of Van Dyck and Hobbema, of Ruysdael and Franz Hals. It heard the first notes of Italian opera, the first strains of Purcell's music and of the Stradivarius violin. It gave the compass and the barometer to the mariner, the telescope and the microscope to the man of science, quinine and the thermometer to the physician, the shot gun to the sportsman. The comfort of daily life was enriched by the invention of the watch and the clock, and gluttony was robbed of half its grossness by the popularization of the fork. It was an age of growing wealth and of an expanding international trade in luxuries. The century of the Puritans and the Jansenists was marked by the discovery of ices and champagne, by the yet more beneficial importation of tea and coffee, and by the introduction of wax candles, the most beautiful of all forms of illumination, into the gorgeous saloons of Versailles. The first formal gardener, the first statistician, the first woman to pursue a professional career on the stage, belong to the later half of the seventeenth century. Yet the age which manifested its energy in these and many other happy ways, such as street lighting, and marine insurance, and the London penny post, was, despite its complex and advancing civilization, a period of almost uninterrupted war. In the policies which provoked war, and in the settlements by which quarrels were composed, little account was taken of public feeling. Democracy was uneducated and unorganized. The newspaper press was in its infancy. After the troubles of the Fronde and the Great Rebellion, the continent of Europe turned as if for safety to governments which became in increasing measure autocratic. In the science and art of hereditary despotism, Louis XIV set an example which was too dazzling for Scandinavia or Germany to resist. Nevertheless, despite everlasting war, the Europe of the seventeenth century held together. The sense of a common civilization and of a common European interest in the maintenance of a balance of power was far too strong to be obliterated by the summer activities of small heterogeneous and mercenary armies. Nine great diplomatic congresses, beginning with Westphalia and ending with Utrecht, attested the growing power of international action, and the passing away of that stage of European history when the office of universal mediator was among Christian people by common consent acknowledged to belong to the Pope.

It is also to be remarked that the wars against France, which fill the reign of Louis XIV, were in no sense waged in a spirit antagonistic to French culture. The intellectual and social prestige of the French monarchy, so far from being lowered in the eyes of its adversaries by the martial ambitions of Louis XIV, received from them an added lustre. French books were not the less read, French science not the less honoured, French fashions not the less followed, because half Europe was coalesced against the French monarchy. French civilization, illustrated by the brilliance and learning of its authors, ruled supreme and gave the law to every social group which aspired to the faintest tincture of culture, from the Russian border to the Atlantic Ocean. Nothing more clearly marks the distinction between the monarchical wars of this age and the national struggles of our own time than the continued spiritual hegemony of France, despite the bitter political opposition provoked by the domineering ambitions of her sovereign.

BOOKS WHICH MAY BE CONSULTED

Macaulay: *History of England*. 1858-62.

G. M. Trevelyan: *England under Queen Anne*. 1932-4.

J. R. Seeley: *Growth of British Policy*. 2 vols. 1895.

E. Lavisse: *Histoire de France*, Vol. VIII.

W. Coxe: *House of Austria*. 1847.

Winston Churchill: *Life of Marlborough*. 1934.

C. T. Atkinson: *Marlborough and the Rise of the British Army*. 1921.

Sainte-Beuve: *Histoire du Port Royal*. 5 vols. 1840-59.

E. Boutroux: *Pascal*. *Tr.* E. M. Creak. 1902.

Von Noorden: *Europaische Geschichte im 18 Jahrhundert. Des Spanische Erbfolge Krieg*. 1870-82.

Ogg: *Europe in the Seventeenth Century*. 1925.

CHRONOLOGICAL TABLE OF ROMAN EMPERORS FROM 27 B.C. *TO* A.D. 476

	Year of Accession		Year of Accession
	B.C.		A.D
Augustus	27	The third Gordian	238
	A.D.	Philip	244
Tiberius	14	Decius	249
Caligula	37	Hostilian, Gallus	251
Claudius	41	Volusian	252
Nero	54	Æmilian, Valerian, Gallienus	253
Galba, Otho, Vitellius, Vespasian	68	Gallienus alone	260
Titus	79	Claudius II	268
Domitian	81	Aurelian	270
Nerva	96	Tacitus	275
Trajan	98	Florian	276
Hadrian	117	Probus	276
Antoninus Pius	138	Carus	282
Marcus Aurelius	161	Carinus, Numerian	284
Commodus	180	Diocletian	284
Pertinax	193	Maximian, associated with Diocletian	286
Didius Julianus	193	Constantius, Galerius	305
Niger	193	Severus	306
Septimus Severus	193	Constantine (the Great)	306
Caracalla, Geta	211	Licinius	307
Opilius Macrinus, Diadumenian	217	Maximin	308
Elagabalus	218	Constantine, Galerius, Licinius, Maximin, Maxentius, and Maximian reigning jointly	309
Alexander Severus	222		
Maximin	235		
The two Gordians, Maximus Pupienus, Balbinus	237	Constantine (the Great) alone	323

H.E. I—23

	Year of Accession A.D.		Year of Accession A.D.
Constantine II, Constantius II, Constans Magnentius.	337	Maximus, Avitus (W.)	455
		Majorian (W.)	455
Constantius alone	353	Leo I (E.)	457
Julian	361	Severus (W.)	461
Jovian	363	Vacancy (W.)	465
Valens and Valentinian I	364	Anthemius (W.)	467
Gratian and Valentinian I	367	Olybrius (W.)	472
Gratian and Valentinian II	375	Glycerius (W.)	473
Theodosius	379	Julius Nepos (W.)	474
Arcadius (in the east), Honorius (in the West)	395	Leo II, Zeno, Basiliscus (all E.)	474
Theodosius II (E.)	408	Romulus Augustulus (W.)	475
Valentinian III (W.)	424	End of the Western line in Romulus Augustus	476
Marcian (E)	450		

(*Henceforth, till* A.D. 800, *Emperors reigning at Constantinople*)

A. *CHARLEMAGNE'S ANCESTRY*

Pippin,
Mayor of Austrasia; *d.* 639.

|

Begga,
m. Ansegisel.

|

Pippin,
Mayor of Austrasia, Neustria and Burgundy; *d.* 714.

|

Charles Martel,
Mayor of all Kingdoms; *d.* 741.

|

Pippin,
Mayor of Neustria, 741; King of Franks, 752.

|

Charlemagne

B. *HOUSE OF TANCRED*
OF HAUTEVILLE
Tancred of Hauteville.

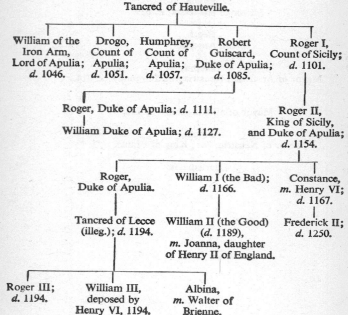

William of the
Iron Arm,
Lord of Apulia;
d. 1046.

Drogo,
Count of
Apulia;
d. 1051.

Humphrey,
Count of
Apulia;
d. 1057.

Robert
Guiscard,
Duke of Apulia;
d. 1085.

Roger I,
Count of Sicily;
d. 1101.

Roger, Duke of Apulia; *d.* 1111.

William Duke of Apulia; *d.* 1127.

Roger II,
King of Sicily,
and Duke of Apulia;
d. 1154.

Roger,
Duke of Apulia.

William I (the Bad);
d. 1166.

Constance,
m. Henry VI;
d. 1167.

Tancred of Lecce
(illeg.); *d.* 1194.

William II (the Good)
(*d.* 1189),
m. Joanna, daughter
of Henry II of England.

Frederick II;
d. 1250.

Roger III;
d. 1194.

William III,
deposed by
Henry VI, 1194.

Albina,
m. Walter of
Brienne.

C. SAXON AND SALIAN EMPERORS

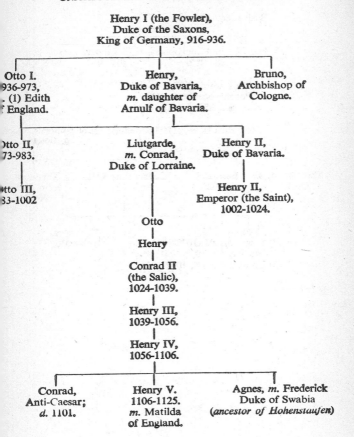

Henry I (the Fowler),
Duke of the Saxons,
King of Germany, 916-936.

Otto I.
936-973,
m. (1) Edith
of England.

Henry,
Duke of Bavaria,
m. daughter of
Arnulf of Bavaria.

Bruno,
Archbishop of
Cologne.

Otto II,
973-983.

Liutgarde,
m. Conrad,
Duke of Lorraine.

Henry II,
Duke of Bavaria.

Otto III,
983-1002

Henry II,
Emperor (the Saint),
1002-1024.

Otto

Henry

Conrad II
(the Salic),
1024-1039.

Henry III,
1039-1056.

Henry IV,
1056-1106.

Conrad,
Anti-Caesar;
d. 1101.

Henry V.
1106-1125.
m. Matilda
of England.

Agnes, m. Frederick
Duke of Swabia
(ancestor of Hohenstaufen)

D. *MACEDONIAN EMPERORS*

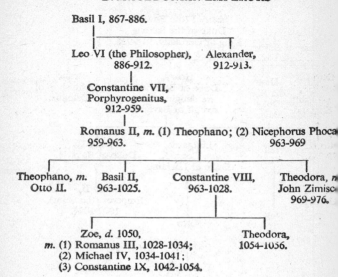

Basil I, 867-886.

Leo VI (the Philosopher),   Alexander,
886-912.   912-913.

Constantine VII,
Porphyrogenitus,
912-959.

Romanus II, *m.* (1) Theophano; (2) Nicephorus Phoca
959-963.   963-969

Theophano, *m.*   Basil II,   Constantine VIII,   Theodora, *m*
Otto II.   963-1025.   963-1028.   John Zimisc
                                                      969-976.

Zoe, *d.* 1050,   Theodora,
m. (1) Romanus III, 1028-1034;   1054-1056.
(2) Michael IV, 1034-1041;
(3) Constantine IX, 1042-1054.

E. *THE GUELFS*
AND HOHENSTAUFEN

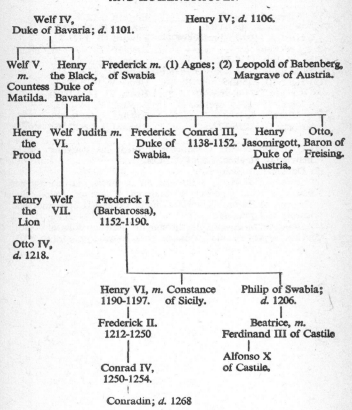

Welf IV,
Duke of Bavaria; *d.* 1101.

Henry IV; *d.* 1106.

Welf V. *m.* Countess Matilda. — Henry the Black, Duke of Bavaria. — Frederick *m.* (1) Agnes; (2) Leopold of Babenberg, of Swabia — Margrave of Austria.

Henry the Proud — Welf VI. — Judith *m.* Frederick Duke of Swabia. — Conrad III, 1138-1152. — Henry Jasomirgott, Duke of Austria. — Otto, Baron of Freising.

Henry the Lion — Welf VII. — Frederick I (Barbarossa), 1152-1190.

Otto IV, *d.* 1218.

Henry VI, *m.* Constance 1190-1197. of Sicily.

Philip of Swabia; *d.* 1206.

Frederick II. 1212-1250

Beatrice, *m.* Ferdinand III of Castile

Conrad IV, 1250-1254.

Alfonso X of Castile.

Conradin; *d.* 1268

F. *THE KINGS OF ENGLAND*
FROM 1066-1485

William I, 1066-87.
William II, 1087-1100.
Henry I, 1100-35, brother of
   William II.
(1) { Stephen, 1135-54.
(2) { Matilda.
(3) Henry II, 1154-89.
Richard I, 1189-99.
John, 1199-1216, brother of
   Richard I.
Henry III, 1216-1272.

Edward I, 1272-1307.
Edward II, 1307-27.
Edward III, 1327-77.
Richard II, 1377-99, grand-
   son of Edward III.
(4) Henry IV, 1399-1413.
Henry V, 1413-22.
Henry VI, 1422-1461.
(5) Edward IV, 1461-83.
Edward V, 1483.
Richard III, 1483-85.

(1) Grandson of the Conqueror through his daughter Adela, married to Stephen, Count of Blois.
(2) Daughter of Henry I.
(3) Grandson of Henry I through his daughter Matilda, by her marriage with Geoffrey Plantagenet. Count of Anjou, and husband to Eleanor, divorced wife of Louis VII of France and heiress of Aquitaine.
(4) Grandson of Edward III, through his third son John of Gaunt.
5) Grandson of Edmund, Duke of York, fourth son of Edward III.

THE KINGS OF FRANCE
FROM 987-1589

Hugues Capet, 987-996.
Robert, 996-1031.
Henry I, 1031-1060.
Philip I, 1060-1108.
Louis VI, 1108-1137.
Louis VII, 1137-1180.
Philip II (Augustus), 1180-1223.
Louis VIII, 1223-1226.
Louis IX, 1226-1270.
Philip III, 1270-1285.
Philip IV, 1285-1314.
Louis X, 1314-1316.
Philip V, 1316-1322.
Charles IV, 1322-1328.

(1) Philip VI, 1328-1350.
John, 1350-1364.
Charles V, 1364-1380.
Charles VI, 1380-1422.
Charles VII, 1422-1461.
Louis XI, 1461-1483.
Charles VIII, 1483-1498.
(2) Louis XII, 1498-1515.
(3) Francis I, 1515-1547.
(4) Henry II, 1547-1559.
Francis II, 1559-1560.
Charles IX, 1560-1574.
(5) Henry III, 1574-1589.
Margaret—Henry IV, son of Anthony of Bourbon.

(1) Son of Charles, Count of Valois, second son of Philip III. First monarch of the Valois House.
(2) Son of Charles, Duke of Orleans, and husband of Jeanne, the sister of Charles VIII. Afterwards married to Anne, Duchess of Brittany.
(3) Son of Charles, Count of Angoulême, married to Claude, daughter of Louis XII.
(4) Married to Catharine de' Medicis.
(5) Children of Henry II and Catherine de' Medicis.

G. *THE SCOTTISH ROYAL LINE*

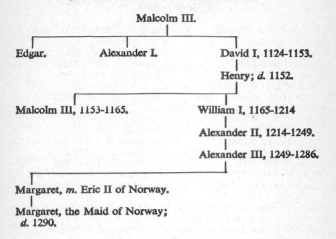

Malcolm III.

Edgar.   Alexander I.   David I, 1124-1153.

Henry; *d.* 1152.

Malcolm III, 1153-1165.   William I, 1165-1214

Alexander II, 1214-1249.

Alexander III, 1249-1286.

Margaret, *m.* Eric II of Norway.

Margaret, the Maid of Norway; *d.* 1290.

H. *CLAIMANTS TO FRENCH THRONE IN 1328 WHEN MAIN CAPET LINE ENDED*

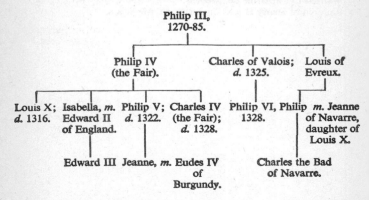

Philip III, 1270-85.

Philip IV (the Fair).   Charles of Valois; *d.* 1325.   Louis of Evreux.

Louis X; *d.* 1316.   Isabella, *m.* Edward II of England.   Philip V; *d.* 1322.   Charles IV (the Fair); *d.* 1328.   Philip VI, 1328.   Philip *m.* Jeanne of Navarre, daughter of Louis X.

Edward III   Jeanne, *m.* Eudes IV of Burgundy.   Charles the Bad of Navarre.

J. THE HOUSE OF HABSBURG
FROM 1273-1519

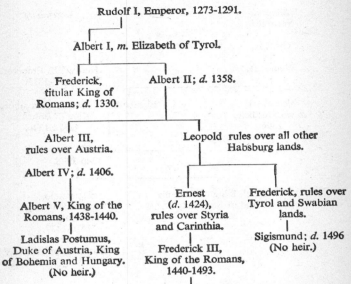

Rudolf I, Emperor, 1273-1291.

Albert I, *m.* Elizabeth of Tyrol.

Frederick,
titular King of
Romans; *d.* 1330.

Albert II; *d.* 1358.

Albert III,
rules over Austria.

Albert IV; *d.* 1406.

Albert V, King of the
Romans, 1438-1440.

Ladislas Postumus,
Duke of Austria, King
of Bohemia and Hungary.
(No heir.)

Leopold rules over all other
Habsburg lands.

Ernest
(*d.* 1424),
rules over Styria
and Carinthia.

Frederick III,
King of the Romans,
1440-1493.

Maximilian I, *m.* Mary of Burgundy
Unites all Habsburg lands.
1493-1519

Frederick, rules over
Tyrol and Swabian
lands.

Sigismund; *d.* 1496
(No heir.)

K. *HOUSE OF LUXEMBURG*
AND SUCCESSION IN BOHEMIA

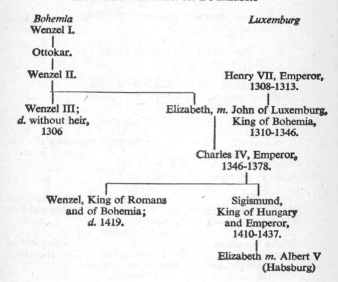

Bohemia   *Luxemburg*
Wenzel I.

Ottokar.

Wenzel II.   Henry VII, Emperor,
                                         1308-1313.

Wenzel III;   Elizabeth, *m.* John of Luxemburg,
d. without heir,   King of Bohemia,
1306   1310-1346.

                          Charles IV, Emperor,
                                1346-1378.

Wenzel, King of Romans   Sigismund,
and of Bohemia;   King of Hungary
d. 1419.   and Emperor,
                                      1410-1437.

                                 Elizabeth *m.* Albert V
                                      (Habsburg)

L. HOUSE OF TUDOR AND STUART:
THE TUDOR AND STUART SUCCESSION

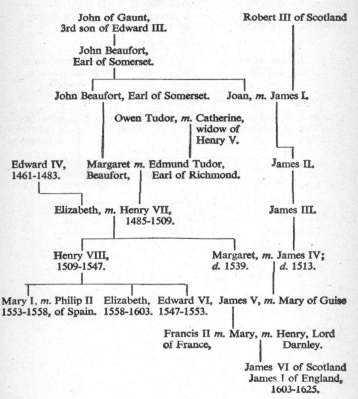

John of Gaunt,
3rd son of Edward III.

Robert III of Scotland

John Beaufort,
Earl of Somerset.

John Beaufort, Earl of Somerset.   Joan, *m.* James I.

Owen Tudor, *m.* Catherine,
widow of
Henry V.

Edward IV,   Margaret *m.* Edmund Tudor,   James II.
1461-1483.   Beaufort, | Earl of Richmond.

Elizabeth, *m.* Henry VII,   James III.
1485-1509.

Henry VIII,   Margaret, *m.* James IV;
1509-1547.   *d.* 1539. | *d.* 1513.

Mary I, *m.* Philip II   Elizabeth,   Edward VI,   James V, *m.* Mary of Guise
1553-1558, of Spain.   1558-1603.   1547-1553.

Francis II *m.* Mary, *m.* Henry, Lord
of France, | Darnley.

James VI of Scotland
James I of England,
1603-1625.

M. *EMPIRE OF CHARLES V*

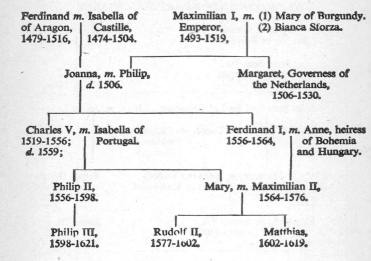

Ferdinand *m.* Isabella of
of Aragon,   Castille,
1479-1516,   1474-1504.

Maximilian I, *m.* (1) Mary of Burgundy.
Emperor,   (2) Bianca Sforza.
1493-1519,

Joanna, *m.* Philip,
d. 1506.

Margaret, Governess of
the Netherlands,
1506-1530.

Charles V, *m.* Isabella of
1519-1556;   Portugal.
d. 1559;

Ferdinand I, *m.* Anne, heiress
1556-1564,   of Bohemia
and Hungary.

Philip II,
1556-1598.

Mary, *m.* Maximilian II,
1564-1576.

Philip III,
1598-1621.

Rudolf II,
1577-1602.

Matthias,
1602-1619.

N. *THE LAST VALOIS KINGS AND*
SUCCESSION OF HENRY OF NAVARRE

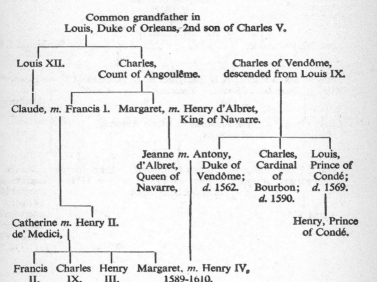

Common grandfather in
Louis, Duke of Orleans, 2nd son of Charles V.

Louis XII.   Charles,
Count of Angoulême.

Charles of Vendôme,
descended from Louis IX.

Claude, *m.* Francis I.   Margaret, *m.* Henry d'Albret,
King of Navarre.

Jeanne *m.* Antony,
d'Albret,   Duke of
Queen of   Vendôme;
Navarre,   *d.* 1562.

Charles,   Louis,
Cardinal   Prince of
of   Condé;
Bourbon;   *d.* 1569.
d. 1590.

Catherine *m.* Henry II.
de' Medici,

Henry, Prince
of Condé.

Francis   Charles   Henry   Margaret, *m.* Henry IV,
II.   IX.   III.   1589-1610.

O. CLAIMANTS TO THE SPANISH THRONE

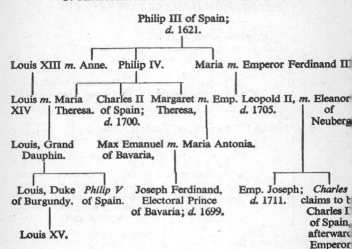

Philip III of Spain;
d. 1621.

Louis XIII *m.* Anne.   Philip IV.   Maria *m.* Emperor Ferdinand III

Louis *m.* Maria   Charles II   Margaret *m.* Emp.   Leopold II, *m.* Eleanor
XIV   Theresa.   of Spain;   Theresa,   *d.* 1705.   of
d. 1700.   Neuberg

Louis, Grand   Max Emanuel *m.* Maria Antonia.
Dauphin.   of Bavaria,

Louis, Duke   *Philip V*   Joseph Ferdinand,   Emp. Joseph;   *Charles
of Burgundy.*   of Spain.   Electoral Prince   *d.* 1711.   claims to b
of Bavaria; *d.* 1699.   Charles I
of Spain,
afterward
Emperor
Charles V
1711-1740

Louis XV.

P. HOUSE OF STUART
AND HANOVERIAN SUCCESSION

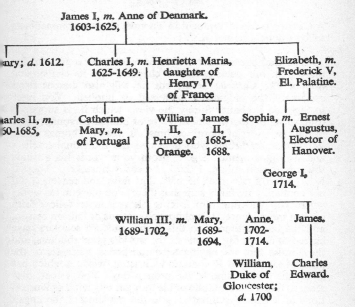

James I, *m.* Anne of Denmark.
1603–1625,

—nry; *d.* 1612.

Charles I, *m.* Henrietta Maria,
1625–1649.   daughter of
Henry IV
of France

Elizabeth, *m.*
Frederick V,
El. Palatine.

—arles II, *m.*
—50–1685,

Catherine
Mary, *m.*
of Portugal

William James
II,   II,
Prince of 1685–
Orange.   1688.

Sophia, *m.* Ernest
Augustus,
Elector of
Hanover.

George I,
1714.

William III, *m.* Mary,
1689–1702,   1689–
1694.

Anne,
1702–
1714.

James.

William,
Duke of
Gloucester;
d. 1700

Charles
Edward.

APPENDIX

A CATHOLIC friend, eminent in Thomist studies, comments as follows upon Chapter XXV:

"The Catholic student will have reason to be grateful for more than one passage in this chapter, with its challenging title of *The Catholic Mind*, but he will also dissent from certain of the judgments expressed or implied. You refer to Siger de Brabant. Surely the views which he is supposed to have supported were destructive of human personality and in the last resort of moral teaching. It was St. Thomas in the *de Unitate Intellectus* who defended the individual intellect and its rights against Siger. From your words his attitude towards reason might, I think, be easily mistaken. Though it is perfectly true that he held that faith and reason could not conflict, I am fairly sure that there is no place in his works where you will find him forcing his reason to follow faith against the evidence. His philosophy stands or falls on reason, and the best testimony to this is that modern scholars have agreed to accept him as one of the world's great thinkers, and they praise him for having accomplished a synthesis of the past, of Greek and Roman and Christian wisdom which has stood the test of time to the present day. You, I fear, may seem to hide the amplitude of his thought by giving as illustrations of it transubstantiation and the rejoicing of the angels and saints over the torments of the damned. I have no space to show that the philosophy of transubstantiation is not the crude, unscientific hocus-pocus one might suppose, but a piece of reasoning of the highest quality. The rejoicing of the saints over the sufferings of the damned has served as a gibe against Aquinas on more than one occasion. It is worth while looking at the chapter or article in which the subject is treated. There St. Thomas asks himself the question whether they rejoice over the suffering of the damned and urges first that it would be a horrible thing to take pleasure in the suffering of others. But he goes on to say that though this is true and no one should take pleasure in the pains of others as such, it is possible and even right to be glad that a villain, for instance, is suffering the punishment deserved for his crimes. We all observe this distinction and are glad if the kidnapper and murderer of children is caught and punished. Why, therefore, this doctrine of Aquinas is held up for reprobation always puzzles me. I think the reason must be that many think in their hearts that the middle ages must have been cruel and superstitious and quite inferior to ourselves in thought and conduct, and so they seize on this text without reflection. Even you say of Dante that 'like all writers of the mediaeval period' he 'draws no clear line between ancient mythology and true history,' forgetting the kind of scholarship required for the verdict on the *de Causis*. If St. Thomas be representative there was a great passion for truth in his time, and it is this passion and the desire for reconciliation of the many-sided aspects of life rather than 'a feeling that the spirit was more important than outward institutions, and faith and intellect than the sacraments or formularies of the Church,' which lay behind the movements and current tendencies.''